W9-CBJ-394

Contemporary Business Mathematics

Brief Edition

Contemporary Business Mathematics

For Colleges 12E

James E. Deitz, Ed.D.
President Emeritus, Heald Colleges

James L. Southam, Ph.D.
San Francisco State University

South-Western College Publishing
an International Thomson Publishing company I(T)P®

Cincinnati • Albany • Boston • Detroit • Johannesburg • London • Madrid • Melbourne • Mexico City
New York • Pacific Grove • San Francisco • Scottsdale • Singapore • Tokyo • Toronto

Team Director: Jack W. Calhoun
Acquisitions Editor: Michael B. Mercier
Developmental Editor: Susanna C. Smart
Production Editor: Sharon L. Smith
Production House: Pre-Press Company, Inc.
Internal and Cover Designer: Meighan Depke Design, Chicago
Cover Illustration: Copyright © 1998 Tony Klassen
Manufacturing Coordinator: Georgina Calderon
Team Assistant: Michael Briggs
Marketing Manager: Lisa L. Lysne

Copyright © 1999
by South-Western College Publishing
Cincinnati, Ohio

All Rights Reserved
The text of this publication, or any part thereof, may not be reproduced or transmitted in any form or by any means, electronic or mechanical, including photocopying, recording, storage in an information retrieval system, or otherwise, without prior written permission from the publisher.

ISBN: 0-538-86883-X

2 3 4 5 6 GP 3 2 1 0 9 8

Printed in the United States of America

Library of Congress Cataloging-in-Publication Data
Deitz, James E.
Contemporary business mathematics for colleges / James E. Deitz, James L. Southam. — 12th ed.
p. cm.
Rev. ed. of: Business mathematics for colleges / James E. Deitz. 11th ed. c1996.
Includes index.
ISBN 0-538-86883-X (brief ed.)
1. Business mathematics. I. Southam, James L. II. Deitz, James E. Business mathematics for colleges. III. Title.
HF5691.D43 1998
650'.01'513—dc21 98-17393
CIP

I(T)P®
International Thomson Publishing
South-Western College Publishing is an ITP Company.
The ITP trademark is used under license.

To the Student

During its previous eleven editions, *Business Mathematics for Colleges* has sold more copies than any other business math textbook. The goal of the twelfth edition is to make a successful book even better. This new edition, now titled *Contemporary Business Mathematics for Colleges,* focuses on *practical, real-world business math, problems,* and *step-by-step solutions* to help you solve these problems. The authors have done this with an eye toward contemporary business issues and the needs of contemporary business students, through new features that make learning easier and more enjoyable. *Contemporary Business Mathematics for Colleges* presents the basic principles of mathematics and immediately applies them in a series of practical business problems. The twelfth edition is designed to provide a balance among conceptual understanding, skill development, and business applications.

Why Study Business Mathematics?

In the business world, everyone—employees and managers alike—needs knowledge of and skill in business mathematics. While computers and calculators are used for many calculations, it is important to understand the concepts behind mechanical computations. The purpose of the business mathematics course is to increase your math knowledge and skill as it applies to many aspects of business and to help make you a more valuable player in the business arena.

New Content and New Organization

COVERAGE. In addition to updating coverage from the previous edition, the authors have added new content and reorganized some chapters. A chapter on computers in business (Chapter 31) has been added, as has a chapter on mathematics in employment tests (Chapter 32 in the full version of the text, and Chapter 24 in the brief version). These practical additions of timely topics will help you better understand and prepare for positions in today's technology-oriented workplaces.

ORGANIZATION. The organization of the twelfth edition has been revised to reflect the need for earlier coverage of some business topics. Coverage of decimals (Chapters 4 and 5) has been placed before the coverage of fractions; coverage of accounting applications (Chapters 8 through 11) has been placed earlier in the text (Part 3) and now includes chapters on taxes, payroll, and banking; and Part 6, on business applications, now contains chapters on insurance, inventory, depreciation, and financial statements. In addition, the chapters on insurance have been combined in this edition into one chapter, "Business and Personal Insurance" (Chapter 20), and the international business chapter (Chapter 26) has been placed in Part 7, "Corporate Finance." These changes are beneficial in that they provide a more logical flow of the important topics to be learned in business mathematics courses.

New and Successful Features

Before you begin your journey through the twelfth edition of *Contemporary Business Mathematics for Colleges,* take our guided tour through the special features that will make your journey a valuable—and memorable—learning experience.

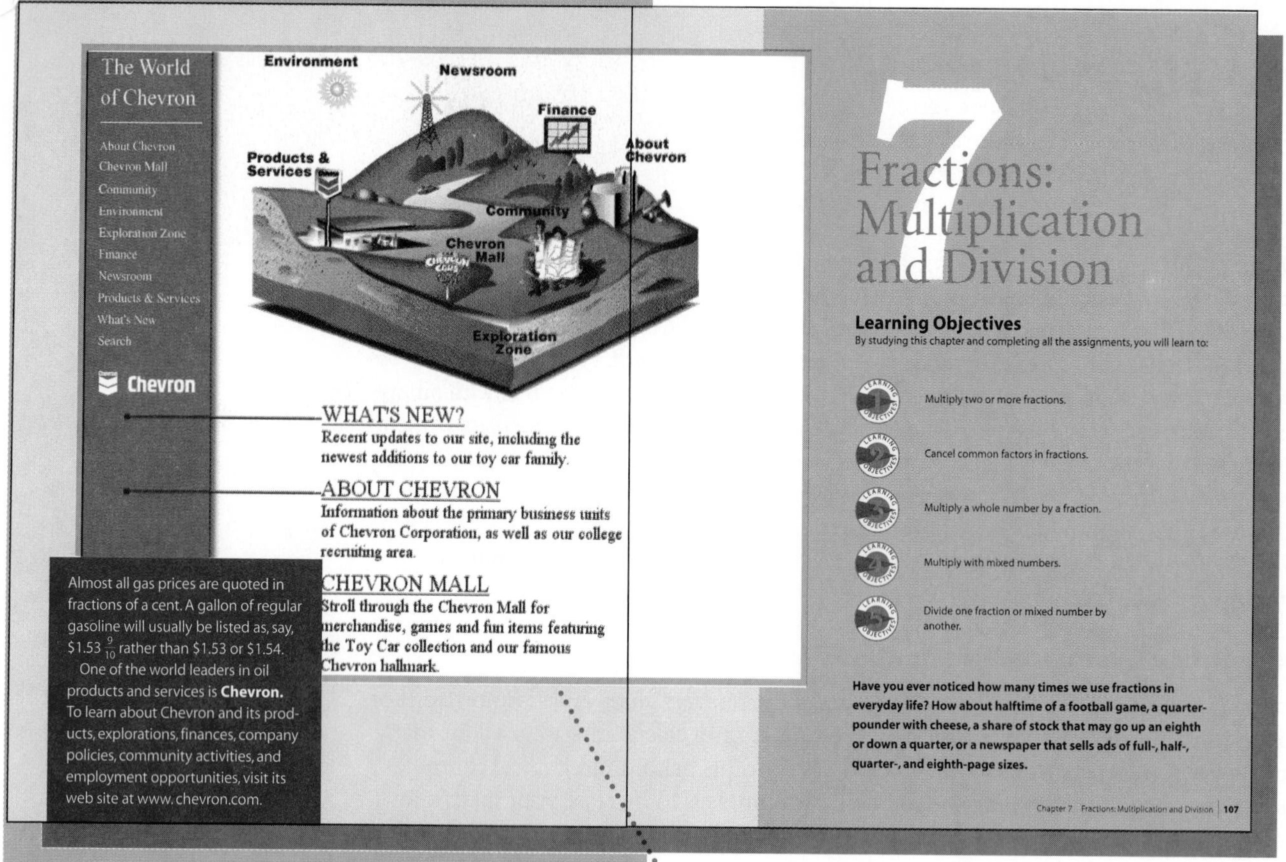

Almost all gas prices are quoted in fractions of a cent. A gallon of regular gasoline will usually be listed as, say, $1.53 \frac{9}{10}$ rather than $1.53 or $1.54.

One of the world leaders in oil products and services is **Chevron.** To learn about Chevron and its products, explorations, finances, company policies, community activities, and employment opportunities, visit its web site at www.chevron.com.

7

Fractions: Multiplication and Division

Learning Objectives

By studying this chapter and completing all the assignments, you will learn to:

1. Multiply two or more fractions.
2. Cancel common factors in fractions.
3. Multiply a whole number by a fraction.
4. Multiply with mixed numbers.
5. Divide one fraction or mixed number by another.

Have you ever noticed how many times we use fractions in everyday life? How about halftime of a football game, a quarter-pounder with cheese, a share of stock that may go up an eighth or down a quarter, or a newspaper that sells ads of full-, half-, quarter-, and eighth-page sizes.

Chapter 7 Fractions: Multiplication and Division | 107

Internet Chapter Openers

The two-page chapter openers include screens from the *Internet sites* of real companies, most of which you may recognize, along with their Internet addresses. These company screens were chosen either to show relationships between the chapter coverage and the companies selected, or to lead you to sites that describe related career opportunities.

In addition, *Learning Objectives* and chapter-opening vignettes give you a preview of what the chapter holds. The learning objectives are repeated in the margins where first discussed, again in the Bottom Line feature, and also are identified for each end-of-chapter assignment. This enables you to find and focus on mastery of the chapter objectives.

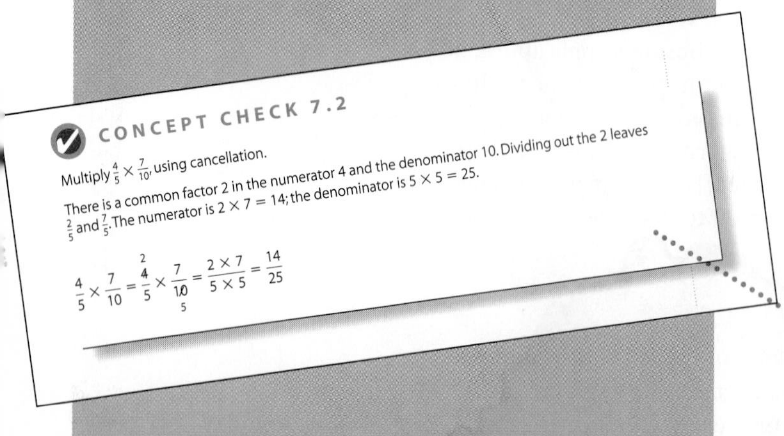

CONCEPT CHECK 7.2

Multiply $\frac{4}{5} \times \frac{7}{10}$, using cancellation.

There is a common factor 2 in the numerator 4 and the denominator 10. Dividing out the 2 leaves $\frac{2}{5}$ and $\frac{7}{5}$. The numerator is $2 \times 7 = 14$; the denominator is $5 \times 5 = 25$.

$$\frac{4}{5} \times \frac{7}{10} = \frac{\overset{2}{\cancel{4}}}{5} \times \frac{7}{\underset{5}{\cancel{10}}} = \frac{2 \times 7}{5 \times 5} = \frac{14}{25}$$

Concept Checks

Throughout the book, *Concept Checks* at the end of each chapter section allow you to test your mastery of the topics just learned. These self-checks let you know immediately if you need more practice, instead of having you wait until assignments are turned in or exams are taken.

The Bottom Line

New *Bottom Line* features, placed before the chapter assignments, are another method of review before beginning chapter assignments. The Learning Objectives are reviewed, an example problem is given, and answers are provided at the end of the feature. This additional self-test helps you review the chapter material. If you had difficulty completing a Concept Check, this is another opportunity to see how well you have mastered the skills covered in the chapter.

Other Important Features:

The twelfth edition again contains many of the features that were useful in making the text a student-friendly book in the previous edition.

- **Step-by-step format for solving word problems.** Chapter 2 presents, step by step, a method for solving word problems. Using this method, you can increase your ability to correctly solve word problems.
- **Illustrated step-by-step solutions.** Short, concise text presentation of topics are followed by examples that show the step-by-step solutions. You will learn mathematical concepts by immediately applying practical solutions to common business problems.
- **Directed assignments.** At specific points within each chapter, you are directed to appropriate end-of-chapter assignments. This allows you to work end-of-chapter problems before completing the entire chapter.
- **End-of-chapter assignments.**

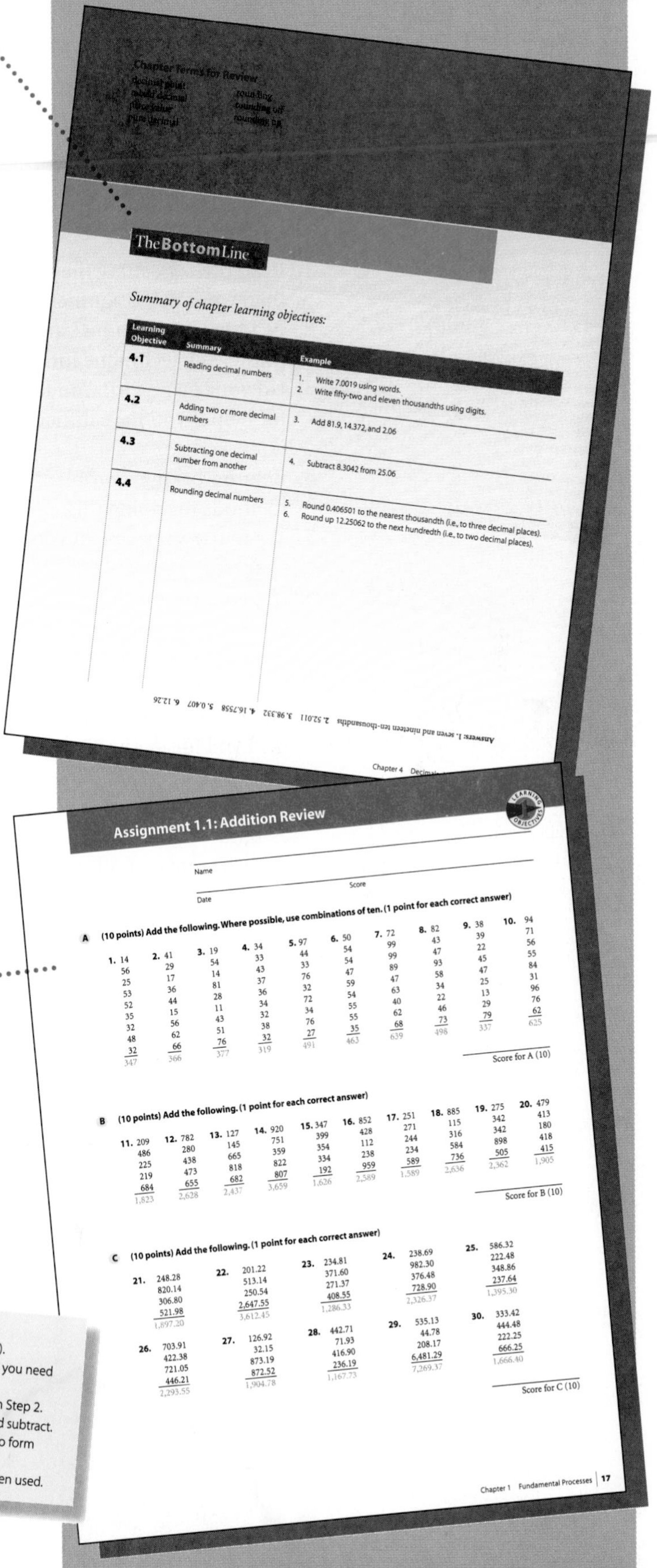

STEPS in Long Division

1. Write the divisor in front of and the dividend inside of a division bracket (⟌).
2. As the first partial dividend, use only as many digits at the left of the dividend as you need in order to have a number that is equal to or larger than the divisor.
3. Write the number of times the divisor will go into the partial dividend selected in Step 2.
4. Multiply the divisor by this answer, write the product under the partial dividend, and subtract.
5. Next to the remainder thus obtained, bring down the next digit of the dividend to form the second partial dividend.
6. Divide as before, and repeat the process until all the digits of the dividend have been used.

Suggestions for Using this Book

1. Read the text, study the step-by-step illustrations and the clear examples carefully, then work the assignments.
2. Read the instructions carefully for each assignment before solving the problems. Master the technique for solving word problems early, as presented in Chapter 2.
3. Do your own work. You learn by doing the calculations yourself. Ask your instructor for help if you have difficulty in understanding what you are asked to do or how to do it.
4. Before working a problem, try to estimate your answer. The early chapters present methods for doing this.
5. Try to use shortcuts in your calculations. You will find shortcuts presented in several chapters.
6. Improve your writing of figures through regular practice so that you will not make errors as a result of mistaking one number for another.
7. Align figures in columns to avoid errors in addition or subtraction.
8. Space is provided on the assignment sheets for you to compute most problems. Show each step in your solution so that if you make an error, your instructor can help you locate the cause of your difficulty.
9. Work the *Concept Checks* and the *Bottom Line* problems. These features give you a comprehensive review of the problems in each chapter, before you get to the assignments.
10. Record your scores for each assignment on the Progress Record at the end of your book.

Supplements to the Text

Contemporary Business Mathematics for Colleges comes with an integrated learning package.

- Business Math Handbook

  The *Business Math Handbook*, by Keith H. Wieland of the University of Cincinnati, Clermont Branch, has been thoroughly revised for this edition. It contains useful materials that you will want to keep for reference long after your business math courses are over.
  ISBN 0-538-86898-8

- Tutorial Software

  Even more problems are available to help you master the mathematical skills you need. This software, prepared by Keith E. Weidkamp of Sierra College and Leland E. Mansuetti, provides you with an opportunity to work math problems on the computer, giving you mathematics and computer practice at the same time. The Tutorial Software is available in both DOS and Windows versions.
  ISBN 0-538-86885-6 (DOS Version)
  ISBN 0-324-00472-9 (Windows Version)

- Spreadsheet Software

Spreadsheet templates are another computer supplement to give you practice with both mathematics and spreadsheet software. The Spreadsheet software, by Adele Stock of Normandale Community College, is available in both DOS and Windows versions, and includes both Lotus 1-2-3 and Excel worksheets.
ISBN 0-538-86890-2 (DOS Version)
ISBN 0-538-89101-7 (Windows Version)

- Topic Review Videos

This video contains twelve major mathematics concepts—including fractions, percents, discounts and markups, and creating graphs—and applies them to a series of practical business problems. These professionally produced, brief video segments can be used by your instructor in class or by you, as an individual review in a lab setting.
ISBN 0-538-86889-9

- Website

Visit *http://deitz.swcollege.com* and learn more about this text. The site provides more information on the learning resources and the text, and you also can contact South-Western College Publishing with comments and questions about the text.

Acknowledgments

We would like to thank the many instructors who have reviewed and assisted with revisions of the numerous earlier editions; it is your suggestions and comments that have helped make this text what it is today.

Linda Johnson
Northern Illinois University

Fran March
Chattanooga State Technical
Community College

Cheryl Macon
Butler County Community College

Steven C. Teeter
Utah Valley State College

Jimmy Anderson
College of the Albemarle

Dale Dean
Athens Area Technical College

Kenneth J. Larson
LDS Business College

Zona J. Elkins
Blue Ridge Community College

Alan Moggio
Illinois Central College

Elizabeth R. King
Heald Business College

Russ Nail
Hernando Community College

Allan L. Sheets
Indiana Business College

Nellie U. Edmundson
Miami Dade Community College

Kay Finlay
Indiana Vocational Technical College

William B. Harrison
DeVry Institute of Technology

Charles Trester
Northeast Wisconsin Technical College

LaVerne Vertrees
St. Louis Community College

Queen Young
DeKalb Technical Institute

We would also like to thank Adele Stock and Keith Wieland for their assistance with the supplements, and the staff at South-Western College Publishing who worked to make this new edition the best business mathematics text possible, especially Sharon L. Smith, our production editor, Mike Mercier, our acquisitions editor, and Susanna C. Smart, our developmental editor. And our appreciation also goes to Sharon Vogt, Audrey Smith, and Suzanne Thomas, our problem verifiers, who worked to make this text as accurate as possible.

James L. Deitz
James E. Southam

Contents

Part 1: Fundamental Review

1 **Fundamental Processes**
Adding 2
Number Combinations 2
Repeated Digits 3
Adding from Left to Right 3
Checking Addition 4
Horizontal Addition 4
Subtracting 5
Checking Subtraction 5
Horizontal Subtraction 5
Subtraction by Changing Numbers 5
Multiplying 6
Checking Multiplication 6
Multiplying Numbers Ending in Zero 7
Multiplying When the Multiplier Contains Zero Not on the End 7
Multiplying the Product of Two Factors 8
Multiplying by 25 8
Multiplying by 50 8
Division 9
Checking Division 10
Dividing by 10 10
Dividing by 100 10
Dividing When Divisor and Dividend End with Zeros 10
Estimating 11
Estimating When Multiplying 11
Estimating When Dividing 12

2 **Word Problems and Equations**
Mental Computations 28
Solving Word Problems 28
Solving Rate, Time, and Distance Problems 30
Solving Simple Numeric Equations 32
Numerical Relationships in a Series 33
Making Quick Calculations by Rounding Numbers 34

3 **Weights and Measurements**
Converting Weights and Measurements 44
Performing Mathematical Operations Using Standard U.S. Weights and Measurements 46
Adding Weights and Measurements 46
Subtracting Weights and Measurements 47
Multiplication of Weights and Measurements 47
Division of Weights and Measurements 48
Business Applications 49

Part 2 Decimals and Fractions

4 **Decimals: Addition and Subtraction**
Fractions versus Decimals 60
Decimals and Electronic Displays 60
Reading Decimal Numbers 61
Reading Large Decimal Numbers Orally 61
Adding Decimal Numbers 62
Subtracting Decimal Numbers 63
Rounding Decimal Numbers 64
Rounding Up 64

5 **Decimals: Multiplication and Division**
Multiplying Decimal Numbers 74
Dividing a Decimal by a Whole Number 75
Dividing a Decimal by Another Decimal Number 76
Multiplying and Dividing by 10, 100, 1,000, etc. 77
Approximating the Product and Quotient 78
Changing Fractions into Decimals 80

6 **Fractions: Addition and Subtraction**
Changing an Improper Fraction to a Mixed Number 90
Changing a Mixed Number to an Improper Fraction 91

Reducing Fractions to Lowest Terms 92
Raising Fractions to Higher Terms 92
Fractions on the New York Stock Exchange 93
Adding Fractions or Mixed Numbers 94
Subtracting Fractions or Mixed Numbers 96

7 Fractions: Multiplication and Division
Multiplying Fractions 106
Canceling Common Factors 106
Multiplying a Whole Number and a Fraction 107
Multiplying Mixed Numbers 108
Spoken Language and Multiplication of Fractions 109
Dividing with Fractions 110

Part 3 Accounting Applications

8 Banking
Using Deposit Slips and Bank Checks 120
Maintaining Checkbooks and Check Registers 122
Reconciling Bank Statements 123

9 Payroll Records
Preparing a Payroll Register 139
Computing Federal Income Tax Withholding Amounts 139
Computing Social Security, Medicare, and Other Withholdings 145
Completing an Employee's Earnings Record 146
Computing an Employer's Quarterly Federal Tax Return 147
Computing an Employer's Federal and State Unemployment Tax Liability 148

10 Federal Income Taxes
Computing Taxable Income Using Standard Form 1940 160
Computation of Taxable Income 164
Computing Taxes Due Using Standard Form 1040 164
Computing Taxes for Businesses 166

11 Sales and Property Taxes
Computing Sales Taxes 176
Sales Tax as a Percent of Price 176
Sales Tax as an Amount per Unit 177
Computing Assessed Valuations and Property Taxes 177
Computing Tax Rates in Percents and Mills 178
Percents 178
Mills 179
Computing Special Assessments, Prorations, and Exemptions 179

Part 4 Percentage

12 Percents in Business
Changing Fractions and Decimals to Percents 190
Changing Percents to Decimals 191
Finding Base, Rate, and Percentage 192
Using Percents in Business 193
Using Percents to Measure Increase and Decrease 194
Using Percents to Allocate Overhead Expenses 195

13 Commissions
Calculating Sales Commissions and Gross Pay 210
Calculating Graduated Sales Commissions 211
Calculating Sales and Purchases for Principals 212

14 Discounts
Calculating Single Trade Discounts 224
Calculating a Series of Trade Discounts 225
Complement Method Shortcut 226

Calculating the Equivalent Single Discount Rate 226
Calculating Cash Discounts for Fully Paid Invoices 227
Returned Merchandise and Freight Charges 229
Calculating Cash Discounts for Partially Paid Invoices 230

15 Markup
Computing Markup Variables 230
Computing Markup Based on Cost 241
Computing Selling Price Directly from Cost 241
Computing Cost from Selling Price 242
Computing Markup Percent Based on Cost 242
Computing Markup Based on Selling Price 243
Computing Cost Directly 244
Computing Selling Price from Cost 244
Computing Markup Percent Based on Selling Price 245

Part 5 Credit and Interest

16 Simple Interest
Computing Simple Interest 256
Computing Ordinary Interest 257
Computing Exact Interest 258
Comparing Ordinary Interest and Exact Interest 258
Use of Calculators 259
Estimating Simple Interest 259
Combinations of Time and Interest That Yield 1% 259
Other Rates and Times 260
Estimation of Exact Interest 260

17 Notes and Interest Variables
Calculating the Number of Interest Days of a Note 272
Determining the Due Date of a Note 273
Computing the Maturity Value of a Note 274
Computing the Interest Variables 275
Finding the Interest Amount, Principal, Rate, or Time 275

18 Borrowing by Business
Borrowing Money to Take a Cash Discount 288
Computing Interest with the Unpaid-Balance Method 289
Analyzing Bank Discounts 291
Discount Rate versus Interest Rate 292
Discounting Non-Interest-Bearing Notes 293
Discounting Interest-Bearing Notes 294

19 Charges for Credit
Converting Interest Rates 306
Computing Simple Interest on a Monthly Basis 306
Computing Finance Charges 307
Computing Costs of installment Purchases 308
Computing Effective Rates 310
Increasing the Effective Rate 310
An Alternative Formula for Estimating the Effective Rate 311
Amortizing a Loan 313
Computing the Monthly Payment 313
Loan Payment Schedule 314

Part 6 Basic Business Applications

20 Business and Personal Insurance
Computing Auto Insurance Costs 328
Computing Low-Risk and High-Risk Rates 329
Computing Short Rates 330
Computing Coinsurance on Property Losses 331
Computing Life Insurance Premiums 332

Computing Cash Surrender and Loan Values 334
Computing Medical Insurance Contributions and Reimbursements 335

21 Business Inventory and Turnover
Accounting for Inventory 348
Inventory Sheets 348
Perpetual Inventory Systems 349
Computing Inventory Using the Average Cost, FIFO, and LIFO Methods 349
The Average Cost Method 349
The FIFO Method 350
The LIFO Method 350
Computing Inventory at the Lower of Cost or Market Value 351
Estimating Inventory Value 352
Computing Inventory Turnover 353

22 Business Depreciation
Computing Depreciation with the Straight-Line Method 366
Book Value 367
Computing Depreciation with the Declining- Balance Method 368
Computing Depreciation with the Sum-of-the-Years-Digits Method 369
Computing Depreciation with the Modified Accelerated Cost Recovery System 370
Computing Partial-Year Depreciation 371

23 Business Financial Statements
Analyzing Balance Sheets 384
Analyzing Income Statements 386
Computing Business Operating Ratios 388
Working Capital Ratio 389
Acid Test Ratio 389
Ratio of Accounts Receivable to Net Sales 389
Inventory Turnover Rate 390
Relationship of Net Income Sales to Net Sales 390
Rate of Return on Investment 390

24 Math in Employment Tests
Solving Rate, Time, and Distance Problems 406
Solving Proportion Problems 407
Solving Time and Work Problems 409
Solving Measurement Problems 410
Solving Percentage Problems 412
Solving Relationship Problems 414
Glossary 428
Answers to Odd-Numbered Problems 435
Index 442
Progress Report 447

Contemporary Business Mathematics

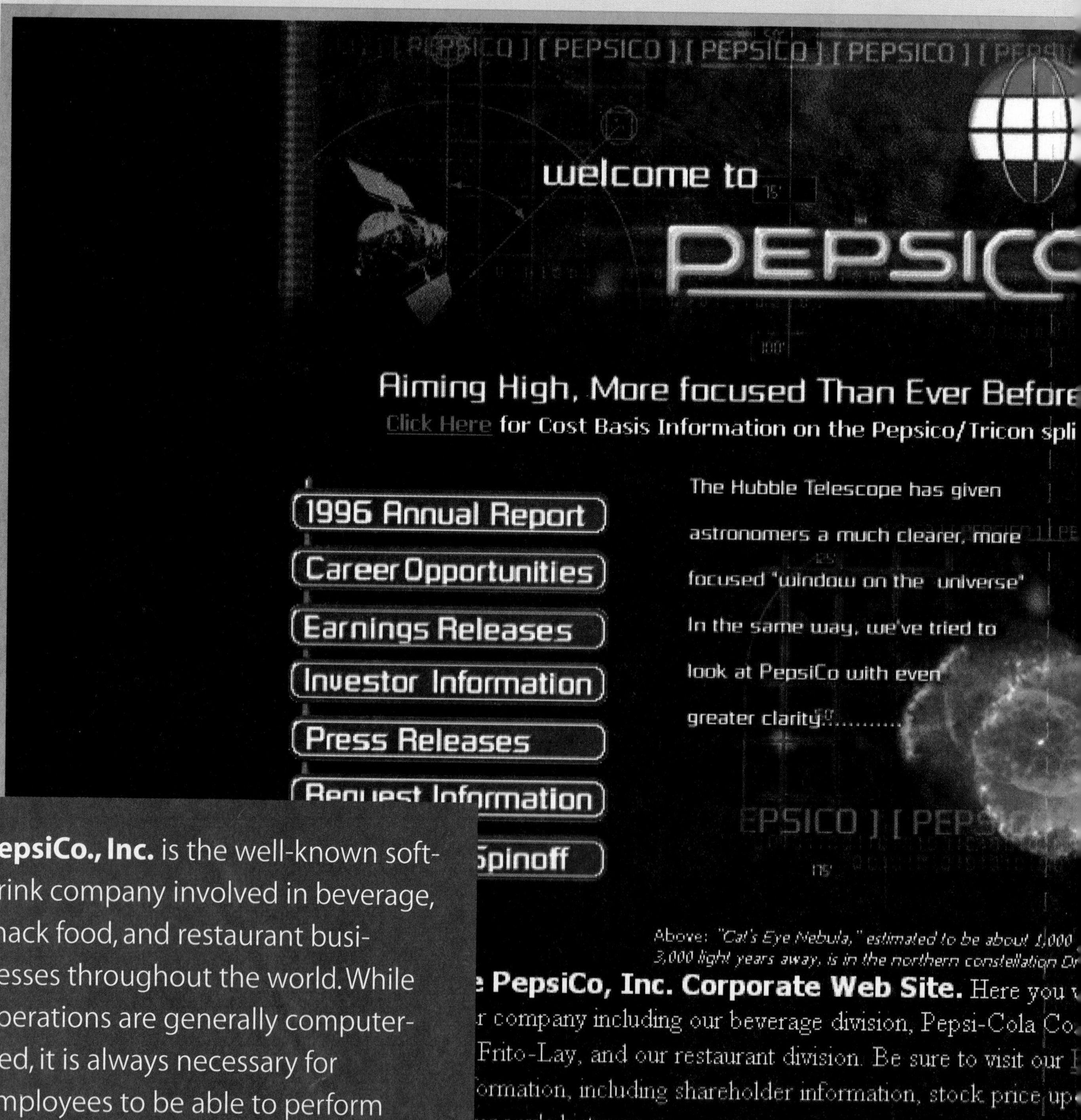
[PEPSICO] [PEPSICO] [PEPSICO]
welcome to
PEPSICO
Aiming High, More focused Than Ever Before
Click Here for Cost Basis Information on the Pepsico/Tricon split
1996 Annual Report
Career Opportunities
Earnings Releases
Investor Information
Press Releases
Request Information
Spinoff
The Hubble Telescope has given
astronomers a much clearer, more
focused "window on the universe"
In the same way, we've tried to
look at PepsiCo with even
greater clarity...........
Above: "Cat's Eye Nebula," estimated to be about 3,000 light years away, is in the northern constellation
PepsiCo, Inc. Corporate Web Site.
company including our beverage division, Pepsi-Cola Co.
Frito-Lay, and our restaurant division. Be sure to visit our
including shareholder information, stock price
history.
Resource Center | Request Information | Press Releases
Restaurant Spinoff | Career Opportunities

PepsiCo., Inc. is the well-known soft-drink company involved in beverage, snack food, and restaurant businesses throughout the world. While operations are generally computerized, it is always necessary for employees to be able to perform fundamental mathematical processes, sometimes in the form of mental estimates or hand calculations. Check out PepsiCo's career opportunities, request that information on the company be sent to you by mail, or see the latest press and news releases, at the PepsiCo site at www.pepsico.com.

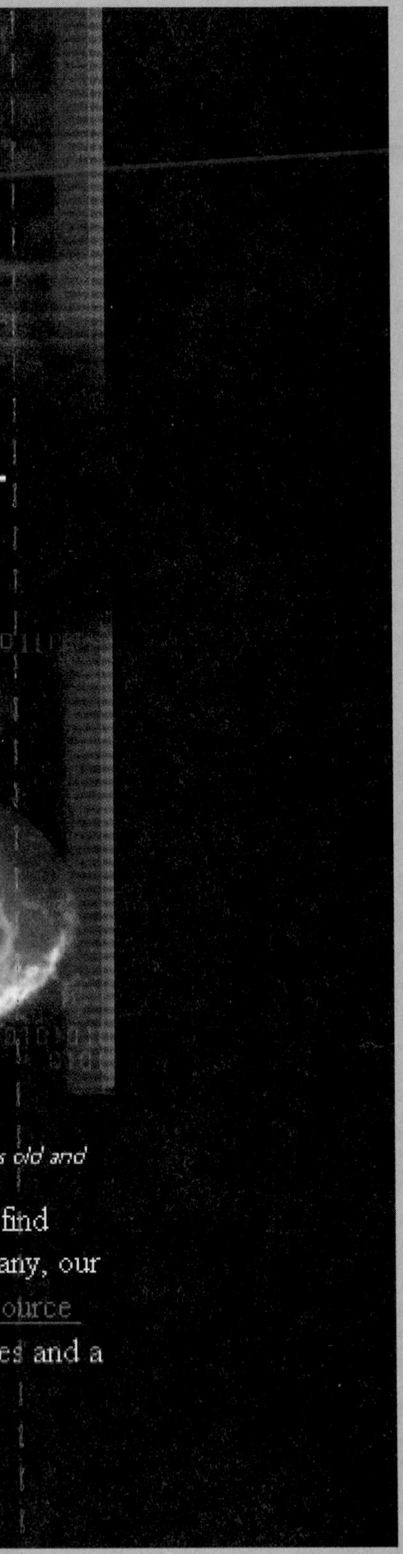

1 Fundamental Processes

Learning Objectives

By studying this chapter and completing all the assignments, you will be able to:

1. Use shortcuts and simplifications to perform the fundamental process of addition rapidly and accurately.
2. Use shortcuts and simplifications to perform the fundamental process of subtraction rapidly and accurately.
3. Use shortcuts and simplifications to perform the fundamental process of multiplication rapidly and accurately.
4. Use shortcuts and simplifications to perform the fundamental process of division rapidly and accurately.
5. Estimate answers before performing operations.

To perfect a skill, you must learn the fundamentals and practice them until you become proficient. In baseball, you learn how to run, slide, and catch until you are a seasoned pro.

It is the same with math in business. First you learn the fundamentals of addition, subtraction, multiplication, and division. Then you practice them over and over through many applications. Finally you can enjoy success in business.

Adding

Use shortcuts and simplifications to perform the fundamental process of addition rapidly and accurately.

About half of all the computations used in business involve addition. The more skilled you become in adding, the more rapidly you will get accurate answers. Addition is the process of finding the *sum* (total) of two or more *addends* (any of a set of numbers to be added).

Number Combinations

Certain aids can help you add more accurately and rapidly. One of the most helpful is to combine any two numbers that total 10. Combinations that total 10 are given below. Practice the combinations until you can identify them instantly.

1	2	3	4	5	9	8	7	6	5
9	8	7	6	5	1	2	3	4	5

When these combinations are found sequentially in any column of numbers, you should add them as 10. In example A, you might add the numbers in the right-hand (ones) column by saying, as you count down the column, "9 plus 4 is 13, plus 6 is 19, plus 3 is 22, plus 7 is 29, plus 8 is 37" (or simply "13, 19, 22, 29, 37"). By using the combinations of 10, however, you can simply add down the column by saying "9 plus 10 is 19, plus 10 is 29, plus 8 is 37" (or "9, 19, 29, 37").

The number 3 is carried over to the top of the next column and written in a small figure above the number 7 in the center column. The combinations of 10 are used in adding the center (tens) column by simply saying "10, 20, 30."

In adding the left-hand (hundreds) column, you carry over the number 3 from the center column total. You can simply say "8, 18, 28, 32."

EXAMPLE A

	3	3	
	5	7	9
	4	2	4
	6	8	6
	9	0	3
	1	5	7
	4	5	8
3,	2	0	7

It is also helpful to recognize the combinations of three numbers that total 10:

1	1	1	1	2	2	2	3
1	2	3	4	2	3	4	3
8	7	6	5	6	5	4	4

The numbers in each combination may appear in any order. For example, the numbers 2, 3, and 5 may appear in any of six arrangements:

2	3	2	3	5	5
3	2	5	5	2	3
5	5	3	2	3	2

When these numbers totaling 10 appear in sequence in a column, they should be combined and added as 10. In example B, you might add the numbers in the ones column as you add down the column, "10, 18, 28, 38, 41." The number 4, which is carried over, is written as a small figure above the 1 in the tens column. The combinations of 10 are used in adding the tens column by saying "5, 15, 25, 35, 43."

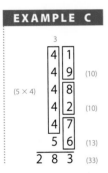

EXAMPLE B

		4		
(5)		1	7	
		6	2	
(15)		4	1	(10)
		2	8	(18)
		2	5	
(25)		6	5	(28)
		5	4	
		2	4	
(35)		3	2	(38)
(43)		8	3	(41)
	4	3	1	

Repeated Digits

When adding a column in which many of the digits are the same, it is often quicker to count the number of repeated digits and then multiply the digit by that number. In example C, the ones column totals 33: 10 + 10 + 13. The tens column shows five 4s, equaling 20: $5 \times 4 = 20$. The 3 that was carried over and the 5 are then added to the 20 for a total of 28 in the tens column. The total for the problem is 283.

EXAMPLE C

		3		
		4	1	
		4	9	(10)
(5 × 4)		4	8	
		4	2	(10)
		4	7	
		5	6	(13)
	2	8	3	(33)

Adding from Left to Right (columns of two-digit numbers)

When adding columns of two-digit numbers, it is easy to count by tens and add the ones column.

EXAMPLE D

Count:

12	12
24	22, 32 + 4 = 36
51	46, 56, 66, 76, 86 + 1 = 87
43	97, 107, 117, 127 + 3 = 130
32	140, 150, 160 + 2 = 162
162	

This technique can be used to add four-digit columns in the same manner.

EXAMPLE E

Count left columns **second**		Count right columns **first**
33	33.28	28
43, 53 + 1 = 54	21.32	38, 48, 58 + 2 = 60
64, 74, 84, 94, 104, 114 + 2 = 116	62.55	70, 80, 90, 100, 110 + 5 = 115
126, 136 + 7 = 143	27.33	125, 135, 145 + 3 = 148
	1.48	
	143.00	
	144.48	

Checking Addition

You should always check the accuracy of your addition. You do this by adding the columns again in the opposite direction—that is, if you added down, add up for the check.

Horizontal Addition

It is sometimes necessary in business records to add numbers horizontally, or across the line, to save the time of recopying the numbers vertically. Several horizontal additions may be checked by adding the columns vertically and then adding these totals horizontally. This is called *cross-checking.* The sums obtained by adding the totals horizontally and vertically should be the same.

EXAMPLE F

282	+	346	+	723	+	409	+	716	=	2,476
113	+	806	+	629	+	916	+	620	=	3,084
240	+	318	+	718	+	312	+	309	=	1,897
716	+	501	+	423	+	716	+	114	=	2,470
872	+	417	+	909	+	704	+	472	=	3,374
2,223	+	2,388	+	3,402	+	3,057	+	2,231	=	13,301

CONCEPT CHECK 1.1

Add horizontally and vertically; compare horizontal and vertical totals to verify accuracy. Use combinations to simplify addition.

1		1		1			
24	+	76	+	63	=	163	(4 + 6)
36	+	24	+	25	=	85	(6 + 4)
27	+	43	+	12	=	82	(7 + 3)
87	+	143	+	100	=	330	

	1	1	
4	76	63	(Note combinations)
6	24	25	
		12	

COMPLETE ASSIGNMENT 1.1.

Subtracting

Subtraction is the process of finding the difference between the *subtrahend* (number being subtracted) and the *minuend* (number from which subtraction is being made); the result is the *difference.* When the subtrahend is greater than the minuend, the result is a negative difference. In business, a negative difference may be called a *credit balance.* A credit balance is frequently shown in parentheses.

LEARNING OBJECTIVES 2

Use shortcuts and simplifications to perform the fundamental process of subtraction rapidly and accurately.

EXAMPLE G

Positive Differences			**Negative Difference (Credit Balance)**
$32.22	$18.88	Minuend	$12.00
−22.22	− 3.63	−Subtrahend	−13.50
$10.00	$15.25	Difference	($ 1.50)

Checking Subtraction

Subtraction is checked with addition. If 209 is subtracted from 317, the difference is 108. This result can be checked by adding the difference (108) to the subtrahend (209). The sum is 317. The same procedure can be used to check subtraction with a negative difference (credit balance).

EXAMPLE H

Subtract:	**Check:**
317	108
−209	+209
108	317

EXAMPLE I

Subtract:	**Check:**
$21.10	($ 3.40)
−24.50	+24.50
($ 3.40)	$21.10

Horizontal Subtraction

Certain business forms make it necessary to subtract numbers horizontally. A number of horizontal subtractions can be checked by adding the columns vertically and then subtracting these totals horizontally. This answer should equal the total of the differences in the column at the right.

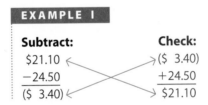

Minuend		**Subtrahend**		**Difference**
$ 120	−	$ 20	=	$100
283	−	10	=	273
440	−	110	=	330
$ 269	−	149	=	120
$1,112	−	$289	=	$823

Subtraction by Changing Numbers

When looking at a subtraction problem, especially one that will involve *borrowing,* it is sometimes easier to alter the problem. If you add the same number to both the minuend and the subtrahend, the difference will remain the same. This will frequently make the answer immediately apparent.

EXAMPLE K

Original Problem	Add:	Changed Problem	
45	+2	47	Minuend
−28	+2	−30	−Subtrahend
17		17	Difference

CONCEPT CHECK 1.2

Subtract:	Check:
276	142
−134	+134
142	276

Subtract horizontally: Check by comparing totals

27	−	13	=	14
24	−	11	=	13
36	−	10	=	26
87	−	34	=	53

COMPLETE ASSIGNMENT 1.2.

Multiplying

Use shortcuts and simplifications to perform the fundamental process of multiplication rapidly and accurately.

Multiplication, stated simply, is repeated addition. When two numbers (called *factors*) are multiplied, one number is repeated as many times as there are units in the other. The factor that is multiplied is called the *multiplicand.* The factor that indicates how many times to multiply is the *multiplier*. The result is the *product.*

STEPS to Multiply Two Numbers

1. Make the smaller factor the multiplier.
2. Multiply from right to left.
3. Add the products to get the final product.

EXAMPLE L

	456	(multiplicand)
STEP 1	×237	(multiplier)
STEP 2	3 192	(product)
STEP 2	13 680	(product)
STEP 2	91 200	(product)
STEP 3	108,072	(final product)

In other words:

7 × 456 =	3,192
30 × 456 =	13,680
200 × 456 =	91,200
237 × 456 =	108,072

Checking Multiplication

The best method of checking multiplication is to divide the product by the multiplier to obtain the multiplicand. Example M shows the relationship between multiplication and division.

EXAMPLE M

multiplicand	22	→ 22
multiplier	×6	→ 6) 132
product	132	→ ↑

Multiplying Numbers Ending in Zero

To multiply a number by 10, simply add a zero onto the end of the number. To multiply a number by 100, add two zeros onto the end: 10 × 46 = 460; 7,689 × 100 = 768,900.

STEPS to Multiply Numbers with Zeros

1. Make the multiplier the factor with the smaller number of digits after ignoring zeros at the right-hand side of the number.
2. Ignore the right-hand zeros and multiply the remaining numbers.
3. Insert the zeros ignored in Step 2 to the right-hand side of the product.

EXAMPLE N

STEP 1 370 × 200: Make 2 the multiplier.

		ignored
	37	(1 zero)
	×2	(2 zeros)
STEP 2	74	(3 zeros)
STEP 3	74 000	= 74,000

EXAMPLE O

STEP 1 1,200 × 160,800: Make 12 the multiplier.

		ignored
	1608	(2 zeros)
	×12	(2 zeros)
	3216	
	1608	
STEP 2	19296	(4 zeros)
STEP 3	19296 0000	= 192,960,000

Multiplying When the Multiplier Contains Zero Not on the End

Often a zero is found in the center of the multiplier rather than at the end. To multiply 42,674 by 401, first multiply the multiplicand by 1 and write down the product. Then multiply by 4 (which is really 400) and write the result two places, instead of one, to the left. In other words, one extra place is left for each zero in the multiplier.

EXAMPLE P

```
   42,674
   × 401
   42 674
17 069 6      (2 places)
17,112,274
```

Whenever more than one zero is found within the multiplier, the multiplication process is similar. To multiply 33,222 by 2,004, as in Example Q, first multiply 33,222 by 4. Then multiply 33,222 by 2, writing the answer three places to the left. Remember, extra places must be left for the two zeros (1 place + 2 extra places = 3 places).

EXAMPLE Q

33,222
×2,004
132 888
66 444 (3 places)
66,576,888

Multiplying the Product of Two Factors

Sometimes in business you will need to multiply two factors, then multiply the product of those factors by a third factor. As shown in example R, you begin by multiplying the first two factors and then multiply that product by the third factor.

EXAMPLE R

21 × 30 × 12 = 7,560

21
×30
630 → 630
×12
1 260
6 30
7 560

Multiplying by 25

A shortcut for multiplying by 25 is to multiply by 100 (increase by two zeros) and divide by 4.

EXAMPLE S

321 × 25
32,100 ÷ 4 = 8,025

EXAMPLE T

828 × 25
82,800 ÷ 4 = 20,700

Multiplying by 50

A shortcut for multiplying by 50 is to multiply by 100 (increase by two zeros) and divide by 2.

EXAMPLE U

732 × 50
73,200 ÷ 2 = 36,600

CONCEPT CHECK 1.3

To multiply by 10, add one zero to the end of the number:
36 × 10 = 360
To multiply by 100, add two zeros to the end of the number:
36 × 100 = 3,600

Multiply:

214 → multiplicand
102 → multiplier
428
21 4 (two places)
21,828 → product

Check:

$102 \overline{)21{,}828}$ = 214

COMPLETE ASSIGNMENT 1.3.

Division

Division is the process of finding how many times one number (the *divisor*) is contained in another (the *dividend*). The result is called the *quotient.* If anything remains after the division is completed, it is called the *remainder*. In example V, 47 ÷ 2 = 23 (with 1 left over), 47 is the dividend, 2 is the divisor, 1 is the remainder, and 23 with a remainder of (1) is the quotient.

Use shortcuts and simplifications to perform the fundamental process of division rapidly and accurately.

EXAMPLE V

```
   23 (1)
2 ) 47
    4
    -
     7
     6
     -
     1
```

STEPS in Long Division

1. Write the divisor in front of and the dividend inside of a division bracket ($\overline{)\quad}$).
2. As the first partial dividend, use only as many digits at the left of the dividend as you need in order to have a number that is equal to or larger than the divisor.
3. Write the number of times the divisor will go into the partial dividend selected in Step 2.
4. Multiply the divisor by this answer, write the product under the partial dividend, and subtract.
5. Next to the remainder thus obtained, bring down the next digit of the dividend to form the second partial dividend.
6. Divide as before, and repeat the process until all the digits of the dividend have been used.

EXAMPLE W

```
          174        STEP 3
164 ) 28,536         STEPS 1 & 2
      164            STEP 4
      ----
      1213           STEP 5
      1148
      ----
        656          STEP 6
        656
        ---
          0
```

When the partial dividend is smaller than the divisor, a zero must be placed in the quotient above that digit. This process is continued until the partial dividend is at least as large as the divisor. Then continue the long division steps, as shown in example X.

EXAMPLE X

```
      20 108
34 ) 683,672
     68
     --
       36
       34
       --
        272
        272
        ---
          0
```

Checking Division

To check division, simply multiply the quotient by the divisor and add any remainder to the product. The result will equal the original dividend. (Examples Y and Z provide checks for examples W and X.)

EXAMPLE Y

```
   174
  ×164
   696
 10 44
 17 4
28,536
```

EXAMPLE Z

```
  20,108
     ×34
  80 432
 603 24
 683,672
```

NOTE: Division is the reverse process of multiplication.

Dividing by 10

To divide by 10, drop the digit at the extreme right of the dividend; the dropped digit will be the remainder.

EXAMPLE AA

790 ÷ 10 = 79 (0 remainder)

EXAMPLE BB

3,652 ÷ 10 = 365 (2 remainder)

Dividing by 100

To divide by 100, drop the two right-hand digits of the dividend—they will be the remainder.

EXAMPLE CC

81,400 ÷ 100 = 814 (0 remainder)

EXAMPLE DD

257,948 ÷ 100 = 2,579 (48 remainder)

Dividing When Divisor and Dividend End with Zeros

When a divisor and dividend both end with zeros, a division shortcut is to delete the ending zeros common to both and then divide.

EXAMPLE EE

Both divisor and dividend end with zeros	Zeros common to divisor and dividend have been dropped	Answer
8,400 ÷ 200	84 ÷ 2	42
46,000 ÷ 2,300	460 ÷ 23	20
42,000 ÷ 100	420 ÷ 1	420
20,000,000 ÷ 4,000	20,000 ÷ 4	5,000
2,760 ÷ 270	276 ÷ 27	10 (6 remainder)
3,200 ÷ 1,000	32 ÷ 10	3 (2 remainder)

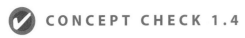

CONCEPT CHECK 1.4

Divide:

```
                21 <—— quotient
divisor ——> 32)683 <—— dividend
               64
                43
                32
                11 <—— remainder
```

Dividing by 10: 860 ÷ 10 = 86

863 ÷ 10 = 86 (3 remainder)

Dividing by 100: 19,300 ÷ 100 = 193

19,346 ÷ 100 = 193 (46 remainder)

Check:

divisor × quotient + remainder = dividend

32 × 21 + 11 = 683

COMPLETE ASSIGNMENT 1.4.

Estimating

Estimating When Multiplying

Estimate answers before performing operations.

Is estimating a final answer necessary when many, if not most, of all office computations are done on a calculator or a computer? **YES.** In using any device to make computations, it is possible to omit keystrokes, accidentally repeat keystrokes, or shift/omit decimal points. There is a great deal of difference between three items at $14.87 each and three items at $1,487 each. When working with calculations in any manner—such as entering items into a spreadsheet, a cash register, or a calculator—the operator should always have a mental estimate of the final product.

Mentally estimating an answer provides a good method for checking whether or not your product is a reasonable answer.

STEPS to Estimate a Multiplication Answer

1. Round the *multiplicand* and *multiplier* to the nearest 10 for two-digit numbers, the nearest 100 for three-digit numbers, the nearest 1,000 for four-digit numbers, etc.
2. Drop the zeros to the right of the non-zero numbers.
3. Mentally multiply the non-zero numbers to determine the base product.
4. Reinsert *all* zeros dropped in Step 2.

EXAMPLE FF

				Reinsert Zeros	
Problem	**Round to**	**Drop Zeros**	**Base Product**	**Estimated Answer**	**Real Answer**
68 × 21	70 × 20	7 × 2	14	1,400	1,428
693 × 1,957	700 × 2,000	7 × 2	14	1,400,000	1,356,201
7,869 × 43,242	8,000 × 40,000	8 × 4	32	320,000,000	340,271,298
9 × 511,739	9 × 500,000	9 × 5	45	4,500,000	4,605,651
882 × 39 × 134	900 × 40 × 100	9 × 4 × 1	36	3,600,000	4,609,332

Estimating When Dividing

Before doing long division problems, estimate a whole-number answer. The process of mentally estimating whole-number answers helps to avoid major and embarrassing errors.

STEPS to Estimate a Long Division Answer

1. Round the *divisor* and *dividend* to the nearest 10 for two-digit numbers, the nearest 100 for three-digit numbers, the nearest 1,000 for four-digit numbers, etc.
2. Drop the number of zeros common to both.
3. Mentally divide the remaining divisor into the remaining dividend.

EXAMPLE GG

Problem	Round to	Drop Zeros	Estimated Answer	Real Answer
77 ÷ 39	80 ÷ 40	8 ÷ 4	2	1.97
196 ÷ 63	200 ÷ 60	20 ÷ 6	3*	3.11*
2,891 ÷ 114	3,000 ÷ 100	30 ÷ 1	30	25.36
592 ÷ 29	600 ÷ 30	60 ÷ 3	20	20.41
18,476 ÷ 384	20,000 ÷ 400	200 ÷ 4	50	48.11
917 ÷ 186	900 ÷ 200	9 ÷ 2	4*	4.93*
21,716,412 ÷ 40,796	20,000,000 ÷ 40,000	2,000 ÷ 4	500	532.32
99,624 ÷ 476	100,000 ÷ 500	1,000 ÷ 5	200	209.29
29,200 ÷ 316	30,000 ÷ 300	300 ÷ 3	100	92.41

CONCEPT CHECK 1.5

ESTIMATING MULTIPLICATION ANSWERS

Problem	Round to	Drop Zeros	Base Product	Reinsert Zeroes Estimated Answer	Real Answer
47 × 31	50 × 30	5 × 3	15	1,500	1,457
498 × 221	500 × 200	5 × 2	10	100,000	110,058

ESTIMATING DIVISION ANSWERS

Problem	Round to	Drop Zeros	Estimated Answer	Real Answer
88 ÷ 29	90 ÷ 30	9 ÷ 3	3	3.03
9,811 ÷ 394	10,000 ÷ 400	100 ÷ 4	25	24.90

COMPLETE ASSIGNMENT 1.5.

Chapter Terms for Review

addend
difference
multiplicand
subtrahend
credit balance
minuend
remainder
sum
factors
quotient
divisor
product
dividend
multiplier

*Since 20 ÷ 6 and 9 ÷ 2 would result in a remainder, it is reasonable to assume the real number will be *larger.*

The Bottom Line

Summary of chapter learning objectives:

Learning Objective	Summary	Example
1.1	Using shortcuts and simplifications to perform addition rapidly and accurately	Add the following, using the technique indicated. **Number combinations** 1. 8, 2, 3, 2, +5 2. 18, 62, 43, 27, +80 **Repeated digits** 3. 52, 58, 57, 52, +51 **Counting by tens** 4. 23, 41, 37, 56, +42 Add and then check by adding both vertically and horizontally. 5. 22 + 54 + 63 + 37 = ____ 27 + 82 + 44 + 19 = ____ 83 + 39 + 72 + 12 = ____ 91 + 71 + 21 + 84 = ____ __ + __ + __ + __ = ____
1.2	Using shortcuts and simplifications to perform subtraction rapidly and accurately	Subtract the following and then check by addition. 6. 228 − 134 = ____ ; ____ + 134 = ____ 7. 335 − 217 = ____ ; ____ + 217 = ____ Subtract horizontally and check. 8. 245 − 130 = ____ 432 − 212 = ____ 381 − 270 = ____ 183 − 111 = ____ ___ − ___ = ____ Subtract by changing numbers. 9. 53 − 18
1.3	Using shortcuts and simplifications to perform multiplication rapidly and accurately	Multiply. 10. 227 × 143 **Multiplying by numbers ending in zero** 11. 437 × 100 12. 879 × 10 **Multiplying by 25** 13. 354 × 25 **Multiplying by 50** 14. 846 × 50

Summary of chapter learning objectives

Learning Objective	Summary	Example
1.4	Using shortcuts and simplifications to perform division rapidly and accurately	Divide and check the answer by multiplication. 15. 27)1,512 27 × ____ **Dividing by numbers ending in 0** 16. 8,430 ÷ 10 = ____ 17. 127,400 ÷ 100 = ____ **Dividing when both divisor and dividend end with zeros** 18. 7,400 ÷ 200 = ____ 19. 53,200 ÷ 400 = ____ 20. 140,000 ÷ 2,000 = ____
1.5	Estimating answers before performing operations	Estimate these multiplication answers. Show your rounding, dropping of zeros with base product, estimated answer, and real answer.

Problem	Round to	Dropped Zeros and Base Product	Estimated Answer	Real Answer
21. 47 × 31	____	____	____	____
22. 498 × 221	____	____	____	____

Estimate these division answers. Show your rounding, dropping of zeros, estimated answer, and real answer.

Problem	Round to	Drop Zeros	Estimated Answer	Real Answer
23. 88 ÷ 29	____	____	____	____
24. 9,811 ÷ 394	____	____	____	____

Answers: 1. 20 **2.** 230 **3.** 270 **4.** 199 **5.** 821 **6.** 94 **7.** 118 **8.** 518 **9.** 35 **10.** 32,461 **11.** 43,700 **12.** 8,790 **13.** 8,850 **14.** 42,300 **15.** 56 **16.** 843 **17.** 1,274 **18.** 37 **19.** 133 **20.** 70 **21.** 50 × 30; 5 × 3 = 15; 1,500, 1457 **22.** 500 × 200; 5 × 2 = 10; 100,000; 110,058 **23.** 90 ÷ 30; 9 ÷ 3; 3; 3.03 **24.** 10,000 ÷ 400; 100 ÷ 4; 25; 24.90

Assignment 1.1: Addition Review

Name

Date Score

A (10 points) Add the following. Where possible, use combinations of ten. (1 point for each correct answer)

1.	2.	3.	4.	5.	6.	7.	8.	9.	10.
14	41	19	34	97	50	72	82	38	94
56	29	54	33	44	54	99	43	39	71
25	17	14	43	33	54	99	47	22	56
53	36	81	37	76	47	89	93	45	55
52	44	28	36	32	59	47	58	47	84
35	15	11	34	72	54	63	34	25	31
32	56	43	32	34	55	40	22	13	96
48	62	51	38	76	55	62	46	29	76
32	66	76	32	27	35	68	73	79	62

Score for A (10)

B (10 points) Add the following. (1 point for each correct answer)

11.	12.	13.	14.	15.	16.	17.	18.	19.	20.
209	782	127	920	347	852	251	885	275	479
486	280	145	751	399	428	271	115	342	413
225	438	665	359	354	112	244	316	342	180
219	473	818	822	334	238	234	584	898	418
684	655	682	807	192	959	589	736	505	415

Score for B (10)

C (10 points) Add the following. (1 point for each correct answer)

21.	22.	23.	24.	25.
248.28	201.22	234.81	238.69	586.32
820.14	513.14	371.60	982.30	222.48
306.80	250.54	271.37	376.48	348.86
521.98	2,647.55	408.55	728.90	237.64

26.	27.	28.	29.	30.
703.91	126.92	442.71	535.13	333.42
422.38	32.15	71.93	44.78	444.48
721.05	873.19	416.90	208.17	222.25
446.21	872.52	236.19	6,481.29	666.25

Score for C (10)

D **(10 points) Add the following. Use the count-by-tens-and-add-the-ones method. (1 point for each correct answer)**

31.	**32.**	**33.**	**34.**	**35.**	**36.**	**37.**	**38.**	**39.**	**40.**
10.76	20.43	33.79	45.86	33.27	11.43	88.71	94.32	55.93	22.79
31.43	82.76	42.56	22.18	98.21	27.43	56.32	74.23	10.70	43.28
88.33	30.42	12.70	33.81	90.01	11.51	83.70	21.44	30.46	12.48
33.08	64.22	21.20	10.04	11.33	21.48	44.12	63.01	47.05	53.20
12.33	56.03	22.19	80.31	33.04	11.80	23.51	34.20	80.11	30.22

Score for D (10)

E **(30 points) Business Application. Below is the first part of a weekly sales summary—the Weekly Sales Report for the computer department. Complete the totals, both horizontal and vertical, and verify your addition by comparing the vertical and horizontal grand totals. (2 points for each column/row; 4 points for grand total)**

DEPARTMENT SALES REPORT
Week of December 11–17, 19XX

Department: COMPUTERS

SALESPERSON	SUN	MON	TUE	WED	THU	FRI	SAT	TOTAL
WHALEN	3,443	———	———	8,643	3,176	7,885	9,378	
TSAO	———	8,772	———	9,483	7,339	8,113	9,771	
CULVER	8,722	2,443	3,114	5,729	6,193	———	———	
HERNANDEZ	6,117	8,783	———	———	5,685	9,473	11,492	
INGAKE	———	3,114	8,492	7,652	3,994	14,119	12,378	
GREENBERG	———	———	5,141	2,739	8,941	2,836	10,242	
TOTALS								

Score for E (30)

F **(30 points) Business Application. Below is the second part of the weekly sales summary—the Consolidated Sales Report for the entire store. Fill in the figures from the above department report and complete the totals, both horizontal and vertical. Verify your addition by comparing the horizontal and vertical grand totals. (2 points for each column/row; 4 points for grand total)**

STORE SALES REPORT
Week of December 11–17, 19XX

DEPARTMENT	SUN	MON	TUE	WED	THU	FRI	SAT	TOTAL
HOME AUDIO	3,465	1,147	1,523	2,403	1,773	2,873	3,432	
AUTO AUDIO	1,278	1,785	1,713	2,117	2,563	3,499	9,971	
VIDEO/TV	15,230	12,377	10,429	9,384	8,773	11,245	13,486	
COMPUTERS								
TELECOMM	849	722	531	733	1,012	1,239	1,375	
GAMES	882	248	379	287	415	978	1,015	
REPAIRS	732	892	384	658	981	1,043	1,774	
TOTALS								

Score for F (30)

Assignment 1.2: Subtraction Review

Name ______________________

Date ______________ Score ______________

A (18 points) Subtract the following. (One point for each correct answer)

1. 77	**2.** 50	**3.** 72	**4.** 63	**5.** 53	**6.** 38	**7.** 92	**8.** 83	**9.** 60
−16	−23	−25	−29	−48	−49	−16	−65	−10

10. 39	**11.** 40	**12.** 13	**13.** 73	**14.** 37	**15.** 68	**16.** 99	**17.** 57	**18.** 91
−36	−31	−26	−14	−22	−39	−27	−43	−69

Score for A (18) ______

B (12 points) Subtract the following. Then check your subtraction by adding the subtrahend and the difference and comparing your total to the minuend. (Two points for each correct answer)

19. 584	**20.** 963	**21.** 92	**22.** 714	**23.** 616	**24.** 7,116
−173	−874	−491	−30	−333	−3,007

Score for B (12) ______

C (6 points) Subtract the following. (1 point for each correct answer)

25. $97.17	**26.** $15.67	**27.** $71.69	**28.** $43.21	**29.** $80.41	**30.** $90.61
−23.19	−0.88	−10.87	−47.18	−41.80	−20.50

Score for C (6) ______

D (9 points) Subtract the following. (One and one-half points for each correct answer)

31. $8,042.88	**32.** $964.38	**33.** $9,011.09	**34.** $7,430.29	**35.** $3,385.03	**36.** $1,029.27
−3,400.07	−201.83	−795.08	−2,597.73	−233.42	−89.27

Score for D (9) ______

E (15 points) Sometimes it is necessary to make a double subtraction. The following problems are of this type. (3 points for each correct final answer)

37. $7,672.18	**38.** $11,739.93	**39.** $734.12	**40.** $745.89	**41.** $1,837,042.03
−564.27	−3,142.18	−672.18	−250.15	−6,218.18
−124.13	−1,694.25	−13.14	−224.13	−39,917.16

Score for E (15) ______

F **(20 points) Business Application. In many cases, multiple subtractions each are required to complete a business transaction. (1 point for each intermediate answer; 2 points for each final answer)**

WINTER CATALOG CLEARANCE SALE ON SOFTWARE AND GAMES
10% REDUCTIONS ON CATALOG ORDERS
10% PREFERRED CUSTOMER DISCOUNTS
MAIL-IN REBATE OFFERS

Item	"Football Pro"	"Nemesis"	"Harpoon 97"	"Mind"	"Formula 1"
List Price	$43.95	$45.70	$42.25	$49.95	$53.75
Less 10% Catalog Rate	−4.40	−4.57	−4.23	−5.00	−5.38
Less 10% Preferred Customer Rate	−3.96	−4.11	−3.80	−4.50	−4.84
Mail-in Rebate	−7.50	−6.25	−7.50	−6.75	−5.75
Your Price					

Score for F (20)

G **(20 points) Business Application. Maintaining a budget involves both addition and subtraction. A budget sometimes keeps a continuous record of cash income and expenses. Study the example, and then complete the balances. (2 points for each balance)**

Date 2/1/98	To	Subtract Expenses	Add Income	Balance
				$1,475.38
2/2/98	Salary Income		$700.00	2,175.38
2/3/98	Hinson Real Estate	$550.00		1,625.38
2/5/98	PG&E	23.22		
2/6/98	Pacific Bell	18.76		
2/6/98	Macy's	43.22		
2/10/98	Chevron	15.75		
2/16/98	Salary Income		$700.00	
2/17/98	Fitness USA	25.00		
2/18/98	John Simms, D.D.S.	30.00		
2/23/98	Prudential Insurance	17.73		
2/25/98	Visa	85.42		
2/27/98	General Motors Finance	257.87		

Score for G (20)

Assignment 1.3: Muiltiplication Review

Name ____________________

Date ____________________ Score

A (20 points) Multiply the following. (Half point for each correct answer)

1. $2 \times 12 =$ ______	**2.** $8 \times 16 =$ ______	**3.** $13 \times 40 =$ ______	**4.** $12 \times 36 =$ ______
5. $9 \times 10 =$ ______	**6.** $5 \times 15 =$ ______	**7.** $15 \times 16 =$ ______	**8.** $70 \times 6 =$ ______
9. $8 \times 9 =$ ______	**10.** $6 \times 12 =$ ______	**11.** $12 \times 12 =$ ______	**12.** $50 \times 8 =$ ______
13. $6 \times 8 =$ ______	**14.** $8 \times 12 =$ ______	**15.** $4 \times 20 =$ ______	**16.** $56 \times 80 =$ ______
17. $6 \times 6 =$ ______	**18.** $7 \times 22 =$ ______	**19.** $8 \times 11 =$ ______	**20.** $11 \times 800 =$ ______
21. $2 \times 14 =$ ______	**22.** $9 \times 22 =$ ______	**23.** $8 \times 17 =$ ______	**24.** $31 \times 50 =$ ______

Score for A (20)

B (24 points) Find the products. (2 points for each correct answer)

25. 1,728 × 42	**26.** 3,026 × 372	**27.** 38,246 × 8,297	**28.** 5,017 × 201	**29.** 3,600 × 300	**30.** 7,179 × 71
31. 8,222 × 509	**32.** 67,406 × 3,006	**33.** 1,236 × 444	**34.** 27,000 × 420	**35.** 8,125 × 279	**36.** 4,017 × 375

Score for B (24)

C (15 points) Multiply by using shortcuts. (3 points for each correct answer)

37. 3,684 × 50	**38.** 4,999 × 50	**39.** 6,642 × 25	**40.** 3,212 × 50	**41.** 1,376 × 25

Score for C (15)

D (9 points) Multiply the three factors. (1 point for each final product)

42. $17 \times 22 \times 31 =$ ______	**43.** $47 \times 16 \times 70 =$ ______	**44.** $33 \times 33 \times 33 =$ ______
45. $14 \times 100 \times 7 =$ ______	**46.** $915 \times 40 \times 20 =$ ______	**47.** $10 \times 10 \times 10 =$ ______
48. $30 \times 30 \times 30 =$ ______	**49.** $1{,}116 \times 3 \times 18 =$ ______	**50.** $2{,}000 \times 7 \times 4 =$ ______

Score for D (9)

E **(20 points) Complete the five multiplication problems, then add the five products. (1 point for each correct answer; 5 points for each correct total)**

51. 12 × 12.00 = ________	**57.** 21 × 7 × 16 = ________
52. 27 × 8.16 = ________	**58.** 13 × 101 × 22 = ________
53. 104 × 3.52 = ________	**59.** 33 × 14 × 7 = ________
54. 6 × 92.92 = ________	**60.** 99 × 11 × 100 = ________
55. 55 × 32.50 = ________	**61.** 3 × 88 × 100 = ________
56. Total = ________	**62.** Total = ________

Score for E (20)

F **(20 points) Business Application. Complete the merchandise inventory TOTAL column. (1 point for each correct total; 4 points for correct grand total)**

MERCHANDISE INVENTORY
JUNE 30, 19xx

Stock Number	Description	Price	# in Stock	Total
G473-2	Blood & Magic	$39.99	58	
G763-4	Circle of Blood	$39.99	172	
G865-A	Time Lapse	$49.95	98	
G2238-1	Nemesis	$34.99	225	
G873-2	Harpoon 97	$42.75	88	
S876-3	Word Perfect Suite Upgrade	$98.77	178	
S4433	Uninstaller 4	$32.59	85	
S887-32	MagnaRAM 97	$45.79	110	
S4536	Netscape Navigator	$38.79	100	
S1322	Norton Utilities 95 2.0	$67.85	68	
S458-2	Quicken 6.0	$27.75	205	
S5382	MS Visual J++	$95.69	80	
E5673-E	Typing Tutor 7	$26.59	108	
E82-18	Corel ChemLab	$52.49	25	
E2442	Encarta 97	$45.29	307	
E3578-1	Perfect Spanish	$44.79	80	
			TOTAL	

Score for F (20)

Assignment 1.4: Division Review

Name ______________________

Date ______________ Score ______________

A (10 points) Divide the following problems mentally. (One-half point for each correct quotient)

1. 72 ÷ 6 = ______ **2.** 90 ÷ 6 = ______ **3.** 96 ÷ 8 = ______

4. 110 ÷ 5 = ______ **5.** 126 ÷ 3 = ______ **6.** 154 ÷ 7 = ______

7. 88 ÷ 22 = ______ **8.** 144 ÷ 12 = ______ **9.** 169 ÷ 13 = ______

10. 135 ÷ 9 = ______ **11.** 990 ÷ 33 = ______ **12.** 187 ÷ 11 = ______

13. 156 ÷ 12 = ______ **14.** 900 ÷ 15 = ______ **15.** 336 ÷ 12 = ______

16. 84 ÷ 12 = ______ **17.** 104 ÷ 2 = ______ **18.** 300 ÷ 20 = ______

19. 119 ÷ 7 = ______ **20.** 225 ÷ 15 = ______

______ Score for A (10)

B (10 points) Divide by shortcut methods. Express remainders in parentheses. (1 point for each correct answer)

21. 3,450 ÷ 487 = ______ **22.** 12,800 ÷ 100 = ______ **23.** 58,700 ÷ 100 = ______

24. 2,200 ÷ 100 = ______ **25.** 7,800 ÷ 20 = ______ **26.** 6,450 ÷ 320 = ______

27. 9,005 ÷ 100 = ______ **28.** 387 ÷ 10 = ______ **29.** 38,500 ÷ 1,000 = ______

30. 3,250,000 ÷ 10,000 = ______

______ Score for B (10)

C (50 points) Divide. Show the remainder in parentheses after the whole number in the quotient. (2 points for each correct answer)

31. 21)478 **32.** 13)2,795 **33.** 23)14,076 **34.** 7)4,919

35. 36)6,436 **36.** 23)478 **37.** 271)50,001 **38.** 33)97,382

39. 926)926,007 **40.** 77)12,770 **41.** 506)10,238 **42.** 9)818,173

43. 700)362,497 **44.** 111)34,173 **45.** 88)97,817 **46.** 13)$67,209

47. 6)$13.20 **48.** 54)78,540 **49.** 51)100 **50.** 26)111,013

51. 66)73,428 **52.** 1,014)20,016 **53.** 66)17,209 **54.** 65)372,000

55. 29)58,004,316

______ Score for C (50)

D (10 points) Divide and check the following problems. (2 points for each correct answer)

56. $22\overline{)1364}$ **57.** $31\overline{)1395}$ **58.** $92\overline{)7284}$ **59.** $21\overline{)2214}$ **60.** $31\overline{)642}$

Check:

× ____ × ____ × ____ × ____ × ____

= ____ = ____ = ____ = ____ = ____

Score for D (10)

E (20 points) Business Applications. As an estimator for a printing company, you must estimate the paper costs for printing jobs. Paper is priced by the ream, which is 500 pages. Compute the paper costs of the jobs below. (1 point for each correct computation)

# of Booklets	# of Pages	Total Pages	Reams of Paper	Cost per Ream	Total Paper Cost
250	66			$2.00	
120	150			$4.25	
75	220			$4.83	
110	250			$3.75	
25	280			$3.15	
30	250			$4.10	
		Total Reams		Total Paper Cost	

Score for E (20)

Assignment 1.5: Estimating

Name ______________________

Date ______________ Score ______________

A **(30 points) Estimate an answer for each of the following problems. Show your rounding, dropping of zeros with base product, and final estimate. ($\frac{1}{2}$ point for each correct answer)**

Problem	Rounding to	Dropped Zeros and Base Product	Estimated Answer
1. 1,095 × 427			
2. 78,221 × 6,099			
3. 34,007 × 80			
4. 56 × 1,528			
5. 18 × 2,855 × 93			
6. 20 × 17 × 19			
7. 2,997 × 13			
8. 41 × 19 × 3			
9. 212 × 101 × 99			
10. 23 × 10,322			
11. 777 × 777			
12. 29,301 × 21			
13. 72,111 × 108			
14. 13 × 100 × 6			
15. 99 × 99 × 99			
16. 28 × 42			
17. 111 × 39			
18. 7 × 99			
19. 204 × 17			
20. 11 × 12 × 13			

____

Score for A (30)

B **(40 points) Estimate an answer for each of the following problems. Show your rounding, dropping of zeros with base product, estimated answer, and real answer. (2 points for each correct answer)**

Problem	Round to	Dropped Zeros and Base Product	Estimated Answer	Real Answer
21. 883 × 294	______	______	______	______
22. 42,100 × 412	______	______	______	______
23. 19,965 × 492	______	______	______	______
24. 89 × 33	______	______	______	______
25. 983 × 204	______	______	______	______

______
Score for B (40)

C **(40 points) Estimate an answer for each of the following division problems. Show your rounding, dropping of zeros, estimated answer, and real answer. Round to two decimal places. ($\frac{1}{2}$ point for each correct answer)**

Problem	Round to	Drop Zeros	Estimated Answer	Real Answer
26. 121 ÷ 41	______	______	______	______
27. 31,500 ÷ 422	______	______	______	______
28. 921 ÷ 78	______	______	______	______
29. 19,779 ÷ 95	______	______	______	______
30. 493 ÷ 28	______	______	______	______
31. 21,973 ÷ 1,132	______	______	______	______
32. 101,753 ÷ 51	______	______	______	______
33. 74 ÷ 42	______	______	______	______
34. 31,793 ÷ 210	______	______	______	______
35. 5,900 ÷ 287	______	______	______	______
36. 99,873 ÷ 994	______	______	______	______

______
Score for C (40)

Notes

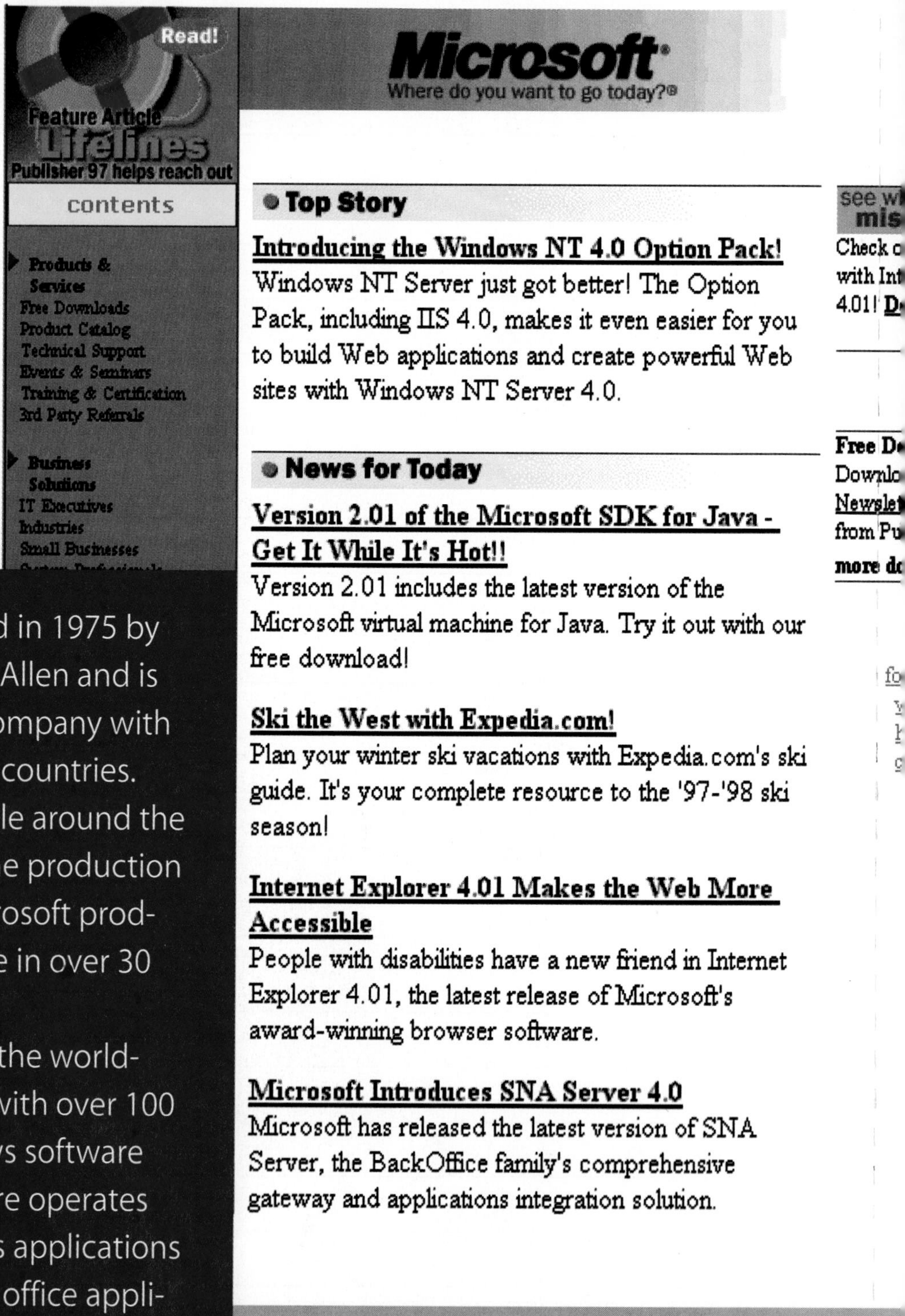
Read!
Feature Article
Lifelines
Publisher 97 helps reach out
contents
Products & Services
Free Downloads
Product Catalog
Technical Support
Events & Seminars
Training & Certification
3rd Party Referrals
Business Solutions
IT Executives
Industries
Small Businesses
Microsoft
Where do you want to go today?
Top Story
Introducing the Windows NT 4.0 Option Pack!
Windows NT Server just got better! The Option Pack, including IIS 4.0, makes it even easier for you to build Web applications and create powerful Web sites with Windows NT Server 4.0.
News for Today
Version 2.01 of the Microsoft SDK for Java - Get It While It's Hot!!
Version 2.01 includes the latest version of the Microsoft virtual machine for Java. Try it out with our free download!
Ski the West with Expedia.com!
Plan your winter ski vacations with Expedia.com's ski guide. It's your complete resource to the '97-'98 ski season!
Internet Explorer 4.01 Makes the Web More Accessible
People with disabilities have a new friend in Internet Explorer 4.01, the latest release of Microsoft's award-winning browser software.
Microsoft Introduces SNA Server 4.0
Microsoft has released the latest version of SNA Server, the BackOffice family's comprehensive gateway and applications integration solution.

Microsoft was founded in 1975 by William Gates and Paul Allen and is now an international company with offices in more than 48 countries. More than 20,000 people around the world are involved in the production and distribution of Microsoft products, which are available in over 30 languages.

Microsoft dominates the worldwide software market, with over 100 million units of Windows software sold. Its systems software operates most computers, and its applications software leads all other office application software in sales.

Visit the Microsoft home page at www.microsoft.com for information on the company, its products, training and education, research, services, and employment.

2 Word Problems and Equations

Learning Objectives

By studying this chapter and completing all the assignments, you will be able to:

1. Use mental computations in simple addition, subtraction, multiplication, and division.
2. Use a systematic approach to solve word problems involving basic mathematical processes.
3. Apply formulas to solve rate, time, and distance problems.
4. Solve simple numeric equations.
5. Recognize numeric relationships in a series.
6. Do quick mental calculations through a process of rounding numbers.

In business, most of the problems to be solved are in the form of word problems. For example, "We need to ship 100 pianos to Chicago. How many trucks do we need, and how much will it cost?" Your job is to find the numbers in the problem and then apply the fundamental processes: add, subtract, multiply, or divide.

Mental Computations

Use mental computations in simple addition, subtraction, multiplication, and division.

Rapid and accurate number computations of a simple nature need to be made frequently in business. Practicing easy computation drills will improve your speed and accuracy in using the four fundamental processes.

In example A you should be able to obtain the ten answers without using pencil, paper, or an electronic calculator. Mentally compute each problem quickly. Each computation is done from left to right. In these problems, addition, subtraction, multiplication, and division are done in the sequence in which they appear.

EXAMPLE A

$7 + 3 + 8 + 4 = 22$
$27 - 2 - 5 + 8 + 2 = 30$
$60 \div 2 \div 3 \div 5 = 2$
$3 + 4 + 2 + 10 = 19$
$3 \times 4 \times 2 \times 10 = 240$
$28 \div 4 \times 5 \times 2 - 7 \div 9 = 7$
$26 \div 2 + 2 \times 2 \times 2 \div 6 + 10 = 20$
$180 \times 2 \div 6 - 20 \div 8 \times 5 = 25$
$100 \times 5 - 20 - 80 - 40 \div 6 = 60$
$4{,}000 \div 2 + 100 \div 7 - 299 = 1$

CONCEPT CHECK 2.1

Practice computations until you can do them mentally without extra copying or writing. Use the simplification techniques in Chapter 1 whenever possible: number combinations, repeated digits, counting by tens and adding ones, subtraction by changing numbers, multiplying numbers ending in zeros, and dividing numbers ending in zeros. Do the following computations mentally:

$7 + 3 + 6 + 6 + 6 \times 20 \div 10 + 31 = 87$
Think: $10 \quad + (3 \times 6 = 18) \quad 28 \quad (2 \times 28) + 0 \quad 560 \quad (560) - 0 \quad 56 \quad (66, 76, 86, 87) = 87$

$78 - 29 + 7 + 7 + 7 \times 40 = 2{,}800$
Think: $(79 - 30 = 49) \quad + (3 \times 7 = 21) \quad 70 \quad (7 \times 4) + 00 = 2{,}800$

Solving Word Problems

Use a systematic approach to solve word problems involving basic mathematical processes.

You might have little difficulty with computations expressed in numbers only. In example B you would quickly answer 350.

EXAMPLE B

$(15 + 15 + 10) \times 10 - 50 = 350$

However, you might not answer $350 as quickly when the business problem in example C appears, even though it uses the same numeric elements as example B.

EXAMPLE C

A company orders carpeting for three offices measuring 15 square yards, 15 square yards, and 10 square yards, respectively. A carpet dealer sells the carpet for $10 a square yard and gives a $50 discount when the sale is for three or more offices. How much would the company pay to have the three offices carpeted?

15 sq yd + 15 sq yd + 10 sq yd = 40 sq yd
40 sq yd × $10 = $400 gross price
$400 − $50 discount = $350 net price

Business problems using computations simply require addition, subtraction, multiplication, and division.

STEPS to Solve Word Problems

Read the entire problem carefully and then

1. Determine what is being requested.
2. Determine the processes to be used to solve the problem.

EXAMPLE D

STEP 1 What is requested: How much money would the company pay?

STEP 2 The process to be used:
Add square yards in the 3 offices: 15 + 15 + 10 = 40
Multiply the $10 per square yard cost by total square yards: 40 × $10 = $400
Subtract the $50 discount: $400 − $50 = $350

Some word problems will involve all four fundamental processes: addition, subtraction, multiplication, and division. Refer to example E.

EXAMPLE E

Phoebe owns half of a small bakery. Last week she baked 6 cakes on Monday, 9 on Tuesday, 11 on Wednesday, 8 on Thursday, and 6 on Friday. She sold all cakes for $9 each. It cost Phoebe $5 to make each cake; the rest was her profit on each cake. Phoebe split her profit evenly with her partner. How much did her partner receive from last week's cakes?

STEP 1 What is requested: How much money did Phoebe's partner receive?

STEP 2 The process to be used:
Add the cakes baked: 6 + 9 + 11 + 8 + 6 = 40
Subtract cost from sales price: $9 − $5 = $4 profit per cake
Multiply the $4 profit per cake by cakes sold: 40 × $4 = $160
Divide total profit by 2: $160 ÷ 2 = $80 received by partner

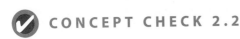

CONCEPT CHECK 2.2

Summary of steps for solving word problems:

1. Determine what is being requested.
2. Determine the processes to be used to solve the problem.

Problem: Maria wants to upholster three chairs. Two chairs will require 4 yards of material each; the third will require 3 yards. One material is $32 per yard; the other is $24 per yard. What is the difference between the costs of the two materials for upholstering the chairs?

STEP 1 What is requested: Difference in cost between the two materials

STEP 2 The process to be used:
Add amount of material needed: 4 yd + 4 yd + 3 yd = 11 yd
Cost of material for three chairs, first material: 11 yd × $32 per yd = $352
Cost of material for three chairs, second material: 11 yd × $24 per yd = $264
Difference in cost between the two materials: $352 − $264 = $88 difference in cost

Solving Rate, Time, and Distance Problems

LEARNING OBJECTIVES 3

Apply formulas to solve rate, time, and distance problems.

In some business word problems, you must determine how much is done in a given amount of time at a specific speed. These rate, time, and distance problems are solved with a simple formula: Rate (speed) × Time = Distance (amount done). Given any two factors, it is easy to find the third.

Rate × Time = **Distance**
Distance ÷ Time = **Rate**
Distance ÷ Rate = **Time**

EXAMPLE F

Jan traveled at 35 miles per hour for 5 hours. How far did Jan travel?
35 mph × 5 hr = 175 mi
(Rate × Time = Distance)

EXAMPLE G

Jan traveled 175 miles in 5 hours. How fast was Jan traveling?
175 mi ÷ 5 hr = 35 mph
(Distance ÷ Time = Rate)

EXAMPLE H

At 35 miles per hour, how long would it take Jan to travel a total of 175 miles?
175 mi ÷ 35 mph = 5 hr
(Distance ÷ Rate = Time)

EXAMPLE I

Jan and Ahmed start traveling toward each other from 300 miles apart. Jan is traveling at 35 miles per hour; Ahmed is traveling at 40 miles per hour. How much time will elapse before they meet?
Distance = 300 mi
Total rate = 35 mph (Jan) + 40 mph (Ahmed) = 75 mph
300 mi ÷ 75 mph = 4 hr
(Distance ÷ Rate = Time)

EXAMPLE J

Jan and Ahmed start traveling toward each other from 300 miles apart. Jan is traveling at 35 miles per hour; Ahmed is traveling at 40 miles per hour. How much distance will Jan travel before they meet?

Total rate = 35 mph (Jan) + 40 mph (Ahmed) = 75 mph

Time = 300 mi ÷ 75 mph = 4 hr

Jan's distance = 35 mph (Jan's Rate) × 4 hr (Time) = 140 mi

EXAMPLE K

Mary needs to type a term paper that will be 30 pages long. Each page contains about 200 words. If Mary can type 40 words per minute, how many minutes will it take her to complete the paper?

Choose a formula: We know distance (amount done) and speed (rate). Therefore, we choose the formula for time.

Distance (amount done) ÷ Rate (speed) = Time

30 pages × 2,000 words = 6,000 words ÷ 40 wpm = 150 min

EXAMPLE L

Flora also had a paper to type, but hers was 9,000 words in length. She was able to type it in 150 minutes. How fast did she type?

Choose formula: We know distance (amount done) and time. Therefore, we choose the formula for rate.

Distance (amount done) ÷ Time = Rate (speed)

9,000 words ÷ 150 min = 60 wpm

EXAMPLE M

It is approximately 400 miles from San Francisco to Los Angeles. Roy's friends tell him he can make the trip in 6 hours if he averages 60 miles per hour. Is this true?

Choose formula: We know the rate and the time, so we choose the formula for distance.

Rate (speed) × Time = Distance (amount done)

60 mph × 6 hr = 360 mi

Can he get there in 6 hours? **No.**

CONCEPT CHECK 2.3

The basic formula:

a. Rate (speed) × Time = Distance (amount done)
   If you know any **two** factors, you can find the **third:**

b. Distance (amount done) ÷ Time = Rate (speed)

c. Distance (amount done) ÷ Rate (speed) = Time

Apply the appropriate formula above to answer the following question: A machine that produces tortillas at the Baja Restaurant can produce 200 tortillas per hour, or 1,600 tortillas in an 8-hour day. A new machine can produce 3,000 tortillas in 6 hours. How many more tortillas per hour can the new machine produce than the old one?

Distance (amount done) ÷ Time = Rate

1,600 tortillas ÷ 8 hr = 200 per hr

3,000 tortillas ÷ 6 hr = 500 per hr

Difference: 500 − 200 = 300 more tortillas per hr

Solving Simple Numeric Equations

LEARNING OBJECTIVES 4

Solve simple numeric equations.

Numeric sentences in which both sides of an equal sign may contain calculations are called *equations.* For example, five plus five equals twelve minus two $(5 + 5 = 12 - 2)$ is an equation, as is seven minus one equals thirty divided by five $(7 - 1 = 30 \div 5)$.

For an equation to be true, the numbers on the left of the equal sign must always compute to the same answer as the numbers on the right of the equal sign. Moving a number from one side of the equation to the other changes its sign. A plus sign will change to minus; a minus sign will change to plus. A multiplication sign will change to division; a division sign will change to multiplication. Note the examples shown below.

EXAMPLE N

$6 + 4 + 5 = 17 - 2$

Change the $+ 5$ and the $- 2$:

$6 + 4 + 2 = 17 - 5$

Check: $6 + 4 + 2 = 12$

$17 - 5 = 12$

Change only the $- 2$:

$6 + 4 + 5 + 2 = 17$

Change only the $+ 5$:

$6 + 4 = 17 - 2 - 5$

$6 + 4 = 10$ and $17 - 2 - 5 = 10$

EXAMPLE O

$3 \times 8 = 48 \div 2$

Change the $\times 8$ and $\div 2$:

$3 \times 2 = 48 \div 8$

Check: $3 \times 2 = 6$

$48 \div 8 = 6$

Change only the $\div 2$:

$3 \times 8 \times 2 = 48$

Change only the $\times 8$:

$3 = 48 \div 2 \div 8$

A numeric equation may be incomplete, with one factor missing, but provide enough information to be completed. Note the examples below.

EXAMPLE P

$6 + 2 = 5 + ?$

$6 + 2 = 8$ so $5 + ? = 8$

Therefore $? = 3$

EXAMPLE Q

$15 - 3 = 2 + ?$

$15 - 3 = 12$ so $2 + ? = 12$

Therefore $? = 10$

EXAMPLE R

$7 + 3 + 6 = 4 + 4 + ?$

$7 + 3 + 6 = 16$ so $4 + 4 + ? = 16$

Therefore $? = 8$

EXAMPLE S

$20 \div 5 = 2 \times ?$

$20 \div 5 = 4$ so $2 \times ? = 4$

Therefore $? = 2$

In business, numeric sentences with equations frequently compare items. Note the following examples.

EXAMPLE T

4 items at \$0.50 each = 10 items at ? each

4 items at \$0.50 each = \$2.00

10 items at ? each = \$2.00

\$2.00 ÷ 10 items = \$0.20

Therefore ? = \$0.20

EXAMPLE U

6 tickets at \$5 each = 15 tickets at ? each

6 tickets at \$5 each = \$30

15 tickets at ? each = \$30

\$30 ÷ 15 tickets = \$2

Therefore ? = \$2

EXAMPLE V

A company had sales of \$25,000 and \$20,000 for January and February of last year, respectively. If January sales this year were \$30,000, what is the amount needed for February in order to equal last year's sales for the two months?

January LY \$25,000 + February LY \$20,000 = \$45,000
January \$30,000 + February (?) = \$45,000
\$45,000 − \$30,000 = \$15,000
Therefore ? = \$15,000

CONCEPT CHECK 2.4

Both sides of a true equation are equal. Each side may contain calculations.

$8 + 4 = 14 - 2$
$3 \times 6 = 36 \div 2$

A number may be moved from one side of an equation to the other by reversing its sign.

$8 = 6 + 2$	$8 - 2 = 6$	$7 + 3 = 10$	$7 = 10 - 3$
$12 = 4 \times 3$	$12 \div 3 = 4$	$24 \div 12 = 2$	$24 = 2 \times 12$

Numerical Relationships in a Series

Learning Objective 5: Recognize numeric relationships in a series.

Relationships in a series of numbers may be found by comparing the first three or four terms in a series and then extrapolating what numbers would most logically come next. For example, examining the series 320, 160, 80, 40 indicates that each term is found by dividing the preceding number by 2. The next two numbers in the series would logically be 20 and 10—that is, $40 \div 2 = 20$ and $20 \div 2 = 10$.

Examining the series 7, 14, 21, 28 suggests the addition of 7 to each preceding number. The next two numbers in this series would logically be 35 and 42 ($28 + 7 = 35$ and $35 + 7 = 42$).

In the series 5, 15, 35, 75, 155, it is difficult to see a relationship; however, a relationship does exist. Each number results from multiplying the preceding number by 2 and then adding 5. In this series, the next number would logically be 315 ($155 \times 2 + 5 = 315$).

Recognizing numeric and series relationships can be important in analyzing, communicating, and computing with numbers. These relationship series are also used frequently in initial employment tests.

CONCEPT CHECK 2.5

In studying relationships in a numeric series, it is necessary to look for patterns. Patterns most commonly fall into categories:

Addition	2, 7, 12, 17, 22, 27	(+ 5)
Alternating addition/subtraction	12, 24, 18, 30, 24, 36, 30	(+ 12, − 6)
Subtraction	39, 32, 25, 18, 11, 4	(− 7)
Alternating subtraction/addition	64, 59, 61, 56, 58, 53, 55	(− 5, + 2)
Multiplication	4, 12, 36, 108, 324, 972	(× 3)
Division	88, 44, 22, 11	(÷ 2)

You can also devise patterns such as multiplication with addition or subtraction, division with addition or subtraction, and many other combinations.

Making Quick Calculations by Rounding Numbers

LEARNING OBJECTIVES 6

Do quick mental calculations through a process of rounding numbers.

Quick calculations frequently are beneficial when working in business situations. *Rounding* odd and difficult-to-compute amounts to even whole numbers that are easier to compute is a technique often used in business. By rounding, you will be able to get quick and accurate answers without having to write out the computations.

EXAMPLE W

How much would 5 items at $2.99 each cost?

To make this computation easily, think "$2.99 is $0.01 less than $3.00." Then think "5 times $3 equals $15." Finally, think "$15.00 less $0.05 (5 × $0.01) is $14.95," which is the correct answer.

EXAMPLE X

The total cost of 3 equally priced items is $119.85. How much does one of these items cost?

To figure out this problem easily, think "$119.85 is $0.15 less than $120.00." Then think "$120 divided by 3 = $40, and $40.00 less $0.05 ($0.15 ÷ 3) is $39.95," the correct answer.

EXAMPLE Y

At 19 miles per gallon, how many miles would a car go on 16 gallons of gas?

To figure out this problem easily, think "19 is just 1 mile less than 20." Then think "16 times 20 = 320, and 320 minus 16 (16 × 1) is 304," the correct answer.

CONCEPT CHECK 2.6

You may have noticed that making quick calculations is quite similar to making estimations, which you did in Chapter 1. In fact, quick calculation is only an additional step. After estimating an answer, you determine the degree to which the estimated, or rounded, answer differs from the actual answer by mentally correcting for the amount of the estimation or rounding.

COMPLETE ASSIGNMENTS 2.1 AND 2.2.

Chapter Terms for Review

equation | numeric sentence | rounding

The Bottom Line

Summary of chapter learning objectives:

Learning Objective	Summary	Example
2.1	Using mental computations in simple addition, subtraction, multiplication, and division problems	Use mental computations. 1. Add: $4 + 3 + 8 + 11 + 9 + 2 + 3 =$ _____ 2. Add by combining numbers: $4 + 6 + 8 + 8 + 8 + 30 + 10 =$ _____ 3. Subtract: $84 - 7 - 12 - 23 =$ _____ 4. Subtract and add: $9 + 4 - 2 - 8 + 4 =$ _____ 5. Multiply and divide: $28 + 4 \times 2 \div 4 + 14 =$ _____ 6. Multiply and divide: $18 \div 3 + 10 - 5 \times 3 =$ _____
2.2	Using a systematic approach to solve world problems	Use the two-step process to solve the word problem. 7. Martha is preparing to make two dresses. One will require 3 yards of material; the other will require 4 yards of material. The material for the first dress is $12.00 per yard; the material for the second is $15.00 per yard. Buttons and trimming will cost $8.00 for each dress. What will be the total cost? Determine what is being requested. Determine the processes to be used to solve the problem. Answer: _____
2.3	Applying formula to solve rate, time, and distance problems	8. At an average rate of 50 miles per hour, how long would it take to drive 650 miles? _____ 9. At an average rate of 60 miles per hour, how far could you drive in 6 hours? _____ 10. If you drove 70 miles per hour and covered 280 miles, how much time did it take? _____
2.4	Solving simple numeric equations	11. $7 + 8 - 2 = 5 + 9 - 1$ — Change the 8 to the opposite side, and test the equation. __________ 12. $5 \times 12 = 120 \div 2$ — Change the 12 to the opposite side, and test the equation. __________ 13. $44 \div 11 = 13 - 9$ — Change the 9 to the opposite side, and test the equation. __________ 14. 18 items at $3.00 each = 6 items at ? ? = __________

The Bottom Line *Continued*

Summary of chapter learning objectives:

Learning Objective	Summary	Example
2.5	Recognizing numeric relationships in a series	Determine the relationships in the following problems, and insert the next two numbers. 15. 4, 7, 6, 9, 8, 11, _____, _____ Pattern: _____ 16. 12, 48, 24, 96, 48, _____, _____ Pattern: _____
2.6	Doing quick mental calculations through a process of rounding numbers	17. What is the cost of 8 items at $3.99 each? 18. At 59 miles per hour, how far would a car go in 20 hours?

Answers: 1. 40 **2.** 74 **3.** 42 **4.** 7 **5.** 30 **6.** 33 **7.** $112 **8.** 13 hr **9.** 360 mi **10.** 4 hr **11.** 7 − 2 = 5 + 9 − 1 − 8 **12.** 5 = 120 ÷ 2 ÷ 12 **13.** 44 ÷ 11 + 9 = 13 **14.** $9.00 **15.** (+ 3, − 1) 10, 13 **16.** (× 4, ÷ 2) 192, 96 **17.** (8 × $4.00) = $32.00 − .08 = $31.92 **18.** (60 × 20) = 1200 − 20 = 1,180 mi

Assignment 2.1: Word Problems, Equations, and Series

LEARNING OBJECTIVES 1, 4, 5

Name ____________________

Date ____________ Score ____________

A (20 points) Do the steps in the order in which they occur. Do not use an electronic calculator. (1 point for each correct answer)

1. $14 + 5 + 3 + 4 =$ ______

2. $6 \times 6 - 4 \div 8 \times 2 =$ ______

3. $17 - 3 - 2 - 5 =$ ______

4. $14 \div 2 \times 5 \times 2 + 5 =$ ______

5. $80 \div 4 \div 2 \div 5 =$ ______

6. $9 \times 2 + 2 \times 6 - 20 \div 4 =$ ______

7. $3 \times 2 \times 5 \times 3 =$ ______

8. $(4 - 3) \times 5 \times 5 \times 5 - 3 =$ ______

9. $25 \div 5 \times 3 + 1 + 11 + 2 - 6 =$ ______

10. $(12 + 12 + 12 + 14) \div 5 \times 3 + 3 =$ ______

11. $100 \times 5 - 50 \div 9 + 5 \div 11 \times 3 =$ ______

12. $(36 \div 3 \div 4 + 10 + 5 - 3) \times 3 =$ ______

13. $(15 \div 3 \times 2 + 8 - 3 + 12) \div 3 =$ ______

14. $(10 \times 8) + (20 \times 3 \div 6 \div 5) + 4 =$ ______

15. $9 \div 3 \times 7 + 4 + 5 \times 4 - 6 =$ ______

16. $680 \div 2 \div 2 + 10 \div 6 \times 2 + 6 =$ ______

17. $32 \times 2 \div 8 \times 100 + 200 \div 4 + 1 =$ ______

18. $12 + 10 + 3 + 26 + 29 \div 4 \times 3 =$ ______

19. $1{,}000 \times 4 \times 2 - 5{,}000 \div 6 =$ ______

20. $3 + 4 + 5 + 6 + 7 \div 5 \times 800 =$ ______

Score for A (20) ______

B (10 points) Do these problems without using scratch paper or an electronic calculator. (2 points for each correct answer)

21. How much would you pay for six gallons of gasoline selling at $1.50 per gallon? ______

22. How many items would you have if you had three books, seven cards, and twenty-one pencils? ______

23. If thirty-three people divided three pizzas so that each person got one piece, how many slices would each pizza have? ______

24. How much would you have if you received $7.00 from one person, $23.00 from a second, $10.50 from a third, and $4.00 from a fourth? ______

25. If 27 people were divided into three equal groups and each group added two additional members, how many members would be in each group? ______

Score for B (10) ______

C (10 points) Do the steps in the order in which they occur. Do these problems without using scratch paper or an electronic calculator. (1 point for each correct answer)

26. 12 items at $3 each plus $2 tax = ______

27. 15 watches at $30 each less a $50 discount = ______

28. 3 lamps at $22 each plus 7 bulbs at $2 each = ______

29. 100 belts at $4 each less discounts of $60 and $30 = ______

30. 3 dozen scissors at $11.20 per dozen plus a $4 shipping charge = ______

31. 8 pounds of pears at $3 per pound plus 50¢ per pound for packaging = ______

32. $38 sale price plus $3 tax less a $12 discount plus a $3 delivery charge = ______

33. 6 bath towels at \$8 each and 4 hand towels at \$3 each plus \$2.50 tax = __________

34. 4 dozen brushes at \$25 per dozen plus \$5 tax plus \$7 shipping charge = __________

35. 2 shirts at \$20 each, 4 ties at \$5 each, and 7 pairs of socks at \$2 each = __________

____
Score for C (10)

D **(20 points) Complete the following equations by supplying the missing items. (1 point for each correct answer)**

36. $21 + 3 =$ __________ $+ 8$

37. $13 +$ __________ $= 7 + 26$

38. __________ $+ 4 = 4 + 12$

39. $400 = 17 - 2 +$ __________

40. $22 - 9 =$ __________ $- 6$

41. $36 -$ __________ $= 17 + 8$

42. $9 + 17 - 3 = 4 \times$ __________ $- 5$

43. $160 \div 4 + 2 = 7 \times 7 -$ __________

44. $13 - 11 \times$ __________ $= 8 \times 8 + 16$

45. __________ $\times 3 \times 3 = 9 \div 3 \times 9$

46. $4 \times 20 =$ __________ $+ 4$

47. __________ $\div 2 = 9 - 1$

48. $64 \div 32 = 900 \div$ __________

49. $15 - 9 - 2 = 25 -$ __________

50. __________ $+ 6 = 43 - 12$

51. $(7 \times 8) - 6 =$ __________

52. $15 \times 2 \times 2 =$ __________

53. $13 \times$ __________ $= 77 - 12$

54. __________ $\times 9 = 81 - 9$

55. $4 \times$ __________ $= 10 \times 6$

____
Score for D (20)

E **(40 points) In each of the following problems, a definite relationship exists among the numbers in each series. Extend each series two items by following the correct process. (8 points for each problem; 2 points for each correct line)**

56. Extend each series below through addition.

a. 4, 8, 12, 16, __________

b. 1, 4, 5, 8, __________

c. 2, 4, 7, 11, 13, __________

d. 5, 10, 20, 35, 55, __________

57. Extend each series below through subtraction.

a. 50, 45, 40, 35, __________

b. 50, 45, 43, 38, __________

c. 100, 90, 81, 73, __________

d. 610, 600, 580, 550, __________

58. Extend each series below through multiplication.

a. 4, 8, 16, 32, __________

b. 5; 25; 125; __________

c. 2, 4, 20, 40, __________

d. 2, 4, 12, 48, __________

59. Extend each series below through division.

a. 15,625; 3,125; 625; 125; __________

b. 729, 243, 81, 27, __________

c. 10,000, 2,000, 1,000, 200, __________

d. 10,000, 5,000, 1,000, 500, __________

60. Extend each series below through combinations of the four processes above.

a. 72, 75, 69, 72, __________

b. 200, 100, 300, 150, __________

c. 6, 9, 18, 21, 42, __________

d. 240, 120, 600, 300, 1,500, __________

____
Score for E (40)

Assignment 2.2: Word Problems, Formulas, and Equations

Name ____________________

Date ____________________ Score

A (40 points) Solve the following word problems. (5 points for each correct answer)

1. A store regularly sold 2 cans of soup for $0.64. It advertised a special sale of 6 cans for $1.56. A customer bought 12 cans at the sale. How much did the customer save over the regular price? ________

2. A sales representative's car gets 18 miles to a gallon of gas. It was driven 120 miles each day for 30 days. Gas cost an average of $1.27 per gallon. What was the sales representative's total 30-day cost for gas? ________

3. A store clerk sold a customer a ruler for $0.67, three pencils for $0.29 each, notebook paper for $0.99, and an eraser for $0.35 and was given $10.00 in payment. How much change did the clerk give the customer from the $10.00? (All prices include tax.) ________

4. A college student worked at a local store for $6.00 per hour, as his class schedule permitted. The student worked 3 hours each Monday, Tuesday, Wednesday, and Thursday. He also worked 2 hours each Friday and 8 hours each Saturday. How many weeks did the student have to work to earn $792 for a new bicycle? ________

5. A box, a crate, and a trunk weigh a total of 370 pounds. The crate weighs 160 pounds. The trunk weighs 4 pounds more than the box. What does the box weigh? ________

6. A hotel has 12 floors. Each floor has 20 single-person rooms and 40 two-person rooms. What is the total guest capacity of the hotel? ________

7. A department store offers its customers socks for $1.50 per pair or $15.00 per dozen. If two customers buy 1 dozen together and each pays half the cost, how much will each customer save by paying the quantity price? ________

8. Supply Clerk A ordered 5 staplers for $27.50 total and 2 large boxes of staples for $1.75 each. Supply Clerk B ordered a box of computer disks for $8.50 and a box of computer paper for $39.95. How much more did Clerk B spend than Clerk A? (All prices include tax.) ________

____
Score for A (40)

B (10 points) Solve the following time, rate, distance problems. (5 points for each correct answer)

9. Wendy leaves Chicago to travel the 2,000 miles to Los Angeles, driving at a speed of 55 miles per hour. Mark leaves Los Angeles to travel the same 2,000-mile route to Chicago, driving at a speed of 45 miles per hour. How many miles will Mark have traveled when they meet? ________

10. Car A traveled to a destination 450 miles away at 50 miles per hour. Car B traveled to a destination 550 miles away at 55 miles per hour. How much longer did Car B travel than Car A? ________

________ Score for B (10)

C (40 points) Solve each of the problems without writing any computations on paper and without using a calculator or a computer. (2 points for each correct answer)

11. 5 items at $1.99 = ________

12. 2 items at $7.98 = ________

13. 4 items at $19.98 = ________

14. 2 items at $49.96 = ________

15. 15 items at $0.99 = ________

16. 10 items at $9.99 = ________

17. 6 items at $3.95 = ________

18. 5 items at $1.02 = ________

19. 19 items at $40 = ________

20. 3 items at $19.99 = ________

21. 20 items at $40.05 = ________

22. 30 items at $1.99 = ________

23. 20 items at $39.98 = ________

24. 2 items at $5.99 = ________

25. 48 items at $5 = ________

26. 5 items at $1.97 = ________

27. 7 items at $7.97 = ________

28. 2 items at $99.98 = ________

29. 30 items at $2.98 = ________

30. 99 items at $1.90 = ________

________ Score for C (40)

D (10 points) In each of the equations below, rewrite the equation by moving the last number on each side of the equal sign to the other side and making appropriate sign changes so that the equation is still true. (Example: Given $13 + 7 + 2 = 10 + 12$: Answer $13 + 7 - 12 = 10 - 2$) (one point for each correct equation)

31. $6 + 4 + 5 = 17 - 2$

32. $6 \times 2 \div 3 = 8 \div 4 \times 2$

33. $9 - 3 - 3 = 2 + 1$

34. $8 \div 2 \times 4 = 24 \div 3 \times 2$

35. $20 + 1 - 7 = 16 - 2$

36. $3 \times 3 \times 3 = 18 \div 2 \times 3$

37. $12 + 3 - 5 = 7 + 3$

38. $7 \times 4 \div 2 = 28 \times 2 \div 4$

39. $64 - 32 - 16 = 8 + 8$

40. $63 \div 7 \times 2 = 3 \times 2 \times 3$

________ Score for D (10)

Notes

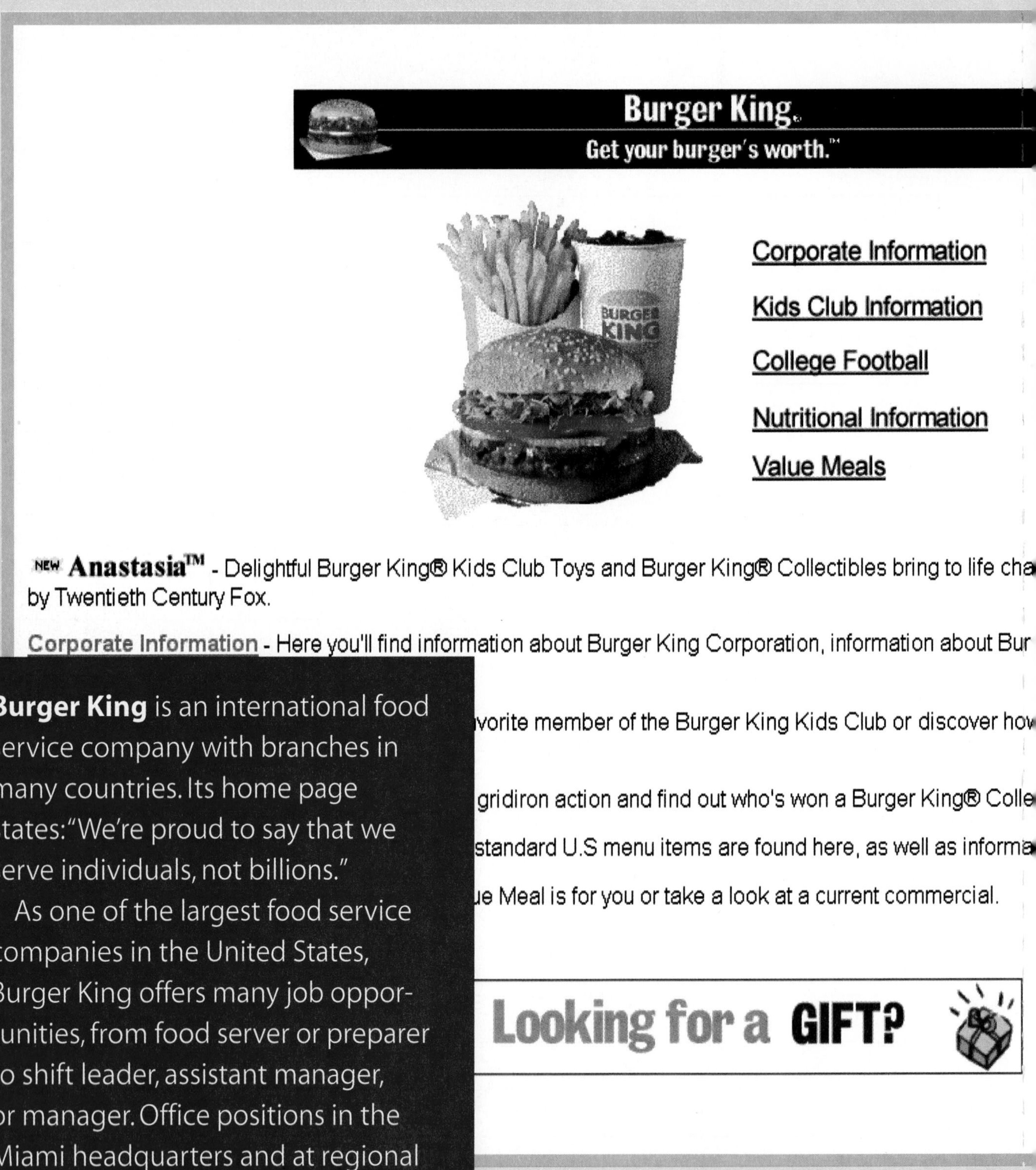
Burger King
Get your burger's worth.
Corporate Information
Kids Club Information
College Football
Nutritional Information
Value Meals
NEW Anastasia™ - Delightful Burger King® Kids Club Toys and Burger King® Collectibles bring to life cha
by Twentieth Century Fox.
Corporate Information - Here you'll find information about Burger King Corporation, information about Bur
vorite member of the Burger King Kids Club or discover how
gridiron action and find out who's won a Burger King® Colle
standard U.S menu items are found here, as well as informa
ue Meal is for you or take a look at a current commercial.
Looking for a GIFT?

Burger King is an international food service company with branches in many countries. Its home page states: "We're proud to say that we serve individuals, not billions."

As one of the largest food service companies in the United States, Burger King offers many job opportunities, from food server or preparer to shift leader, assistant manager, or manager. Office positions in the Miami headquarters and at regional offices require a thorough grounding in mathematics and accounting.

Burger King's home page stresses feedback on customer satisfaction as part of the company's quality control program. Visit Burger King at www.burgerking.com.

EXAMPLE B

Convert the following liquid units into the requested liquid units:

Problem	Information Needed		Solution
12 gal = ? qt	4 qt = 1 gal	so	12 gal = 48 qt
24 oz = ? c	8 oz = 1 c	so	24 oz = 3 c
10 qt = ? pt	1 qt = 2 pt	so	10 qt = 20 pt
4 qt = ? c	1 qt = 2 pt and		
	1 pt = 2 c	so	4 qt = 16 c

EXAMPLE C

Convert the following weight units into the requested weight units:

Problem	Information Needed		Solution
80 oz = ? lb	1 lb = 16 oz	so	80 oz = 5 lb
1 t = ? oz	2,000 lb = 1 t and		
	1 lb = 16 oz	so	1 t = 32,000 oz

EXAMPLE D

Convert the following volume units into the requested volume units:

Problem	Information Needed		Solution
3 cu yd = ? cu ft	1 cu yd = 27 cu ft	so	3 cu yd = 81 cu ft
2 cu ft = ? cu in.	1 cu ft = 1,728 cu in.	so	2 cu ft = 3,456 cu in.
216 cu ft = ? cu yd	1 cu yd = 27 cu ft	so	216 cu ft = 8 cu yd

EXAMPLE E

Convert the following area units into the requested area units:

Problem	Information Needed		Solution
4 sq ft = ? sq in.	1 sq ft = 144 sq in.	so	4 sq ft = 576 sq in.
864 sq in. = ? sq ft	1 sq ft = 144 sq in.	so	864 sq in. = 6 sq ft
6 sq yd = ? sq ft	1 sq yd = 9 sq ft	so	6 sq yd = 54 sq ft
130,680 sq ft = ? a	1 a = 43,560 sq ft	so	130,680 sq ft = 3 a
3,200 a = ? sq mi	1 sq mi = 640 a	so	3,200 a = 5 sq mi

CONCEPT CHECK 3.1

Complete the following conversions.

	Original	Process		Solution
Converting Distance Measurements				
Change inches to feet	48 in.	48 ÷ 12	=	4 ft
Feet to inches	5 ft	5 × 12	=	60 in.
Feet to yards	15 ft	15 ÷ 3	=	5 yd
Yards to feet	6 yd	6 × 3	=	18 ft
Miles to feet	2 mi	2 × 5,280	=	10,560 ft
Feet to miles	5,280 ft	5,280 ÷ 5,280	=	1 mi
Miles to yards	4 mi	4 × 1,760	=	7,040 yd
Yards to miles	10,560 yd	10,560 ÷ 1,760	=	6 mi

	Original	Process		Solution
Converting Liquid Measurements				
Ounces to cups	24 oz	24 ÷ 8	=	3 c
Cups to ounces	6 c	6 × 8	=	48 oz
Cups to pints	8 c	8 ÷ 2	=	4 pt
Pints to cups	5 pt	5 × 2	=	10 c
Pints to quarts	10 pt	10 ÷ 2	=	5 qt
Quarts to pints	8 qt	8 × 2	=	16 pt
Quarts to gallons	12 qt	12 ÷ 4	=	3 gal
Gallons to quarts	3 gal	3 × 4	=	12 qt
Converting Weights				
Ounces to pounds	48 oz	48 ÷ 16	=	3 lb
Pounds to ounces	5 lb	5 × 16	=	80 oz
Converting Volume Measurements				
Cubic inches to cubic feet	5,184 cu in.	5,184 ÷ 1,728	=	3 cu ft
Cubic feet to cubic inches	5 cu ft	5 × 1,728	=	8,640 cu in.
Cubic feet to cubic yards	135 cu ft	135 ÷ 27	=	5 cu yd
Cubic yards to cubic feet	50 cu yd	50 × 27	=	1,350 cu ft
Converting Area Measurements				
Square inches to square feet	1,584 sq in.	1,584 ÷ 144	=	11 sq ft
Square feet to square inches	24 sq ft	24 × 144	=	3,456 sq in.
Square feet to square yards	180 sq ft	180 ÷ 9	=	20 sq yd
Square yards to square feet	30 sq yd	30 × 9	=	270 sq ft

Performing Mathematical Operations Using Standard U.S. Weights and Measurements

Learning Objectives 2

Perform mathematical operations of addition, subtraction, multiplication, and division using standard U.S. weights and measurements.

Adding Weights and Measurements

When adding weights and measurements, first arrange units in a right-to-left sequence of smallest to largest. In expressing a final answer, convert smaller units into larger units whenever possible—for example, ounces into pounds, quarts into gallons, feet into yards.

EXAMPLE F

Add and convert, where possible, the following distance measurements. Refer to Figure 3-1 as necessary.

7 yd	2 ft	11 in.
+2 yd	1 ft	6 in.

7 yd	2 ft	11 in.
+2 yd	1 ft	6 in.
9 yd	3 ft	17 in.
	(+1) ⟵	(−12)
9 yd	4 ft	5 in.
(+1) ⟵	(−3)	
10 yd	1 ft	5 in.

EXAMPLE G

Add and convert, where possible, the following liquid measurements. Refer to Figure 3-1 as necessary.

2 gal	3 qt	1 pt
3 gal	2 qt	1 pt
+4 gal		1 pt

2 gal	3 qt	1 pt
3 gal	2 qt	1 pt
+4 gal		1 pt
9 gal	5 qt	3 pt
	(+1) ⟵	(−2)
9 gal	6 qt	1 pt
(+1) ⟵	(−4)	
10 gal	2 qt	1 pt

Subtracting Weights and Measurements

When subtracting weights and measurements, first arrange units in a right-to-left sequence of smallest to largest. When subtracting weights and measurements, "borrow" quantities needed from the next higher unit. In expressing a final answer, convert smaller units into larger units whenever possible.

EXAMPLE H

Subtract the following distance measurements.

13 yd	2 ft	5 in.
−3 yd	2 ft	9 in.

13 yd	2 ft	5 in.
	1 (2 − 1) ⟶	17 (5 + 12)
12 (13 − 1) ⟶	4 (1 + 3)	
−3 yd	2 ft	9 in.
9 yd	2 ft	8 in.

EXAMPLE I

Subtract the following liquid measurements.

6 gal	2 qt	1 pt
−2 gal	3 qt	

6 gal	2 qt	1 pt
5 (6 − 1) ⟶	6 (2 + 4)	
−2 gal	3 qt	
3 gal	3 qt	1 pt

EXAMPLE J

Subtract the following area measurements.

28 sq yd	3 sq ft
−15 sq yd	8 sq ft

28 sq yd	3 sq ft
27 (28 − 1) ⟶	12 (3 + 9)
−15 sq yd	8 sq ft
12 sq yd	4 sq ft

Multiplication of Weights and Measurements

Businesses use multiplication of weights and measurements most frequently to compute the square feet, square yards, or cubic measurement of a given area and to compute prices for various quantities and measurements of merchandise.

To find the total square inches, square feet, or square yards of an area, multiply its width times its length.

EXAMPLE K

How many square feet are there in an office 12 feet wide and 15 feet long?
12 ft × 15 ft = 180 sq ft

EXAMPLE L

How many square yards are there in an exhibit area 30 yards wide and 66 yards long?
30 yd × 66 yd = 1,980 sq yd

To find a total cubic measurement, multiply length times width times height.

EXAMPLE M

How many cubic feet are there in a warehouse that measures 100 feet by 60 feet by 12 feet?
100 ft × 60 ft × 12 ft = 72,000 cu ft

EXAMPLE N

How many cubic yards are there in a room measuring 21 feet long by 18 feet wide by 9 feet high?
21 ft × 18 ft × 9 ft = 3,402 cu ft
3,402 cu ft ÷ 27 cu ft per cu yd = 126 cu yd

Division of Weights and Measurements

EXAMPLE O

A store wants to divide its building totaling 30,000 square feet into 6 equal department spaces. How many square feet will each department have?
30,000 sq ft ÷ 6 = 5,000 sq ft per department

EXAMPLE P

A contractor wants to excavate a pit containing 720 cubic yards of dirt. If he has 6 customers who want to purchase the dirt and he wishes to allocate an even amount to each customer, how much will each receive?
720 cu yd ÷ 6 = 120 cu yd each

CONCEPT CHECK 3.2

Adding and Converting Weights and Measurements

5 yd	2 ft	9 in.
+4 yd	2 ft	11 in.
9 yd	4 ft	20 in.
	5 (4 + 1) ⟵	8 (20 − 12)
10 (9 + 1) ⟵	2 (5 − 3)	
10 yd	2 ft	8 in.

Subtracting and Converting Weights and Measurements

10 gal	3 qt	1 pt
	2 (3 − 1) ⟶	3 (1 + 2)
−3 gal	2 qt	2 pt
7 gal	0 qt	1 pt

Multiplying and Converting Weights and Measurements

How many cubic feet are there in a storage cabinet measuring 8 feet wide by 6 feet deep by 9 feet high?
8 ft × 6 ft × 9 ft = 432 cu ft

Dividing and Converting Weights and Measurements

A contractor is excavating for three swimming pools in the same neighborhood. The first is 5 yards wide, 10 yards long, and 3 yards deep. The second is 6 yards wide, 10 yards long, and 4 yards deep. The third is 5 yards wide, 14 yards long, and 3 yards deep. His largest truck will haul 5 cubic yards on each trip. How many trips will it require to haul away the dirt?

1st pool	= 5 yd × 10 yd × 3 yd =	150 cu yd
2nd pool	= 6 yd × 10 yd × 4 yd =	240 cu yd
3rd pool	= 5 yd × 14 yd × 3 yd =	210 cu yd
Total cu yd		600 cu yd

600 cu yd ÷ 5 = 120 trips

Business Applications

Businesses constantly use measurement computations in transactions. They use gross weight to determine the price of commodities sold by ounces, pounds, tons, etc. They use square yards to price carpet installations. They use cubic yards to determine the cost of removing dirt for a basement or swimming pool. They use gallons to compute the cost per mile of gasoline or other fuels used to operate cars and trucks.

LEARNING OBJECTIVES 3

Use mathematical processes to solve business problems involving standard U.S. weights and measurements.

EXAMPLE Q

What is the total dollar value for the following sales of a group of spices selling at $9.60 per pound?

Sale A = 2 lb 4 oz
Sale B = 2 lb 10 oz
Sale C = 1 lb 2 oz

Add:	2 lb	4 oz
	2 lb	10 oz
	1 lb	2 oz
	5 lb	16 oz

Convert: 5 lb 16 oz = 6 lb
Multiply: 6 lb × $9.60 = $57.60 total value

EXAMPLE R

A liquid spray sells for $6.40 per gallon.

1. How much will 1 quart cost?
   Divide: $6.40 per gal ÷ 4 qt per gal = $1.60 per qt
2. How much will 1 pint cost?
   Divide: $1.60 per qt ÷ 2 pt per qt = $0.80 per pt
3. How much will 3 gallons, 3 quarts, and 1 pint cost?

Multiply and add:	3 gal	× $6.40 =	$19.20
	3 qt	× $1.60 =	4.80
	1 pt	× $0.80 =	.80
		Total Cost	$24.80

EXAMPLE S

A homeowner wants to build a swimming pool requiring dirt removal to a depth of 9 feet, for an area that is 15 feet wide and 45 feet long. At a removal cost of $40 per cubic yard, how much will the homeowner pay?

Multiply: 45 ft × 15 ft × 9 ft = 6,075 cu ft
Divide: 6,075 cu ft ÷ 27 cu ft per cu yd = 225 cu yd
Multiply: 225 cu yd × $40 = $9,000

EXAMPLE T

How much will it cost to carpet a room that measures 15 feet by 21 feet if the installed carpet costs $22 per square yard?

21 ft × 15 ft = 315 sq ft
315 sq ft ÷ 9 sq ft per sq yd = 35 sq yd
35 sq yd × $22 per sq yd = $770

EXAMPLE U

A business plans to recarpet its office, which is 27 feet wide by 45 feet long. Supplier A charges $30 per square yard installed; Supplier B charges $26 per square yard installed. How much will the business save by using Supplier B?

27 ft × 45 ft = 1,215 sq ft
1,215 sq ft ÷ 9 sq ft per sq yd = 135 sq yd
Supplier A: 135 sq yd × $30 per sq yd = $4,050
Supplier B: 135 sq yd × $26 per sq yd = $3,510
Supplier A − Supplier B: $4,050 − $3,510 = $540 savings
or
$30 − $26 = $4 × 135 sq yd = $540

EXAMPLE V

Land sells for $2 per square foot. How much will 3 acres cost?

1 a = 43,560 sq ft
43,560 sq ft per a × 3 a = 130,680 sq ft
130,680 sq ft × $2 per sq ft = $261,360

CONCEPT CHECK 3.3

Review steps in solving word problems:

1. Determine what is being requested.
2. Determine the processes to be used to solve the problem.

A homeowner wants to carpet a room that measures 18 feet by 24 feet. The carpet will cost $27 per square yard, installed. In addition to the carpet, he will put a baseboard around all four sides of the room, less one 6-foot open archway. The cost of the baseboard is $6 per yard. What will be the total cost?

What is requested: Total cost of carpeting and baseboard
The process to be used:

Multiply:	18 ft × 24 ft = 432 sq ft
Divide:	432 sq ft ÷ 9 = 48 sq yd of carpet needed
Multiply:	48 sq yd carpet × \$27 per sq yd = \$1,296, cost of carpet
Add:	18 ft + 18 ft + 24 ft + 24 ft = 84 ft around room
Subtract:	84 ft − 6 ft (open archway) = 78 ft
Divide:	78 ft ÷ 3 = 26 yd of baseboard needed
Multiply:	26 yd of baseboard × \$6 per yd = \$156
Add:	Cost of carpet \$1,296
	Cost of baseboard 156
	\$1,452, total cost of project

A manufacturer of computer chips packs them into cartons, allowing exactly one cubic inch (1 in. × 1 in. × 1 in.) per chip. She has boxes that measure 2 feet by 3 feet by 4 feet. How many packed chips can she ship in 8 boxes?

What is requested: Number of cubic inches in 8 boxes
The process to be used:

Multiply:	2 ft × 3 ft × 4 ft = 24 cu ft per box
Multiply:	24 cu ft per box × 8 boxes = 192 cu ft in all boxes
Multiply:	192 cu ft × 1,728 cu in. per cu ft = 331,776 cu in., or 331,776 chips

COMPLETE ASSIGNMENTS 3.1 AND 3.2.

Chapter Terms for Review

acre	ounce
cubic foot	pint
cubic inch	pound
cubic yard	quart
cup	square foot
fluid ounce	square inch
foot	square mile
gallon	square yard
inch	ton
mile	yard

The Bottom Line

Summary of chapter learning objectives:

Learning Objective	Summary	Example
3.1	Converting weights and measurements between units on the same scale	Convert the following weights and measurements to the requested units. 1. 2,448 in. = ______ ft 2. 56 fl oz = ______ c 3. 240 oz = ______ lb 4. 8,640 cu in. = ______ cu ft 5. 8,640 sq in. = ______ sq ft 6. 21 yd = ______ ft 7. 4 pt = ______ c 8. 8 t = ______ lb 9. 5 cu yd = ______ cu ft 10. 12 sq yd = ______ sq ft 11. 36,960 ft = ______ mi 12. 8 qt = ______ pt 13. 130,680 sq ft = ______ a
3.2	Performing mathematical operations of addition, subtraction, multiplication, and division using standard U.S. weights and measurements	14. 5 yd 3 ft 9 in. + 1 yd 2 ft 4 in. 17. 9 yd 3 ft 7 in. − 2 yd 4 ft 6 in. 15. 5 gal 3 qt 1 pt + 2 gal 2 qt 1 pt 18. 3 gal 3 qt 1 pt − 1 gal 1 qt 2 pt 16. 30 sq yd 8 sq ft + 12 sq yd 7 sq ft 19. 42 sq yd 3 sq ft − 17 sq yd 4 sq ft 20. How many square yards are there in a classroom that is 30 feet wide and 42 feet long? ______ 21. How many cubic yards are there in a room 18 feet by 12 feet by 9 ft? ______ 22. A contractor has 36 cubic yards of gravel that he wants to distribute equally among 4 work sites. How many cubic yards of gravel will go to each work site? ______
3.3	Using mathematical processes to solve business problems involving standard U.S. weights and measurements	23. How much will it cost to carpet a room that measures 27 feet by 21 feet if the carpet costs $28.00 per square yard and an extra 6 square yards are needed for matching? ________

Answers: 1. 204 ft **2.** 7 c **3.** 15 lb **4.** 5 cu ft **5.** 60 sq ft **6.** 63 ft **7.** 8 c **8.** 16,000 lb **9.** 135 cu ft **10.** 108 sq ft **11.** 7 mi **12.** 16 pt **13.** 3 a **14.** 8 yd 1 in. **15.** 8 gal 2 qt **16.** 43 sq yd 6 sq ft **17.** 6 yd 2 ft 1 in. **18.** 2 gal 1 qt 1 pt **19.** 24 sq yd 8 sq ft **20.** 140 sq yd **21.** 72 cu yd **22.** 9 cu yd **23.** $1,932

Assignment 3.1: Weights and Measurements

Name ______________________

Date ______________________ Score ______________________

A (6 points) Use Figure 3-1 to convert the following weights and measures into the requested units. (1 point for each correct answer)

1. 4 miles	=	________	feet	**4.** 8 square feet	=	________	square inches
2. 168 inches	=	________	feet	**5.** 6 gallons	=	________	pints
3. 45 yards	=	________	inches	**6.** 360 square feet	=	________	square yards

________ Score for A (6)

B (66 points) Add, subtract, multiply, and divide the following standard U.S. weights and measurements. (6 points for each correct answer)

7.

5 yd	2 ft	11 in.
18 yd	1 ft	4 in.
+2 yd	2 ft	7 in.

8.

5 yd	1 ft	10 in.
2 yd		6 in.
+4 yd	2 ft	11 in.

9.

3 lb	15 oz
82 lb	4 oz
+24 lb	1 oz

10.

2 t	1,100 lb
+4 t	1,700 lb

11.

2 gal	3 qt	1 pt
+6 gal	2 qt	1 pt

12.

3 sq yd	7 sq ft
+27 sq yd	8 sq ft

13. Undeveloped land in Utah is offered for sale at $1.50 per square foot. How much will 5 acres cost?

____

14. If 8 acres of land sells for $696,960, what is its cost per square foot? ________

15. Cheese sells for $7 per pound. What is the total cost of three packages that weigh, respectively, 2 lb 11 oz, 1 lb 6 oz, and 4 lb 15 oz? ________

16. Which costs more: 5 gallons of gasoline priced at $1.62 per gallon or 7 quarts of oil priced at $1.17 per quart?

____

17. Twenty acres of land sold for $5,227,200. What was the selling price per square foot? ________

________ Score for B (66)

C **(28 points) Use Figure 3-1 to do the following problems. In the final answers, convert smaller units into larger units whenever possible. (4 points for each correct answer)**

18. How many cubic yards of air are contained in a room measuring 18 feet long, 12 feet wide, and 9 feet high?

____

19. Liquid soap sells for $38.40 per gallon. How much will it cost to fill 64 dispensers if each dispenser holds 4 fluid ounces? __________

20. If a cargo of rice weighs 44 tons, what would its value be if rice were priced at $0.05 per pound? __________

21. A toy manufacturer packages tiny cars in boxes 4 inches long, 3 inches wide, and 2 inches high. How many cubic feet of storage space would be required to store 18,000 boxed cars? __________

22. If a liquid lawn spray sells for $12.80 per gallon, how much will a merchant pay for 2 gallons, 3 quarts, and 1 pint?

____

23. The Astoria Park swimming pool is 90 feet long and 30 feet wide and averages 6 feet in depth. The water flows through the pipe that fills the pool at the rate of 18 cubic feet per minute. How long will be required to fill the Astoria Park pool? __________________

24. An office has 30 workers in a room that is 60 feet in length by 24 feet in width and 12 feet high. What is the number of cubic feet of air available for each person in the room? __________________

____
Score for C (28)

Assignment 3.2: Business Applications

Name ______________________

Date ______________ Score ______________

A (100 points) Solve the following word problems and business applications involving weights and measurements. (10 points for each correct answer)

1. A room is 30 feet long and 24 feet wide. How much will it cost to cover the floor with carpet costing $12 a square yard (9 square feet) if 4 extra square yards are purchased for matching? __________

2. A company packs its fish in cans. Each can weighs 1 ounce empty and is filled with 12 ounces of fish. An empty carton weighs 8 ounces. Two dozen cans are packed in a carton. A customer orders 5 cartons. How many pounds does the shipment weigh? __________

3. A state is building a freeway. It needs a 1,936-foot length of property owned by a citizen. The width of the area needed is 90 feet. If an acre is 43,560 square feet, how much would the owner receive for the land at the rate of $972 per acre? __________

4. Carpet costs $31 per square yard. Carpet padding costs $6 per square yard. Carpet installation charges are $3 per square yard. How much will it cost to cover two areas with carpet and pad if area A measures 20 feet by 30 feet and area B measures 30 feet by 40 feet? __________

5. Room A measures 15 feet by 15 feet and is being carpeted with carpet that costs $22 per square yard installed. Room B measures 12 feet by 21 feet and is being carpeted with carpet that costs $20 per square yard installed. Which room will be cheaper to carpet? __________

6. In an effort to improve his general health, the president of Farrell Machine Company has begun exercising regularly. One Sunday he walks at an average pace of three miles an hour. He starts his walk at 3:30 and returns at 6:00. During that time he stops to talk to a friend for 12 minutes. He also stops to jump rope for 15 minutes and spends 3 minutes giving directions to a stranger. How far does he walk? ___________

7. In developing a machine model for a client, an engineer uses 9 inches of black wire, 6 inches of green wire, 21 inches of white wire, and 12 inches of yellow wire. How many feet of wire does she use? ___________

8. A lifeguard buys rope to tie up boats at the Community Sailing Center. He needs 12 feet for boat A, 14 feet for boat B, 17 feet for boat C, and 14 feet for boat D. How many yards of rope does he need?

____

9. The captain of a commercial cruise ship walks around the deck (a distance of 1,056 feet) 15 times each day for 8 days. How many miles does she walk during that time? ___________

10. A florist shop owner waters the plants in his greenhouse once a week. He puts three pints of water on each of the 16 plants in row A and two quarts of water on each of the 14 plants in row B. How many gallons of water does he use? ___________

____

Score for A (100)

Notes

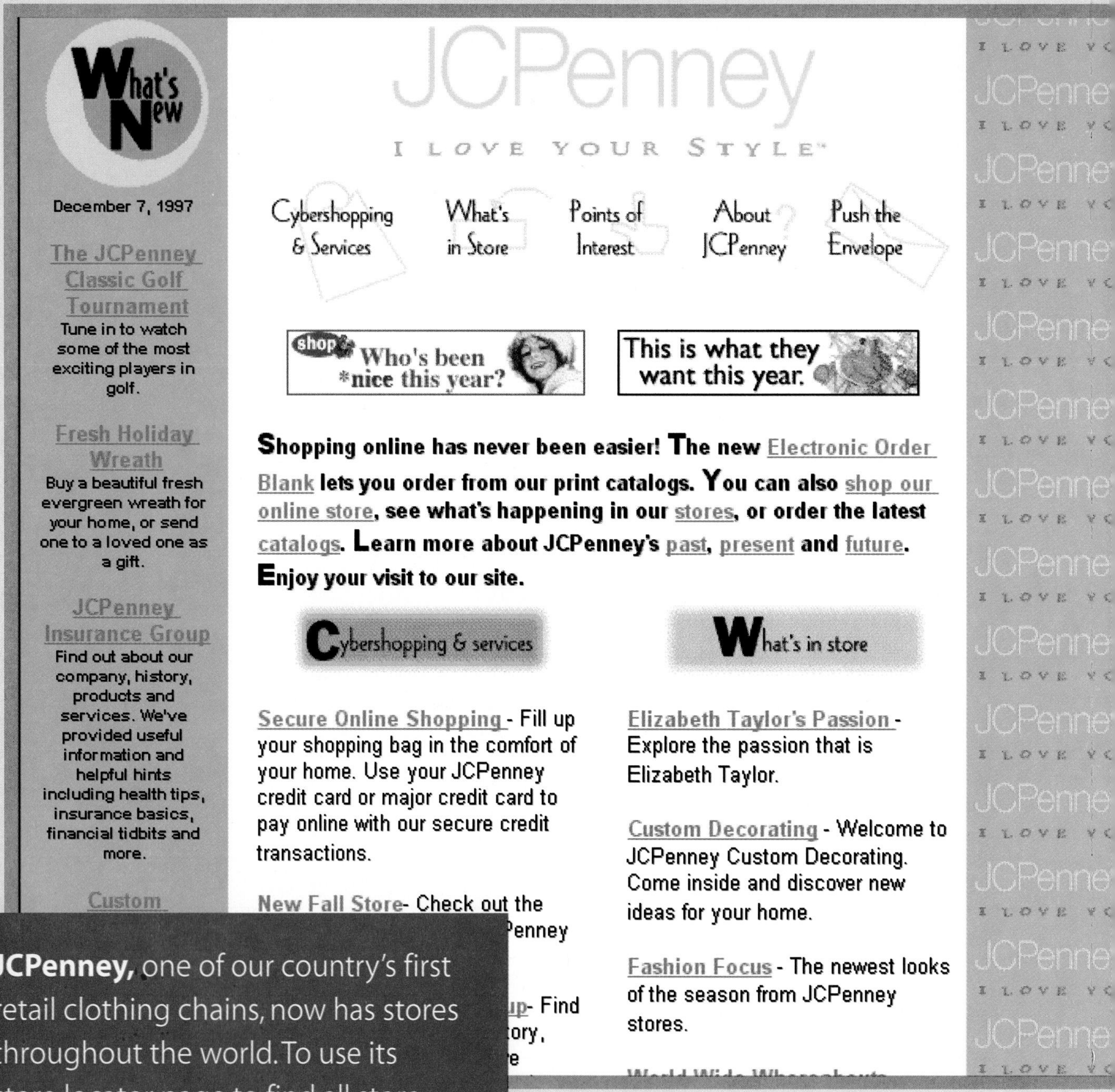

What's New
December 7, 1997
The JCPenney Classic Golf Tournament
Tune in to watch some of the most exciting players in golf.
Fresh Holiday Wreath
Buy a beautiful fresh evergreen wreath for your home, or send one to a loved one as a gift.
JCPenney Insurance Group
Find out about our company, history, products and services. We've provided useful information and helpful hints including health tips, insurance basics, financial tidbits and more.
Custom
JCPenney
I LOVE YOUR STYLE
Cybershopping & Services
What's in Store
Points of Interest
About JCPenney
Push the Envelope
Who's been *nice this year?
This is what they want this year.
Shopping online has never been easier! The new Electronic Order Blank lets you order from our print catalogs. You can also shop our online store, see what's happening in our stores, or order the latest catalogs. Learn more about JCPenney's past, present and future. Enjoy your visit to our site.
Cybershopping & services
What's in store
Secure Online Shopping - Fill up your shopping bag in the comfort of your home. Use your JCPenney credit card or major credit card to pay online with our secure credit transactions.
New Fall Store- Check out the
Elizabeth Taylor's Passion - Explore the passion that is Elizabeth Taylor.
Custom Decorating - Welcome to JCPenney Custom Decorating. Come inside and discover new ideas for your home.
Fashion Focus - The newest looks of the season from JCPenney stores.

JCPenney, one of our country's first retail clothing chains, now has stores throughout the world. To use its store locator page to find all store locations or to learn more about employment opportunities, company history, and many special programs, visit the JCPenney web site at www.JCPenney.com.

JCPenney is famous for its catalog. In the catalog you will find many uses of decimals. Contact the web site and find out how to request the latest catalog for your area.

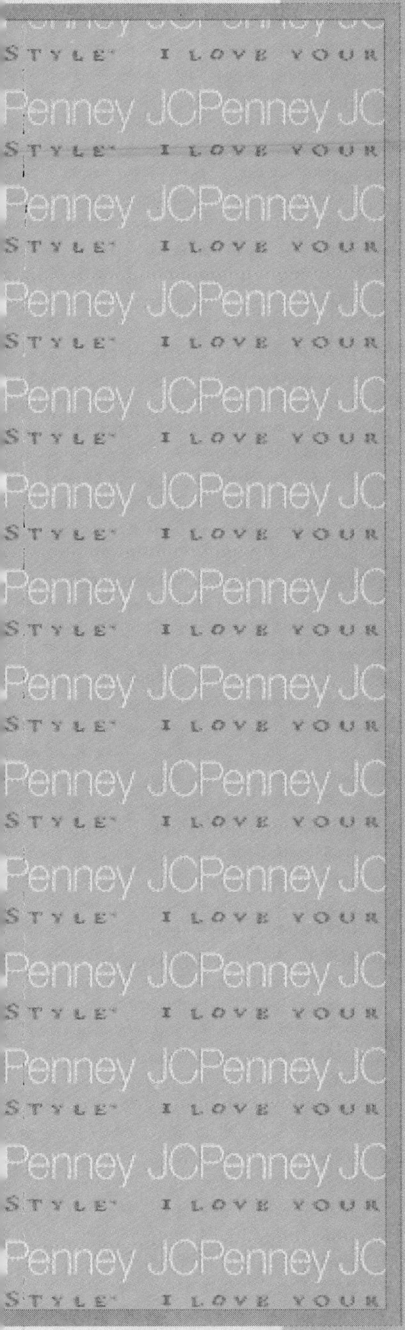

4 Decimals: Addition and Subtraction

Learning Objectives

By studying this chapter and completing all the assignments, you will be able to:

1. Read decimals numbers.
2. Add two or more decimal numbers.
3. Subtract one decimal number from another.
4. Round decimal numbers.

The U.S. monetary system is based on the decimal system, which we use for its ease of computation. You can see examples of the use of decimals in many everyday situations, especially on electronic digital displays in retail stores, on gas pumps, and in electronic banking.

Fractions versus Decimals

McDonald's restaurant sells a hamburger sandwich called the Quarter Pounder. The sandwich is named for the amount of meat: one quarter of a pound of ground beef. McDonald's—or anyone—can describe the same amount of meat in four different ways: 4 ounces, ¼ pound, 0.25 pound, or 25% of a pound. To express less than one pound, McDonald's could use smaller units, fractions, decimals, or percents.

All four expressions are useful, but which one is best? It depends on what you are doing: whether you are buying or selling, whether you are speaking or writing, whether you are just estimating or making accurate financial records, whether you are working with large volumes of something cheap or small quantities of something very expensive. For McDonald's, a Four Ouncer would not sell as well as a Quarter Pounder, but Bloomingdale's sells perfume by the (fluid) ounce rather than by the gallon, quart, pint, or even cup.

You reviewed units of measure in Chapter 3. Fractions, such as ¼ and ¾, are useful in speech and in estimating. Some fractions will always be used in verbal expression because they are so intuitive. Children learn some fractions before they can read. Computations in fractions are sometimes cumbersome, but they are still used in a few types of businesses. You may review computations with fractions in Chapters 6 and 7. Decimals, which permit easy and accurate computations and record keeping, with or without a calculator, are reviewed here and in Chapter 5. Percents, to be studied in Chapter 12, are a hybrid of mostly decimals and a few fractions; they have some of the ease of verbal expression that fractions have.

Decimals and Electronic Displays

A customer in a delicatessen might ask for a fourth of a pound of salami or maybe four ounces. However, the electronic scale in the delicatessen will display 0.25 or 0.250 or even 0.2500. To indicate one fourth as a fraction, we write ¼; three fourths is ¾. In the U.S. monetary system, a *quarter* is the actual name of the coin worth twenty-five cents; three quarters are worth seventy-five cents. But when we write monetary amounts, we use either whole numbers or decimals instead of fractions. We write either 25¢ and 75¢ or $0.25 and $0.75. We do not normally write $¼ or $¾.

For most business transactions and record keeping, decimals are much better than fractions. Calculations in decimals are both easy and accurate. The development of modern electronic digit displays, such as that on your calculator, has also helped decrease the importance of fractions. Photo 4-1 shows the electronic digital display on a gasoline pump. Service stations such as Exxon and Shell use gasoline pumps to measure gasoline

Photo 4-1

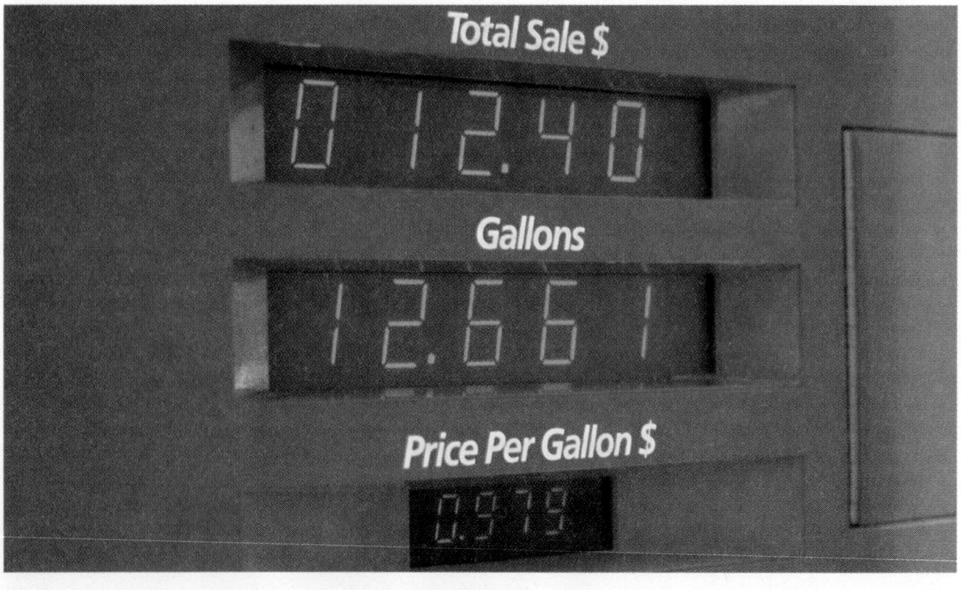

accurately to three decimal places. The pump in the photo displays a purchase of 12.661 gallons of gasoline. The number 12.661 is sometimes called a *mixed decimal.* The 12 is the whole number part of the number; the 661 is the *pure decimal* part. The period that separates the 12 from the 661 is the *decimal point.*

Reading Decimal Numbers

Reading decimal numbers is just like reading whole numbers: each place represents a different value. Starting at the decimal point and reading to the left, the places represent ones, tens, hundreds, etc.; starting at the decimal point and reading to the right, the places represent tenths, hundredths, thousandths, etc.

LEARNING OBJECTIVES 1

Read decimal numbers.

To read the pure decimal part of a number, read the numbers as if they were not a decimal; then, attach the name of the *place value* where the last digit on the right appears. In the 12.661 of the gasoline pump in Photo 4-1, the last digit is the 1 in the thousandths place. The .661 is read as "six hundred sixty-one thousandths." The decimal point is read as the word *and.* The entire number 12.661 is read as "twelve **and** six hundred sixty-one **thousandths.**"

Figure 4-1 illustrates the number system on both sides of the decimal point for the number 607,194.35824. The place value for each digit is given.

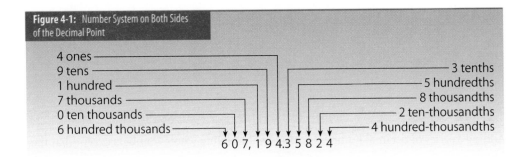

Figure 4-1: Number System on Both Sides of the Decimal Point

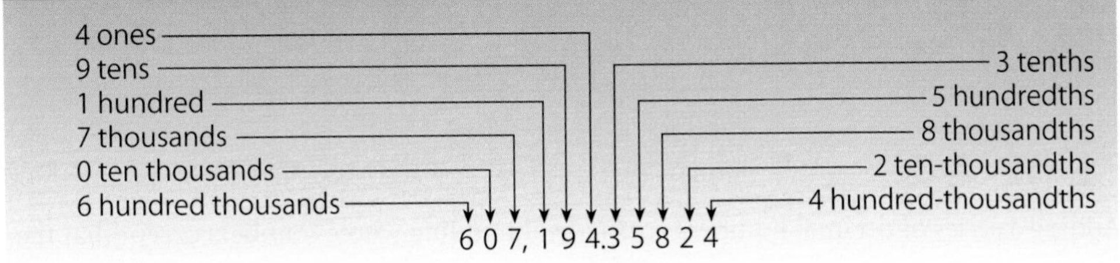

EXAMPLE A

The decimal part of the number in Figure 4-1 is .35824. With the digits in the figure, you can write several decimal numbers, including 0.3, 0.35, 0.008, 0.0082, and 0.35824. These numbers are read as shown below.

Decimal	Words
0.3	three tenths
0.35	thirty-five hundredths
0.008	eight thousandths
0.0082	eighty-two ten-thousandths
0.35824	thirty-five thousand eight hundred twenty-four hundred-thousandths

Reading Large Decimal Numbers Orally

The entire number in Figure 4-1—607,194.35824—is read as "six hundred seven thousand one hundred ninety-four and thirty-five thousand eight hundred twenty-four hundred-thousandths." For a large number, reciting such a description orally is inefficient, and it can be confusing to the listener.

It is often necessary for two employees to double-check long lists of important numbers—payroll data, for example. In such situations, it is most common for one employee to simply read the digits and commas, from left to right. The word *point* is used for the decimal point.

EXAMPLE B

Recite orally the numbers 0.35824 and 607,194.35824.

Number	Oral Recitation
0.35824	zero point three five eight two four
607,194.35824	six zero seven comma one nine four point three five eight two four

Comments: Decimals and fractions are not different numerically; they are merely two different ways to write the same number. The 3 in 607,194.35824 represents three tenths. But when someone speaks, without writing anything, it is impossible to know whether that person is thinking of *three tenths* as $\frac{3}{10}$ or as 0.3.

Enter the number .35 into your calculator, pressing the decimal point first. Notice that your calculator automatically writes a 0 in front of the decimal point. This book uses the same convention. Each of the pure decimals in example A is preceded by a 0.

No comma is used to separate groups of digits to the right of the decimal point.

CONCEPT CHECK 4.1

a. Write 28.074 using words: Twenty-eight and seventy-four thousandths
b. Write thirteen and five hundredths using digits: 13.05

Adding Decimal Numbers

LEARNING OBJECTIVES 2

Add two or more decimal numbers.

Adding a series of decimal numbers is exactly like adding whole numbers except that the numbers are first aligned (lined up) on their decimals points.

STEPS to Add Decimal Numbers

1. Arrange the numbers in columns, with the decimal points in a vertical line.
2. Add each column, from right to left, as with whole numbers. Insert the decimal point.

Option: You may want to write zeros in the right-hand columns of decimals so that each number has the same number of decimal places.

EXAMPLE C

Add 3.42, 218.6004, 9.423, 32, and 0.87782

STEP 1	STEP 2		STEP 2 WITH OPTION
3.42	3.42		3.42000
218.6004	218.6004		218.60040
9.423	9.423	or	9.42300
32.	32.		32.00000
0.87782	+ 0.87782		+ 0.87782
	264.32122		**264.32122**

CONCEPT CHECK 4.2

Add these decimal numbers: 6.4, 13.791, 0.58

First align:	Then add:
6.4	6.4
13.791	13.791
0.58	+ 0.58
	20.771

Subtracting Decimal Numbers

Subtracting one decimal number from another is very similar to subtracting whole numbers. When you are not using a calculator, it is advisable to write enough zeros so that both numbers have the same number of places.

LEARNING OBJECTIVES 3

Subtract one decimal number from another.

STEPS to Subtract Decimal Numbers

1. Arrange the numbers in columns, with the decimal points in a vertical line.
2. If necessary, write enough extra zeros so that both numbers have the same number of decimal places.
3. Subtract each column, from right to left, as with whole numbers. Insert the decimal point.

EXAMPLE D

Subtract 4.935 from 12.8.

STEP 1	STEPS 2 & 3
12.8	12.800
−4.935	−4.935
	7.865

EXAMPLE E

Subtract 9.4 from 82.113.

STEP 1	STEPS 2 & 3
82.113	82.113
−9.4	−9.400
	72.713

CONCEPT CHECK 4.3

Subtract 53.784 from 207.6

Align:	Write zeros and subtract:
207.6	207.600
53.784	−53.784
	153.816

COMPLETE ASSIGNMENT 4.1.

Rounding Decimal Numbers

Round decimal numbers.

In business transactions involving money, the smallest amount of money that can actually be paid is 1 cent. It is impossible to pay the amount $5.268. Thus the amount to be paid can have at most two decimal places. Sometimes businesses will pay the amount to the nearest cent, which is called *rounding off,* or just *rounding,* the number. For example, $5.268 would be rounded to $5.27.

Decimals can be rounded to any number of decimal places. The procedure is the same.

STEPS to Round Decimals

1. Find the last place, or digit, to be retained.
2. Examine the digit to the right of the last digit to be retained.
3. **a.** If it is equal to or greater than 5, increase the digit to be retained by 1. Drop all digits to the right of the ones retained.
   b. If it is less than 5, leave the digit to be retained unchanged. Drop all digits to the right of the ones retained.

EXAMPLE F

Round 7.3951 and 35.2149 to one decimal place, to two decimal places, and to three decimal places.

Round to the nearest tenth	7.3951 ⟶ 7.4	35.2149 ⟶ 35.2
Round to the nearest hundredth	7.3951 ⟶ 7.40	35.2149 ⟶ 35.21
Round to the nearest thousandth	7.3951 ⟶ 7.395	35.2149 ⟶ 35.215

Rounding Up

Retail businesses, such as grocery stores, often use a different method of rounding to a whole number of cents. Suppose a grocery store has lemons priced at 3 for $1.00. Usually the store will charge $0.34 for one lemon, even though $1.00 divided by 3 is $0.3333 (to four places). The store has *rounded up* to the next larger whole cent. To round up monetary amounts, always increase any partial cent to the next whole cent. For example, $27.842 would round up to $27.85.

CONCEPT CHECK

Round 3.4681 to the nearest hundredth (i.e., to two decimal places).

Step 1	Find the hundredths digit:	3.4681	(The 6)
Step 2	Examine the digit to the right of the 6.	3.4681	(It is greater than 5.)
Step 3a	Increase the 6 to a 7 and drop the digits 81 at the right	3.47	(The answer)

Round up 8.5014 to the nearest tenth (i.e., to one decimal place).

Step 1	Find the tenths digit:	8.5014	(The 5)
Step 2	Increase the 5 to a 6 and drop the digits 014 at the right.	8.6	(The answer)

COMPLETE ASSIGNMENT 4.2.

Chapter Terms for Review

decimal point
mixed decimal
place value
pure decimal
rounding
rounding off
rounding up

The Bottom Line

Summary of chapter learning objectives:

Learning Objective	Summary	Example
4.1	Reading decimal numbers	1. Write 7.0019 using words. 2. Write fifty-two and eleven thousandths using digits.
4.2	Adding two or more decimal numbers	3. Add 81.9, 14.372, and 2.06
4.3	Subtracting one decimal number from another	4. Subtract 8.3042 from 25.06
4.4	Rounding decimal numbers	5. Round 0.406501 to the nearest thousandth (i.e., to three decimal places). 6. Round up 12.25062 to the next hundredth (i.e., to two decimal places).

Answers: 1. seven and nineteen ten-thousandths **2.** 52.011 **3.** 98.332 **4.** 16.7558 **5.** 0.407 **6.** 12.25

Notes

Assignment 4.1: Addition and Subtraction of Decimals

Name ____________________

Date ____________________ Score

A (12 points) Use digits to write each number that is expressed in words. Use words to write each number that is expressed in digits. (1 point for each correct answer)

1. Six hundred thirteen thousandths ____________________

2. Nineteen ten-thousandths ____________________

3. Forty-two hundredths ____________________

4. Seventy-four and twelve thousandths ____________________

5. Eight hundred sixty and ninety-eight hundred-thousandths ____________________

6. Sixty and six ten-thousandths ____________________

7. 15.73 ____________________

8. 0.004 ____________________

9. 492.3 ____________________

10. 0.0081 ____________________

11. 58.909 ____________________

12. 2,403.07 ____________________

____
Score for A (12)

B (36 points) Write the following numbers in columns, and then add. (3 points for each correct answer)

13. 3.84, 42.81, 604.927

14. 24.78, 71.402, 8.3176

15. 337.51, 15.8042, 0.452

16. 0.7323, 4.084, 17.42

17. 6.084, 0.005, 48.2007

18. 36.7, 208.51, 3.992

19. 15.4, 32.574, 9.51, 74.0822

20. 6.4, 3.211, 12.6, 28.59

21. 0.592, 1.82, 0.774, 6.5

22. 0.380, 0.68, 1.156, 0.4

23. 804.7, 14.623, 7.1959, 211.14

24. 44.63, 3.828, 19.118, 0.0419

______ Score for B (36)

C (42 points) Subtract the following. (3 points for each correct answer)

25. $\begin{array}{r} 0.829 \\ -0.37 \\ \hline \end{array}$

26. $\begin{array}{r} 0.7212 \\ -0.034 \\ \hline \end{array}$

27. $\begin{array}{r} 5.0739 \\ -2.843 \\ \hline \end{array}$

28. $\begin{array}{r} 4.37 \\ -1.9055 \\ \hline \end{array}$

29. $\begin{array}{r} 0.04264 \\ -0.00497 \\ \hline \end{array}$

30. $\begin{array}{r} 32. \\ -4.37 \\ \hline \end{array}$

31. $\begin{array}{r} 708.932 \\ -419.058 \\ \hline \end{array}$

32. $\begin{array}{r} 8.432 \\ -5.947 \\ \hline \end{array}$

33. $\begin{array}{r} 26.04 \\ -9.108 \\ \hline \end{array}$

34. $\begin{array}{r} 804.07 \\ -167.1 \\ \hline \end{array}$

35. $\begin{array}{r} 0.395 \\ -0.296 \\ \hline \end{array}$

36. $\begin{array}{r} 1.0045 \\ -1.003 \\ \hline \end{array}$

37. $\begin{array}{r} 122.704 \\ -54.8061 \\ \hline \end{array}$

38. $\begin{array}{r} 8.402 \\ -6.501 \\ \hline \end{array}$

______ Score for C (42)

D (10 points) Business Applications. Solve the following. (5 points for each correct answer)

39. The foreman in a machine shop says to a head machinist, "This shaft has a diameter of four hundred sixteen thousandths of an inch. You need to reduce it by another forty-one thousandths." What will be the new diameter?

______

40. On an automobile, it may be necessary to adjust the spark plug gap. The manufacturer's repair manual says that the gap should be 0.030 inch. A mechanic finds that a spark plug gap needs to be increased by about five thousandths. How wide is this spark plug gap before it gets increased? ______

______ Score for D (10)

Assignment 4.2: Decimals in Business

LEARNING OBJECTIVES 2 · 3 · 4

Name ______________________

Date __________ Score __________

A (24 points) In Problems 1–6, round each number to the nearest tenth. In Problems 7–12, round amounts to the nearest cent. In Problems 13–18, round numbers to the nearest thousandth. In Problems 19–24, round each amount UP to the next cent. (1 point for each correct answer)

Nearest Tenth			Nearest Cent		
1.	6.3499 gal	______	**7.**	$5.426	______
2.	48.53 mi	______	**8.**	$0.068	______
3.	3.824 qt	______	**9.**	$942.3749	______
4.	374.29 yd	______	**10.**	$3.1077	______
5.	4.25 ft	______	**11.**	$0.0449	______
6.	6.375 in.	______	**12.**	$72.625	______

Nearest Thousandth			UP to the NEXT Cent		
13.	4.37275 pt	______	**19.**	$4.621	______
14.	0.00549 qt	______	**20.**	$0.159	______
15.	12.6325 oz	______	**21.**	$42.525	______
16.	5.040603 in.	______	**22.**	$2.0917	______
17.	8.9989 yd	______	**23.**	$11.4485	______
18.	0.100499 lb	______	**24.**	$0.6545	______

______ Score for A (24)

B (36 points) Round each decimal as indicated by the column heading, and then add or subtract as indicated. (3 points for each correct answer)

Nearest Tenth		Nearest Hundredth		Nearest Thousandth	
25.	251.325 +12.49	**29.**	5.9275 +35.4149	**33.**	34.00349 −8.00351
26.	24.74 −14.76	**30.**	624.913 −188.766	**34.**	16.48288 +51.7314
27.	8.7137 −6.8702	**31.**	22.527 −17.214	**35.**	0.4205 +0.038241
28.	0.317 +4.0619	**32.**	84.166 +199.284	**36.**	0.037499 −0.007501

______ Score for B (36)

C **(40 points) Solve the following. Do not round your final answers. (5 points for each correct answer)**

37. Ken Davis sold three apples that weighed 7.5, 6.3, and 5.8 ounces, respectively. What was the total weight of the apples?

____

38. Eastside Meat Market sold 9.8 pounds of steak, 8.4 pounds of roast, and 13.7 pounds of ground beef to Alicia Montero. What was the total weight of the meat products that she purchased?

____

39. Tim Wong had 18.5 feet of rope. He cut off a piece 12.75 feet long. How much did he have left?

____

40. A jeweler had only 2.8 ounces of gold on hand. So, she bought 12.5 ounces more to make Christmas items. She used 9.7 ounces for gold rings. How much gold did she have left?

____

41. Carol Avis reads meters for the electric company. She walked 2.4 miles on Monday; 3.8 miles on Tuesday, 2.9 miles on Wednesday, 3.25 miles on Thursday, and 3.1 miles on Friday. What was her total distance for the week?

____

42. Four drivers bring their cars in to a service station to buy gasoline. Individually, they buy 10.4, 8.3, 13.6, and 15.9 gallons. How much did they purchase all together?

____

43. World Jewelers had 50.8 ounces of gold on hand. After they received 120 ounces and used 117.9 ounces, how much gold was on hand?

____

44. Central Paving Co. delivered 7.3 tons of asphalt. They used 5.2 tons for a parking lot in a shopping center and 1.4 tons for an access road. How many tons of asphalt were left?

____

____

Score for C (40)

Notes

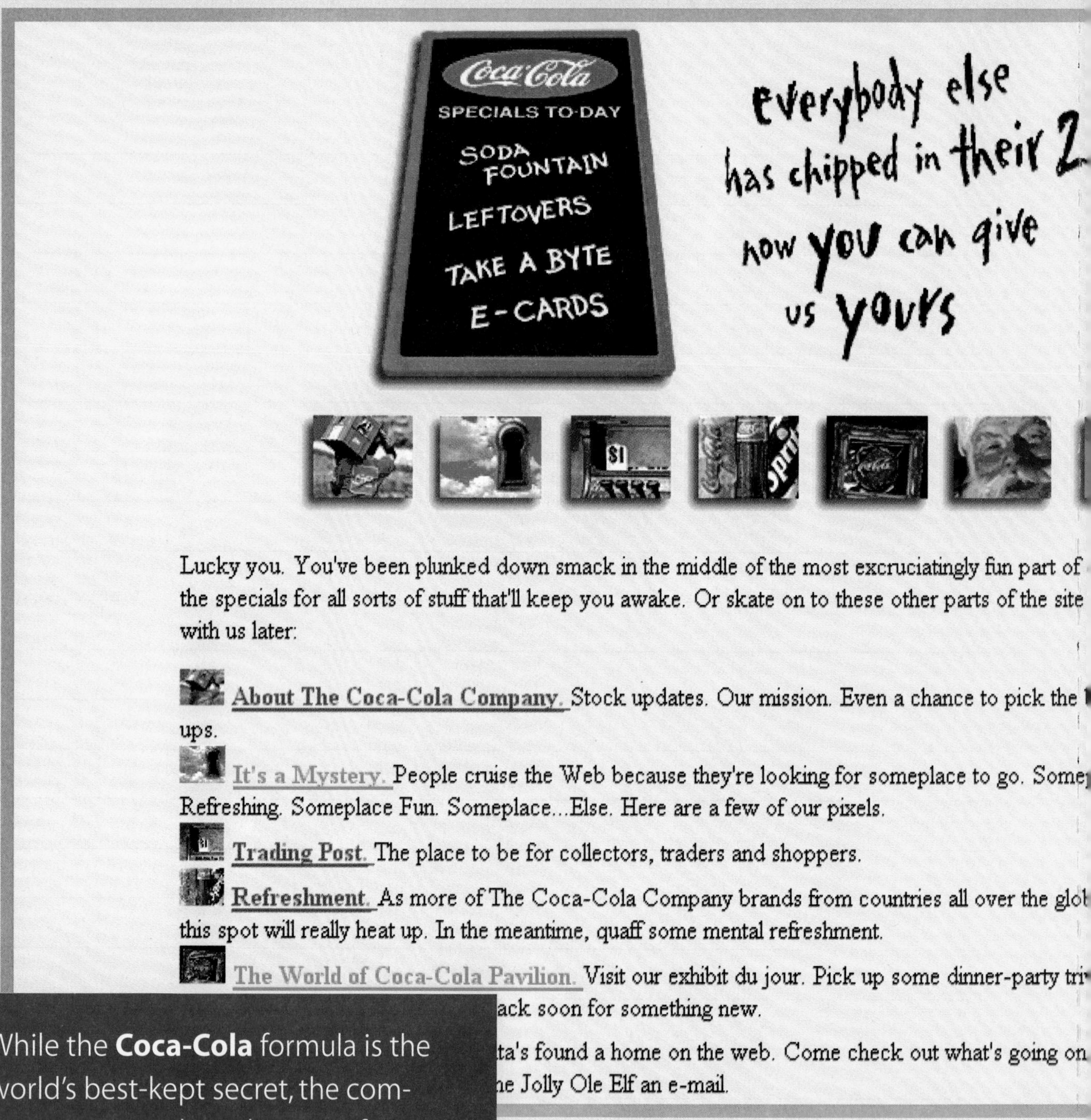
Coca-Cola
SPECIALS TO-DAY
SODA FOUNTAIN
LEFTOVERS
TAKE A BYTE
E-CARDS
everybody else has chipped in their 2
now you can give us yours
$1
Lucky you. You've been plunked down smack in the middle of the most excruciatingly fun part of
the specials for all sorts of stuff that'll keep you awake. Or skate on to these other parts of the site
with us later:
About The Coca-Cola Company. Stock updates. Our mission. Even a chance to pick the
ups.
It's a Mystery. People cruise the Web because they're looking for someplace to go. Some
Refreshing. Someplace Fun. Someplace...Else. Here are a few of our pixels.
Trading Post. The place to be for collectors, traders and shoppers.
Refreshment. As more of The Coca-Cola Company brands from countries all over the glob
this spot will really heat up. In the meantime, quaff some mental refreshment.
The World of Coca-Cola Pavilion. Visit our exhibit du jour. Pick up some dinner-party tri
ack soon for something new.
ta's found a home on the web. Come check out what's going on
he Jolly Ole Elf an e-mail.

While the **Coca-Cola** formula is the world's best-kept secret, the company name and products are famous throughout the world. Coca-Cola products are sold in more than 170 countries.

What are the employment opportunities at Coca-Cola? What is the company's mission? What is the current price for a share of Coca-Cola stock? Coke is worth a visit, at www.cocacola.com.

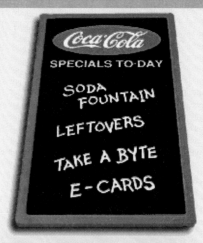

5 Decimals: Multiplication and Division

Learning Objectives

By studying this chapter and completing all the assignments, you will learn to:

1. Multiply two decimal numbers.
2. Divide one decimal number by a whole number.
3. Divide one decimal number by another decimal number.
4. Multiply and divide decimals by 10, 100, 1,000, etc.
5. Approximate products and quotients.
6. Change a fraction into a decimal.

If you visit another country, you need to exchange your money for local currency. You'll be able to determine the best rates if you can multiply and divide in decimals. Decimal coinage means money is divided and multiplied by tens.

Multiplying Decimal Numbers

LEARNING OBJECTIVES 1

Multiply two decimal numbers.

Almost every business owner and employee multiplies decimal numbers. Daily wages equal the hourly rate multiplied by the hours worked in a day. Annual salary equals the monthly salary times the months worked in a year. Multiplication with one or more decimals is the same as multiplication with whole numbers except that you need to put the decimal point in the correct position in the product.

STEPS to Multiply with Decimals

1. Multiply the two numbers as if they were whole numbers.
2. Count the *total* number of decimal places in the two numbers.
3. **a.** In the product, place the decimal point so that the number of decimal places is the same as the number in Step 2. (Count from right to left.)
   b. If necessary, insert zeros in front of the left-hand digit to provide enough decimal places. (See example B.)

EXAMPLE A

3.764×21

	3.764	(3 places)
	× 21	(0 places)
STEP 1	3 764	
	75 28	STEP 2
STEP 3	79.044	(3 + 0 = 3 places)

EXAMPLE B

3.764×0.0021

	3.764	(3 places)
	× 0.0021	(4 places)
STEP 1	3764	
	7528	STEP 2
STEP 3	0.0079044	(3 + 4 = 7 places; insert 2 zeros)

In business applications, zeros that come at the right end of the decimal part of the product are often omitted (example C). Of course, do not omit zeros that come at the end of the whole-number part (example D). When the product is written in dollars and cents, two decimal places are written, including zeros at the end (example E).

EXAMPLE C

$0.76 \times 0.5 = 0.380$ (3 places)
may be written as 0.38

EXAMPLE D

$12.5 \times 0.8 = 10.00$ (2 places)
may be written as 10

EXAMPLE E

$8.40 × 6.5 = $54.600 (3 places)
written as $54.60

CONCEPT CHECK 5.1

a. Multiply 3.15×2.4

3.15	(2 places)
× 2.4	(1 place)
1260	
630	
7.560	(3 places)

may be written as 7.56

b. Multiply 0.315×0.24

0.315	(3 places)
× 0.24	(2 places)
1260	
630	
0.07560	(5 places; insert 1 zero)

may be written as 0.0756

Dividing a Decimal Number by a Whole Number

Division with a decimal number is the same as with two whole numbers except for placement of the decimal point. Three steps may be required to divide correctly.

LEARNING OBJECTIVES 2

Divide one decimal number by a whole number.

STEPS to Divide a Decimal by a Whole Number

1. Write the decimal point in the quotient directly above the decimal point in the divisor.
2. If necessary, insert zeros in the quotient between the decimal point and the other digits (example G).
3. Divide as you would for whole numbers.

EXAMPLE F

STEP 1 | STEP 3

12) 40.8 (quotient: .) = 12) 40.8 (quotient: 3.4)

− 36

48

− 48

0

EXAMPLE G

STEP 1 | STEPS 2 & 3

4) 0.056 (quotient: .) = 4) 0.056 (quotient: 0.014)

− 4

16

− 16

0

To complete the division process or to carry it out to more places, it may be necessary to add zeros to the right end of the dividend (examples H, I, and J).

For a larger divisor and a small dividend, it may be necessary to insert zeros in the quotient between the decimal point and the other digits (example I).

When the dividend is also a whole number, the procedure is the same except that the decimal point in the divisor is understood to be at the right end of the dividend (example J).

EXAMPLE H

STEP 1 | STEPS 2 & 3

8) 24.4 (quotient: .) = 8) 24.40 (quotient: 3.05)

24

40

40

0

EXAMPLE I

STEP 1 | STEPS 2 & 3

25) 0.06 (quotient: .) = 25) 0.0600 (quotient: 0.0024)

50

100

100

0

EXAMPLE J

STEP 1 | STEPS 2 & 3

20) 70 (quotient: .) = 20) 70.0 (quotient: 3.5)

60

100

100

0

Note: In decimal division, there are no remainders, as there are in whole-number division. Instead, the division process is continued to compute one or more digits to the right of the decimal point. In example J, $70 \div 20 = 3.5$ rather than 3R10 (3 with a remainder 10).

CONCEPT CHECK 5.2

Divide 1.026 by 15

STEP 1 | STEPS 2 & 3

$$15\overline{)1.026} = 15\overline{)1.0260}$$

$$\begin{array}{r} 0.0684 \\ 15\overline{)1.0260} \\ \underline{90} \\ 126 \\ \underline{120} \\ 60 \\ \underline{60} \\ 0 \end{array}$$

Dividing a Decimal Number by Another Decimal Number

LEARNING 3 OBJECTIVES

Divide one decimal number by another decimal number.

When the divisor is a decimal, first change the divisor into a whole number and then divide as described in Section 5.2.

STEPS to Divide a Decimal by Another Decimal

1. Move the decimal point in the divisor to the right until the divisor is a whole number.
2. Move the decimal point in the dividend to the right exactly the same number of decimal places as in Step 1. (It may first be necessary to write more zeros to the right end of the dividend—see example K.)
3. Write the decimal point in the quotient directly above the new decimal point in the dividend.
4. Divide as described in Section 5.2.

EXAMPLE K

STEP 1 STEP 2 | STEP 3 | STEP 4

$$2.4 \div 0.16 \text{ is } 0.16\overline{)2.4} = 0.16.\overline{)2.40.} = 16\overline{)240.} = \begin{array}{r} 15. \\ 16\overline{)240.} \\ \underline{16} \\ 80 \\ \underline{80} \\ 0 \end{array}$$

CONCEPT CHECK 5.3

Divide 0.007 by 0.4

STEPS 1 & 2 STEPS 3 & 4

```
                     0.0175
0.4.)0.0.07  =  4)0.0700
                  4
                  30
                  28
                   20
                   20
                    0
```

Multiplying and Dividing by 10, 100, 1,000, etc.

The numbers 10, 100, 1,000, etc., are called *powers of ten.* To multiply a decimal number by a power of ten, simply move the decimal point to the **right.** To divide a decimal number by a power of ten, move the decimal point to the **left.**

LEARNING OBJECTIVES 4

Multiply and divide decimals by 10, 100, 1,000, etc.

Rule: To Multiply a Decimal Number by a Power of Ten
Move the decimal point to the RIGHT the same number of places as the number of zeros in the power of ten. If necessary, add zeros to the right of the decimal number before moving the decimal point (example M).

EXAMPLE L

$0.56 \times 10 = 0.5.6 = 5.6$
(1 place)

EXAMPLE M

$4.73 \times 1{,}000 = 4.730. = 4{,}730$
(3 places)

If the multiplier has zero digits like 100 or 1,000 but has a first digit that is not 1, you can still multiply quickly. First, move the decimal point the appropriate number of places to the **right;** then, multiply by the non-zero digit.

EXAMPLE N

Multiply 3.431 by 2,000

Move the decimal point three places to the right: 3.431 ⟶ 3,431.
Multiply by 2: $3{,}431 \times 2 = 6{,}862$

Rule: To Divide a Decimal Number by a Power of Ten
Move the decimal point to the LEFT the same number of places as the number of zeros in the power of ten. If necessary, insert zeros to the left of the decimal (dividend) before moving the decimal point (example P).

EXAMPLE O

735.1 ÷ 100
735.1 ÷ 100 = 7.35.1 = 7.351
(2 places)

EXAMPLE P

9.64 ÷ 1,000
9.64 ÷ 1,000 = .009.64 = 0.00964
(3 places)

If the divisor has zero digits like 100 or 1,000 but has a first digit that is not 1, you can still divide quickly. First, move the decimal point the appropriate number of places to the **left;** then, divide by the non-zero digit.

EXAMPLE Q

Divide 615.24 by 300

Move the decimal point two places to the left: 615.24 ⟶ 6.1524
Divide by 3: 6.1524 ÷ 3 = 2.0508

CONCEPT CHECK 5.4

a. Multiply 0.413 by 300

Move the decimal point two places to the right:

0.413 ⟶ 41.3
41.3 × 3 = 123.9

b. Divide 4.375 by 10

Move the decimal point one place to the left:

4.375 ÷ 10 = .4375 = 0.4375

COMPLETE ASSIGNMENT 5.1.

Approximating the Product and Quotient

LEARNING OBJECTIVES 5

Approximate products and quotients.

Business people today use calculators almost exclusively to do important computations. But calculators are only perfect if every single key is pressed correctly. You can find many calculator errors by doing some simple mental approximations. Follow the steps below. The objective is to determine whether the answer is approximately the right size—whether the decimal point is in the correct position.

STEPS to Approximate a Multiplication Problem

1. In each factor, increase the first digit by 1 if the second digit is greater than or equal to 5; otherwise, leave the first digit the same.
2. In each factor, change all digits to the right of the first digit to zero.
3. Multiply the two new factors.
4. Place the decimal point correctly in the product.

EXAMPLE R

Approximate 3.764 × 7.1

		STEPS 1 & 2	STEPS 3 & 4
3.764	⟶	4.000	4
× 7.1	⟶	× 7.0	× 7
			28

EXAMPLE S

Approximate 0.089 × 61.18

		STEPS 1 & 2	STEPS 3 & 4
0.089	⟶	0.090	0.09
× 61.18	⟶	× 60.00	× 60
			5.40

The estimates shown in examples R and S are relatively close to the exact answers of 26.7244 and 5.44502.

For division, the mental arithmetic is easier if you round the two numbers so that the division will end in only one step. This will happen if the divisor has one non-zero digit at the left and the dividend has two non-zero digits at the left.

STEPS to Approximate a Division Problem

1. Change the divisor to a **single non-zero digit,** followed by all zeros, as described above.
2. Change the dividend to a **two-digit number,** followed by all zeros. Select the two-digit number so that it is evenly divisible by the one-digit divisor.
3. Divide the new dividend by the new divisor.
4. Place the decimal point correctly in the quotient.

EXAMPLE T

Approximate 3.764 ÷ 7.1

		STEP 1		STEP 2		STEPS 3 & 4
$7.1\overline{)3.764}$	⟶	$7.0\overline{)3.764}$	⟶	$7.\overline{)3.500}$	⟶	$\begin{array}{r} 0.5 \\ 7.\overline{)3.5} \\ \underline{3\,5} \\ 0 \end{array}$

Note that 0.5 is an approximation; the correct answer to four decimal places is 0.5301.

EXAMPLE U

Approximate 61.18 ÷ 0.089

		STEP 1		STEP 2		STEPS 3 & 4
$0.089\overline{)61.18}$	⟶	$0.090\overline{)61.18}$	⟶	$0.09\overline{)63.00}$	⟶	$\begin{array}{r} 700. \\ 9.\overline{)6300.} \\ \underline{63} \\ 0 \end{array}$

For example U, the correct answer to four decimal places is 687.4157.

Vocabulary note: In example U, we say that 0.089 has two *significant digits,* 0.090 has one *significant digit,* and 6,300 has two *significant digits.* Significant digits are non-zero digits that are either preceded or followed by all zeros.

CONCEPT CHECK 5.5

a. Approximate 5.932 × 0.407

5.932 ⟶ 6.000
0.407 ⟶ 0.400

$$\begin{array}{rl} 0.4 & \text{(1 place)} \\ \times\ 6 & \text{(0 places)} \\ \hline 2.4 & \text{(1 place)} \end{array}$$

Compare with 5.932 × 0.407 = 2.414324.

b. Approximate 0.0738 ÷ 92.65

Remember to round off the divisor first.

92.65 ⟶ 90.00
0.0738 ⟶ 0.0720

$$90\overline{)0.072} \longrightarrow \begin{array}{r} .0008 \\ 90\overline{)0.0720} \\ \underline{720} \\ 0 \end{array}$$

Compare with 0.0738 ÷ 92.65 = 0.000796546.

Changing Fractions into Decimals

LEARNING OBJECTIVES 6

Change a fraction into a decimal.

In example J, we divided the whole number 70 by the whole number 20. The quotient was 3.5. Earlier, we mentioned that 75 cents, or \$0.75, is $\frac{3}{4}$ of a dollar. You may recall that in the fraction $\frac{3}{4}$, the whole numbers 3 and 4 are called the numerator and the denominator, respectively. Any fraction can be changed into its decimal form by dividing its numerator by its denominator.

EXAMPLE V

Change $\frac{3}{4}$ to a decimal.

$$3 \div 4 \longrightarrow 4\overline{)3.} \longrightarrow \begin{array}{r} 0.75 \\ 4\overline{)3.00} \\ \underline{2\,8} \\ 20 \\ \underline{20} \\ 0 \end{array}$$

EXAMPLE W

Change $\frac{3}{5}$ to a decimal.

$$3 \div 5 \longrightarrow 5\overline{)3.} \longrightarrow \begin{array}{r} 0.6 \\ 5\overline{)3.0} \\ \underline{3\,0} \\ 0 \end{array}$$

Vocabulary note: The fractions $\frac{3}{4}$ and $\frac{3}{5}$ in examples V and W are called *fractional equivalents* of 0.75 and 0.6. And the 0.75 and 0.6 are called *decimal equivalents* of $\frac{3}{4}$ and $\frac{3}{5}$. Sometimes the division of the numerator by the denominator does not end evenly. In this book, round the division to four decimal places unless instructed to do otherwise. For example, $\frac{1}{3}$ will be 0.3333, and $\frac{2}{3}$ will be 0.6667.

Chapters 6 and 7 will review how to add, subtract, multiply, and divide fractions. However, there are only a few industries in which such calculations, in fractions, remain mandatory. With your calculator, you can quickly change any fractions to decimals and then add, subtract, multiply, or divide the decimals.

EXAMPLE X

Add $\frac{3}{4}$ and $\frac{3}{5}$

From example V, $\frac{3}{4} = 0.75$.

From example W, $\frac{3}{5} = 0.6$.

$$\begin{array}{rr} \frac{3}{4} = & 0.75 \\ +\frac{3}{5} = & +0.6 \\ \hline & 1.35 \end{array}$$

EXAMPLE Y

Multiply $\frac{3}{4}$ and $\frac{3}{5}$

From example V, $\frac{3}{4} = 0.75$.

From example W, $\frac{3}{5} = 0.6$.

$$\begin{array}{rr} \frac{3}{4} = & 0.75 \\ \times\frac{3}{5} = & \times\ 0.6 \\ \hline & 0.450 \end{array}$$

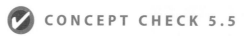

CONCEPT CHECK 5.6

Change $\frac{3}{8}$ and $\frac{1}{4}$ to decimals and then calculate $\frac{3}{8} - \frac{1}{4}$ as a decimal.

$$\frac{3}{8} \longrightarrow 8\overline{)3.} \longrightarrow \begin{array}{r} 0.375 \\ 8\overline{)3.000} \\ \underline{2\,4} \\ 60 \\ \underline{56} \\ 40 \\ \underline{40} \\ 0 \end{array} \qquad \frac{1}{4} \longrightarrow 4\overline{)1.} \longrightarrow \begin{array}{r} 0.25 \\ 4\overline{)1.00} \\ \underline{8} \\ 20 \\ \underline{20} \\ 0 \end{array}$$

$$\begin{array}{rr} \frac{3}{8} = & 0.375 \\ -\frac{1}{4} = & -0.250 \\ \hline & 0.125 \end{array}$$

COMPLETE ASSIGNMENT 5.2.

Chapter Terms for Review

decimal equivalents
fractional equivalents
powers of ten
significant digits

The Bottom Line

Summary of chapter learning objectives:

Learning Objective	Summary	Example
5.1	Multiplying two decimal numbers	1. Multiply 4.68 × 3.5 _____
5.2	Dividing one decimal number by a whole number	2. Divide 0.076 ÷ 4 _____
5.3	Dividing one decimal number by another decimal number	3. Divide 0.046 ÷ 2.5 _____
5.4	Multiplying and dividing decimals by 10, 100, 1,000, etc.	4. Multiply 0.049765 × 1,000 _____ 5. Divide 9.462 by 100 _____ 6. Multiply 0.0623 × 30 _____ 7. Divide 84.8 by 200 _____
5.5	Approximating products and quotients	8. Approximate 48.79 × 0.47 _____ 9. Approximate 0.2688 ÷ 0.713 _____
5.6	Changing a fraction into a decimal	10. Change $\frac{1}{2}$ and $\frac{2}{5}$ to decimals and then calculate $\frac{1}{2} + \frac{2}{5}$ as a decimal. _____

Answers: 1. 16.38 **2.** 0.019 **3.** 0.0184 **4.** 49.765 **5.** 0.09462 **6.** 1.869 **7.** 0.424 **8.** 25 **9.** 0.4 **10.** 0.5; 0.4; 0.9

Assignment 5.1: Multiplication and Division of Decimals

Name

Date Score

A (32 points) Multiply the following. Round monetary products to the nearest cent. Do not round non-monetary products. (4 points for each correct answer)

1. $\$14.25 \times 56$

2. $\$24.60 \times 3.5$

3. $\$410.00 \times 0.706$

4. $\$57.80 \times 0.25$

5. 107.21×0.84

6. 51.97×0.43

7. 285.70326

8. 916.03×0.402

Score for A (32)

B (32 points) Divide the following. Round monetary quotients to the nearest cent. Round non-monetary quotients to two decimals places. (4 points for each correct answer)

9. $7\overline{)\$12.95}$

10. $0.36\overline{)\$6.75}$

11. $1.2\overline{)\$54.30}$

12. $2.25\overline{)\$18.36}$

13. $1.5\overline{)2.57}$ **14.** $0.11\overline{)0.6735}$ **15.** $0.09\overline{)0.7888}$ **16.** $0.007\overline{)0.003548}$

_________ _________ _________ _________

____
Score for B (32)

C **(26 points) Multiply and/or divide by just moving the decimal point or by doing some simple multiplication/division and moving the decimal point. Round monetary answers to the nearest cent. Do not round non-monetary answers. (2 points for each correct answer)**

17. 0.0425×100 = _________
18. $\$72.41 \times 20$ = _________
19. $3.0608 \times 1{,}000$ = _________
20. $\$32.25 \times 300$ = _________
21. $0.0972 \times 10{,}000$ = _________
22. $\$0.06 \times 8{,}000$ = _________
23. $\$2.50 \times 600$ = _________
24. $863 \div 10$ = _________
25. $\$42.60 \div 20$ = _________
26. $0.571 \div 100$ = _________
27. $\$9{,}216 \div 300$ = _________
28. $369.512 \div 1{,}000$ = _________
29. $\$832.56 \div 4{,}000$ = _________

____
Score for C (26)

D **(10 points) Business Applications and Critical Thinking. Solve the following business problems. If necessary, round monetary amounts to the nearest cent. (2.5 points for each correct answer)**

30. Keri Sosa operates a restaurant in a hotel. She purchased 45.5 pounds of beef at $4.84 per pound and 16 pounds of lamb priced at $3.56 per pound. What was the total that she spent on the meat?

____

31. At Midtown Market, oranges are priced at $1.29 per pound. Ken Graves buys 10 oranges that have a total weight of 4.82 pounds. What is the average price per orange that Ken pays? _________

32. A hardware store sells roofing nails by weight. Fifteen pounds of nails cost $11.85. What is the price per pound? _________

33. Doug Warren gets paid $8.70 per hour. Yesterday he worked 6.5 hours. What will be his pay, assuming that he gets paid for exactly the time that he works?

____

____
Score for D (20)

Assignment 5.2: Estimates, Equivalents, and Applications

LEARNING OBJECTIVES 5
LEARNING OBJECTIVES 6

Name

Date Score

A (32 points) For each of the following problems, underline the estimate that is most nearly correct. (2 points for each correct answer)

1. 0.079×0.053	**(a)** 4.0	**(b)** 0.4	**(c)** 0.04	**(d)** 0.004
2. 7.65×0.8499	**(a)** 0.064	**(b)** 0.64	**(c)** 6.4	**(d)** 64
3. 3.8×66.758	**(a)** 0.28	**(b)** 2.8	**(c)** 28	**(d)** 280
4. 0.00867×642	**(a)** 0.054	**(b)** 0.54	**(c)** 5.4	**(d)** 54
5. 0.8388×0.5503	**(a)** 0.0048	**(b)** 0.048	**(c)** 0.48	**(d)** 4.8
6. 0.00389×0.0957	**(a)** 0.04	**(b)** 0.004	**(c)** 0.0004	**(d)** 0.00004
7. 278.25×93.99	**(a)** 27,000	**(b)** 2,700	**(c)** 270	**(d)** 27
8. 0.00058×0.0049	**(a)** 0.000003	**(b)** 0.00003	**(c)** 0.0003	**(d)** 0.003
9. 0.21×5987	**(a)** 120	**(b)** 1,200	**(c)** 12,000	**(d)** 120,000
10. $7.958 \div 0.0544$	**(a)** 16	**(b)** 160	**(c)** 1,600	**(d)** 16,000
11. $3.865 \div 873.12$	**(a)** 0.004	**(b)** 0.04	**(c)** 0.4	**(d)** 4
12. $0.00612 \div 0.00358$	**(a)** 0.15	**(b)** 1.5	**(c)** 15	**(d)** 150
13. $83.72 \div 0.6186$	**(a)** 0.14	**(b)** 1.4	**(c)** 14	**(d)** 140
14. $0.5447 \div 0.00585$	**(a)** 900	**(b)** 90	**(c)** 9	**(d)** 0.9
15. $43.85 \div 6.397$	**(a)** 70	**(b)** 7	**(c)** 0.7	**(d)** 0.07
16. $0.02655 \div 0.09481$	**(a)** 300	**(b)** 30	**(c)** 3	**(d)** 0.3

Score for A (32)

B (28 points) Solve the following problems, first changing each fraction to a decimal. If necessary, round the decimals to three places. Leave the answer as a decimal. (4 points for each correct answer)

17. $\frac{1}{4} + \frac{3}{8}$

18. $\frac{3}{4} + \frac{2}{3}$

19. $\frac{7}{8} - \frac{1}{3}$

20. $\frac{5}{6} - \frac{3}{5}$

21. $\frac{3}{4} \times \frac{1}{2}$

22. $\frac{3}{8} \times \frac{4}{5}$

23. $\frac{3}{8} \div \frac{1}{4}$

Score for B (28)

C (40 points) Business Applications and Critical Thinking. Solve the following business problems. Change any fractions to decimals. Use shortcuts where possible. If necessary, round answers to three decimal places. (5 points for each correct answer)

24. A plumbing supply store sells a large-diameter plastic pipe for $0.08 per foot and copper pipe for $1.02 per foot. How much will Margaret Trent save by using plastic pipe if she needs 250 feet of pipe?

____

25. Benoit Landscaping sent three truckloads of topsoil to a job. The soil cost $21.50 per cubic yard. Two trucks carried $7\frac{1}{4}$ cubic yards; the third carried $6\frac{3}{4}$. What was the total cost of all the topsoil?

____

26. Wholesale, 1,000 two-ounce plastic bottles cost $3\frac{1}{2}$ cents each, and 2,000 four-ounce bottles cost $4\frac{1}{2}$ cents each. What is the total cost of all 3,000 bottles?

____

27. Connie commutes to work. On Monday, she bought 14.62 gallons of regular gasoline at $1.279 per gallon. On Thursday, she bought 15.51 gallons at $1.319. How much did she pay for gasoline that week? __________

28. David Carson paid $24.60 for 300 feet of nylon rope. The rope was $\frac{1}{4}$ inch in diameter. What was David's cost per foot for this particular rope? __________

29. A pizza chef has 24 pounds of flour on hand. He needs $3\frac{3}{4}$ pounds of flour for one large recipe of pizza dough. How many recipes can he make with the flour on hand? (Round to the nearest tenth.)

____

30. Paint thinner costs $1.29 per gallon. How many gallons can a painting contractor buy for $10? (Round to the nearest tenth.) __________

31. Evelyn Griner earns $17.48 per hour. How many hours did she work during a partial day for which her pay was $109.25? __________

____

Score for C (40)

Notes

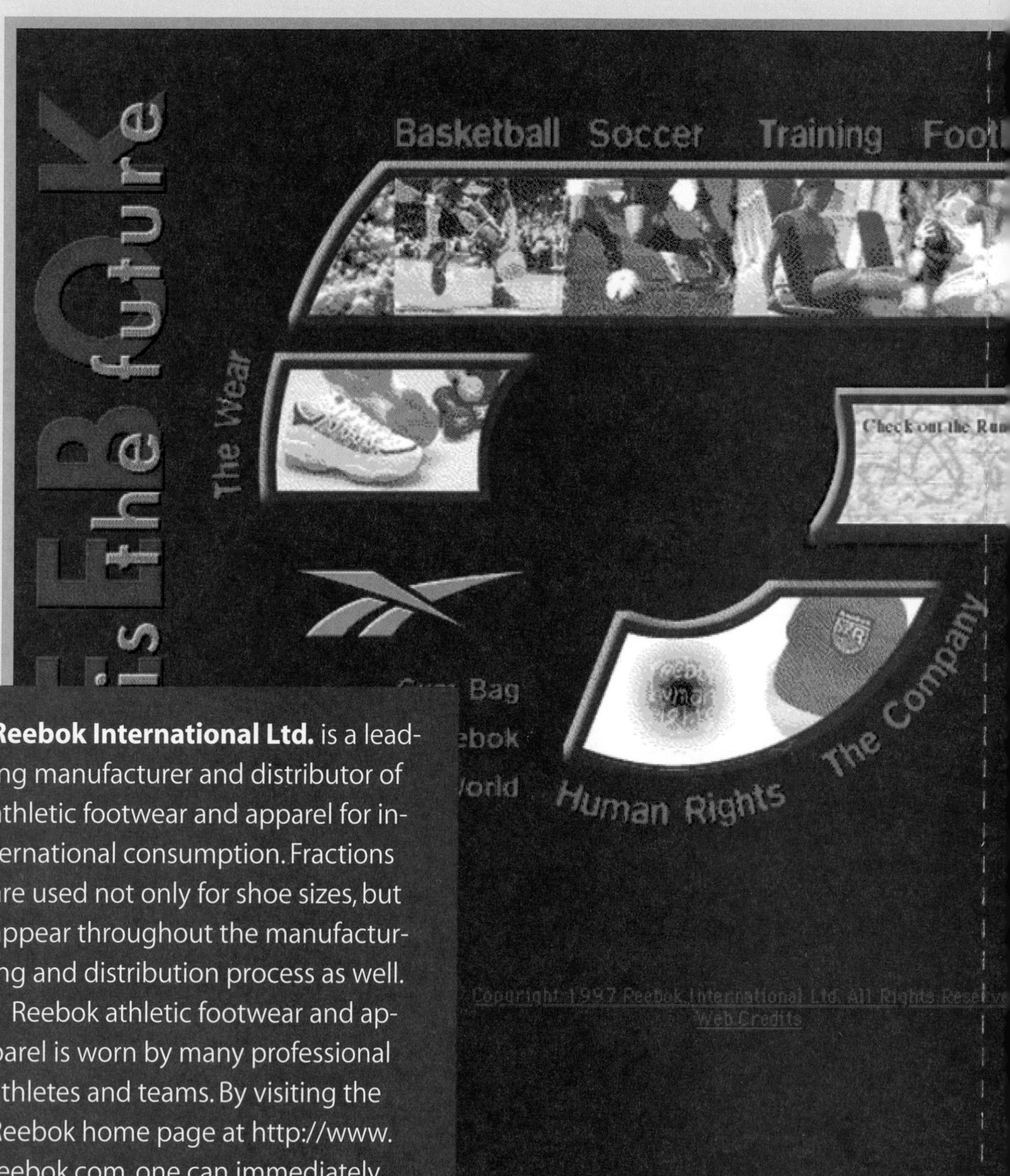

Reebok International Ltd. is a leading manufacturer and distributor of athletic footwear and apparel for international consumption. Fractions are used not only for shoe sizes, but appear throughout the manufacturing and distribution process as well.

Reebok athletic footwear and apparel is worn by many professional athletes and teams. By visiting the Reebok home page at http://www.reebok.com, one can immediately learn about the products available from, athletes affiliated with and history of this world-famous company.

Image courtesy of Reebok International Ltd. Any unauthorized duplication is strictly prohibited.

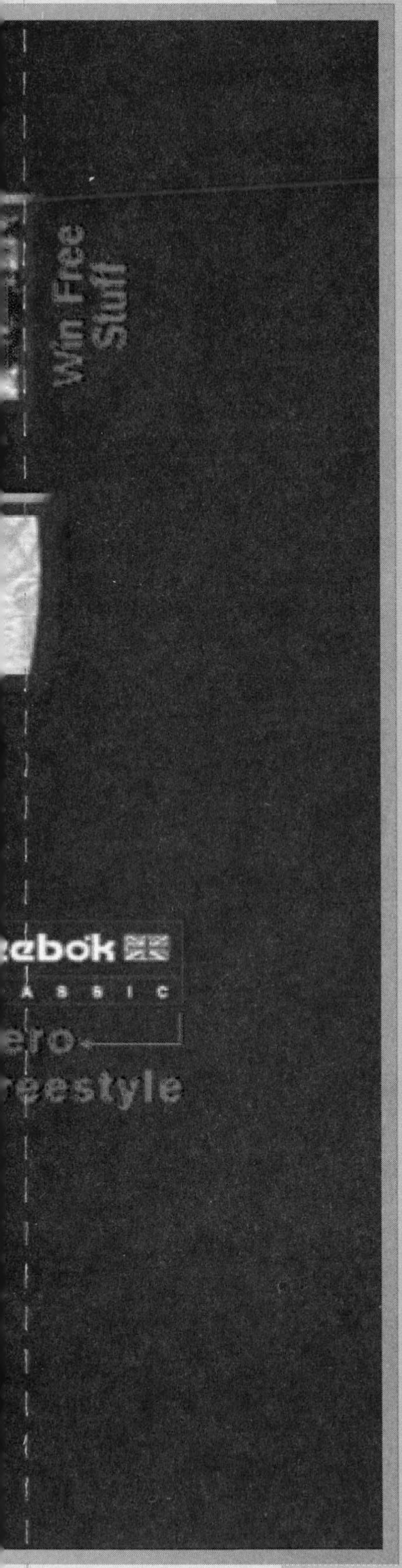

6 Fractions: Addition and Subtraction

Learning Objectives

By studying this chapter and completing all the assignments, you will be able to:

1. Change improper fractions to mixed numbers.
2. Change mixed numbers to improper fractions.
3. Reduce fractions to lowest terms.
4. Raise fractions to higher terms.
5. Add two or more fractions or mixed numbers.
6. Subtract one fraction or mixed number from another.

Nearly every job and profession uses fractions at one time or another. It's important to understand what they mean and how to combine them. Mastering the basic rules of fractions will help you do your job better, faster, and more productively.

A *fraction* expresses one or more equal parts of a whole unit, such as $\frac{3}{5}$ (three-fifths of a unit) or $\frac{1}{3}$ (one-third of a unit).

In a fraction, the number below the line, called the *denominator*, shows the number of equal parts into which the unit is divided. The number above the line, the *numerator*, shows how many equal parts are expressed.

$\frac{3}{4}$ $\frac{\text{numerator}}{\text{denominator}}$ $\frac{\text{number of equal parts}}{\text{total parts}}$

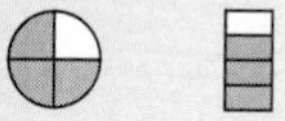

The example above is known as a proper fraction. A *proper fraction* is smaller than one whole unit; its value is less than one. In all proper fractions, the numerator is smaller than the denominator. Here is another example:

$\frac{2}{3}$ $\frac{\text{numerator is smaller number}}{\text{denominator is larger number}}$

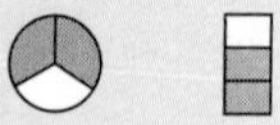

An *improper fraction* is one whole unit or more. The numerator of an improper fraction is larger than or equal to the denominator.

$\frac{5}{3}$ $\frac{\text{numerator is larger (or equal)}}{\text{denominator is smaller (or equal)}}$

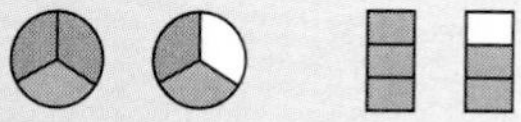

Look back at the diagram illustrating improper fractions. Notice that there are two whole units drawn to represent $\frac{5}{3}$. The diagram shows one whole unit shaded plus $\frac{2}{3}$ of another unit shaded. This is a diagram of a *mixed number*. A mixed number is actually the sum of a whole number and a proper fraction. We do not, however, write the plus sign. Other examples are $6\frac{1}{4}$, $3\frac{5}{6}$, and $2\frac{3}{5}$. You can change any improper fraction to a mixed number and vice versa.

Changing an Improper Fraction to a Mixed Number

LEARNING OBJECTIVES 1

Change improper fractions to mixed numbers.

STEPS to Change an Improper Fraction to a Mixed Number

1. Divide the numerator by the denominator.
2. Put the quotient in the whole-number position.
3. Put the remainder in the numerator position of the fraction part.
4. Put the original denominator in the denominator position of the fraction part.

EXAMPLE A

Change $\frac{11}{8}$ to a mixed number.

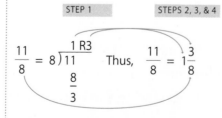

STEP 1

$$\frac{11}{8} = 8\overline{)11} = 1 \text{ R3} \quad \begin{array}{r} 11 \\ -8 \\ \hline 3 \end{array}$$

STEPS 2, 3, & 4

$$\text{Thus, } \frac{11}{8} = 1\frac{3}{8}$$

Note: Refer to Point A in Figure 6-1 to see where this mixed number appears on a ruler.

Figure 6-1: On a ruler, it's easy to see how an improper fraction equates to a mixed number—see points A and B.

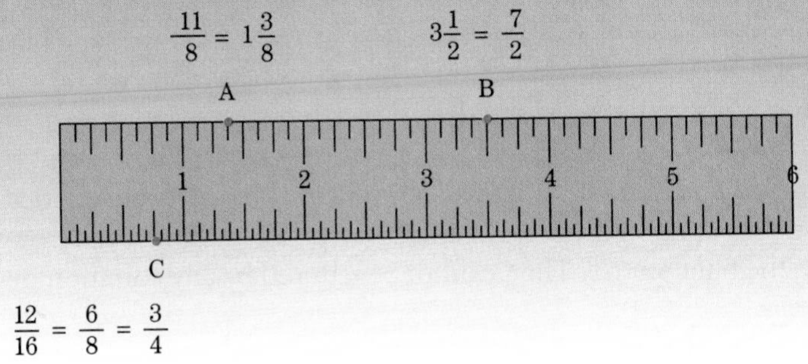

CONCEPT CHECK 6.1

Change $\frac{19}{5}$ to a mixed number.

Divide 19 by 5. The quotient is 3, so the whole number is 3; the remainder is 4, so the new numerator is 4.

$5\overline{)19}$ = 3 R4

$\frac{19}{5} = 3\frac{4}{5}$

Changing a Mixed Number to an Improper Fraction

STEPS to Change a Mixed Number to an Improper Fraction

1. Multiply the denominator of the fraction by the whole number.
2. Add the numerator of the fraction to the product of Step 1. Put the sum in the numerator position of the improper fraction.
3. Put the denominator of the fraction of the mixed number in the denominator position of the improper fraction.

LEARNING OBJECTIVES 2

Change mixed numbers to improper fractions.

EXAMPLE B

Change $3\frac{1}{2}$ to an improper fraction.

STEP 1 | STEPS 2 & 3

$2 \times 3 = 6$ Thus, $3\frac{1}{2} = \frac{6+1}{2} = \frac{7}{2}$

See Point B in Figure 6-1.

CONCEPT CHECK 6.2

Change $2\frac{3}{4}$ to an improper fraction.

Multiply 4 by 2; the product is 8. Add 3 to 8; the sum is 11. Therefore, the new numerator is 11. The denominator is still 4.

$4 \times 2 = 8$
$8 + 3 = 11$

$2\frac{3}{4} = \frac{11}{4}$

Reducing Fractions to Lowest Terms

LEARNING OBJECTIVES 3

Reduce fractions to lowest terms.

Simpler fractions are easier to use. Look carefully at Point C on the tape measure in Figure 6-1. It measures $\frac{12}{16}$ inch, $\frac{6}{8}$ inch, or $\frac{3}{4}$ inch. But almost everyone would say that the distance is $\frac{3}{4}$ inch. The other fractions are also correct, but they seem more complicated. The fraction $\frac{6}{8}$ is in lower terms than $\frac{12}{16}$, and $\frac{3}{4}$ is in lower terms than both $\frac{6}{8}$ and $\frac{12}{16}$. In each fraction except $\frac{3}{4}$, the numerator and the denominator can be evenly divided by the same number called the common divisor. For example, in $\frac{6}{8}$ both 6 and 8 can be evenly divided by 2 to reduce the fraction to $\frac{3}{4}$. The $\frac{3}{4}$ cannot be reduced by any common divisor. Thus, $\frac{3}{4}$ is in *lowest terms.*

STEPS to Reduce a Fraction to Lowest Terms

1. Divide both the numerator and the denominator by a common divisor greater than 1 to arrive at a reduced fraction.
2. If necessary, repeat Step 1 until the fraction is in lowest terms.

Rule: If a fraction's numerator and denominator have no common divisor greater than 1, the fraction is in lowest terms.

EXAMPLE C

Reduce $\frac{12}{16}$ to lowest terms.

$$\frac{12}{16} = \frac{12 \div 2}{16 \div 2} = \frac{6}{8} = \frac{6 \div 2}{8 \div 2} = \frac{3}{4} \quad \text{or} \quad \frac{12}{16} = \frac{12 \div 4}{16 \div 4} = \frac{3}{4}$$

Notice that it is faster to divide by 4 once than to divide by 2 twice. Always try to use the greatest common divisor that you can find.

CONCEPT CHECK 6.3

Reduce $\frac{30}{45}$ to lowest terms.

Divide both the numerator and the denominator by 3 and then by 5, or divide them both by 15:

$30 \div 15 = 2$ and $45 \div 15 = 3$. So, $\frac{30}{45} = \frac{2}{3}$

Raising Fractions to Higher Terms

LEARNING OBJECTIVES 4

Raise fractions to higher terms.

A fraction is raised to *higher terms* by multiplying both the numerator and the denominator by the *same* number. **The new numerator and denominator will be exact multiples of the old numerator and denominator.**

STEPS to Raise a Fraction to Higher Terms

1. Divide the new denominator by the old denominator. The quotient is the *common multiplier.*
2. Multiply the old numerator by the multiplier.
3. Multiply the old denominator by the multiplier.

EXAMPLE D

Raise $\frac{3}{4}$ to twenty-fourths.

STEP 1

$$\frac{3}{4} = \frac{?}{24} \qquad 24 \div 4 = 6$$

STEPS 2 & 3

$$\text{So, } \frac{3}{4} = \frac{3 \times 6}{4 \times 6} = \frac{18}{24}$$

EXAMPLE E

Raise $\frac{5}{6}$ to twenty-fourths.

STEP 1

$$\frac{5}{6} = \frac{?}{24} \qquad 24 \div 6 = 4$$

STEPS 2 & 3

$$\text{So, } \frac{5}{6} = \frac{5 \times 4}{6 \times 4} = \frac{20}{24}$$

In examples D and E, the new fractions, $\frac{18}{24}$ and $\frac{20}{24}$, have the same denominator, 24, which is called a *common denominator* of $\frac{3}{4}$ and $\frac{5}{6}$. The most important reason for learning to raise fractions to higher terms is to create new fractions with common denominators. In examples D and E, 12 is also a common denominator, and 12 is smaller than 24. Thus, 12 is called the *least common denominator* of $\frac{3}{4}$ and $\frac{5}{6}$—it is the least, or lowest, number divisible by both 4 and 6.

CONCEPT CHECK 6.4

Raise $\frac{5}{8}$ to twenty-fourths.

Divide 24 by 8. The quotient 3 is the common multiplier.
Multiply 5 by 3, giving 15; multiply 8 by 3, giving 24.

$$\frac{5}{8} = \frac{5 \times 3}{8 \times 3} = \frac{15}{24}$$

Fractions on the New York Stock Exchange

Today, the New York Stock Exchange is the most important stock exchange in America and is among the most important in the world. Like other American stock exchanges, it continues to quote prices of American stocks as mixed numbers, in dollars. The fractional part of the stock price will be in either halves, quarters, eighths, or sixteenths of a dollar. For example, the price of one share of General Motors stock might be quoted as $61\frac{1}{2}$, one share of Ford as $46\frac{3}{4}$, and one share of Chrysler as $33\frac{7}{8}$. Some of the fractions used to quote stock prices appear below.

Fraction	Meaning	Fraction	Meaning	Fraction	Meaning
$\frac{1}{2}$	50 cents	$\frac{1}{8}$	$12\frac{1}{2}$ cents	$\frac{1}{16}$	$6\frac{1}{4}$ cents
$\frac{1}{4}$	25 cents	$\frac{3}{8}$	$37\frac{1}{2}$ cents	$\frac{3}{16}$	$18\frac{3}{4}$ cents
$\frac{3}{4}$	75 cents	$\frac{5}{8}$	$62\frac{1}{2}$ cents	$\frac{5}{16}$	$31\frac{1}{4}$ cents
		$\frac{7}{8}$	$87\frac{1}{2}$ cents	$\frac{11}{16}$	$68\frac{3}{4}$ cents

Price	Interpretation
$35\frac{1}{2}$	The price is \$35.50 per share of stock.
$8\frac{3}{4}$	The price is \$8.75 per share of stock.

It is normal for us to say "a quarter" to mean $\frac{1}{4}$ of a dollar, or 25 cents, and "a half dollar" to mean 50 cents. It is less normal to say "three quarters" or "three fourths" instead of 75 cents, and it would be downright unusual for anyone to say "five eighths" to mean $\frac{5}{8}$ of a dollar, or $62\frac{1}{2}$ cents, unless the reference was to the stock market.

COMPLETE ASSIGNMENT 6.1.

Adding Fractions or Mixed Numbers

LEARNING OBJECTIVES 5

Add two or more fractions or mixed numbers.

Fractions and mixed numbers are all numbers—they can be added and subtracted just like whole numbers. However, **before fractions and mixed numbers can be added or subtracted, they must have common denominators.** The product of the denominators is always a common denominator, but there may be a smaller one.

STEPS to Add Two or More Fractions

1. If necessary, change the fractions to fractions with a common denominator. Put the common denominator in the denominator position of the answer.
2. Add the numerators of the new fractions. Put the sum of the numerators in the numerator position of the answer.
3. Reduce the answer, or write it as a mixed number in lowest terms.

EXAMPLE F

Add $\frac{7}{8}$ and $\frac{5}{8}$.

STEP 1

The denominator 8 is already common to both fractions.

STEP 2 STEP 3

$$\frac{7}{8} + \frac{5}{8} = \frac{12}{8} = 1\frac{4}{8} = 1\frac{1}{2}$$

EXAMPLE G

Add $\frac{5}{6}$ and $\frac{3}{4}$.

The least common denominator is 12.

$$\frac{5}{6} + \frac{3}{4} = \frac{5 \times 2}{6 \times 2} + \frac{3 \times 3}{4 \times 3} = \frac{10}{12} + \frac{9}{12} = \frac{19}{12} = 1\frac{7}{12}$$

EXAMPLE H

Add $\frac{3}{10}$, $\frac{4}{5}$, and $\frac{2}{3}$.

A common denominator is $10 \times 5 \times 3 = 150$.

$$\frac{3}{10} + \frac{4}{5} + \frac{2}{3} = \frac{3 \times 15}{10 \times 15} + \frac{4 \times 30}{5 \times 30} + \frac{2 \times 50}{3 \times 50} = \frac{45}{150} + \frac{120}{150} + \frac{100}{150} = \frac{265}{150} = 1\frac{115}{150} = 1\frac{23}{30}$$

Note: Example H could have been solved more easily by using a common denominator smaller than 150—30, 60, 90, and 120 are all common denominators smaller than 150. The solution is correct, but there is less reducing needed if you use a smaller common denominator. Compare the solution in H with the solution in example I below.

EXAMPLE I

Add $\frac{3}{10}$, $\frac{4}{5}$, and $\frac{2}{3}$

The least common denominator is 30.

$$\frac{3}{10}+\frac{4}{5}+\frac{2}{3}=\frac{3\times 3}{10\times 3}+\frac{4\times 6}{5\times 6}+\frac{2\times 10}{3\times 10}=\frac{9}{30}+\frac{24}{30}+\frac{20}{30}=\frac{53}{30}=1\frac{23}{30}$$

The procedure for adding mixed numbers is almost identical to that for adding only fractions. First, the fraction parts and whole-number parts are added separately; then, the totals are combined.

STEPS to Add Two or More Mixed Numbers

1. If necessary, change the fraction parts to fractions with a common denominator.
2. Add the whole-number parts; add the fraction parts.
3. Combine the two sums to form a mixed-number answer.
4. Reduce the fraction part to a proper fraction in lowest terms (increasing the whole-number part if necessary).

EXAMPLE J

Add $1\frac{1}{12}$ and $4\frac{3}{4}$

The least common denominator is 12.

STEP 1

$$1\frac{1}{12} = 1\ \frac{1}{12}$$

$$+\,4\frac{3}{4} = +\,4\ \frac{9}{12}$$

STEPS 2, 3, & 4

$$5\ \frac{10}{12} = 5\frac{5}{6}$$

EXAMPLE K

Add $3\frac{3}{8}$, $7\frac{5}{6}$, and $\frac{1}{4}$

The least common denominator is 24.

STEP 1

$$3\frac{3}{8} = 3\ \frac{9}{24}$$

$$7\frac{5}{6} = 7\ \frac{20}{24}$$

$$+\,\frac{1}{4} = +\ \frac{6}{24}$$

STEP 2

$$10\ \frac{35}{24}$$

STEPS 3 & 4

$$10 + 1\frac{11}{24} = 11\frac{11}{24}$$

CONCEPT CHECK 6.5

a. Add $\frac{3}{5}$, $\frac{1}{3}$, and $\frac{7}{9}$

The least common denominator is 45.

$$\frac{3}{5}=\frac{3\times 9}{5\times 9}=\frac{27}{45}$$

$$\frac{1}{3}=\frac{1\times 15}{3\times 15}=\frac{15}{45}$$

$$+\,\frac{7}{9}=\frac{7\times 5}{9\times 5}=+\,\frac{35}{45}$$

$$\frac{77}{45}=1\frac{32}{45}$$

b. Add $1\frac{5}{6}$ and $2\frac{4}{9}$

A common denominator is 18.

$$1\frac{5}{6}=1\frac{15}{18}$$

$$+\,2\frac{4}{9}=+\,2\frac{8}{18}$$

$$3\frac{23}{18}=4\frac{5}{18}$$

Subtracting Fractions or Mixed Numbers

LEARNING OBJECTIVES 6

Subtract one fraction or mixed number from another

The procedure for subtracting one fraction from another is essentially the same as the procedure for adding one fraction to another.

STEPS to Subtract One Fraction From Another

1. If necessary, change the fractions to fractions with a common denominator. Put the common denominator in the denominator position of the answer.
2. Subtract one numerator of the new fractions from the other. Put the difference of the numerators in the numerator position of the answer.
3. Reduce the answer, if necessary.

EXAMPLE L

STEP 2, STEP 3

$$\frac{7}{8} - \frac{5}{8} = \frac{2}{8} = \frac{1}{4}$$

EXAMPLE M

STEP 1, STEP 2

$$\frac{3}{4} - \frac{1}{5} = \frac{3 \times 5}{4 \times 5} - \frac{1 \times 4}{5 \times 4} = \frac{15}{20} - \frac{4}{20} = \frac{11}{20}$$

When you subtract one mixed number from another, you may need to follow a slightly different procedure. If the fraction part of the subtrahend (the number being subtracted) is larger than the fraction part in the minuend (the number from which you are subtracting), you need to borrow from the whole-number part of the minuend.

STEPS to Subtract Mixed Numbers

1. If necessary, rewrite the mixed numbers so the fraction parts have a common denominator.
2. If the fraction part in the subtrahend is larger than the fraction part in the minuend (example O) borrow 1 from the whole-number part of the minuend. Otherwise, skip to Step 3.
3. Subtract the whole-number parts; subtract the fraction parts.
4. Combine the two differences to form the mixed-number answer.
5. If necessary, reduce the fraction part of the answer to lowest terms.

EXAMPLE N

STEP 1

$$5\frac{3}{4} = 5\frac{9}{12}$$

$$-2\frac{1}{3} = -2\frac{4}{12}$$

STEPS 3 & 4 $\quad 3\frac{5}{12}$

EXAMPLE O

STEP 1, STEP 2

$$4\frac{2}{9} = 4\frac{4}{18} = 3\frac{18}{18} + \frac{4}{18} = 3\frac{22}{18}$$

$$-1\frac{5}{6} = -1\frac{15}{18} = -1\frac{15}{18} = -1\frac{15}{18}$$

STEPS 3 & 4 $\quad 2\frac{7}{18}$

CONCEPT CHECK 6.6

a. Subtract $\frac{5}{6}$ from $\frac{7}{8}$
The least common denominator is 24.

$$\begin{array}{r} \frac{7}{8} = \frac{21}{24} \\ -\frac{5}{6} = -\frac{20}{24} \\ \hline \frac{1}{24} \end{array}$$

b. Subtract $2\frac{7}{10}$ from $5\frac{4}{15}$
The least common denominator is 30.

$$\begin{array}{rcrcr} 5\frac{4}{15} & = & 5\frac{8}{30} & = & 4\frac{38}{30} \\ -2\frac{7}{10} & = & -2\frac{21}{30} & = & -2\frac{21}{30} \\ \hline & & & & 2\frac{17}{30} \end{array}$$

Applications

Examples P and Q illustrate applications of the addition and subtraction of fractions.

EXAMPLE P

Buddy George, a chef, had $3\frac{1}{3}$ cups of fresh herbs. He used $\frac{3}{4}$ cup in a meat sauce and another $1\frac{1}{2}$ cups as a garnish on the serving platters. How much herb was left?

$\frac{3}{4} + 1\frac{1}{2} = \frac{3}{4} + \frac{3}{2} = \frac{3}{4} + \frac{6}{4} = \frac{9}{4}$ cups used $\quad 3\frac{1}{3} - \frac{9}{4} = \frac{10}{3} - \frac{9}{4} = \frac{40}{12} - \frac{27}{12} = \frac{13}{12} = 1\frac{1}{12}$ cups left

EXAMPLE Q

Shelly Evans remodeled her office. The old office subfloor was $\frac{3}{4}$ inch thick. She had it covered with new $\frac{1}{4}$-inch-thick plywood to make a smooth surface. Then she had vinyl tile installed. If the vinyl tiles were $\frac{3}{16}$ inch thick, what was the total thickness of the three layers of flooring?

$\frac{3}{4} + \frac{1}{4} + \frac{3}{16} = \frac{12}{16} + \frac{4}{16} + \frac{3}{16} = \frac{19}{16} = 1\frac{3}{16}$ inches thick

COMPLETE ASSIGNMENT 6.2.

Chapter Terms for Review

common denominator
common divisor
common multiplier
denominator
fraction
higher terms
improper fraction
least common denominator
lowest terms
mixed number
numerator
proper fraction

The Bottom Line

Summary of chapter learning objectives:

Learning Objective	Summary	Example
6.1	Changing improper fractions to mixed numbers	1. Change $\frac{26}{7}$ to a mixed number.
6.2	Changing mixed numbers to improper fractions	2. Change $3\frac{2}{5}$ to an improper fraction.
6.3	Reducing fractions to lower terms	3. Reduce $\frac{30}{42}$ to lowest terms.
6.4	Raising fractions to higher terms	4. Raise $\frac{7}{12}$ to sixtieths; that is, $\frac{7}{12} = \frac{?}{60}$.
6.5	Adding two or more fractions or mixed numbers	5. Add $\frac{7}{8}$, $\frac{5}{6}$, and $\frac{1}{4}$.
6.6	Subtracting one fraction or mixed number from another	6. Subtract $1\frac{3}{4}$ from $4\frac{2}{5}$.

Answers: 1. $3\frac{5}{7}$ **2.** $\frac{17}{5}$ **3.** $\frac{5}{7}$ **4.** $\frac{35}{60}$ **5.** $1\frac{23}{24}$ **6.** $2\frac{13}{20}$

Assignment 6.1: Fractions and Mixed Numbers

LEARNING OBJECTIVES 1 2 3 4

Name ______________________

Date ______ Score ______

A (20 points) Change the improper fractions to whole numbers or to mixed numbers. Reduce the answers to lowest terms. (1 point for each correct answer)

1. $\frac{13}{7}$ ____ **2.** $\frac{32}{10}$ ____ **3.** $\frac{4}{4}$ ____ **4.** $\frac{8}{5}$ ____

5. $\frac{18}{8}$ ____ **6.** $\frac{20}{15}$ ____ **7.** $\frac{15}{4}$ ____ **8.** $\frac{9}{2}$ ____

9. $\frac{11}{6}$ ____ **10.** $\frac{25}{5}$ ____ **11.** $\frac{48}{15}$ ____ **12.** $\frac{7}{3}$ ____

13. $\frac{12}{7}$ ____ **14.** $\frac{8}{3}$ ____ **15.** $\frac{27}{12}$ ____ **16.** $\frac{35}{16}$ ____

17. $\frac{60}{45}$ ____ **18.** $\frac{9}{5}$ ____ **19.** $\frac{33}{25}$ ____ **20.** $\frac{16}{11}$ ____

Score for A (20) ______

B (20 points) Change the mixed numbers to improper fractions. (1 point for each correct answer)

21. $1\frac{2}{3}$ ____ **22.** $3\frac{7}{10}$ ____ **23.** $2\frac{11}{15}$ ____ **24.** $5\frac{3}{5}$ ____

25. $2\frac{8}{15}$ ____ **26.** $4\frac{5}{8}$ ____ **27.** $3\frac{1}{4}$ ____ **28.** $1\frac{6}{11}$ ____

29. $5\frac{5}{6}$ ____ **30.** $6\frac{3}{5}$ ____ **31.** $1\frac{2}{7}$ ____ **32.** $2\frac{4}{9}$ ____

33. $3\frac{8}{13}$ ____ **34.** $1\frac{7}{12}$ ____ **35.** $4\frac{10}{21}$ ____ **36.** $6\frac{3}{8}$ ____

37. $4\frac{2}{7}$ ____ **38.** $2\frac{6}{11}$ ____ **39.** $5\frac{9}{10}$ ____ **40.** $3\frac{1}{6}$ ____

Score for B (20) ______

C (20 points) Reduce each fraction to lowest terms. (1 point for each correct answer)

41. $\frac{9}{15}$ ____ **42.** $\frac{15}{25}$ ____ **43.** $\frac{12}{20}$ ____ **44.** $\frac{8}{24}$ ____ **45.** $\frac{10}{15}$ ____

46. $\frac{6}{21}$ ____ **47.** $\frac{14}{35}$ ____ **48.** $\frac{32}{48}$ ____ **49.** $\frac{27}{45}$ ____ **50.** $\frac{18}{22}$ ____

51. $\frac{24}{30}$ ____ **52.** $\frac{42}{56}$ ____ **53.** $\frac{4}{18}$ ____ **54.** $\frac{17}{34}$ ____ **55.** $\frac{39}{65}$ ____

56. $\frac{33}{55}$ ____ **57.** $\frac{12}{42}$ ____ **58.** $\frac{28}{35}$ ____ **59.** $\frac{6}{27}$ ____ **60.** $\frac{49}{63}$ ____

Score for C (20)

D (20 points) Raise each fraction to higher terms, as indicated. (1 point for each correct answer)

61. $\frac{1}{6} = \frac{}{18}$ **62.** $\frac{3}{4} = \frac{}{20}$ **63.** $\frac{4}{5} = \frac{}{15}$ **64.** $\frac{7}{8} = \frac{}{24}$ **65.** $\frac{2}{3} = \frac{}{9}$

66. $\frac{5}{12} = \frac{}{36}$ **67.** $\frac{3}{7} = \frac{}{28}$ **68.** $\frac{8}{9} = \frac{}{36}$ **69.** $\frac{1}{2} = \frac{}{6}$ **70.** $\frac{9}{10} = \frac{}{50}$

71. $\frac{8}{11} = \frac{}{44}$ **72.** $\frac{3}{8} = \frac{}{40}$ **73.** $\frac{11}{12} = \frac{}{48}$ **74.** $\frac{5}{6} = \frac{}{12}$ **75.** $\frac{4}{9} = \frac{}{27}$

76. $\frac{1}{4} = \frac{}{28}$ **77.** $\frac{7}{10} = \frac{}{30}$ **78.** $\frac{1}{3} = \frac{}{12}$ **79.** $\frac{6}{7} = \frac{}{42}$ **80.** $\frac{2}{5} = \frac{}{45}$

Score for D (20)

E (20 points) Business Applications and Critical Thinking. Solve the following. (5 points for each correct answer)

81. Bri-Tex Fabrics sells fabric by the yard. To finish a project, a tailor needs only 54 more inches of fabric. How much fabric does he need, measured in yards? Write your answer as a mixed number in lowest terms. ____

82. Pompei's Pizza cuts each small pizza into six equal slices. Each slice is $\frac{1}{6}$ of a whole pizza. Rebecca has $\frac{2}{3}$ of a pizza on a plate. How many slices of pizza does she have? (*Hint:* Raise the fraction $\frac{2}{3}$ to sixths.) ____

83. The local True Value Hardware Store arranged a display of five drill bits on its counter. (Drill bits are used in power drills to drill holes in wood and metal.) A customer bumped into the display and knocked the drill bits onto the floor. The drill bits were marked with their diameters:, $\frac{9}{64}, \frac{3}{16}, \frac{1}{4}, \frac{7}{32}, \frac{1}{8}$. Arrange the drill bit sizes in order, from smallest to largest. (*Hint:* It may be useful to raise some of the fractions to common denominators, then reduce them back to lowest terms. ____

84. Kathryn Martinez of Martinez Paint Store needed to mix eighteen quarts of paint, so she poured all eighteen quarts into a five-gallon container. How many gallons of paint were in the container? Write your answer as a mixed number in lowest terms. ____

Score for E (20)

Assignment 6.2: Addition and Subtraction

LEARNING OBJECTIVES 5
LEARNING OBJECTIVES 6

Name ______________________

Date ______________ Score ______________

A (36 points) Add the following fractions and mixed numbers. Write the answers as fractions or mixed numbers, with fractions in lowest terms. (3 points for each correct answer)

1. $\dfrac{5}{8} + \dfrac{1}{8}$

2. $\dfrac{7}{10} + \dfrac{3}{10}$

3. $\dfrac{7}{16} + 2\dfrac{11}{16}$

4. $1\dfrac{2}{3} = $; $+\ 2\dfrac{3}{4} = $

5. $\dfrac{4}{5} = $; $+\ \dfrac{9}{10} = $

6. $\dfrac{5}{6} = $; $+\ \dfrac{2}{3} = $

7. $2\dfrac{3}{10} = $; $2\dfrac{1}{2} = $; $+\ \dfrac{3}{5} = $

8. $\dfrac{1}{3} = $; $\dfrac{1}{4} = $; $+\ \dfrac{1}{6} = $

9. $1\dfrac{1}{4} = $; $\dfrac{3}{8} = $; $+\ 4\dfrac{11}{12} = $

10. $4\dfrac{1}{2} = $; $3\dfrac{2}{3} = $; $+\ \dfrac{5}{6} = $

11. $\dfrac{3}{5} = $; $3\dfrac{5}{6} = $; $+\ 5\dfrac{1}{3} = $

12. $5\dfrac{8}{9} = $; $4\dfrac{8}{15} = $; $+\ 1\dfrac{1}{5} = $

______________ Score for A (36)

B (36 points) Subtract the following fractions and mixed numbers. Write the answers as proper fractions or mixed numbers, with fractions in lowest terms. (3 points for each correct answer)

13. $\dfrac{7}{8} - \dfrac{3}{8}$

14. $3\dfrac{11}{12} - 1\dfrac{1}{12}$

15. $\dfrac{3}{4} = $; $-\ \dfrac{7}{16} = $

16. $1\dfrac{3}{4} = $; $-\ 1\dfrac{2}{3} = $

17. $2\dfrac{7}{8} = $; $-\ 2\dfrac{1}{4} = $

18. $8\dfrac{1}{3} = $; $-\ 3\dfrac{1}{5} = $

19. $3\dfrac{3}{10} = $; $-\ \dfrac{7}{10} = $

20. $5\dfrac{1}{4} = $; $-\ 2\dfrac{3}{4} = $

21. $3\frac{2}{3} = \quad =$

$-\ 2\frac{5}{6} = \quad =$

22. $4\frac{2}{5} =$

$-\ 1\frac{3}{4} =$

23. $6\frac{7}{8} =$

$-\ 2\frac{2}{3} =$

24. $8\frac{1}{10} =$

$-\ 4\frac{3}{4} =$

Score for B (36)

C **(28 points) Business Applications and Critical Thinking. Solve the following. (4 points for each correct answer)**

25. On the first of the month, the price of one share of Reebok stock was $36\frac{5}{8}$. During the month, the stock decreased in value by $2\frac{3}{4}$ per share. What was the price of the stock at the end of the month? ______

26. Cathy Keeler bought some stock in Microsoft that was priced at $136\frac{3}{4}$. She sold it after two months, because the stock increased in price by $3\frac{1}{2}$ during the first month and by another $4\frac{7}{8}$ during the second month. What was the price of the stock when Cathy sold it? ______

27. To teach his children about financial investments, Bradley Carter gave each of them a share of stock. Bradley gave his daughter Sarah a share of General Motors that was priced at $54\frac{5}{8}$. After one week, the stock dropped by $\frac{3}{4}$. The stock price then rose, finishing the second week at $55\frac{1}{2}$. By how much did the stock price increase during that second week? ______

28. Desmond Green has a top board that is $\frac{13}{16}$ inch thick. He wants to use wood screws to attach it to a bottom board. If a wood screw is $1\frac{1}{2}$ inches long, how much of the screw will be left over to go into the bottom board? ______

29. Leslie Bishop is planning to attach a plywood panel to the wall with nails that are $1\frac{3}{4}$ inches long. The panel is $\frac{3}{8}$ inch thick. Beneath the panel will be a layer of sheetrock that is $\frac{1}{2}$ inch thick. How many inches of the nail will go into the wood frame that is underneath the sheetrock? ______

30. A dress manufacturer has a piece of fabric that is $15\frac{1}{2}$ yards long. She cuts off one piece that is $3\frac{3}{4}$ yards long and another piece that is $3\frac{2}{3}$ yards long. How many yards of fabric remain? ______

31. London Fabric Center sold four pieces of wool fabric to a tailor. The pieces measure $3\frac{2}{3}$ yards, $2\frac{3}{4}$ yards, 3 yards, and $4\frac{1}{2}$ yards. How many yards of wool did the tailor purchase? ______

Score for C (28)

Notes

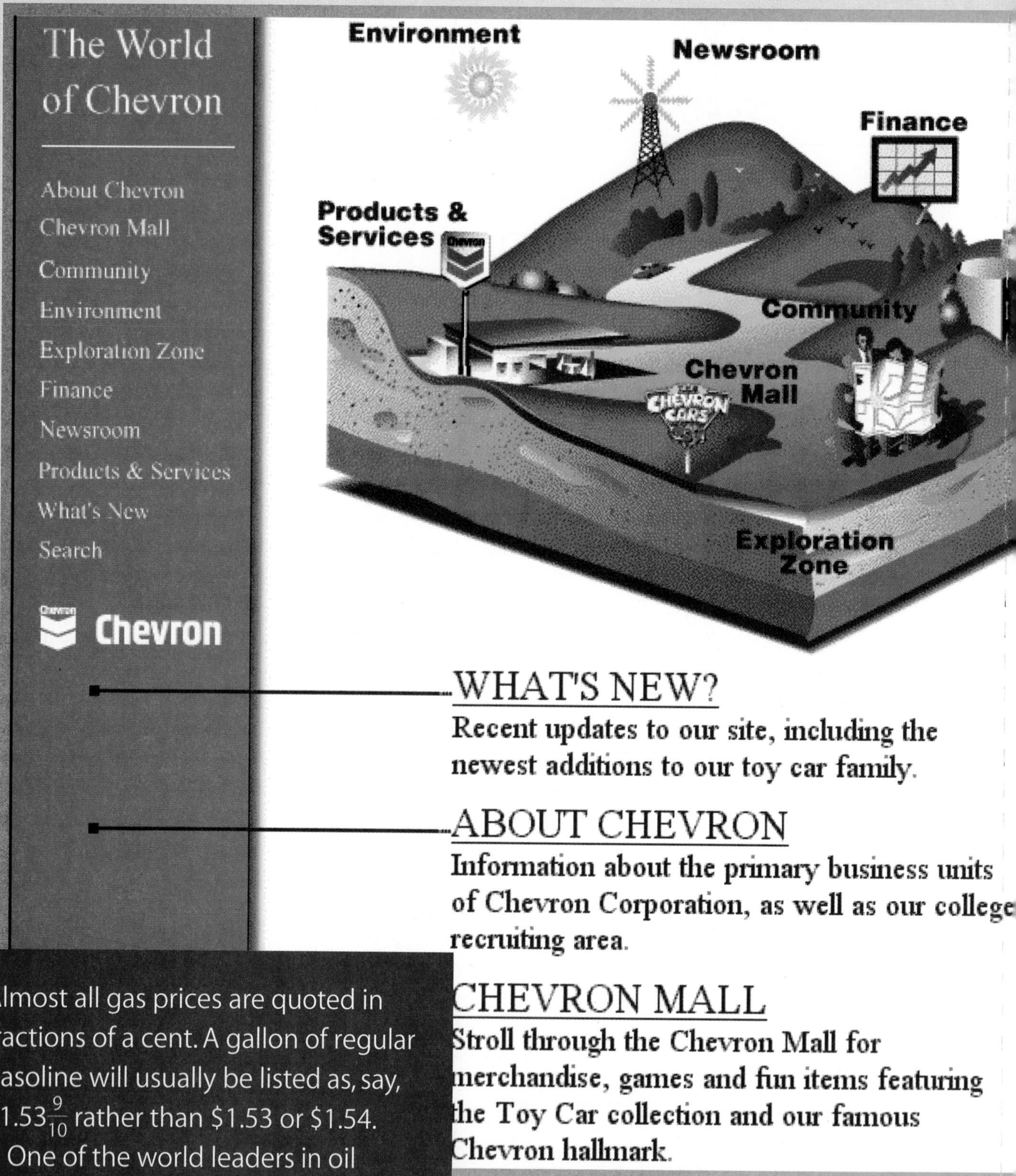
The World of Chevron
About Chevron
Chevron Mall
Community
Environment
Exploration Zone
Finance
Newsroom
Products & Services
What's New
Search
Chevron
Environment
Newsroom
Finance
Products & Services
Community
Chevron Mall
Chevron Cars
Exploration Zone
WHAT'S NEW?
Recent updates to our site, including the newest additions to our toy car family.
ABOUT CHEVRON
Information about the primary business units of Chevron Corporation, as well as our college recruiting area.
CHEVRON MALL
Stroll through the Chevron Mall for merchandise, games and fun items featuring the Toy Car collection and our famous Chevron hallmark.

Almost all gas prices are quoted in fractions of a cent. A gallon of regular gasoline will usually be listed as, say, $\$1.53\frac{9}{10}$ rather than \$1.53 or \$1.54.

One of the world leaders in oil products and services is **Chevron.** To learn about Chevron and its products, explorations, finances, company policies, community activities, and employment opportunities, visit its web site at www. chevron.com.

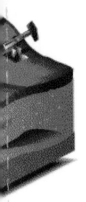

7 Fractions: Multiplication and Division

Learning Objectives

By studying this chapter and completing all the assignments, you will learn to:

1. Multiply two or more fractions.
2. Cancel common factors in fractions.
3. Multiply a whole number by a fraction.
4. Multiply with mixed numbers.
5. Divide one fraction or mixed number by another.

Have you ever noticed how many times we use fractions in everyday life? How about halftime of a football game, a quarter-pounder with cheese, a share of stock that may go up an eighth or down a quarter, or a newspaper that sells ads of full-, half-, quarter-, and eighth-page sizes.

Multiplying Fractions

Multiply two or more fractions.

Multiplication of fractions is the simplest operation with fractions. For multiplication, you do not need common denominators. The steps below explain how to multiply fractions.

STEPS to Multiply Fractions

1. Multiply the numerators to get the numerator of the product.
2. Multiply the denominators to get the denominator of the product.
3. Reduce the product to lowest terms.

EXAMPLE A

STEPS 1 & 2

$$\frac{2}{3} \times \frac{4}{5} = \frac{2 \times 4}{3 \times 5} = \frac{8}{15}$$

EXAMPLE B

STEPS 1 & 2 — STEP 3

$$\frac{2}{3} \times \frac{4}{5} \times \frac{5}{6} = \frac{2 \times 4 \times 5}{3 \times 5 \times 6} = \frac{40}{90} = \frac{4}{9}$$

CONCEPT CHECK 7.1

Multiply $\frac{4}{5} \times \frac{7}{10}$

Multiply the numerators:	$4 \times 7 = 28$	(The numerator of the product)
Multiply the denominators:	$5 \times 10 = 50$	(The denominator of the product)

The product is $\frac{28}{50}$, which reduces to $\frac{14}{25}$.

Canceling Common Factors

Cancel common factors in fractions.

When you reduce a fraction to lower terms, you are dividing out some common factor that is in both the numerator and the denominator. When you multiply one fraction by another, you can divide out any common factor that is in the numerator of one fraction and in the denominator of the other fraction. This process is sometimes called *cancellation*. It simplifies the multiplication process by making the products smaller.

EXAMPLE C

$$\frac{2}{3} \times \frac{4}{5} \times \frac{5}{6} = \frac{2}{3} \times \frac{4}{\underset{1}{5}} \times \frac{\overset{1}{5}}{6} = \frac{2 \times 4 \times 1}{3 \times 1 \times 6} = \frac{8}{18} = \frac{4}{9}$$

In example C, notice that only the factor *5* was canceled originally. There is also a *2* that could have been canceled. If every possible common factor is canceled before multiplication is done, the product will already be in lowest terms, as shown in example D.

EXAMPLE D

$$\frac{2}{3} \times \frac{4}{5} \times \frac{5}{6} = \frac{\overset{1}{\cancel{2}}}{3} \times \frac{4}{\underset{1}{\cancel{5}}} \times \frac{\overset{1}{\cancel{5}}}{\underset{3}{\cancel{6}}} = \frac{1 \times 4 \times 1}{3 \times 1 \times 3} = \frac{4}{9}$$

In example D, there was a choice of how to cancel the 2. The example illustrated canceling the 2 in $\frac{2}{3}$ and $\frac{5}{6}$. We could have canceled the 2 in $\frac{4}{5}$ and $\frac{5}{6}$, as shown in example E.

EXAMPLE E

$$\frac{2}{3} \times \frac{4}{5} \times \frac{5}{6} = \frac{2}{3} \times \frac{\overset{2}{\cancel{4}}}{\underset{1}{\cancel{5}}} \times \frac{\overset{1}{\cancel{5}}}{\underset{3}{\cancel{6}}} = \frac{2 \times 2 \times 1}{3 \times 1 \times 3} = \frac{4}{9}$$

CONCEPT CHECK 7.2

Multiply $\frac{4}{5} \times \frac{7}{10}$, using cancellation.

There is a common factor 2 in the numerator 4 and the denominator 10. Dividing out the 2 leaves $\frac{2}{5}$ and $\frac{7}{5}$. The numerator is $2 \times 7 = 14$; the denominator is $5 \times 5 = 25$.

$$\frac{4}{5} \times \frac{7}{10} = \frac{\overset{2}{\cancel{4}}}{5} \times \frac{7}{\underset{5}{\cancel{10}}} = \frac{2 \times 7}{5 \times 5} = \frac{14}{25}$$

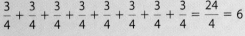

Multiplying a Whole Number and a Fraction

When learning arithmetic, students are taught that multiplication is a shortcut for repeated addition. We know that $8 \times 4 = 32$. But 8×4 means eight 4s and can be written as $4 + 4 + 4 + 4 + 4 + 4 + 4 + 4 = 32$. The same is true when one number is a fraction: $8 \times \frac{3}{4}$ means eight $\frac{3}{4}$s and can be written as

Multiply a whole number by a fraction.

$$\frac{3}{4} + \frac{3}{4} + \frac{3}{4} + \frac{3}{4} + \frac{3}{4} + \frac{3}{4} + \frac{3}{4} + \frac{3}{4} = \frac{24}{4} = 6$$

However, since we can write the whole number 8 as the fraction $\frac{8}{1}$, we can multiply the numbers as two fractions to get the same answer more quickly.

STEPS to Multiply a Whole Number by a Fraction

1. Write the whole number as a fraction by making the whole number the numerator and 1 the denominator.
2. Multiply the fractions.
3. Write the product as a mixed number in lowest terms.

EXAMPLE F

$$8 \times \frac{3}{4} = \frac{8}{1} \times \frac{3}{4} = \frac{\overset{2}{\cancel{8}}}{1} \times \frac{3}{\underset{1}{\cancel{4}}} = \frac{2 \times 3}{1 \times 1} = \frac{6}{1} \quad \text{or} \quad 6$$

CONCEPT CHECK 7.3

Multiply $5 \times \frac{2}{3}$

$$5 = \frac{5}{1}, \quad \text{so} \quad 5 \times \frac{2}{3} = \frac{5}{1} \times \frac{2}{3} = \frac{10}{3} = 3\frac{1}{3}$$

Multiplying Mixed Numbers

Multiply with mixed numbers.

If any of the numbers in a multiplication problem are mixed numbers, they must first be changed to improper fractions. Refer to the steps below.

STEPS to Multiply Mixed Numbers

1. Change all mixed numbers to improper fractions.
2. Multiply fractions (cancel if possible).
3. Write the product as a mixed number or proper fraction in lowest terms.

EXAMPLE G

STEP 1 | STEP 2

$$\frac{2}{5} \times 1\frac{3}{4} = \frac{2}{5} \times \frac{7}{4} = \frac{\overset{1}{\cancel{2}}}{5} \times \frac{7}{\underset{2}{\cancel{4}}} = \frac{1 \times 7}{5 \times 2} = \frac{7}{10}$$

EXAMPLE H

STEP 1 | STEP 2 | STEP 3

$$\frac{1}{4} \times 3 \times 2\frac{2}{3} = \frac{1}{4} \times \frac{3}{1} \times \frac{8}{3} = \frac{1}{\underset{1}{\cancel{4}}} \times \frac{\overset{1}{\cancel{3}}}{1} \times \frac{\overset{2}{\cancel{8}}}{\underset{1}{\cancel{3}}} = \frac{1 \times 1 \times 2}{1 \times 1 \times 1} = \frac{2}{1} = 2$$

CONCEPT CHECK 7.4

Multiply $3\frac{3}{5} \times 3\frac{3}{4}$

Change both mixed numbers to improper fractions: $\frac{18}{5} \times \frac{15}{4}$

Multiply, canceling the 2 and the 5: $\frac{18}{5} \times \frac{15}{4} = \frac{\overset{9}{\cancel{18}}}{\underset{1}{\cancel{5}}} \times \frac{\overset{3}{\cancel{15}}}{\underset{2}{\cancel{4}}} = \frac{9 \times 3}{1 \times 2} = \frac{27}{2} = 13\frac{1}{2}$

Spoken Language and Multiplication of Fractions

Examples of multiplication with fractions occur frequently in everyday speech, making multiplication possibly more important than addition, subtraction, and division. In mathematics, speech is converted to word problems, which often can be as imprecise as speech itself. Students just learning fractions may think they are having trouble mastering the subject when the real problem is in interpreting poorly phrased problems. A hint for understanding word problems: The key word *of* can be interpreted as "multiply." Following are three examples of oral communications involving fractions, each written three different ways.

1. a. "The eight-foot board is too long. Let's use three fourths of it." (i.e., $\frac{3}{4}$ of 8)
   b. "The eight-foot board is too long. Let's use three fourths as much." (i.e., $\frac{3}{4}$ of 8)
   c. "The eight-foot board is too long. Let's use one fourth less." (i.e., $\frac{1}{4}$ of 8 subtracted from 8)
2. a. "The gap under the door is nine sixteenths inch, which looks too wide. What if we make it two thirds of that?" (i.e., $\frac{2}{3}$ of $\frac{9}{16}$)
   b. "The gap under the door is nine sixteenths inch, which looks too wide. What if we make it two thirds as wide?" (i.e., $\frac{2}{3}$ of $\frac{9}{16}$)
   c. "The gap under the door is nine sixteenths inch, which looks too wide. What if we make it one third narrower?" (i.e., $\frac{1}{3}$ of $\frac{9}{16}$ subtracted from $\frac{9}{16}$)
3. a. "These screws are one and a quarter inches long, but they should be half of that again." (i.e., $\frac{1}{2}$ of $1\frac{1}{4}$ added to $1\frac{1}{4}$)
   b. "These screws are one and a quarter inches long, but they should be half again longer." (i.e., $\frac{1}{2}$ of $1\frac{1}{4}$ added to $1\frac{1}{4}$)
   c. "These screws are one and a quarter inches long, but they should be one and a half times as long." (i.e., $1\frac{1}{2} \times 1\frac{1}{4}$)

Figures 7-1a, 7-1b, and 7-1c illustrate graphically the various fractional parts described in the sentences above. Below each figure are the mathematical computations.

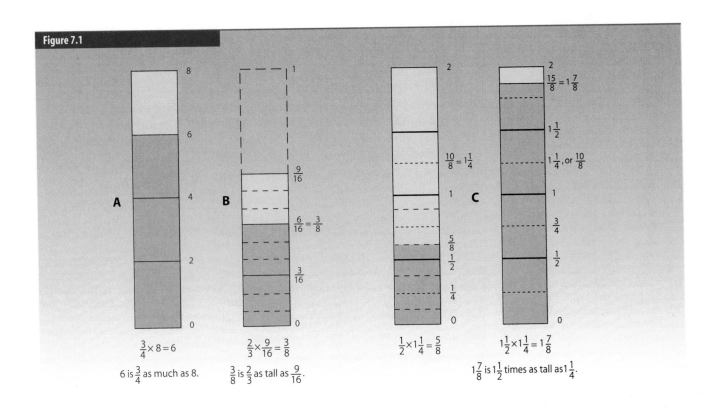

Figure 7.1

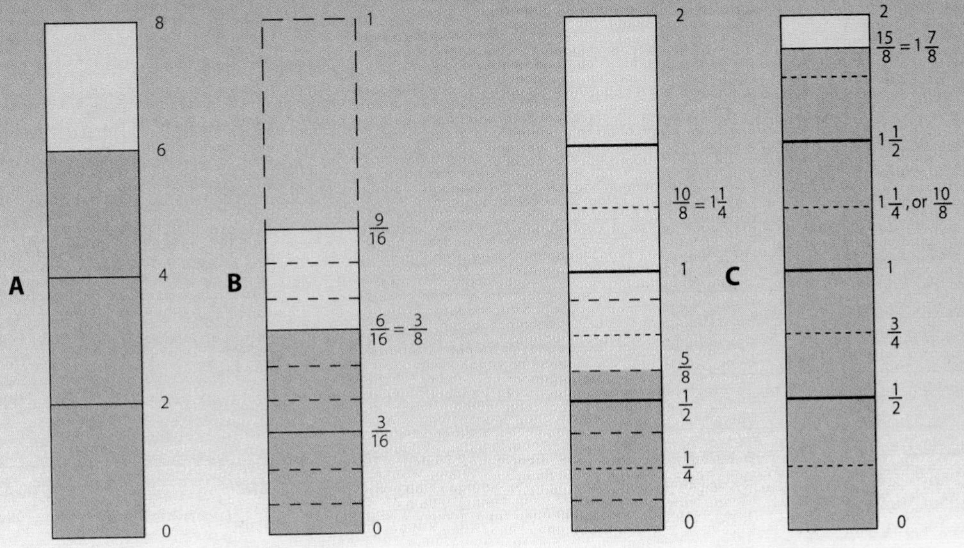

$\frac{3}{4} \times 8 = 6$ — 6 is $\frac{3}{4}$ as much as 8.

$\frac{2}{3} \times \frac{9}{16} = \frac{3}{8}$ — $\frac{3}{8}$ is $\frac{2}{3}$ as tall as $\frac{9}{16}$.

$\frac{1}{2} \times 1\frac{1}{4} = \frac{5}{8}$

$1\frac{1}{2} \times 1\frac{1}{4} = 1\frac{7}{8}$ — $1\frac{7}{8}$ is $1\frac{1}{2}$ times as tall as $1\frac{1}{4}$.

The following sentences relate Figures 7-1A, 7-1B, and 7-1C to oral communications 1, 2, and 3, respectively.

1. a. The column is 8 feet tall. $\frac{3}{4}$ of the column is 6 feet tall. $\frac{3}{4}$ of $8 = \frac{3}{4} \times \frac{8}{1} = 6$ feet.

   b. The column is 8 feet tall. A column 6 feet tall is $\frac{3}{4}$ as tall as the original 8-foot column.

   c. The column is 8 feet tall. $\frac{1}{4}$ of the column is 2 feet tall. If the original column is reduced by 2 feet, it will be 6 feet tall. $\frac{1}{4}$ of $8 = \frac{1}{4} \times 8 = 2$, and $8 - 2 = 6$ feet.

2. a. The column is $\frac{9}{16}$ inch tall. $\frac{2}{3}$ of $\frac{9}{16}$ is $\frac{6}{16}$, or $\frac{3}{8}$ inch tall. $\frac{2}{3}$ of $\frac{9}{16} = \frac{2}{3} \times \frac{9}{16} = \frac{6}{16} = \frac{3}{8}$ inch.

   b. The column is $\frac{9}{16}$ inch tall. A column $\frac{3}{8}$ inch tall is $\frac{2}{3}$ as tall as the original column.

   c. The column is $\frac{9}{16}$ inch tall. $\frac{1}{3}$ of the column is $\frac{3}{16}$ inch. If the original column is reduced by $\frac{3}{16}$ inch, it will be $\frac{6}{16}$ inch. $\frac{1}{3} \times \frac{9}{16} = \frac{3}{16}$, and $\frac{9}{16} - \frac{3}{16} = \frac{6}{16}$, or $\frac{3}{8}$ inch.

3. a. & b. The column is $1\frac{1}{4}$ inches tall. $\frac{1}{2}$ of $1\frac{1}{4}$ is $\frac{1}{2} \times 1\frac{1}{4} = \frac{1}{2} \times \frac{5}{4} = \frac{5}{8}$ inch. $1\frac{1}{4} + \frac{5}{8} = \frac{5}{4} + \frac{5}{8} = \frac{10}{8} + \frac{5}{8} = \frac{15}{8} = 1\frac{7}{8}$ inches.

   c. The column is $1\frac{1}{4}$ inches tall. $1\frac{1}{2}$ times as large is $1\frac{1}{2} \times 1\frac{1}{4} = \frac{3}{2} \times \frac{5}{4} = \frac{15}{8} = 1\frac{7}{8}$ inches.

COMPLETE ASSIGNMENT 7.1.

Dividing with Fractions

LEARNING OBJECTIVES 5

Divide one fraction or mixed number by another.

When we want to find $\frac{1}{2}$ of 8, we multiply $\frac{1}{2} \times 8$ to get 4:

$$\frac{1}{2} \times \frac{8}{1} = \frac{1}{\cancel{2}_{1}} \times \frac{\cancel{8}^{4}}{1} = \frac{1 \times 4}{1 \times 1} = \frac{4}{1} = 4$$

In the cancellation step, we actually "divided out" a 2 in the numerator and denominator. In other words, we divided the 8 by 2 to get 4. Instead of multiplying by $\frac{1}{2}$ we can divide by 2, and instead of dividing by 2 we can multiply by $\frac{1}{2}$. The numbers 2 and $\frac{1}{2}$ are called *reciprocals* (or *inverses*) of each other. You can always choose to either divide by a number or multiply by its reciprocal. In fact, in early lessons about fractions, you may have memorized the instruction to "invert the divisor and multiply."

STEPS to Divide by a Fraction or Mixed Number

1. If either the divisor or the quotient is a whole or mixed number, change it to an improper fraction.
2. *Invert* the divisor (exchange the numerator and denominator).
3. Change the division symbol to a multiplication symbol.
4. Solve the multiplication problem, simplifying if possible.
5. Write the answer as a proper fraction or mixed number, with the fraction in lowest terms.

EXAMPLE I

STEP 1 STEPS 2 & 3 STEP 4

$$\frac{3}{4} \div 2 = \frac{3}{4} \div \frac{2}{1} = \frac{3}{4} \times \frac{1}{2} = \frac{3 \times 1}{4 \times 2} = \frac{3}{8}$$

EXAMPLE J

STEPS 2 & 3 STEP 4

$$\frac{3}{10} \div \frac{2}{5} = \frac{3}{10} \times \frac{5}{2} = \frac{3}{\underset{2}{\cancel{10}}} \times \frac{\overset{1}{\cancel{5}}}{2} = \frac{3 \times 1}{2 \times 2} = \frac{3}{4}$$

EXAMPLE K

STEP 1 STEPS 2 & 3 STEP 4

$$\frac{7}{12} \div 2\frac{2}{3} = \frac{7}{12} \div \frac{8}{3} = \frac{7}{12} \times \frac{3}{8} = \frac{7}{\underset{4}{\cancel{12}}} \times \frac{\overset{1}{\cancel{3}}}{8} = \frac{7 \times 1}{4 \times 8} = \frac{7}{32}$$

In the previous examples, the dividend was a proper fraction. The same procedure is also followed when the dividend is a whole or mixed number.

EXAMPLE L

STEP 1 STEPS 2 & 3 STEP 4

$$9 \div \frac{3}{5} = \frac{9}{1} \div \frac{3}{5} = \frac{9}{1} \times \frac{5}{3} = \frac{\overset{3}{\cancel{9}}}{1} \times \frac{5}{\underset{1}{\cancel{3}}} = \frac{3 \times 5}{1 \times 1} = \frac{15}{1} = 15$$

EXAMPLE M

STEP 1 STEPS 2 & 3 STEP 4

$$2\frac{2}{5} \div \frac{3}{4} = \frac{12}{5} \div \frac{3}{4} = \frac{12}{5} \times \frac{4}{3} = \frac{\overset{4}{\cancel{12}}}{5} \times \frac{4}{\underset{1}{\cancel{3}}} = \frac{4 \times 4}{5 \times 1} = \frac{16}{5} = 3\frac{1}{5}$$

EXAMPLE N

STEP 1 STEPS 2 & 3 STEP 4

$$3\frac{3}{4} \div 1\frac{1}{2} = \frac{15}{4} \div \frac{3}{2} = \frac{15}{4} \times \frac{2}{3} = \frac{\overset{5}{\cancel{15}}}{\underset{2}{\cancel{4}}} \times \frac{\overset{1}{\cancel{2}}}{\underset{1}{\cancel{3}}} = \frac{5 \times 1}{2 \times 1} = \frac{5}{2} = 2\frac{1}{2}$$

CONCEPT CHECK 7.5

Divide: $3\frac{3}{4} \div 1\frac{1}{2}$

Change both mixed numbers to improper fractions: $\frac{15}{4} \div \frac{3}{2}$

Invert the divisor $\frac{3}{2}$ to $\frac{2}{3}$ and multiply:

$$\frac{15}{4} \times \frac{2}{3} = \frac{\overset{5}{\cancel{15}}}{\underset{2}{\cancel{4}}} \times \frac{\overset{1}{\cancel{2}}}{\underset{1}{\cancel{3}}} = \frac{5 \times 1}{2 \times 1} = \frac{5}{2} = 2\frac{1}{2}$$

COMPLETE ASSIGNMENT 7.2.

Chapter Terms for Review

cancel (cancellation)
reciprocals
inverses
invert

The Bottom Line

Summary of chapter learning objectives:

Learning Objective	Summary	Example
7.1	Multiplying two or more fractions	1. Multiply: $\frac{2}{5} \times \frac{3}{7}$
7.2	Canceling common factors in fractions	2. Cancel, then multiply: $\frac{9}{10} \times \frac{4}{7} \times \frac{5}{6}$
7.3	Multiplying a whole number by a fraction	3. Multiply: $\frac{2}{3} \times 6$
7.4	Multiplying with mixed numbers	4. Multiply: $4\frac{1}{6} \times 1\frac{7}{15}$
7.5	Dividing one fraction or mixed number by another	5. Divide: $1\frac{1}{5} \div 2\frac{2}{3}$

Answers: 1. $\frac{6}{35}$ **2.** $\frac{3}{7}$ **3.** 4 **4.** $6\frac{1}{9}$ **5.** $\frac{9}{20}$

Assignment 7.1: Multiplication of Fractions

Name

Date Score

A (40 points) Multiply the fractions. Cancel if possible. Where the word *of* appears, replace it by the multiplication symbol. Reduce the products to lowest terms. (4 points for each correct answer)

1. $\frac{1}{3} \times \frac{2}{5} =$ ________

2. $\frac{5}{6}$ of $\frac{9}{20} =$ ________

3. $\frac{3}{5} \times \frac{11}{12} =$ ________

4. $\frac{2}{3} \times \frac{1}{2} \times \frac{2}{5} =$ ________

5. $\frac{5}{6} \times \frac{4}{15} =$ ________

6. $\frac{3}{10} \times \frac{4}{7} \times \frac{5}{6} =$ ________

7. $\frac{3}{4}$ of $\frac{5}{6} =$ ________

8. $\frac{5}{18} \times \frac{4}{9} \times \frac{3}{10} =$ ________

9. $\frac{2}{3}$ of $\frac{5}{8} =$ ________

10. $\frac{5}{12} \times \frac{5}{6} \times \frac{27}{50} =$ ________

Score for A (40)

B (40 points) Change whole or mixed numbers to improper fractions and multiply. Cancel if possible. Where the word *of* appears, replace it by the multiplication symbol. Write the answers as mixed numbers or proper fractions in lowest terms. (4 points for each correct answer)

11. $1\frac{1}{2} \times 1\frac{5}{9} =$ ________

12. $\frac{3}{8}$ of $10 =$ ________

13. $3\frac{1}{3} \times 1\frac{11}{16} =$ ________

14. $2\frac{1}{2} \times 1\frac{5}{6} \times 2\frac{2}{5} =$ ________

15. $2\frac{5}{8} \times 6 =$ ________

16. $2\frac{1}{4} \times \frac{5}{6} \times 4\frac{2}{3} =$ ________

17. $\frac{2}{3}$ of $4\frac{4}{5} =$ ________

18. $1\frac{7}{8} \times 12 \times \frac{3}{10} =$ ________

19. $\frac{5}{6}$ of $5\frac{1}{3} =$ ________

20. $1\frac{1}{3} \times 1\frac{7}{8} \times 1\frac{4}{5} =$ ________

____
Score for B (40)

C (20 points) Business Applications. Use fractions and mixed numbers to solve each of the following. (5 points for each correct answer)

21. Last week Devlin Contracting built a small driveway that required $7\frac{1}{3}$ cubic yards of concrete. This week they must build another one that is $2\frac{1}{2}$ times larger. How much concrete will be required? ____________

22. Teddy Wilson bought eight pieces of copper tubing that were each $6\frac{3}{4}$ inches long. What was the total length of tubing that Teddy bought? (Give the answer in inches.) ____________

23. Wanda Yu trains employees to assemble door bells. The assembly time for the old bell is 8 minutes. Wanda estimates that it will take $1\frac{1}{2}$ times longer to assemble a newly designed one. How many minutes does she think the new bell will take to assemble? ____________

24. Coreen Jacobs had $2\frac{1}{4}$ quarts of liquid fertilizer in a container. Her supervisor asked her to mix $\frac{2}{3}$ of the fertilizer with water and save the remainder. How many quarts of fertilizer did Coreen mix with water? ____________

____
Score for C (20)

Assignment 7.2: Division of Fractions

Name

Date

Score

A (40 points) Divide the fractions. Cancel where possible. Write the quotients as mixed numbers or proper fractions in lowest terms. (4 points for each correct answer)

1. $\frac{2}{3} \div \frac{3}{5} =$ ________

2. $\frac{4}{5} \div \frac{1}{8} =$ ________

3. $\frac{5}{8} \div \frac{3}{4} =$ ________

4. $\frac{7}{10} \div \frac{8}{15} =$ ________

5. $\frac{3}{4} \div \frac{5}{8} =$ ________

6. $\frac{10}{21} \div \frac{5}{12} =$ ________

7. $\frac{5}{12} \div \frac{1}{6} =$ ________

8. $\frac{9}{16} \div \frac{3}{4} =$ ________

9. $\frac{5}{12} \div \frac{2}{3} =$ ________

10. $\frac{15}{16} \div \frac{5}{24} =$ ________

____

Score for A (40)

B (40 points) Change the mixed numbers to improper fractions and divide. Cancel where possible. Write the quotients as mixed numbers or proper fractions in lowest terms. (4 points for each correct answer)

11. $1\frac{3}{4} \div \frac{3}{8} =$ ________

12. $1\frac{1}{3} \div 1\frac{2}{5} =$ ________

13. $3\frac{1}{3} \div \frac{4}{5} =$ ________

14. $\frac{3}{10} \div 3\frac{3}{5} =$ ________

15. $3\frac{3}{4} \div 2\frac{1}{2} =$ ________

16. $\frac{4}{9} \div \frac{5}{6} =$ ________

17. $4\frac{4}{5} \div 1\frac{3}{5} =$ ________

18. $1\frac{3}{4} \div 2\frac{1}{3} =$ ________

19. $6\frac{1}{4} \div 1\frac{7}{8} =$ ________

20. $3\frac{5}{6} \div 1\frac{7}{12} =$ ________

____
Score for B (40)

C (20 points) Business Applications. Use fractions and mixed numbers to solve each of the following. State the answers as whole numbers, proper fractions, or mixed numbers. (5 points for each correct answer)

21. Western Landscapers needs several pieces of PVC irrigation pipe, each 3 feet 4 inches long. PVC pipe comes in 20-foot lengths. How many pieces can Western cut out of one length of pipe? *Hint:* 4 inches equals $\frac{1}{3}$ foot.

____

22. Tara Campbell has a diesel-powered generator on her ranch. The generator has a tank that holds $3\frac{3}{4}$ gallons of diesel fuel. Tara stores the diesel fuel in 55-gallon drums (barrels). How many times can Tara refill her generator from one drum of fuel? ________

23. To replant her collection of geraniums, Kathryn Bogen had 35 cubic feet of planting mix delivered. Kathryn's son is going to move the planting mix, using a wheelbarrow that holds $4\frac{2}{3}$ cubic feet. How many wheelbarrow loads will he have? ________

24. Brian Melvin, a home builder, is planning a narrow stairway to an attic. The stairs will each be 2 feet 3 inches long. Brian will cut the stairs from boards that are 12 feet long. How many whole stairs can he cut from one 12-foot board? *Hint:* 3 inches is $\frac{1}{4}$ foot. ________

____
Score for C (20)

Notes

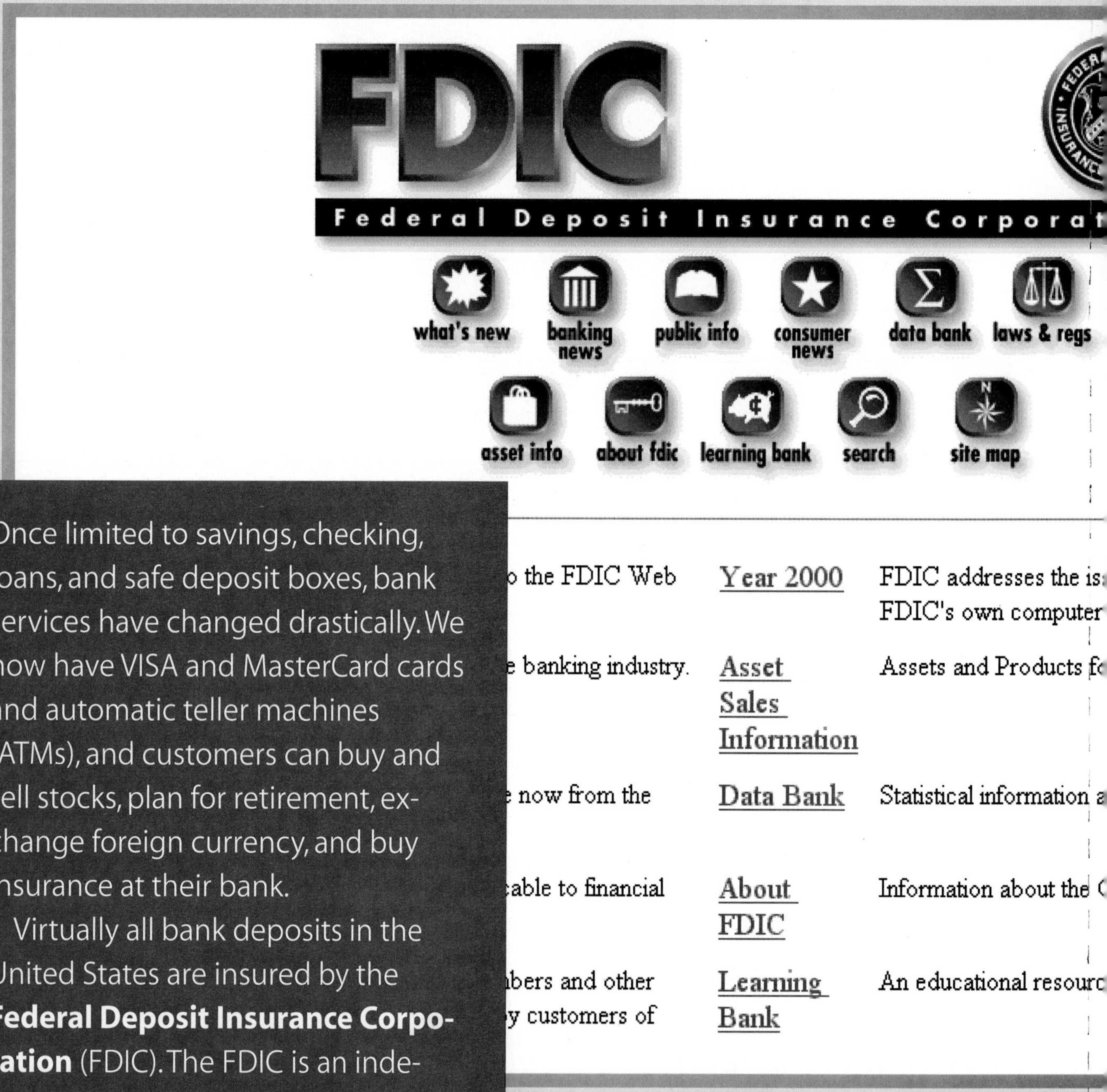

Once limited to savings, checking, loans, and safe deposit boxes, bank services have changed drastically. We now have VISA and MasterCard cards and automatic teller machines (ATMs), and customers can buy and sell stocks, plan for retirement, exchange foreign currency, and buy insurance at their bank.

Virtually all bank deposits in the United States are insured by the **Federal Deposit Insurance Corporation** (FDIC). The FDIC is an independent government agency created to stabilize and secure our nation's banking system. It insures most U.S. bank deposits by individuals and companies to a maximum of $100,000 per account.

The FDIC has a highly skilled and diverse workforce. Visit the home page at www.fdic.gov to see the many job opportunities that exist at the FDIC.

8 Banking

Learning Objectives

By studying this chapter and completing all the assignments, you will learn to:

1. Use a deposit slip and bank check.
2. Maintain a checkbook and check register.
3. Reconcile a bank statement with a checkbook balance.

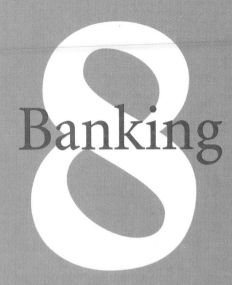

Practically all people and all U.S. businesses deal with banks and other financial institutions that offer traditional banking services (all called "banks" in this chapter). Most bank customers have accounts to which they make deposits in the form of cash, checks, electronic transfers, and, in the case of businesses, receipts from charge cards and other business transactions. Bank customers then draw checks (drafts) or make electronic withdrawals against their balances on deposit, generally to get cash, make purchases, pay bills, or submit taxes.

Using Deposit Slips and Bank Checks

LEARNING OBJECTIVES 1

Use a deposit slip and bank check.

Bank customers usually make deposits to their checking accounts by using *deposit slips.* Figure 8-1 shows a typical deposit slip, with spaces to list cash and checks being deposited.

In most businesses, each deposit will include a number of checks. Each check is individually listed on each deposit slip. Deposits are also made electronically. Many employees have their pay electronically transmitted directly from their employer's bank account to their individual bank account.

Bank *checks* are written orders directing the bank to pay a certain sum to a designated party, called the *payee.* Banks normally provide checkbooks to their members. Figures 8-2 and 8-3 show typical bank checks, one with the stub on the left and the other with the stub on the top.

Today, many bank transactions are completed electronically. Funds that are transmitted electronically are called *electronic fund transfers (EFT).* EFT transactions include *automatic teller machine (ATM)* transactions. Computer programs also initiate many electronic fund transfers. These transactions are processed through the Automated Clearing House Association and include such transactions as direct deposits of payroll checks and Social Security and other government and pension benefit payments.

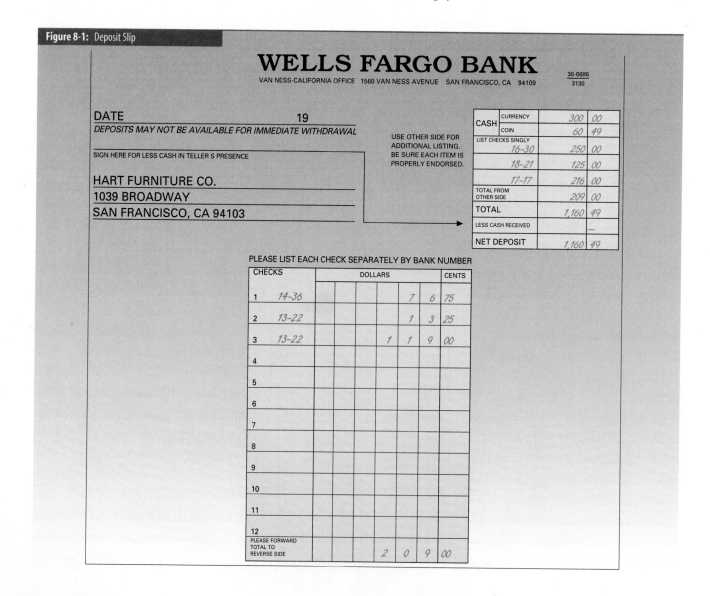

Figure 8-1: Deposit Slip

WELLS FARGO BANK

VAN NESS-CALIFORNIA OFFICE 1560 VAN NESS AVENUE SAN FRANCISCO, CA 94109

35-6686
3130

DATE 19

DEPOSITS MAY NOT BE AVAILABLE FOR IMMEDIATE WITHDRAWAL

SIGN HERE FOR LESS CASH IN TELLER S PRESENCE

HART FURNITURE CO.
1039 BROADWAY
SAN FRANCISCO, CA 94103

USE OTHER SIDE FOR ADDITIONAL LISTING. BE SURE EACH ITEM IS PROPERLY ENDORSED.

CASH	CURRENCY	300	00
	COIN	60	49
LIST CHECKS SINGLY	16-30	250	00
	18-21	125	00
	17-17	216	00
TOTAL FROM OTHER SIDE		209	00
TOTAL		1,160	49
LESS CASH RECEIVED			—
NET DEPOSIT		1,160	49

PLEASE LIST EACH CHECK SEPARATELY BY BANK NUMBER

CHECKS		DOLLARS	CENTS
1	14-36	76	75
2	13-22	13	25
3	13-22	119	00
4			
5			
6			
7			
8			
9			
10			
11			
12			
PLEASE FORWARD TOTAL TO REVERSE SIDE		209	00

Figure 8-2: Check with Check Stub on Left

No. 2506 $ 124.35
September 24 19--
To Ace Auto Repair
For Delivery truck

	$	¢
Balance Bro't Fwd	1,332	80
Amount Deposited	1,160	49
Total	2,493	29
Amount This Check	124	35
Balance Car'd Fwd	2,368	94

HART FURNITURE CO.
1039 Broadway
San Francisco, CA 94103

No. 2506
September 24 19--
35-6686
3130

Pay to the order of Ace Auto Repair $ 124.35

One hundred twenty - four and 35/100 DOLLARS

WELLS FARGO BANK
VAN NESS-CALIFORNIA OFFICE 1560 VAN NESS AVENUE SAN FRANCISCO, CA 94109

For Delivery truck repair

Robert S. Hart

⑆313066861⑆ 2506⑈ 117⑈020⑈8

Figure 8-3: Check with Check Stub on Top

BAL. FOR'D	997	03
DEPOSITS	— 451	04
	— 107	01
NEW BAL.	1,555	08

DATE 10-1-19--
TO: Men's Wearhouse
FOR: Suit-Slacks

3500

NEW BAL.	1,555	08
THIS CHECK	300	00
BAL. FOR'D	1,255	08

3500

VALUED CUSTOMER SINCE 1976

WELLS FARGO BANK

91-119
1221(1)

October 1, 19--

Pay to the order of Men's Wearhouse $ 300.00

Three hundred no/100------------------------------------ DOLLARS

MARY MAHEW
40 ACELA DR.
TIBURON, CA 94920

For Suit-Slacks

Mary Mayhew

⑆122101191⑆3500 0255 355521⑈

CONCEPT CHECK 8.1

Fill in the total (as necessary) and balance on each check stub. Carry each balance forward to the next

No. 1 $ 65.00
May 1 19--
To Citizens News
For Advertising

	$	¢
Balance Bro't Fwd	890	00
Amount Deposited		
Total		
Amount This Check	65	00
Balance Car'd Fwd	825	00

No. 2 $ 79.00
May 4 19--
To District Utilities
For Gas & electric

	$	¢
Balance Bro't Fwd	825	00
Amount Deposited		
Total		
Amount This Check	79	00
Balance Car'd Fwd	746	00

No. 3 $ 25.00
May 5 19--
To U.S Postal Service
For Stamps

	$	¢
Balance Bro't Fwd	746	00
Amount Deposited	100	00
Total	846	00
Amount This Check	25	00
Balance Car'd Fwd	821	00

Maintaining Checkbooks and Check Registers

Maintain a checkbook and check register.

Bank *checkbooks* provide check stubs or a special page on which to record deposits, withdrawals, check numbers, dates, check amounts, other additions and subtractions, and the account balance.

The check in Figure 8-2 shows that check number 2506 was written against the account of Hart Furniture Co. on September 24 to Ace Auto Repair. The check was for $124.35 for repairs to the delivery truck. The stub shows a balance brought forward of $1,332.80, a deposit on September 24 of $1,160.49, the amount of this check ($124.35), and a balance carried forward of $2,368.94.

Today, most small businesses and many individuals use a *check register*. The check register, like the check stub, provides a place to record information about each bank transaction. Figure 8-4 shows a typical check register. Note that a continuous balance is maintained.

Figure 8-4: Check Register

CHECK REGISTER			DEDUCT ALL PER CHECK OR SERVICE CHARGES THAT APPLY			BALANCE
DATE		CHECK NUMBER	CHECKS ISSUED TO OR DEPOSITS RECEIVED FROM	AMOUNT OF CHECK	AMOUNT OF DEPOSIT	$1,332.80
Sept	24		Deposit cash receipts		1,160.49	2,493.29
	24	2506	Ace Auto Repair	124.35		2,368.94
	24	2507	Morton Window Decorators	450.00		1,918.94
	24	2508	Donation to Guide Dogs	100.00		1,818.94
	25	2509	Secure Alarm Systems	150.00		1,668.94
Oct	19	2517	Best Janitorial Service	325.00		855.94
	20		Deposit cash receipts		980.00	1,835.94

CONCEPT CHECK 8.2

In the check register below, fill in the cash balance resulting from each transaction.

CHECK REGISTER			DEDUCT ALL PER CHECK OR SERVICE CHARGES THAT APPLY			BALANCE
DATE		CHECK NUMBER	CHECKS ISSUED TO OR DEPOSITS RECEIVED FROM	AMOUNT OF CHECK	AMOUNT OF DEPOSIT	$304.36
Mar	27	123	Replenish petty cash	$ 20.00		284.36
	31	124	Jiffy Janitorial Service	100.00		184.36
Apr	01	125	Sun County Water District	132.50		51.86
	03	-	Deposit weekly receipts		$2,470.80	2,522.66
	03	126	Midtown Mortgage Co.	475.00		2,047.66
	03	127	Sun Gas and Electric Co.	48.32		1,999.34
	04	128	Midtown Weekly Advertiser	29.80		1,969.54
	04	129	Trash Disposal, Inc.	60.00		1,909.54
	04	130	Pacific Plumbing Supplies	1,743.00		166.54
	10	-	Deposit weekly receipts		2,942.50	3,109.04

Reconciling Bank Statements

Checking account customers receive a printed *bank statement* every month. The bank statement shows an opening balance; deposits and credits, including EFTS; checks paid; withdrawals, including EFTs; service charges; general information about the account; and the balance at the end of the period. In addition, most banks today provide electronic banking through your personal computer. In this case, you can view your current bank statement at any time. Figure 8-5 shows a typical bank statement.

LEARNING 3 OBJECTIVES

Reconcile a bank statement with a checkbook balance.

The balance shown in the checkbook or check register is usually different from the balance on the bank statement. The items that cause this difference are used in reconciling the two balances. These items are as follows:

Figure 8-5: Bank Statement

WELLS FARGO BANK

VAN NESS-CALIFORNIA
1560 VAN NESS AVE.
SAN FRANCISCO CA 94109

#307

HART FURNITURE CO.
1039 BROADWAY
SAN FRANCISCO, CA 94103

CALL (415) 456-9081
24 HOURS/DAY, 7 DAYS/WEEK
FOR ASSISTANCE WITH
YOUR ACCOUNT.

PAGE 1 OF 1 THIS STATEMENT COVERS: 09/21/– – THROUGH 10/20/– –

WELLS FARGO NEWSLINE

NEW! GET STAMPS AT EXPRESS ATMS WHEN YOU STOP BY FOR CASH. AND, PLEASE NOTE THAT THE COMBINED TOTAL OF CASH WITHDRAWN AND STAMP PURCHASES CANNOT EXCEED YOUR DAILY CASH LIMIT.

REWARD ACCOUNT
31306686

SUMMARY

PREVIOUS BALANCE	$1,332.80
DEPOSITS	1,560.49
WITHDRAWALS	1,081.23
INTEREST	6.30
MONTHLY CHECKING FEE AND OTHER CHARGES	13.00
▸ **NEW BALANCE**	$1,805.36

MINIMUM BALANCE	$980.17
AVERAGE BALANCE	$1,336.91

CHECKS AND WITHDRAWALS

CHECK	DATE PAID	AMOUNT
2506	9/26	124.35
2507	9/26	450.00
2508	9/26	100.00
2509	9/27	150.00
2510	10/03	50.00
2511	10/10	132.50
2512	10/20	74.38

DEPOSITS

CUSTOMER DEPOSIT	DATE POSTED	AMOUNT
CUSTOMER DEPOSIT	9/25	1,160.49
EFT CREDIT	9/26	400.00

Outstanding checks Almost always there are some checks that have been written and recorded by the customer but have not yet been presented to or processed by the bank for payment and charged to the customer's account.

Bank charges to the customer At the time the bank statement is made up, the customer's account may have been charged for bank service fees, for printing checks, for bad checks returned, and for EFTs not yet recorded by the customer. These charges would therefore not yet be deducted from the customer's checkbook or check register balance.

Credits to customer's account In many cases, the bank has credited the customer's account for an item such as an EFT deposited into the account or interest earned on the account. Since the customer does not know the amount of these credits until the bank statement arrives, the credits are not yet entered in the customer's checkbook or check register.

Outstanding deposits A deposit made near the end of the statement period by the customer would have been recorded in the customer's checkbook or check register but not recorded by the bank in time to appear on the statement.

Because of these items that cause a difference between the bank statement balance and the customer's checkbook or check register balance, a reconciliation is done by the customer immediately upon receipt of the statement.

To start the reconciliation, a bank customer compares the check stubs or check register, all deposit slips, and any company records of ATM transactions with the bank statement. Such a comparison is called a *reconciliation of the bank balance.*

When Hart received its monthly bank statement, the bookkeeper noted that the ending balance was $1,805.36, but the balance in the company checkbook was $1,835.94. The bookkeeper noted the following differences: an EFT credit for $400 had been made to the account and not recorded by Hart; a bank service charge of $13 had been subtracted; interest earnings of $6.30 had been added; an October 20 deposit of $980 had not yet been recorded by the bank; and checks for $27.92, $10, $48.95, $144.25, and $325 had not yet been processed and deducted by the bank.

Most bank statements have printed on the back of the statement a form that can be used to quickly and easily reconcile the customer's checkbook or check register balance with the statement balance. Figure 8-6 shows this form as completed by the Hart Furniture bookkeeper.

STEPS to Reconcile Bank Balances

1. Reconcile the checkbook (check register) balance. Start with the last balance as recorded in the checkbook.
   a. Subtract any charges or debits made by the bank, such as service charges, check printing charges, returned-check charges, or EFT charges not yet recorded in the checkbook.
   b. Add any bank-statement credits, such as interest earned or EFT deposits not yet recorded in the checkbook.

   This gives you your ***adjusted checkbook balance.***
2. Reconcile the bank balance. Start with the balance as presented on the statement.
   a. Add any deposits or other credits not yet recorded by the bank.
   b. Subtract all outstanding checks.

   This gives you your ***adjusted bank balance.***
3. Ensure that the two adjusted balances agree.

Figure 8-6: Reconciliation Form

Balance Your Account

DATE *10/20/--*

Checks Outstanding

Check No.	Amount	
2513	*27*	*92*
2514	*10*	*00*
2515	*48*	*95*
2516	*144*	*25*
2517	*325*	*00*
TOTAL	*556*	*12*

1 Check off (✓) checks appearing on your statement. Those checks not checked off (✓) should be recorded in the checks outstanding column.

2

Enter your checkbook balance	*$ 1,835*	*94*
Add any credits made to your account through interest, etc. as shown on this statement. (Be sure to enter these in your checkbook).	*6*	*30*
	400	*00*
SUBTOTAL	*2,242*	*24*
Subtract any debits made to your account through bank charges, account fees, etc. as shown on this statement. (Be sure to enter these in your checkbook).	*– 13*	*00*
Adjusted checkbook balance.	*$ 2,229*	*24* **A**

3

Bank balance shown on this statement.	*$ 1,805*	*36*
Add deposits shown in your checkbook but not shown on this statement, because they were made and received after date on this statement.	*980*	*00*
Subtotal	*2,785*	*36*
Subtract checks outstanding	*556*	*12*
Adjusted bank balance.	*$ 2,229*	*24* **B**

Your checkbook is in balance if line **A** agrees with line **B**.

CONCEPT CHECK 8.3

At month end, Johnson Hardware received the following bank statement. Use the forms that follow the statement to reconcile the check register used in Concept Check 8.2 and the bank statement.

MIDTOWN BANK

MIDTOWN BANK

JOHNSON HARDWARE COMPANY
346 POPLAR STREET
MIDTOWN, CA 94872
THIS STATEMENT COVERS: 3/27/9- THROUGH 4/08/9-

SUMMARY	
PREVIOUS BALANCE	$ 304.36
DEPOSITS	2,470.80+
WITHDRAWALS	2,416.12-
INTEREST	5.60+
SERVICE CHARGES	7.00-
NEW BALANCE	$ 357.64

CHECKS AND WITHDRAWALS	CHECK	DATE PAID	AMOUNT	CHECK	DATE PAID	AMOUNT
	123	3/29	20.00	130*	4/06	1,743.00
	124	4/02	100.00			
	126*	4/03	475.00			
	127	4/05	48.32			
	128	4/05	29.80			

DEPOSITS	CUSTOMER DEPOSIT	DATE POSTED	AMOUNT
	CUSTOMER DEPOSIT	4/05	2,470.80

Enter your checkbook balance	$ 3,109	04
Add any credits made to your account through interest, etc. as shown on this statement. (Be sure to enter these in your checkbook).	5	60
SUBTOTAL	3,114	64
Subtract any debits made to your account through bank charges, account fees, etc. as shown on this statement. (Be sure to enter these in your checkbook).	7	00
Adjusted checkbook balance.	$ 3,107	64

Bank balance shown on this statement.	$ 357	64
Add deposits shown in your checkbook but not shown on this statement, because they were made and received after date on this statement.	2,942	50
Subtotal	3,300	14
Subtract checks outstanding	192	50
Adjusted bank balance.	$ 3,107	64

Your checkbook is in balance if line **A** agrees with line **B**.

Checks Outstanding

Check No.	Amount	
125	$ 132	50
129	60	00
TOTAL	$ 192	50

COMPLETE ASSIGNMENTS 8.1, 8.2, and 8.3.

Chapter Terms for Review

- adjusted bank balance
- adjusted checkbook balance
- automatic teller machine (ATM)
- bank statement
- check
- checkbook
- check register
- deposit slip
- electronic fund transfer (EFT)
- FDIC
- payee
- reconciliation of the bank balance

The Bottom Line

Summary of chapter learning objectives:

Learning Objective	Summary	Example
8.1	Using a deposit slip and bank check	1. Fill in the New Bal and Bal For'd on each check stub. Carry Bal For'd to the next stub.

#1				#2			
Bal For'd	$100.00	Date	01/17	Bal For'd	______	Date	01/22
Deposit	350.50	To	Store	Deposit	375.00	To	Store
New Bal	______		______	New Bal	______		______
This Ck	175.09	For	Misc	This Ck	78.88	For	Misc
Bal For'd	______		______	Bal For'd	______		______

Learning Objective	Summary	Example
8.2	Maintaining a checkbook and check register	2. Fill in the cash balance for each date.

CHECK REGISTER

DATE	CHECK NUMBER	CHECK TO—DEPOSIT INFORMATION	DEPOSIT AMOUNT	CHECK AMOUNT	BALANCE
					$2,077.50
12/11	100	MacDonalds		$ 77.14	
12/12		Monthly Salary Check	$782.17		
12/13	101	R.J. Maples–Rent		$1,000.00	
12/14	102	Macy's		$ 99.97	
12/15	103	True Value		$ 107.16	
12/17		Income from Stocks	$222.24		

Learning Objective	Summary	Example
8.3	Reconciling a bank statement with a checkbook balance	3. Robert Mark's monthly bank statement balance was $1,200. His checkbook balance was $1,440. He noted the following checks outstanding: #119 for $500; #125 for $197. He noted the following deposit as not recorded by the bank: $1,800. The bank had charged him $17 for checks and $20 for a bad check he had deposited. The bank had credited his account with an electronic transfer for $900. Reconcile the bank and checkbook balances.

Checkbook balance:		$1,440
Add electronic transfer:		______
Subtotal		______
Less bank charges:	______	
	______	______
Adjusted checkbook balance:		______
Bank balance on statement:		$1,200
Add unrecorded deposit:		______
Subtotal		______
Less outstanding checks: #119	______	
#125	______	______
Adjusted bank balance		______

Answers: 1. $450.50; $275.41; $650.41; $571.53 **2.** $2,000.36; $2,782.53; $1,782.53; $1,682.56; $1,575.40; $1,797.64
3. $2,303

Notes

Assignment 8.1: Check Register and Check Stubs

Name

Date Score

A (20 points) In the check register below, fill in the cash balance resulting from each transaction. (2 points for each correct answer)

1.

CHECK REGISTER			DEDUCT ALL PER CHECK OR SERVICE CHARGES THAT APPLY			BALANCE
DATE		CHECK NUMBER	CHECKS ISSUED TO OR DEPOSITS RECEIVED FROM	AMOUNT OF CHECK	AMOUNT OF DEPOSIT	$980.00
Apr	04	842	Central Mortgage Company	775.00		
	04	–	Deposit weekly cash receipts		3,987.50	
	05	843	Internal Revenue Service	1,743.00		
	06	844	State Income Tax	990.00		
	07	845	Olympic Telephone	45.00		
	08	846	Cash Register Repair Service	72.00		
	12	–	Deposit weekly cash receipts		2,995.75	
	12	847	Central Utilities	87.00		
	12	848	Central Advertising, Inc.	850.00		
	12	849	Tax Services, Inc.	425.00		

Score for A (20)

B (15 points) Fill in the new balance (New Bal) and balance forward (BalFor'd) on each check stub, carrying each balance forward to the next stub. ($1\frac{1}{2}$ points for each correct answer)

2.

#101
BalFor'd 806.12 Date 6-1 New Bal ______
Deposit 300.00 To ACE This Ck 29.30
New Bal ______ For REPAIR BalFor'd ______

3.

#102
BalFor'd ______ Date 6-5 New Bal ______
Deposit ______ To DON This Ck 312.80
New Bal ______ For NOTE BalFor'd ______

4.

#103
BalFor'd ______ Date 6-8 New Bal ______
Deposit 862.13 To NEC This Ck 740.12
New Bal ______ For COMPUTER BalFor'd ______

5.

#104
BalFor'd ______ Date 6-10 New Bal ______
Deposit 2,160.00 To CHRON This Ck 83.16
New Bal ______ For AD BalFor'd ______

6.

#105
BalFor'd ______ Date 6-15 New Bal ______
Deposit 907.16 To B/A This Ck 294.28
New Bal ______ For CAR PAYMENT BalFor'd ______

Score for B (15)

C (20 points) According to the check register of the ABC Advertising Company, the cash balance on July 1 was $1,072.16. During the month, deposits were made of $129.67, $681.10, and $100.50. Checks were recorded for $98.99, $307.53, $19.56, $212.40, $4.77, and $88.62. (15 points for a correct answer in 7; 5 points for a correct answer in 8)

7. What was the cash balance shown in the check register on July 31? ________

8. After entering all of the items in the check register, the bookkeeper found that the check recorded as $212.40 was actually written as $224.20. What is the correct cash balance? ________

____
Score for C (20)

D (45 points) The following problems show the deposits and checks that were recorded on a series of check stubs. In each problem, find the bank balance after each deposit or check. (3 points for each correct answer)

9.

Balance	$4,300	00
Check #1	279	10
Balance		
Check #2	148	20
Balance		
Deposit	976	80
Balance		
Check #3	814	00
Balance		
Check #4	285	17
Balance		

10.

Balance	$205	55
Check #21	25	00
Balance		
Deposit	876	43
Balance		
Check #22	188	14
Balance		
Check #23	314	82
Balance		
Check #24	72	38
Balance		

11.

Balance	$1,401	36
Deposit	277	00
Balance		
Check #31	136	41
Balance		
Check #32	364	18
Balance		
Deposit	1,124	85
Balance		
Check #33	775	10
Balance		

____
Score for D (45)

Assignment 8.2: Check Register and Bank Statements

Name

Date Score

A (40 points) Solve the following problems. (10 points for a correct final balance in 1; 30 points for a correct final answer in 2)

1. On October 31, the balance of the account of Toyland, Inc., at the Citizens Bank was $922.10. This amount was also the balance on the check register at that time. Company checks written and deposits made during November are shown on the check register. Fill in the cash balance for each transaction.

CHECK REGISTER			DEDUCT ALL PER CHECK OR SERVICE CHARGES THAT APPLY			BALANCE
DATE		CHECK NUMBER	CHECKS ISSUED TO OR DEPOSITS RECEIVED FROM	AMOUNT OF CHECK	AMOUNT OF DEPOSIT	$922.10
Nov	01	551	Muni. Water, Inc. (2 mos)	119.60		
	06	552	Columbia Gas	49.60		
	07	553	Olympia Telephone	74.19		
	07	-	Deposit cash receipts		225.50	
	21	554	City Trash Disposal (3 mos)	112.32		
	21	555	Jack's Janitorial Service	33.33		
	24	556	United Fund	12.00		
	24	557	Guide Dogs for the Blind	67.77		
	26	558	Wilson Insurance	212.00		
	28	559	Security Systems, Inc.	138.00		
	28	-	Deposit cash receipts		94.00	

2. On December 3, Toyland, Inc., whose check register you completed in Problem 1, received the bank statement shown below. Reconcile the balance on the check register at the end of the month with the final balance on the bank statement. In reconciling the bank statement, you can find which of the checks are outstanding by comparing the list of checks on the statement with the register. Interest and a service charge were recorded on the statement.

CB CITIZEN'S BANK

STATEMENT OF ACCOUNT

ACCOUNT NUMBER: 072 4736

TOYLAND, INC.
4617 GILMORE ROAD
WHEATLAND, WI 54828-6075

DATE OF STATEMENT: 11/30/--

Balance From Previous Statement	Number of Debits	Amount of Checks and Debits	No. of Credits	Amount of Deposits and Credits	Service Charge	Statement Balance
922.10	8	594.81	2	229.70	9.00	547.99

DATE	CHECKS - DEBITS	CHECKS - DEBITS	DEPOSITS - CREDITS	BALANCE
11/03	119.60			802.50
11/05	49.60			752.90
11/09	9.00 SC			743.90
11/09	74.19			669.71
11/09			225.50 ATM	895.21
11/23	112.32	33.33		749.56
11/26	67.77			681.79
11/30	138.00			543.79
11/30			4.20 INT	547.99

PLEASE EXAMINE AND REPORT ANY DISCREPANCIES WITHIN 10 DAYS — DM-Debit Memo, OD-Overdraft, ATM-Automated Teller Machine, INT-Interest Paid, CM-Credit Memo, SC-Service Charge

TOYLAND, INC.
Reconciliation of Bank Statement
November 30

Bank balance on statement

Plus deposit not recorded by bank

Minus outstanding checks:

Checkbook balance

Minus service charge

Plus bank interest paid

Score for A (40)

B (60 points) Solve the following problems. (12 points for each correct answer)

3. Compute the reconciled balance for each of the problems from the information given.

	Bank Statement Balance	Checkbook Balance	Other Information	Reconciled Balance
a.	$ 956.15	$ 974.30	Outstanding checks: $8.75, $29.10	
			Automatic transfer to savings: $50.00	________
			Automatic charge, safety deposit box: $6.00	
b.	$1,559.39	$1,617.94	Outstanding checks: $84.62, $14.20, $55.00	
			Outstanding deposit: $224.70	________
			Automatic transfer to savings: $25.00	
			Bank interest credited: $37.33	
c.	$ 893.17	$1,007.13	Outstanding checks: $7.50, $4.18	
			Outstanding deposits: $12.32, $120.00	________
			Bank interest credited: $24.18	
			Charge for printing new checks: $17.50	
d.	$ 984.32	$ 944.39	Outstanding checks: $42.00	________
			Deposit of $76.89 shown in check register as $78.96	
e.	$ 797.65	$1,259.83	Outstanding checks: $150.00, $37.82	________
			Outstanding deposit: $325.00	
			Deposit of $325.00 shown twice in check register	

____
Score for B (60)

Assignment 8.3: Bank Balance Reconciliation Statements

Name

Date Score

A (50 points) Using the data provided, prepare a bank reconciliation statement in each of the following problems. Space is provided for your solutions. (25 points for each correct reconciliation)

1. The balance shown in the bank statement of Central Heating, Inc., on November 30 was $1,132.46. The balance shown on the check register was $896.91. The following checks were outstanding:

No. 148	$ 26.62	No. 161	77.17
No. 156	100.16	No. 165	29.10

There was a bank interest credit of $12.00 and a service charge of $9.50 that had not been entered on Central Heating's check register.

2. The June 30 bank statement for Franklin Chemical Company shows that a customer's bad check in the amount of $960 was returned and charged against the Franklin Chemical Company's account by the bank. This is the first knowledge the company had that one of the checks deposited was no good.

The balance shown on the Franklin Chemical Company's bank statement was $22,367.14. The balance shown on the check register was $24,696.83. The following checks were outstanding:

No. 363	$1,066.20	No. 396	$1,544.14
No. 387	1,972.81	No. 397	772.86

The following items required adjustment on the bank reconciliation statement:

Outstanding deposit:	$3,001.87
Automatic transfer to note payment:	$4,000.00
Bad check returned and charged to Franklin Chemical Company's account by the bank:	$ 960.00
Bank interest credit:	$ 276.17

Score for A (50)

B (50 points) Using the data provided, prepare a bank reconciliation statement in each of the following problems. Space is provided for your solutions. (25 points for each correct reconciliation)

3. The balance shown on the July 31 bank statement of Davis and Davis, Inc., was $17,464.54. The balance shown by the check register was $17,940.44. A deposit of $2,004.35 had not been credited by the bank, and the following checks were outstanding:

No. 730	$ 78.60	No. 753	556.25	No. 761	97.73
No. 749	2,765.23	No. 757	271.84	No. 768	958.60

The following items required adjustment on the bank reconciliation statement:

Charge for printing checks:	$ 18.00
Automatic insurance payment charged to depositor's account by the bank:	$1,765.00
Check deposited by Davis and Davis, returned to bank as bad check:	$1,500.00
Interest on bank account credited by the bank:	$ 83.20

4. The balance shown on the March 31 bank statement of Melody Music, Inc., was $9,686.56. The balance shown on the check register was $6,855.74. The following checks were outstanding:

No. 1243	$ 640.70	No. 1267	87.30	No. 1270	143.90
No. 1258	1,225.20	No. 1268	221.12	No. 1272	462.70

The following items were listed on the bank statement:

Charge made by the bank for safe deposit box:	$ 13.86
AA Realty's check incorrectly charged to the Melody Music account by the bank:	$ 65.00
Interest on bank account credited by the bank:	$128.76

Score for B (50)

Notes

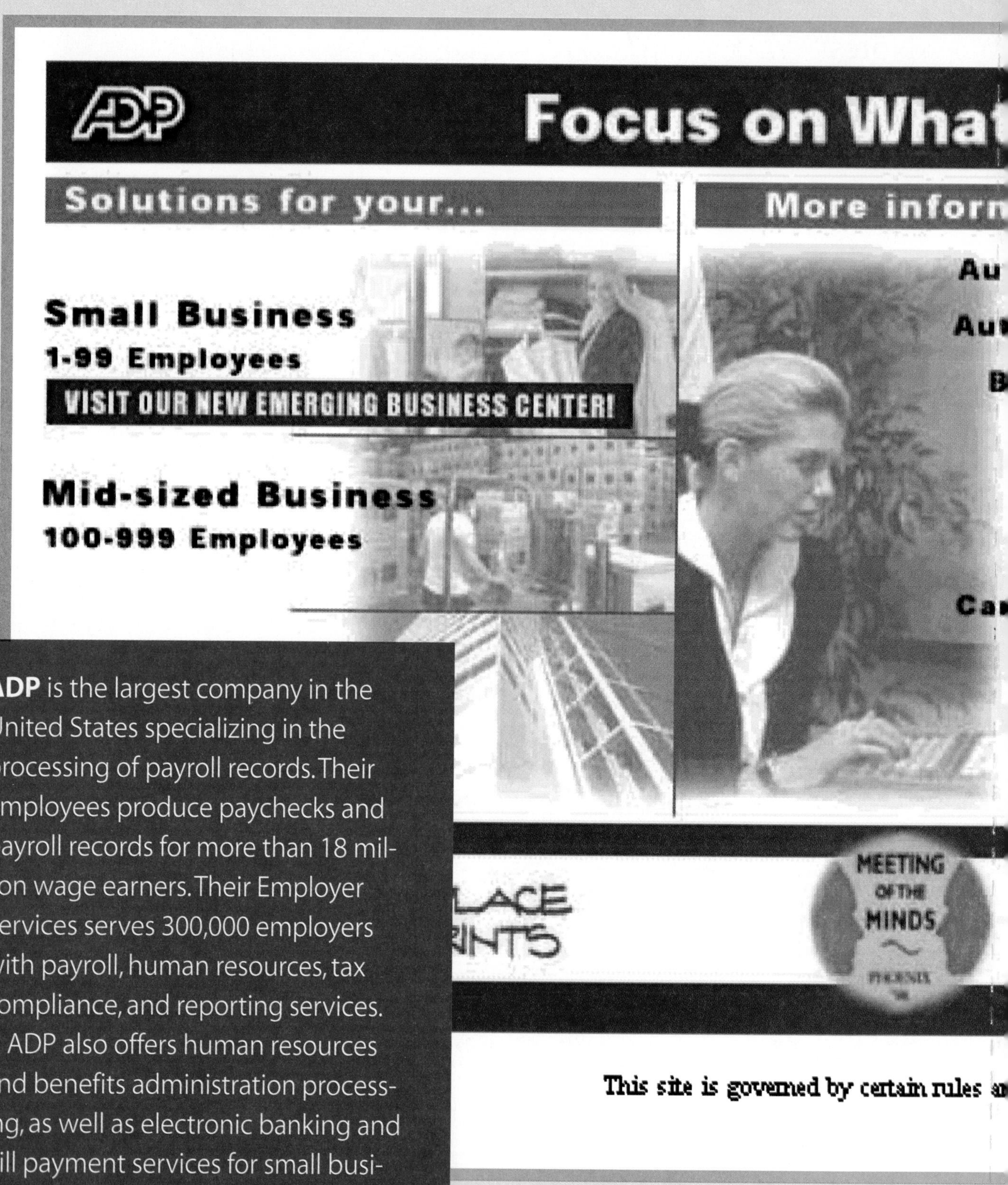

ADP is the largest company in the United States specializing in the processing of payroll records. Their employees produce paychecks and payroll records for more than 18 million wage earners. Their Employer Services serves 300,000 employers with payroll, human resources, tax compliance, and reporting services.

ADP also offers human resources and benefits administration processing, as well as electronic banking and bill payment services for small businesses. Their on-line *Career Magazine*, featuring articles on job search techniques, career changes, and employee concerns, is available through links from their home page at www.adp.com.

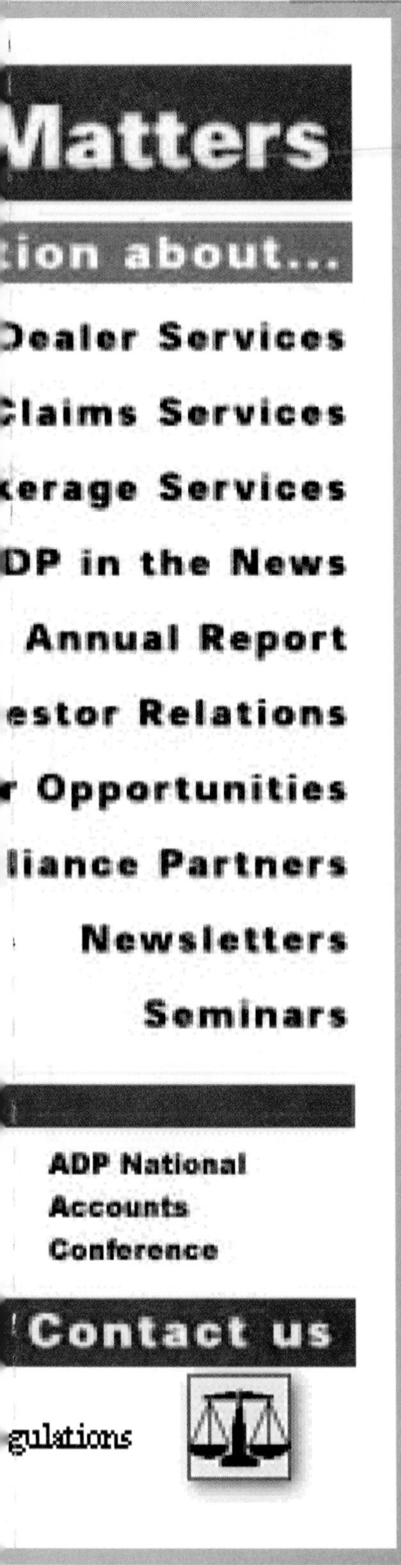

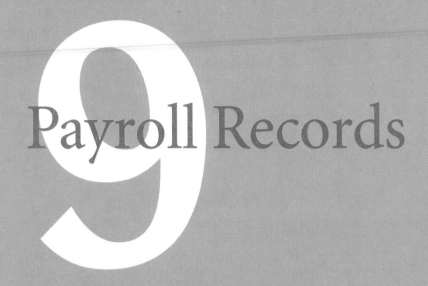

9 Payroll Records

Learning Objectives

By studying this chapter and completing all the assignments, you will learn to:

1. Prepare a payroll register.
2. Compute federal income tax withholding amounts.
3. Compute Social Security, Medicare, and other withholdings.
4. Complete an employee's earnings record.
5. Compute an employer's quarterly federal tax return.
6. Compute an employer's federal and state unemployment tax liability.

Keeping track of time, computing earnings, and computing net pay after taxes and deductions are part of every business.

Although much of the processing is done by specialized firms with large computers, the original data are developed by payroll personnel in business, professional, and government offices.

Employers must keep payroll records, withhold and pay payroll taxes, and file quarterly reports with state and federal government offices. The payroll records and processes described in this chapter are common to all employers.

Federal taxes paid by all employees include the federal income tax and the two taxes required by the Federal Insurance Contributions Act (FICA): old-age, survivors, and disability insurance, commonly called Social Security, and the hospital insurance, commonly called Medicare.

When hiring new employees, employers must verify each employee's eligibility to work in the United States, get the employee's Social Security number, and have the employee complete a Form W-4 (Figure 9-1). The W-4 in Figure 9-1 indicates that Harry Allen is married and claims four dependents.

Figure 9-1: Form W-4 (1996)

Personal Allowances Worksheet

A Enter "1" for **yourself** if no one else can claim you as a dependent . . . . . A 1

B Enter "1" if: • You are single and have only one job; or • You are married, have only one job, and your spouse does not work; or • Your wages from a second job or your spouse's wages (or the total of both) are $1,000 or less. . . B ____

C Enter "1" for your **spouse.** But, you may choose to enter -0- if you are married and have either a working spouse or more than one job. (This may help you avoid having too little tax withheld.). . . . . C 1

D Enter number of **dependents** (other than your spouse or yourself) you will claim on your tax return . . . . D 2

E Enter "1" if you will file as **head of household** on your tax return (see conditions under **Head of household** above) . E ____

F Enter "1" if you have at least $1,500 of **child or dependent care expenses** for which you plan to claim a credit . . F ____

G **New—Child Tax Credit:** • If your total income will be between $16,500 and $47,000 ($21,000 and $60,000 if married), enter "1" for each eligible child. • If your total income will be between $47,000 and $80,000 ($60,000 and $115,000 if married), enter "1" if you have two or three eligible children, or enter "2" if you have four or more . . . . G ____

H Add lines A through G and enter total here. **Note:** This amount may be different from the number of exemptions you claim on your return. ► H 4

For accuracy, complete all worksheets that apply.
- If you plan to **itemize or claim adjustments to income** and want to reduce your withholding, see the Deductions and Adjustments Worksheet on page 2.
- If you are **single,** have **more than one job,** and your combined earnings from all jobs exceed $32,000 OR if you are **married** and have a **working spouse or more than one job,** and the combined earnings from all jobs exceed $55,000, see the Two-Earner/Two-Job Worksheet on page 2 to avoid having too little tax withheld.
- If **neither** of the above situations applies, **stop here** and enter the number from line H on line 5 of Form W-4 below.

- - - - - - - **Cut here and give the certificate to your employer. Keep the top part for your records.** - - - - - - -

Form **W-4** Department of the Treasury Internal Revenue Service

Employee's Withholding Allowance Certificate

► **For Privacy Act and Paperwork Reduction Act Notice, see page 2.**

OMB No. 1545-0010 **1998**

1 Type or print your first name and middle initial: Harry — Last name: ALLEN — 2 Your social security number: 123 45 6789

Home address (number and street or rural route): 4043 Sixth Street

3 ☐ Single ☒ Married ☐ Married, but withhold at higher Single rate.
Note: *If married, but legally separated, or spouse is a nonresident alien, check the Single box.*

City or town, state, and ZIP code: Anytown USA 90001

4 If your last name differs from that on your social security card, check here and call 1-800-772-1213 for a new card . . . . ► ☐

5 Total number of allowances you are claiming (from line H above or from the worksheets on page 2 if they apply) . 5 4

6 Additional amount, if any, you want withheld from each paycheck . . . . . 6 $

7 I claim exemption from withholding for 1998, and I certify that I meet **BOTH** of the following conditions for exemption:
- Last year I had a right to a refund of **ALL** Federal income tax withheld because I had **NO** tax liability **AND**
- This year I expect a refund of **ALL** Federal income tax withheld because I expect to have **NO** tax liability.

If you meet both conditions, enter "EXEMPT" here . . . . . ► 7

Under penalties of perjury, I certify that I am entitled to the number of withholding allowances claimed on this certificate or entitled to claim exempt status.

Employee's signature ► Harry Allen **Date** ► 12/17, 19XX

8 Employer's name and address (Employer: Complete 8 and 10 only if sending to the IRS) | 9 Office code (optional) | 10 Employer identification number

Cat. No. 10220Q

Preparing a Payroll Register

A *payroll register* is a summary of employee status information, wages earned, payroll deductions, and take-home pay. Whether they do it manually or by computer, all employers maintain some form of payroll register.

A payroll register is prepared for each payroll period. Payroll periods are weekly, biweekly, semi-monthly, or monthly. Figure 9-2 shows a payroll register for one weekly period ending March 29. The line for Harry Allen shows he is married, claims four withholding allowances, and is paid on an hourly basis at the rate of $11 per hour ($16.50 for overtime hours). For the current week, he worked 40 regular hours and 6 overtime hours, for gross earnings of $539. From his gross pay he had deductions for Social Security taxes ($33.42), Medicare ($7.82), Federal Income Tax ($31.10), Group Medical Insurance ($39), Group Dental Insurance ($12), and Other ($42), totaling $165.34. His net pay was $373.66.

LEARNING OBJECTIVES 1

Prepare a payroll register.

Figure 9-2: Weekly Payroll Register

NAME	MARITAL STATUS	WITHHOLDING ALLOWANCES	W=WEEKLY H=HOURLY	RATE	HOURS REG	HOURS O/T	GROSS EARNINGS	DEDUCTIONS: SOCIAL SECURITY	MEDICARE	FEDERAL INCOME TAX	GROUP MED. INS.	GROUP DENTAL INS.	OTHER	TOTAL DEDUCTIONS	NET EARNINGS
Allen, Harry	M	4	H	11.00	40	6	539.00	33.42	7.82	31.10	39.00	12.00	42.00	165.34	373.66
Garcia, Fran	S	2	W	680.00	40		680.00	42.16	9.86	86.46	18.00	9.00	—	165.48	514.52
Parker, Marie	S	1	H	6.90	32		220.80	13.69	3.20	17.68	18.00	—	—	52.57	168.23
Thomas, Robert	M	3	H	9.40	40	4	432.40	26.81	6.27	22.90	39.00	12.00	13.10	120.08	312.32
Weber, James	S	1	H	13.50	40		540.00	33.48	7.83	65.56	18.00	9.00	—	133.87	406.13
Totals							2,412.20	149.56	34.98	223.70	132.00	42.00	55.10	637.34	1,774.86

CONCEPT CHECK 9.1

When the payroll register entries have been completed, one way to check on the accuracy of computations is to subtract the Total Deductions column from the Gross Pay total; the difference should equal the total of the Net Earnings column. From the payroll register shown in Figure 9-2, check the accuracy of the column totals:

Total of Gross Earnings column	$2,412.20
Less total of Deductions column	637.34
Total of Net Earnings column	$1,774.86

Computing Federal Income Tax Withholding Amounts

The federal income tax is a payroll tax that the employer must withhold from the employee's pay and turn over to the Internal Revenue Service (IRS). The amount of the deduction varies with the amount of earnings, the employee's marital status, and the number of withholding allowances claimed.

LEARNING OBJECTIVES 2

Compute federal income tax withholding amounts.

The *Employer's Tax Guide*, published annually by the Internal Revenue Service, gives employers two primary methods to figure how much income tax to withhold from their employees. These two methods are the *percentage method* and the *wage-bracket method.*

In Figure 9-2, Harry Allen's federal income tax withholding amount was $31.10, computed by the percentage method. With the percentage method, a deduction is granted for each withholding allowance claimed, based on a chart in the *Employer's Tax Guide*. The amount for each withholding allowance is provided in a table labeled Income Tax Withholding Percentage Method Table. Figure 9-3 illustrates a recent table. This table shows that for weekly pay, a deduction of $51.92 is allowed for each withholding allowance. (For monthly pay, a deduction of $225.00 is allowed for each withholding allowance.)

Figure 9-3: Percentage Method Amount for One Withholding Allowance

Payroll Period	One Withholding Allowance
Weekly	$51.92
Biweekly	$103.85
Semimonthly	$112.50
Monthly	$225.00

After subtracting the total withholding allowance from an employee's gross earnings, you compute the amount to be withheld by taking a percentage of the difference. The percentage to be used is given by the IRS in the Tables for Percentage Method of Withholding. Figure 9-4 illustrates a recent table for weekly, biweekly, semimonthly, and monthly payroll periods.

STEPS to Figure the Amount of Federal Income Tax Withholding Using the Percentage Method

1. Determine the employee's gross earnings.
2. Multiply the appropriate (weekly/monthly) "one withholding allowance" amount (from the Withholding Table) by the number of allowances the employee claims.
3. Subtract that amount from the employee's gross earnings.
4. From the appropriate (weekly/monthly and single/married) Percentage Method table, subtract the "of excess over" figure to get the amount subject to the tax.
5. Multiply the amount from step 4 by the appropriate percentage from the Percentage Method table.
6. If required, add the base tax amount (if any) shown next to the percentage from the Percentage Method Table. (For example, see Table 1, WEEKLY Payroll Period, Married, the second line of the chart: $116.25 plus 28% of excess over $899.)

EXAMPLE A

Using the six steps given above, Harry Allen's withholding is computed as follows:

STEP 1 $539.00 (gross earnings from payroll register)

STEP 2

	$ 51.92	(one withholding allowance)
	×4	(number of withholding allowances claimed)
	$207.68	(total withholding allowance)

Figure 9-4: Tables for Percentage Method of Withholding (For Wages Paid in 1998)

Tables for Percentage Method of Withholding

(For Wages Paid in 1998)

TABLE 1—WEEKLY Payroll Period

(a) SINGLE person (including head of household)—

If the amount of wages (after subtracting withholding allowances) is: Not over $51 . . . . . The amount of income tax to withhold is: $0

Over—	But not over—		of excess over—
$51	—$517	15%	—$51
$517	—$1,105	$69.90 plus 28%	—$517
$1,105	—$2,493	$234.54 plus 31%	—$1,105
$2,493	—$5,385	$664.82 plus 36%	—$2,493
$5,385	. . . . . .	$1,705.94 plus 39.6%	—$5,385

(b) MARRIED person—

If the amount of wages (after subtracting withholding allowances) is: Not over $124 . . . . The amount of income tax to withhold is: $0

Over—	But not over—		of excess over—
$124	—$899	15%	—$124
$899	—$1,855	$116.25 plus 28%	—$899
$1,855	—$3,084	$383.93 plus 31%	—$1,855
$3,084	—$5,439	$764.92 plus 36%	—$3,084
$5,439	. . . . . .	$1,612.72 plus 39.6%	—$5,439

TABLE 2—BIWEEKLY Payroll Period

(a) SINGLE person (including head of household)—

If the amount of wages (after subtracting withholding allowances) is: Not over $102 . . . . The amount of income tax to withhold is: $0

Over—	But not over—		of excess over—
$102	—$1,035	15%	—$102
$1,035	—$2,210	$139.95 plus 28%	—$1,035
$2,210	—$4,987	$468.95 plus 31%	—$2,210
$4,987	—$10,769	$1,329.82 plus 36%	—$4,987
$10,769	. . . . . .	$3,411.34 plus 39.6%	—$10,769

(b) MARRIED person—

If the amount of wages (after subtracting withholding allowances) is: Not over $248 . . . . The amount of income tax to withhold is: $0

Over—	But not over—		of excess over—
$248	—$1,798	15%	—$248
$1,798	—$3,710	$232.50 plus 28%	—$1,798
$3,710	—$6,167	$767.86 plus 31%	—$3,710
$6,167	—$10,879	$1,529.53 plus 36%	—$6,167
$10,879	. . . . . .	$3,225.85 plus 39.6%	—$10,879

TABLE 3—SEMIMONTHLY Payroll Period

(a) SINGLE person (including head of household)—

If the amount of wages (after subtracting withholding allowances) is: Not over $110 . . . . The amount of income tax to withhold is: $0

Over—	But not over—		of excess over—
$110	—$1,121	15%	—$110
$1,121	—$2,394	$151.65 plus 28%	—$1,121
$2,394	—$5,402	$508.09 plus 31%	—$2,394
$5,402	—$11,667	$1,440.57 plus 36%	—$5,402
$11,667	. . . . . .	$3,695.97 plus 39.6%	—$11,667

(b) MARRIED person—

If the amount of wages (after subtracting withholding allowances) is: Not over $269 . . . . The amount of income tax to withhold is: $0

Over—	But not over—		of excess over—
$269	—$1,948	15%	—$269
$1,948	—$4,019	$251.85 plus 28%	—$1,948
$4,019	—$6,681	$831.73 plus 31%	—$4,019
$6,681	—$11,785	$1,656.95 plus 36%	—$6,681
$11,785	. . . . . .	$3,494.39 plus 39.6%	—$11,785

TABLE 4—MONTHLY Payroll Period

(a) SINGLE person (including head of household)—

If the amount of wages (after subtracting withholding allowances) is: Not over $221 . . . . The amount of income tax to withhold is: $0

Over—	But not over—		of excess over—
$221	—$2,242	15%	—$221
$2,242	—$4,788	$303.15 plus 28%	—$2,242
$4,788	—$10,804	$1,016.03 plus 31%	—$4,788
$10,804	—$23,333	$2,880.99 plus 36%	—$10,804
$23,333	. . . . . .	$7,391.43 plus 39.6%	—$23,333

(b) MARRIED person—

If the amount of wages (after subtracting withholding allowances) is: Not over $538 . . . . The amount of income tax to withhold is: $0

Over—	But not over—		of excess over—
$538	—$3,896	15%	—$538
$3,896	—$8,038	$503.70 plus 28%	—$3,896
$8,038	—$13,363	$1,663.46 plus 31%	—$8,038
$13,363	—$23,571	$3,314.21 plus 36%	—$13,363
$23,571	. . . . . .	$6,989.09 plus 39.6%	—$23,571

STEP 3	$539.00	(gross earnings)
	−207.68	(total withholding allowance)
	$331.32	(amount subject to withholding)
STEP 4	$331.32	(amount subject to withholding)
	−124.00	(less $124, "excess amount" in Fig. 9-4)
	$207.32	(amount subject to percentage computation)
STEP 5	$207.32	(amount subject to percentage computation)
	×0.15	(15% computation)
	$ 31.10	(amount of tax withheld)

STEP 6 The wage range $124–$899 does not have a base tax amount and, therefore, does not apply in the case of Harry Allen.

The second method of figuring the amount of tax to be withheld from an employee's pay, the wage-bracket method, uses a series of wage-bracket tables published in the IRS *Employer's Tax Guide*. Figures 9-5 and 9-6 illustrate the tables for single and married persons who are paid on a weekly basis.

Using the tables from Figure 9-6, we see that a married employee earning a weekly wage of between $530 and $540 and claiming four withholding allowances will have $30 withheld. Note that the amount of federal income tax withheld from Harry Allen's pay using the wage-bracket method is approximately the same as the amount withheld using the percentage method: $30 vs. $31.10. Small differences will frequently result because the wage-bracket method uses tables based on $10 divisions and rounded amounts. Over a period of a year, these differences tend to be relatively insignificant and are accepted by the IRS.

CONCEPT CHECK 9.2

Using the percentage method steps shown above, verify the federal income tax withholding for Fran Garcia as given in the payroll register.

STEP 1	$680.00	(gross earnings from payroll register)
STEP 2	$ 51.92	(one withholding allowance)
	×2	(number of withholding allowances claimed)
	$103.84	(total withholding allowance)
STEP 3	$680.00	(gross earnings)
	−103.84	(total withholding allowance
	$576.16	(amount subject to withholding)
STEP 4	$576.16	(amount subject to withholding)
	−517.00	(less $517; excess amount in Fig. 9-4)
	$ 59.16	(amount subject to percentage computation)
STEP 5	$ 59.16	(amount subject to percentage computation)
	×0.28	(28% computation)
	$ 16.56	(amount of tax withheld on percentage computation)
STEP 6	$ 16.56	(amount of tax withheld on percentage computation)
	+69.90	(base tax amount)
	$ 86.46	(total amount of tax withheld)

Use the wage-bracket method to find the federal income tax withholding for Fran Garcia. Then compute the difference between the percentage method and the wage bracket method.

Percentage method (Step 6 above)	$86.46
Wage-bracket method (Fig. 9-5, since she is single)	88.00
Difference	$ 1.54

Figure 9-5: Single Persons—Weekly Payroll Period

SINGLE Persons—WEEKLY Payroll Period

(For Wages Paid in 1998)

If the wages are–		And the number of withholding allowances claimed is—										
At least	But less than	0	1	2	3	4	5	6	7	8	9	10
		The amount of income tax to be withheld is—										
$0	$55	0	0	0	0	0	0	0	0	0	0	0
55	60	1	0	0	0	0	0	0	0	0	0	0
60	65	2	0	0	0	0	0	0	0	0	0	0
65	70	2	0	0	0	0	0	0	0	0	0	0
70	75	3	0	0	0	0	0	0	0	0	0	0
75	80	4	0	0	0	0	0	0	0	0	0	0
80	85	5	0	0	0	0	0	0	0	0	0	0
85	90	5	0	0	0	0	0	0	0	0	0	0
90	95	6	0	0	0	0	0	0	0	0	0	0
95	100	7	0	0	0	0	0	0	0	0	0	0
100	105	8	0	0	0	0	0	0	0	0	0	0
200	210	23	15	8	0	0	0	0	0	0	0	0
210	220	25	17	9	1	0	0	0	0	0	0	0
220	230	26	18	11	3	0	0	0	0	0	0	0
230	240	28	20	12	4	0	0	0	0	0	0	0
240	250	29	21	14	6	0	0	0	0	0	0	0
250	260	31	23	15	7	0	0	0	0	0	0	0
260	270	32	24	17	9	1	0	0	0	0	0	0
270	280	34	26	18	10	2	0	0	0	0	0	0
280	290	35	27	20	12	4	0	0	0	0	0	0
290	300	37	29	21	13	5	0	0	0	0	0	0
300	310	38	30	23	15	7	0	0	0	0	0	0
310	320	40	32	24	16	8	1	0	0	0	0	0
320	330	41	33	26	18	10	2	0	0	0	0	0
330	340	43	35	27	19	11	4	0	0	0	0	0
340	350	44	36	29	21	13	5	0	0	0	0	0
350	360	46	38	30	22	14	7	0	0	0	0	0
360	370	47	39	32	24	16	8	0	0	0	0	0
370	380	49	41	33	25	17	10	2	0	0	0	0
380	390	50	42	35	27	19	11	3	0	0	0	0
390	400	52	44	36	28	20	13	5	0	0	0	0
400	410	53	45	38	30	22	14	6	0	0	0	0
410	420	55	47	39	31	23	16	8	0	0	0	0
420	430	56	48	41	33	25	17	9	2	0	0	0
430	440	58	50	42	34	26	19	11	3	0	0	0
440	450	59	51	44	36	28	20	12	5	0	0	0
450	460	61	53	45	37	29	22	14	6	0	0	0
460	470	62	54	47	39	31	23	15	8	0	0	0
470	480	64	56	48	40	32	25	17	9	1	0	0
480	490	65	57	50	42	34	26	18	11	3	0	0
490	500	67	59	51	43	35	28	20	12	4	0	0
500	510	68	60	53	45	37	29	21	14	6	0	0
510	520	70	62	54	46	38	31	23	15	7	0	0
520	530	72	63	56	48	40	32	24	17	9	1	0
530	540	75	65	57	49	41	34	26	18	10	3	0
540	550	78	66	59	51	43	35	27	20	12	4	0
550	560	81	68	60	52	44	37	29	21	13	6	0
560	570	83	69	62	54	46	38	30	23	15	7	0
570	580	86	72	63	55	47	40	32	24	16	9	1
580	590	89	74	65	57	49	41	33	26	18	10	2
590	600	92	77	66	58	50	43	35	27	19	12	4
600	610	95	80	68	60	52	44	36	29	21	13	5
610	620	97	83	69	61	53	46	38	30	22	15	7
620	630	100	86	71	63	55	47	39	32	24	16	8
630	640	103	88	74	64	56	49	41	33	25	18	10
640	650	106	91	77	66	58	50	42	35	27	19	11
650	660	109	94	79	67	59	52	44	36	28	21	13
660	670	111	97	82	69	61	53	45	38	30	22	14
670	680	114	100	85	70	62	55	47	39	31	24	16
680	690	117	102	88	73	64	56	48	41	33	25	17
690	700	120	105	91	76	65	58	50	42	34	27	19

Figure 9-6: Married Persons—Weekly Payroll Period

MARRIED Persons—**WEEKLY** Payroll Period

(For Wages Paid in 1998)

If the wages are–		And the number of withholding allowances claimed is—										
At least	But less than	0	1	2	3	4	5	6	7	8	9	10
		The amount of income tax to be withheld is—										
$0	**$125**	0	0	0	0	0	0	0	0	0	0	0
125	**130**	1	0	0	0	0	0	0	0	0	0	0
130	**135**	1	0	0	0	0	0	0	0	0	0	0
135	**140**	2	0	0	0	0	0	0	0	0	0	0
140	**145**	3	0	0	0	0	0	0	0	0	0	0
145	**150**	4	0	0	0	0	0	0	0	0	0	0
150	**155**	4	0	0	0	0	0	0	0	0	0	0
155	**160**	5	0	0	0	0	0	0	0	0	0	0
160	**165**	6	0	0	0	0	0	0	0	0	0	0
165	**170**	7	0	0	0	0	0	0	0	0	0	0
170	**175**	7	0	0	0	0	0	0	0	0	0	0
175	**180**	8	0	0	0	0	0	0	0	0	0	0
180	**185**	9	1	0	0	0	0	0	0	0	0	0
185	**190**	10	2	0	0	0	0	0	0	0	0	0
190	**195**	10	2	0	0	0	0	0	0	0	0	0
195	**200**	11	3	0	0	0	0	0	0	0	0	0
200	**210**	12	4	0	0	0	0	0	0	0	0	0
210	**220**	14	6	0	0	0	0	0	0	0	0	0
220	**230**	15	7	0	0	0	0	0	0	0	0	0
230	**240**	17	9	1	0	0	0	0	0	0	0	0
240	**250**	18	10	3	0	0	0	0	0	0	0	0
250	**260**	20	12	4	0	0	0	0	0	0	0	0
260	**270**	21	13	6	0	0	0	0	0	0	0	0
270	**280**	23	15	7	0	0	0	0	0	0	0	0
280	**290**	24	16	9	1	0	0	0	0	0	0	0
290	**300**	26	18	10	2	0	0	0	0	0	0	0
300	**310**	27	19	12	4	0	0	0	0	0	0	0
310	**320**	29	21	13	5	0	0	0	0	0	0	0
320	**330**	30	22	15	7	0	0	0	0	0	0	0
330	**340**	32	24	16	8	0	0	0	0	0	0	0
340	**350**	33	25	18	10	2	0	0	0	0	0	0
350	**360**	35	27	19	11	3	0	0	0	0	0	0
360	**370**	36	28	21	13	5	0	0	0	0	0	0
370	**380**	38	30	22	14	6	0	0	0	0	0	0
380	**390**	39	31	24	16	8	0	0	0	0	0	0
390	**400**	41	33	25	17	9	2	0	0	0	0	0
400	**410**	42	34	27	19	11	3	0	0	0	0	0
410	**420**	44	36	28	20	12	5	0	0	0	0	0
420	**430**	45	37	30	22	14	6	0	0	0	0	0
430	**440**	47	39	31	23	15	8	0	0	0	0	0
440	**450**	48	40	33	25	17	9	1	0	0	0	0
450	**460**	50	42	34	26	18	11	3	0	0	0	0
460	**470**	51	43	36	28	20	12	4	0	0	0	0
470	**480**	53	45	37	29	21	14	6	0	0	0	0
480	**490**	54	46	39	31	23	15	7	0	0	0	0
490	**500**	56	48	40	32	24	17	9	1	0	0	0
500	**510**	57	49	42	34	26	18	10	3	0	0	0
510	**520**	59	51	43	35	27	20	12	4	0	0	0
520	**530**	60	52	45	37	29	21	13	6	0	0	0
530	**540**	62	54	46	38	30	23	15	7	0	0	0
540	**550**	63	55	48	40	32	24	16	9	1	0	0
550	**560**	65	57	49	41	33	26	18	10	2	0	0
560	**570**	66	58	51	43	35	27	19	12	4	0	0
570	**580**	68	60	52	44	36	29	21	13	5	0	0
580	**590**	69	61	54	46	38	30	22	15	7	0	0
590	**600**	71	63	55	47	39	32	24	16	8	1	0
600	**610**	72	64	57	49	41	33	25	18	10	2	0
610	**620**	74	66	58	50	42	35	27	19	11	4	0
620	**630**	75	67	60	52	44	36	28	21	13	5	0
630	**640**	77	69	61	53	45	38	30	22	14	7	0
640	**650**	78	70	63	55	47	39	31	24	16	8	0
650	**660**	80	72	64	56	48	41	33	25	17	10	2
660	**670**	81	73	66	58	50	42	34	27	19	11	3
670	**680**	83	75	67	59	51	44	36	28	20	13	5
680	**690**	84	76	69	61	53	45	37	30	22	14	6
690	**700**	86	78	70	62	54	47	39	31	23	16	8
700	**710**	87	79	72	64	56	48	40	33	25	17	9
710	**720**	89	81	73	65	57	50	42	34	26	19	11
720	**730**	90	82	75	67	59	51	43	36	28	20	12
730	**740**	92	84	76	68	60	53	45	37	29	22	14

Computing Social Security, Medicare, and Other Withholdings

The *Federal Insurance Contributions Act* (FICA) provides for a federal system of old-age, survivors, disability, and hospital insurance. The old-age, survivors, and disability insurance part of FICA is financed by the *Social Security tax*. The hospital insurance part of FICA is financed by the *Medicare tax*. Each of these taxes is reported separately. Social Security and Medicare taxes are levied on both the employer and the employee. These taxes have different rates, and only the Social Security tax has a wage base, which is the **maximum** wage that is subject to the tax for the year.

LEARNING OBJECTIVES 3

Compute Social Security, Medicare, and other withholdings.

The tax rate for Social Security is 6.2%, levied on both the employer and the employee. For 1998, the wage base was $68,400.

The tax rate for Medicare is 1.45%, levied on both the employer and the employee. There is no wage base limit for Medicare; all covered wages are subject to Medicare tax.

Both of these rates are subject to change by legislation, but they are given here because they were current at the time of compiling this payroll register. All amounts are rounded for the nearest cent. The amounts for Harry Allen were $33.42 for Social Security and $7.82 for Medicare.

EXAMPLE B

Social Security deduction:

$539.00	(gross earnings)
×0.062	(Social Security rate)
$ 33.42	(Social Security amount)

EXAMPLE C

Medicare deduction:

$539.00	(gross earnings)
×.0145	(Medicare rate)
$ 7.82	(Medicare amount)

Many employers today provide some form of group medical insurance for their employees. Frequently, the employee is asked to pay a portion of the premium charged for such insurance, based on the number of dependents the employee has named to be insured. For the payroll register in Figure 9-1, we assume the weekly rates for medical and dental plans shown in Figure 9-7.

Figure 9-7: Weekly Medical and Dental Plan Rates

	Weekly Medical Plan Premium Paid by Employee	Weekly Dental Plan Premium Paid by Employee
Employee only	$18.00	$9.00
Employee plus one dependent	$22.00	$10.00
Employee plus 2 or more dependents	$39.00	$12.00

The payroll register in Figure 9-2 showed that Harry Allen subscribed to both the medical and the dental program. Because of his three dependents, the amounts of his deductions were $39 and $12, respectively.

Frequently, employees will arrange to have special payroll deductions made by the employer to pay union dues, put money into special retirement or savings plans, or make contributions to charitable organizations.

In addition, 42 of the 50 states have some form of state income tax, which normally requires withholding in the same manner as the federal income tax. In such states, state income tax withholding columns are added to the payroll register and withholdings are made according to wage-bracket or percentage charts established by the state, in the same manner as federal income tax withholdings.

The payroll register illustrated in Figure 9-2 reflects a $42 weekly deduction Harry Allen had requested be made for payment of his union dues (other).

CONCEPT CHECK 9.3

Using the format in examples B and C, compute Social Security and Medicare amounts for Fran Garcia, based on her gross weekly earnings of $680.

Social Security		**Medicare**	
$ 680	(gross earnings)	$ 680	(gross earnings)
×0.062	(Social Security rate)	×0.0145	(Medicare rate)
$ 42.16	(Social Security amount)	$ 9.86	(Medicare amount)

Completing an Employee's Earnings Record

LEARNING OBJECTIVES 4

Complete an employee's earnings record.

An employer must submit quarterly and annual reports to the federal and state government and pay the amount of taxes withheld from employees' earnings for the period. To obtain the necessary information, most employers keep an *employee's earnings record* for each employee. The employee's earnings record summarizes by quarter the employee's gross earnings, deductions, and net pay.

EXAMPLE D

Figure 9-8: Employee's Earnings Record

Name **Harry Allen** Social Security No. **123-45-6789**

Address **4043 Sixth Street** No. of Allowances **4** Marital Status **Married**

Period Ending	Total Wages	Cumulative Total	Deductions: Social Security	Medicare	Federal Inc. Tax	Other Deductions	Total	Net Pay
1/4	$ 440.00	$ 440.00	$ 27.28	$ 6.38	$ 16.25	$ 93.00	$ 142.91	$ 297.09
1/11	440.00	880.00	27.28	6.38	16.25	93.00	142.91	297.09
3/29	539.00	$6,952.00	33.42	7.82	31.10	93.00	165.34	373.66
Quarter Total	$6,952.00		$431.20	$ 99.87	$486.13	$908.70	$1,925.90	$5,026.10

The employee's earnings record in Figure 9-8 shows that Harry Allen is married, claims four allowances, and for the first quarter of the year earned total wages of $6,952. His net pay was $5,026.10 after first quarter withholdings as follows:

Federal income tax withholding	$ 486.13
Social Security withholding	431.20
Medicare withholding	99.87
Other deductions	908.70
Total deductions	$1,925.90

CONCEPT CHECK 9.4

Assuming that Fran Garcia's weekly earnings and deductions have remained constant for each of the 13 weeks in the first quarter of the year, compute the following totals, which would appear on her employee's earnings record for the first quarter:

Total wages	$8,840.00
Federal income tax withholding	1,123.98
Social Security withholding	548.08
Medicare withholding	128.18
Group medical insurance deductions	234.00
Group dental insurance deductions	117.00
Total deductions	2,151.24
Net pay	6,688.76

Computing an Employer's Quarterly Federal Tax Return

Every employer who withholds federal income tax and FICA taxes (Social Security and Medicare) must file a quarterly return, Form 941—*Employer's Quarterly Federal Tax Return.* Figure 9-9 shows the data that the employer must include on Form 941 (the completed form has been slightly abbreviated here). The return is filed with the IRS within one month after the end of the quarter.

LEARNING OBJECTIVES 5

Compute an employer's quarterly federal tax return.

The employer obtains Social Security and Medicare amounts by multiplying the taxable wages paid by 12.4% and 2.9%, respectively. This represents the employee's deductions and a matching amount required to be paid by the employer.

Figure 9-9: Form 941—Employer's Quarterly Federal Tax Return (extract)

1	Number of employees in the pay period that includes March 12th . ▶ 1 5		
2	Total wages and tips, plus other compensation	2	60,138 12
3	Total income tax withheld from wages, tips, and sick pay	3	4,997 45
4	Adjustment of withheld income tax for preceding quarters of calendar year	4	—
5	Adjusted total of income tax withheld (line 3 as adjusted by line 4—see instructions)	5	4,997 45
6	Taxable social security wages . . . 6a 60,138 12 × 12.4% (.124) =	6b	7,457 13
	Taxable social security tips . . . 6c — × 12.4% (.124) =	6d	—
7	Taxable Medicare wages and tips . . . 7a 60,138 12 × 2.9% (.029) =	7b	1,744 01
8	Total social security and Medicare taxes (add lines 6b, 6d, and 7b). Check here if wages are not subject to social security and/or Medicare tax . ▶ ☐	8	9,201 14
9	Adjustment of social security and Medicare taxes (see instructions for required explanation) Sick Pay $ ______ ± Fractions of Cents $ ______ ± Other $ ______ =	9	—
10	Adjusted total of social security and Medicare taxes (line 8 as adjusted by line 9—see instructions)	10	9,201 14
11	**Total taxes** (add lines 5 and 10)	11	14,198 59
12	Advance earned income credit (EIC) payments made to employees	12	—
13	Net taxes (subtract line 12 from line 11). **This should equal line 17, column (d) below (or line D of Schedule B (Form 941))**	13	14,198 59
14	Total deposits for quarter, including overpayment applied from a prior quarter	14	14,107 58
15	**Balance due** (subtract line 14 from line 13). See instructions	15	91 01

EXAMPLE E

For the first quarter of 1998, Merck Medical paid total wages of $2,132,684.27. The company withheld $372,486.20 for federal income tax. All wages paid were subject to Social Security and Medicare taxes. If during the quarter Merck had deposited $680,000 toward its taxes due, how much would it be required to send in with its first-quarter Form 941?

Gross wages $2,132,684.27 × 12.4% (Social Security)	$264,452.85
Gross wages $2,132,684.27 × 2.9% (Medicare)	61,847.84
Subtotal	326,300.69
Income taxes withheld	372,486.20
Total	698,786.89
Less deposit	680,000.00
Balance due	$ 18,786.89

CONCEPT CHECK 9.5

As displayed in Figure 9-9, the total taxes due to the IRS consist of the $4,997.45 in federal income taxes withheld from employees, plus $7,457.13 and $1,744.01 for Social Security and Medicare taxes, respectively, half of which is withheld from employees and half of which is paid by the employer. Although the employer files Form 941 quarterly, the amount of taxes due is usually deposited in a qualified depository (bank) monthly, and it is only the difference between the monthly deposits and the total taxes due that is sent with the Form 941 report.

Computing an Employer's Federal and State Unemployment Tax Liability

LEARNING OBJECTIVES 6

Compute an employer's federal and state unemployment tax liability.

In the last section, we learned that the employer must match the employee's contributions to Social Security and Medicare taxes. In addition, employers must pay two payroll taxes for federal and state unemployment programs.

The Federal Unemployment Tax Act (FUTA) requires the employer to pay a 6.2% tax on the first $7,000 paid to each employee. Most states have also passed a State Unemployment Tax Act (SUTA), requiring the employer to pay 5.4% tax on the first $7,000 paid to each employee. This 5.4% state tax is **deductible** from the federal tax payment. Thus, in most cases, employers pay the federal government just 0.8% FUTA tax: 6.2% FUTA − 5.4% SUTA = 0.8% requirement.

EXAMPLE F

During the first quarter, Johnson and Johnson paid wages of $976,550.80. Of this amount, $172,400.60 was paid to employees who had been paid $7,000 earlier in the quarter. What was the employer's liability for FUTA and SUTA taxes, assuming that the state rate was 5.4%?

$976,550.80 − $172,400.60 = $804,150.20 subject to FUTA and SUTA taxes
$804,150.20 × 0.008 = $6,433.20 FUTA tax payment
$804,150.20 × 0.054 = $43,424.11 SUTA tax payment
$6,433.20 + $43,424.11 = $49,857.31

CONCEPT CHECK 9.6

Warner-Lambert Company employed Rojas Perez for 13 weeks during the period from January 1 through March 31, 1998. His salary was $1,350 per week. At the end of the quarter, how much in FUTA and SUTA taxes was required to be paid to the federal and state governments based on Rojas's income?

$1,350 per week × 13 weeks = $17,550 total wage
$7,000 maximum × 0.008 = $56 FUTA tax
$7,000 maximum × 0.054 = $378 SUTA tax
$378 + $56 = $434 total federal and state unemployment taxes

COMPLETE ASSIGNMENTS 9.1 AND 9.2.

Chapter Terms for Review

employee's earnings record
Employer's Quarterly Federal Tax Return
Federal Insurance Contributions Act (FICA)
Federal Unemployment Tax Act (FUTA)
Form W-4
Medicare tax
payroll register
percentage method
Social Security tax
State Unemployment Tax Act (SUTA)
wage-bracket method

The Bottom Line

Summary of chapter learning objectives:

Learning Objective	Summary	Example
9.1	Preparing a payroll register	Based on the data presented, complete the payroll register below. Fill out the total wages section and then compute the federal income tax, Social Security, Medicare, and other withholdings. Total all columns and check. Use the percentage method.
9.2	Computing federal income tax withholding amounts	1. G. Lee is paid $14.20 per hour. He works 40 regular hours and 6 overtime hours during the week ending January 7. He is single and claims one withholding allowance. He takes a weekly medical deduction of $7. 2. E. Berg is paid $13 per hour. He worked 40 regular hours and 8 overtime hours during the week of January 7. He is married and claims 4 withholding allowances. He takes a weekly medical deduction of $15.
9.3	Computing Social Security, Medicare, and other withholdings	

Name	Marital Status	W/H Allow	Total Hours	Regular Earnings		Overtime Earnings			Total Wages	Deductions					Net Pay
				Rate per Hour	Amt	Hours Worked	Rate per Hour	Amt		Social Security	Medi-care	Fed. Inc. Tax	Med. Insurance	Total	

The Bottom Line *Continued*

Summary of chapter learning objectives:

Learning Objective	Summary	Example
9.4	Completing an employee's earnings record	3. Complete the earnings record for D. Chan. Use 6.2% for Social Security and 1.45% for Medicare taxes. Use the percentage method for federal income tax withholding.

Name D. Chan Social Security No. 125-11-3296

Address 7821 Oak Ave. No. of Allowances 1 Marital Status Married

Period Ending	Total Wages	Cumulative Total	Deductions: Social Security	Deductions: Medicare	Deductions: Federal Inc. Tax	Deductions: Other Deductions	Deductions: Total	Net Pay
1/31	$ 3,100	$ 3,100				$ 18.00		
2/28	3,000	6,100				18.00		
3/31	3,450	$9,550				18.00		
Quarter Total	$9,550					$ 54.00		

Learning Objective	Summary	Example
9.5	Computing an employer's quarterly federal tax return	4. The Frazer Company had a total payroll of $279,440 for the first quarter of the year. It withheld $29,700 for federal income tax. It made monthly tax deposits of $24,100. Frazer is now filing its quarterly Form 941. Complete the following to determine the amount of the check that Frazer must send to the IRS for undeposited taxes due. a. Social Security tax due for the quarter _____ b. Medicare tax due for the quarter _____ c. Total taxes due for the quarter _____ d. Total deposits for the quarter _____ e. Undeposited taxes due IRS _____
9.6	Computing an employer's federal and state unemployment tax liability	5. Miller Outfitters employed R. Rehnquist for the period from January 1 through March 31, 13 weeks, at a salary of $1,230 per week. At the end of the quarter, how much in FUTA and SUTA taxes are owed to the federal and state governments if the state had a 0.8% FUTA rate and a 5.4% SUTA rate? a. Total wages b. FUTA tax c. SUTA tax d. Total federal and state unemployment taxes paid

Answers: 1 and 2. Lee: Reg Earn $568; O/T Earnings $127.80; Total $695.80; Deductions: SS–$43.14; MC–$10.09; FIT–$105.43; MI–$7. Total Deductions $165.66; Net pay $530.14 Berg: Reg Earn $520; O/T Earnings 156.00; Total $676.00; Deductions: SS–$41.91; MC–$9.80; FIT–$51.64; MI–$15. Total Deductions 118.36; Net Pay $557.64 **3.** 1/31: $192.20; $44.95; $350.55; $605.70; $2,494.30 2/28: $186.00; $43.50; $335.55; $583.05; $2,416.95 3/31: $213.90; $50.03; $403.05; $684.98; $2,765.02 Totals: $592.10; $138.48; $1,089.15; $54.00; $1,873.73; $7,676.27 **4. a.** $34,650.56 **b.** 8,103.76 **c.** 72,454.32 **d.** 72,300.00 **e.** $154.32 **5. a.** $15,990.00 **b.** 56.00 **c.** 378.00 **d.** $434.00

Assignment 9.1: Payroll Problems

Name

Date Score

A (52 points) Complete the payroll. (1 point for each correct answer)

1. In this company, employees are paid 1½ times their regular rate for overtime hours between 40 and 48 and 2 times their regular rate for overtime hours over 48.

Name	Total Hours	Regular Rate Per Hour	Regular Earnings Hours	Regular Earnings Amount	Time and a Half Hours	Time and a Half Amount	Double Time Hours	Double Time Amount	Total Earnings
Abrams, John	52	9.00	40		8		4		
Aguilar, Ralph	40	8.00	40		—		—		
Kula, Mary	50	7.50	40		8		2		
Murphy, Tom	45	9.00	40		5		—		
Norton, Alice	40	8.80	40		—		—		
Payton, Alan	40	8.00	40		—		—		
Perry, Lance	47	8.00	40		7		—		
Polar, Barbara	41	9.00	40		1		—		
Quinn, Carl	49	8.80	40		8		1		
Reston, Sally	40	8.80	40		—		—		
Sacco, Dom	50	7.50	40		8		2		
Warren, Bill	44	8.80	40		4		—		
TOTALS									

Score for A (52)

B (28 points) Solve the following problems. (7 points for each correct answer)

2. Joy Agliano is employed at a monthly salary of $3,000. How much is deducted from her monthly salary for FICA taxes (Social Security and Medicare)? __________

3. Coleen Klein is employed by a company that pays her $2,900 a month. She is single and claims one withholding allowance. What is her net pay after Social Security, Medicare, and federal income tax withholding? Use the percentage method. __________

4. On April 1, the company in Problem 3 changed its pay plan from monthly to weekly and began paying Coleen $700 per week. What is her net weekly pay after Social Security, Medicare, and income tax deductions? Use the percentage method. __________

5. James Cox is married and claims four withholding allowances. His weekly wages are $725. Calculate his Social Security and Medicare deductions and, using the wage-bracket method, his federal income tax withholding. Find his weekly net pay. __________

____
Score for B (28)

C (20 points) Compute and compare the federal income tax withholding amounts for each of the following individuals using the percentage method and the wage-bracket method. (Follow the steps in Section 9.2 for the percentage method.) (5 points for each correct difference)

6. Ralph Carson: weekly wages, $275; single; 1 withholding allowance
Percentage method: __________
Wage-bracket method: __________
Difference: __________

7. George Wilson: weekly wages, $320; married; 3 withholding allowances
Percentage method: __________
Wage-bracket method: __________
Difference: __________

8. Mary Suizo: weekly wages, $292; single; 2 withholding allowances
Percentage method: __________
Wage-bracket method: __________
Difference: __________

9. Josephine Creighton: weekly wages, $375; married; 1 withholding allowance
Percentage method: __________
Wage-bracket method: __________
Difference: __________

____
Score for C (20)

Assignment 9.2: Payroll, Earnings Record, Payroll Tax Returns

LEARNING OBJECTIVES 4 5 6

Name

Date Score

A (40 points) Solve the following problems. (1 point for each correct answer in the Total Wages column in 1; 2 points for each correct answer in the Net Pay column in 1 and 2)

1. Complete the following weekly payroll register. Workers receive overtime pay for any time worked in excess of 40 hours per week at the rate of time and a half. There is a 6.2% deduction for Social Security and 1.45% for Medicare taxes. Use the wage-bracket method for federal income tax withholding. Be sure to use the correct withholding table, based on the marital status of each employee.

				Regular Earnings		Overtime Earnings				Deductions					
Name	Marital Status	W/H Allow.	Total Hours	Rate Per Hour	Amount	Hours Worked	Rate Per Hour	Amount	Total Wages	Social Security	Medi-care	Fed. Inc. Tax	Med Ins.	Total	Net Pay
Black, J.	M	3	40	$10.00		–							$ 15.00		
Burns, E.	S	0	45	8.80		5							12.00		
Dawson, R.	M	2	40	9.20		–							15.00		
Frey, W. R.	M	4	40	10.50		–							21.00		
Muldez, T.	S	1	44	9.80		4							12.00		
Nations, B.	M	3	41	9.00		1							15.00		
Odell, L. O.	M	4	40	9.80		–							18.00		
Rayder, D.	M	4	48	10.50		8							18.00		
Ridem, G.	S	1	40	8.80		–							12.00		
TOTALS													$138.00		

2. The total weekly wages of four employees are listed below. Determine the amount of the deductions and the net pay due to each employee. Use 6.2% for Social Security and 1.45% for Medicare tax deductions, and use the percentage method for federal income tax withholding. Determine the deductions and totals.

				Deductions				
Name	Marital Status	W/H Allow.	Total Wages	Social Security	Medicare	Federal Income Tax	Total	Net Pay
Alvarez, George	S	1	$ 450.00					
Coburn, Carol	M	3	480.00					
Garnett, Mildred	S	1	505.00					
Kline, Marvin	M	2	430.00					
TOTALS			$1,865.00					

Score for A (40)

B (20 points) Solve the following problems. (1 point for each correct weekly answer in the Net Pay column and 2 points for the correct quarter total of that column in 1; 1 point for each correct answer in 2)

3. Complete the employee's earnings records for J. R. Collins. Use 6.2% for Social Security and 1.45% for Medicare taxes. Use the percentage method for federal income tax withholding.

Name J. R. Collins Social Security No. 125-11-3290

Address 7821 Oak Ave. No. of Allowances 2 Marital Status Married

			Deductions					
Period Ending	Total Wages	Cumulative Total	Social Security	Medicare	Federal Inc. Tax	United Fund	Total	Net Pay
1/6	$ 286.50	$ 286.50				$ 4.00		
1/13	318.40	604.90				4.00		
1/20	318.40	923.30				4.00		
1/27	309.00	1,232.30				4.00		
2/3	320.50	1,552.80				4.00		
2/10	322.40	1,875.20				4.00		
2/17	318.60	2,193.80				4.00		
2/24	318.00	2,511.80				4.00		
3/3	320.14	2,831.94				4.00		
3/10	361.00	3,192.94				4.00		
3/17	305.00	3,497.94				4.00		
3/24	316.20	3,814.14				4.00		
3/31	306.50	4,120.64				4.00		
Quarter Totals	$4,120.64					$52.00		

4. Shown below is a summary of quarterly earnings of employees. Determine the information requested for the employer's quarterly federal tax return.

Name	Total Wages	Taxes Withheld		
		Social Security	Medicare	Fed. Inc. Tax
Collins, J.	$ 4,120.64	$ 255.48	$ 59.75	$ 337.58
Doyle, L.	4,828.00	299.34	70.01	400.18
Gordon, J.	4,772.60	295.90	69.20	317.80
McBride, C.	4,748.70	294.42	68.86	412.90
Taggert, L.	4,787.00	296.79	69.41	500.24
Walton, N.D.	4,791.90	297.10	69.48	319.80
TOTALS				

a. Total earnings paid __________

b. Federal income tax withheld __________

c. Total Social Security tax paid __________

d. Total Medicare tax paid __________

e. Total taxes __________

__________ Score for B (20)

C (40 points) Solve the following problems. (4 points for each correct answer in 5 and 6; 1 point for each correct answer in 7)

5. The quarterly earnings of the employees of the Zulu Company are listed below. Determine the information needed for the employer's quarterly federal tax return (Form 941).

Name	Total Wages	Taxes Withheld		
		Social Security	Medicare	Fed. Inc. Tax
Caldwell, Janice	$ 3,420.00	$ 212.04	$ 49.59	$ 423.90
Dorman, J.A.	3,600.00	223.20	52.20	473.67
Eagie, T.W.	4,016.50	249.04	58.24	433.33
Fortune, Mark	3,774.90	234.02	54.74	410.05
Morris, Regina	3,605.40	223.53	52.28	399.83
Tracy, Joseph	4,111.60	254.92	59.62	360.17
TOTALS				

a. Total earnings paid ________

b. Employee's contribution of Social Security tax ________

c. Employee's contribution of Medicare tax ________

d. Federal income tax withheld from wages ________

e. Total taxes ________

6. The Primo Company had a total payroll of $148,600.34 for the first quarter of the current year. It has withheld $28,531.27 from the employees for federal income tax during this quarter. The company has made the following deposits in a qualified bank depository for the amount of the income and Social Security and Medicare taxes withheld from the employees and for the company's contribution to FICA tax: $17,050 on February 6; $17,050 on March 4; and $17,050 on April 5. Primo Company is now filling out Form 941 (quarterly return), which is due by the end of April. Complete the following to determine the amount of the check that the company must send to the IRS for the undeposited taxes due.

a. Total Social Security and Medicare taxes to be paid for quarter ________

b. Total taxes ________

c. Total deposits for quarter (sent to qualified bank depository) ________

d. Undeposited taxes due IRS ________

7. Jordan Mills employed Ruth Liebowitz for the period January 1 through March 31 (13 weeks), at a salary of $1,500 per week. At the end of the first quarter of the year, how much in FUTA and SUTA taxes were owed to the federal and state governments if the state had an 0.8% FUTA rate and a 5.4% SUTA rate?

a. Total wages and taxable wages ________

b. FUTA tax ________

c. SUTA tax ________

d. Total federal and state unemployment taxes paid ________

____
Score for C (40)

Notes

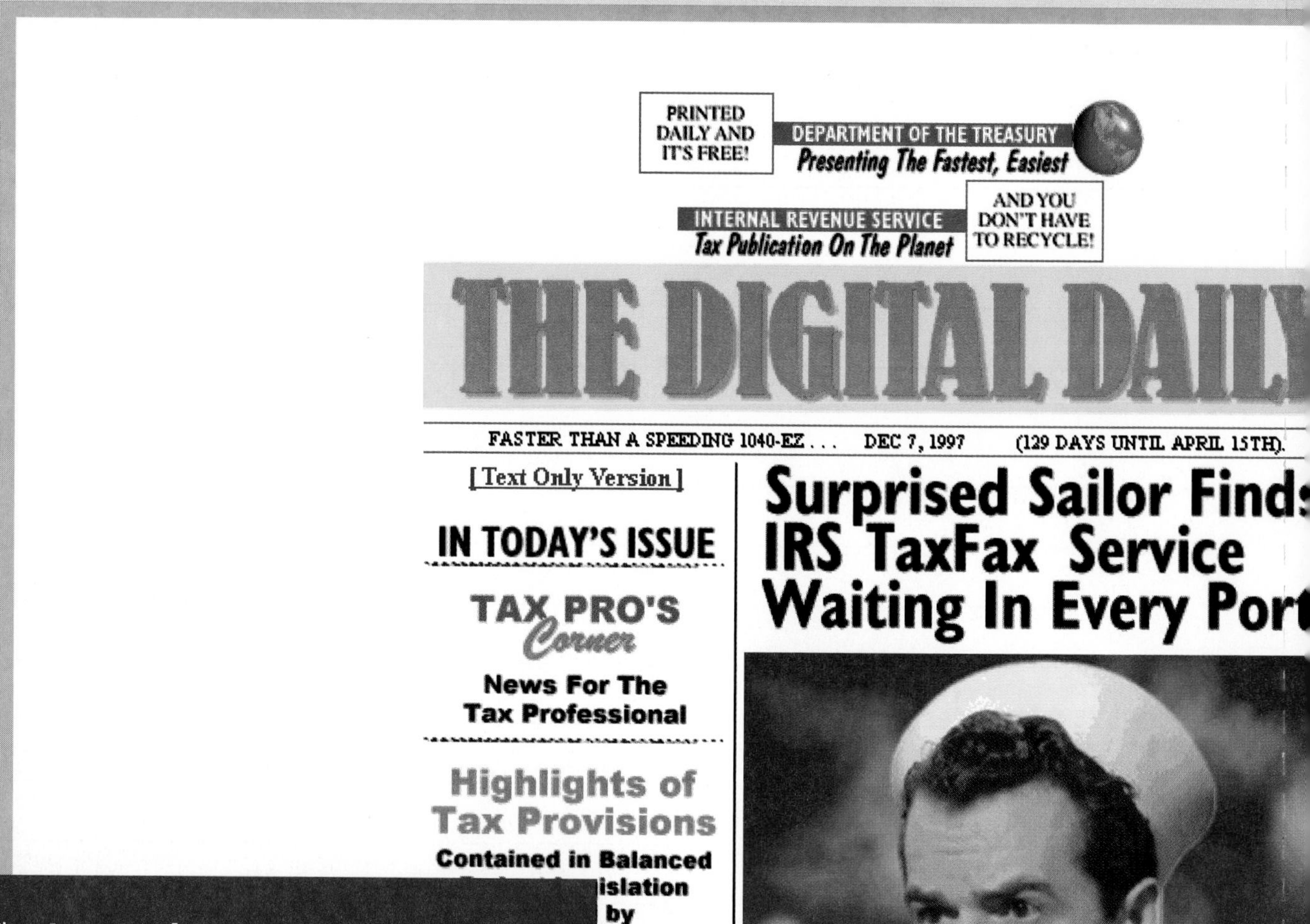

PRINTED DAILY AND IT'S FREE!

DEPARTMENT OF THE TREASURY
Presenting The Fastest, Easiest

INTERNAL REVENUE SERVICE
Tax Publication On The Planet

AND YOU DON'T HAVE TO RECYCLE!

THE DIGITAL DAIL

FASTER THAN A SPEEDING 1040-EZ . . .   DEC 7, 1997   (129 DAYS UNTIL APRIL 15TH).

[Text Only Version]

IN TODAY'S ISSUE

TAX PRO'S Corner

News For The Tax Professional

Highlights of Tax Provisions

Contained in Balanced

Surprised Sailor Find
IRS TaxFax Service
Waiting In Every Port

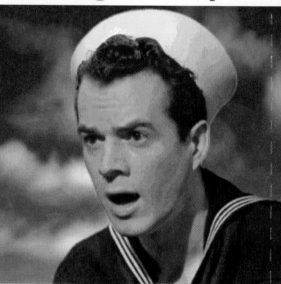

AGANA, GUAM   When Seaman Barry Barkent needed a few extra Federal Income Tax forms he thought he would have to wait until his parents cou mail them from home. Hard to tell how long that mi take; you see, Barry was somewhere near 15 degr North Latitude, 175 degrees East Longitude aboar

The **Internal Revenue Service** (IRS) is the federal department with which working adults have the most contact—through the income tax return.

The IRS has made efforts to simplify the tax-paying process. Taxpayers can receive over 100 forms by fax or find answers to questions at the IRS home page at www.irs.ustreas.gov. In addition, the IRS provides prerecorded telephone information 24 hours a day, 7 days a week and telephone assistance 10 hours each business day.

One of the features of the IRS home page is "The Digital Daily," a daily Internet publication that assists taxpayers in finding information.

10

Federal Income Taxes

Learning Objectives

By studying this chapter and completing all the assignments, you will learn to:

1. Compute taxable income for taxpayers who use the standard Form 1040.

2. Compute taxes due for taxpayers who use the standard Form 1040.

3. Compute taxes due for corporations and other businesses, given the taxable income.

In 1913, the U.S. Congress enacted the original Revenue Act, which imposed a tax on the income of American individuals and corporations. The federal income tax, which began to be collected in the United States in the next year, has now become the dominant tax in the U.S. federal tax system.

Personal income taxes provide 39% of all income of the federal government. Social Security and Medicare taxes, which were studied in Chapter 9, provide another 32%. Together these two taxes make up 71% of all government income. Since all taxes combined do not cover the entire cost of government, 11% of government operating expenses come from borrowed money (see Figure 10-1).

Outlays for Social Security, Medicare, and retirement programs constitute 36% of all government expenditures. Payment of interest on government debt represents 15% of all government expenditures (Figure 10-1).

Computing Taxable Income Using Standard Form 1040

Compute taxable income for taxpayers who use the standard Form 1040.

Form 1040 is the basic form filed by the majority of taxpayers. There are two simplified variations of this form: Form 1040A and Form 1040EZ. The income tax calculation process is illustrated for Form 1040, shown in Figures 10-2 through 10-7. The label in Figure 10-2 contains spaces for names, address, and Social Security numbers, as well as boxes to check to donate $3 to finance presidential elections.

A taxpayer's current *filing status* is indicated in the second section of Form 1040, shown in Figure 10-3. There are five choices given. The one selected determines the tax rates the taxpayer uses, as well as many of the taxpayer's deductions.

Personal exemptions, shown in Figure 10-4, are reductions to taxable income for the primary taxpayer and a spouse. One *dependency exemption* is granted for each depen-

Figure 10-1: Income and Outlays. These pie charts show the relative sizes of the major categories of federal income and outlays for fiscal year 1995.

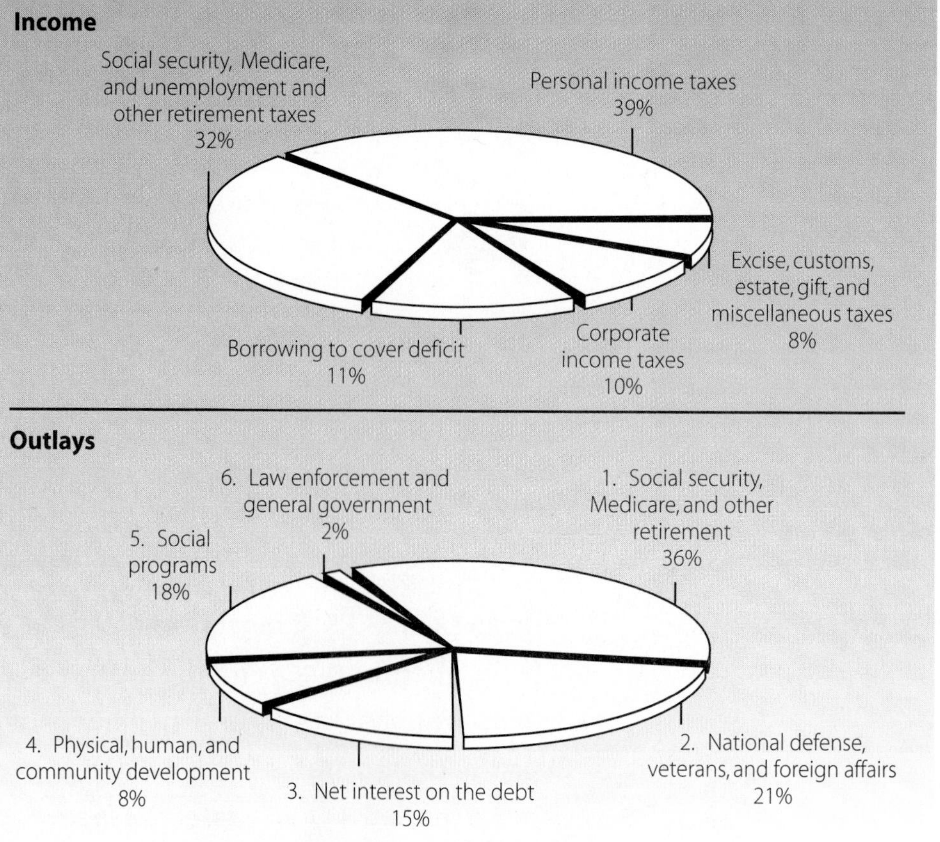

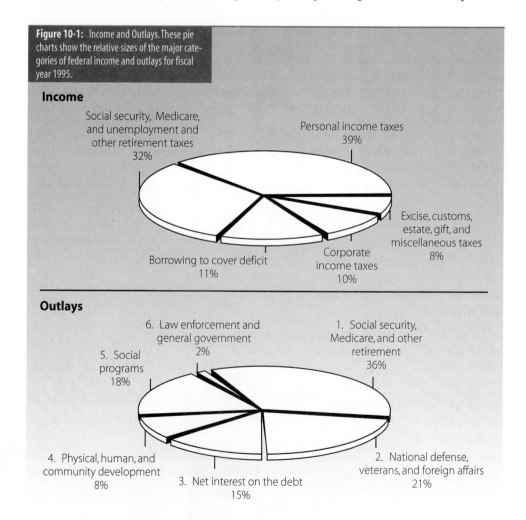

dent. Exemptions are phased out for individuals with higher incomes: adjusted gross incomes above $90,900 for a married person filing separately, $121,200 for a single person, or $181,800 for a married couple filing jointly. The amount deducted for each exemption is currently $2,650. This amount is usually adjusted for inflation each year.

Taxable income, shown in Figure 10-5, includes wages, salaries, tips, dividends, interest, commissions, back pay, bonuses and awards, refunds of state and local taxes, alimony received, property received for services, severance pay, accrued leave payments, sick pay, unemployment compensation payments, and capital gains. Taxable income may include a portion of Social Security payments, IRA distributions, and pensions and annuities. It also includes income from businesses, professions, farming, partnerships, rents, royalties, estates, trusts, and other sources. It does not include income from gifts, inheritances, bequests, interest on tax-exempt state and local municipal bonds, life insurance proceeds at death, workers' compensation benefits, and certain income items for veterans.

The Adjustments to Income section, shown in Figure 10-6, allows the taxpayer to list certain items that are allowed as reductions to the total income. These adjustments include payments by the taxpayer or spouse to an individual retirement account (IRA), moving expenses, one-half of self-employment tax paid, payments to a retirement plan for the self-employed, penalty on early withdrawal of savings, and alimony paid. *Adjusted gross income (AGI)* is a taxpayer's income after subtracting adjustments to income from total income. (See lines 31 and 32 of Adjusted Gross Income in Figure 10-6.)

Figure 10-2: Form 1040 Label Section

Form **1040** Department of the Treasury—Internal Revenue Service
U.S. Individual Income Tax Return **1997** (99) IRS Use Only—Do not write or staple in this space.

For the year Jan. 1–Dec. 31, 1997, or other tax year beginning , 1997, ending , 19 OMB No. 1545-0074

Label (See instructions on page 10.) **Use the IRS label.** Otherwise, please print or type.

LABEL HERE

Your first name and initial: John J.	Last name: Sample	Your social security number: 345 : 67 : 8901
If a joint return, spouse's first name and initial: Mary M.	Last name: Sample	Spouse's social security number: 456 : 78 : 9012
Home address (number and street). If you have a P.O. box, see page 10.: 210 Elm Street	Apt. no.	For help in finding line instructions, see pages 2 and 3 in the booklet.
City, town or post office, state, and ZIP code. If you have a foreign address, see page 10.: Anytown Mo 83817-2402		

Presidential Election Campaign (See page 10.)

	Yes	No	Note: *Checking "Yes" will not change your tax or reduce your refund.*
Do you want $3 to go to this fund?	X		
If a joint return, does your spouse want $3 to go to this fund?	X		

Figure 10-3: Form 1040 Filing Status Section

Filing Status

Check only one box.

1		Single
2	X	Married filing joint return (even if only one had income)
3		Married filing separate return. Enter spouse's social security no. above and full name here. ▶
4		Head of household (with qualifying person). (See page 10.) If the qualifying person is a child but not your dependent, enter this child's name here. ▶
5		Qualifying widow(er) with dependent child (year spouse died ▶ 19). (See page 10.)

Figure 10-4: Form 1040 Exemptions Section

Exemptions

6a ☒ **Yourself.** If your parent (or someone else) can claim you as a dependent on his or her tax return, **do not** check box 6a.

b ☒ **Spouse**

c **Dependents:**

(1) First name	Last name	(2) Dependent's social security number	(3) Dependent's relationship to you	(4) No. of months lived in your home in 1997
Johnny	Sample	567 : 89 : 0123	Son	12
Maria	Sample	678 : 90 : 1234	daughter	12

If more than six dependents, see page 10.

d Total number of exemptions claimed

No. of boxes checked on 6a and 6b: 2
No. of your children on 6c who:
• lived with you: 2
• did not live with you due to divorce or separation (see page 11)
Dependents on 6c not entered above
Add numbers entered on lines above ▶ 4

Figure 10-5: Form 1040 Income Section

Income	Line	Description	Box	Amount
Attach Copy B of your Forms W-2, W-2G, and 1099-R here.	7	Wages, salaries, tips, etc. Attach Form(s) W-2	7	62,000 00
	8a	**Taxable** interest. Attach Schedule B if required	8a	500 00
	b	**Tax-exempt** interest. DO NOT include on line 8a . . . 8b		
	9	Dividends. Attach Schedule B if required	9	
	10	Taxable refunds, credits, or offsets of state and local income taxes (see page 12)	10	
If you did not get a W-2, see page 12.	11	Alimony received	11	
	12	Business income or (loss). Attach Schedule C or C-EZ	12	
	13	Capital gain or (loss). Attach Schedule D	13	
	14	Other gains or (losses). Attach Form 4797	14	
	15a	Total IRA distributions . 15a — b Taxable amount (see page 13)	15b	
	16a	Total pensions and annuities 16a — b Taxable amount (see page 13)	16b	
Enclose but do not attach any payment. Also, please use **Form 1040-V.**	17	Rental real estate, royalties, partnerships, S corporations, trusts, etc. Attach Schedule E	17	500 00
	18	Farm income or (loss). Attach Schedule F	18	
	19	Unemployment compensation	19	
	20a	Social security benefits . 20a — b Taxable amount (see page 14)	20b	
	21	Other income. List type and amount—see page 15	21	
	22	Add the amounts in the far right column for lines 7 through 21. This is your **total income** ▶	22	63,000 00

Figure 10-6: Form 1040 Adjustments to Income Section/Adjusted Gross Income

Adjusted Gross Income						
	23	IRA deduction (see page 16)	23	3,000 00		
	24	Medical savings account deduction. Attach Form 8853	24			
	25	Moving expenses. Attach Form 3903 or 3903-F	25			
	26	One-half of self-employment tax. Attach Schedule SE	26			
If line 32 is under $29,290 (under $9,770 if a child did not live with you), see EIC inst. on page 21.	27	Self-employed health insurance deduction (see page 17)	27			
	28	Keogh and self-employed SEP and SIMPLE plans	28			
	29	Penalty on early withdrawal of savings	29			
	30a	Alimony paid b Recipient's SSN ▶	30a			
	31	Add lines 23 through 30a			31	3,000 00
	32	Subtract line 31 from line 22. This is your **adjusted gross income** ▶			32	60,000 00

For Privacy Act and Paperwork Reduction Act Notice, see page 38. Cat. No. 11320B Form **1040** (1997)

Figure 10-7: Form 1040 Taxable Income and Tax Due Section

Form 1040 (1997) Page **2**

Tax Computation				
	33	Amount from line 32 (adjusted gross income)	33	60,000 00
	34a	Check if: ☐ **You** were 65 or older, ☐ Blind; ☐ **Spouse** was 65 or older, ☐ Blind. Add the number of boxes checked above and enter the total here ▶ 34a		
	b	If you are married filing separately and your spouse itemizes deductions or you were a dual-status alien, see page 18 and check here ▶ 34b ☐		
	35	Enter the **larger** of your: **Itemized deductions** from Schedule A, line 28, **OR** **Standard deduction** shown below for your filing status. **But** see page 18 if you checked any box on line 34a or 34b **or** someone can claim you as a dependent. • Single—$4,150 • Married filing jointly or Qualifying widow(er)—$6,900 • Head of household—$6,050 • Married filing separately—$3,450	35	6,900 00
If you want the IRS to figure your tax, see page 18.	36	Subtract line 35 from line 33	36	53,100 00
	37	If line 33 is $90,900 or less, multiply $2,650 by the total number of exemptions claimed on line 6d. If line 33 is over $90,900, see the worksheet on page 19 for the amount to enter	37	10,600 00
	38	**Taxable income.** Subtract line 37 from line 36. If line 37 is more than line 36, enter -0-	38	42,500 00
	39	**Tax.** See page 19. Check if any tax from **a** ☐ Form(s) 8814 **b** ☐ Form 4972 ▶	39	6,544 00

After the adjusted gross income figure is computed, *deductions*—either the standard deduction or itemized deductions—are subtracted in order to figure taxable income in Figure 10-7. The standard deductions for most taxpayers are shown in Figure 10-8. There are higher standard deductions for individuals who are 65 or over and for individuals who are blind; these are shown in Figure 10-9.

Some taxpayers choose to itemize deductions rather than use the IRS-approved standard deduction. *Itemized deductions* are deductions allowed for specific payments made by the taxpayer during the tax year. These deductions include charitable contributions,

Figure 10-8: Standard Deduction Chart for Most People

Table 7. **Standard Deduction Chart for Most People***

If Your Filing Status is:	Your Standard Deduction is:
Single	$4,150
Married filing joint return or Qualifying widow(er) with dependent child	6,900
Married filing separate return	3,450
Head of household	6,050

*DO NOT use this chart if you were 65 or older or blind, OR if someone else can claim an exemption for you (or your spouse if married filing jointly).

Figure 10-9: Standard Deduction Chart for People Age 65 and Older or Blind (Line 35)

Table 8. **Standard Deduction Chart for People Age 65 or Older or Blind***

Check the correct number of boxes below. Then go to the chart.

You 65 or older ☐ Blind ☐

Your spouse, if claiming spouse's exemption 65 or older ☐ Blind ☐

Total number of boxes you checked ☐

If Your Filing Status is:	And the Number in the Box Above is:	Your Standard Deduction is:
Single	1	$5,150
	2	6,150
Married filing joint return or Qualifying widow(er) with dependent child	1	7,700
	2	8,500
	3	9,300
	4	10,100
Married filing separate return	1	4,250
	2	5,050
	3	5,850
	4	6,650
Head of household	1	7,050
	2	8,050

*If someone else can claim an exemption for you (or your spouse if married filing jointly), use Table 9, instead.

certain interest payments, state and local taxes, a portion of medical and dental expenses, casualty and theft losses, tax preparation fees, and other annually identified deductions. Illustrations, examples, and problems in this book assume that all state and local taxes and all donations to charity are deductible.

Computation of Taxable Income

Line 38 of Form 1040 shows "taxable income." *Taxable income* is the amount of income on which the income tax is based. Taxable income for most taxpayers is computed as follows (amounts from the preceding figures):

Total income (income from all sources) (Line 22)	$63,000
Less adjustments to income (reductions of Total Income) (Line 31)	3,000
Adjusted gross income (Line 32)	60,000
Less deductions (from Figure 10-8 or 10-9)	6,900
Less exemptions (Line 6d × $2,650, per Line 37)	10,600
Taxable income (the amount on which taxes are computed) (Line 38)	$42,500

CONCEPT CHECK 10.1

Catherine, a 72 -year-old blind widow, had an annual adjusted gross income of $28,000. She filed a return claiming a single exemption and standard deduction. No income tax had been withheld during the year. What was the total income tax due?

Adjusted gross income	$ 28,000
Standard deduction: single, over 65, blind	6,150
	21,850
Minus 1 exemption	2,650
Taxable income	$ 19,200
From Schedule X:	
$19,200 × (0.15)	$ 2,880

Computing Taxes Due Using Standard Form 1040

Compute taxes due for taxpayers who use the standard Form 1040.

Taxes are computed using taxable income (Line 38). *Tax Rate Schedules* (Figure 10-10) show the tax rate for (1) single, (2) married filing joint return (even if only one had income), (3) married filing separate return, (4) head of household, and (5) qualifying widow or widower. The Tax Rate Schedules in Figure 10-10 are used for all illustrations, examples, and problems in this book.

The remaining sections of Form 1040 permit listing of special credits, other taxes, and payments, to arrive at the final refund or amount owed, and have spaces for signatures of the taxpayers, and of paid preparers.

EXAMPLE A

For the illustrated Form 1040, the tax is computed as follows:

Line 38—Taxable income	$42,500
From Schedule Y-1 (married):	
Tax on $41,200	$ 6,180
Plus 28% of amount over $41,200	
$42,500 − $41,200 = $1,300 × 0.28	$ 364
Total tax	$ 6,544

EXAMPLE B

Larry, filing as head of household, has an adjusted gross income of $107,000. He itemizes the following deductions: $700 to Salvation Army, $900 to his church, $2,900 interest on

Figure 10-10: Tax Rate Schedules

Schedule X—Use if your filing status is **Single**

If the amount on Form 1040, line 38, is: Over—	But not over—	Enter on Form 1040, line 39	of the amount over—
$0	$24,650	----- 15%	$0
24,650	59,750	$3,697.50 + 28%	24,650
59,750	124,650	13,525.50 + 31%	59,750
124,650	271,050	33,644.50 + 36%	124,650
271,050	-----	86,348.50 + 39.6%	271,050

Schedule Y-1—Use if your filing status is **Married filing jointly** or **Qualifying widow(er)**

If the amount on Form 1040, line 38, is: Over—	But not over—	Enter on Form 1040, line 39	of the amount over—
$0	$41,200	----- 15%	$0
41,200	99,600	$6,180.00 + 28%	41,200
99,600	151,750	22,532.00 + 31%	99,600
151,750	271,050	38,698.50 + 36%	151,750
271,050	-----	81,646.50 + 39.6%	271,050

Schedule Y-2—Use if your filing status is **Married filing separately**

If the amount on Form 1040, line 38, is: Over—	But not over—	Enter on Form 1040, line 39	of the amount over—
$0	$20,600	----- 15%	$0
20,600	49,800	$3,090.00 + 28%	20,600
49,800	75,875	11,266.00 + 31%	49,800
75,875	135,525	19,349.25 + 36%	75,875
135,525	-----	40,823.25 + 39.6%	135,525

Schedule Z—Use if your filing status is **Head of household**

If the amount on Form 1040, line 38, is: Over—	But not over—	Enter on Form 1040, line 39	of the amount over—
$0	$33,050	----- 15%	$0
33,050	85,350	$4,957.50 + 28%	33,050
85,350	138,200	19,601.50 + 31%	85,350
138,200	271,050	35,985.00 + 36%	138,200
271,050	-----	83,811.00 + 39.6%	271,050

his mortgage, and $3,300 state taxes. He claims two exemptions. Compute his federal tax. Round to the nearest dollar.

Adjusted gross income	$107,000
Minus itemized deductions	7,800
	99,200
Minus 2 exemptions	5,300
Taxable income	$ 93,900
From Schedule Z:	
Tax on $85,350–$138,200	$ 19,601.50
Plus 31% (0.31) of excess over $85,350	
$93,900 − $85,350 = $8,550 × 0.31	2,650.50
Total tax	$ 22,252.00

EXAMPLE C

Robert and Rosemary file a joint return. Their adjusted gross income is $52,000. They take the standard deduction. They have three children and claim five exemptions. Compute their federal income tax.

Adjusted gross income	$52,000
Standard deduction	6,900
	45,100
Minus 5 exemptions × $2,650 each	13,250
Taxable income	$31,850
From Schedule Y-1:	
$31,850 × 0.15 =	$ 4,777.50, rounded $4,778

CONCEPT CHECK 10.2

Chris and Sue had wages of $43,200, interest income of $2,400, dividend income of $3,900, and business income of $9,500. They put $2,000 into an IRA. They filed a joint return, claiming 5 exemptions and using the standard deduction. During the year, $4,600 in federal income tax had been withheld for them. What was the total income tax due with the return?

Total income	$ 59,000
Adjustments to income: $2,000 IRA deduction	2,000
Adjusted gross income	57,000
Standard deduction: married, filing jointly	6,900
	50,100
Minus 5 exemptions: 5 × $2,650	13,250
Taxable income	$ 36,850
From Schedule Y-1:	
$36,850 × 0.15 =	$ 5,527.50, rounded $5,528
Less federal income tax withheld	4,600
Total tax due	$ 928

Computing Taxes for Businesses

LEARNING OBJECTIVES 3

Compute taxes due for corporations and other businesses, given the taxable income.

For a *sole proprietorship*—a business that has only one owner and is not incorporated—the owner includes the net income or loss from the business on Form 1040 and attaches a substantiating form: Schedule C, Profit or Loss from Business.

For a *partnership*—a business that is not incorporated and has more than one owner—each partner must include his or her share of the income or loss on his or her individual Form 1040.

For-profit corporations—businesses that operate for a profit and whose owners are stockholders—must file special corporate returns regardless of the amount of taxable income or loss, even if no tax is due or refundable. The form most commonly used is IRS Form 1120. Most corporations figure their tax by using a Tax Rate Schedule. Figure 10-11 shows the latest Corporate Tax Rate Schedule used for this book.

EXAMPLE D

In 199X, Steel Structures Corp. had taxable income of $72,000. What was the company's total income tax for the year?

Tax on $50,000–$75,000	$ 7,500
Plus $72,000 − $50,000 = $22,000 × 0.25	5,500
Total income tax	$13,000

Figure 10-11: Tax Rate Schedule—Corporate

Tax Rate Schedule

If taxable income (line 30, Form 1120, or line 26, Form 1120–A) on page 1 is:

Over—	*But not over—*	*Tax is:*	*Of the amount over—*
$0	$50,000	15%	$0
50,000	75,000	$ 7,500 + 25%	50,000
75,000	100,000	13,750 + 34%	75,000
100,000	335,000	22,250 + 39%	100,000
335,000	10,000,000	113,900 + 34%	335,000
10,000,000	15,000,000	3,400,000 + 35%	10,000,000
15,000,000	18,333,333	5,150,000 +38%	15,000,000
18,333,333	- - - - -	35%	0

EXAMPLE E

In the following year, Steel Structures Corp. had taxable income of $13,546,753. What was the income tax? Round to the nearest dollar.

Tax on $10,000,000–$15,000,000	$3,400,000
Plus $13,546,753 − $10,000,000 = $3,546,753 × 0.35	$1,241,363.55
Total income tax	$4,641,363.55
Rounded to	$4,641,364

CONCEPT CHECK 10.3

a. If the Digby Construction Company had taxable income of $22,250,500 last year, what was their income tax?

$22,250,500 × 0.35% = $7,787,675

b. The Pearl Diving Corporation had a taxable income of $82,100 last year. What was their income tax?

Tax on $75,000–$100,000	$13,750
Plus $82,100 − $75,000 = $7,100 × 0.34	$ 2,414
Income tax	$16,164

COMPLETE ASSIGNMENTS 10.1 AND 10.2.

Chapter Terms for Review

adjusted gross income (AGI)
deductions
dependency exemption
filing status
Form 1040
for-profit corporation
itemized deductions
partnership
personal exemption
sole proprietorship
Tax Rate Schedule
taxable income

The Bottom Line

Summary of chapter learning objectives:

Learning Objective	Summary	Example
10.1	Computing taxable income for taxpayers who use the standard Form 1040	1. Gary Champagne is 28 years old and single. He claimed one exemption. In 199X he earned $47,000 in wages and $300 in taxable interest income. He also received dividend income of $375. During the year he invested $1,800 in an individual retirement account. Because of a change of jobs, he also had $1,200 in moving expenses, which qualified as an adjustment to income. He had qualifying deductions of $1,000 in medical bills, $300 in church donations, and $9,600 in interest on the condominium he owned. He also paid $150 in state taxes. He had $2,500 in federal income tax withheld during the year. What was the tax due with his return? Income: Adjustments to income: Adjusted gross income Less deductions: Less exemptions: Taxable income Tax computation Less tax withheld during the year Tax due with return
10.2	Computing taxes due for taxpayers who use the standard Form 1040	2. John and Julia Fishman are 72 and 70 years of age, respectively. Julia is blind. They filed as married, filing jointly. Last year they had a total income of $38,000 from investments. They filed a return and claimed the standard deduction. During the year they made quarterly payments of estimated tax in the amount of $2,400. What was the amount of tax due with their return? Adjusted gross income Less standard deduction Less exemptions: Taxable income Tax computation Less payments made during the year on estimated tax Tax due with return
10.3	Computing taxes due for corporations and other businesses, given the taxable income	3. The SED Corporation earned taxable income of $110,000 in 199X. How much federal income tax did it owe?

Answers: 1. $2,969 **2.** $1,110 **3.** $26,150

Assignment 10.1: Federal Income Tax

Name

Date Score

A (52 points) Complete all problems, using the exemptions, deductions, and tax rates given in the chapter. Round all amounts to the nearest dollar. (This is allowed as long as it is done consistently.) (12 points for correct answers to 2a and 3a; 4 points for other correct answers)

1. Determine the taxable income for each of the following taxpayers.

Adjusted Gross Income	Number of Exemptions	Type of Return	Deductions	Taxable Income
a. $19,700	1	single	standard	________
b. $52,450	4	head of household	standard	________
c. $23,900	2	joint	standard	________
d. $12,464	1	single	$4,218	________
e. $43,700	6	joint	$7,023	________

2. Mary Rogers is a 70-year-old single person who lives alone. She takes the standard deduction. Her income during the year was $16,500.

a. What is Mary's taxable income? ________

b. What is Mary's tax? ________

3. George Sampson is 82 years old, and his wife Marcia is 83. Marcia is blind. They have $19,000 taxable income, including dividends from investments. They file a joint return and take the standard deduction.

a. What is the Sampsons' taxable income? ________

b. What is the Sampsons' income tax? ________

Score for A (52)

B (48 points) Solve the following problems. (12 points for correct taxable income; 4 points for correct income tax)

4. Jim Paul is 66 years old; his wife Ann is 64. They file a joint return. Jim's salary for the year was $30,000. Ann's salary was $24,500. They paid mortgage interest of $3,900 and property tax of $950 on their home. They paid state income tax of $3,200 during the year. They itemize their deductions.

a. What is their taxable income? __________

b. What is their income tax? __________

5. Walter and Louise Cross have two children. Both Walter's and Louise's mothers live with them and have no income. Walter's salary for the year was $23,000. Louise's salary was $24,000. They received taxable stock dividends of $1,200. They also received $500 from a state bond. They take the standard deduction and file a joint return.

a. What is their taxable income? __________

b. What is their income tax? __________

6. Arnold and Rita Stewart have three children. Arnold's father lives with them and has no income. Arnold earned a salary of $36,000 during the year. Rita is not employed. They received taxable stock dividends of $3,000. They paid $3,100 property tax and $4,100 mortgage interest on their home. They paid $2,600 principal on their mortgage. They paid state income tax of $2,175. They donated $500 to their church and $500 to the Salvation Army. They spent $5,600 on groceries and $1,100 on utilities. They itemize their deductions.

a. What is their taxable income? __________

b. What is their income tax? __________

____
Score for B (48)

Assignment 10.2: Federal Income Tax

Name ______________________

Date ______________ Score ______________

A (55 points) Solve the following problems. (25 points for a correct answer in 1; 3 points for each correct answer in 2)

1. Tara St. Clair, who is single, is employed at a salary of $15,500. She reported receiving tips amounting to $5,650. She collected $475 interest on her savings account and $2,000 interest on state bonds. She pays $350 a month rent for her apartment. Her itemized deductions total $2,280. During the year her employer withheld $1,220 from her pay for income tax purposes. She also made four estimated tax payments of $250 each within the year. How much more will she have to remit with her tax return? __________

2. Ben Hardy's salary is $24,000 a year, and his wife Gail earns $14,400 at a part-time job. They have two children, ages 13 and 16.

a. If they file a joint return, what is their tax? __________

b. If they file separately and Ben takes both children as exemptions, how much tax will they pay?
Ben: $__________; Gail $__________; Total $__________

c. If they file separately and each takes one child as an exemption, how much tax will they pay?
Ben: $__________; Gail $__________; Total $__________

d. If they file separately and Gail takes both children as exemptions, how much tax will they pay?
Ben: $__________; Gail $__________; Total $__________

____
Score for A (55)

B (45 points) Solve the following problems. (25 points for a correct answer in 3; 10 points for correct answers in 4 and 5)

3. The Allen and Day families live on the same street and work for the same company. Each has a salary of $32,000 a year. Mr. Allen also receives $5,000 a year as the village treasurer and $280 a year nontaxable dividends from a veterans' insurance policy. The family consists of Mr. Allen, his wife, and a daughter, age 17. The Allens own their own home and pay real estate taxes of $2,900 annually. Interest payments on their mortgage total $3,450 for the year, and charitable contributions total $900.

The Days have five children, all below high school age. They pay $500 a month rent for their home, and their charitable contributions are $900.

If each family files a joint return, which pays more federal income tax and by how much? (25 points)

____

4. The Green Laundry Corporation had income of $169,400 and expenses of $134,300. How much income tax should it pay? __________

5. A corporation had taxable income of $85,000. During the year it paid $1,865 for Social Security and $1,245 for unemployment compensation tax. What was the total it paid in taxes? __________

____
Score for B (45)

Notes

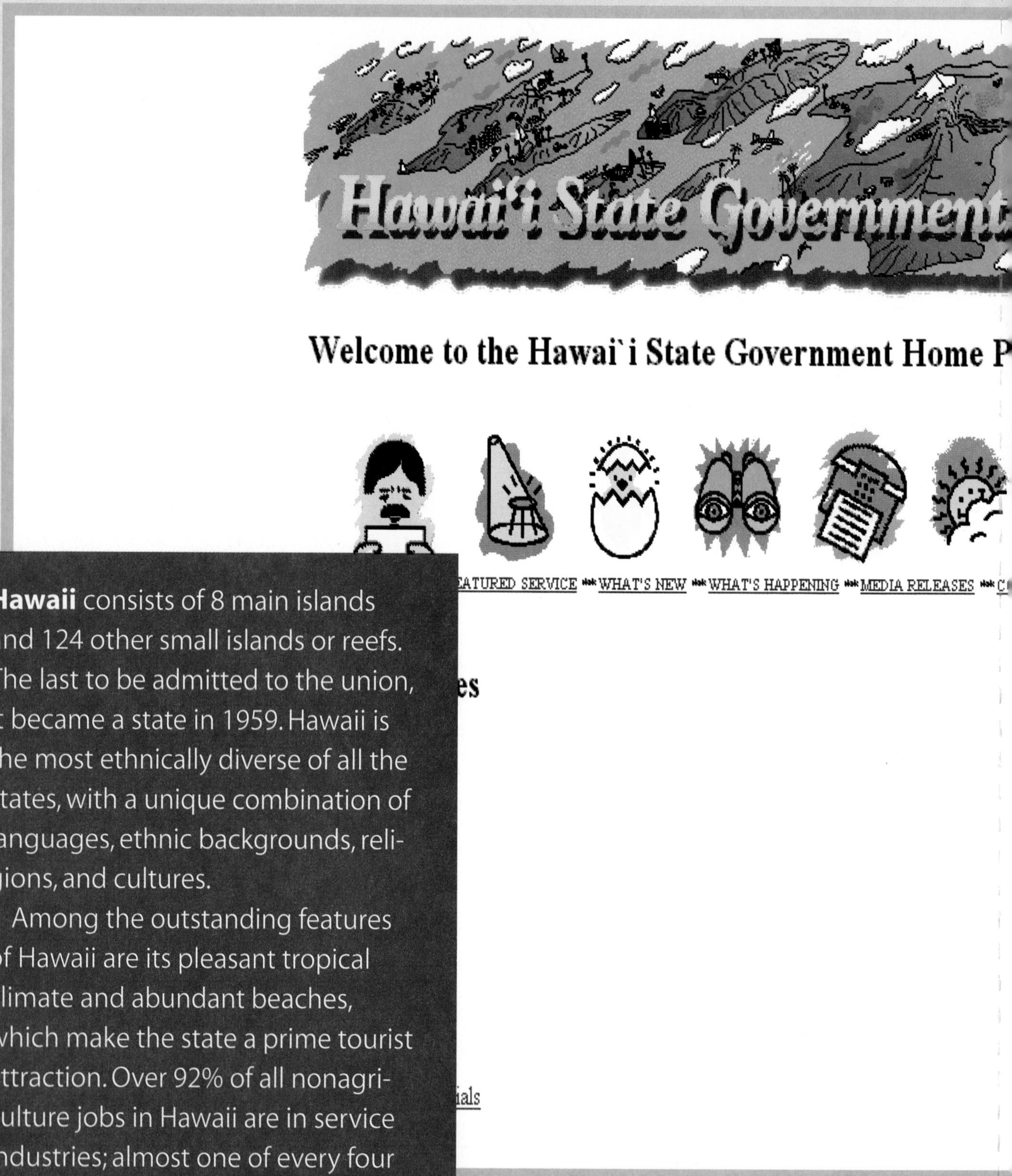

Hawaii consists of 8 main islands and 124 other small islands or reefs. The last to be admitted to the union, it became a state in 1959. Hawaii is the most ethnically diverse of all the states, with a unique combination of languages, ethnic backgrounds, religions, and cultures.

Among the outstanding features of Hawaii are its pleasant tropical climate and abundant beaches, which make the state a prime tourist attraction. Over 92% of all nonagriculture jobs in Hawaii are in service industries; almost one of every four jobs is directly related to tourism, air transportation, food service establishments, and hotels, serving over six million people each year.

Hawaii's home page can be seen at www.hawaii.gov.

11 Sales and Property Taxes

Learning Objectives

By studying this chapter and completing all the assignments, you will learn to:

1. Compute sales taxes using rate tables and percents.
2. Compute assessed valuations and property taxes based on assessed valuation.
3. Compute tax rates in percents and mills.
4. Compute tax payments involving special assessments, prorations, and exemptions.

Sales and property taxes are imposed by states, counties, cities, and special tax districts. Sales taxes are the most common of the state taxes. Property taxes are the most common revenue source for cities and special districts and support most elementary and secondary schools.

Most retail businesses collect a sales tax from customers when a sale occurs. The tax money must be turned over to the government. Persons and companies owning property usually pay taxes on the property's value. This chapter explains calculations involving sales and property taxes.

Computing Sales Taxes

LEARNING OBJECTIVES 1

Compute sales taxes using rate tables and percents.

A *sales tax* is a government *levy,* or charge, on retail sales of certain goods and services. Most states and many cities levy sales taxes. The state *tax rate*—the percent used to compute the amount of sales tax—currently ranges from 3% to 8%, while city and county rates range from 0.925% to 6%.

Sales Tax as a Percent of Price

Sales taxes generally are rounded to the nearest cent. For example, sales taxes of 4% and 5% on amounts of up to $1 are charged as shown in Figure 11-1.

Figure 11-1: Sales Taxes

4% on Sales of	Tax Due	5% on Sales of	Tax Due
$0.01 to $0.12	none	$0.01 to $0.09	none
$0.13 to $0.37	$0.01	$0.10 to $0.29	$0.01
$0.38 to $0.62	$0.02	$0.30 to $0.49	$0.02
$0.63 to $0.87	$0.03	$0.50 to $0.69	$0.03
$0.88 to $1.00	$0.04	$0.70 to $0.89	$0.04
		$0.90 to $1.00	$0.05

STEPS to Compute Sales Tax and Total Sales Amount

1. Multiply the taxable sales amount by the tax rate.
2. Add the sales tax amount to the taxable sales amount to get the total sales amount.

EXAMPLE A

If taxable merchandise of $60.39 is sold in a state with a 5% sales tax, what are the amount of tax and the total amount to be paid?

Amount of tax: $60.39 × 0.05 = $3.019, which rounds to $3.02
Total amount to be paid: $60.39 + $3.02 = $63.41

Today, total sales and taxes are generally computed automatically and displayed on the receipt, with total sales shown as a subtotal and sales plus tax as the total. Usually, discounts on a sale are subtracted from the sale price before the tax is figured. Shipping and installation labor charges are generally not taxed.

EXAMPLE B

A customer living in a city with a 6% state sales tax and a 1.5% city sales tax purchased a refrigerator regularly priced at $850. He was given a 10% discount. Delivery charges were $45. What were the amount of tax and the total cost to the buyer?

Price after discount: $850 × 0.90 = $765.00 discount price
Sales tax: $765 × (0.06 + 0.015) = $57.38
Cost to buyer: $765 + $57.38 tax + $45 delivery = $867.38

State laws regarding the items subject to sales tax vary. Most states do not tax groceries; however, most do tax meals served in restaurants. Certain nonfood items also sold in grocery stores (such as laundry detergent) are generally taxed. When nontaxable and taxable items are purchased together, the register usually computes the total price of items purchased and automatically adds the correct amount of tax for each taxable item. The taxable items are clearly marked on the register tape along with the total amount of tax charged.

EXAMPLE C

A customer living in a state in which the tax rate is 4% went to a grocery store and purchased a quart of milk at $1.11, a loaf of bread at $1.73, potatoes at $2.25, and two taxable items, laundry detergent at $3.69 and fabric softener at $2.87. What was her total charge at the checkout counter?

Taxable items: $3.69 + $2.87 = $6.56
Tax: $6.56 × 0.04 = $0.26
Total: $1.11 + $1.73 + $2.25 + $6.56 + $0.26 = $11.91

Sales Tax as an Amount per Unit

All of the states and the District of Columbia levy special taxes on gasoline and cigarettes, usually stated in cents per unit (gallon or pack). State taxes on gasoline vary widely, from $0.075 in Georgia to $0.37 in Connecticut; in addition, there is a federal tax that is currently $0.19 per gallon. State taxes on cigarettes currently range from $0.02 to $0.24 per pack; the federal tax is currently $0.16 per pack.

CONCEPT CHECK 11.1

In a state in which the combined state and city sales tax rate is 6%, a customer went to a convenience store and purchased the following items: bread, $1.95; ground meat, $6.79; cheese, $4.79; light bulbs, $4.25; and motor oil, $1.79. Only the last two items are taxable. Rounding the tax to the nearest cent, compute the total cost of all items and tax.

Nontaxable items: $1.95 + $6.79 + $4.79 = $13.53
Taxable items: $4.25 + $1.79 = $6.04
Total tax: $6.04 × 0.06 tax rate = $0.36

$13.53	Nontaxable items
6.04	Taxable items
0.36	Tax
$19.93	Total

Computing Assessed Valuations and Property Taxes

LEARNING OBJECTIVES 2

Compute assessed valuations and property taxes based on assessed valuation.

A *property tax* for a business is a tax on real estate or other property, such as machinery, owned by the business. Businesses usually pay property tax bills semiannually. Taxes are based on a value, known as the *assessed valuation,* determined by a representative of the local or state government.

Assessed valuation ordinarily is based on a current *market value* of the property (what the property could be sold for). While in many states it is fixed by law at 100%, it is a fraction of that value in other states. Thus, a particular community may use 60%

of property values as the basis for tax billing. In most instances, land and buildings are assessed separately.

EXAMPLE D

The Smith family lives in a town in which assessed valuation is 60% of market value. The Bradley family lives in a town in which assessed valuation is 75% of market value. Each home has a market value of $120,000. What is the assessed valuation of each home?

Smith: $120,000 × 0.60 = $72,000
Bradley: $120,000 × 0.75 = $90,000

Assessed valuation often is increased by improvements to the property, such as the addition of an enclosed porch or expensive shrubbery. Ordinary maintenance—new coat of paint, for instance, or repairs to the roof—is not justification for an increased assessment.

EXAMPLE E

The Robertson family and the Atherton family live in a town in which assessed valuation is set by law at 80% of market value. They live in identical houses having a market value of $130,000. The Robertson family added an enclosed deck costing $6,500 and a family room costing $17,000. The Atherton family made extensive repairs and repainted the house a new color at a total cost of $12,000. What was the assessed valuation on each home the following year?

Robertson: $130,000 + $6,500 + $17,000 = $153,500 × 0.8 = $122,800
Atherton: $130,000 × 0.8 = $104,000 (repairs and painting are not considered improvements)

CONCEPT CHECK 11.2

a. The Farrago family owns a home with a market value of $300,000 in a community that assesses property at 100% of market value. The Nikko family owns a home with a market value of $400,000 in a community that assesses property at 60% of market value. What is the difference between the actual assessments of the two homes?

$300,000 × 1 = $300,000
$400,000 × 0.6 = $240,000
Difference = $60,000

b. The Chen family home has a present market value of $200,000 in a community that assesses property at 80% of market value. If they add a family room and an additional bathroom at a cost of $30,000, what will be the new assessed valuation?

Revised market value: $200,000 + $30,000 = $230,000
New assessed value: $230,000 × 0.8 = $184,000

Computing Tax Rates in Percents and Mills

LEARNING OBJECTIVES 3

Compute tax rates in percent and mills.

Percents

For a city, county, or special assessment district, the tax rate is found by dividing the amount of money the governmental unit needs to raise by the total assessed valuation of the particular governmental unit.

EXAMPLE F

The town of Lakeside has a total assessed valuation of \$570,000,000. The amount to be raised by taxation is \$9,975,000. What is the tax rate?

The tax rate is

\$9,975,000 ÷ \$570,000,000 = 0.0175, or 1.75%

This rate is usually written as 1.75% of value, or \$1.75 on each \$100 of value.

EXAMPLE G

If a property in Lakeside is assessed for \$20,000, what is the tax?

The tax can be found by multiplying the amount by the rate:

\$20,000 × 0.0175 = \$350

Mills

To assess property taxes, some government entities still use mills. A *mill* is one tenth of one cent, or \$0.001 (one thousandth of a dollar). To convert mills into cents, divide by 10—for example, 30 mills equals 3¢, or \$0.03. To convert cents into mills, multiply by 10. Thus, a rate of \$0.15, or 15¢, on \$1.00 is 150 mills.

EXAMPLE H

Marshall County assesses property at the rate of 160 mills per \$100 of assessed value. How much tax would be due on property assessed at \$650,000?

\$650,000 ÷ 100 = \$6,500 to assess millage
160 mills = \$0.16
0.16 × \$6,500 = \$1,040 tax

CONCEPT CHECK 11.3

a. A town has a total assessed valuation of \$960,000,000. A total of \$12,000,000 must be raised by taxation for the operating expenses of the town. What will the tax rate be?

\$12,000,000 ÷ \$960,000,000 = 0.0125, or 1.25%
Convert \$0.57 into mills: 57 × 10 = 570

b. If property in a town is assessed at the rate of 140 mills per \$100 of assessed value, how much tax will be due on property assessed at \$475,000?

\$475,000 ÷ 100 = \$4,750 to assess millage
140 mills = \$0.14

Computing Special Assessments, Prorations, and Exemptions

Special assessments can be levied for improvements in a community, such as sewers, roads, or sidewalks. Sometimes the cost is spread over a period of years and added to the annual property tax bill of each property owner.

LEARNING OBJECTIVES 4

Compute tax payments involving special assessments, prorations, and exemptions.

EXAMPLE I

The residents of Porterville voted to widen their roads and add sidewalks, at a cost of $240 per residence, with the cost to be spread over a 12-year period. The Young family had an annual tax bill of $345 before the improvements. If they pay their property taxes semiannually, what will be the amount of their next tax payment?

Annual cost for improvement: $\$240 \div 12 \text{ years} = \$20$
Annual property tax and improvement payment:
$\$345 + \$20 = \$365$
Next semiannual tax payment: $\$365 \div 2 = \$182.50$

Whenever property is sold, it is customary to *prorate,* or distribute, the taxes between seller and buyer as of the date of the settlement.

EXAMPLE J

A home having an annual tax bill of $360 was sold at the end of the seventh month of the taxable year. The seller had already paid the entire tax for the year. How much tax was the seller reimbursed on proration of taxes at the time of the sale?

Months prepaid by seller: $12 - 7 = 5$

Tax reimbursed by buyer: $\$360 \times \frac{5}{12} = \$150$

In almost all states, property used exclusively by nonprofit organizations, such as schools, churches, governments, and charities, is exempt from taxation. Some states also allow partial exemptions for veterans and elderly persons.

EXAMPLE K

The town of Brookside assesses property at 75% of market value. The tax rate is 1.9%. A church has a total market value of $560,000. How much does the church save by being exempt from property taxes?

$\$560{,}000 \times 0.75 = \$420{,}000$ $\quad$ $\$420{,}000 \times 0.019 = \$7{,}980$ saved

EXAMPLE L

A veteran living in Tucson receives a partial exemption of 15% of regular property taxes. The veteran owns property valued at $240,000. If the property is assessed at 75% of value and the current rate is 1.3%, how much tax is due each six months?

Assessed value: $\$240{,}000 \times 0.75 = \$180{,}000$
Regular taxes: $\$180{,}000 \times 0.013 = \$2{,}340$
Taxes due after exemption: $\$2{,}340 \times 0.85 = \$1{,}989$
Taxes due each six months: $\$1{,}989 \div 2 = \$994.50$

CONCEPT CHECK 11.4

a. The city of Marshaltown voted to add decorative street lighting and landscaping to the median strips at a cost of $450 per residence, to be spread over a period of 15 years. If the Evarts family presently has a yearly tax bill of $730, paid semiannually, what will be the amount of their next tax payment?

$450 per residence $\div$ 15 years = $30 per year
$730 present yearly tax amount + $30 = $760 new yearly tax amount
$760 $\div$ 2 = $380 new semiannual tax amount

b. If a home with an annual tax bill of $480 is sold at the end of the second month of the tax year, after taxes have already been paid, how much will the buyer reimburse the seller when taxes are prorated?

$12 - 2 = 10$ months prepaid by seller

$\$480 \times \frac{10}{12} = \$400$ reimbursed by buyer

c. A 70-year-old man lives in a state that grants senior citizens a 10% exemption from property taxes. If his home has a market value of $150,000 and the tax rate is 1.5%, how much will his yearly taxes be? The county in which he resides assesses property at 80% of market value.

$150,000 market value × 0.8 = $120,000 assessed valuation
$120,000 assessed valuation × 0.015 = $1,800 regular taxes
$1,800 regular taxes × 0.10 = $180 reduction
$1,800 regular taxes − $180 reduction = $1,620 revised taxes

COMPLETE ASSIGNMENTS 11.1 AND 11.2.

Chapter Terms for Review

assessed valuation
levy
market value
mill
property tax
prorate
sales tax
tax rate

The Bottom Line

Summary of chapter learning objectives:

Learning Objective	Summary	Example
11.1	Computing sales taxes using rate tables and percents	1. The Farley family lives in a state in which the sales tax rate is 8%. When they purchased a dining room table and chairs regularly priced at $1,400, they were given a discount of 15%. Shipping charges were $50. What was the total cost to the Farleys? 2. Ms. Carrow lives in a state in which the state tax on gasoline is $0.18 a gallon. Federal tax is $0.19 a gallon. If she purchased an average of 8 gallons a week during the 52-week year, how much did she pay in state and federal taxes combined? Standard Five and Dime Store is in a state with a tax rate of 4%. Using Figure 11-1, on page 176, compute the amount of tax, total sale, and change given for each transaction listed below.

	Amount of Sale	Sales Tax	Total	Cash Paid	Amount of Change
3.	$ 8.90	______	______	$ 10.00	______
4.	4.62	______	______	5.00	______
5.	13.08	______	______	15.00	______
6.	26.41	______	______	30.00	______
7.	47.05	______	______	50.00	______
8.	64.70	______	______	100.00	______
9.	3.05	______	______	5.00	______
10.	1.37	______	______	2.00	______
11.	4.10	______	______	5.26	______
12.	0.55	______	______	5.00	______

The Bottom Line *Continued*

Summary of chapter learning objectives:

Learning Objective	Summary	Example
11.2	Computing assessed valuations and property taxes based on assessed valuation	13. The Mercer family lives in a town in which the assessed valuation on property is 65% of market value. The Parker family lives in a town in which the assessed valuation on property is 80% of market value. Each home has a market value of $162,000. How much is the assessed valuation of each home?
11.3	Computing tax rates in percents and mills	14. The town of Bayview has a total assessed valuation of $880,000,000. For the coming year the city must raise $14,520,000 for operating expenses. a. What will the tax rate be? b. What will the semiannual taxes be on a home with an assessed valuation of $180,000? 15. a. Convert 400 mills into its equivalent in dollars. b. Convert $0.90 into mills.
11.4	Computing tax payments involving special assessments, prorations, and exemptions.	16. The town of Bayview decides to develop a series of neighborhood playgrounds funded by a special assessment of $480 on each piece of property, spread over a 10-year period. Using the tax rate figure for Bayview from question 14 above, determine the semiannual taxes on the home assessed at $180,000, including the special assessment. 17. A home with annual tax payments of $420 was sold at the end of the third month of the taxable year. What was the amount of tax prorated to the buyer? 18. A veteran living in Newtown receives a partial exemption of 10% of regular property taxes. The veteran owns property valued at $190,000. If the property is assessed at 80% of value and the current rate is 1.5%, how much tax is due each six months?

Answers: 1. $1,335.20 **2.** $153.92 **3.** $0.36, $9.26, $0.74 **4.** $0.18, $4.80, $0.20 **5.** $0.52, $13.60, $1.40 **6.** $1.06, $27.47, $2.53 **7.** $1.88, $48.93, $1.07 **8.** $2.59, $67.29, $32.71 **9.** $0.12, $3.17, $1.83 **10.** $0.05, $1.42, $0.58 **11.** $0.16, $4.26, $1.00 **12.** $0.02, $0.57, $4.43 **13.** $105,300 (Mercer), $129,600 (Parker) **14.** a. 1.65% b. $1,485 **15.** a. $0.40 b. 900 mills **16.** $1,509 **17.** $315 **18.** $1,026

Assignment 11.1: Sales Tax

LEARNING OBJECTIVES 1

Name

Date Score

A (50 points) Solve the following problems. (1 point for each correct answer)

1. Paiolies fast-food restaurant is in a state with a tax rate of 5%. Compute the sales tax, the total sale, and the change given for each transaction below.

Amount of Sale	Sales Tax	Total Sale	Cash Paid	Amount of Change
$ 5.89			$10.00	
3.07			4.00	
14.12			20.00	
7.97			10.37	
0.85			1.00	
23.15			30.00	
9.60			20.08	
28.35			50.00	
13.21			15.00	
17.49			19.00	

2. Giramonte's clothing store is in a city where the state tax is 3% and the city tax is 1%. Determine the sales tax, the total sale, and the change given for each transaction below. Then compute the total sales taxes and total sales.

Amount of Sale	Sales Tax	Total Sale	Cash Paid	Amount of Change
$317.20			$350.00	
29.30			31.00	
72.85			80.00	
9.95			20.35	
109.40			120.00	
299.95			500.00	
Total				

Score for A (50)

B (30 points) Solve the following problems. Use Figure 11-1 for problems 3 and 4. (points for correct answers as marked)

3. A candy store, operating in a state with a sales tax of 4%, made 868 sales at 10¢; 946 sales at 45¢; 457 sales at 50¢; 921 sales at 75¢; and 815 sales at 90¢. How much did the store receive in taxes? (8 points) ________

4. If the candy store in problem 3 computed the amount of state sales tax submitted to the state based on 4% of gross sales, what would be the difference between the amount of tax the store collected and the amount it submitted to the state? (8 points) ________

5. Gems, Inc., and the Jewelry Co. each bought a new car. Gems is located in a state that has a 4% sales tax and paid the regular price of $12,487 plus tax. Jewelry is located in a state that has a 5% sales tax and got a special discount of $150 off the regular $12,487 price.

a. Including sales tax, which company paid more for its car? (8 points) ____________

b. How much more? (6 points) ________

____
Score for B (30)

C (20 points) Solve the following problems. (points for correct answers as marked)

6. Pianos Plus has stores in four states. Sales tax rates for the four states are as follows: state A, 8%; state B, $6\frac{1}{2}$%; state C, $5\frac{1}{2}$%; and state D, 3%. Annual sales for the four states last year were as follows: state A, $742,000; state B, $837,000; state C, $491,000; and state D, $987,000.

a. How much did Pianos Plus collect in sales taxes during the year? (10 points) ________

b. If all four states had the same lower sales tax rate of 3%, how much would Pianos Plus have collected in sales taxes during the year? (5 points) ________

c. If all four states had the same higher tax rate of 8%, how much would Pianos Plus have collected in sales taxes during the year? (5 points) ________

____
Score for C (20)

Assignment 11.2: Property Taxes

Name ______________________________

Date ______________ Score ______________

A (40 points) Solve the following problems. (4 points for each correct answer)

1. Find the assessed valuation for each of the following towns.

Town	Property Value	Basis for Tax Billing	Assessed Valuation
A	$940,000,000	100%	________
B	515,625,000	80%	________
C	424,000,000	75%	________

2. Find the tax rate for each of the following towns. Show your answer as a percent.

Town	Assessed Valuation	Amount to Be Raised	Tax Rate
F	$940,000,000	$16,920,000	________
G	412,500,000	7,095,000	________
H	876,000,000	11,826,000	________

3. Convert the following percentage tax rates into dollars and cents per $100 of assessed valuation.

Tax Rate	Dollars and cents
1.8%	________
1.75%	________

4. Convert the following percent tax rates into mills per $1 of assessed valuation.

Tax Rate	Mills
1.8%	________
1.75%	________

________ Score for A (40)

B (24 points) Solve the following problems. (6 points for each correct answer)

5. The Parson Company is located in a state in which assessed valuation is 100% of market value. The tax rate this year is $1.35 on each $100 of market value. The market value of the company building is $190,000. How much property tax will Parson pay this year? ________

6. The Raulston Corporation is located in an area in which assessed valuation is 70% of market value. The tax rate this year is 1.6%. The market value of Raulston's property is $310,000. How much property tax will Raulston pay this year? ________

7. Next year, the assessed valuation in Raulston's area (problem 6) will decrease to 65% of market value and the tax rate will remain the same as this year. How much less tax will Raulston pay next year than it paid this year? ____________

8. Perez Inc. is headquartered in an area in which assessed valuation is 80% of market value. The tax rate this year is \$1.40 on each \$100 of assessed valuation. Its property has a market value of \$320,000. How much property tax will Perez pay this year? ____________

____
Score for B (24)

C (24 points) Solve the following problems. Round to the nearest dollar. (3 points for each correct answer)

9. a. There are four towns in Foothill county: Gateway, Hilltop, Skyview, and Bellevue. Using the total assessed valuations given and the amount of money the town must raise for operating expenses, compute the necessary tax rate for each town.

Town	Total Assessed Valuation	Money That Must Be Raised	Tax Rate as a Percent
Gateway	\$200,000,000	\$3,200,000	____________
Hilltop	\$340,000,000	\$5,780,000	____________
Skyview	\$280,000,000	\$3,920,000	____________
Bellevue	\$450,000,000	\$6,750,000	____________

b. Convert each of the above percentage rates to mills.

Gateway ____________ mills
Hilltop ____________ mills
Skyview ____________ mills
Bellevue ____________ mills

____
Score for C (24)

D (12 points) Solve the following problems. Round to the nearest dollar. (6 points for each correct answer)

10. A home with annual tax payments of \$780 was sold at the end of the ninth month of the taxable year. The seller had already paid the entire tax for the year. How much tax was the seller reimbursed on proration of taxes at the time of the sale? ____________

11. A senior citizen lives in a state that grants a 20% partial exemption on property taxes. Her property is valued at \$180,000 and is assessed at 75% of value. The current tax rate is 1.8%. How much tax is due each six months?

____

____
Score for D (12)

Notes

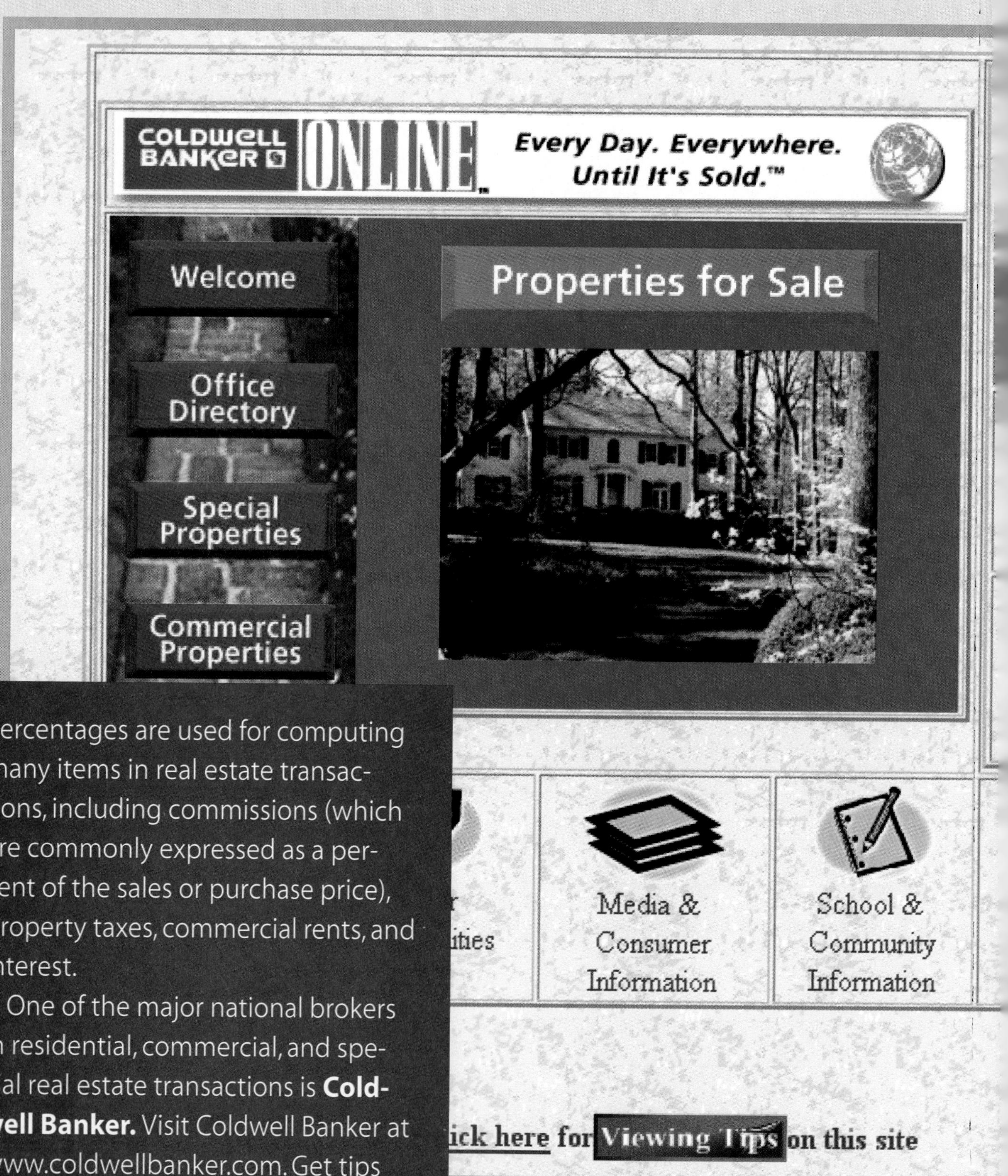

Percentages are used for computing many items in real estate transactions, including commissions (which are commonly expressed as a percent of the sales or purchase price), property taxes, commercial rents, and interest.

One of the major national brokers in residential, commercial, and special real estate transactions is **Coldwell Banker.** Visit Coldwell Banker at www.coldwellbanker.com. Get tips on buying or selling a home or on financing a real estate purchase. Learn about the past, present, and future of the Coldwell Banker company, as well as career opportunities offered by a major player in real estate brokerage.

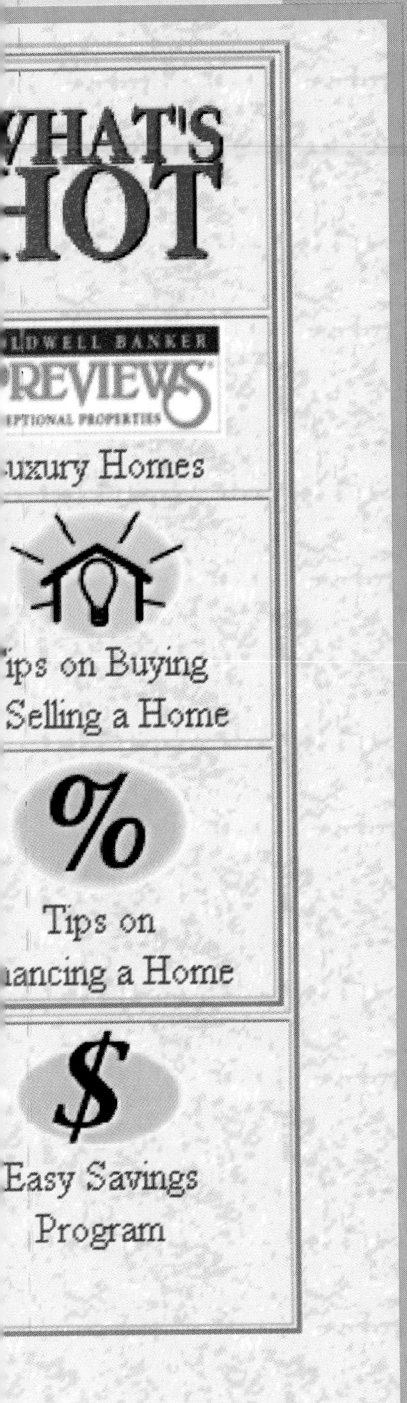

12 Percents in Business

Learning Objectives

By studying this chapter and completing all the assignments, you will learn to:

1. Change fractions and decimals to percents.
2. Change percents to decimals.
3. Find base, rate, and percentage.
4. Use percents to measure increase and decrease.
5. Use percents to allocate overhead expenses.

Do you know what profession has one of the lowest percentages of success in the nation? Show business! In the best of times, 93 percent of union actors are out of work. For writers, unemployment hovers at 80 percent year-round.

Percents and percentages are used extensively in a wide variety of applications. The National Football League (NFL) computes the completion percentage for each quarterback. The National Basketball Association (NBA) calculates field goal percentages for all of the players. When the Bank of America loans money, the interest is quoted as a percentage rate. Almost every container of food has a label with nutritional information printed on it, and much of the information is written in percents.

Changing Fractions and Decimals to Percents

LEARNING OBJECTIVES 1

Change fractions and decimals to percents.

A *percent* is a number equal to a fraction whose denominator is 100. Since every fraction can be written as a decimal, every percent can be written three ways: (1) as a percent, with the % symbol following the number, (2) as a fraction, and (3) as a decimal. For example, 15 percent = $15\% = \frac{15}{100} = 0.15$.

A percent, such as 15%, that is smaller than 100% is equal to a fraction smaller than 1. Because $100\% = \frac{100}{100}$, 100% is equal to 1. A percent, such as 150%, that is larger than 100% is larger than 1: $150\% = \frac{150}{100} = 1.50$. People use percents in their speech and writing instead of fractions. A state sales tax rate of 5% would probably never be quoted as "five one hundredths" or as "one twentieth." Calculations with percents are often done in decimals or on a calculator using a percent key. To work with percents, you need to be able to change among fractions, decimals, and percents.

STEPS to Change a Fraction or a Decimal to a Percent

1. If the number is a fraction, change it to a decimal (round to four places if it does not terminate).
2. In the decimal, move the decimal point two places to the *right* (add zeros if necessary).
3. Write a percent sign at the *right* end of the new number.

EXAMPLE A

	STEP 2	STEP 3
0.75 →	0.75. →	75%

EXAMPLE B

	STEP 2	STEP 3
0.005 →	0.00.5 →	0.5%

EXAMPLE C

	STEP 2	STEP 3
0.3 →	0.30. →	30%

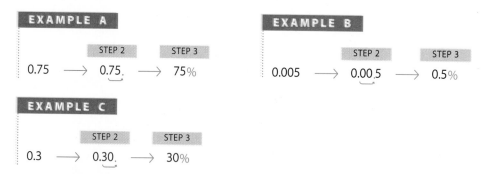

Use the same rule if the number is a mixed decimal or a whole number.

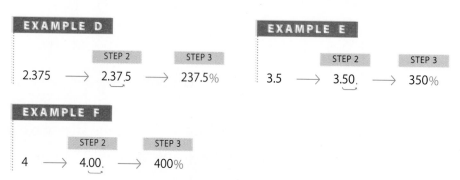

EXAMPLE D

	STEP 2	STEP 3
2.375 →	2.37.5 →	237.5%

EXAMPLE E

	STEP 2	STEP 3
3.5 →	3.50. →	350%

EXAMPLE F

	STEP 2	STEP 3
4 →	4.00. →	400%

EXAMPLE G

STEP 1	STEP 2	STEP 3
$\frac{4}{5} = 0.8$ ⟶	0.80. ⟶	80%

EXAMPLE H

STEP 1	STEP 2	STEP 3
$2\frac{5}{8} = 2.625$ ⟶	2.62.5 ⟶	262.5%

CONCEPT CHECK 12.1

a. Change $2\frac{3}{5}$ to a percent.

$2\frac{3}{5} = 2.6$ ⟶ 2.60. ⟶ 260%

b. Change 0.025 to a percent.

0.025 ⟶ 0.02.5 ⟶ 002.5 = 2.5%

Changing Percents to Decimals

STEPS to Change a Percent to a Decimal

1. Remove the percent sign.
2. Move the decimal point two places to the *left* (insert zeros if needed).

LEARNING OBJECTIVES 2

Change percents to decimals.

EXAMPLE I

	STEP 1	STEP 2
35% ⟶	35 ⟶	.35. = 0.35

EXAMPLE J

	STEP 1	STEP 2
1.5% ⟶	1.5 ⟶	.01.5 = 0.015

EXAMPLE K

	STEP 1	STEP 2
200% ⟶	200 ⟶	2.00. = 2

STEPS to Change a Percent Containing a Fraction to a Decimal

1. Convert the fraction in the percent to its decimal equivalent.
2. Drop the percent sign.
3. Move the decimal point two places to the *left* (insert zeros if needed).

EXAMPLE L

STEP 1	STEP 2	STEP 3
$\frac{1}{2}\% = 0.5\%$ ⟶	0.5 ⟶	.00.5 = 0.005

EXAMPLE M

STEP 1	STEP 2	STEP 3
$2\frac{3}{4}\% = 2.75\%$ ⟶	2.75 ⟶	.02.75 = 0.0275

CONCEPT CHECK 12.2

a. Change 126% to a decimal.

126% ⟶ 126 ⟶ 1.26. = 1.26

b. Change $\frac{1}{4}$% to a decimal.

$\frac{1}{4}$% = 0.25% ⟶ 0.25 ⟶ .00.25 = 0.0025

Finding Base, Rate, and Percentage

LEARNING OBJECTIVES 3

Find base, rate, and percentage.

Suppose you have \$5 and you spend \$4 for lunch. Example G shows that the fraction $\frac{4}{5}$ equals 80%. We can say that you spent 80% of your money for lunch. Every percentage problem will always have three numbers similar to these. In this book we will call 80% the *Rate (R),* \$5 the *Base* amount *(B),* and \$4 the *Percentage* amount *(P).* The Base and the Percentage amount will always have the same units, like dollars, feet, or pounds. The Rate will be the percent. (The word *rate* comes from the word *ratio*—in this case, $\frac{4}{5}$.)

Note: In practice, the terms percent and percentage are used interchangeably. Sometimes you will see the word *percentage* used to mean a rate and the word *percent* used to mean an amount. You will even see the two words *percentage rate* to mean the rate. In this book, however, we will use only one meaning for each word.

EXAMPLE N

80% of \$5 = \$4
80% is the Rate
\$5 is the Base
\$4 is the Percentage

EXAMPLE O

25% of 12 ft = 3 ft
25% is the Rate
12 ft is the Base
3 ft is the Percentage

EXAMPLE P

50% of 40 lb = 20 lb
50% is the Rate
40 lb is the Base
20 lb is the Percentage

Figure 12-1

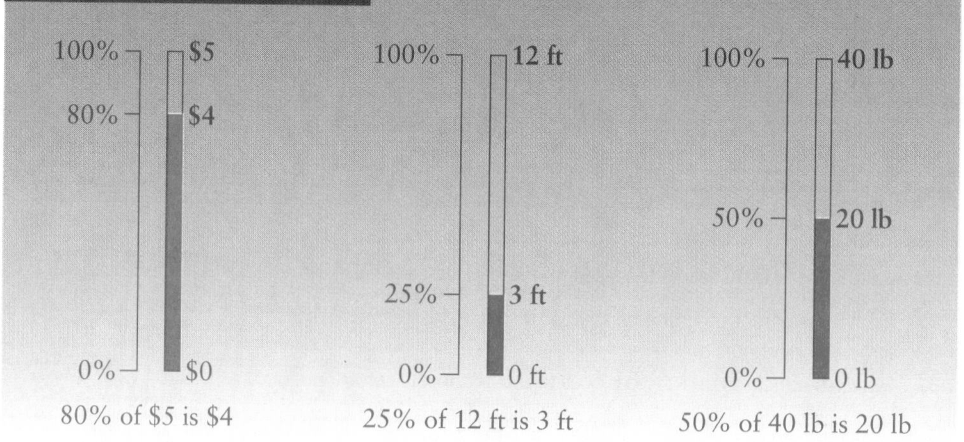

In the diagrams above, the Rate (or percent) is shown in the left-hand column; the Percentage is represented by the shaded portion of the right-hand column. The Base is represented by the entire right-hand column.

The word *of* appears in most situations in which percents are used. (Look back at the previous examples.) In fractions, the word *of* often means "multiply," as in $\frac{1}{2}$ of 40 lb =

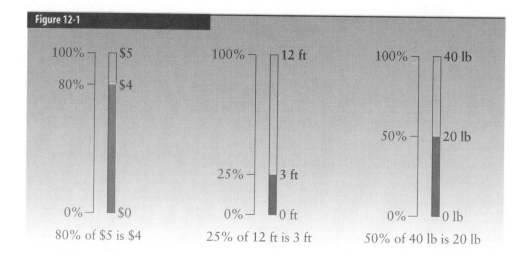

$\frac{1}{2} \times 40$ lb = 20 lb. The same is true with percents—for example, 50% of 40 lb = 0.5×40 lb = 20 lb, and 80% of \$5 = $0.8 \times \$5$ = \$4.

The previous two examples illustrate the basic relationship among the Rate, Base, and Percentage: Rate × Base = Percentage. As a formula, it is written as $R \times B = P$ or as $P = R \times B$.

When you know any two of these three numbers, you can calculate the third by changing the formula:

If you want to find B, the formula becomes $B = P \div R$ or $P \div R = B$.
If you want to find R, the formula becomes $R = P \div B$ or $P \div B = R$.

EXAMPLE Q

Find P when $R = 50\%$ and $B = 200$ qt

EXAMPLE R

Find R when $B = \$50$ and $P = \$10$

EXAMPLE S

Find B when $P = 60$ yd and $R = 75\%$

Figure 12-2

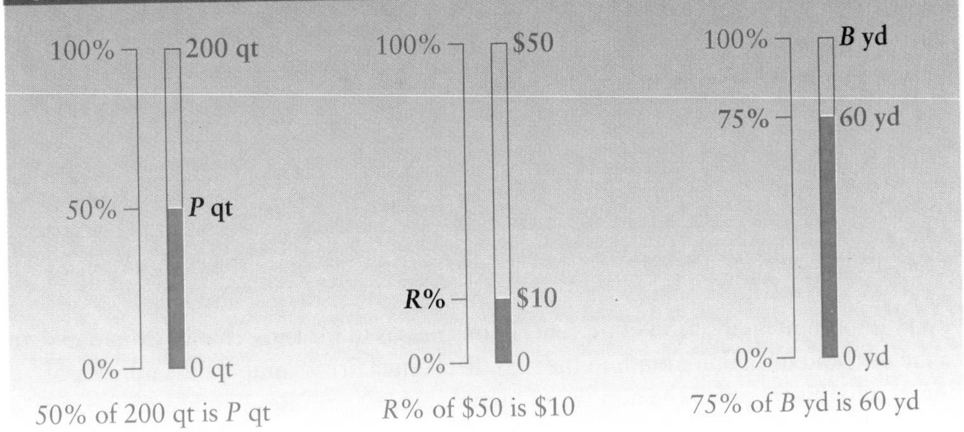

$P = R \times B$
$P = 50\% \times 200$ qt
$P = 0.50 \times 200$ qt
$P = 100$ qt

$R = P \div B$
$R = \$10 \div \$50$
$R = 0.20$
$R = 20\%$

$B = P \div R$
$B = 60$ yd $\div 75\%$
$B = 60$ yd $\div 0.75$
$B = 80$ yd

CONCEPT CHECK 12.3

a. Find the Base when the Rate is 15% and the Percentage amount is \$60.
$B = P \div R = \$60 \div 15\% = \$60 \div 0.15 = \$400$

b. Find the Rate when the Base is 96 feet and the Percentage amount 72 feet.
$R = P \div B = 72 \text{ ft} \div 96 \text{ ft} = 0.75 = 75\%$

COMPLETE ASSIGNMENT 12.1.

Using Percents in Business

Percent problems occur frequently in business. Examples T and U are typical fundamental applications, in which we solve for the Base amount (B) and the Rate (R), respectively.

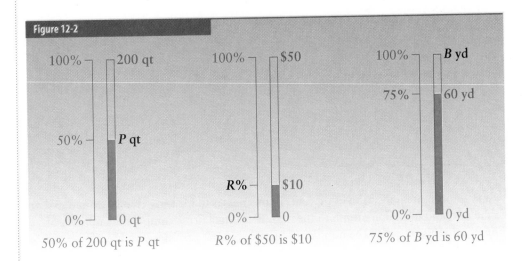

EXAMPLE T

Judith Cruz is a computer programmer. In December, she received a $900 bonus, which equaled 20% of her monthly salary. What was her monthly salary?

P = amount of bonus = \$900
R = rate of bonus = 20%
B = monthly salary = ?
Since $P \div R = B$,
$P \div R = \$900 \div 20\% = \$900 \div 0.20 = \$4{,}500$ monthly salary

EXAMPLE U

Last year Coastal Coffee Stop had total expenses of $250,000. Of that total, $150,000 was the expense for employee salaries. At Coastal, employee salary expense is what percent of total expenses?

P = employee salaries = \$150,000
R = ?
B = total expenses = \$250,000
Since $P \div B = R$,
$P \div B = \$150{,}000 \div \$250{,}000 = 0.60 = 60\%$

Using Percents to Measure Increase and Decrease

Use percents to measure increase and decrease.

A very important application of percents in business is to measure change from one year to the next and from one month to the next. Real estate firms compare the number of homes sold this year with the number of homes sold last year. Read and carefully compare the following four statements about home sales last year and this year:

Lipski Realty sold 50% more homes this year than it did last year, when it sold 36 homes.

Kilby & Cohn Real Estate sold 30 more homes this year than last year. This represents 25% more homes this year than last year.

Real estate agent Jane Wu sold 3 fewer homes this year than she did last year, when she sold 12 homes.

Devon Shively, a real estate broker, sold 20 homes last year; this year he sold 26 homes.

The number of homes sold last year is the Base amount (B) (last year is called the *base year*). The change in homes can be reported as a number, which would be the Percentage amount (P), or as a percent, which would be the Rate (R). If any two of the three values are given, the third can be determined using one of the three formulas in this chapter. The following examples are based on the statements above.

EXAMPLE V

Find the number of additional homes (P) that Lipski Realty sold this year.

$B = 36$ and $R = 50\%$. Since $P = R \times B$,
$P = 50\% \times 36 = 0.50 \times 36 = 18$ more homes this year

EXAMPLE W

Find the number of homes that Kilby & Cohn Real Estate sold last year (B).

$P = 30$ and $R = 25\%$. Since $B = P \div R$,
$B = 30 \div 25\% = 30 \div 0.25 = 120$ homes sold last year

EXAMPLE X

Find Jane Wu's Rate of decrease (R) from last year's sales.

$P = 3$ and $B = 12$. Since $R = P \div B$,
$R = 3 \div 12 = 0.25 = 25\%$ decrease

To find the percent change when the only numbers reported are the amounts for last year (B) and this year, the first step is to find the amount (P), of *increase* or *decrease.* P is the difference between the two years. Then, use $R = P \div B$ to find the *rate of increase* or *decrease.*

EXAMPLE Y

Find Devon Shively's Rate of change (R).

Shively sold 20 homes last year (B) and 26 this year. The amount of his change is

$P = 26 - 20 = 6$ more homes this year.

The Rate of change is

$R = P \div B = 6 \div 20 = 0.30 = 30\%$ increase

CONCEPT CHECK 12.4

A company had sales of \$144,000 this year and \$120,000 last year (B). Find both the amount of increase (P) and the rate of increase (R).

The Amount of increase is
$P = \$144,000 - \$120,000 = \$24,000$
The Rate of increase is
$R = P \div B = \$24,000 \div \$120,000 = 0.20 = 20\%$

COMPLETE ASSIGNMENTS 12.2 AND 12.3.

Using Percents to Allocate Overhead Expenses

LEARNING OBJECTIVES 5

Use percents to allocate overhead expenses.

Many businesses are organized into divisions or departments. Suppose JUMP! Inc., a retailer of sportswear, has three departments: women's clothes, men's clothes, and children's clothes. It is helpful to the management and owners of JUMP! to measure the profitability of each department. JUMP! also knows the amounts that it paid for the merchandise sold and the salaries of employees in each department. JUMP! can subtract these departmental costs from the departmental revenues.

But what about rent and other general costs such as electricity? These costs that are not directly related to the types of merchandise sold are called *overhead costs.* For example, JUMP!'s monthly rental expense might be \$12,000 for the entire building. How should that single amount be divided among the three departments? Should each department be assigned $\frac{1}{3}$, or \$4,000, of the total rent?

Most businesses *allocate,* or distribute, the rent based on a measurement that is related to the total cost. Rent is a cost of using the building; it could be allocated on the basis of floor space, since each department occupies some of that space.

STEPS to Allocate an Overhead Cost Based on Total Floor Space (or Some Other Measurement)

1. Find the total square feet of floor space.
2. Divide the floor space of each department by the total floor space and change to percents.
3. Multiply each percent (in fractional or decimal form) times the total rent (or other overhead value).

EXAMPLE Z

Determine the amount of rent to allocate to the respective departments of Jump! Inc.

	STEP 1	STEP 2	STEP 3
Department	**Floor Space**	**Percent of Total**	**Distribution of Rent**
Children's	25 ft × 20 ft = 500 sq ft	500 ÷ 2,500 = 20%	\$12,000 × 0.20 = \$ 2,400
Women's	25 ft × 50 ft = 1,250 sq ft	1,250 ÷ 2,500 = 50%	\$12,000 × 0.50 = \$ 6,000
Men's	25 ft × 30 ft = 750 sq ft	750 ÷ 2,500 = 30%	\$12,000 × 0.30 = \$ 3,600
Total	2,500 sq ft	100%	\$12,000

This same method is used for many other business expenses, such as utilities, fire insurance, and salaries of office personnel. Examples of other bases that might be used for allocation are number of employees, hours worked, and units produced.

CONCEPT CHECK 12.5

A building maintenance company has two different divisions: commercial and residential. Employees spend 980 hours working in commercial buildings and 420 hours working in residences. The company has an office expense of \$10,000 that it wants to allocate between the two divisions, based on the percent of employee hours used by each division.

Total hours worked: 980 + 420 = 1,400

Commercial: 980 ÷ 1,400 = 0.70, or 70% of employee hours
70% of \$10,000 = 0.70 × \$10,000 = \$7,000 of office expense

Residential: 420 ÷ 1,400 = 0.30, or 30% of employee hours
30% of \$10,000 = 0.30 × \$10,000 = \$3,000 of office expense

COMPLETE ASSIGNMENT 12.4.

Chapter Terms for Review

allocate
amount of decrease
amount of increase
Base (B)
"of"
overhead costs
percent
Percentage (P)
Rate (R)
rate of decrease
rate of increase

The Bottom Line

Summary of chapter learning objectives:

Learning Objective	Summary	Example
12.1	Changing fractions and decimals to percents	1. Change 0.35 to a percent. 2. Change $\frac{5}{8}$ to a percent.
12.2	Changing percents to decimals	3. Change 3.75% to a decimal.
12.3	Finding base, rate, and percentage	4. Find the percentage: 15% of 36 = P 5. Find the rate: R% of 140 = 28 6. Find the base: 75% of B = 150
12.4	Using percents to measure increase and decrease	7. Increase a $3,000 salary by 30%. 8. From 300 to 240 is a decrease of what percent?
12.5	Using percents to allocate overhead expenses	9. A company has three stores, A, B and C, with 4, 6, and 10 employees, respectively. Based on the number of employees, allocate a $3,000 expense among the stores.

Answers: 1. 35% **2.** 62.5% **3.** 0.0375 **4.** 5.4 **5.** 20% **6.** 200 **7.** $3,900 **8.** 20% **9.** Store A: $600, Store B: $900, Store C: $1,500

Notes

Assignment 12.1: Base, Rate, and Percentage

LEARNING OBJECTIVES 1 2 3

Name ______________________

Date ______________ Score ______________

A (20 points) Change the percents to decimals. Change the nonpercents to percents. (1 point for each correct answer)

1. 21% = ________ **2.** 100% = ________ **3.** $3\frac{2}{3}$% = ________

4. 0.375 = ________ **5.** 4 = ________ **6.** $33\frac{1}{3}$% = ________

7. 0.12 = ________ **8.** 0.3 = ________ **9.** $1\frac{1}{4}$ = ________

10. 3.2% = ________ **11.** 324.5% = ________ **12.** 0.0004% = ________

13. 0.52 = ________ **14.** 250% = ________ **15.** $0.08\frac{1}{3}$ = ________

16. $\frac{1}{2}$ = ________ **17.** 5.0 = ________ **18.** 0.000075 = ________

19. 0.1% = ________ **20.** 1,000% = ________

____
Score for A (20)

B (30 points) Solve each of the following problems for the Percentage. (2 points for each correct answer)

21. 0.375% of 64 = ________ **22.** 0.25% of 1,200 = ________ **23.** 100% of 13.19 = ________

24. 62.5% of 16 = ________ **25.** 40% of 0.96 = ________ **26.** 250% of $24 = ________

27. 25% of $1.12 = ________ **28.** 120% of $42 = ________ **29.** 2.5% of $200 = ________

30. 50% of $284 = ________ **31.** 8% of 20 = ________ **32.** 15% of 0.06 = ________

33. 187.5% of 32 = ________ **34.** 1.5% of $96 = ________ **35.** 0.2% of 560 = ________

____
Score for B (30)

C (50 points) Solve each of the following for the Percentage, the Rate, or the Base. Write rates as percents. Round dollars to the nearest cent. (2 points for each correct answer)

36. $33\frac{1}{3}$% of ________ = $15

37. ________ of $24 = $6

38. ________ of 0.12 = 0.36

39. ________ of 26.9 = 26.9

40. ________ of 500 = 12.5

41. 80% of .60 = $0.48

42. 1.25% of 144 = 1.8

43. 225% of 60 = 135

44. ________ of 0.048 = 0.012

45. 150% of $44.00 = $66

46. 2.5% of $2,460 = 61.50

47. 0.75% of 4,000 = $30

48. 250% of 5.76 = 14.4

49. 37.5% of 88 = 33

50. 0.025% of $12,800 = $3.20

51. 120% of 400 = 480

52. 120% of ________ = $39

53. ________ of 5.4 = 2.16

54. ________ of $2,340 = $46,800

55. 15% of $140 = $933.33

56. 120% of $91 = $75.83

57. 1.4 of 75 = 105

58. 175% of 320 = $560

59. 12% of 25 = 3

60. 0.16 of 2.1 = 0.336

____

Score for C (50)

Assignment 12.2: Rate of Increase and Rate of Decrease

LEARNING 4 OBJECTIVES

Name ____________________

Date ____________________ Score ____________________

A (40 points) Calculate the missing values. ($2\frac{1}{2}$ points for each correct answer)

1. Increasing the base value of 240 by 25% gives the new value ________.

2. Decreasing the base value of 140 by 60% gives the new value ________.

3. Start with 65; increase it by 60%; end up with ________.

4. Start with 90; decrease it by 12%; end up with ________.

5. Sales were $8,000 last month. There was a 3% decrease this month. Sales were ________ this month.

6. Profits were $4,400 last month. There was a 4% increase this month. Profits were ________ this month.

7. Base value = 271; increase = 100%; new (final) value = ________

8. Base value = 350; decrease = 100%; new (final) value = ________

9. A $12 decrease is 20% of the base value of ________.

10. An increase of 40 units is 8% of the base value of ________ units.

11. The price increased from $150 to $165; the percent increase was ________.

12. Production decreased from 5,000 units to 4,000 units; the percent decrease was ________.

13. $300 is what percent less than $400? ________

14. 320 is what percent greater than 160? ________

15. Sales were $500,000 in June but only $400,000 in July. The rate of decrease was ________.

16. Profits were $11,000 last month and $10,000 the previous month. The rate of increase was ________.

Score for A (40) ________

B (30 points) The table below shows the volumes of various items sold by Auto Parts Emporium during the past two years. Compute the amount of change and the rate of change between this year and last year. Compute the rates to the nearest tenth of a percent. If the amount and rate are increases, write a + in front of them; if they are decreases, enclose them in parentheses ( ). (1 point for each correct amount; 2 points for each correct rate)

Auto Parts Emporium
Volume Sold (number of units)

Description of Item	This Year	Last Year	Amount of Change	Rate of Change
17. Batteries	513	439	______	______
18. Brake fluid (pints)	1,784	1,942	______	______
19. Coolant (gallons)	2,045	1,815	______	______
20. Headlight lamps	4,907	4,084	______	______
21. Oil (quarts)	12,458	10,743	______	______
22. Mufflers	439	525	______	______
23. Shock absorbers	895	1,084	______	______
24. Tires, Auto	6,742	5,866	______	______
25. Tires, Truck	2,195	2,803	______	______
26. Wiper blades	1,920	1,842	______	______

______ Score for B (30)

C (30 points) During May and June, Stewart's Paint Store had sales in the amounts shown in the table below. Compute the amount of change and the rate of change between May and June. Compute the rates of change to the nearest tenth of a percent. If the amount and rate are increases, write a + in front of them; if they are decreases, then enclose them in parentheses ( ). (1 point for each correct amount; 2 points for each correct rate)

Stewart's Paint Store
Volume Sold (in dollars)

Description of Item	June	May	Amount of Change	Rate of Change
27. Brush, 2" wide	$711.14	$594.67	______	______
28. Brush, 3" wide	564.20	512.51	______	______
29. Brush, 4" wide	229.87	244.27	______	______
30. Drop cloth, 9 × 12	143.50	175.66	______	______
31. Drop cloth, 12 × 15	174.29	151.55	______	______
32. Paint, latex (gal)	35,506.24	37,382.19	______	______
33. Paint, latex (qt)	4,072.35	4,878.96	______	______
34. Paint, oil (gal)	8,308.44	7,864.41	______	______
35. Paint, oil (qt)	3,358.35	4,074.96	______	______
36. Paint scraper	274.10	238.82	______	______

______ Score for C (30)

Assignment 12.3: Business Applications

LEARNING OBJECTIVES 3

Name ____________

Date ____________ Score ____________

A (50 points) Solve the following problems. Round dollar amounts to the nearest cent. Round other amounts to the nearest tenth. Write rates as percents to the nearest tenth of a percent. (5 points for each correct answer)

1. Midwestern Electric shipped 4,500 capacitors in April. Clients eventually returned 6% of the capacitors. How many of the April capacitors were eventually returned? ____________

2. The chief executive officer (CEO) at Midwestern Electric wants the company to reduce the percent of capacitors that customers return. In May, the company shipped 4,000 capacitors, and 200 were eventually returned. What percent of the May shipment was eventually returned? ____________

3. By June of the following year, Midwestern Electric had reduced the percent of capacitors returned to 4% of the number shipped. If there were 220 capacitors returned from that month's shipment, how many had been shipped? ____________

4. A food importer called Tastes of Europe imports 60% of its vinegars from France, 30% from Italy, and 10% from Spain. The total value of all the vinegars that it imports is $72,000. What is the value of the vinegars that are *not* imported from France? ____________

5. Next year, Tastes of Europe is planning to import $44,000 worth of vinegars from France, $20,000 worth of vinegars from Italy, and $16,000 worth of vinegars from Spain. If next year's imports occur as currently being planned, what percent of the total imports will be from France? ____________

6. Parker Parka Products, Inc. manufactures only parkas for adults and children. Last year, Parker manufactured all its children's parkas in Asia. Those children's parkas represented 38% of all the Parker production. If the company made a total of 235,000 parkas, how many children's parkas did it produce? ____________

7. This year, Parker again plans to manufacture all its children's parkas in Asia, and Parker will expand the children's product line to 40% of the total number of parkas produced. If Parker plans to produce 96,000 children's parkas, how many parkas does the company plan to produce in total? ____________

8. Next year, Parker plans to keep the percent of children's parkas at 40% but increase the number of children's parkas produced to 100,000. How many parkas does the company plan to produce for adults? (Hint: First you need to calculate the total number of all parkas to be produced next year.) ____________

9. Toby Hudson is a single father. He tries to save 15% of his monthly salary for his son's education. In August, Toby's salary was $2,800. How much should Toby save to meet his objective? ____________

10. In September, Toby Hudson got a promotion and a raise. Because his monthly expenses did not increase very much, Toby was able to save more dollars. Toby saved $800, which was 25% of his new salary. How much was Toby's new salary? ____________

____
Score for A (50)

B (50 points) Solve the following problems. Round dollar amounts to the nearest cent. Round other amounts to the nearest tenth. Write rates as percents to the nearest tenth of a percent. (5 points for each correct answer)

11. Bradley Grayson, a paralegal, will receive a 3% salary increase this month. Hence, he will receive $90 more salary this month than he received last month. What was Bradley's salary last month? __________

12. Cindy Wells works in the market research department of a soft drink company. Last month Cindy received a $125 raise, which means that she now earns 5% more than she did before the raise. How much does Cindy earn now? __________

13. There is a farmers' market held downtown every Saturday. The volume has been increasing by about 4% every week. If the volume was $24,000 this week, what should the volume be next week? __________

14. Alicia Sanchez works as a sales analyst for a toy manufacturer. She predicts that toy sales will decrease 6% between May and June. If the amount of the sales decrease is $165,000, what sales is she predicting for June? __________

15. Last month, James Fraenkel started working as an apprentice machinist. One of his first projects was to reduce the diameter of a metal shaft from 0.160 inch to 0.136 inch. By what percent did he reduce the diameter of the shaft? __________

16. Zorica Gregory, a mechanical engineer, was able to increase the efficiency of a manufacturing facility. By doing so, she decreased the cost to manufacture a commercial-quality lawnmower by $21, which was 12% of the former cost. What will be the new reduced cost to manufacture the lawnmower? __________

17. Richard Altman is the purchasing agent for a janitorial service. He orders all the supplies used by his company. Because of new contracts to clean three new office buildings, Richard ordered an additional $6,000 worth of supplies this month. This was a 12% increase from last month. What was the value of the supplies that Richard ordered last month? __________

18. Nancy Yamamoto owns a gift ship that had sales of $65,000 in November. Because of the Christmas holiday season, Nancy predicts that the shop will double its monthly sales in December. What percent increase is Nancy predicting for December over November? __________

19. Suppose that Nancy Yamamoto's gift shop had had sales of $125,000 in November and had doubled its sales in December. What would be the percent increase for December over November? __________

20. Because of Father's Day, a men's clothing store had sales of $250,000 in June. Sales decreased by 50% in July. What were the sales in July? __________

____

Score for B (50)

Assignment 12.4: Distribution of Overhead

Name

Date Score

A (20 points) Complete the square feet, percent, and distribution columns below. Round percents to the nearest whole number. (1 point for each correct answer in column 1; 2 points for each correct answer in columns 2 and 3)

1. Carla Viberti owns restaurants in four districts of town: (a) Pineview, (b) Oakhurst, (c) Laurel Glen, and (d) Citrus Heights. She buys all of the food through a central office, which she maintains at the Pineview restaurant. Monthly expenses for the office are distributed among the four restaurants based on the floor space of each. Complete the distribution table for monthly expenses of $12,000.

	Store	Space Occupied	Square Feet	Percent of Total	Distribution of Expense
a.	Pineview	30 ft × 70 ft			
b.	Oakhurst	40 ft × 45 ft			
c.	Laurel Glen	40 ft × 60 ft			
d.	Citrus Heights	30 ft × 40 ft			
	Total		7,500	100%	$12,000

Score for A (20)

B (16 points) Complete the percent and distribution columns below. Before computing the distribution, round each percent to the nearest whole number. (2 points for each correct answer)

2. Mary Lou Fechtig owns a temporary services company. She employs four types of employees whom she places into temporary positions: (a) accountants, (b) secretaries, (c) food service people, and (d) hotel service people. Mary Lou rents office space for $4,200 per month. She distributes the rent among the four labor groups, according to the number of people from each group placed into jobs. Calculate the percents and the resulting distributions.

		Number of Employees	Percent of Total	Distribution of Rent
a.	Accountants	18		
b.	Secretaries	42		
c.	Food Service	36		
d.	Hotel Service	24		
	Total	120	100%	$4,200

Score for B (16)

C (64 points) The following situations provide practice in distributing monthly overhead expenses at a central office. From the information given in the table, complete the distributions indicated in problems 3 through 6. Remember: Answers for each problem should sum to the total monthly overhead expense. (4 points for each correct answer)

Monthly Overhead Expense		Basis of Distribution	Location				
			East	West	North	South	TOTAL
Rent	$25,000	Square feet	16,800	9,600	14,400	19,200	60,000
Janitorial	12,000	Machine hours worked	14,400	18,000	10,800	28,800	72,000
Utilities	16,000	Units produced	5,700	7,800	10,200	6,300	30,000
Insurance	10,000	Number of employees	90	75	105	30	300

3. Distribute rent based on the number of square feet at each location.
East ________; West ________; North ________; South ________ Check.

4. Distribute janitorial expense based on the number of machine hours worked in each location.
East ________; West ________; North ________; South ________ Check.

5. Distribute utilities expense based on the units produced at each location.
East ________; West ________; North ________; South ________ Check.

6. Distribute insurance expense based on the number of employees at each location.
East ________; West ________; North ________; South ________ Check.

____
Score for C (64)

Notes

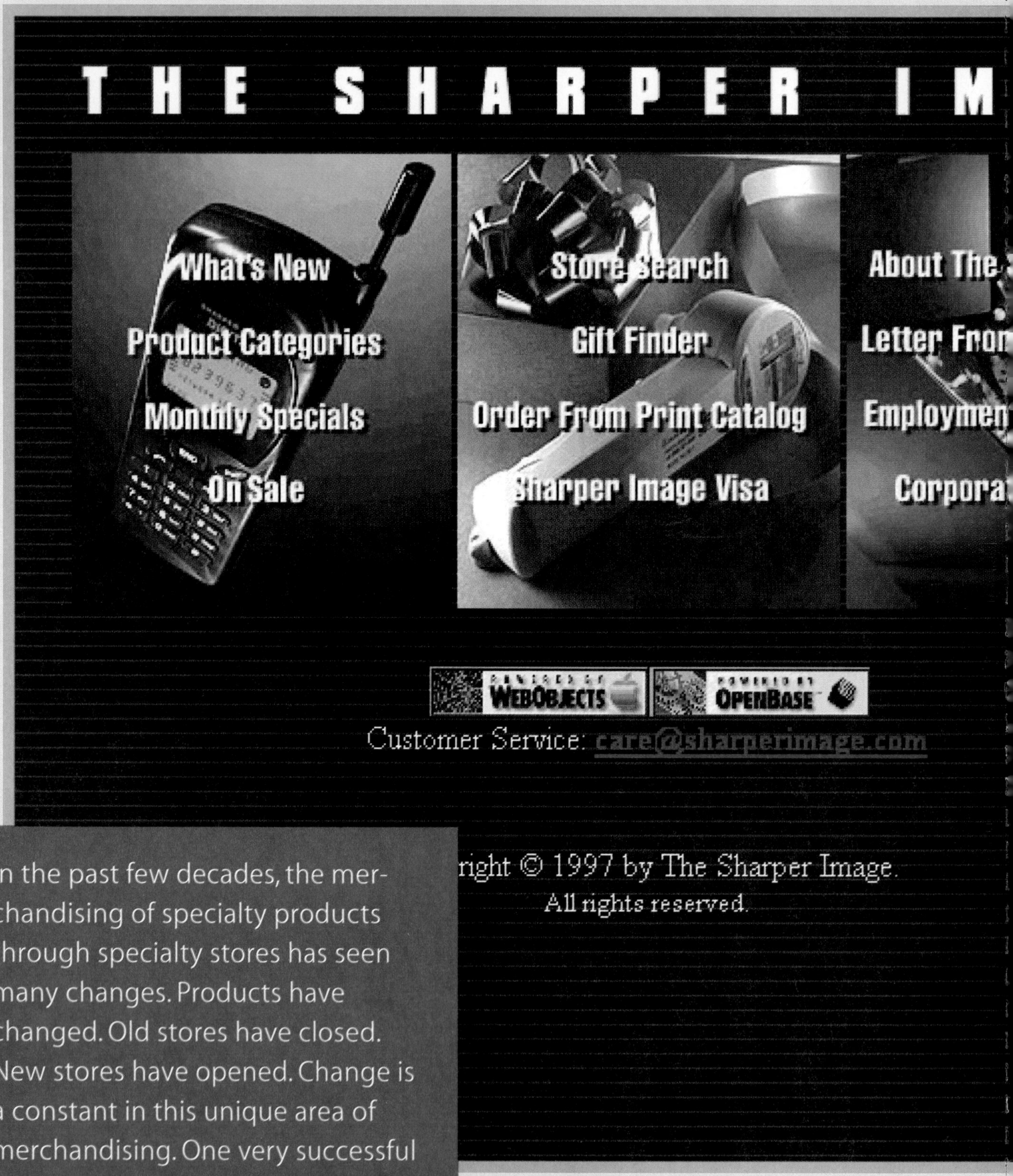

In the past few decades, the merchandising of specialty products through specialty stores has seen many changes. Products have changed. Old stores have closed. New stores have opened. Change is a constant in this unique area of merchandising. One very successful specialty store is **The Sharper Image.** To learn more about this fascinating and unusual specialty store, including current employment opportunities, visit its web site at www.sharperimage.com.

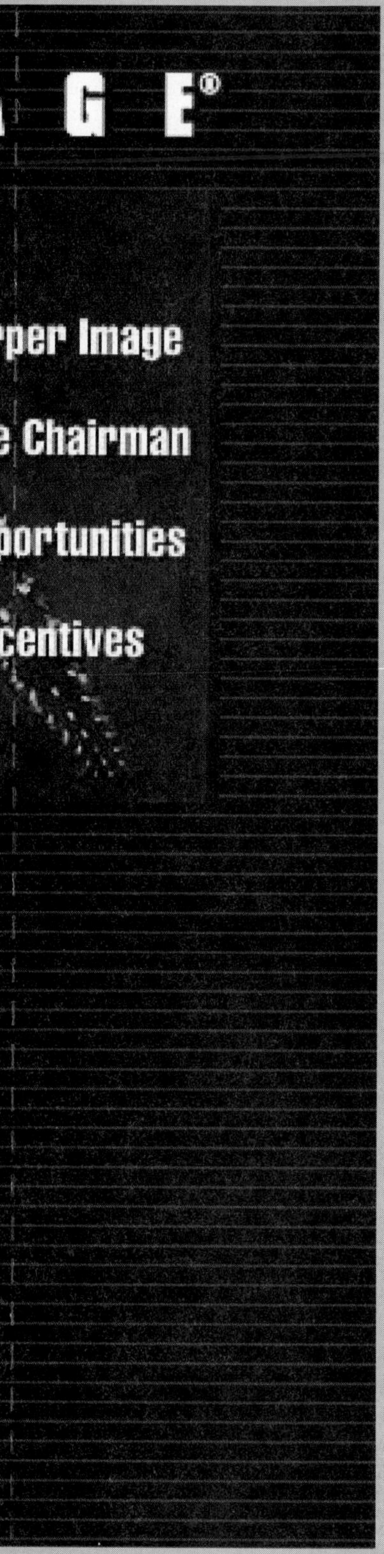

13 Commissions

Learning Objectives

By studying this chapter and completing all the assignments, you will learn to:

1. Calculate sales commissions and gross pay.
2. Calculate graduated sales commissions.
3. Calculate sales and purchases for principals.

Some of the highest earning professionals do it without a salary, working on commission as salespeople. On every sale, they are paid a percentage of the sales price. They can sell real estate, cars, insurance, and stocks and bonds, as well as high-ticket goods that can result in a six-figure commission.

Commission is payment to an employee or to an agent for performing a business transaction or service. The most familiar type of commission is that received by a salesperson. Many companies have employees who are paid either totally or partially on a commission basis. Persons who sell insurance, real estate, and automobiles typically are in this category.

For a business owner, one advantage of using the commission method to pay employees is that the commission is an incentive. Employees are paid on the basis of the volume of business they produce for the company. The advantage to the employee is that she or he can earn more by being more productive.

Besides typical salespeople, there are other businesspersons who provide selling and buying services. These include commission merchants, agents, and brokers, all of whom are paid a commission for their services. The person for whom the services are provided is called the *principal.* A commission merchant will normally take actual possession of the merchandise and make the sales transaction in his or her name. A *broker,* however, will usually make the transaction in the principal's name and does not take possession of the merchandise.

Calculating Sales Commissions and Gross Pay

LEARNING OBJECTIVES 1

Calculate sales commissions and gross pay.

A sales commission paid to a salesperson is usually a stated percent of the dollar value of the goods or services sold. Whether the commission is based on the wholesale or retail value of the goods will depend on the type of business and merchandise sold. The rate that is used to calculate the commission will also vary among different businesses. In some companies, the salesperson receives both a salary and a commission.

STEPS to Compute Commission and Total Pay

1. Multiply the commission rate by the amount sold to get the commission amount.
2. If there is a salary, add it to the commission to get the total gross pay.

EXAMPLE A

Dana Ayers works for Trans Bay Yacht Sales. She receives a base salary of $2,500 per month and earns a commission that is 2% of the value of all boating equipment that she sells during the month. Find her commission and total pay during September, a month in which she sold $106,000 worth of equipment.

STEP 1 $2\% \times \$106{,}000 = 0.02 \times \$106{,}000 = \$2{,}120$ commission

STEP 2 $\$2{,}120$ commission $+ \$2{,}500$ base salary $= \$4{,}620$ total pay

Commissions normally are paid only on actual sales. Thus, goods that are returned or orders that are canceled are not subject to commission. The reason for this policy is to protect the business owner. Suppose Trans Bay Yacht Sales in the preceding example pays the 2% commission whether or not the goods are returned. When Dana Ayers got an order for $10,000, her commission would be $2\% \times \$10{,}000 = \$200$. If the goods were all returned but the commission was still paid, then the owner would have to pay $200 to Dana. Since no goods were sold, the owner actually would lose $200 on this transaction.

STEPS to Compute Commission When Sale Involves Returned Goods

1. Subtract the value of the returned goods from the total ordered to determine the amount sold.
2. Multiply the commission rate by the amount sold to get the commission amount.

EXAMPLE B

Kevin Thompson is a salesperson for Topanga Office Supply. He works on a *commission-only* basis—he receives a commission of 2.5% on his monthly sales, but no base salary. What are his commission and total pay during a month when he sells $167,500 worth of office products, but one of his customers cancels an order for $15,000 and returns the merchandise that had already been delivered?

STEP 1 $\quad \$167{,}500 - \$15{,}000 = \$152{,}500$

STEP 2 $\quad 2.5\% \times \$152{,}500 = 0.025 \times \$152{,}500 = \$3{,}812.50$ commission

Total Pay = $3,812.50, since he is paid on a commission-only basis

CONCEPT CHECK 13.1

Calculate the commission and gross pay for a salesperson who is paid a $1,600 salary and earns a 4% commission. Total sales were $96,000, but there were returns of $8,000.

$\$96{,}000 - \$8{,}000 = \$88{,}000$ net sales

$0.04 \times \$88{,}000 =$	$3,520	commission
	+1,600	salary
	$5,120	gross pay

Calculating Graduated Sales Commissions

Commission plans provide incentives for employees because they can earn more money by selling more products. A company can provide additional incentive for even greater productivity by using *graduated commission rates.* As the level of sales increases, so does the commission rate.

LEARNING OBJECTIVES 2

Calculate graduated sales commissions.

STEPS to Compute Commission Under a Graduated Rates Plan

1. Compute the dollar amount at each rate level by using subtraction.
2. Multiply each level's commission rate by the level's sales dollars.
3. Add the products computed in Step 2 to determine the total commission.

EXAMPLE C

Melody Chiu has a monthly commission plan under which she receives 2% on the first $40,000 of sales during the month and 3% on sales above $40,000 for the month. If Melody has sales of $73,000 during a month, compute her commission for that month.

STEP 1

$73,000	total sales
− 40,000	at 2%
$33,000	at 3%

STEP 2

$\$40{,}000 \times 0.02 = \$\ 800$

$33{,}000 \times 0.03 = \ \ 990$

STEP 3

Total commission = $1,790

EXAMPLE D

Assume Melody has a monthly commission plan under which she receives 2% on the first $40,000 of sales during the month, 3% on sales between $40,000 and $80,000, and 4% on all sales over $80,000. If Melody has sales of $106,500 during a month, compute her commission for that month.

STEP 1

$106,500	total sales
− 40,000	at 2%
$ 66,500	
− 40,000	at 3%
$ 26,500	at 4%

STEP 2

$40,000 × 0.02	=	$ 800
40,000 × 0.03	=	1,200
26,500 × 0.04	=	1,060

STEP 3

Total commission = $3,060

The same graduated incentive plan can be defined in terms of bonus rates. The calculations are similar.

EXAMPLE E

Dale Crist has a monthly commission plan under which he receives 2% on all sales during the month. If Dale has sales over $40,000, he receives a bonus of 1% of everything over $40,000. If he sells more than $80,000, he receives a "super bonus" of an additional 1% of everything over $80,000. What is Dale's commission for a month during which he sold $96,500?

	0 – $40,000	$40,000 – $80,000	$80,000 – $96,500	
Base	$40,000			0.02 × $96,500 = $1,930
Bonus		$96,500 − $40,000 = $56,500		0.01 × $56,500 = 565
Super Bonus			$96,500 − $80,000 = $16,500	0.01 × $16,500 = 165

Total commission (add the three commission amounts) = $2,660

CONCEPT CHECK 13.2

Calculate the total commission on sales of $182,400. The commission is graduated: 1% on sales to $60,000, 2% on sales from $60,000 to $120,000, and 3% on sales above $120,000.

0.01 × $60,000	=	$ 600
0.02 × $60,000	=	1,200
0.03 × $62,400	=	1,872
Total commission	=	**$3,672**

Calculating Sales and Purchases for Principals

LEARNING OBJECTIVES 3

Calculate sales and purchases for principals.

A producer may send goods to an agent, called a *commission merchant,* for sale at the best possible price. Such a shipment is a *consignment.* The party who sends the shipment is the *consignor;* the party to whom it is sent—that is, the commission merchant—is the *consignee.*

Whatever price the commission merchant gets for the consignment is the *gross proceeds.* The commission is generally a certain percent of the gross proceeds. Sometimes it is a certain amount per unit of weight or measure of the goods sold. The commission and any other sales expenses, such as transportation, advertising, storage, insurance, etc., are the *charges.* The charges are deducted from the gross proceeds. The resulting amount, which is sent to the consignor, is the *net proceeds.*

EXAMPLE F

Ernest Dawkins Ranch has been trying to sell a used truck for hauling livestock and a tractor. Unsuccessful after a month, Dawkins consigns the pieces to Carson Equipment Brokers. They agree on commission rates of 6% on the gross proceeds from the truck and 9% on the tractor. Carson sells the truck for $34,600 and the tractor for $41,800. Carson also pays $380 to deliver the truck and $625 to deliver the tractor. What are the net proceeds due to Dawkins Ranch from the sale of the equipment?

Truck:	Commission: 0.06 × $34,600 =	$2,076	Gross Proceeds:	$34,600
	Freight:	+ 380	less charges	− 2,456
	Total Charges	$2,456	Net Proceeds:	$32,144
Tractor:	Commission: 0.09 × $41,800 =	$3,762	Gross Proceeds:	$41,800
	Freight:	+ 625	less charges	− 4,387
	Total Charges	$4,387	Net Proceeds:	$37,413

$32,144 + $37,413 = $69,557 Total Net Proceeds

Along with the net proceeds, the commission merchant sends the consignor a form known as an *account sales.* This is a detailed statement of the amount of the sales and the various deductions. Figure 13-1 is a typical account sales.

Figure 13-1: Account Sales

CARSON EQUIPMENT BROKERS

August 16, 19-- NO. 67324

309 Sule Road, Wilbraham, MA 01095-2073

BELOW ARE ACCOUNT SALES OF Consignment No. 76
RECEIVED August 1, 19--
and sold for account of Same

NAME Ernest Dawkins Ranch
ADDRESS 127 N. Kaye
Albany, GA 31704-5606

DATE	CHARGES	AMOUNT	DATE	SALES	AMOUNT
Aug. 1	Freight (truck)	$380	Aug. 10	Truck	$34,600
16	6% Commission (truck)	2,076			
	Net proceeds (truck)	32,144	13	Tractor	41,800
				Gross proceeds	$76,400
	Freight (tractor)	625			
	9% Commission (tractor)	3,762			
	Net proceeds (tractor)	37,413			
	Total	$76,400			

When commission merchants purchase goods for their principals, the price that they pay for the merchandise is the *prime cost.* The prime cost and all charges are the *gross cost,* or the cost that the principal pays.

EXAMPLE G

Asia-Pacific Tours commissioned Specialty Marketing Group to purchase 10,000 vinyl travel bags that will be labeled with Asia-Pacific's logo and used as promotional items. For this size order, Specialty Marketing purchased the bags for $4.29 each. Charges include the commission, which is 6% of the prime cost; storage, $42.50; and freight, $24.40. What is the gross cost that Asia-Pacific should pay to Specialty Marketing?

$ 4.29		$42,900	prime cost
× 10,000	units	× 0.06	
$ 42,900	prime cost	$ 2,574	commission

$2,574 commission + $42.50 storage + $24.40 freight = $2,640.90 charges
$42,900 prime cost + $2,640.90 charges = $45,540.90 gross cost

An *account purchase* is a detailed statement from the commission merchant to the principal. It shows the cost of goods purchased, including charges. Figure 13-2 is a typical account purchase, for the transaction in example G.

Figure 13-2: Account Purchase

SPECIALTY MARKETING GROUP
4445 Mission
San Francisco, CA 94112

ACCOUNT PURCHASE
NO. 1311

October 26 19 --

Bought on Consignment for
Asia-Pacific Tours
7300 Harbor Place
San Francisco, CA 94104

DATE	DESCRIPTION	CHARGES	AMOUNT
Oct. 23	10,000 units stock #T805 @ $4.29		42,900.00
23	6% commission	2,574.00	
	Storage	42.50	
	Freight	24.40	2,640.90
	Gross Cost		45,540.90

CONCEPT CHECK 13.3

a. Compute the commission and the net proceeds on a consignment sale of $6,500. The commission rate is 4%, local delivery charges are $328.16, and storage charges are $125.
0.04 × $6,500 = $260 commission
$6,500 − $260 − $328.16 − $125 = $5,786.84 net proceeds

b. Compute the commission and gross cost on a $12,500 purchase for a principal. The commission rate is 6%, air freight is $138.70, and local delivery charges are $64.60.
0.06 × $12,500 = $750 commission
$12,500 + $750 + $138.70 + $64.60 = $13,453.30

COMPLETE ASSIGNMENTS 13.1 AND 13.2.

Chapter Terms for Review

account purchase
account sales
broker
charges
commission
commission merchant
commission only
consignee
consignment
consignor
graduated commission rates
gross cost
gross proceeds
net proceeds
prime cost
principal

The **Bottom** Line

Summary of chapter learning objectives:

Learning Objective	Summary	Example
13.1	Calculating sales commissions and gross pay	1. A salesperson gets a $2,240 salary and a 2% commission. Find the commission and the gross pay when sales are $58,200 and returns are $6,500.
13.2	Calculating graduated sales commissions	2. A salesperson has a graduated commission rate: 1% on sales up to $100,000; 1.5% on sales from $100,001 to $200,000; and 2% on sales above $200,000. Find the commission when sales are $245,000.
13.3	Calculating sales and purchases for principals	3. A broker sells a principal's merchandise at a gross sales price of $15,600 and a commission rate of 3.5%. There are sales costs of $300 for storage and $119 for delivery. Find the commission and net proceeds. 4. A commission merchant purchases merchandise for a principal at a prime cost of $6,250. The commission rate is 8%, air freight is $139, and local delivery is $65. Find the commission and gross cost.

Answers: 1. Commission: $1,034; Gross pay: $3,274 **2.** $3,400 **3.** Commission: $546; Net proceeds: $14,635
4. Commission: $500; Gross cost: $6,954

Notes

Assignment 13.1: Commission

Name ______________________________

Date ______________ Score ______________

A (24 points) Find the commission and the total gross pay. (2 points for each correct answer)

Employee	Monthly Salary	Commission Rate	Monthly Sales	Commission	Gross Pay
1. Cagan, D.	$ 0	9%	$42,000	______	______
2. Jao, R.	2,000	2%	36,000	______	______
3. Merrill, T.	1,600	4.5%	38,000	______	______
4. Prestrelski, J.	2,400	2%	40,000	______	______
5. Roensch, P.	1,200	5%	52,000	______	______
6. Strickland, A.	1,500	4%	36,000	______	______

____
Score for A (24)

B (36 points) Calculate the total commission for the following commission payment plans. (6 points for each correct answer)

Graduated Commission Rates	Sales	Commission
7. 2% on sales to $50,000 4% on sales above $50,000	$ 92,000	______
8. 1% on sales to $150,000 2% on sales above $150,000	$195,000	______
9. 3% on sales to $40,000 5% on sales above $40,000	$ 82,200	______
10. 1% on sales to $80,000 2% on sales from $80,001 to $160,000 3% on sales above $160,000	$225,000	______
11. 3% on sales to $40,000 4% on sales from $40,001 to $100,000 5% on sales above $100,000	$116,000	4,400

12. 2% on sales to $65,000 — $134,800 — ________
3% on sales from $65,001 to $150,000
4% on sales above $150,000

Score for B (36)

C **(20 points) Katrina Vallente is a commission merchant. She charges different commission rates to sell different types of merchandise. During May, she completed the following consignment sales for consignors. Find Katrina's commission on each sale and the net proceeds sent to each consignor. (2 points for each correct answer)**

	Gross Sales	Comm. Rate	Commission	Local Delivery	Storage	Air Freight	Net Proceeds
13.	$28,400	3%	________	$68.75	$ 0	173.50	________
14.	1,600	3.5%	________	51.35	75.00	0	________
15.	8,400	6%	________	284.65	0	0	________
16.	12,880	2.5%	________	0	0	248.00	________
17.	5,600	4%	________	0	85.00	115.00	________

Score for C (20)

D **(20 points) Greg Boesch, a commission merchant in Chicago, buys merchandise exclusively for principals. Listed below are five recent transactions. Calculate Greg's commission on each purchase and the gross cost. (2 points for each correct answer)**

	Prime Cost	Comm. Rate	Commission	Local Delivery	Storage	Air Freight	Gross Cost
18.	$14,200	4%	________	$ 89.50	$88.00	0	________
19.	4,975	12%	________	0	0	195.00	________
20.	8,400	6%	________	62.00	0	96.00	________
21.	2,850	8%	________	0	110	108.80	________
22.	19,700	9%	________	150.00	0	0	________

Score for D (20)

Assignment 13.2: Applications with Commission

LEARNING OBJECTIVES 3

Name ____________________

Date ____________ Score ____________

A (56 points) Solve each of the following business application about salespersons who are paid partly or entirely on a commission basis. Solve the problems in order, because some of the questions are sequential. (8 points for each correct answer)

1. Loren Miller sells memberships to an athletic club. He receives a monthly salary of $1,500 plus a commission of 12% on new membership fees. What was Loren's monthly pay for May, when he sold new memberships valued at $32,500? __________

2. Roberta Reavis sells commercial restaurant supplies and equipment. She is paid on a commission-only basis. She receives 2% for her sales up to $60,000. For the next $90,000 of sales, she is paid 3%, and for any sales above $150,000 she is paid 4%. How much commission would she earn in a month when her sales were $165,000? __________

3. Roberta Reavis (Problem 2) is not paid commission on any restaurant supplies or equipment that is later returned. If an item is returned, its price is deducted from Roberta's total sales to get her net sales. The commission-only rate is applied to her net sales. Suppose that Roberta sold merchandise worth $165,000 but that $20,000 of that was later returned. What would be Roberta's commission on net sales? __________

4. Peggy Covey works for Southwest Appliance Depot. She receives a monthly salary of $2,500 for which she must sell $20,000 worth of appliances. She also receives a commission of 4% on net sales above $20,000. What will Peggy's pay for October be when her net appliance sales were $42,000? __________

5. Southwest Appliance Depot (Problem 4) offers service contracts with all appliance sales. To encourage salespersons like Peggy to sell more service contracts, the company pays a commission of 20% on all service contracts. What will Peggy's total pay for a month be if she sells $42,000 worth of appliances and $1,200 worth of service contracts? __________

6. Stock brokers for companies like Paine Webber are normally paid a commission on the stocks that they buy and sell for their clients. Suppose that the commission rate is 5% of the value of the stock. What will the commission be on 5,000 shares of General Motors stock that is selling for $67.31 per share? __________

7. Bonnie Johnson works in telemarketing. Her job is to make telephone calls from a computerized list of names and try to convince people to make an appointment with a life insurance salesperson. Bonnie receives 30¢ for each completed telephone call, $6.00 for each appointment made and kept, and 0.75% of any initial revenue that results from the appointment. How much would Bonnie earn if she completed 862 calls, 137 persons made and kept appointments, and $23,500 in revenue resulted from the appointments? __________

Score for A (56)

B (24 points) Solve each of the following business applications about consignment sales and commission merchants. (8 points for each correct answer)

8. Teresa Gomez is a commission merchant specializing in consignment sales of antique furniture. Alan Kimmel, a furniture owner, sets the price of his antique furniture at $5,000. He agrees to pay Teresa a 15% commission plus $145 shipping from his home to her showroom. He also agrees to reimburse Teresa $188 for shipping the antiques from her showroom to the buyer's home. What will be Alan's net proceeds from the sale? __________

9. What would net earnings for Teresa Gomez (Problem 8) be if she were required to pay the shipping expenses from her showroom to the buyer's home? __________

10. Heather Kruse makes artistic weavings that are used as wall hangings. She sells her weavings primarily at open-air art shows and street fairs through her agent, Stella Chow. Stella charges 20% on all sales, plus the fees to operate a sales booth and transportation expenses. What will Heather's net proceeds be if Stella sells weavings worth $22,400 at four different art shows? Each art show charged a booth fee of $450, and Stella's total transportation expenses were $375. __________

Score for B (24)

C (20 points) The following problems involve the purchase of a home. (10 points for each correct answer)

11. Joseph Carter has a home that he would like to sell and he asks real estate agent Deanna Souza to sell it. Deanna works for Coldwell Banker Real Estate, which advises Joseph that he should be able to sell his house for $150,000. The commission rate for selling a home is 6%. If the house goes for the expected price, what will be the total commission amount that Joseph pays? __________

12. See Problem 11. To sell his home, Joseph Carter must pay some additional fees for termite inspection and title insurance, as well as fees to the county to record the transaction. These fees total $2,500 and are added to the 6% commission. What will Joseph's net proceeds be from the sale of his $150,000 home? __________

Score for C (20)

Notes

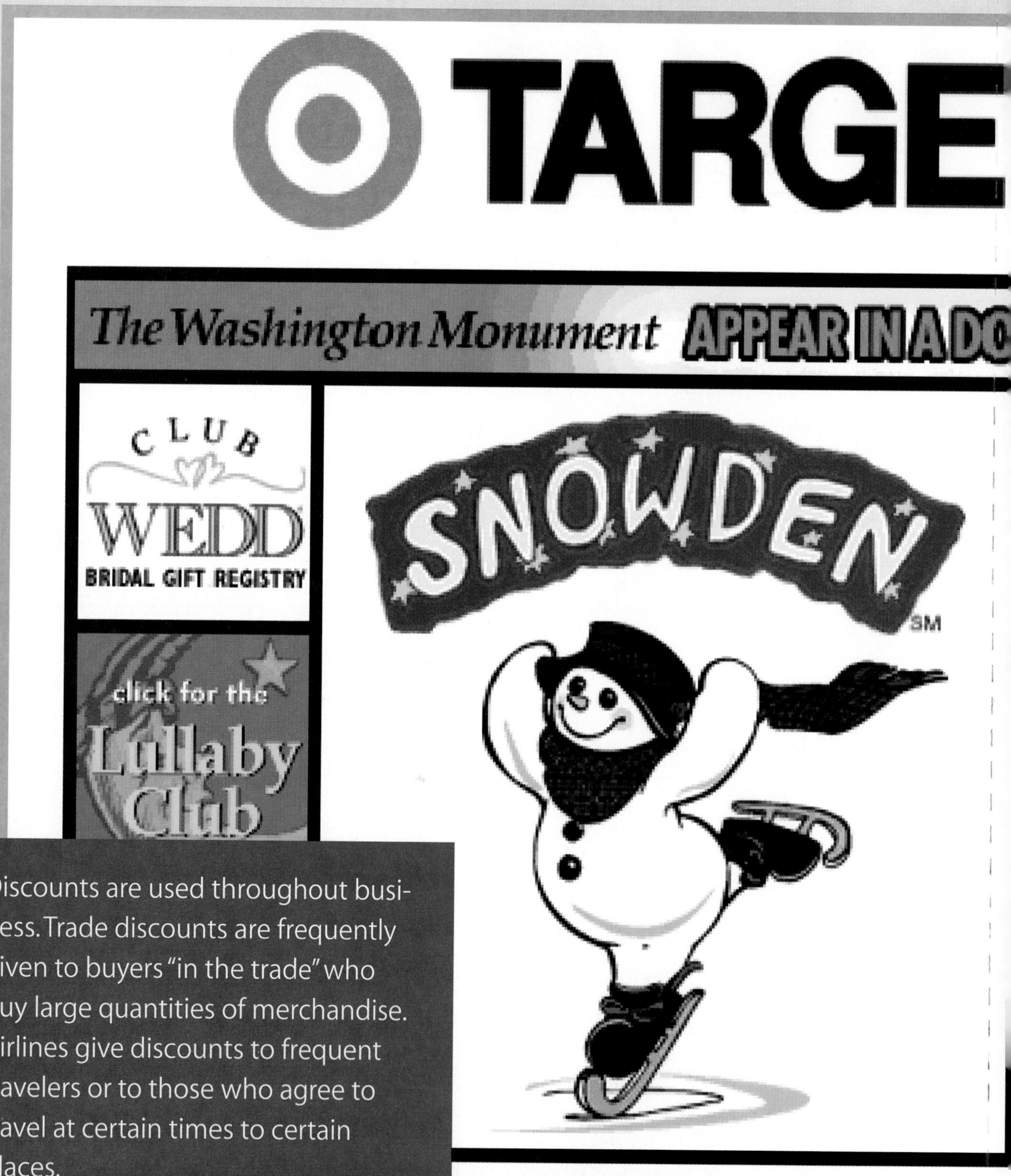

Discounts are used throughout business. Trade discounts are frequently given to buyers "in the trade" who buy large quantities of merchandise. Airlines give discounts to frequent travelers or to those who agree to travel at certain times to certain places.

Some stores and many wholesalers and distributors give a discount for cash. The **Target** stores provide quality merchandise at reasonable, often discounted, prices. Visit their web site at www.target.com.

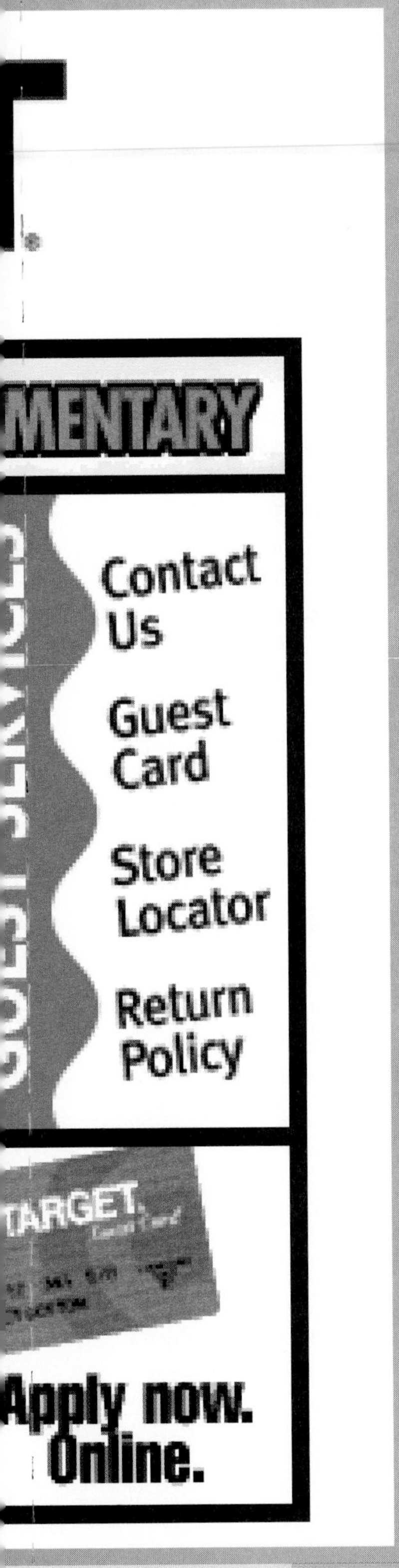

14 Discounts

Learning Objectives

By studying this chapter and completing all the assignments, you will learn to:

1. Calculate single trade discounts.
2. Calculate a series of trade discounts.
3. Calculate the equivalent single discount rate for a series of trade discounts.
4. Calculate cash discounts and remittance amounts for fully paid invoices.
5. Calculate cash discounts and remittance amounts for partially paid invoices.

Smart travelers and theater-goers are able to see top shows for half price by taking advantage of a discount known as the "Twofer," which entitles you to purchase two seats for the price of one. But travelers must be wary: "Discount" and "Going Out of Business" signs can actually mean higher prices.

When one business sells merchandise to another business, the seller usually offers two types of discounts: trade discounts and cash discounts. Trade discounts affect the agreed-upon selling price **before** the sale happens. Cash discounts affect the amount actually paid **after** the transaction.

Calculating Single Trade Discounts

LEARNING OBJECTIVES 1

Calculate single trade discounts.

Businesses that sell products want to attract and keep customers who make repeated, large-volume purchases. Manufacturers, distributors, and wholesalers frequently offer *trade discounts* to buyers "in the trade," generally based on the quantity purchased. For example, Federated Food Supply gives a 40% discount to Cajun Hot, a local chain of 34 sidewalk sandwich carts that sell hot dogs and sausages. Another Federated customer is Clarita Nicholson, founder and owner of Clarita's Muffins. Clarita's business is still small. She bakes her muffins between 11 p.m. and 2 a.m. in oven space that she leases from a bakery. Federated gives Clarita only a 25% discount because she does not do as much business as Cajun Hot does with Federated. Federated also sells to persons who are not "in the trade." These retail customers pay the regular *list price.*

Large restaurant chains like McDonald's can go directly to the manufacturer for most items or even do their own manufacturing. They can have items manufactured to their exact specifications for a contracted price. They reduce their costs by eliminating the distributors (the "middle men").

There are two traditional methods for calculating trade discounts: the discount method and the complement method. Both can be used to find the *net price* that the distributor will charge to the customer after the discount. The *discount method* is useful when you want to know both the net price and the actual amount of the trade discount. The *complement method* is used to find only the net price. It get its name because you use the *complement rate,* which is 100% minus the discount rate. Each method has only two steps.

STEPS to Compute Net Price with the Discount Method

1. Multiply the discount rate (expressed as a decimal) by the list price to get the discount amount:
   Discount = Trade discount rate × List price
2. Subtract the discount from the list price to get the net price:
   Net price = List price − Discount

EXAMPLE A

Federated Food Supply sells a set of stainless steel trays to Clarita's Muffins. The list price is $240, and Clarita qualifies for a 25% trade discount. Compute the net price using the discount method.

STEP 1 Discount = 0.25 × $240 = $60

STEP 2 Net price = $240 − $60 = $180

STEPS to Compute Net Price with the Complement Method

1. Subtract the discount rate (expressed as a percentage) from 100% to get the complement rate:
   Complement rate = 100% − Trade discount rate
2. Multiply the complement rate (expressed as a decimal) by the list price to get the net price:
   Net price = Complement rate × List price

EXAMPLE B

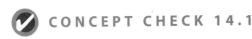

Using the data in example A, compute the net price using the complement method.

STEP 1	Complement rate	= 100% − 25% = 75%
STEP 2	Net price	= 0.75 × $240 = $180

CONCEPT CHECK 14.1

a. Calculate the trade discount amount and the net price using the **discount method.**

List price = $230 Trade discount = 30%
Discount amount = 0.30 × $230 = $69
Net price = $230 − $69 = $161

b. Calculate the complement rate and the net price using the **complement method.**

List price = $750 Trade Discount = 40%
Complement rate = 100% − 40% = 60%
Net price = 0.60 × $750 = $450

Calculating a Series of Trade Discounts

LEARNING OBJECTIVES 2

Calculate a series of trade discounts.

A distributor or manufacturer may give additional discounts to those customers who actually buy the largest volumes. Suppose that Federated gives all food preparation businesses a 25% discount for being in the trade. However, if one business buys twice as much from Federated, it may be rewarded with an **additional discount.** For example, Clarita's Muffins may receive its first discount of 25% automatically. Then, Clarita gets an additional 20% discount if its accumulated purchases were between $10,000 and $25,000 during the previous year and another 10% if accumulated purchases were over $25,000 during the previous year. Therefore, Clarita could have discounts of 25%, 20%, and 10%. This is called a *series of discounts.*

Both the discount method and the complement method can be used to compute the net price with a series of discounts. **The two methods are the same as shown above except that the steps are repeated for each discount in the series.** For example, if there are three discounts, repeat the steps three times. Apply the first *discount rate* to the list price. For the second and third discounts, compute intermediate prices and then apply the discount rates to them.

EXAMPLE C

Federated Food Supply sells a set of mixing bowls for a list price of $480. Clarita's Muffins qualifies for the series of discounts: 25%, 20%, 10%. Compute the net price using the discount method.

	1st discount	2nd discount	3rd discount
STEP 1	0.25 × $480 = $120	0.20 × $360 = $72	0.10 × $288 = $28.80
STEP 2	$480 − $120 = $360	$360 − $72 = $288	$288 − $28.80 = $259.20

EXAMPLE D

Using the data in example C, compute the net price using the complement method.

	1st discount	2nd discount	3rd discount
STEP 1	100% − 25% = 75%	100% − 20% = 80%	100% − 10% = 90%
STEP 2	0.75 × $480 = $360	0.80 × $360 = $288	0.90 × $288 = $259.20

Complement Method Shortcut

When you use complement rates, an efficient shortcut eliminates all of the intermediate prices:

Multiply the list price by the product of all the complement rates.

EXAMPLE E

Repeat example D using the shortcut. The list price is \$480, and the discounts are 25%, 20%, and 10%. The complement rates are 75%, 80%, and 90%.

Net price = \$480 × 0.75 × 0.80 × 0.90 = \$259.20

Note: Remember that there should be **no rounding** until you reach the final net price. It should then be rounded to the nearest cent.

CONCEPT CHECK 14.2

a. A wholesaler offers a series of trade discounts: 30%, 25%, and 10%. Find each of the discount amounts and the final net price on a \$1,200 purchase.

First discount amount:	\$1,200 × 0.30 = \$360
Second discount amount:	\$1,200 − \$360 = \$840; \$840 × 0.25 = \$210
Third discount amount:	\$840 − \$210 = \$630; \$630 × 0.10 = \$63
Net price:	\$630 − \$63 = \$567

b. A series of trade discounts is 40%, 20%, and 5%. Find each of the complement rates, and use the shortcut to calculate the final net price on a purchase of \$650.

First complement rate:	100% − 40% = 60%
Second complement rate:	100% − 20% = 80%
Third complement rate:	100% − 5% = 95%
Net price:	\$650 × 0.60 × 0.80 × 0.95 = \$296.40

Calculating the Equivalent Single Discount Rate

LEARNING OBJECTIVES 3

Calculate the equivalent single discount rate for a series of trade discounts.

Suppose that North Coast Hotel Supply Company offers a single discount of 45% to Clarita's Muffins. How does that rate compare with the series of discounts from Federated: 25%, 20%, and 10%? Clarita could check by computing the *equivalent single discount rate.*

The most efficient way to find the single discount rate that is equivalent to a series of discounts is essentially the shortcut used in example E.

STEPS to Compute the Equivalent Single Discount Rate

1. Compute the complement of each rate.
2. Compute the product of the complements by multiplying all complement rates together.
3. Compute the equivalent single discount rate by subtracting the product (Step 2) from 100%.

EXAMPLE F

Find the equivalent single discount rate for Federated's series of discounts: 25%, 20%, and 10%.

STEP 1 1st Complement rate $= 100\% - 25\% = 75\%$
2nd Complement rate $= 100\% - 20\% = 80\%$
3rd Complement rate $= 100\% - 10\% = 90\%$

STEP 2 Product of complements $= 0.75 \times 0.80 \times 0.90 = 54\%$

STEP 3 Equivalent single discount $= 100\% - 54\% = 46\%$

CONCEPT CHECK 14.3

A series of trade discounts is 40%, 20%, and 5%. Find the three complement rates, and then find the equivalent single trade discount rate.

Complement rates: $100\% - 40\% = 60\%, 100\% - 20\% = 80\%, 100\% - 5\% = 95\%$
Product of the complement rates: $0.60 \times 0.80 \times 0.95 = 0.456$, or 45.6%
Equivalent single discount rate: $100\% - 45.6\% = 54.4\%$

COMPLETE ASSIGNMENT 14.1.

Calculating Cash Discounts for Fully Paid Invoices

LEARNING OBJECTIVES 4

Calculate cash discounts and remittance amounts for fully paid invoices.

When a seller sends merchandise to a buyer, the seller often wants to get its payment quickly and the buyer often tries to delay payment as long as possible. Sellers can encourage early payment by offering a *cash discount;* they can discourage late payment by assessing an extra interest payment; or they can do both. These stipulations are called the *terms of payment,* or simply the *terms.* The terms describe details about cash discounts and/or penalty periods.

After shipping merchandise to a buyer, the seller usually sends a document called an *invoice,* requesting payment. The invoice lists each product, its cost, and the total cost. Additional costs such as packaging or freight are also listed. The invoice will state the terms of payment. The amount the buyer pays is called the *remittance.* The buyer uses the following steps to calculate the remittance.

STEPS to Compute the Remittance

1. Multiply the discount rate (expressed as a decimal) times the net purchase amount to get the cash discount:
   Cash discount = Discount rate × net purchase
2. Subtract the cash discount from the net purchase amount to get the remittance:
   Remittance = Net purchase − Cash discount

Figure 14-1 shows an invoice from National Automotive Supply, which sold car wax to Speedway Auto Detailers for $480. The wax will be sent via UPS, and National will pay for the shipping. The invoice lists terms of 2/10, n/30. The *invoice date* is May 23.

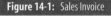

Figure 14-1: Sales Invoice

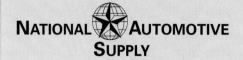

NATIONAL AUTOMOTIVE SUPPLY

INVOICE NO. 782535

SOLD TO Speedway Auto Detailers
730 W. Columbia Dr.
Peoria, IL 62170-1184

DATE May 23, 199-
TERMS 2/10, n/30
SHIP VIA UPS

QUANTITY	DESCRIPTION	UNIT PRICE	GROSS AMOUNT	NET AMOUNT
24 gals.	Car wax	$20.00	$480.00	$480.00

The expression 2/10, n/30 means that Speedway can get a 2% discount if it pays the invoice within 10 days of the invoice date. Ten days after May 23 is June 2, which is called the *discount date.* The 10-day period between May 23 and June 2 is called the *discount period.* The n/30 is short for net 30, which means that if Speedway does not pay within 30 days, National will charge an interest penalty. Thirty days after May 23 is June 22, which is called the *due date.* (See Figure 14-2)

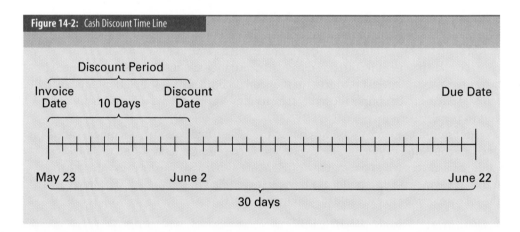

Figure 14-2: Cash Discount Time Line

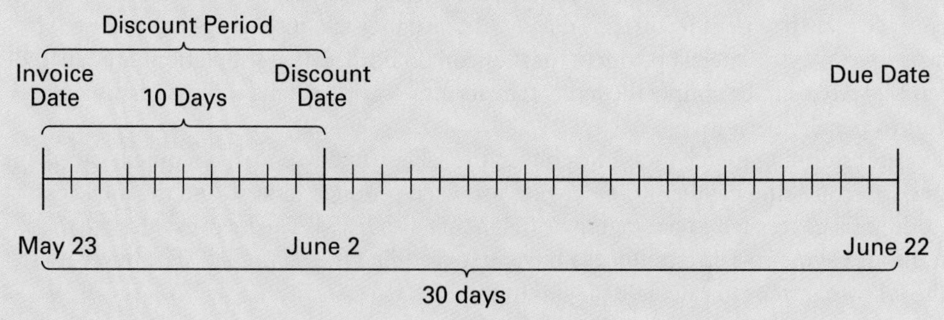

EXAMPLE G

Calculate the remittance due if Speedway pays National within the 10-day discount period.

STEP 1 Cash discount $= 2\%$ of $\$480 = 0.02 \times \$480 = \$9.60$

STEP 2 Remittance $= \$480 - \$9.60 = \$470.40$

All companies do not use exactly the same notation for writing their terms; 2/10, n/30 is also written as 2/10, net 30 or as 2-10, n-30. Likewise, there can be more than one discount rate and discount period. For example 2/5, 1/15, n/30 means that the seller gets a 2% discount by paying within 5 days, gets a 1% discount by paying between 6 and 15 days, and must pay a penalty after 30 days.

Returned Merchandise and Freight Charges

The seller gives a discount only on merchandise that is actually purchased—the *net purchases.* For example, there is no discount on returned items. Likewise, there is no discount on charges from a third party, such as freight. Use the following steps to calculate the cash discount when there are merchandise returns and/or freight charges.

STEPS to Compute the Remittance When There Are Merchandise Returns and/or Freight Charges:

1. Net purchase = Invoice amount − Merchandise returns − Freight
2. Cash discount = Discount rate × Net purchase
3. Cost of merchandise = Net purchase − Cash discount
4. Remittance = Cost of merchandise + Freight, if any

EXAMPLE H

National Automotive Supply sells merchandise to Speedway Auto Detailers. The invoice amount is $510, which includes $30 in freight charges. The invoice date is August 13, and the terms are 2/10, n/30. Speedway returns $200 worth of merchandise and pays the rest of the invoice before the discount date. Compute the cash discount and the remittance. Also, determine the discount date and due date.

STEP 1 Net purchase = $510 − $200 − $30 = $280

STEP 2 Cash discount = 0.02 × $280 = $5.60

STEP 3 Cost of merchandise = $280 − $5.60 = $274.40

STEP 4 Remittance = $274.40 + $30 = $304.40

Discount date = August 13 + 10 days = August 23
Due date = August 13 + 30 days = September 12

If you don't need to know the actual cost of the merchandise, you can eliminate Step 3 and calculate the remittance directly:

Remittance = $280.00 − $5.60 + $30.00 = $304.40

There is also a complement method for cash discounts, but it is not used as often as the discount method because most businesses want to know the amount of the cash discount before deciding whether or not to pay the invoice early. In the complement method for cash discounts, only Steps 2 and 3 change.

STEPS to Compute the Remittance with the Complement Method

1. Net purchase = Invoice amount − Merchandise returns − Freight
2. Complement rate = 100% − Cash discount rate
3. Cost of merchandise = Net purchase × Complement rate
4. Remittance = Cost of merchandise + Freight, if any

EXAMPLE I

Solve example H using the complement method for cash discounts. The invoice amount is $510, merchandise returns are $200, and freight is $30.

STEP 1 Net purchase = $510 − $200 − $30 = $280

STEP 2 Complement rate = 100% − 2% = 98%

STEP 3 Cost of merchandise = $280 × 0.98 = $274.40

STEP 4 Remittance = $274.40 + $30 = $304.40

CONCEPT CHECK 14.4

a. Use the given information to compute the discount date, due date, cash discount, and remittance.

Terms:	1/10, n/60	Discount date = July 22 + 10 days = August 1
Invoice date:	July 22	Due date = July 22 + 60 days = September 20
Invoice amount:	$842.17	
Returned goods:	$195.67	Net purchases = $842.17 − $195.67 − $51.50 = $595.00
Freight:	$51.50	Cash discount = 0.01 × $595 = $5.95
		Remittance = $595 − $5.95 + $51.50 = $640.55

b. Compute the remittance for the problem in part a using the complement method.

Net purchases = $842.17 − $195.67 − $51.50 = $595.00
Complement rate = 100% − 1% = 99%
Cost of merchandise = $595 × 0.99 = $589.05
Remittance = $589.05 + $51.50 = $640.55

Calculating Cash Discounts for Partially Paid Invoices

LEARNING OBJECTIVES 5

Calculate cash discounts and remittance amounts for partially paid invoices.

Sometimes a buyer wants to take some advantage of the cash discount but can afford to pay only part of the invoice within the discount period. The invoice will be reduced by the amount paid (remittance) plus the amount of the discount. The total of the amount paid plus the amount of cash discount is called the *amount credited* to the buyer's account. To calculate the amount credited, you need to know the complement rate: 100% − discount rate.

STEPS to Compute the Unpaid Balance

1. Compute the complement of the discount rate (100% − discount rate).
2. Compute the amount credited by dividing the amount paid (remittance) by the complement rate.
3. Compute the unpaid balance by subtracting the amount credited (Step 2) from the invoice amount.

EXAMPLE J

Farnoush Jacobson operates a shop called The Space Enhancers, a do-it-yourself center for closets and storage. Farnoush buys shelving materials with an invoice price of $392 and terms of 2/10, net 60. Within the 10-day discount period, she sends in a check for $200. How much credit should Farnoush receive, and what is her unpaid balance?

STEP 1 Complement rate = 100% − 2% = 98%

STEP 2 Amount credited = \$200 ÷ 0.98 = \$204.0816 = \$204.08

STEP 3 Unpaid balance = \$392.00 − \$204.08 = \$187.92

Notice that in the example, Farnoush receives \$1.00 credit for every \$0.98 paid. In other words, the \$200 actually remitted is 98% of the total amount credited. Check your work by multiplication:

Cash discount = 0.02 × \$204.08 = \$4.0816 or \$4.08
Remittance = \$204.08 − \$4.08 = \$200.00

A slightly different situation, which arises less frequently, is when the buyer decides in advance the total amount that she wants to have credited to the account. This problem is exactly like the original cash discount problems.

EXAMPLE K

Farnoush Jacobson buys \$392 worth of shelving materials for use in her closet and storage shop. The terms are 2/10, net 60. Farnoush wants to pay enough money within the 10-day discount period to reduce her unpaid balance by exactly \$200. What amount should she remit to the seller? What will be her unpaid balance?

STEP 1 Cash discount = 2% × \$200 = \$4

STEP 2 Remittance = \$200 − \$4 = \$196

STEP 3 Unpaid balance = \$392 − \$200 = \$192

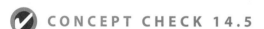

CONCEPT CHECK 14.5

a. An invoice for \$476 has terms of 1/15, net 25. How much is the unpaid balance after a \$350 remittance is made within the discount period?

Complement rate = 100% − 1% = 99%
Amount credited = \$350 ÷ 0.99 = \$353.54
Unpaid balance = \$476.00 − \$353.54 = \$122.46

b. An invoice for \$476 has terms of 1/15, net 25. What size remittance should be made in order to have a total of \$350 credited to the account?

Cash discount = \$350 × 0.01 = \$3.50
Remittance = \$350.00 − \$3.50 = \$346.50

COMPLETE ASSIGNMENT 14.2.

Chapter Terms for Review

amount credited
cash discount
complement method
complement rate
discount date
discount method
discount period
discount rate
due date
equivalent single discount rate
invoice
invoice date
list price
net price
net purchase
remittance
series of discounts
terms of payment (terms)
trade discount

The Bottom Line

Summary of chapter learning objectives:

Learning Objective	Summary	Example
14.1	Calculating single trade discounts	1. Find the net price on a list price of $450 with a 20% trade discount, using the discount and the complement methods.
14.2	Calculating a series of trade discounts	2. Find the net price on a list price of $800 with a series of trade discounts of 25% and 10%. Use both the discount method and the complement method.
14.3	Calculating the equivalent single discount rate for a series of trade discounts	3. A series of trade discounts is 20%, 10%, 5%. Use complement rates to find the equivalent single discount rate.
14.4	Calculating cash discounts and remittance amounts for fully paid invoices	An invoice is dated December 26 and has terms of 1.5/10, n/25. The total amount is $964.24, with $141.34 of returned goods and $82.90 freight. 4. Calculate the discount date, due date, cash discount, and remittance. 5. Calculate the remittance using the complement rate.
14.5	Calculating cash discounts and remittance amounts for partially paid invoices	An invoice for $500 has terms of 3-10, n-30. 6. Calculate the unpaid balance after a $400 payment within the discount period. 7. Calculate the remittance required within the discount period in order to have $400 credited to the account.

Answers: 1. Discount method: $450 − $90 = $360; Complement method: 0.80 × $450 = $360 **2.** Discount method: $800 − $200 = $600, $600 − $60 = $540; Complement method: 0.75 × 0.90 × $800 = $540 **3.** 31.6% **4.** Discount date: Jan. 5; Due date: Jan. 20; Cash discount: $11.10; Remittance: $811.80 **5.** $811.80 **6.** $87.63 **7.** $388.00

Assignment 14.1: Trade Discounts

Name ______________________________

Date ______________________ Score ______________________

A (24 points) Problems 1–3: Find the dollar amount of the trade discount and the net price using the discount method. Problems 4–6: Find the complement rate and the net price using the complement method. (2 points for each correct answer)

Trade Discount	List Price	Discount Amount	Net Price
1. 30%	$1,250	________	________
2. 40%	$2,800	________	________
3. 35%	$3,400	________	________

Trade Discount	List Price	Complement Rate	Net Price
4. 15%	$1,600	________	________
5. 34%	$3,000	________	________
6. 40%	$4,750	________	________

____
Score for A (24)

B (16 points) Find the amount of each discount in the given series of trade discounts. Then find the net price. Where a discount does not exist, place a dash. (2 points for each correct answer)

List Price	Trade Discounts	Trade Discount Amounts			Net Price
		First	Second	Third	
7. $2,200	40%, 25%	________	________	________	________
8. $1,650	30%, 20%	________	________	________	________

____
Score for B (16)

C (20 points) Find the complement rate for each discount in the given series of trade discounts. Then find the net price using the complement method. Where a complement rate does not exist, place a dash. (2.5 points for each correct answer)

List Price	Trade Discounts	Complement Rates First	Second	Third	Net Price
9. $1,800	30%, 15%	_______	_______	_______	_______
10. $2,040	35%, 25%	_______	_______	_______	_______

____
Score for C (20)

D (20 points) Find the complement rate for each discount in the given series of trade discounts. Then find the equivalent single discount rate, to the nearest $\frac{1}{10}$ of a percent. (2.5 points for each correct answer)

Trade Discounts	Complement Rates First	Second	Third	Equivalent Single Discount Rate
11. 30%, 20%, 5%	_______	_______	_______	_______
12. 20%, 10%, 5%	_______	_______	_______	_______

____
Score for D (20)

E (20 points) Solve each of the following business applications about trade discounts. Use either the discount method or the complement method. (10 points for each correct answer)

13. Modern Landscaping Inc. purchased $425 worth of plants and $180 worth of soil and fertilizer from a garden supply wholesaler. The wholesaler gives Modern Landscaping a 20% trade discount on the plants and a 30% trade discount on the other items. Compute the net price that Modern Landscaping will be required to pay. _______

14. Bill Blevins Roofing Contractor is purchasing redwood shakes to re-roof a house. The shakes have a list price of $14,400. The Northwest Roofing Supply Company gives Bill the normal trade discount of 20%. In addition, Northwest gives Bill two further trade discounts of 10% and 5% because of the large volume of business that Bill has already done with Northwest so far this year. What is Bill's net price on the order of redwood shakes? _______

____
Score for E (20)

Assignment 14.2: Cash Discounts

LEARNING OBJECTIVES 4

LEARNING OBJECTIVES 5

Name ______________________

Date ______________________ Score ______________________

A (60 points) For the following problems, find the discount date, the due date, the amount of the cash discount, and the amount of the remittance. (1 point for each correct date and 2 points for each correct amount)

1.

Terms:	3/5, n/25	Discount date:	________
Invoice date:	March 28	Due date	________
Invoice amount:	$518.30	Discount amount:	________
		Remittance:	________

2.

Terms:	2/10, n/30	Discount date:	________
Invoice date:	October 24	Due date	________
Invoice amount:	$482.86	Discount amount:	________
Freight:	$25.00	Remittance:	________

3.

Terms:	1/15, net 45	Discount date:	________
Invoice date:	May 21	Due date	________
Invoice amount:	$781.50	Discount amount:	________
Returned goods:	$184.00	Remittance:	________

4.

Terms:	1.5/20, N/60	Discount date:	________
Invoice date:	March 29	Due date	________
Invoice amount:	$1,095.55	Discount amount:	________
Returned goods:	$298.88	Remittance:	________
Freight:	$80.00		

____

Score for A (60)

B (20 points) For the following problems, find the discount date, the complement rate, and the amount of the remittance. (1 point for each date and rate; 2 points for each correct remittance)

5. Terms: 1/7, n/25
Invoice date: January 25
Invoice amount: $482.80

Discount date: ________
Complement rate: ________
Remittance: ________

6. Terms: 1/25, net 55
Invoice date: July 9
Invoice amount: $295.20
Freight: $45.00

Discount date: ________
Complement rate: ________
Remittance: ________

____
Score for B (20)

C (20 points) The following problems involve partial payments made within the discount period. Solve for the items indicated. (2 points for each correct answer)

7. Terms: 1.5/7, n/30
Invoice date: June 2
Invoice amount: $848

Amount credited: ________
Remittance: $500
Unpaid balance: ________

8. Terms: 2/15, net 35
Invoice date: April 9
Invoice amount: $532.90
Returned goods: $184.00

Amount credited: ________
Remittance: $300
Unpaid balance: ________

____
Score for C (20)

Notes

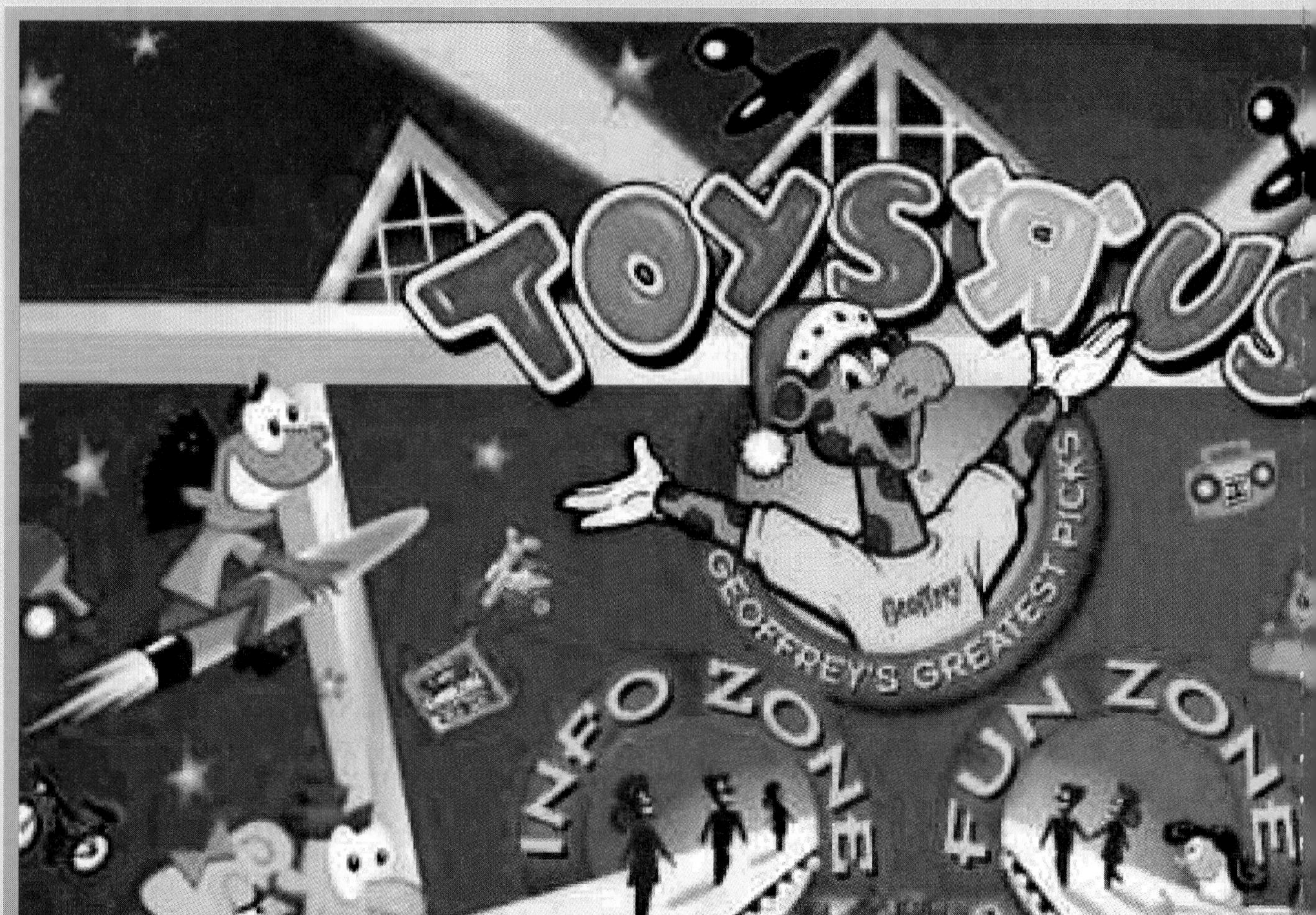

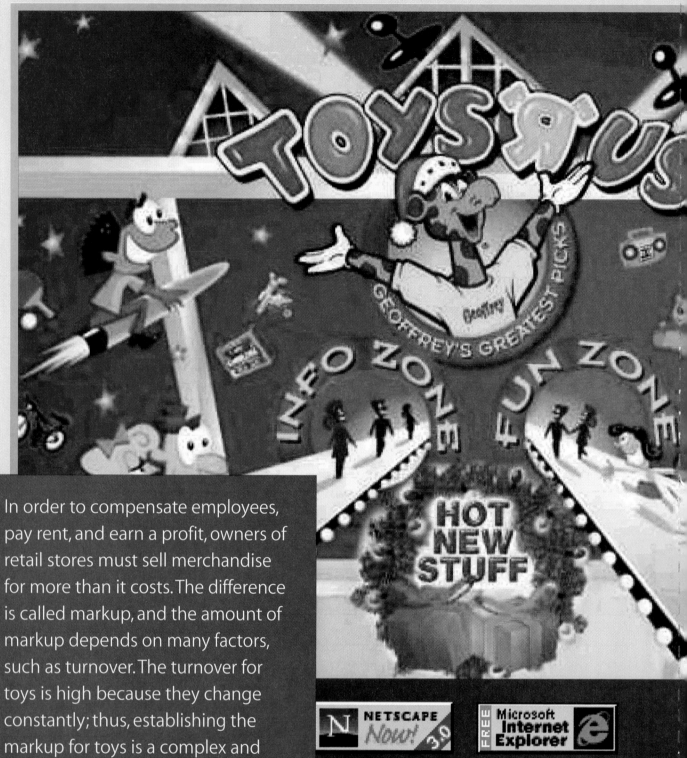

In order to compensate employees, pay rent, and earn a profit, owners of retail stores must sell merchandise for more than it costs. The difference is called markup, and the amount of markup depends on many factors, such as turnover. The turnover for toys is high because they change constantly; thus, establishing the markup for toys is a complex and continuously changing process.

Toys "Я" Us has toy stores around the world. A significant part of its success is due to its expertise in determining and computing markups. To learn about this successful company, visit www.toysrus.com.

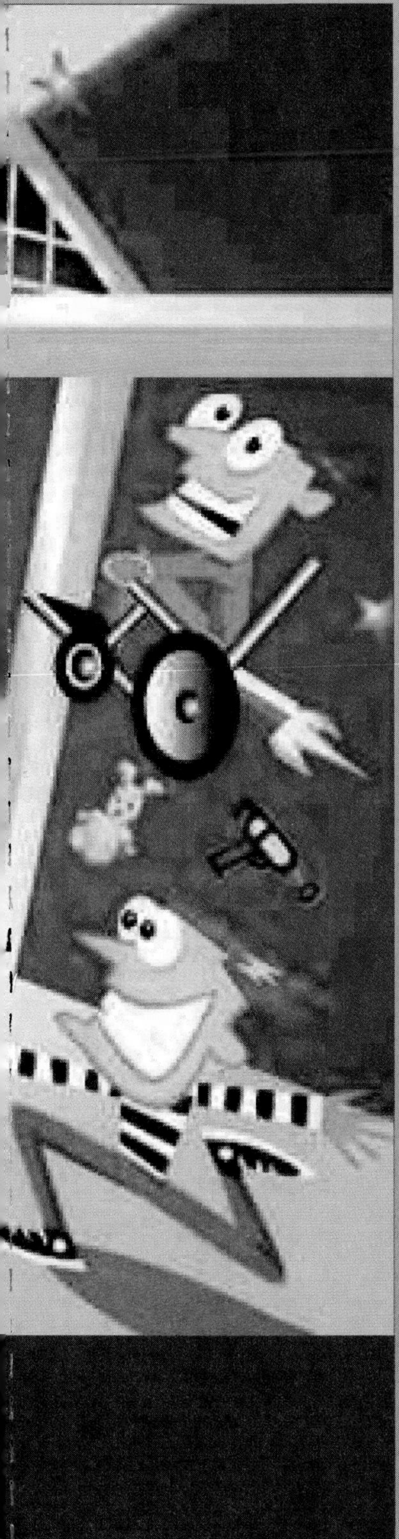

15 Markup

Learning Objectives

By studying this chapter and completing all the assignments, you will learn to:

1. Compute the variables in the basic markup formula.
2. Compute the markup variables when the markup percent is based on cost.
3. Compute markup percent based on cost.
4. Compute the markup variables when the markup percent is based on selling price.
5. Compute markup percent based on selling price.

When you read an ad for a sale, you may see the words "Marked down from . . ." This means the price was marked up from what it cost the store and now has been lowered to sell goods faster. Goods are marked up high enough to allow for markdowns to stimulate sales.

Computing Markup Variables

LEARNING OBJECTIVES 1

Compute the variables in the basic markup formula.

Some businesses manufacture products and sell them. Other businesses buy products from someone else and then resell them. Both types of businesses must sell their products for more than it costs to produce or purchase them. This price increase is called the *markup.*

The Athletic Advantage is a retail store that sells athletic equipment and athletic clothing. The store buys running shoes directly from a manufacturer. Suppose the manufacturer charges $21.50 per pair for one particular type of running shoes and an additional $0.25 to deliver them to the store. The total cost of a pair of the shoes, with delivery, is $21.75; this is called the *cost of goods sold* or just the *cost.*

If The Athletic Advantage sells the shoes for exactly the cost, $21.75, it will lose money on the sale. The store has many other expenses—such as rent, utilities, and salaries—that are not part of the cost of acquiring the shoes. The Athletic Advantage must mark up the selling price high enough above the cost of the shoes to cover all of these additional costs—and also leave some profit for the owners.

The total amount that The Athletic Advantage marks up the selling price is called the *dollar markup.* (Note: Markup is expressed both in dollars and in percents. To eliminate confusion, this book will use two separate terms: *dollar markup* and *markup percent.*)

Suppose that The Athletic Advantage estimates that $9.40 of additional expenses should be allocated to a pair of running shoes. Also, suppose that the store would like a profit of $8.00 on the pair of shoes. Then the total dollar markup that it should give the shoes is $9.40 + $8.00 = $17.40

To determine the selling price of the shoes, The Athletic Advantage adds the dollar markup to the cost of goods sold (cost), using the basic markup formula:

Selling price = Cost + Dollar markup = $21.75 + $17.40 = $39.15

Since the dollar markup is the difference between the selling price and the cost of goods sold, it is often useful to rewrite the formula:

Dollar markup = Selling price − Cost = $39.15 − $21.75 = $17.40

Likewise, cost is the difference between selling price and dollar markup. Thus,

Cost = Selling price − Dollar markup = $39.15 − $17.40 = $21.75

CONCEPT CHECK 15.1

Compute the missing terms in the basic markup formula: Selling price = Cost + Dollar markup

a. Cost = $417.82; Dollar markup = $204.20

Selling price = Cost + Dollar markup
= $417.82 + $204.20 = $622.02

b. Cost = $154.40; Selling price = $392.12

Dollar markup = Selling price − Cost
= $392.12 − $154.40 = $237.72

c. Dollar markup = $41.26; Selling price = $93.20

Cost = Selling price − Dollar markup
= $93.20 − $41.26 = $51.94

Computing Markup Based on Cost

Compute the markup variables when the markup percent is based on cost.

The Athletic Advantage computed its markup directly by determining the expenses and the desired profit. However, this method is not practical when a business has hundreds or thousands of items. Allocating expenses and profit to each item would be too tedious. A more practical method is for the owner, an employee, or an accountant to analyze prior sales of the company or a similar company. She or he can look at the costs of goods, additional expenses, and desired profit to determine a percent to use to mark up various items. This is called the *markup percent.*

One company may use different markup percents for different types of items. For example, an appliance store typically also performs repair services and sells replacement parts for the appliances that it sells. The store may have one markup percent for the actual appliance, a second markup percent for repair services, and a third markup percent for replacement parts.

In Chapter 12 on percents, three terms were introduced: Rate, Base, and Percentage. In this chapter, Rate is the markup percent, or *markup rate.* Percentage is the *dollar markup.* Determining the Base is more challenging, because sometimes *cost* is the base and sometimes *selling price* is the base. For some businesses, cost may be the more logical base for calculating dollar markup. However, calculating dollar markup based on selling price is an advantageous method for many retail stores.

The accountant for The Athletic Advantage says that in order to pay all expenses and have a reasonable profit, the company should have an 80% *markup based on cost.* The running shoes cost $21.75. When you know the cost and the markup percent, you can compute the dollar markup and the selling price.

STEPS to Compute the Selling Price Based on Cost

1. Multiply the cost by the markup percent to get the dollar markup.
2. Add the dollar markup to the cost to get the selling price.

For The Athletic Advantage's running shoes,

STEP 1 Dollar markup = Markup percent × Cost = 0.80 × $21.75 = $17.40

STEP 2 Selling price = Cost + Dollar markup = $21.75 + $17.40 = $39.15

EXAMPLE A

Using markup based on cost, what are the dollar markup and the selling price on merchandise that costs $40 and has a 25% markup?

STEP 1 Dollar markup = Markup percent × Cost = 0.25 × $40 = $10

STEP 2 Selling price = Cost + Dollar markup = $40 + $10 = $50

Computing Selling Price Directly from Cost

You can compute the selling price directly from the cost, without computing the dollar markup.

STEPS to Compute the Selling Price Directly from the Cost

1. Add 100% to the markup percent.
2. Multiply this sum by the cost to get the selling price.

EXAMPLE B

What is the selling price of an item that has a cost of $200 and a markup percent of 30% based on cost?

STEP 1 Markup percent + 100% = 30% + 100% = 130%

STEP 2 Selling price = (Markup percent + 100%) × Cost = 1.30 × $200 = $260

Computing Cost from Selling Price

When you know the selling price and the markup percent, the procedure for computing cost is just the reverse of that for computing selling price.

STEPS to Compute the Cost from the Markup Percent

1. Add the markup percent to 100%.
2. Divide the selling price by this sum to get the cost.

EXAMPLE C

The selling price of a pair of shoes is $70. The markup percent based on cost is 40%. Find the cost.

STEP 1 100% + Markup percent = 100% + 40% = 140%

STEP 2 Cost = Selling price ÷ (100% + Markup percent) = $70 ÷ 1.40 = $50

You can always check your work in markup problems.

Cost is $50, and markup percent is 40%.
Dollar markup = Cost × Markup percent = $50 × 0.40 = $20
Selling Price = Cost + Dollar markup = $50 + $20 = $70

It checks!

CONCEPT CHECK 15.2

Compute the required values when the markup percent is based on cost.

a. Cost = $1,340; Markup percent = 30% Find dollar markup, and then find selling price.	Dollar markup = $1,340 × 0.30 = $402 Selling price = $1,340 + $402 = $1,742
b. Cost = $430; Markup percent = 60% Find 100% + Markup percent, and then find selling price directly.	100% + Markup percent = 100% + 60% = 160% Selling price = $430 × 1.60 = $688
c. Selling price = $780; Markup percent = 25% Find 100% + Markup percent, and then find cost directly.	100% + Markup percent = 100% + 25% = 125% Cost = $780 ÷ 1.25 = $624

Computing Markup Percent Based on Cost

LEARNING OBJECTIVES 3

Compute markup percent based on cost.

In the illustration with The Athletic Advantage, the accountant determined that the markup percent needed to be 80% of cost, which meant that the selling price needed to be $39.15. However, the store owner may prefer to price the shoes at $39.95. Now, the markup percent is no longer 80% of cost. The markup percent based on cost can be computed in two steps.

STEPS to Compute the Markup Percent Based on Cost

1. Subtract the cost from the selling price to get the dollar markup.
2. Divide the dollar markup by the cost to get the markup percent.

For The Athletic Advantage's running shoes,

STEP 1 Dollar markup = Selling price − Cost = \$39.95 − \$21.75 = \$18.20

STEP 2 Markup percent = Dollar markup ÷ Cost = \$18.20 ÷ \$21.75 = 0.837, or 83.7% (rounded to one decimal place)

EXAMPLE D

What is the markup percent based on cost when the selling price is \$80 and the cost is \$50?

STEP 1 Dollar markup = Selling price − Cost = \$80 − \$50 = \$30

STEP 2 Markup percent = Dollar markup ÷ Cost = \$30 ÷ \$50 = 0.60, or 60%

EXAMPLE E

What is the markup percent based on cost when the dollar markup is already known to be \$15 and the cost is \$75? (Step 1 is not necessary.)

STEP 2 Markup percent = Dollar markup ÷ Cost = \$15 ÷ \$75 = 0.20, or 20%

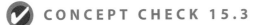

CONCEPT CHECK 15.3

Cost = \$1,800; Selling price = \$3,150
Find the markup percent based on cost.

Dollar markup = \$3,150 − \$1,800 = \$1,350
Markup percent = \$1,350 ÷ \$1,800 = 0.75, or 75%

COMPLETE ASSIGNMENT 15.1.

Computing Markup Based on Selling Price

LEARNING OBJECTIVES 4

Compute the markup variables when the markup percent is based on selling price.

Although many businesses base their markup on cost, it is common for the markup percent in retail business to be a percent of selling price—that is, for businesses to use *markup based on selling price.* This does not mean that selling price is determined without considering cost or even before considering cost. It merely means that the dollar markup can be computed by multiplying the markup percent by the selling price.

Many people start a business when they observe another successful business selling a product. New owners believe that they can acquire the product, pay all expenses, and still sell it for less than the existing business sells its product. Instead of basing the selling price on costs, expenses, and satisfactory profit, the new owners may price their product just under the competition's price. They base their selling price on the competition rather than marking up from their costs.

Basing markup calculations on selling price can be an advantage in a retail store where the salesperson or sales manager has the authority to lower the sales price immediately in order to make a sale.

STEPS to Compute the Dollar Markup and Cost from the Markup Percent

1. Multiply the selling price by the markup percent to get the dollar markup.
2. Subtract the dollar markup from the selling price to get the cost.

EXAMPLE F

Robert Landles enters an appliance store to buy a washing machine. He finds one with a selling price of $400. He knows he can buy it for $375 at another store, but he prefers this store because of its reputation for good service. He tells the salesperson, "I would buy it for $375." Kristin Beaver, the store manager, knows that the markup percent is 25% of the selling price. What is the cost of the washing machine?

STEP 1 Dollar markup = Markup percent × Selling price = 0.25 × $400 = $100

STEP 2 Cost = Selling price − Dollar markup = $400 − $100 = $300

Kristin can then decide whether she prefers no sale at all or one in which she gets only $75 markup. Although it would be helpful if Kristin knew how much markup she would need to pay for expenses, at least she would know the cost.

EXAMPLE G

Find the dollar markup and the cost of an item that sells for $120 and has a markup percent that is 40% of the selling price.

STEP 1 Dollar markup = Markup percent × Selling price = 0.40 × $120 = $48

STEP 2 Cost = Selling price − Dollar markup = $120 − $48 = $72

Computing Cost Directly

You can compute the cost directly from the selling price, without computing the dollar markup.

STEPS to Compute the Cost from the Markup Percent and Selling Price

1. Subtract the markup percent from 100%.
2. Multiply this difference by the selling price.

EXAMPLE H

What is the cost of an item that has a selling price of $200 and a markup percent of 30% based on selling price?

STEP 1 100% − Markup percent = 100% − 30% = 70%

STEP 2 Cost = (100% − Markup percent) × Selling price = 0.70 × $200 = $140

Computing Selling Price from Cost

When you know the cost and the markup percent, the procedure for computing cost is just the reverse of that for computing selling price.

STEPS to Compute the Selling Price from the Cost

1. Subtract the markup percent from 100%.
2. Divide the cost by this difference to get the selling price.

EXAMPLE I

The cost of a bicycle is $90. The markup percent based on selling price is 25%. Find the selling price.

STEP 1 100% − Markup percent = 100% − 25% = 75%

STEP 2 Selling price = Cost ÷ (100% − Markup percent) = $90 ÷ 0.75 = $120

You can always check your work in markup problems:

Selling price is $120, and markup percent is 25%.
Dollar markup = Selling price × Markup percent = $120 × 25% = $30
Cost = Selling price − Dollar markup = $120 − $30 = $90

It checks!

CONCEPT CHECK 15.4

Compute the required values when the markup percent is based on selling price.

a. Selling price = $640; Markup percent = 40%
Find dollar markup, and then find cost.

Dollar markup = $640 × 0.40 = $256
Selling price = $640 − $256 = $384

b. Selling price = $40; Markup percent = 30%
Find 100% − Markup percent, and then find cost directly.

100% − Markup percent = 100% − 30% = 70%
Cost = $40 × 0.70 = $28

c. Cost = $160; Markup percent = 25%
Find 100% − Markup percent, and then find selling price directly.

100% − Markup percent = 100% − 25% = 75%
Cost = $160 ÷ 0.75 = $213.33

Computing Markup Percent Based on Selling Price

In the illustration with The Athletic Advantage, the pair of running shoes had a cost of $21.75. The store owner decided that the selling price of the running shoes would be $39.95. The markup percent based on selling price can be calculated in two steps.

LEARNING OBJECTIVES 5

Compute markup percent based on selling price.

STEPS to Compute the Markup Percent from the Selling Price

1. Subtract the cost from the selling price to get the dollar markup.
2. Divide the dollar markup by the selling price to get the markup percent.

For The Athletic Advantage's running shoes,

STEP 1 Dollar markup = Selling price − Cost = $39.95 − $21.75 = $18.20

STEP 2 Markup percent = Dollar markup ÷ Selling price = $18.20 ÷ $39.95
= 0.455, or 45.5% (rounded to one decimal place)

EXAMPLE J

What is the markup percent based on selling price when the selling price is \$80 and the cost is \$50?

STEP 1 Dollar markup = Selling price − Cost = \$80 − \$50 = \$30

STEP 2 Markup percent = Dollar markup ÷ Selling price = \$30 ÷ \$80 = 0.375, or 37.5%

EXAMPLE K

What is the markup percent based on selling price when the dollar markup is already known to be \$15 and the selling price is \$60? (Step 1 is not necessary.)

STEP 2 Markup percent = Dollar markup ÷ Selling price = \$15 ÷ \$60 = 0.25, or 25%

CONCEPT CHECK 15.5

Cost = \$1,800; Selling price = \$3,150
Find the markup percent based on selling price.

Dollar markup = \$3,150 − \$1,800 = \$1,350
Markup percent = \$1,350 ÷ \$3,150 = 0.429, or 42.9%

COMPLETE ASSIGNMENT 15.2.

Chapter Terms for Review

cost
cost of goods sold
dollar markup
markup
markup based on cost
markup based on selling price
markup percent
markup rate
selling price

The Bottom Line

Summary of chapter learning objectives:

Learning Objective	Summary	Example
15.1	Computing the variables in the basic markup formula	Find the missing variables in the basic formula: Selling price = Cost + Dollar markup 1. Cost = $231.50; Dollar markup = 109.12 2. Cost = $35.20; Selling price = $58.95 3. Dollar markup = $475; Selling price = $900
15.2	Computing the markup variables when the markup percent is based on cost	4. Cost = $750; Markup percent = 40% Find dollar markup, and then find selling price. Find 100% + Markup percent, and then find selling price. 5. Selling price = $2,400; Markup percent = 50% Find 100% + Markup percent, and then find cost.
15.3	Computing the markup percent based on cost	6. Cost = $80; Selling price = $108 Find the markup percent based on cost.
15.4	Computing the markup variables when the markup percent is based on selling price	7. Selling price = $820; Markup percent = 25% Find dollar markup, and then find cost. Find 100% − Markup percent, and then find cost. 8. Cost = $1,350; Markup percent = 40% Find 100% − Markup percent, and then find selling price.
15.5	Computing the markup percent based on selling price	9. Cost = $440; Selling price = $800 Find the markup percent based on selling price.

Answers: 1. Selling price = $340.62 **2.** Dollar markup = $23.75 **3.** Cost = $425 **4.** $300, $1,050, 140%; $1,050 **5.** 150%, $1,600 **6.** 35% **7.** $205, $615; 75%, $615 **8.** 60%, $2,250 **9.** 45%

Notes

Assignment 15.1: Markup Based on Cost

Name ______

Date ______ Score ______

A **(12 points) Calculate the missing terms. (2 points for each correct answer)**

	Cost	Dollar Markup	Selling Price
1.	$482.43	$175.25	______
2.	$48.51	______	$69.95
3.	______	$284.11	$529.99
4.	$175.50	$57.50	______
5.	$629.12	______	$909.59
6.	______	$384.75	$784.11

Score for A (12) ______

B **(32 points) In the following problems, the markup percent is based on *cost*. Find the missing terms. (2 points for each correct answer)**

	Cost	Markup Percent	Dollar Markup	Selling Price
7.	$750	30%	______	______
9.	$1,200	80%	______	______
11.	$620	25%	______	______
13.	$2,500	100%	______	______

	Cost	Markup Percent	100% + Markup Percent	Selling Price
8.	$48	75%	______	______
10.	$275	125%	______	______
12.	$824	60%	______	______
14.	$88	120%	______	______

Score for B (32) ______

C (32 points) In the following problems, the markup percent is based on cost. Find the missing terms. Round all percents to the nearest tenth of a percent. (2 points for each correct answer)

	Selling Price	Markup Percent	100% + Markup Percent	Cost
15.	$1,300	30%	________	________
17.	$110	100%	________	________
19.	$860	25%	________	________
21.	$1,050	150%	________	________

	Selling Price	Cost	Dollar Markup	Markup Percent
16.	$24	$20	________	________
18.	$1,922	$1,240	________	________
20.	$675	$388	________	________
22.	$216	$96	________	________

____
Score for C (32)

D (24 points) Business Applications. In the following problems, the markup percent is based on cost. Round all percents to the nearest tenth of a percent. (3 points for each correct answer)

23. Betty Chew owns a firm that sells office furniture to other businesses. One matched set of six pieces costs Betty $2,465. To cover her own business expenses and allow a reasonable profit, Betty marks up this set by 60% of the cost. Find the dollar markup and the selling price.

Dollar markup ________
Selling price ________

24. Jerry Alvarez manufactures a hand-held heart monitoring device. He sells it for $840, which represents a markup of 275% on his production cost. Jerry marks it up this much to cover additional business expenses and profit as well as product development. Find Jerry's production cost and the dollar markup.

Cost ________
Dollar markup ________

25. Rotweiller Security Systems sells burglar and fire alarm systems for homes and small businesses. One basic system costs Rotweiller $380. Rotweiller charges an installation price and also marks up the alarm system by $190. Find the selling price, and find the markup percent based on cost.

Selling price ________
Markup percent ________

26. After Randy Bennett drove his car with no oil, he needed a new engine. Randy's car dealer charged Randy $1,740 for an engine that cost $1,200. The labor was additional. Compute the dollar markup and the markup percent based on cost.

Dollar markup ________
Markup percent ________

____
Score for D (24)

Assignment 15.2: Markup Based on Selling Price

Name ______________________

Date ______________ Score ______________

A (12 points) Calculate the missing terms. (2 points for each correct answer)

	Cost	Dollar Markup	Selling Price
1.	$171.38	$82.15	________
2.	$293.11	________	$452.28
3.	________	$1,356.88	$3,947.00
4.	$789.75	$476.50	________
5.	$62.50	________	$99.99
6.	________	$307.15	$978.95

Score for A (12) ______________

B (32 points) In the following problems, the markup percent is based on selling price. Find the missing terms. (2 points for each correct answer)

	Selling Price	Markup Percent	Dollar Markup	Cost
7.	$64	45%	________	________
9.	$368	60%	________	________
11.	$1,480	35%	________	________
13.	$824	50%	________	________

	Selling Price	Markup Percent	100% − Markup Percent	Cost
8.	$180	25%	________	________
10.	$1,260	20%	________	________
12.	$66	80%	________	________
14.	$926	55%	________	________

Score for B (32) ______________

C (32 points) In the following problems, the markup percent is based on selling price. Find the missing terms. (2 points for each correct answer)

	Cost	Markup Percent	100% − Markup Percent	Selling Price
15.	$400	20%	________	________
17.	$64	75%	________	________
19.	$2,460	40%	________	________
21.	$612	25%	________	________

	Selling Price	Cost	Dollar Markup	Markup Percent
16.	$220	$143	________	________
18.	$45	$27	________	________
20.	$1,480	$518	________	________
22.	$840	$462	________	________

Score for C (32)

D (24 points) Business Applications. In the following problems, the markup percent is based on selling price. Round all percents to the nearest tenth of a percent. (3 points for each correct answer)

23. At the end of winter, Red River Hardware features garden equipment specials. One leaf mulcher has a selling price of $248. The markup to cover expenses and profit is 40% of the selling price. Calculate the dollar markup and the cost.

Dollar markup ________

Cost ________

24. Dave's Two-Wheelers is a retail bicycle store. For last Christmas season, Dave purchased one model of mountain bike to use as a Christmas promotion. The bicycles cost $126 each. For this promotion, Dave's markup was only 20% of selling price. Find Dave's selling price and the dollar markup.

Selling price ________

Dollar markup ________

25. Fine Tune Stereo sells cordless telephones. A two-line model with a speaker phone base and an answering machine is priced at $182.40. This price includes a markup of $109.44. If a phone sells at this price, what are the cost and the markup percent based on selling price?

Cost ________

Markup percent ________

26. Arizona Patio Supply Store purchased a large volume of redwood lounge chairs for $246 each. Upholstered pads were included in the price. To sell the chairs and pads quickly, the store priced the chairs at $328. Compute the dollar markup and the markup percent based on selling price.

Dollar markup ________

Markup percent ________

Score for D (24)

Notes

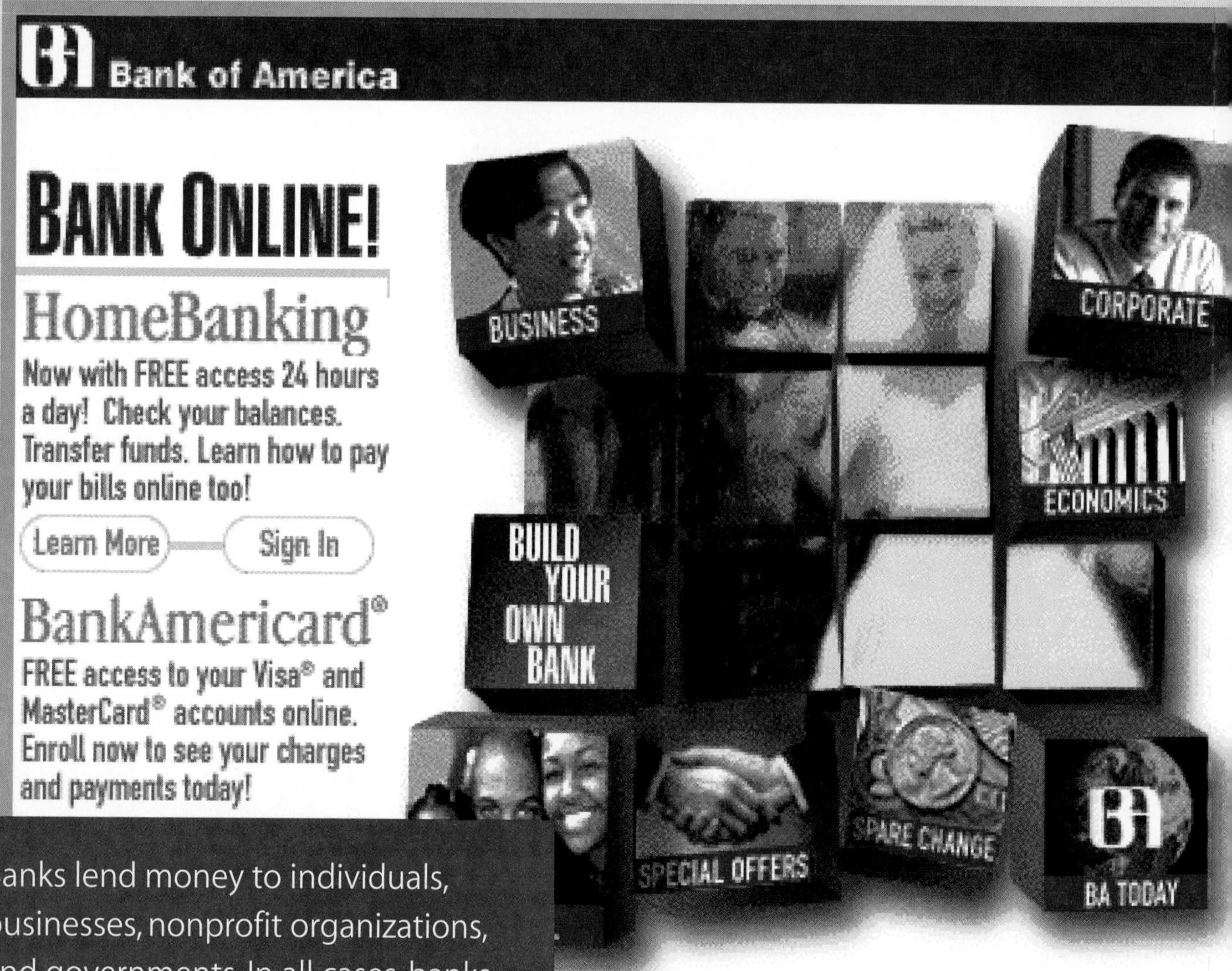

Bank of America
BANK ONLINE!
HomeBanking
Now with FREE access 24 hours a day! Check your balances. Transfer funds. Learn how to pay your bills online too!
Learn More
Sign In
BankAmericard®
FREE access to your Visa® and MasterCard® accounts online. Enroll now to see your charges and payments today!
BUSINESS
CORPORATE
ECONOMICS
BUILD YOUR OWN BANK
SPECIAL OFFERS
SPARE CHANGE
BA TODAY

Banks lend money to individuals, businesses, nonprofit organizations, and governments. In all cases, banks charge interest on these loans. Most of the money that banks lend comes from depositors. To entice customers to deposit their money, banks pay interest. While banks provide many additional services, borrowing and lending are still their primary activities, and interest is always involved in these transactions.

One of the world's leading full-service banks is the **Bank of America.** To learn more about its services, lending processes, and current interest rates, visit the web site at www.bofa.com.

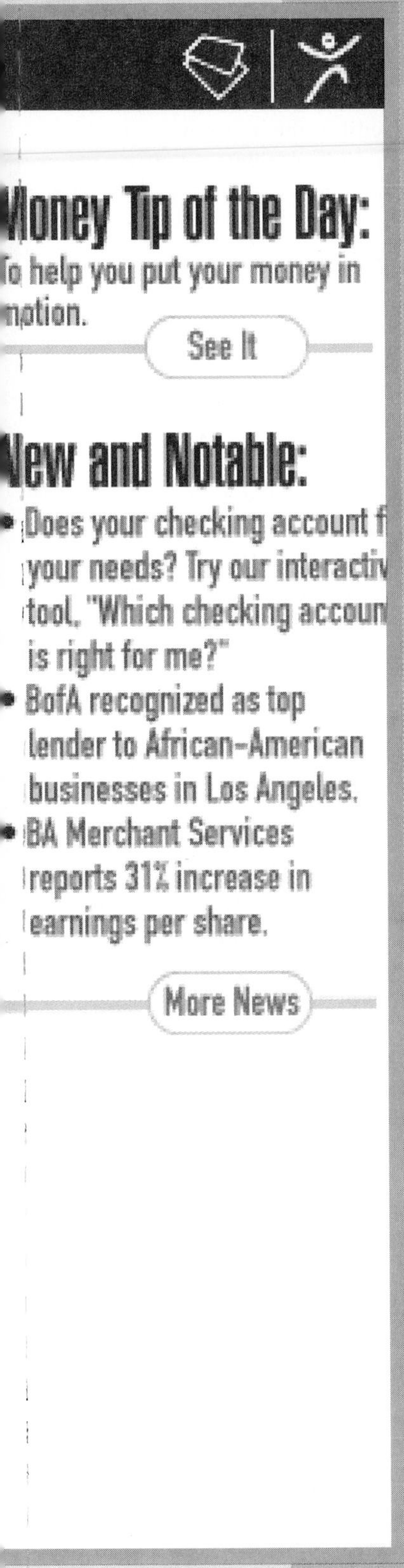

Money Tip of the Day:
To help you put your money in motion.
See It
New and Notable:
Does your checking account fit your needs? Try our interactive tool, "Which checking account is right for me?"
BofA recognized as top lender to African-American businesses in Los Angeles.
BA Merchant Services reports 31% increase in earnings per share.
More News

16 Simple Interest

Learning Objectives

By studying this chapter and completing all the assignments, you will learn to:

1. Compute simple interest with Time in years or months.
2. Compute ordinary simple interest using a 360-day year.
3. Compute exact simple interest using a 365-day year.
4. Compare ordinary simple interest and exact simple interest.
5. Estimate simple interest calculations.

To understand the concept of simple interest, consider the money a bank makes on loaning—or renting—money. The more it can rent, the more it can make. That's the beauty of interest from the lender's standpoint. From the borrower's standpoint, interest is an added cost beyond the money being rented.

Most businesses and individuals buy at least some assets without making full payment at the time of the purchase. The seller gives immediate possession to the buyer, but does not require payment until some later date. For example, large retailers such as Macy's Department Store may receive merchandise for the Christmas season, but not be required to pay the seller until January. The seller, who **extends credit** to the buyer, may or may not charge for this privilege. The charge is called *interest,* and it is usually quoted as a percent of the amount of credit extended (the *principal*). When part of the price is paid at the time of purchase, that part is called a **down payment.**

If the seller charges too much interest or does not extend any credit at all, the buyer might borrow money from a third party such as a bank. A retailer like Macy's could then buy the merchandise and sell it to repay the bank loan. The amount borrowed is called the *principal,* and the interest charged is a percent of the principal. The bank will charge interest between the loan date and the repayment date. This period of time is called the *interest period* or the *term of the loan.*

The promise to repay a loan or pay for merchandise may be oral or written. If it is written, it may be in the form of a letter or it could be one of several special documents known collectively as *commercial paper. Short-term credit* or transactions are those for between one day and one year. *Long-term credit* transactions are those for longer than one year. Normally, long-term credit transactions involve major items such as new buildings or equipment rather than supplies or merchandise for sale.

Computing Simple Interest

Compute simple interest with Time in years or months.

The easiest type of interest to calculate is called *simple interest.* The calculations are the same for both a loan and a purchase on credit. The interest is a percent of the principal for the period of the loan or credit. The quoted percent usually is an **annual** (yearly) rate. A rate of 10% means that the interest payment for one year will be 10% of the principal.

To compute the simple interest on a one-year loan, simply multiply the Principal by the Rate.

EXAMPLE A

Della Jacobs borrows \$1,200 for 1 year at a rate of 10% simple interest. Compute the interest.

The principal is \$1,200. The interest for 1 year is 10% of \$1,200, or $0.10 \times \$1{,}200 = \$120$.

Most loans, however, are not for a period of exactly 1 year. Loans for longer periods will require the borrower to pay more interest. Likewise, loans for shorter periods will earn less interest. To compute the simple interest on loans of any period, multiply the Principal by the Rate and then multiply by the Time, with Time stated in years or in fractions of years. Therefore, the fundamental formula for simple interest is

> Interest = Principal × Rate × Time
> abbreviated as $I = P \times R \times T$ or, even more simply, $I = PRT$.

EXAMPLE B

Find the simple interest on loans of \$1,000 when the rate is 8% and the loan periods are $\frac{1}{2}$ year and 3 years.

$\frac{1}{2}$ year	**3 years**
$I = P \times R \times T$	$I = P \times R \times T$
$= \$1{,}000 \times 0.08 \times \frac{1}{2}$	$= \$1{,}000 \times 0.08 \times 3$
$= \$40$	$= \$240$

The time period often will be measured in months instead of years. Before computing the interest, change the time into years by dividing the number of months by 12 (the number of months in one year).

EXAMPLE C

Compute the interest on credit purchases of $2,000 at 10% for periods of 9 months and 18 months.

9 months	**18 months**
$I = P \times R \times T$	$I = P \times R \times T$
$= \$2{,}000 \times 0.10 \times \frac{9}{12}$	$= \$2{,}000 \times 0.10 \times \frac{18}{12}$
$= \$150$	$= \$300$

CONCEPT CHECK 16.1

The Principal is $1,500, the Rate is 6%, and Interest = Principal × Rate × Time, or $I = P \times R \times T$. Find the interest both for 4 years and for 4 months.

a. If Time is 4 years: $I = P \times R \times T = \$1{,}500 \times 0.06 \times 4 = \$360$
b. If Time is 4 months: $I = P \times R \times T = \$1{,}500 \times 0.06 \times \frac{4}{12} = \$30$

Computing Ordinary Interest

If the term of the loan is stated as a certain number of days, computing interest involves dividing the number of days by the number of days in one year—either 360 or 365. Before computers and calculators, interest was easier to compute by assuming that every year had 360 days and that every month had 30 days. The 360-day method, called the *ordinary interest method,* is still used by many businesses and individuals.

LEARNING OBJECTIVES 2

Compute ordinary simple interest using a 360-day year.

EXAMPLE D

Compute the ordinary interest on $800 at 9% for 90 days.

$$I = P \times R \times T$$
$$= \$800 \times 0.09 \times \frac{90}{360}$$
$$= \$18$$

CONCEPT CHECK 16.2

The Principal is $3,000, the Rate is 7%, and the Time is 180 days. Compute the ordinary simple interest.

Ordinary interest uses a 360-day year: $I = P \times R \times T = \$3{,}000 \times 0.07 \times \frac{180}{360} = \$105.00$

Computing Exact Interest

Compute exact simple interest using a 365-day year.

Banks, savings and loan institutions, credit unions, and the federal government use a 365-day year (366 days for leap years) to compute interest. This method is called the *exact interest method.* The calculations are the same, except 365 days is used instead of 360 days.

EXAMPLE E

Compute the exact interest on \$800 at 9% for 90 days.

$$I = P \times R \times T$$
$$= \$800 \times 0.09 \times \frac{90}{365}$$
$$= \$17.7534, \text{or } \$17.75$$

CONCEPT CHECK 16.3

The Principal is \$2,400, the Rate is 8%, and the Time is 30 days. Compute the exact simple interest.

Exact interest uses a 365-day year: $I = P \times R \times T = \$2{,}400 \times 0.08 \times \frac{30}{365} = \$15.78$

Comparing Ordinary Interest and Exact Interest

Compare ordinary simple interest and exact simple interest.

Since the 360-day year was very useful before the age of calculators, there is a long tradition of using it. However, the 365-day year is more realistic than the 360-day year. Also, the 365-day year is financially better for the borrower, because the interest amounts are always smaller. (Why? Because a denominator of 365 gives a smaller quotient than a denominator of 360).

Re-examine examples D and E above. The difference between ordinary interest and exact interest is only \$18.00 − \$17.75, or \$0.25. When businesses borrow money, however, the principal may be very large and then the difference will be more significant. Example F is similar to examples D and E, except the principal is in millions of dollars rather than hundreds.

EXAMPLE F

Find the difference between ordinary interest and exact interest on \$8,000,000 at 9% for 90 days.

Ordinary Interest

$$I = P \times R \times T$$
$$= \$8{,}000{,}000 \times 0.09 \times \frac{90}{360}$$
$$= \$180{,}000$$

Exact Interest

$$I = P \times R \times T$$
$$= \$8{,}000{,}000 \times 0.09 \times \frac{90}{365}$$
$$= \$177{,}534.2466, \text{or } \$177{,}534.25$$

The difference is \$180,000 − \$177,534.25, or \$2,465.75.

CONCEPT CHECK 16.4

The Principal is \$6,000, the Rate is 12%, and the Time is 120 days. Find the difference between the amounts of simple interest calculated using the ordinary method (360-day year) and the exact method (365-day year).

Ordinary interest: $I = P \times R \times T = \$6{,}000 \times 0.12 \times \frac{120}{360} = \$240.00$

Exact interest: $I = P \times R \times T = \$6{,}000 \times 0.12 \times \frac{120}{365} = \$236.71$

Difference = Ordinary interest − Exact interest = \$240.00 − \$236.71 = \$3.29

Use of Calculators

Today, calculators or computers are used in almost every interest application. The numbers are often large and are always important. The steps are performed on the calculator in the same order as they are written in the formula.

EXAMPLE G

Write the calculator steps to compute the exact interest on \$8,000,000 at 9% for 90 days.

$$I = P \times R \times T = \$8{,}000{,}000 \times 0.09 \times \frac{90}{365}$$

8 000 000 [×] .09 [×] 90 [÷] 365

[=] 177 534.2466, or \$177,534.25

With the percent key [%], the steps would be

8 000 000 [×] 9 [%] [×] 90 [÷] 365 [=] 177 534.2466, or \$177,534.25

Estimating Simple Interest

LEARNING OBJECTIVES 5

Estimate simple interest calculations.

Although calculators are used to compute interest, approximation remains as useful as ever. The following calculator solution requires a minimum of 19 key entries.

8 000 000 [×] .09 [×] 90 [÷] 365 [=] 177 534.2466

If any one of the 19 keys is pressed incorrectly, there will be a large error. By making an estimate of the interest in advance, you may spot a significant calculator error.

Combinations of Time and Interest That Yield 1%

To make simple mental approximations, you can round the rate and time to numbers that are easy to compute mentally. For ordinary interest, several combinations of rate and time are easy to use because their product is 1%. For example, $12\% \times \frac{30}{360} = 12\% \times \frac{1}{12} = 1\%$ and $6\% \times \frac{60}{360} = 6\% \times \frac{1}{6} = 1\%$.

EXAMPLE H

Approximate the ordinary interest on \$1,500 at 6.25% for 59 days.

Round 6.25% to 6% and 59 days to 60 days.

Estimate: $\$1{,}500 \times 0.06 \times \frac{60}{360} = \$1{,}500 \times 0.01 = \$15$

Actual interest: $\$1{,}500 \times 0.0625 \times \frac{59}{360} = \$15.3646$, or \$15.36

Other Rates and Times

Table 16-1 shows several combinations of rate and time whose products are useful for estimating interest.

Table 16-1: Rate and Time

$6\% \times \frac{60}{360} = 6\% \times \frac{1}{6} = 1\%$	$10\% \times \frac{36}{360} = 10\% \times \frac{1}{10} = 1\%$
$8\% \times \frac{45}{360} = 8\% \times \frac{1}{8} = 1\%$	$12\% \times \frac{30}{360} = 12\% \times \frac{1}{12} = 1\%$
$9\% \times \frac{40}{360} = 9\% \times \frac{1}{9} = 1\%$	$18\% \times \frac{20}{360} = 18\% \times \frac{1}{18} = 1\%$
$12\% \times \frac{60}{360} = 12\% \times \frac{1}{6} = 2\%$	$12\% \times \frac{90}{360} = 12\% \times \frac{1}{4} = 3\%$
$8\% \times \frac{90}{360} = 8\% \times \frac{1}{4} = 2\%$	$9\% \times \frac{120}{360} = 9\% \times \frac{1}{3} = 3\%$

Estimation of Exact Interest

The goal in approximating interest is just to get an estimate. Even though exact interest requires 365 days in a year, you can make a reasonable estimate by assuming that the number of days in a year is 360.

EXAMPLE I

Compute the estimate and exact interest on \$1,200 at 11.8% for 62 days.

First, round 11.8% to 12% and 62 days to 60 days.
Second, assume that a year has 360 days.

Estimate: $\$1{,}200 \times 0.12 \times \frac{60}{360} = \$1{,}200 \times 0.02 = \$24$

Actual interest: $\$1{,}200 \times 0.118 \times \frac{62}{365} = \$24.0526$, or \$24.05

CONCEPT CHECK 16.5

The Principal is \$3,650, the Rate is 11.7%, and the Time is 31 days. Calculate the actual exact simple interest. Then, make an estimate by using a 360-day year and simpler values for *R* and *T*. Compare the results.

Actual value: $I = P \times R \times T = \$3{,}650 \times 0.117 \times \frac{31}{365} = \$36.27$

Estimate: $I = P \times R \times T = \$3{,}650 \times 0.12 \times \frac{30}{360} = \$3{,}650 \times 0.01 = \$36.50$

Difference: Estimate − Actual = \$36.50 − \$36.27 = \$0.23

COMPLETE ASSIGNMENTS 16.1 AND 16.2.

Chapter Terms for Review

commercial paper
exact interest method
interest
interest period
long-term credit
ordinary interest method
principal
short-term credit
simple interest
term of the loan
time

The **Bottom** Line

Summary of chapter learning objectives:

Learning Objective	Summary	Example
16.1	Computing simple interest with Time in years or months	Find the simple interest using the basic formula: **Interest = Principal × Rate × Time**, or $I = P \times R \times T$. 1. Principal = \$2,500; Rate = 9%; Time = 1.5 years 2. Principal = \$975; Rate = 8%; Time = 9 months
16.2	Computing ordinary simple interest using a 360-day year	3. Find the ordinary simple interest using a 360-day year: Principal = \$3,250; Rate = 10%; Time = 90 days
16.3	Computing exact simple interest using a 365-day year	4. Find the exact simple interest using a 365-day year: Principal = \$1,800; Rate = 11%; Time = 45 days
16.4	Comparing ordinary and exact simple interest	5. Find the difference between ordinary simple interest and exact simple interest: Principal = \$5,000; Rate = 6%; Time = 75 days
16.5	Estimating simple interest calculations	6. Estimate the exact interest using a 360-day year and simpler values for rate and time: Principal = \$2,100; Rate = 5.8%; Time = 62 days

Answers: 1. \$337.50 **2.** \$58.50 **3.** \$81.25 **4.** \$24.41 **5.** \$62.50 − \$61.64 = \$0.86 **6.** $\$2,100 \times 0.06 \times \frac{60}{360} = \$21$

Notes

Assignment 16.1: Simple Interest

Name ______________________

Date ______________ Score ______________

A (20 points) Compute the simple interest. If the time is given in months, let one month be $\frac{1}{12}$ of a year. If the time is in days, let one year be 360 days. (2 points for each correct answer)

	Principal	Rate	Time	Interest		Principal	Rate	Time	Interest
1.	$400	7.0%	1 year	________	**2.**	$2,000	8%	4 years	________
3.	$640	9%	3 months	________	**4.**	$960	4%	15 months	________
5.	$8,250	6%	$\frac{1}{2}$ year	________	**6.**	$3,600	12%	30 months	________
7.	$12,800	7%	2.5 years	________	**8.**	$750	3%	6 years	________
9.	$4,860	10%	21 months	________	**10.**	$24,000	5.5%	4 months	________

________ Score for A (20)

B (40 points) Compute the ordinary interest, the exact interest, and their difference. Round answers to the nearest cent. (2 points for each correct interest; 1 point for each correct difference)

	Principal	Rate	Time	Ordinary Interest	Exact Interest	Difference
11.	$780	9%	90 days	______	______	______
12.	$2,350	6%	150 days	______	______	______
13.	$85	12%	270 days	______	______	______
14.	$12,400	7%	225 days	______	______	______
15.	$985	10%	180 days	______	______	______
16.	$1,400	15%	60 days	______	______	______
17.	$20,000	11%	300 days	______	______	______
18.	$365	4%	30 days	______	______	______

______

Score for B (40)

C (40 points) In each problem, make an estimate of the interest. Assume a 360-day year, and round each rate and time to the nearest numbers that will permit the shortcuts in Table 16-1. Then find the actual interest (ordinary interest in Problems 19–22, exact interest in Problems 23–26) and find the difference. If the estimate is larger than the actual interest, write a "+" in front of the difference; if the estimate is smaller than the actual interest, write a "−" in front of the difference. Round answers to the nearest cent. (2 points for each correct estimate and actual interest; 1 point for each correct difference)

	Principal	Rate	Time	Estimate	Actual Interest	Difference
	Ordinary Interest					
19.	$850	6%	60 days	______	______	______
20.	$1,300	11.8%	91 days	______	______	______
21.	$700	8.25%	88 days	______	______	______
22.	$2,500	12.1%	31 days	______	______	______

Principal	Rate	Time	Estimate	Actual Interest	Difference
Exact Interest					
23. $625	8.1%	44 days	________	________	________
24. $900	11.9%	62 days	________	________	________
25. $2,000	8.95%	123 days	________	________	________
26. $10,000	6%	60 days	________	________	________

____
Score for C (40)

Assignment 16.2: Simple Interest Applications

Name ______________________

Date ______________ Score ______________

A (50 points) Solve each of the following ordinary simple interest problems using a 360-day year. Find both the interest dollars and the total amount (i.e., principal plus interest) of the loan. (7 points for each correct interest; 3 points for each correct amount)

1. Tom Titus plans to lend $750 to his friend Bill White so that Bill can fly with him to Canada for vacation. Tom is charging Bill only 4% ordinary simple interest. Bill repays everything, interest plus principal, to Tom 90 days later. How much does Bill pay?

Interest ________

Amount ________

2. Francis Koo is planning to start a business that will export American foods to China. He estimates that he will need $50,000 to pay for organizational costs, get product samples, and make three trips to Shanghai. He can borrow the money from his relatives for 3 years. Since they are his relatives, he is willing to pay them 10% ordinary simple interest. Compute the amount that Francis will owe them in 3 years.

Interest ________

Amount ________

3. Carolyn Wilfert owns a temporary services employment agency. Businesses call her when they need to hire various types of workers for a short period of time. The businesses pay a fee to Carolyn, who pays the salaries and benefits to the employees. One benefit is that Carolyn will make small, short-term loans to her employees. After a flood, an employee named Judy Hillstrom needed to borrow $3,600 to have her house cleaned and repainted. Judy repaid the loan in 6 months. If Carolyn charged 5% ordinary simple interest, how much did Judy repay?

Interest ________

Amount ________

4. Several years ago, Ed Velure and Lee Oman formed a partnership to rent musical instruments to school districts that do not want to own and maintain the instruments. In the spring, they investigate borrowing $50,000 to buy trumpets and trombones. Since they collect their rental fees in advance, they anticipate being able to repay the loan in 105 days. How much will they need to repay if the ordinary simple interest rate is 9.5%?

Interest ________

Amount ________

5. With her husband, Ruby Williams owns and manages a video game arcade. A manufacturer developed a new line of games and offered very low interest financing to encourage arcade operators like Ruby to install the new games. Ruby was able to finance $75,000 worth of games for 8 months for 3.2% ordinary simple interest. Calculate how much Ruby will repay.

Interest ________

Amount ________

____

Score for A (50)

B (50 points) Solve each of the following exact simple interest problems using a 365-day year. Find both the interest dollars and the total amount (i.e., principal plus interest) of the loan. (7 points for each correct interest; 3 points for each correct amount)

6. Charles Peterson, managing partner of a local transportation company, thinks that the company should borrow money to upgrade its truck repair facility. After investigating several sources of short-term loans, Charles determines that the company can borrow $250,000 for 180 days at 7.5% exact simple interest. If the company agrees to this loan, how much will it need to repay at the end of the 180 days?

Interest ________

Amount ________

7. Claudia Ortega is a former teacher who now has a business that sells educational materials such as books and computer software to parents and schools. In June, she borrowed $25,000 from her bank to buy some new educational computer games that she hopes to sell during August and September. The bank's rate is 8.25% exact simple interest as long as the time does not exceed half a year. If Claudia repays everything in 100 days, how much will she pay?

Interest ________

Amount ________

8. After working in construction for five years, Gale Holfert had saved almost enough money to buy a fishing boat and move to Alaska to become a commercial fisherman. He still needed $15,000, which his wife could borrow from her parents until the end of the first fishing season. The parents charged 6% exact simple interest, and Gale repaid them after 175 days. How much interest did he pay, and what was the total amount?

Interest ________

Amount ________

9. Bill and Carol Campbell need to purchase two new saws for their retail lumber yard. The company that sells the saws offers them some short-term financing at the relatively high rate of 11% exact simple interest. They decide to accept the financing offer, but only for $5,000 and only for 45 days. How much will Bill and Carol repay at the end of the 45 days?

Interest ________

Amount ________

10. After working for a large accounting firm for ten years, Jackie Wong, C.P.A., decided to open her own office. She borrowed $30,000 at 8% exact simple interest. She made enough during the first income tax season to repay the loan in 150 days. How much did Jackie repay?

Interest ________

Amount ________

____

Score for B (50)

Notes

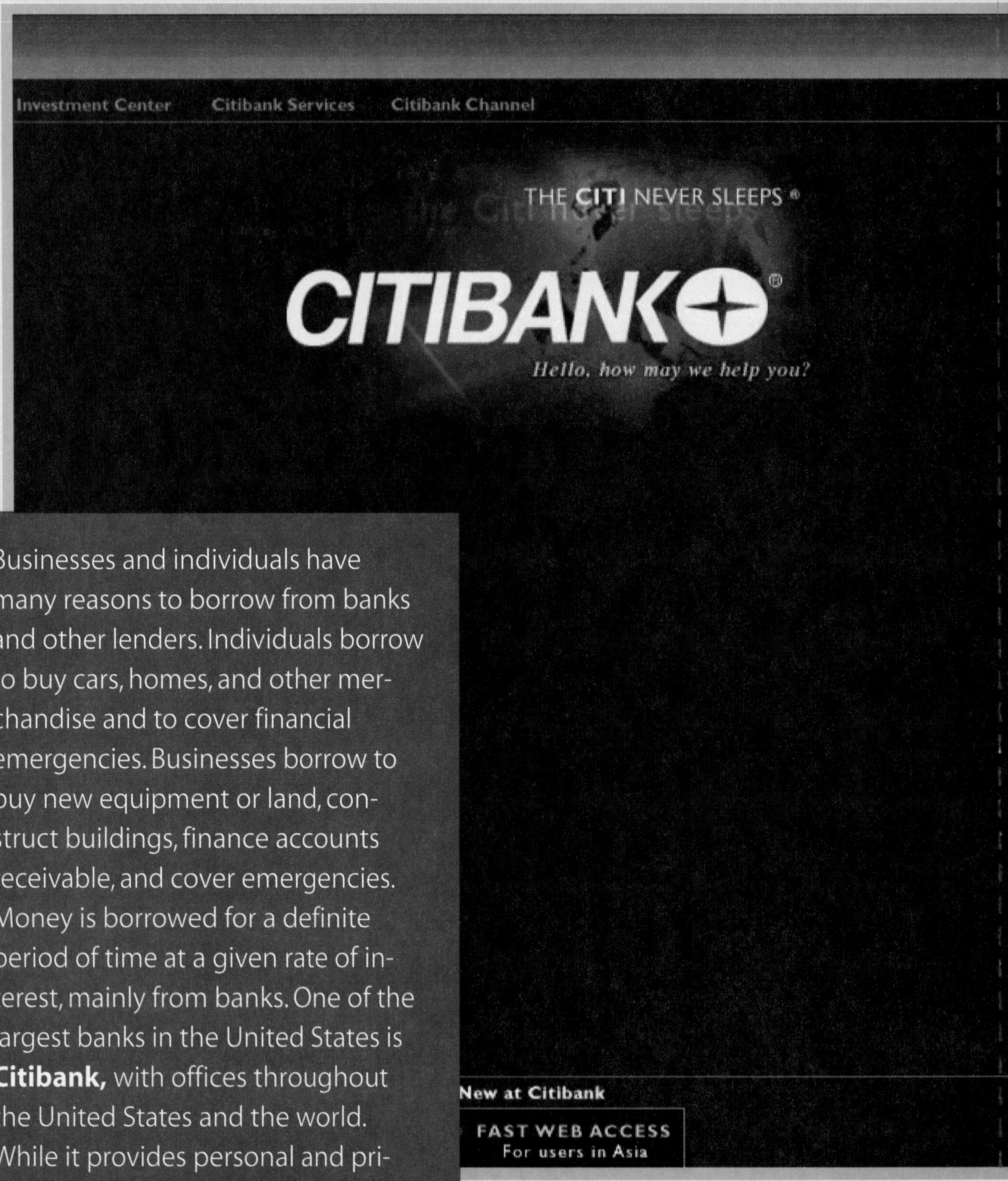

Businesses and individuals have many reasons to borrow from banks and other lenders. Individuals borrow to buy cars, homes, and other merchandise and to cover financial emergencies. Businesses borrow to buy new equipment or land, construct buildings, finance accounts receivable, and cover emergencies. Money is borrowed for a definite period of time at a given rate of interest, mainly from banks. One of the largest banks in the United States is **Citibank,** with offices throughout the United States and the world. While it provides personal and private banking for individuals and corporate banking for large and small corporations, it specializes in business and professional banking services. For a look at Citibank's services, visit www.citibank.com.

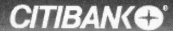

17 Notes and Interest Variables

Learning Objectives

By studying this chapter and completing all the assignments, you will learn to:

1. Calculate the number of interest days of a note.
2. Determine the due date of a promissory note.
3. Compute the maturity value of a promissory note.
4. Compute the Principal, Rate, and Time from the basic interest formula.

Businesses often take out short-term loans by signing promissory notes. How much does it cost to borrow money for various lengths of time? Whether you own a business or work for one, you'll have to know how to compute interest on a promissory note to make good decisions about financing.

Businesses use many different methods and documents to charge interest. One of the fundamental documents is the *promissory note,* which is an unconditional promise made in writing by one party to another. The maker of the promise agrees to pay on demand—or at a particular time—a certain sum of money to the bearer. It is called a *negotiable promissory note* when it may be sold to a third party.

The dollar amount written on the note is called the *face value* of the note. The face value is the same as the *principal (P),* or amount borrowed. Promissory notes may be either interest-bearing or non-interest-bearing. If a note is interest-bearing, the sum of the face value and the *interest dollars (I)* is the *maturity value (MV).* It is the total amount that must be paid by the borrower when the note becomes due. The date when a note is due is called the *due date* or *maturity date.* Figure 17-1 is an illustration of a simple promissory note.

Figure 17-1: Promissory Note

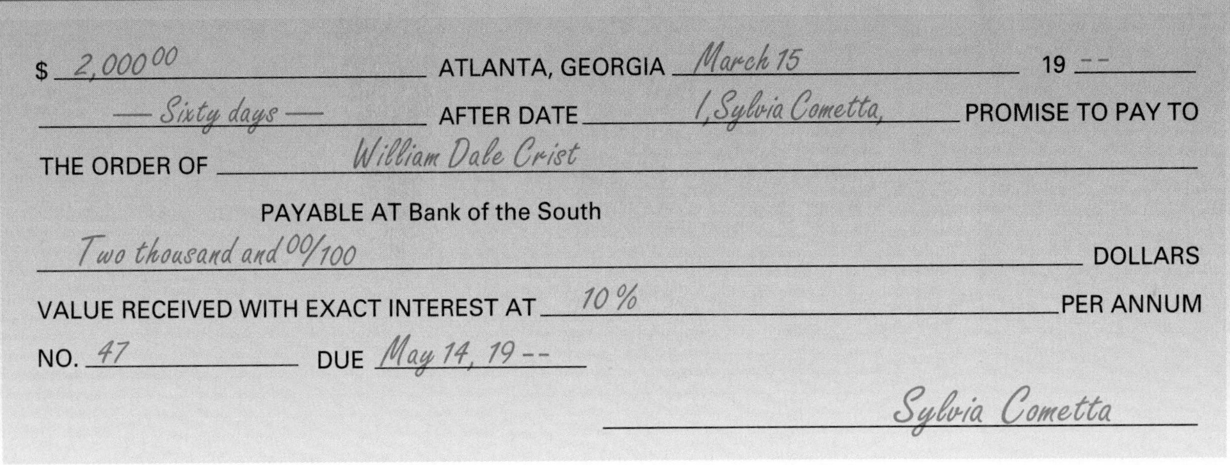
$ 2,000 00 ATLANTA, GEORGIA March 15 19 --

— Sixty days — AFTER DATE I, Sylvia Cometta, PROMISE TO PAY TO

THE ORDER OF William Dale Crist

PAYABLE AT Bank of the South

Two thousand and 00/100 DOLLARS

VALUE RECEIVED WITH EXACT INTEREST AT 10 % PER ANNUM

NO. 47 DUE May 14, 19 --

Sylvia Cometta

Calculating the Number of Interest Days of a Note

LEARNING 1 OBJECTIVES

Calculate the number of interest days of a note.

To define the *interest period,* or *term,* of a promissory note, the lender either specifies the due date of the note or states the number of interest days. When the due date is given, you must calculate the number of interest days before you can compute the interest charge.

You need the number of days in each month, as shown in Table 17-1. February has 29 days in leap years. A leap year is any year that is evenly divisible by 4, except for years ending in 00, like 1900 and 2000. In order to be leap years, such years must be evenly divisible by 400; 2000 is a leap year, but 1900 was not.

STEPS to Compute the Number of Interest Days Between Two Dates

1. Determine the number of interest days in the beginning month.
2. Determine the number of interest days in the middle months.
3. Add the numbers from Steps 1 and 2 to the number of interest days in the final month. (For the final month, the number of interest days is equal to the number of the due date.)

EXAMPLE A

A promissory note is made on July 25. The due date is October 8. Determine the number of interest days between July 25 and October 8

Table 17-1: Days in Each Month (non–leap years)

Month	Number of Days	Month	Number of Days	Month	Number of Days
January	31 days	May	31 days	September	30 days
February	28 days	June	30 days	October	31 days
March	31 days	July	31 days	November	30 days
April	30 days	August	31 days	December	31 days

STEP 1

31 days in July
−25 days of note
6 days of interest in July

STEP 2

August has 31 days
September has 30 days

STEP 3

6 days in July
31 days in August
30 days in September
+8 days in October
75 total interest days in the promissory note

CONCEPT CHECK 17.1

A promissory note is dated October 20. The maturity date (due date) is February 20. Determine the number of interest days.

Since October has 31 days and the note is dated October 20, there are 31 − 20 = 11 days of interest in October. Since the note is due on February 20, there are 20 interest days in February. The total can be expressed as

October		November		December		January		February		Total Interest Days
11	+	30	+	31	+	31	+	20	=	123

Determining the Due Date of a Note

When the promissory note explicitly states the number of interest days, then you must determine the due date. The procedure is somewhat the reverse of finding the number of interest days.

LEARNING OBJECTIVES 2

Determine the due date of a promissory note.

STEPS to Determine the Due Date

1. Determine the number of interest days in the beginning month.
2. Determine the number of interest days that remain after the first month.
3. Determine the number of interest days remaining at the end of each succeeding month by subtracting. Continue subtracting until less than one month remains. The due date is the number of interest days remaining in the final month.

EXAMPLE B

A promissory note is made on July 25. The note is for 75 days. Determine the due date.

STEP 1

31	days in July
−25	days of note
6	days of interest in July

STEP 2

75	days of interest in the note
−6	days of interest in July
69	days left in term after end of July

STEP 3

69	days of interest left after July
−31	days in August
38	days of interest left after August
−30	days in September
8	days of interest left after end of September, or 8 days of interest in October

The due date is October 8.

Although the procedure looks somewhat cumbersome on paper, it goes very quickly on a calculator. You can subtract repeatedly to deduct the days of each month, and after each subtraction, the calculator will display the number of interest days remaining. You do not need to write down all of the intermediate results.

When the length of the interest period is expressed in months, the date is advanced by the number of months given. The due date is the same day of the month as the date of the note. For example, a 3-month note dated July 3 will be due on September 3. The exact number of interest days must then be computed, as shown previously. If the note is dated the 31st of a month and the month of maturity is April, June, September, or November, then the due date is the 30th. If the month of maturity is February, the due date is the 28th (or 29th in a leap year).

EXAMPLE C

Find the due date of a 3-month note dated January 31 (the last day of the month).

Maturity month:	April (count "February, March, April")
Last day:	30 (last day of April)
	Therefore, the due date is April 30

CONCEPT CHECK 17.2

a. A 90-day promissory note is dated February 5 in a non–leap year. Determine the due date. Since February has 28 days, the note has 28 − 5 = 23 days of interest in February.

Total Interest Days		February		March		April
90	−	23	−	31	−	30
	=	67	=	36	=	6 days remaining after April.

The due date is May 6.

b. A 4-month promissory note is dated April 30. Determine the due date.

Four months after April 30 is August 30. The due date is August 30.

Computing the Maturity Value of a Note

LEARNING OBJECTIVES 3

Compute the maturity value of a promissory note.

The maturity value (*MV*) of a promissory note is the sum of the face value (principal) of the note and the interest:

Maturity value = Principal + Interest, or, briefly, $MV = P + I$

EXAMPLE D

Compute the maturity value of the interest-bearing promissory note illustrated in Figure 17-1.

The face value (P) of the note is \$2,000. The interest rate (R) is 10% exact interest per year. The loan period of the note is 60 days, so the time in years (T) is $\frac{60}{365}$.

$$I = P \times R \times T = \$2{,}000 \times 0.10 \times \frac{60}{365} = \$32.88$$

$$MV = P + I = \$2{,}000 + \$32.88 = \$2{,}032.88$$

CONCEPT CHECK 17.3

A 90-day promissory note has a face value of \$2,800 and an exact simple interest rate of 7.5%. Compute the maturity value.

$$I = P \times R \times T = \$2{,}800 \times 0.075 \times \frac{90}{365} = \$51.78 \qquad MV = P + I = \$2{,}800 + \$51.78 = \$2{,}851.78$$

Computing the Interest Variables

Every simple interest problem has four variables: Interest, Principal, Rate, and Time. In Chapter 16, we solved for the amount of Interest (I) when the Principal (P), Rate (R), and Time (T) were all given. However, as long as any three variables are given, the fourth always can be computed by just changing the formula $I = P \times R \times T$ into one of its possible variations, shown in Table 17-2.

LEARNING OBJECTIVES 4

Compute the Principal, Rate, and Time from the basic interest formula.

Table 17-2: *PRT* formulas

To find	You must know	Use this formula
I	P, R, and T	$I = P \times R \times T$
P	I, R, and T	$P = \frac{I}{(R \times T)}$
R	I, P, and T	$R = \frac{I}{(P \times T)}$
T	I, P, and R	$T = \frac{I}{(P \times R)}$

You should assume the use of ordinary interest (a 360-day year) unless the use of exact interest (a 365-day year) is indicated. The stated or computed interest rate is the rate for one full year. Also, the length of time used for computing interest dollars must be stated in terms of all or part of a year.

Finding the Interest Amount, Principal, Rate, or Time

When any three variables are known, you can solve for the fourth variable, using a formula from Table 17-2.

EXAMPLE E

Find the Principal if the Interest is \$45, the Rate is 9%, and the Time is 60 days.

$P = ?;\quad I = \$45;\quad R = 9\%;\quad T = \frac{60}{360}$ year

$$P = \frac{I}{(R \times T)} = \frac{\$45}{\left(0.09 \times \frac{60}{360}\right)} = \frac{\$45}{0.015} = \$3{,}000$$

EXAMPLE F

Find the Rate if the Interest is \$22, the Principal is \$2,000, and the Time is 30 days.

$R = ?;\quad I = \$22;\quad P = \$2{,}000;\quad T = \frac{30}{360}$ year

$$R = \frac{I}{(P \times T)} = \frac{\$22}{\left(\$2{,}000 \times \frac{30}{360}\right)} = \frac{\$22}{\$166.67} = 0.132, \text{ or } 13.2\%$$

EXAMPLE G

Find the Time if the Interest is \$54, the Principal is \$1,800, and the Rate is 12%. Express Time in days, based on a 360-day year.

$T = ?;\quad I = \$54;\quad P = \$1{,}800;\quad R = 12\%$

$$T = \frac{I}{(P \times R)} = \frac{\$54}{(\$1{,}800 \times 0.12)} = \frac{\$54}{\$216} = 0.25 \text{ year}$$

Based on a 360-day year, 0.25 year = 0.25 × 360 days = 90 days.

CONCEPT CHECK 17.4

Each of the following problems gives three of the four variables. Find the missing variable. All rates are ordinary simple interest (360-day year). Round *P* and *I* to the nearest cent; round *R* to the nearest $\frac{1}{10}\%$; round *T* to the nearest whole day, assuming that one year has 360 days. Use one of the four formulas:

$$I = P \times R \times T \qquad P = \frac{I}{(R \times T)} \qquad R = \frac{I}{(P \times T)} \qquad T = \frac{I}{(P \times R)}$$

a. Principal = \$840; Rate = 8%; Time = 120 days
Find Interest:

$$I = P \times R \times T = \$840 \times 0.08 \times \frac{120}{360} = \$22.40$$

c. Principal = \$1,280; Interest = \$64; Rate = 10%
Find Time:

$$T = \frac{I}{(P \times R)} = \frac{\$64}{(\$1{,}280 \times 0.10)} = 0.5 \text{ year}$$

In a 360-day year, *T* = 0.5 year = 0.5 × 360 days = 180 days.

b. Principal = \$8,000; Interest = \$50; Time = 45 days
Find Rate:

$$R = \frac{I}{(P \times T)} = \frac{\$50}{\left(\$8{,}000 \times \frac{45}{360}\right)} = 0.05, \text{ or } 5\%$$

d. Interest = \$90; Rate = 12%; Time = 75 days
Find Principal:

$$P = \frac{I}{(R \times T)} = \frac{\$90}{\left(0.12 \times \frac{75}{360}\right)} = \$3{,}600$$

COMPLETE ASSIGNMENTS 17.1 AND 17.2.

Chapter Terms for Review

due date
face value
interest dollars (I)
interest period
maturity date
maturity value (MV)
negotiable promissory note
principal (P)
promissory note
term of note

The Bottom Line

Summary of chapter learning objectives:

Learning Objective	Summary	Example
17.1	Calculating the number of interest days of a note	1. Find the number of days between December 20 and February 25.
17.2	Determining the due date of a promissory note	2. Find the due date of a 60-day note written on April 20.
17.3	Computing the maturity value of a promissory note	3. Find the maturity value of a 75-day promissory note with a face value of \$8,100 and an exact interest rate of 11%.
17.4	Computing the Principal, Rate, and Time from the basic interest formula	Solve for Principal, Rate, and Time using a 360-day year and the following formulas: $P = \frac{I}{(R \times T)}$ $R = \frac{I}{(P \times T)}$ $T = \frac{I}{(P \times R)}$ 4. Interest = \$42; Rate = 6%; Time = 105 days 5. Principal = \$1,600; Interest = \$30; Time = 75 days 6. Principal = \$7,200; Interest = \$135; Rate = 15%

Answers: 1. 67 days **2.** June 19 **3.** \$8,283.08 **4.** \$2,400 **5.** 0.09, or 9% **6.** 45 days

Notes

Assignment 17.1: Dates, Times, and Interest

Name

Date Score

A (20 points) Problems 1–5: Find the number of interest days. Problems 6–10: Find the due date. Be sure to check for leap years. (2 points for each correct answer)

Date of Note	Due Date	Days of Interest
1. August 31, 1999	December 7, 1999	________
2. June 15, 1999	September 15, 1999	________
3. March 6, 2000	September 11, 2000	________
4. December 8, 2000	April 9, 2001	________
5. January 9, 2001	May 15, 2001	________

Date of Note	Interest Days	Due Date
6. July 16, 1999	180 days	________
7. December 3, 1999	90 days	________
8. January 28, 2000	45 days	________
9. August 24, 2001	75 days	________
10. December 31, 2001	2 months	________

____

Score for A (20)

B **(48 points) For each of the following promissory notes, find the missing entry for days of interest or maturity date (due date). Then compute the amount of interest due at maturity and the maturity value. For problems 11–14, use a 360-day year. For problems 15–18, use a 365-day year and consider leap years if necessary. (2 points for each correct answer)**

	Face Value	Date of Note	Days of Interest	Maturity Date	Rate	Interest	Maturity Value
360-day year							
11.	$8,000	Oct. 5, 1999	90	________	6%	________	________
12.	$960	Mar. 30, 2000	_____	July 10, 2000	8%	________	________
13.	$24,000	Sept. 8, 2000	75	________	7%	________	________
14.	$1,180	April 10, 2000	_____	Aug. 23, 2000	10%	________	________
365-day year							
15.	$845	July 15, 1999	_____	Oct. 28, 1999	9%	________	________
16.	$16,400	Jan. 24, 2001	65	________	5.1%	________	________
17.	$9,250	Feb. 9, 2001	_____	Aug. 28, 2001	8.4%	________	________
18.	$3,200	Nov. 5, 2002	125	________	6.5%	________	________

____

Score for B (48)

C (32 points) Determine the missing variable by using one of the following formulas:

$$I = P \times R \times T \qquad P = \frac{I}{(R \times T)} \qquad R = \frac{I}{(P \times T)} \qquad T = \frac{I}{(P \times R)}$$

For problems 19–26, use a 360-day year. For problems 27–34, use a 365-day year. Round dollar amounts to the nearest cent. Round interest rates to the nearest $\frac{1}{10}$ of a percent. Find the time in days, rounded to the nearest whole day. (2 points for each correct answer)

	Principal	Rate	Time	Interest
	360-day year			
19.	$6,000	6%	180 days	________
20.	$840	________	75 days	$14.00
21.	________	11%	120 days	$88.00
22.	$12,000	5%	________	$50.00
23.	$400	________	60 days	$6.00
24.	$2,480	6%	75 days	________
25.	$24,890	3%	________	$280.00

26. _______	8%	270 days	$510.00

Principal	**Rate**	**Time**	**Interest**
365-day year			
27. $325	7.1%	90 days	_______
28. $34,950	5.5%	_______	$395.00
29. $18,600	_______	45 days	$195.00
30. _______	4.9%	135 days	$50.00
31. $4,080	8.2%	_______	$55.00
32. $200,000	_______	50 days	$1,700.00
33. _______	6.8%	105 days	$25.00
34. $875	10.6%	100 days	_______

____
Score for C (32)

Assignment 17.2: Using Interest in Business

LEARNING 1 OBJECTIVES

LEARNING 2 OBJECTIVES

LEARNING 4 OBJECTIVES

Name ______________________

Date ______________ Score ______________

A (50 points) The following problems involve ordinary simple interest, using a 360-day year. Find the due date or the number of interest days, as required. Find the missing variable by using one of the following formulas:

$$I = P \times R \times T \qquad P = \frac{I}{(R \times T)} \qquad R = \frac{I}{(P \times T)} \qquad T = \frac{I}{(P \times R)}$$

Compute time to the nearest day; compute rates to the nearest $\frac{1}{10}$ of a percent. (5 points for each correct answer)

1. Roger Sundahl is opening a new bakery. On June 18, 1999, Roger signs a promissory note to borrow $9,500 for 60 days to help pay for some new dough-mixing equipment. The rate is 6% ordinary simple interest. Find the amount of interest that Roger will pay and the due date.

Interest amount ______________

Due date ______________

2. Kathleen Donaldson and her husband raise wild birds—including pheasants and ducks—for sale only to restaurants. On March 13, 2000, they borrow money at 10% ordinary simple interest to pay for some new holding pens. On July 26, 2000, they pay back the loan principal and also $150 in interest. First compute the number of interest days between the two dates. Then compute the principal.

Interest days ______________

Principal ______________

3. Michelle Fong inherited a jewelry store from her father. On September 21, 2000, she borrowed $36,000 for new items for the Christmas holiday season. Ninety days later, she repaid a total of $36,540, which was the principal plus interest. After determining the amount of interest, compute the ordinary simple interest rate. Then find the due date.

Interest rate ______________

Due date ______________

4. Jack Hacket bought a roofing company. On February 21, 2001, Jack borrowed $75,000 to help finance a machine to hydraulically lift materials, workers, and equipment onto roofs. On the due date, when Jack repaid the principal, he also paid $1,250 in interest. If the ordinary simple interest rate was 8%, compute the number of interest days. Then determine the due date.

Interest days ______________

Due date ______________

5. Rebecca Crist is planning to write an economics book for high school students, but to do so she needs a new computer and printer. On April 6, 2001, she borrows money from her father at 5% ordinary simple interest. She repays the principal and $45 interest 180 days later. Compute the principal and the due date.

Principal ______________

Due date ______________

____
Score for A (50)

B (50 points) The following problems involve exact simple interest using a 365-day year. Find the due date or the number of interest days, as required. Find the missing variable by using one of the following formulas:

$$I = P \times R \times T \qquad P = \frac{I}{(R \times T)} \qquad R = \frac{I}{(P \times T)} \qquad T = \frac{I}{(P \times R)}$$

Compute time to the nearest day; compute rates to the nearest $\frac{1}{10}$ of a percent. (5 points for each correct answer)

6. Wilson Ma, a contractor, needed a short-term loan of $10,000 to pay one of his suppliers. Wilson signed a promissory note at 8.7% exact simple interest on January 19, 1999. He repaid the principal and interest on March 5, 1999. First find the number of interest days. Then compute the dollars of interest that Wilson paid.

Interest days ____________

Interest amount ____________

7. A few months after graduating from medical school, Angelina Hernandez borrowed $16,500. The exact simple interest rate was 6.2%; the date of the promissory note was November 29, 2000. On the due date, when Angelina repaid the principal, she also paid $420.41 interest. Compute the number of interest days. Then determine the due date of the note.

Interest days ____________

Due date ____________

8. On May 3, 2000, Vikosh Singh signed a promissory note to borrow a small amount of money for 105 days. The rate on the loan was 7.7% exact simple interest. On the due date, Vikosh repaid the entire principal and $32.34 interest. Calculate the amount of money that Vikosh borrowed, and then determine the due date of the note.

Principal ____________

Due date ____________

9. On October 12, 2001, Melvin Counts loaned $830 to Roy Brainard, one of his friends from high school. On the due date, 270 days later, Roy repaid the principal and $30.70 interest. Compute the exact simple interest rate and the due date.

Interest rate ____________

Due date ____________

10. Five days after starting the fall semester, Dennis Mateski had an automobile accident. He needed to buy a replacement car, so he borrowed $4,000 on September 12, 2001. On November 11, 2001, Dennis received a gift from his grandfather and repaid the $4,000, along with $61.15 interest. First, determine the number of interest days; then compute the exact simple interest rate.

Interest days ____________

Interest rate ____________

____

Score for B (50)

Notes

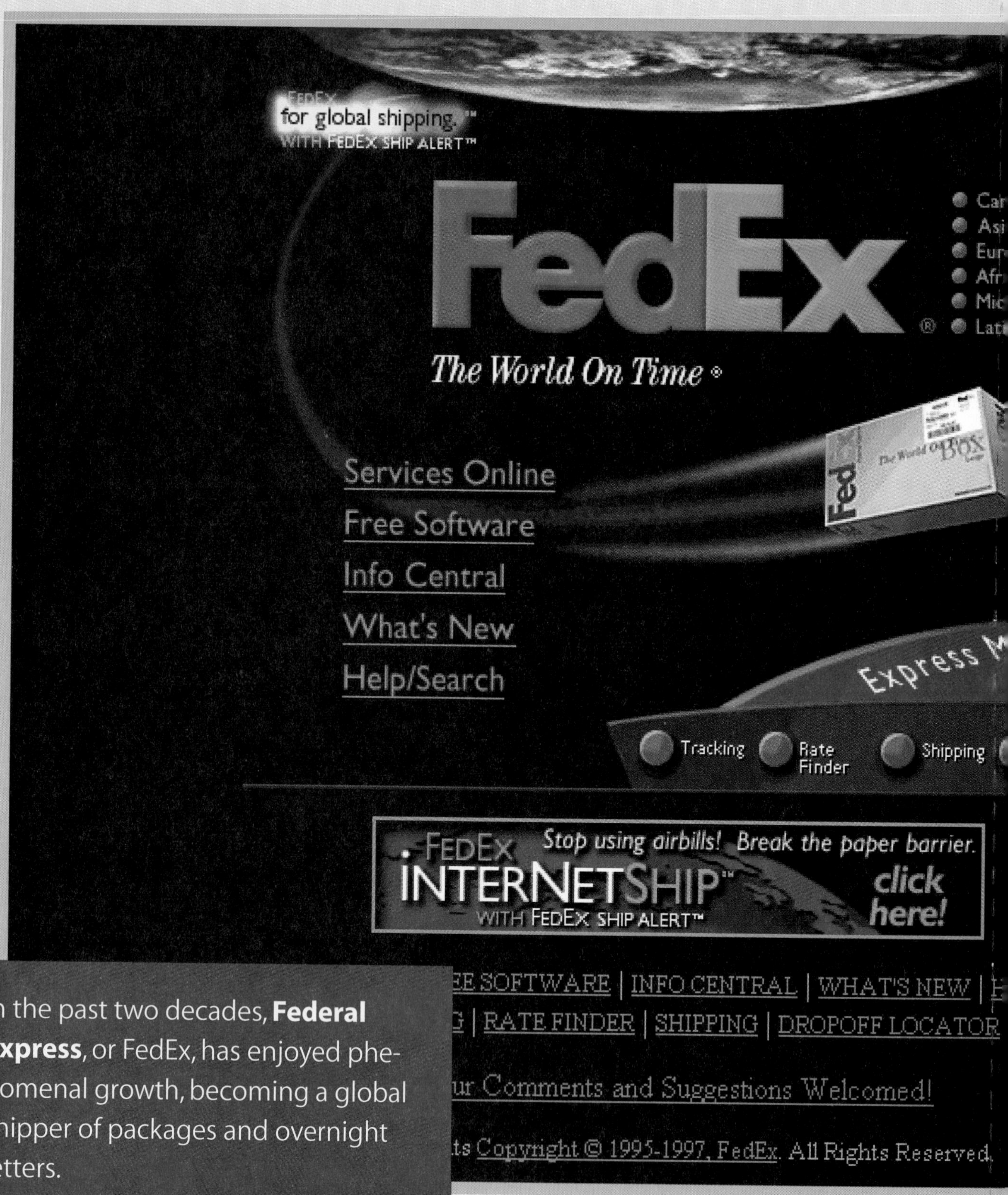

In the past two decades, **Federal Express**, or FedEx, has enjoyed phenomenal growth, becoming a global shipper of packages and overnight letters.

The FedEx web site provides company information, as well as a means to track a letter or package, find the addresses of dropoff locations, and check rates. Visit FedEx at www.FedEx.com.

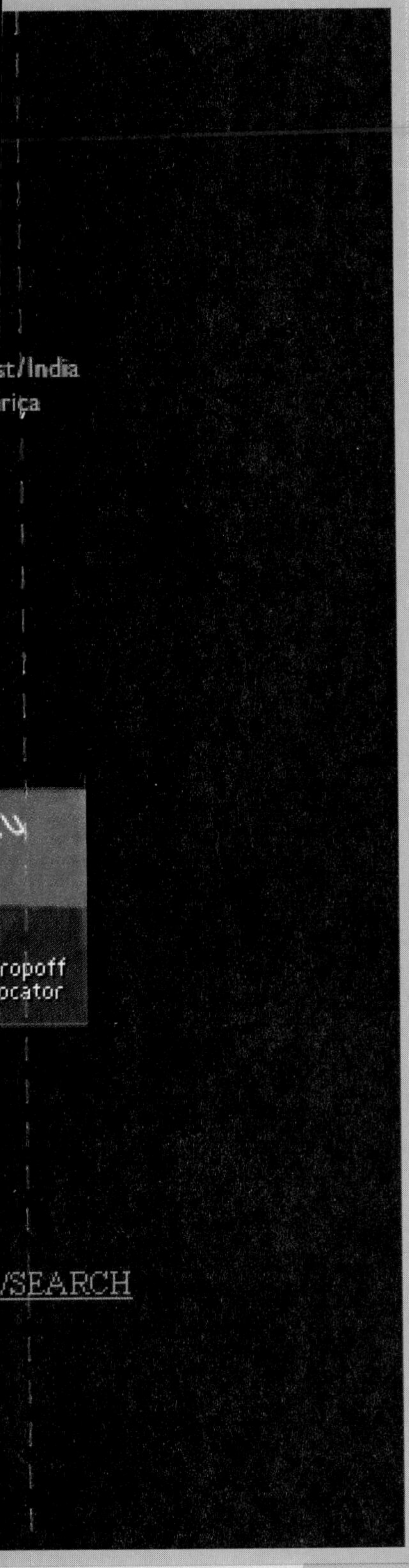

18 Borrowing By Business

Learning Objectives

By studying this chapter and completing all the assignments, you will learn to:

1. Compute the savings from borrowing money to take a cash discount.
2. Compute interest using the unpaid-balance method.
3. Compute the proceeds and actual interest rate on a bank discount loan.
4. Discount a non-interest-bearing note.
5. Discount an interest-bearing note.

To stay competitive, businesses must borrow for everything from current inventory to major capital investments in new equipment, buildings, and retooling for new products. Knowing when and how to borrow can make the difference between thriving and closing down.

Businesses, just like individuals, use long-term loans (more than one year) to purchase large items such as new equipment or buildings. Unlike individuals, though, businesses often borrow money for very short periods—even for only a few days. When retail businesses such as Stereo Depot or CD Max buy merchandise from manufacturers and wholesalers, often they know in advance that they cannot sell the merchandise in time to pay the supplier's invoice. If they do not have sufficient cash on hand, they must borrow money until they have made enough sales. If the supplier offers a cash discount (see Chapter 14), it is usually possible to save money by borrowing enough cash to take advantage of the discount.

In Chapters 16 and 17, all of the interest was single payment. The lender gave money to the borrower; after a specified period of time, the borrower made a single payment, repaying the principal and all of the interest. For loans that are longer than a few days or weeks, banks and other financial institutions usually require the borrower to make some intermediate partial payments of principal and/or interest. There are several borrowing and repayment methods, some specific to individuals and others more common for businesses. Chapter 19 describes some examples of loans that are consumer-oriented; here we will discuss borrowing and repayments by businesses.

Borrowing Money to Take a Cash Discount

LEARNING OBJECTIVES 1

Compute the savings from borrowing money to take a cash discount.

Chapter 14 described how the wholesalers and manufacturers use cash discounts to encourage their customers to pay quickly. The terms 2/10, net 30 mean that the buyer will receive a discount of 2% by paying the invoice within 10 days and that the entire invoice is due within 30 days.

EXAMPLE A

CD Max purchased $100,000 worth of CDs, videotapes, and laser discs. The invoice was dated October 4 with terms of 2/10, net 30. Compute the due date, the discount date, the cash discount, and the total remittance required to get the cash discount. (Review Chapter 14 if necessary.)

Due date = October 4 + 30 days = November 3

Discount date = October 4 + 10 days = October 14

If paid by October 14:
  Cash discount = $100,000 × 0.02 = $2,000
  Total remittance: $100,000 − $2,000 = $98,000

Regardless of whether it takes the discount, CD Max needs to pay $100,000 by November 3. The company may want to save the $2,000, but perhaps it does not have the $98,000 now. Or maybe it has the money, but wants to spend it on something else. In either situation, CD Max might be able to borrow the money from October 14 until November 3. Before borrowing, CD Max should compare the savings from the cash discount with the interest on a loan.

EXAMPLE B

CD Max can borrow $98,000 for 20 days (October 14 to November 3) by paying 10% exact simple interest (365-day year). Compute the interest on the loan and the savings for CD Max if it borrows to take the discount.

$$\text{Interest} = P \times R \times T = \$98{,}000 \times 0.10 \times \frac{20}{365} = \$536.99$$

$$\text{Savings} = \$2{,}000 \text{ discount} - \$536.99 \text{ interest} = \$1{,}463.01$$

The reason for borrowing only between the discount date and the due date is to delay making payments as long as possible, whether to get discounts or to avoid penalties. The discount date is the latest possible date to pay and get the discount; the due date is the latest possible date to pay and avoid a penalty.

Although it is almost always cheaper to borrow and take the discount, the actual dollar amount may determine what CD Max decides. If the original purchase were only $1,000, then the savings would be only $14.63. Such an amount may not be worth the effort of getting a loan. On the other hand, for borrowing small amounts on a regular basis, businesses often have "revolving lines of credit." These allow them to borrow and repay frequently, without always making a new loan application.

CONCEPT CHECK 18.1

A retailer purchases merchandise under the terms 1.5/20, net 45. The invoice is for $45,000 and is dated July 22. For the cash discount, calculate the due date, the discount date, the amount of the cash discount, and the total remittance required. The retailer borrows enough money to pay the entire remittance. The interest rate is 12% exact simple interest, and the loan is for the length of time between the discount date and the due date. Calculate the amount of the interest and the savings gained by borrowing the remittance to take the discount.

Discount:	Due date:	July 22 + 45 days = September 5
	Discount date:	July 22 + 20 days = August 11
	Cash discount:	$\$45{,}000 \times 0.015 = \$675$
	Remittance:	$\$45{,}000 - \$675 = \$44{,}325$
Loan:	Interest days:	August 11 to September 5 = 25 days
	$\text{Interest} = P \times R \times T = \$44{,}325 \times 0.12 \times \frac{25}{365} = \$364.32$	
Savings:	$675 cash discount − $364.32 interest = $310.68	

Computing Interest with the Unpaid-Balance Method

LEARNING OBJECTIVES 2

Compute interest using the unpaid-balance method.

Lenders charge interest on the *principal,* which is the amount of money that the borrower owes to the lender. Many loans require the borrower to repay the loan in regular monthly payments. The payments may or may not be equal every month. Usually the borrower pays all of the interest for that month and also repays part of the principal. The amount of the principal that has not been repaid is called the *unpaid balance.* Since the borrower repays part of the principal, the unpaid balance decreases. The new unpaid balance will be the principal in the interest calculation for the next month.

In this chapter, interest for each month will be computed using the basic unpaid-balance method, based on the formula $I = P \times R \times T$. P is the unpaid balance for that month; I is the annual interest rate; and T, the time, is expressed as a fraction of a 365-day year. Recall from Chapter 16 that this is *exact interest.*

Chapter 19 describes slightly different versions of the unpaid-balance method, more common in credit purchases and consumer loans.

STEPS to Compute Interest and the New Unpaid Balance Using the Unpaid-Balance Method

1. Determine P, R, and T.
   a. P is the unpaid balance for the month.
   b. R is the quoted annual interest rate.
   c. T, the time, is a fraction of a 365-day year, where the numerator is the exact number of days in that particular month and the denominator is 365.
2. Compute the interest payment for the month using $I = P \times R \times T$.
3. Compute the principal payment by subtracting the interest payment from the total monthly payment.
4. Compute the new unpaid balance by subtracting the principal payment from the former unpaid balance (P in Step 1a).
5. Repeat Steps 1 through 4 until the last month. For the last month, compute the total payment by adding the interest due to the unpaid balance.

EXAMPLE C

On October 13, Ladera Service Station borrows \$30,000 for some new oil-changing equipment. The interest rate is 11% exact (365-day year). Ladera makes payments of \$10,000 on November 13 and December 13. Each payment includes interest on the unpaid balance from the preceding month. The rest of the \$10,000 is used to repay the principal. On January 13, Ladera makes a final payment to repay the balance plus the interest since December 13. Compute the interest and principal payment for each month. Also, show the new unpaid balance for each month and the total payment for January 13.

STEP 1	P, R & T:	$P = \$30{,}000$ (loan amount); $R = 11\%$; $T = \frac{31}{365}$ (31 days between October 13 and November 13)
STEP 2	Interest payment:	$I = P \times R \times T = \$30{,}000 \times 0.11 \times \frac{31}{365} = \$280.27$
STEP 3	Principal payment:	$\$10{,}000 - \$280.27 = \$9{,}719.73$
STEP 4	Unpaid balance:	$\$30{,}000 - \$9{,}719.73 = \$20{,}280.27$

STEP 1	P, R & T:	$P = \$20{,}280.27$ (unpaid balance from November 13); $R = 11\%$; $T = \frac{30}{365}$ (30 days between November 13 and December 13)
STEP 2	Interest payment:	$I = P \times R \times T = \$20{,}280.27 \times 0.11 \times \frac{30}{365} = \$183.36$
STEP 3	Principal payment:	$\$10{,}000 - \$183.36 = \$9{,}816.64$
STEP 4	Unpaid balance:	$\$20{,}280.27 - \$9{,}816.64 = \$10{,}463.63$

STEP 1	P, R & T:	$P = \$10{,}463.63$ (unpaid balance from December 13); $R = 11\%$; $T = \frac{31}{365}$ (31 days between December 13 and January 13)
STEP 2	Interest payment:	$I = P \times R \times T = \$10{,}463.63 \times 0.11 \times \frac{31}{365} = \$97.76$
STEP 3	Principal payment:	\$10,463.63 (repay the entire unpaid balance)
STEP 4	Unpaid balance:	$\$10{,}463.63 - \$10{,}463.63 = \$0.00$
STEP 5	Total payment:	$\$10{,}463.63 + \$97.76 = \$10{,}561.39$

CONCEPT CHECK 18.2

On January 25, 1999, a bank loaned $4,000 to a business for two months at 12% exact simple interest (365-day year). On February 25, 1999, the borrower made a total payment of $2,000, which included interest on the unpaid balance. On March 25, 1999, the borrower paid the remaining principal and interest on the balance. Calculate the amount of interest and principal paid each month. (Check for leap years.)

There are 31 days between January 25 and February 25. There are 28 days between February 25 and March 25.

	February 25, 1999		**March 25, 1999**	
Unpaid balance:	Original principal	$4,000.00	From February 25	$2,040.77
Interest payment:	$\$4,000.00 \times 0.12 \times \frac{31}{365}$	$= \$40.77$	$\$2,040.77 \times 0.12 \times \frac{28}{365}$	$= \$18.79$
Total payment:		$2,000.00	Add: $2,040.77 + $18.79 =	$2,059.56
Principal payment:	$2,000 − $40.77 =	$1,959.23		$2,040.77
New balance:	$4,000 − $1,959.23 =	$2,040.77	$2,040.77 − $2,040.77 =	$0.00

COMPLETE ASSIGNMENT 18.1.

Analyzing Bank Discounts

As you learned in Chapter 16, the simplest loan situation is where the borrower goes to a lender, borrows some money, and then repays the money plus some interest. The interest is the lender's fee for making the loan.

Compute the proceeds and actual interest rate on a bank discount loan.

EXAMPLE D

Bob Wilson, owner/operator of a McDonald's Restaurant, borrows $8,000 from his bank for 60 days at 9% ordinary interest. Using a 360-day year, compute the interest and amount due at maturity.

$$P = \$8{,}000;\ R = 9\%;\ T = \frac{60}{360}$$

$$\text{Interest} = P \times R \times T = \$8{,}000 \times 0.09 \times \frac{60}{360} = \$120$$

$$\text{Amount due} = P + I = \$8{,}000 + \$120 = \$8{,}120$$

Bob will keep the entire $8,000 principal for the entire 60 days and then repay $8,120 on the due date.

In order to get a loan, a borrower is often required to sign a document called a *promissory note* (see Chapter 17). If there were a promissory note for the loan in example D, the $8,000 would be the face value of the note and the $8,120 would be the maturity value of the note.

Another lending method that banks sometimes use is to *subtract* the loan fee from the face value at the time the loan is made. In example D, instead of giving Bob Wilson $8,000 for 60 days, the bank would subtract $120 from $8,000 and give him only $7,880. Then, on the due date, he would repay a total amount of $8,000.

To help avoid confusion, some different vocabulary words are useful. The procedure is called *discounting.* The calculation is the same: $\$8{,}000 \times 9\% \times \frac{60}{360} = \$120$. The 9% is called the *discount rate.* The 60 days is called the *discount period.* The $120 is called the *discount amount* or the *bank discount.* The $7,880 is called the *proceeds* of the loan.

The \$8,000 is both the *face value* and the *maturity value.* Notice that the \$8,000 is not really the "principal," because \$8,000 is not the amount that is actually borrowed. To distinguish the calculations, use different symbols:

$$\text{Discount} = FV \times R \times T, \text{ where } FV = \text{Face value and } R = \text{Discount rate}$$

and

$$\text{Proceeds} = FV - D, \text{ where } D = \text{Discount}$$

EXAMPLE E

Compute the discount and the proceeds on a 60-day loan that has a face value of \$8,000 and a bank discount rate of 9%. (Use a 360-day year.)

$$FV = \$8{,}000; R = 9\%; T = \frac{60}{360}$$

$$\text{Discount} = FV \times R \times T = \$8{,}000 \times 0.09 \times \frac{60}{360} = \$120$$

$$\text{Proceeds} = FV - D = \$8{,}000 - \$120 = \$7{,}880$$

Some people refer to this type of loan as non-interest-bearing, because the borrower repays only the face value. However, the term *non-interest-bearing* is probably misleading because the borrower is not really getting an "interest-free loan." There is a charge of \$120 to borrow \$7,880 for 60 days.

Discount Rate versus Interest Rate

When a bank uses the discount method, the discount rate is not the interest rate. In example E, the discount rate was 9%, and the borrower had to pay \$120 to borrow \$7,880 for 60 days. To compute the actual interest rate, use the formula $R = I/(P \times T)$ from Chapter 17, letting $I = \$120$, $P = \$7{,}880$, and $T = \frac{60}{360}$.

$$R = \frac{I}{(P \times T)} = \frac{\$120}{\left(\$7{,}880 \times \frac{60}{360}\right)} = 0.09137, \text{ or } 9.14\%$$

The interest rate is actually 9.14%, whereas the discount rate is 9%. Since the two rates do not represent the same thing, a borrower must understand which rate is used in the loan.

CONCEPT CHECK 18.3

A bank made a 90-day loan on a discount basis. The face value was \$6,400, and the discount rate was 11%. Compute the discount amount and the proceeds. Then compute the actual interest rate, using the proceeds as the principal of the loan instead of the face value. Use a 360-day year in all calculations.

$$\text{Discount} = FV \times R \times T = \$6{,}400 \times 0.11 \times \frac{90}{360} = \$176$$

$$\text{Proceeds} = \text{Face value} - \text{Discount} = \$6{,}400 - \$176 = \$6{,}224$$

$$\text{Actual interest rate} = \frac{T}{(P \times T)} = \frac{\$176}{\left(\$6{,}224 \times \frac{90}{360}\right)} = 0.1131, \text{ or } 11.31\%$$

Discounting Non-Interest-Bearing Notes

In example E, the bank made the loan on a discount basis. Although there was a $120 charge for the loan, the promissory note might be said to be a *non-interest-bearing note* because the maturity value is equal to the face value. This also occurs when the loan truly has no interest charge, as might happen when an individual lends money to a relative or close friend.

LEARNING OBJECTIVES 4

Discount a non-interest-bearing note.

When a lender holds a non-interest-bearing promissory note, the lender may be able to "sell" the note to someone else. Such a note is said to be *negotiable.* A lender would sell a note to get cash immediately instead of having to wait until the maturity date. Of course, whoever buys the note will not pay the entire maturity value to the original lender, because there is risk involved. The risk depends on both the reputation (credit rating) of the borrower and the length of time until the maturity date. Since the buyer of the note will pay less than the maturity value, the buyer is said to be *discounting* the note. The discount amount is calculated just like a bank discount. The original lender, who is now selling the note, receives the proceeds.

Discount $= FV \times R \times T$, where R is the discount rate
Proceeds $= FV - D$

STEPS to Compute the Discount and the Proceeds of a Non-Interest-Bearing Note

1. Determine the maturity (due) date of the note.
2. Compute the length of the discount period—the number of days between the discount date and the due date. Divide the number of days by 360 (or 365) to get T.
3. Compute the amount of the discount using $D = FV \times R \times T$.
4. Compute the proceeds using $FV - D$.

EXAMPLE F

Rob Wegner, owner of a True-Value Hardware Store, is holding a 45-day non-interest-bearing note for $5,000, dated April 2. On April 11, Rob sells the note to Marshfield Finance Company. The finance company discounts the note at 15%. Find the amount of the discount and the proceeds. (Use a 360-day year.)

STEP 1 Due date: April 2 + 45 days = May 17

STEP 2 Discount period: April 11 to May 17 = 36 days

STEP 3 Amount of discount: Face value × Discount rate × Time

$$= \$5{,}000.00 \times 0.15 \times \frac{36}{360}$$

$$= \$75.00$$

STEP 4 Proceeds: Face value − Discount

$$= \$5{,}000.00 - \$75.00$$

$$= \$4{,}925$$

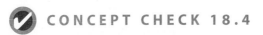

CONCEPT CHECK 18.4

A 90-day non-interest-bearing promissory note dated March 19 has a face value of \$2,500. On April 14, a finance company discounts the note at a rate of 11%. Find the discount amount and the proceeds. Note: the maturity date and the days of discount must first be determined. Use a 365-day year for the discount calculation.

Maturity date:	March 19 + 90 days = June 17
Days of discount:	April 14 to June 17 = 64 days
Discount amount:	$\$2{,}500 \times .011 \times \frac{64}{365} = \$48.22$
Proceeds:	\$2,500 − \$48.22 = \$2,451.78

Discounting Interest-Bearing Notes

LEARNING 5 OBJECTIVES

Discount an interest-bearing note.

Most promissory notes, such as the one in example G, are *interest-bearing.*

EXAMPLE G

On September 20, Redbourne Medical Supply borrowed \$120,000 from a private investor, John White. In return for the \$120,000, Redbourne Medical gave John a 90-day promissory note at an ordinary interest rate of 10%. Compute the due date and maturity value of the note.

Due date:	September 20 + 90 days = December 19
Interest:	$I = P \times R \times T = \$120{,}000 \times 0.10 \times \frac{90}{360} = \$3{,}000$
Maturity value:	MV = Principal + Interest = \$120,000 + \$3,000 = \$123,000

In example G, Redbourne Medical will not pay the \$123,000 to John White until December 19. During the 90 days, John has only the promissory note. If the note is *negotiable,* John can sell it for cash to a third party before December 19.

Suppose that John decides to sell the note on November 19. The note will be worth \$123,000 on December 19. Whoever buys the note wants to earn a profit, so the buyer will pay less than \$123,000 for the note. We again say that the new buyer *discounts* the note or buys the note at a discount. The amount that John White receives is called the *proceeds.* The decrease in value of the note is the *discount amount.*

This discount is computed the same way as that on a non-interest-bearing note.

Amount of discount = Maturity value × Discount rate × Time
Proceeds = Maturity value − Discount

STEPS to Discount an Interest-Bearing Note

1. Compute the interest and maturity value of the original note.
2. Determine the maturity (due) date of the original note.
3. Compute the number of days in the discount period. The time, T, is the number of days in the discount period divided by 360 (or 365).
4. Compute the discount amount using $D = MV \times R \times T$.
5. Compute the proceeds by subtracting the discount amount (Step 4) from the maturity value (Step 1).

EXAMPLE H

John White held the 90-day promissory note signed by Redbourne Medical Supply on September 20. On November 19, John sold the note to Central Finance Company. Central discounted the note at a discount rate of 15%. Compute the due date of the note, the maturity value, the discount amount, and the proceeds. (Use a 360-day year throughout.)

Maturity value: $MV = \text{Principal} + \text{Interest}$ (from example G)
$= \$120{,}000 + \$3{,}000 = \$123{,}000$

Due date: December 19 (from example G)

Discount period: November 19 to December 19 = 30 days

Discount amount: Maturity value × Discount rate × Time

$$= \$123{,}000 \times 0.15 \times \frac{30}{360} = \$1{,}537.50$$

Proceeds: Maturity value − discount
$= \$123{,}000 - \$1{,}537.50 = \$121{,}462.50$

CONCEPT CHECK 18.5

A 75-day promissory note, bearing interest at 10%, is dated December 11 and has a face value of $5,000. On January 24, the note is discounted at 14%. Find the discount amount and the proceeds. Note: The interest amount, the maturity value, the maturity date, and the days of discount must first be determined. Use a 365-day year for all interest and discount calculations.

Interest amount: $\$5{,}000 \times 0.10 \times \frac{75}{365} = \$102.74$

Maturity value: $5,000 + $102.74 = $5,102.74

Maturity date: Dec. 11 + 75 days = Feb. 24

Days of discount: Jan. 24 to Feb. 24 = 31 days

Discount amount: $\$5{,}102.74 \times 0.14 \times \frac{31}{365} = \$60.67$

Proceeds: $5,102.74 − $60.67 = $5,042.07

COMPLETE ASSIGNMENTS 18.2 AND 18.3.

Chapter Terms for Review

bank discount
borrowing to take a cash discount
discount amount
discounting a note
discount period
discount rate
discounting
face value
interest-bearing note
maturity date (or due date)
maturity value
negotiable note
non-interest-bearing note
principal
proceeds
unpaid balance
unpaid-balance method

The Bottom Line

Summary of chapter learning objectives:

Learning Objective	Summary	Example
18.1	Computing the savings from borrowing money to take a cash discount	1. A $20,000 invoice dated March 15 has terms of 2/5, net 25. Find the due date, discount date, cash discount, and required remittance. Then calculate the savings realized by borrowing the remittance at 9% exact interest for the time between the discount date and the due date.
18.2	Computing interest using the unpaid-balance method	2. A business borrows $20,000 on July 17 at 11% exact simple interest. On August 17, September 17, and October 17, it will make equal payments of $5,000. Each payment will include interest on the unpaid balance. On November 17, it will pay the remaining balance and interest on the unpaid balance. Compute the payments and balances for the first month.
18.3	Computing the proceeds and actual interest rate on a bank discount loan	3. A 60-day bank loan with a face value of $3,900 is made on a discount basis at a discount rate of 12%. Use a 360-day year to compute the discount amount, the proceeds, and the actual interest rate, based on the proceeds rather than on the face value.
18.4	Discounting a non-interest-bearing note	4. A 45-day non-interest-bearing note has a face value of $1,600 and is dated May 13. On June 3, the note is discounted at 13%. Use a 365-day year to find the discount amount and the proceeds.
18.5	Discounting an interest-bearing note	5. A 30-day note, bearing an interest rate of 9%, is dated November 6 and has a face value of $8,000. On November 15, the note is discounted at 12%. Use a 365-day year to find the discount amount and the proceeds.

Answers: 1. Due date, April 9; discount date, March 20; cash discount, $400; remittance, $19,600; savings, $303.34 **2.** Unpaid balance, $20,000; interest payment, $186.85; principal payment, $4,813.15; new balance, $15,186.85 **3.** Discount, $78; proceeds, $3,822; interest rate, 12.24% **4.** Discount, $13.68; proceeds, $1,586.32 **5.** Discount, $55.64; proceeds, $8,003.54

Assignment 18.1: Single and Multiple Payment Interest

LEARNING OBJECTIVES 1

LEARNING OBJECTIVES 2

Name

Date Score

A **(64 points) Pedrezzetti Construction Company made several purchases from vendors, who offered various terms of payment. How much can Pedrezzetti save on each invoice if it borrows the money so as to pay the invoice early and receive the cash discount? The loan interest rates are all exact simple interest (365-day year). Assume that the number of interest days is the time between the due date and the last day to take advantage of the cash discount. (2 points for each correct answer)**

	Invoice	Terms	Cash Discount	Interest Rate on Loan	Interest Days	Amount of Interest	Savings
1.	$3,000	2/10, n/30	________	12%	________	________	________
2.	$420	1/15, n/45	________	7.25%	________	________	________
3.	$17,500	3/5, n/25	________	8%	________	________	________
4.	$880	1.5/15, n/30	________	11%	________	________	________
5.	$9,200	1/30, n/60	________	9%	________	________	________
6.	$1,380	2/10, n/30	________	10%	________	________	________
7.	$26,000	2.5/5, n/25	________	8.5%	________	________	________
8.	$695	3/10, n/25	________	9.75%	________	________	________

Score for A (64)

B (36 points) Complete the tables below. Compute the exact simple interest (365-day year) on the unpaid balance each month. Reduce the principal accordingly, and compute the new unpaid balance. (1 point for each correct answer)

9. On March 20, Sampson Hardware financed $12,000 worth of new garden equipment and gardening supplies at an exact simple interest rate of 9.8%. On April 20, it will pay $7,000, which will include the interest for the first month. On May 20, Sampson will repay the entire unpaid balance plus the interest for the last month.

Payment Date	Interest Days	Unpaid Balance	Interest Payment	Total Payment	Principal Payment	New Balance
April 20	______	______	______	______	______	______
May 20	______	______	______	______	______	______

10. Chang Electrical Supply purchased $16,000 worth of electrical supplies from one manufacturer on June 5. The manufacturer offered Chang an exact simple interest rate of 7.5%, and Chang agreed to pay $4,000 on July 5, August 5, and September 5. The $4,000 payments will include the interest on the unpaid balance and reduce the principal accordingly. On October 5, Chang will repay the remaining unpaid balance and the interest for the final month.

Payment Date	Interest Days	Unpaid Balance	Interest Payment	Total Payment	Principal Payment	New Balance
July 5	______	______	______	______	______	______
August 5	______	______	______	______	______	______
September 5	______	______	______	______	______	______
October 5	______	______	______	______	______	______

____
Score for B (36)

Assignment 18.2: Bank Discount and Discounting Notes

Name ______________________

Date ______________ Score ______________

A (36 points) Suppose that a small finance company made four new loans on a discount basis. Compute the dollar amount of the discount and the proceeds. Then compute the actual interest rate, based on the proceeds rather than the face value. Use a 360-day year for all calculations. Round the actual interest rate to the nearest $\frac{1}{100}$ of a percent. (3 points for each correct answer)

	Face Value	Discount Rate	Time	Discount Amount	Proceeds	Actual Interest Rate
1.	$6,600	7%	60 days	________	________	________
2.	$24,000	6%	90 days	________	________	________
3.	$2,850	12%	30 days	________	________	________
4.	$12,840	8%	120 days	________	________	________

____
Score for A (36)

B (16 points) Assume that you are a loan officer in a finance company. Discount the following non-interest-bearing notes using a 360-day year. (2 points for each correct answer)

5.

Face value:	$4,600
Date of note:	July 15
Length of note:	120 days
Discount date:	September 10
Discount rate:	9%
Maturity date:	________
Days of discount:	________
Discount amount:	________
Proceeds:	________

6.

Face value:	$6,500
Date of note:	March 1
Length of note:	90 days
Discount date:	April 15
Discount rate:	10%
Maturity date:	________
Days of discount:	________
Discount amount:	________
Proceeds:	________

____
Score for B (16)

C (48 points) A loan company discounts interest-bearing promissory notes. Compute the requested information for the following notes. Use a 360-day year for all interest and discount computations. (2 points for each correct answer)

7. Face value: $4,200
Date of note: June 3
Interest rate: 8%
Length of note: 75 days
Discount date: July 1
Discount rate: 10%

Interest amount: ________
Maturity value: ________
Maturity date: ________
Days of discount: ________
Discount amount: ________
Proceeds: ________

8. Face value: $960
Date of note: April 4
Interest rate: 9%
Length of note: 60 days
Discount date: April 20
Discount rate: 12%

Interest amount: ________
Maturity value: ________
Maturity date: ________
Days of discount: ________
Discount amount: ________
Proceeds: ________

9. Face value: $6,480
Date of note: October 9
Interest rate: 7%
Length of note: 105 days
Discount date: November 1
Discount rate: 10%

Interest amount: ________
Maturity value: ________
Maturity date: ________
Days of discount: ________
Discount amount: ________
Proceeds: ________

10. Face value: $1,170
Date of note: July 17
Interest rate: 6%
Length of note: 90 days
Discount date: August 20
Discount rate: 9%

Interest amount: ________
Maturity value: ________
Maturity date: ________
Days of discount: ________
Discount amount: ________
Proceeds: ________

____
Score for C (48)

Assignment 18.3: Discounting Notes Using a 365-Day Year

Name ______________________________

Date ______________ Score ______________

A (36 points) Compute the missing information for the following applications, which involve discounting non-interest-bearing notes. Use a 365-day year for all discount calculations. (3 points for each correct discount amount; 2 points for all other correct answers)

1. Jean Millspaugh held a 60-day, $2,100 non-interest-bearing note dated July 20. On August 10, she took the note to a finance company, which discounted it at 10%.

Maturity date: __________
Days of discount: __________
Discount amount: __________
Proceeds: __________

2. Chris Keylock was holding a $750, 90-day non-interest-bearing note from her brother. The note is dated October 13. On November 24, Chris sold the note to a loan company, which charged a 13% discount rate.

Maturity date: __________
Days of discount: __________
Discount amount: __________
Proceeds: __________

3. Jim Elliott was holding a 75-day, $3,500 non-interest-bearing note dated December 3. He needed money for Christmas, so on December 20 he took the note to a local finance company, which discounted it at 12%.

Maturity date: __________
Days of discount: __________
Discount amount: __________
Proceeds: __________

4. Terry Shore had a 120-day non-interest-bearing note. The face value is $925; the date of the note is March 29. On May 3, Terry sold the note to a loan company at a discount rate of 15%.

Maturity date: __________
Days of discount: __________
Discount amount: __________
Proceeds: __________

____
Score for A (36)

B **(64 points) Compute the missing information for the following applications, which involve discounting interest-bearing notes. Use a 365-day year for all interest and discount calculations. (4 points for each correct interest amount and discount amount; 2 points for all other correct answers)**

5. Karen Kaiser was holding a $5,600, 120-day note with an interest rate of 9%. The note is dated May 10. On June 15, a finance company bought the note from Karen, discounting it at a rate of 13%.

Interest amount: ________
Maturity value: ________
Maturity date: ________
Days of discount: ________
Discount amount: ________
Proceeds: ________

6. On July 28, David Eng needed cash and sold a 60-day promissory note at a 14% discount rate. The note had a face value of $820, was dated June 25, and carried an interest rate of 10%.

Interest amount: ________
Maturity value: ________
Maturity date: ________
Days of discount: ________
Discount amount: ________
Proceeds: ________

7. Pedro Gomez had been holding a 75-day, $1,800 note that had an 8% interest rate and had been written on April 14. Pedro decided to sell the note on May 20 to a loan company, which discounted it at 12%.

Interest amount: ________
Maturity value: ________
Maturity date: ________
Days of discount: ________
Discount amount: ________
Proceeds: ________

8. On September 9, Simona Fogliati decided to sell a 150-day note to an agency that used a 13% discount rate. Simona's note had a face value of $6,000, was dated July 17, and carried a 9% interest rate.

Interest amount: ________
Maturity value: ________
Maturity date: ________
Days of discount: ________
Discount amount: ________
Proceeds: ________

____
Score for B (64)

Notes

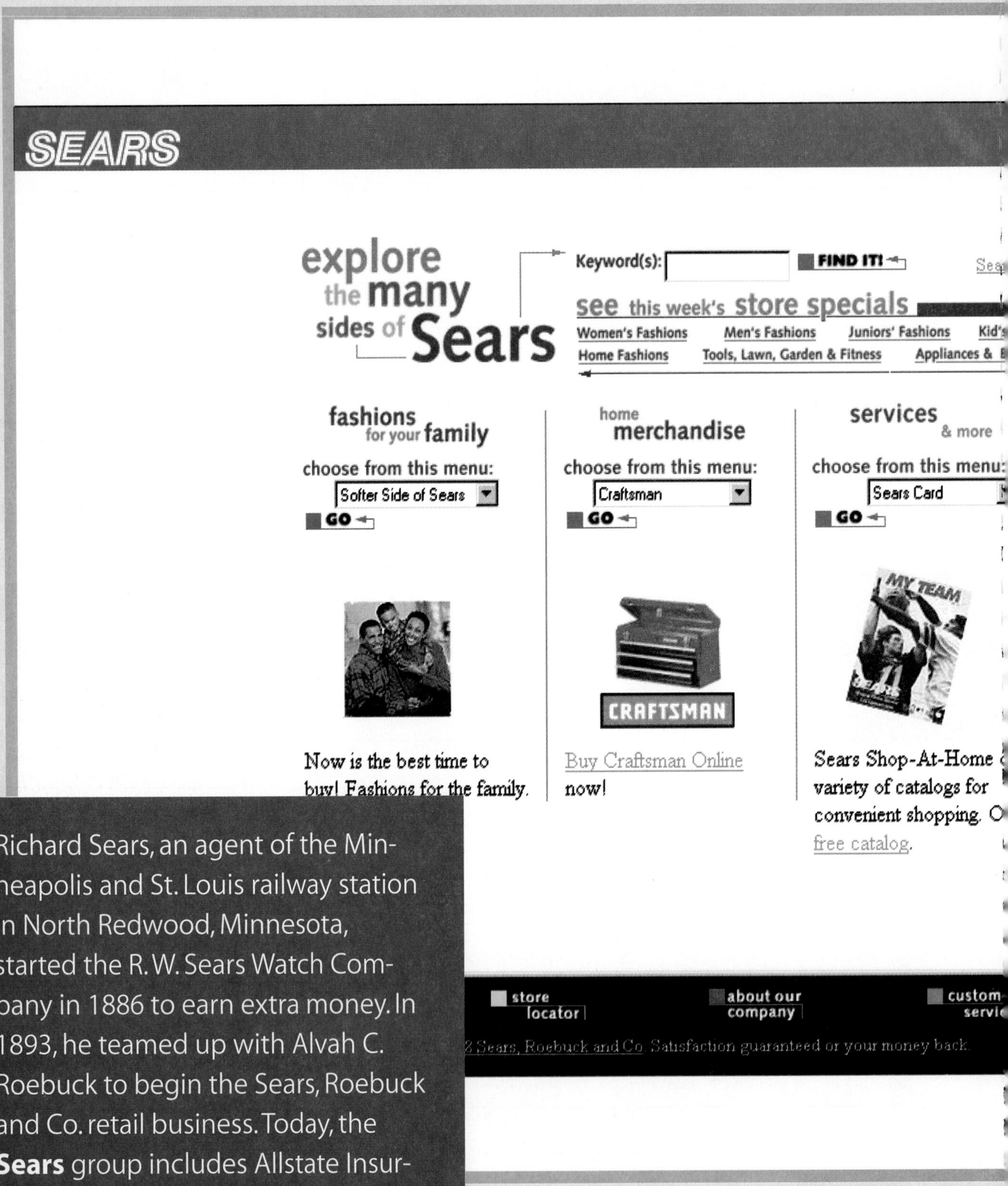

Richard Sears, an agent of the Minneapolis and St. Louis railway station in North Redwood, Minnesota, started the R. W. Sears Watch Company in 1886 to earn extra money. In 1893, he teamed up with Alvah C. Roebuck to begin the Sears, Roebuck and Co. retail business. Today, the **Sears** group includes Allstate Insurance, Dean Witter Financial Services, Coldwell Banker Real Estate, and the Discover Card. Check the Sears site at www.sears.com for information on the company and its products, services, and locations.

products & services

19 Charges for Credit

Learning Objectives

By studying this chapter and completing all the assignments, you will learn to:

Learning Objectives 1 — Convert between annual and monthly interest rates.

Learning Objectives 2 — Compute simple interest on a monthly basis.

Learning Objectives 3 — Compute finance charges for credit account purchases.

Learning Objectives 4 — Compute costs of installment purchases.

Learning Objectives 5 — Compute effective rates.

Learning Objectives 6 — Amortize a loan.

Today, credit is part of an increasingly "cashless" economic system. As a medium of exchange, it has speeded up the production, exchange, and consumption of goods. This, in turn, has brought about a higher standard of living.

home page

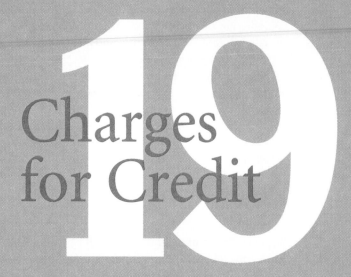

Most individuals today can purchase goods or services on credit. The buyer gets immediate possession or immediate service, but delays the payment. Either the seller offers credit or the buyer uses a *credit card* from a third party.

Credit may be offered for an interest charge, often called a *finance charge*. This charge is usually computed each month, and a summary (the statement) is sent to the buyer (borrower). It can be difficult to compare the finance charges of two competing creditors. The statement itself may be confusing because more than one interest rate may be mentioned. Also, there may be additional charges such as administrative fees, annual membership fees, and insurance fees. Finally, the borrower may not understand the method the creditor uses to compute the finance charges.

Converting Interest Rates

LEARNING OBJECTIVES 1

Convert between annual and monthly interest rates.

The general concept behind charging for credit purchases is to compute finance charges on the unpaid balance each month. The formula is still $I = P \times R \times T$, where P is basically the unpaid balance. However, T is not years or a fraction of a year (Chapters 16–18) —T is in months, and R, the rate, is a monthly rate. For example, the rate might be 1.5% **per month.**

It is important to understand the relationship between monthly and annual rates.

Rule: To convert an annual rate to a monthly rate, divide the annual rate by 12; to convert a monthly rate to an annual rate, multiply the monthly rate by 12.

EXAMPLE A

a. Convert 18% per year to the equivalent monthly rate.

18% annually ÷ 12 = 1.5% monthly

b. Convert 0.5% per month to the equivalent annual rate.

0.5% monthly × 12 = 6% annually

CONCEPT CHECK 19.1

a. Convert a 9% annual rate to the equivalent monthly rate.

Divide the annual rate by 12 to get the monthly rate: 9% ÷ 12 = 0.75% per month

b. Convert a 1.25% monthly rate to the equivalent annual rate.

Multiply the monthly rate by 12 to get the annual rate: 1.25% × 12 = 15% per year

Computing Simple Interest on a Monthly Basis

LEARNING OBJECTIVES 2

Compute simple interest on a monthly basis.

In terms of single-payment simple interest, 1.5% **per month** is identical to 18% **per year,** as shown in the following example.

EXAMPLE B

Compute the simple interest on $1,000 for 2 months at 18% per year, on an annual basis and on a monthly basis.

Annual: $I = P \times R \times T = \$1{,}000 \times 0.18 \text{ per year} \times \frac{2}{12} = \$30 \text{ for 2 months}$

Monthly: $18\% \text{ per year} = 18\% \div 12 = 1.5\% \text{ per month}$

$I = P \times R \times T = \$1{,}000 \times 0.015 \text{ per month} \times 2 \text{ months}$

$= \$30 \text{ for 2 months}$

REMINDER: Both computations differ from those in Chapter 16, where you counted the exact number of days and divided by either 360 or 365.

CONCEPT CHECK 19.2

Compute the simple interest on $800 for 3 months at 0.5% per month.

$I = P \times R \times T = \$800 \times 0.5\% \text{ per month} \times 3 \text{ months} = \$800 \times 0.005 \times 3 = \$12$

Computing Finance Charges

LEARNING OBJECTIVES 3

Compute finance charges for credit account purchases.

To help consumers learn the total cost of credit, the federal government has passed several laws, beginning with the Consumer Credit Protection Act of 1968. This was the beginning of *Truth in Lending.* Creditors must tell consumers these three things:

1. The total of all finance charges, including interest, carrying charges, insurance, and special fees
2. The *annual percentage rate (APR)* of the total finance charge
3. The method by which they compute the finance charge

The annual percentage rate (APR) is the monthly rate multiplied by 12. However, the quoted APR considers only the interest computation; it does not include other charges such as membership fees, loan fees, and insurance. The total of all finance charges is easy to find on the statement, because usually it is well labeled. The method for computing the finance charge is easy to find, but it may not be easy to understand. One difficulty is determining what balance is used in the computation. A wide variety of methods may be applied:

1. The finance charge may be based on the amount owed at the beginning of the current month, ignoring payments and purchases.
2. The finance charge may be based on the amount owed at the beginning of the month, after subtracting any payments during the month and ignoring purchases.
3. The finance charge may be based on the *average daily balance.* (Add the unpaid balance each day; divide the total by the number of days in the month.) Payments are usually included; new purchases may or may not be included.
4. A variation of the average daily balance method is to compute the interest charge each day, on a daily basis, and then add up all of the daily interest charges for the month.

Even with the same interest rate and exactly the same daily payments and purchases, these four methods could lead to different results. Some of these methods, although easy for a computer, are tedious for a consumer to check, even with a calculator. Truth in Lending does not require creditors to use a particular method, nor does Truth in Lending limit the rate or the amount that the creditor may charge. However, the creditor must tell consumers the annual percentage rate, the total finance charge, and the method by which the finance charge is computed. If a borrower doesn't understand the description on the statement, he or she can write to the creditor for a more detailed explanation.

Figure 19-1 is the lower portion of a typical statement of a retail store. Examples C and D below illustrate two methods used to compute finance charges.

Figure 19-1: Retail Statement of Account

PREVIOUS BALANCE	FINANCE CHARGE	PAYMENTS	CREDITS	PURCHASES	NEW BALANCE	MINIMUM PAYMENT	CLOSING DATE
624.00	9.36	500.00	62.95	364.57	434.98	45.00	10-16-99

IF WE RECEIVE PAYMENT OF THE FULL AMOUNT OF THE NEW BALANCE BEFORE THE NEXT CYCLE CLOSING DATE, SHOWN ABOVE, YOU WILL AVOID A FINANCE CHARGE NEXT MONTH. THE FINANCE CHARGE, IF ANY, IS FIGURED ON THE PREVIOUS BALANCE BEFORE DEDUCTING ANY PAYMENTS OR CREDITS SHOWN ABOVE. THE PERIODIC RATES USED ARE 1-1/2% OF THE BALANCE ON AMOUNTS UNDER $1,000 AND 1% OF AMOUNTS IN EXCESS OF $1,000 WHICH ARE ANNUAL PERCENTAGE RATES OF 18% AND 12% RESPECTIVELY.

EXAMPLE C

Compute the finance charge and the new balance for the statement shown in Figure 19-1 based on the previous balance, $624, ignoring all payments, credits, and purchases.

Finance charge = $624 × 1.5% × 1 month = $9.36
New balance = $624.00 + $9.36 − $500.00 − $62.95 + $364.57 = $434.98

EXAMPLE D

Assume that the finance charge in Figure 19-1 is based on the previous balance less any payments or credits, but ignore subsequent purchases. Compute the finance charge and the new balance.

The finance charge is based on $624.00 − $500.00 − $62.95 = $61.05.
Finance charge = $61.05 × 1.5% × 1 month = $0.91575, or $0.92
New balance = $624.00 + $0.92 − $500.00 − $62.95 + $364.57 =$426.54

CONCEPT CHECK 19.3

The finance terms given in the charge account statement of Figure 19-1 indicate that the finance charge, if any, is charged on the previous balance, before deducting payments or credits or adding purchases. Calculate the finance charge and the unpaid balance if the previous balance was $2,425.90, the payment was $1,200, there were no credits, and there were $572.50 in new purchases.

An interest rate of 1.5% applies to the first $1,000 and 1% applies to the excess:
$2,425.90 − $1,000 = $1,425.90
0.015 × $1,000 = $15.00
0.01 × $1,425.90 = $14.26
Finance charge = $15.00 + $14.26 = $29.26
New balance = $2,425.90 − $1,200 + $29.26 + $572.50 = $1,827.66

COMPLETE ASSIGNMENT 19.1.

Computing Costs of Installment Purchases

LEARNING OBJECTIVES 4

Compute costs of installment purchases.

In a credit sale, the buyer may pay the purchase price plus credit charges in monthly payments, called installments. The method of computing the interest is just as important as the interest rate. The interest may be computed just once on the principal or it may be computed monthly on the unpaid balance. In Chapter 18, the unpaid balance method used exact interest (365-day year). For consumer credit, the unpaid balance method is normally applied on a monthly basis, using a monthly interest rate that is the same for all months.

EXAMPLE E

Compute the total interest on purchases of $2,400 for 4 months at 15%, when interest is paid equally over 4 months. The principal is also repaid equally over 4 months, in payments of $600 each.

$\$2,400 \times 15\% \times \frac{4}{12} = \$120$ total interest

$\$120 \div 4 = \$30$ per month for interest

Month	Unpaid Balance	Monthly Interest	Principal Payment	Total Payment	New Balance
1	$2,400	$ 30.00	$ 600.00	$ 630.00	$1,800
2	1,800	30.00	600.00	630.00	1,200
3	1,200	30.00	600.00	630.00	600
4	600	30.00	600.00	630.00	0
Total		$120.00	$2,400.00	$2,520.00	

EXAMPLE F

Compute the total interest on purchases of $2,400 for 4 months at 15%, when interest is computed on the unpaid balance each month. The principal is repaid at $600 per month.

For the monthly interest of 15% per year, $15\% \div 12 = 1.25\%$ per month.

Month 1: $\$2,400 \times 1.25\% = \$30$
Month 2: $\$1,800 \times 1.25\% = \$22.50$
Month 3: $\$1,200 \times 1.25\% = \$15$
Month 4: $\$600 \times 1.25\% = \$7.50$

Total interest $= \$30 + \$22.50 + \$15 + \$7.50 = \$75$

Month	Unpaid Balance	Monthly Interest	Principal Payment	Total Payment	New Balance
1	$2,400	$30.00	$ 600.00	$ 630.00	$1,800
2	1,800	22.50	600.00	622.50	1,200
3	1,200	15.00	600.00	615.00	600
4	600	7.50	600.00	607.50	0
Total		$75.00	$2,400.00	$2,475.00	

CONCEPT CHECK 19.4

A kitchen stove has a price of $600. It is purchased with a $100 down payment. The $500 remaining balance is paid in two successive monthly payments of $250 each. Compute interest using the following methods.

a. Simple interest is calculated on the entire $500 for 2 months at 1.5% per month (18% annual rate).

$\$500 \times 0.015$ per month $\times$ 2 months $= \$15.00$

b. Interest of 1.5% is calculated on the unpaid balance each month (18% annual rate).

Month 1: $\$500 \times 0.015 = \$7.50$
Month 2: New balance is $250. $\$250 \times 0.015 = \$3.75$
Total interest $= \$7.50 + \$3.75 = \$11.25$

Computing Effective Rates

Compute effective rates.

The accounts in examples E and F are similar, but not identical. Both have purchases of \$2,400; both repay the principal in four equal payments of \$600; both use 15% to compute the interest. But the total interest in example E is \$120, while it is \$75 in example F. The problem is that although both loans quote a 15% interest rate, in example E, 15% is not the true interest rate. The true interest rate is called the *effective rate.* To find the effective rate, we can use $R = I/(P \times T)$, where I is the interest amount, T is the time of the loan, and P is the *average principal*, or the *average unpaid balance*, over the period of the loan.

In Chapter 17, the formula $I = P \times R \times T$ was written as $R = I/(P \times T)$ to solve for R, the interest rate. For examples E and F, T is $\frac{4}{12}$ of a year, and I is the interest amount: \$120 in E and \$75 in F. In Chapter 17, the borrower had the **entire** principal for the **entire** time, T. In the loans of examples E and F, the borrower does not have the entire \$2,400 for the entire four months. The principal decreases monthly, from \$2,400 down to \$600.

EXAMPLE G

Compute the effective interest rate on the purchases of examples E and F.

a. The average P is (\$2,400 + \$1,800 + \$1,200 + \$600) ÷ 4 = \$1,500. Therefore, $P = \$1{,}500$, $I = \$120$, and $T = \frac{4}{12}$ of a year.

$$R = \frac{I}{(P \times T)} = \frac{\$120}{\left(\$1{,}500 \times \frac{4}{12}\right)} = \frac{\$120}{\$500} = 0.24\text{, or } 24\%$$

b. The average P is (\$2,400 + \$1,800 + \$1,200 + \$600) ÷ 4 = \$1,500. Therefore, $P = \$1{,}500$, $I = \$75$, and $T = \frac{4}{12}$ of a year.

$$R = \frac{I}{(P \times T)} = \frac{\$75}{\left(\$1{,}500 \times \frac{4}{12}\right)} = \frac{\$75}{\$500} = 0.15\text{, or } 15\%$$

When interest is computed on the unpaid balance each month, the quoted rate and the effective rate will be the same. When interest is computed only on the original principal but the unpaid balance decreases each month, the true interest rate is always higher than the quoted rate.

Increasing the Effective Rate

Some credit purchasers do not consider the cost of credit when they make credit purchases. Other purchasers consider only the stated interest rate. Examples E, F, and G illustrate how creditors can increase the true interest rate by manipulating the method of computing interest and requiring payments.

Another method of increasing the true interest rate is to charge additional fees for the credit purchase or loan. There may be a credit application fee, a transaction fee, or an insurance fee on the merchandise purchased. Recall that Truth in Lending does not require these to be included in the computation of the stated APR, but they are certainly part of the increased cost of buying an item on credit instead of paying cash.

Even when interest is computed on the unpaid balance, if additional fees are charged, the effective rate will be higher than the quoted rate. The result is practically the same whether the extra charges are paid in advance, paid equally over the repayment period, or all paid at the end. Consider the following variation to the credit purchase in example F and part b of example G, where interest was computed on the unpaid balance.

EXAMPLE H

A loan of \$2,400 is for four months at 15% with interest computed on the unpaid balance each month. The principal is repaid in four monthly payments of \$600 each. There is also a loan origination fee of 1% of the purchase price and a \$1 per month insurance premium on the merchandise. Compute the effective rate using $R = I/(P \times T)$ where P is the average principal over the four months and I is the total of all finance charges.

The loan origination fee is 1% × \$2,400 = \$24.00.
The insurance premiums are \$1 per month, or \$4.00 total.
From example F, the total interest is \$75.00.
From part b of example G, the average principal, P, is \$6,000/4 = \$1,500.
The time, T, is $\frac{4}{12}$ year (4 months).

$$I = \text{Total finance charge} = \text{Interest} + \text{Loan origination fee} + \text{Insurance}$$
$$= \$75 + \$24 + \$4 = \$103$$

$$R = \frac{I}{(P \times T)} = \frac{\$103}{\left(\$1{,}500 \times \frac{4}{12}\right)} = \frac{\$103}{\$500} = 0.206\text{, or } 20.6\%$$

Recall that in part b of example G, the effective rate was 15%, the same as the quoted rate. By adding the additional charges, the creditor has increased the effective rate from 15% to 20.6%.

An Alternative Formula for Estimating the Effective Rate

One difficulty with using the formula $R = I/(P \times T)$ to find the effective rate is that P is the average unpaid balance. Sometimes the payment plan is stated without reference to interest rates, making the calculation of the monthly unpaid balance impossible. The formula discussed below gives exactly the same results as $R = I/(P \times T)$—if the principal is repaid **equally** during each month of the loan. The P in this new formula is just the original amount that is financed or borrowed.

$$R = \frac{2 \times M \times I}{[P \times (n + 1)]}$$

where

R = Effective annual interest rate
M = 12 months in one year (use 12 for all problems in this book; see note below)
I = Total finance charge (interest plus additional fees, if any)
P = Amount of the credit purchase or amount of the loan
n = Number of payments in the credit plan

NOTE ABOUT M: M is the number of payment periods in exactly one year—regardless of the length of the credit plan. If payments are weekly, $M = 52$; if payments are quarterly, $M = 4$; etc.

EXAMPLE I

Use the alternative formula to find the effective rate in example H.

M = 12
I = Total finance charge = \$75 + \$24 + \$4 = \$103
P = Amount of the purchase = \$2,400 (instead of the average unpaid balance)
n = 4 payments

$$R = \frac{2 \times M \times I}{[P \times (n + 1)]} = \frac{2 \times 12 \times \$103}{[\$2{,}400 \times (4 + 1)]} = \frac{\$2{,}472}{\$12{,}000} = 0.206\text{, or } 20.6\%$$

This formula gives the same result, without the need to calculate the average unpaid balance. In example H, however, coming up with the total interest charge, I, still requires a computation for every month. Therefore, not much time has been saved.

A more useful application of the alternative formula is when it is not possible to compute the average unpaid balance but it is possible to find the total finance charge, as in the following example. Although we don't know that the principal is being paid equally each month, the alternative formula will *approximate the effective rate.*

Use the alternative formula in the following example.

EXAMPLE J

An advertisement reads: "Buy this big-screen television today for $2,200. Or, make a $200 down payment and 11 equal monthly payments of $200 each." The buyer does not know how the principal is being repaid.

The total cost of the television using credit equals the down payment plus 11 × $200: $200 + $2,200 = $2,400.

The finance charge is the total cost less the cash price: I = $2,400 − $2,200 = $200. The amount that is financed, P, is the cash price less the down payment: P = $2,200 − $200 = $2,000. The number of monthly payments is 11: $n = 11$ monthly payments.

$$R = \frac{2 \times M \times I}{P \times (n + 1)} = \frac{2 \times 12 \times \$200}{[\$2{,}000 \times (11 + 1)]} = \frac{\$4{,}800}{\$24{,}000} = 0.2, \text{ or } 20\%$$

R is the *approximate* effective rate. We do not know whether or not the $2,000 is being repaid in 11 equal parts, but we assume so in order to estimate R.

CONCEPT CHECK 19.5

a. A kitchen stove priced at $600 is purchased with a $100 down payment. The $500 remaining balance may be financed over 2 months with either of the following installment payment plans (see Concept Check 19.4).

Plan 1: Two monthly principal payments of $250 each and a total interest amount of $15.00
Plan 2: Two monthly principal payments of $250 each and a total interest amount of $11.25

Calculate the effective annual rate of each plan using $R = \frac{I}{(P \times T)}$, where P is the average unpaid monthly balance and T is $\frac{2}{12}$ of a year. In each plan, the monthly unpaid balances are $500 in month 1 and $250 in month 2.

The average unpaid balance is $\frac{(\$500 + \$250)}{2} = \frac{\$750}{2} = \$375$, so $P = \$375$.

Plan 1: $$R = \frac{I}{(P \times T)} = \frac{\$15.00}{\left(\$375 \times \frac{2}{12}\right)} = \frac{\$15.00}{\$62.50} = 0.24, \text{ or } 24\% \text{ effective annual rate}$$

Plan 2: $$R = \frac{I}{(P \times T)} = \frac{\$11.25}{\left(\$375 \times \frac{2}{12}\right)} = \frac{\$11.25}{\$62.50} = 0.18, \text{ or } 18\% \text{ effective annual rate}$$

b. A kitchen stove priced at $600 can be purchased on an installment plan for a $100 down payment and five equal monthly payments of $105 each. Calculate the approximate effective rate using the formula

$R = \frac{2 \times M \times I}{[P \times (n + 1)]}$, where $M = 12$, the number of months in 1 year; I = the total finance charge; P = $500, the amount financed; and $n = 5$, the actual number of payments.

The total charge to finance the stove is the difference between the total amount paid and the cash price.

Total paid = $100 down payment + 5 × $105 = $100 + $525 = $625; I = $625 − $600 = $25

$$\frac{2 \times M \times I}{P \times (n + 1)} = \frac{2 \times 12 \times \$25}{\$500 \times (5 + 1)} = \frac{\$600}{\$3{,}000}$$

The effective annual rate is 20%.

COMPLETE ASSIGNMENT 19.2.

Amortizing a Loan

In example F, interest was computed on the unpaid balance, but the total monthly payments were unequal. In example E, the total payments were equal, but the interest was not computed on the unpaid balance. It is easier for both borrower and lender if the monthly payments are equal, but the quoted rate does not equal the true effective rate unless the interest is computed on the unpaid balance.

LEARNING OBJECTIVES 6

Amortize a loan.

By using a computer, a financial calculator, or special tables (such as Table 19-1), it is possible to determine monthly payments that will always be equal and still have the interest computed on the unpaid balance. This is called *amortization;* it is usually used for loans to purchase homes, cars, and other long-term, high-cost items. In a credit purchase, the buyer may make a down payment and amortize the balance.

The combined principal and interest are paid in equal monthly payments. Each of the equal monthly payments includes the interest on the unpaid balance of the loan and a payment on the principal. With each successive payment, the unpaid balance decreases. Thus, the subsequent interest payments decrease, and the corresponding payments on the principal increase. Because of rounding, the final monthly payment may be a few cents different from the others.

Computing the Monthly Payment

Companies that amortize loans compute the monthly payment by using computers, financial calculators, or special tables. Table 19-1 has only five interest rates (columns) and twelve loan time periods (rows), but it illustrates the concept. The numbers in the table are called *amortization payment factors.* Multiply the amount of the loan or the finance purchase by the amortization payment factor to find the monthly payment.

Table 19-1: Amortization Payment Factors (for monthly payments)

Term of Loan	Annual Interest Rate					
	6%	9%	12%	15%	18%	21%
1 month	1.00500	1.00750	1.01000	1.01250	1.01500	1.01750
2 months	0.50375	0.50563	0.50751	0.50939	0.51128	0.51316
3 months	0.33667	0.33835	0.34002	0.34170	0.34338	0.34507
4 months	0.25313	0.25471	0.25628	0.25786	0.25944	0.26103
5 months	0.20301	0.20452	0.20604	0.20756	0.20909	0.21062
6 months	0.16960	0.17107	0.17255	0.17403	0.17553	0.17702
1 year	0.08607	0.08745	0.08885	0.09026	0.09168	0.09311
2 years	0.04432	0.04568	0.04707	0.04849	0.04992	0.05139
3 years	0.03042	0.03180	0.03321	0.03467	0.03615	0.03768
4 years	0.02349	0.02489	0.02633	0.02783	0.02937	0.03097
5 years	0.01933	0.02076	0.02224	0.02379	0.02539	0.02705
10 years	0.01110	0.01267	0.01435	0.01613	0.01802	0.01999

EXAMPLE K

Find the monthly payment to amortize a $4,000 loan over 4 months at 12% (1% per month).

STEP 1 Find the intersection of the 12% column and the 4-month row. The amortization payment factor is 0.25628.

STEP 2 Multiply the amount amortized by the payment factor:
$4,000 × 0.25628 = $1,025.12 monthly payment

EXAMPLE L

Karen Davidson agrees to purchase an automobile for $18,300. Karen will pay a $2,000 down payment and amortize the balance over 4 years at 15% (1.25% per month). Determine Karen's monthly payment.

STEP 1 $18,300 − $2,000 = $16,300 amortized

STEP 2 Find the intersection of the 15% column and the 4-year row. The amortization payment factor is 0.02783.

STEP 3 Multiply the amount amortized by the payment factor:
$16,300 × 0.02783 = $453.63 monthly payment

Loan Payment Schedule

After determining the amount of the monthly payments, a lender can prepare a schedule of loan payments called an *amortization schedule*. The payment for the last month is determined in the schedule, and it may be slightly different from the payment in the other months. To create an amortization schedule, follow these steps.

STEPS to Create an Amortization Schedule

For each row except the last:

1. Interest payment = Unpaid balance × Monthly interest rate
2. Principal payment = Monthly payment − Interest payment
3. New unpaid balance = Old unpaid balance − Principal payment

For the last row (i.e., for the final payment):

1. Interest payment = Unpaid balance × Monthly interest rate
2. (Then **add**) Monthly payment = Unpaid balance + Interest payment
3. Principal payment = Unpaid balance

EXAMPLE M

Create the amortization schedule for the loan in example K, a $4,000 loan amortized at 12% over 4 months. The interest rate is 1% per month.

Table 19-2: Amortization Schedule

Month	Unpaid Balance	Interest Payment	Principal Payment	Total Payment	New Balance
1	$4,000.00	$ 40.00	$ 985.12	$1,025.12	$3,014.88
2	3,014.88	30.15	994.97	1,025.12	2,019.91
3	2,019.91	20.20	1,004.92	1,025.12	1,014.99
4	1,014.99	10.15	1,014.99	1,025.14	0
Totals		$100.50	$4,000.00	$4,100.50	

NOTE: The last monthly payment is 2 cents larger than the others. Because the interest payments need to be rounded off, there will often be a small rounding error in the final payment.

The alternative formula for effective rate gives

$$R = \frac{2 \times M \times I}{[P \times (n + 1)]} = \frac{2 \times 12 \times \$100.50}{[\$4,000 \times (4 + 1)]} = \frac{\$2,412}{\$20,000} = 0.1206, \text{ or } 12.06\%$$

You get 12.06% instead of 12% because the alternative formula requires that the amount paid on the principal be equal every period. Examine Table 19-2 and you will see that the amounts paid on principal are slightly different each month. Therefore, the rate from this formula is slightly different from the true effective rate of 12%.

CONCEPT CHECK 19.6

A $500 purchase is amortized over 2 months at an annual rate of 18%. First use Table 19-1 to calculate the monthly payment. Then show the calculations to construct a 2-month amortization schedule.

Amortization payment factor from Table 19-1: 0.51128 × $500 principal = $255.64 monthly payment

Month	1		2	
Unpaid balance	Original principal	$500.00	From end of month 1	$251.86
Monthly rate	0.18 ÷ 12 = 0.015			
Interest payment	$500.00 × 0.015 =	$7.50	$251.86 × 0.015 =	$3.78
Total payment	From table	$255.64	$251.86 + $3.78 =	$255.64
Principal payment	$255.64 − $7.50 =	$248.14		$251.86
New balance	$500 − $248.14 =	$251.86	$251.86 − $251.86 =	$0.00

COMPLETE ASSIGNMENT 19.3.

Chapter Terms for Review

amortization
amortization payment factor
amortization schedule
amortizing a loan
annual percentage rate (APR)
approximating the effective rate
average daily balance
average principal
average unpaid balance
credit card
effective interest rate
finance charge
Truth in Lending

The Bottom Line

Summary of chapter learning objectives:

Learning Objective	Summary	Example
19.1	Converting between annual and monthly interest rates	1. Convert 0.5% per month to an annual rate. 2. Convert 21% per year to a monthly rate.
19.2	Computing simple interest on a monthly basis	3. Compute the simple interest on \$1,200 for 5 months at 0.75% per month (9% per year).
19.3	Computing finance charges for credit account purchases	4. Charge account terms apply a 1.25% finance charge to the previous balance less any payments and credits, ignoring purchases. Find the finance charge and new balance when the previous balance is \$1,683.43, payments plus credits total \$942.77, and purchases are \$411.48.
19.4	Computing costs of installment purchases	5. Furniture worth \$1,800 is paid for with a \$300 down payment and three payments of \$500, plus monthly interest of 1% on the unpaid balance. Find the total interest paid. The monthly balances are \$1,500, \$1,000, and \$500.
19.5	Computing effective rates	6. A \$2,400 loan is repaid in 12 payments of \$210 each. Find the approximate annual effective rate. $M = 12$ months in one year; Interest = (\$210 × 12) − \$2,400 = \$120; $P =$ \$2,400 financed; $n = 12$ payments.
19.6	Amortizing a loan	7. A \$2,400 loan will be amortized over 12 months at an annual rate of 9%. Find the payment using Table 19-1, and calculate the unpaid balance after the first month.

Answers: 1. 6% per year **2.** 1.75% per month **3.** \$45 **4.** Finance charge, \$9.26; new balance, \$1,161.40 **5.** \$30 **6.** 9.2% **7.** Payment, \$209.88; unpaid balance, \$2,208.12

Assignment 19.1: Monthly Finance Charges

Name ______________________

Date ______________ Score ______________

A **(22 points) Problem 1: Change the rates from annual to monthly. Problem 2: Change the rates from monthly to annual. (1 point for each correct answer)**

1. a. 12% = ________ **b.** 15% ________ **c.** 16% ________ **d.** 8% ________

e. 6% ________ **f.** 20% ________ **g.** 24% ________ **h.** 18% ________

i. 9% ________ **j.** 21% ________ **k.** 10% ________

2. a. 1.5% = ________ **b.** 1% = ________ **c.** 1.75% = ________ **d.** 2% = ________

e. $1\frac{2}{3}$% = ________ **f.** 1.25% = ________ **g.** $1\frac{1}{3}$% = ________ **h.** 0.75% = ________

i. $\frac{7}{12}$% = ________ **j.** $\frac{2}{3}$% = ________ **k.** 0.5% = ________

____

Score for A (22)

B **(30 points) Atherton Furniture Store offers the credit terms shown below to its retail customers. Problems 3–6: Compute the finance charge, if any, and the new balance. Assume that all payments are made within the current billing cycle. Problems 7–8: Judith Carey has an account at Atherton Furniture Store. Compute the missing values in Judith's accounts summary for the months of July and August. The Previous Balance in August is the same as the New Balance in July. ($2\frac{1}{2}$ points for each correct answer)**

TERMS: There will be no finance charge if the full amount of the new balance is received within 25 days after the cycle-closing date. The finance charge, if any, is based upon the entire previous balance **before** any payments or credits are deducted. The rates are 1.5% per month on amounts up to $1,000 and 1.25% on amounts in excess of $1,000. These are annual percentage rates of 18% and 15%, respectively.

Cycle Closing	Previous Balance	Payment Amount	Credits	Finance Charge	Purchases	New Balance
3. 3/20/—	$1,539.75	$750.00	$195.50	________	$520.16	________
4. 6/20/—	$743.72	$0.00	$15.00	________	$609.88	________
5. 9/20/—	$3,208.46	$2,500.00	$158.12	________	$851.72	________
6. 12/20/—	$2,061.14	$2,061.14	$0.00	________	$1,488.34	________

	Cycle Closing	Previous Balance	Payment Amount	Credits	Finance Charge	Purchases	New Balance
7.	7/20/—	$1,636.55	$900.00	$36.00	________	$844.25	________
8.	8/20/—		$1,250.00	$88.50	________	$609.88	________

Score for B (30)

C **(48 points) Devlin's Feed & Fuel offers the credit terms shown below to its retail customers. Problems 9–12: Compute the missing values in the charge accounts shown. Assume that all payments are made within 30 days of the billing date. Problems 11–12: Compute the missing values in Jimmy Petrasek's charge account summary at Devlin's for the months of January and February. The Previous Balance in February is the same as the New Balance in January. (4 points for each correct answer)**

TERMS: Finance Charge is based on the Net Balance, if payment is received within 30 days of the billing date. If payment is made after 30 days, then the Finance Charge is based on the Previous Balance. Net Balance equals Previous Balance less Payments and Credits. In either case, the monthly rate is 1.25% on the first $500 and 1% on any amount over $500. These are annual percentage rates of 15% and 12%, respectively.

	Billing Date	Previous Balance	Payment Amount	Credit	Net Balance	Finance Charge	New Purchases	Balance
9.	4/25/—	$2,056.42	$1,500.00	$0.00	________	________	$937.20	________

	Billing Date	Previous Balance	Payment Amount	Credit	Net Balance	Finance Charge	New Purchases	Balance
10.	8/25/—	$1,727.95	$1,000.00	$23.75	________	________	$499.06	________
11.	1/25/—	$1,352.12	$500.00	$52.00	________	________	$375.21	________
12.	2/25/—	$1,184.58	$500.00	$0.00	________	________	$508.14	________

____

Score for C (48)

Assignment 19.2: Installment Sales and Effective Rates

LEARNING OBJECTIVES 4
LEARNING OBJECTIVES 5

Name ____________________

Date ____________________ Score ____________________

A **(24 points) Karen Ann Senter makes a credit purchase of $2,000 for dining room furniture. She agrees to pay simple interest for 4 months at 9% of the purchase price. (Use $T = \frac{4}{12}$ year.) Each month Karen will pay $\frac{1}{4}$ of the total interest and $\frac{1}{4}$ of the $2,000 principal. Compute the answer to each of the following questions. (6 points for each correct answer)**

1. a. What is the simple interest on $2,000 at 9% for 4 months? __________

b. Over the 4-month period, what is the average unpaid balance? __________

c. What is the effective annual rate of interest (to the nearest $\frac{1}{10}$%)? Use the formula $R = I/(P \times T)$, where P is the average unpaid balance, I is the total interest paid, and T is $\frac{4}{12}$ year. __________

2. What is the effective annual rate of interest (to the nearest $\frac{1}{10}$%)? Use the formula $R = 2 \times M \times I/[P \times (n + 1)]$, where P is the amount of the credit purchase, I is the amount of interest, M is the number of months in one year, and n is the number of actual payments. __________

Score for A (24) __________

B **(40 points) Rework the problem from Part A with a different method of calculating interest. As above, Karen Ann Senter makes a $2,000 credit purchase. And, as above, she agrees to repay the $2,000 principal in 4 equal monthly payments of $500. This time, however, calculate her interest each month at 0.75% per month (9% annual rate) on the unpaid balance. Complete the table below. (2 points for each correct answer)**

	Month	Unpaid Balance	Interest Payment	Principal Payment	Total Payment	New Balance
3.	1	________	________	________	________	________
4.	2	________	________	________	________	________
5.	3	________	________	________	________	________
6.	4	________	________	________	________	________

Score for B (40) __________

C (24 points) Use the information from the table you completed in Part B to solve problems 7 and 8. (6 points for each correct answer)

7. Compute the effective annual interest rate (to the nearest $\frac{1}{10}$%) for Karen Ann Senter's credit purchase in Part B. Use $R = I/(P \times T)$. Use the table to find P, the average unpaid principal over the 4-month period, and I, the total interest paid; $T = \frac{4}{12}$ year.

a. Total interest: __________ **b.** Average unpaid balance: __________ **c.** Effective rate: __________

8. For the same credit purchase, compute the effective annual rate (to the nearest $\frac{1}{10}$%) using the formula $R = 2 \times M \times I/[P \times (n + 1)]$, where P is the amount of the credit purchase, I is the total amount of interest, M is the number of months in one year, and n is the actual number of payments. __________

____
Score for C (24)

D (12 points) Approximate the effective annual rate of interest using the formula $R = 2 \times M \times I/[P \times (n + 1)]$, where P is the amount of the purchase that is charged, I is the total finance charge, M is the number of months in one year, and n is the actual number of payments. Give the rate to the nearest $\frac{1}{10}$%. (6 points for each correct answer)

9. Belva Warren has decided to buy a rototiller from a catalog. She can purchase the rototiller for $1,150 cash, or she can choose a 1-year credit purchase with a $50 down payment and 12 monthly payments of $100 each. What is the approximate effective rate of the credit purchase plan? __________

10. Western States TV & Stereo is offering a special credit purchase of new big screen television sets. The customer can pay $250 down and make 24 payments of $150 each. There is also a $10 fee to set up the credit plan and a $12 charge for insurance on the TV set (50 cents per month). The cash price of the television set is $3,495. Find the approximate effective rate of interest. __________

____
Score for D (12)

Assignment 19.3: Amortization

Name ______________________

Date ______________ Score ______________

A (20 points) Midwest National Bank amortizes most of its personal loans on a monthly basis. The total monthly payments include both interest and principal, and the payments are the same each month. Use Table 19-1 to find the amortization payment factor for the following loans. Then compute the monthly payment for each loan. (2 points for each correct answer)

Loan and Terms of Amortization	Amortization Payment Factor	Monthly Payment
1. \$3,500 over 4 months at 18%	________	________
2. \$45,000 over 5 years at 9%	________	________
3. \$12,400 over 2 years at 12%	________	________
4. \$150,000 over 10 years at 6%	________	________
5. \$7,650 over 1 year at 15%	________	________

Score for A (20)

B (32 points) On April 13, Ryan English borrowed \$6,000 from his bank to help pay his federal income taxes for the previous year. The bank amortized the loan over 4 months at a rate of 9%. Find the amortization payment factor from Table 19-1. The interest payment is 0.75% (9%/12) times the unpaid balance each month. Subtract the interest from the total payment to get the principal payment. Subtract the principal payment from the unpaid balance to get the new balance. In the last (fourth) month, add the interest payment to the unpaid balance to get the total payment. (2 points for each correct answer)

6. Amortization factor from Table 19-1: ________
Multiply the amortization factor by \$6,000 to get the total payment shown for months 1, 2, and 3.

	Month	Unpaid Balance	Interest Payment	Total Payment	Principal Payment	New Balance
7.	1	\$6,000.00	________	\$1,528.26	________	________
8.	2	________	________	1,528.26	________	________
9.	3	________	________	1,528.26	________	________
10.	4	________	________	________	________	0.00

Score for B (32)

C **(30 points) Refer to Part B, in which Ryan English borrowed $6,000 to help pay his federal income taxes. Now suppose that Ryan agreed to make payments of $1,200 in months 1, 2, and 3. The bank will compute the interest on the unpaid balance at a rate of 0.75% (9%/12) each month and deduct the interest from the $1,200. In the last (fourth) month, Ryan will pay all of the remaining unpaid balance plus the interest for the last month. Complete the table using the same procedure as in Part B. (2 points for each correct answer)**

	Month	Unpaid Balance	Interest Payment	Total Payment	Principal Payment	New Balance
11.	1	$6,000.00	________	$1,200.00	________	________
12.	2	________	________	1,200.00	________	________
13.	3	________	________	1,200.00	________	________
14.	4	________	________	________	________	0.00

____
Score for C (30)

D **(18 points) The following questions are about amortized loans. To answer the questions, you will need to compute one or two rows of the amortization schedule. Do only the work necessary to answer the questions. (3 points for each correct answer)**

15. Jennifer Brown and her husband purchased a duplex apartment (two units) so that they could live in one unit and rent the other. To complete the purchase, they decided to borrow $75,000. Their bank amortized the loan over 10 years at 9% interest.

a. How much did the Browns pay in interest during the first month? ________

b. How much did the Browns pay in principal during the first month? ________

c. What was the unpaid balance at the end of the first month? ________

16. Doyle Bransom bought a new Ford pickup truck. He traded in his old truck, used some of his savings, and got a loan from the Ford agency for $8,000. The Ford agency amortized the loan over 3 years at 6%.

a. What was Doyle's monthly payment? ________

b. How much total interest did Doyle pay during the first two months? ________

c. What was the unpaid balance at the end of the second month? ________

____
Score for D (18)

Notes

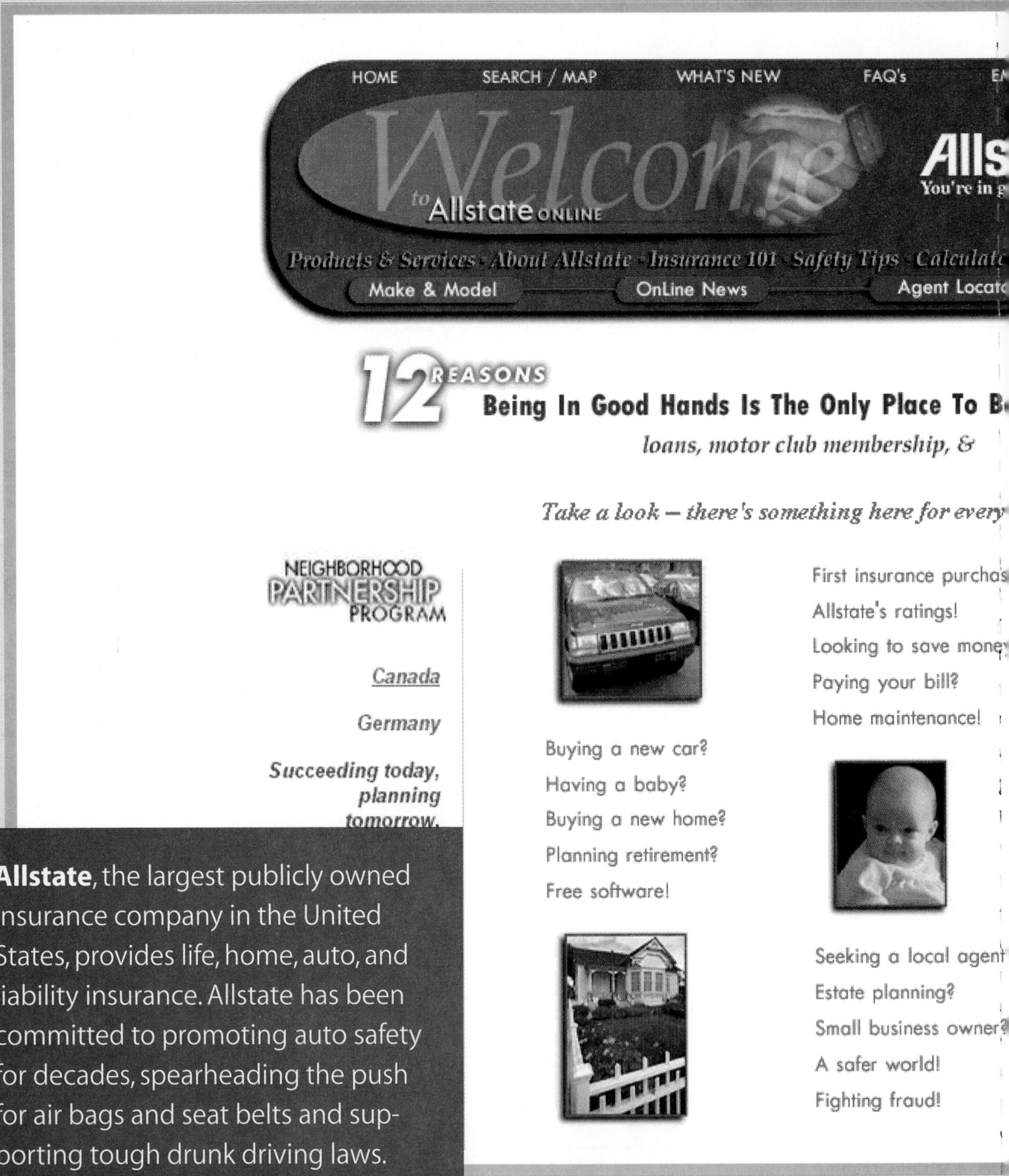

Allstate, the largest publicly owned insurance company in the United States, provides life, home, auto, and liability insurance. Allstate has been committed to promoting auto safety for decades, spearheading the push for air bags and seat belts and supporting tough drunk driving laws. Allstate has many claim offices and drive-in centers in the United States and Canada, supported by up to 14,000 knowledgeable insurance agents. Visit Allstate at www.allstate.com.

20 Business and Personal Insurance

Learning Objectives

By studying this chapter and completing all the assignments, you will learn to:

1. Compute costs and savings for auto insurance.
2. Compute auto insurance premium rates for high- and low-risk drivers.
3. Compute short-rate refunds.
4. Compute coinsurance on property losses.
5. Compute life insurance premiums.
6. Compute cash surrender and loan values.
7. Compute medical insurance contributions and reimbursements.

In early colonial times, mainly just sea captains and other ocean travelers purchased life insurance. No medical examination was required, and the cost was high. Today, about two out of three Americans have life insurance. Many have property and auto insurance as well.

Computing Auto Insurance Costs

LEARNING OBJECTIVES 1

Compute costs and savings for auto insurance.

Auto insurance falls into three classifications: liability and property damage, comprehensive, and collision. A policy that fully protects the insured will contain all three classifications.

Liability and property damage insurance protects the insured against claims resulting from personal injuries and property damage. Some states require all drivers to carry auto liability and property damage insurance. The amount of protection generally ranges from $50,000 to $1,000,000 per accident.

Comprehensive insurance protects the vehicle of the insured against water, theft, vandalism, falling objects, and other damage that is not caused by collision.

Collision insurance protects the vehicle of the insured against collision damage. Such damage may result from a collision with another vehicle or a one-car accident, such as hitting a tree.

The payment for an insurance policy is called a *premium.* Premium rates for auto insurance depend on the coverage included in the policy and the driving record of the insured.

Auto collision insurance policies usually contain a *deductible clause,* which stipulates that the insured will pay the first portion of collision damage, usually $50 to $500, and the insurance company will pay the remainder up to the value of the insured vehicle. A deductible clause not only reduces the amount of damages for which the insurance company must pay but also keeps the insurance company from having to get involved in and do paperwork for small repairs costing less than the deductible. Therefore, a deductible clause lowers the premium for collision insurance.

EXAMPLE A

A car was insured for collision damage with a $500 deductible. The premium was $1,250 per year. The insured hit a tree, causing $2,700 damage to his car. How much more did the insured receive than he paid in premiums for that year?

$2,700 damage − $500 deductible = $2,200 paid by insurance
$2,200 received by insured − $1,250 premium paid = $950

EXAMPLE B

The driver of car A carried auto liability and property damage insurance only. She struck car B, causing $1,400 damage to car B and $700 in injuries to the driver. Car A suffered $940 damage.

a. How much did the insurance company pay for this accident?

$1,400 for damage to car B + $700 for injuries to driver = $2,100

b. How much did this accident cost the driver of car A?

$940 in uncovered damage to her own car

No-fault insurance requires that the driver of each vehicle involved in an injury accident submit a claim to **his or her own insurance company** to cover medical costs for injuries to the driver and passengers in that person's own vehicle. No-fault insurance is mandatory in some states. No-fault insurance does not cover damage to either vehicle involved in an accident.

EXAMPLE C

Drivers A and B live in a state in which no-fault insurance is mandatory. Their two cars collided. Driver A and his passengers incurred medical expenses of $3,500. Driver B and her passengers incurred $1,700 in medical expenses. Car A required $1,400 in repairs. Car B required $948 in repairs. How much did the insurance companies pay under the no-fault insurance coverage?

Driver A's insurance company paid $3,500 in medical expenses.
Driver B's insurance company paid $1,700 in medical expenses.
Car repairs are not covered under no-fault insurance.

CONCEPT CHECK 20.1

Driver A lives in a state in which no-fault insurance is mandatory. He carries all three classifications of insurance to be fully protected. His total insurance premium is $2,400, with a collision deductible of $500. Driver A is involved in a major accident when he loses control of his car and hits two parked cars (cars B and C) before colliding with an oncoming car (car D) containing a driver and three passengers. Driver A is alone.

Damage to Driver A's car is $3,200.
Damages to cars B, C, and D total $8,600.
Medical expenses for driver A are $2,800.
Medical expenses for the driver and passengers of car D are $7,300.

a. How much does driver A's insurance company pay?
   Damage to car A: $3,200 − $500 deductible = $2,700 covered by collision
   Damage to cars B, C, and D: $8,600 covered by liability
   Medical expenses for driver A under no-fault: $2,800
   $2,700 + $8,600 + $2,800 = $14,100 paid by driver A's insurance
b. How much does driver D's insurance company pay?
   Medical expenses paid for driver D and passengers (no-fault): $7,300
c. How much more did driver A's insurance company pay to him and on his behalf for this accident than he paid in insurance expenses for the year? (This is the amount driver A saved this year by being fully insured.)
   $2,400 premium + $500 deductible = $2,900 paid by Driver A
   $14,100 from insurance − $2,900 = $11,200
   Driver A saved $11,200 this year by being fully insured.

Computing Low-Risk and High-Risk Rates

Auto insurance premium rates reflect the risk involved. Insurance companies study the statistics on automobile accidents relative to driving records. Premium rates are adjusted according to the driving record of the insured. A driver with a clear record of long standing is considered to be a *low-risk driver* and may be rewarded with a discount in the premium rate. Conversely, a driver with a record of numerous citations or accidents is considered to be a *high-risk driver* and may pay double or triple the normal premium rate.

LEARNING OBJECTIVES 2

Compute auto insurance premium rates for high- and low-risk drivers.

EXAMPLE D

Drivers A and B have identical automobiles and amounts of insurance coverage. The normal premium rate for each is $950 per year. Driver A is a low-risk driver and receives a 10% discount on the premium rate. Driver B is a high-risk driver and must pay double the normal rate. How much more does driver B pay for insurance than driver A?

Driver A pays $950 × 90% = $855
Driver B pays $950 × 2 = $1,900
Driver B pays $1,900 − $855 = $1,045 more

CONCEPT CHECK 20.2

Driver A, a very careful driver, has had the same insurance company for 5 years and has not had a ticket during that 5-year period. Each year, driver A has received a 10% reduction in her premium. Driver B has a record of speeding tickets. He has had one or more every year for 5 years. His premium for year 1 was normal, for years 2 and 3 it was 150%, and for years 4 and 5 it was 200%. The normal annual premium rate for each driver would be $980.

a. How much did driver A pay in premiums over the 5-year period?
   $\$980 \times 90\% = \$882$
   $\$882 \times 5 = \$4{,}410$

b. How much did driver B pay in premiums over the 5-year period?
   Year 1: $980
   Years 2 and 3: $\$980 \times 1.5 \times 2 = \$2{,}940$
   Years 4 and 5: $\$980 \times 2 \times 2 = \$3{,}920$
   $\$980 + \$2{,}940 + \$3{,}920 = \$7{,}840$

c. How much more did driver B pay during the 5-year period than driver A?
   $\$7{,}840 - \$4{,}410 = \$3{,}430$

Computing Short Rates

LEARNING OBJECTIVES 3

Compute short-rate refunds.

Short rates are rates charged for less than a full term of insurance. If an insurance policy is canceled by the *insured* (the person who receives the benefit of the insurance) before the policy's full term is complete, the insured will receive a short-rate return of premium. If a policy is canceled by the insurance company rather than by the insured, the company must refund the entire unused premium.

EXAMPLE E

A driver paid an annual premium of $980 for auto insurance. After 3 months, the vehicle was sold and the insurance canceled. The insurance company refunded the remaining portion of the premium at the short rate, based on a 10% penalty. What was the refund?

Unused premium: $\$980 \times \frac{3}{4} = \$735$

Penalty: $\$980 \times 10\% = \$98$

Short-rate refund: $\$735 - \$98 = \$637$

CONCEPT CHECK 20.3

A company purchased two cars. Each car was insured at an annual premium of $890. At the end of 6 months, the company sold one car and canceled the insurance on that car. At the end of 9 months, the insurance company decided to cancel the insurance on the second car. The insurance company imposes a 10% penalty for short-rate premiums. Compute the refunds the insurance company paid for car 1 and car 2.

Car 1: $\$890 \times \frac{1}{2}$ year $= \$445$ unused premium
$\$890 \times 10\%$ penalty $= \$89$
$\$445 - \$89 = \$356$ refunded

Car 2: $\$890 \times \frac{1}{4}$ year $= \$222.50$ unused and refunded premium

COMPLETE ASSIGNMENT 20.1.

Computing Coinsurance on Property Losses

Property insurance is insurance against loss of or damage to property. A policy can be written to protect the insured against one or more of the following: fire, casualty, liability, and theft.

Premium rates, which are quoted in terms of the number of dollars per $1,000 of insurance, depend on the nature of the risk, the location of the property, and the length of time covered by the policy. Short rates and short-rate penalties for less than a full term of insurance apply to property insurance as they do to auto insurance.

LEARNING OBJECTIVES 4

Compute coinsurance on property losses.

EXAMPLE F

A building worth $300,000 is insured for $225,000. The annual premium for the policy is $5,000. A fire causes $220,000 in damage.

a. How much does the insurance company pay?
   $220,000 in damage is less than the $225,000 policy. The insurance company pays the entire $220,000.

b. How much does the property owner pay?
   The property owner pays no damages.

c. How much does the property owner pay that year in damages and insurance?
   $5,000 for the insurance premium only.

In an ordinary fire insurance policy, the insured will be paid for the loss up to the amount of the insurance. Policies may be obtained at lower rates if they contain a *coinsurance clause.* This clause specifies that if a property is not insured up to a certain percentage of its value, the owner is responsible for part of the insurance and will not be covered for the full amount of damages.

It is common for a policy to have an 80% coinsurance clause. Under this clause, the full amount of the loss will not be paid by the insurance company unless the policy amount equals 80% of the property value. It is important to note that the amount of the loss is not necessarily the total value of the property. For example, suppose only a part of a building valued at $300,000 were damaged in a fire. The loss would not be the entire value of the building; rather, it would be the cost of repairing the partial damage.

STEPS to Determine the Owner's Share of Property Loss Under Coinsurance

1. Compute the amount of insurance required by multiplying the entire value of the property by the coinsurance percentage.
2. Compute the *recovery amount,* the maximum amount the insurance company will pay, by using the following formula:

$$\frac{\text{Amount of insurance carried}}{\text{Amount of insurance required}} \times \text{Loss} = \text{Recovery amount}$$

3. Compare the recovery amount with the amount of the insurance policy.
   a. If the recovery amount is greater than the amount of the policy, the insurance company will pay the amount of the policy.
   b. If the recovery amount is less than the amount of the policy, the insurance company will pay the recovery amount.
   NOTE: The insurance company will not pay more than the amount of the loss.
4. Determine the owner's share of the property loss by subtracting the amount the insurance company will pay from the loss amount.

EXAMPLE G

A building worth $300,000 is insured for $225,000, and the policy carries an 80% coinsurance clause. The annual premium is $3,500. A fire causes $220,000 in damage.

a. How much will the insurance company pay?

STEP 1 $\quad \$300{,}000 \times 80\% = \$240{,}000$ insurance required

STEPS 2 & 3 $\quad \dfrac{\$225{,}000}{\$240{,}000} \times \$220{,}000 = \$206{,}250$ insurance pays

b. How much must the owner pay if the building is repaired for $220,000?

STEP 4 $\quad \$220{,}000 - \$206{,}250 = \$13{,}750$ owner pays

c. How much does the property owner pay that year for damages and insurance?

$13,750 damages + $3,500 premium = $17,250

EXAMPLE H

If the amount of insurance carried in example G had been $240,000, how much would the insured have paid for damages and insurance that year?

$3,500 premium only (the 80% coinsurance requirement would have been met)

CONCEPT CHECK 20.4

A building worth $100,000 is insured for $60,000 with an 80% coinsurance clause. A fire causes $70,000 in damage. How much will the insurance company pay, and how much will the insured pay?

$\$100{,}000 \times 80\% = \$80{,}000$ insurance required

$\dfrac{\$60{,}000}{\$80{,}000} \times \$70{,}000 = \$52{,}500$ insurance pays

$\$70{,}000 - \$52{,}500 = \$17{,}500$ insured pays

COMPLETE ASSIGNMENT 20.2.

Computing Life Insurance Premiums

LEARNING OBJECTIVES 5

Compute life insurance premiums.

The policies most commonly issued by life insurance companies are straight life (sometimes called ordinary life), limited-payment life, term, endowment, and annuity.

On a *straight (ordinary) life insurance policy,* a certain premium, or fee, is paid every year **until the death of the insured.** The policy then becomes payable to the *beneficiary.* A policy beneficiary can be a person, a company, or an organization.

On a *limited-payment life insurance* policy (such as 20-payment life), a certain premium is paid every year **for a certain number of years** specified at the time of insuring or until the death of the insured, should that occur during the specified period. The policy is payable on the death of the insured.

A *term insurance* policy is insurance protection issued for a limited time. A certain premium is paid every year **during the specified time period,** or term. The policy is payable only in case of death of the insured during the term. Otherwise, neither the insured nor the specified beneficiaries receive any payment, and the protection stops at the end of the term.

An *endowment insurance* policy provides insurance payable on the insured's death if it occurs within a specified period. If the insured is alive at the end of the specified period, an endowment of the same amount as the policy is payable.

An *annuity insurance* policy pays a certain sum of money to the insured every year after the insured reaches a specified age, until the insured's death.

An *additional death benefit (ADB)*,sometimes referred to as an accidental death benefit, accompanies some policies. ADB allows the insured to purchase, at a low rate per thousand dollars of coverage, additional insurance up to the full face value of the policy. In case of death of the insured by accident, both the full value of the policy and the ADB are paid to the beneficiaries. If death occurs other than by accident, the full value of the policy is paid, but no ADB is paid.

Figure 20-1 shows typical annual, semiannual, and quarterly premiums (ages 25–28) for straight life, 20-payment life, and 20-year endowment policies. Premiums vary from company to company because of such differences as the exact type of coverage and participation in dividends.

Figure 20-1: Insurance Premiums per $1,000

	Straight Life			20-Payment Life			20-Year Endowment		
Age	**Annual**	**Semi-annual**	**Quarterly**	**Annual**	**Semi-annual**	**Quarterly**	**Annual**	**Semi-annual**	**Quarterly**
25	$17.20	$ 8.94	$4.73	$31.20	$16.26	$8.26	$52.00	$27.04	$14.30
26	17.85	9.28	4.91	31.81	16.52	8.45	52.60	27.35	14.47
27	18.60	9.67	5.11	32.41	16.83	8.64	53.20	27.66	14.63
28	19.30	10.04	5.31	33.06	17.31	8.85	53.86	28.01	14.81

EXAMPLE I

Using the premiums shown in Figure 20-1, determine the yearly premiums for each of the following $50,000 life insurance policies purchased at the age of 26.

Type of Insurance	Method of Payment	Premium Computation
Straight Life	Annual	$17.85 × 50 = $892.50
20-Year Endowment	Quarterly	$14.47 × 4 × 50 = $2,894
20-Payment Life	Semiannual	$16.52 × 2 × 50 = $1,652
20-Year Endowment	Semiannual	$27.35 × 2 × 50 = $2,735
Straight Life	Quarterly	$4.91 × 4 × 50 = $982

CONCEPT CHECK 20.5

a. If a person at the age of 27 purchases a straight life insurance policy having a face value of $75,000 with quarterly premiums, what is the yearly premium?
$5.11 × 4 × 75 = $1,533

b. If a person at the age of 28 purchases a 20-payment life insurance policy having a face value of $100,000 with semiannual premiums, what is the yearly premium?
$17.31 × 2 × 100 = $3,462

c. If a person at the age of 25 purchases a 20-year endowment insurance policy having a face value of $25,000 with annual premiums, what is the yearly premium?
$52 × 25 = $1,300

Computing Cash Surrender and Loan Values

LEARNING OBJECTIVE 6

Compute cash surrender and loan values.

Except for term insurance, insurance usually has a *cash surrender value,* which is the amount of cash that the company will pay the insured on the surrender, or "cashing in," of the policy. The *loan value* of a policy is the amount that the insured may borrow on the policy from the insurance company. Interest is charged on such loans. The values, often quoted after the third year of the policy, are stated in the policy and increase every year. Figure 20-2 shows typical cash surrender and loan values for policies issued at age 25 per $1,000 of life insurance.

Figure 20-2: Insurance Values per $1,000

End of Policy Year	Cash Surrender and Loan Values		
	Straight Life	20-Payment Life	20-Year Endowment
3	$ 10	$ 43	$ 88
4	22	68	130
5	35	93	173
10	104	228	411
15	181	380	684
20	264	552	1,000

EXAMPLE J

Using the figures shown in Figure 20-2, determine the cash surrender or loan value for each of the following policies.

Policy Year	Type of Policy	Amount of Policy	Cash Surrender or Loan Value
10	Straight Life	$ 30,000	$104 × 30 = $3,120
5	20-Year Endowment	$ 15,000	$173 × 15 = $2,595
10	20-Payment Life	$ 10,000	$228 × 10 = $2,280
4	Straight Life	$100,000	$22 × 100 = $2,200
15	20-Year Endowment	$ 50,000	$684 × 50 = $34,200

CONCEPT CHECK 20.6

Using the figures shown in Figure 20-2 determine the cash surrender or loan value for each of the following policies.

a. Third policy year of a $50,000 20-year endowment policy
$88 × 50 = $4,400

b. Twentieth policy year of a $100,000 straight life policy
$264 × 100 = $26,400

c. Tenth policy year of a $25,000 20-payment life policy
$228 × 25 = $5,700

Computing Medical Insurance Contributions and Reimbursements

Today, most employers subscribe to a group plan on behalf of their employees. *Group insurance* plans provide medical insurance coverage to large numbers of people at lower premium rates than individuals could obtain separately. Employers generally pay all of the premium for employees and pay a portion of the premium for family members of employees. Most employers now use a group plan known as an *HMO (health maintenance organization)* or a *PPO (preferred provider organization).*

LEARNING OBJECTIVES 7

Compute medical insurance contributions and reimbursements.

EXAMPLE K

Employer A selected a basic health care plan to cover employees who wish to participate. Monthly premiums are as follows: employee only, $350; employee with one dependent, $450; and employee with multiple dependents, $530. Employees pay a portion of the premium as follows: employee only, $0; employee with one dependent, $80; and employee with multiple dependents, $120. How much does the employer pay during the year for each category of employee?

Employee only: $350 × 12 = $4,200
Employee with one dependent: ($450 − $80) × 12 = $4,440
Employee with multiple dependents: ($530 − $120) × 12 = $4,920

EXAMPLE L

Employer B selected a total care health plan to cover employees who wish to participate. Monthly premiums are as follows: employee only, $300; employee with one dependent, $400; and employee with multiple dependents, $480. The employer pays most of the premium, but employees pay a portion as follows: employee only, $30; employee with one dependent, $80; and employee with multiple dependents, $120. What percent of the premium will be paid by a single employee, an employee with 1 dependent, and an employee with 6 dependents?

A single employee: $30 ÷ 300 = 0.10, or 10%
An employee with 1 dependent: $80 ÷ 400 = 0.20, or 20%
An employee with 6 dependents: $120 ÷ 480 = 0.25, or 25%

Many group plans include a provision for an annual deductible, which is the cost that must be paid by the employee before any cost is paid by the insurance company. Group medical plans also frequently provide for the payment by the insurance company of a percent of costs over the deductible, usually 70% to 90%, with the remaining 10% to 30% paid by the insured.

EXAMPLE M

Employer C provides group health coverage that includes a $500 annual deductible per family and payment of 70% of the medical charges over the deductible. How much would an employee with three dependents pay if her year's medical bills were $1,500?

$1,500 − $500 deductible = $1,000
$1,000 × 30% paid by employee = $300
$500 deductible + $300 = $800 paid by the employee

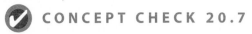

CONCEPT CHECK 20.7

An employer provides group health coverage that includes a \$300 annual deductible per family and payment of 80% of costs over the deductible.

a. How much would an employee with two dependents pay if his year's medical bills were \$460?
   \$460 − \$300 deductible = \$160
   \$160 × 20% = \$32
   \$300 deductible + \$32 = \$332 paid by the employee

b. How much would that employee have paid if total medical bills for the year had been \$4,300?
   \$4,300 medical costs − \$300 deductible = \$4,000
   \$4,000 × 20% = \$800
   \$300 deductible + \$800 = \$1,100

c. How much of the \$4,300 in medical bills would that employee have paid if his employer did not provide medical insurance?
   \$4,300

d. How much did the employer pay if the monthly premium for an employee with multiple dependents was \$480?
   \$480 × 12 = \$5,760

COMPLETE ASSIGNMENT 20.3.

Chapter Terms for Review

additional death benefit (ADB)
annuity insurance
auto collision insurance
auto comprehensive insurance
auto liability and property damage insurance
beneficiary
cash surrender value
coinsurance clause
deductible clause
endowment insurance
group insurance
health maintenance organization (HMO)
high-risk driver
insured
limited-payment life insurance
loan value
low-risk driver
no-fault insurance
preferred provider organization (PPO)
premium
property insurance
recovery amount
short rates
straight (ordinary) life insurance
term insurance

The Bottom Line

Summary of chapter learning objectives:

Learning Objective	Summary	Example
20.1	Computing costs and savings for auto insurance	Drivers A and B live in a state in which no-fault insurance is mandatory. Both drivers carry all three classifications of insurance. Driver A has a deductible of $500; driver B has a deductible of $200. Driver A crashes into driver B. Neither auto has any passengers. Car A has $1,800 in damages; car B has $2,000 in damages. Driver A is not hurt; driver B has $900 in medical bills. 1. How much does driver A's insurance company pay? 2. How much does driver B's insurance company pay?
20.2	Computing auto insurance premium rates for high- and low-risk drivers	3. Driver A has an excellent driving record and receives a 10% discount on her annual premium. Driver B has a record of numerous tickets and must pay one and a half times the normal annual premium rate. If the normal premium for both drivers is $1,500, how much more does driver B pay for his insurance than driver A pays?
20.3	Computing short-rate refunds	4. XYZ company purchased a delivery truck and paid an annual insurance premium of $3,200. XYZ company sold the truck at the end of 3 months. The insurance company has a policy of charging a 10% penalty for short-rate refunds. What was the amount of the short-rate refund to XYZ company?
20.4	Computing coinsurance on property losses	5. A building worth $200,000 is insured for $120,000 with an 80% coinsurance clause. Fire causes $140,000 in damage. How much does the insurance company pay?
20.5	Computing life insurance premiums	6. Premiums per $1,000 of straight life insurance at the age of 25 are as follows: annual, $17.20; semiannual, $8.94; and quarterly, $4.73. What will be the total premiums for the following three policies: $50,000, annual; $25,000, semiannual; and $20,000, quarterly?
20.6	Computing cash surrender and loan values	7. If cash surrender values for year 15 of a policy are $181 per thousand dollars of coverage for straight life and $380 per thousand dollars of coverage for 20-payment life, what is the total cash surrender value of these two policies: $50,000 straight life and $30,000 20-payment life?
20.7	Computing medical insurance contributions and reimbursements	8. An employer provides group health coverage that includes a $200 annual deductible per family and payment of 80% of costs over deductible. How much would an employee with four dependents pay if his year's medical bills were as follows: self, $240; dependent 1, $170; dependent 2, $640; dependent 3, $460; and dependent 4, $1,360?

Answers: 1. $3,300 **2.** $900 **3.** $900 **4.** $2,080 **5.** $105,000 **6.** $1,685.40 **7.** $20,450 **8.** $734

Notes

Assignment 20.1: Auto Insurance

Name ____________________

Date ____________________ Score ____________________

A (50 points) Solve the following problems. (5 points for each correct answer)

1. Mary Johnson had full insurance coverage. Her liability and property damage coverage was $100,000 per accident. Her collision insurance had a $500 deductible clause. She struck two cars. Damages to the cars were $640 and $320. Damage to her own car was $470. Her annual insurance premium was $1,180.

a. What are the total costs to the insurance company for Mary Johnson's accident? __________

b. If this was the only accident Mary Johnson had this year, how much money did the insurance company make on her? __________

c. What are Mary Johnson's total costs this year for insurance and the accident? __________

d. What would Mary Johnson's total costs for the accident have been without insurance? __________

2. John Allen has auto collision insurance with a $300 deductible clause. His steering went out, and he hit a tree. Damage to his car totaled $1,957. His annual insurance premium was $1,260. How much did he save this year by having insurance? __________

3. Roger Smith received his driver's license one year ago. He has had three citations for speeding, but no accidents. His insurance premium last year was $1,250. This year his premium will be 50% higher because of his driving record.

a. What will be the amount of his premium this year? __________

b. Four months into the next year, Roger Smith has continued his unsafe driving habits. The insurance company is canceling his policy. What will be the amount of the refund? __________

c. Roger Smith has found an insurance company that will insure him as a high-risk driver at triple the standard annual rate of $1,425. What will be his average monthly insurance premium for the first 28 months of his driving career? (Round your answer to the nearest dollar.) __________

d. If Roger Smith had been a careful driver and kept the amount of his premium unchanged, how much would he have saved in these first 28 months? (Round your computations to the nearest dollar.) __________

4. Drivers A and B have identical insurance coverage. Driver A has an excellent driving record and receives a 15% discount on the standard premium. Driver B has numerous citations and pays double the standard rate. The standard rate in both cases is $1,240. How much more does driver B pay for insurance than driver A? __________

____
Score for A (50)

B (50 points) Solve the following problems. (5 points for each correct answer)

5. Tom Barton carries liability and property damage insurance coverage up to $50,000 per accident, comprehensive insurance, and collision insurance with a $100 deductible clause. He lost control of his car and drove through the display window of a furniture store. Damage to the building was $17,200 and to the inventory was $34,300. Damage to a bike rack on the sidewalk and three bicycles in the rack was $1,840. Damage to his own car was $6,100.

a. What was the total property damage, excluding damage to Tom's car? __________

b. How much did the insurance company pay for property damage, excluding damage to Tom's car? __________

c. How much did the insurance company pay for damage to Tom Barton's car? __________

d. How much did the accident cost Tom Barton? __________

e. If Tom Barton had been in a previous accident this year in which there had been property damage to a parked car of $12,700, how much would the insurance company have paid for damages to everything in the current accident, including Tom Barton's car? __________

6. Lucy Peters and John Rogers live in a state in which no-fault insurance is mandatory. They have identical full coverage of $50,000 liability and property damage per accident, comprehensive insurance, and collision insurance with a $200 deductible. John lost control of his car on an icy street and struck Lucy's car, a parked motorcycle, and a fence. Lucy had medical expenses of $780. John had medical expenses of $560. Lucy's car had damages of $1,350. John's car had damages of $1,750. Damage to the parked motorcycle was $650 and to the fence was $320.

a. What did Lucy's insurance company pay under the no-fault provision? __________

b. What did John's insurance company pay under the no-fault provision? __________

c. How much did John's insurance company pay under his liability and property damage coverage? __________

d. How much did John's insurance company pay under his comprehensive coverage? __________

e. How much would John's insurance company have paid under his liability and property damage if he had hit Lucy's car and five parked cars, with total damage to the six cars of $56,700? __________

____
Score for B (50)

Assignment 20.2: Property Insurance

Name ______________________

Date ______________ Score ______________

A (42 points) Solve the following problems. (6 points for each correct answer)

1. A building valued at $250,000 is insured for its full value. The annual premium is $12 per thousand dollars of coverage.

a. How much does the insured pay to insure his building? __________

b. If the insurance company cancels the policy at the end of 3 months, how much refund does the insured receive? __________

c. If the insurance company has a 10% penalty clause for short-rate refunds and the insured cancels the policy after 6 months, how much refund does the insured receive? __________

2. If a company pays an annual premium of $2,400 and the insurance company charges $12 per thousand dollars of insurance, how much insurance does the company carry? __________

3. A company carries property insurance of $200,000. A fire causes $170,000 in damage. How much does the insurance company pay the insured? __________

4. A company carries property insurance of $100,000. A fire causes $120,000 in damage.

a. How much does the insurance company pay the insured? __________

b. How much does the insured pay? __________

__________ Score for A (42)

B (58 points) Solve the following problems. (points for correct answers as marked)

5. A building worth $300,000 is insured for $150,000, and the policy carries an 80% coinsurance clause. A fire causes $220,000 in damage.

a. How much will the insurance company pay? (10 points) ________

b. How much will the insured pay if the building is repaired for $220,000? (6 points) ________

c. How much would the insurance company pay if damage to the building totaled $300,000? (10 points)

____

d. If the damage totaled $300,000, how much would the insured pay if the building were rebuilt for $300,000? (6 points) ________

6. A building worth $350,000 is insured for $280,000, and the policy carries an 80% coinsurance clause. A fire causes $300,000 in damage.

a. How much does the insurance company pay if the building is repaired for $300,000? (10 points) ________

b. How much does the insured pay? (6 points) ________

7. If an insurance company issues insurance on property valued at $400,000 with a 90% coinsurance clause, what is the amount required to be carried by the insured? (5 points) ________

8. If an insurance company issues insurance on property valued at $200,000 with a 70% coinsurance clause, what is the amount required to be carried by the insured? (5 points) ________

____
Score for B (58)

Assignment 20.3: Life and Medical Insurance

Name ______________________

Date ______________ Score ______________

A **(50 points) Refer to Figures 20-1 and 20-2 in solving the following problems. Assume every year is a full 12 months long. (points for correct answers as marked)**

1. Find the rates per thousand dollars and the premiums on the following policies. (1 point for each correct answer)

Age	Type	Payments Made	Face Value of Policy	Rate per $1,000	Premium Paid Each Year
28	Straight Life	Annually	$ 15,000	______	______
25	20-Payment Life	Quarterly	12,000	______	______
25	20-Year Endowment	Semiannually	20,000	______	______
26	Straight	Quarterly	100,000	______	______
27	20-Payment Life	Semiannually	50,000	______	______
28	20-Year Endowment	Annually	75,000	______	______

2. Find the cash surrender or loan value for each of the following policies issued at age 25. (1 point for each correct answer)

Policy Year	Type of Policy	Amount of Policy	Cash Surrender or Loan Value
20	Straight Life	$50,000	______
15	20-Payment Life	$25,000	______
10	20-Year Endowment	$30,000	______
3	Straight Life	$20,000	______
5	20-Payment Life	$75,000	______
4	20-Year Endowment	$60,000	______

3. When Alice Jones was 27 years old, she took out a $50,000, 20-year endowment policy. She paid the premiums annually and survived the endowment period. How much more did she pay in annual premiums than she received from the insurance company at the end of 20 years? (4 points) ______

4. Roger Johnson purchased a $50,000 ordinary life policy and an ADB for 50% of the value of the policy. In addition, he purchased a 5-year, $50,000 term policy. He died in an accident 3 years later.

a. How much money did Roger's beneficiaries receive? (4 points) ______

b. How much money would Roger's beneficiaries have received if he had died in an accident 7 years after purchasing the policies? (4 points) ______

c. How much money would Roger's beneficiaries have received if he had died of natural causes 10 years after purchasing the policies? (4 points) ______

5. At the age of 25, George Beacon purchased a $50,000 straight life policy, with premiums payable annually. He also purchased a $25,000 20-payment life policy, with premiums payable semiannually. At the end of 15 years, he decided to cash in both policies.

a. How much did he receive for the straight life policy? (4 points) ________

b. How much did he receive for the 20-payment life policy? (4 points) ________

c. How much more did he pay in premiums than the total amount received for both policies?(8 points) ________

____
Score for A (50)

B (50 points) Solve the following problems. (10 points for a correct answer to problem 6; 8 points for each other correct answer)

6. An employer provides group health coverage that includes a $400 annual deductible per family and payment of 80% of costs over the deductible. How much would an employee with two dependents pay if her year's medical bills were $420 for herself; $730 for dependent 1; and $640 for dependent 2? ________

7. An employer provides group health coverage that includes a $400 annual deductible per family and 70% of costs over the deductible.

a. How much would an employee with no dependents pay if her medical bills were $980 this year? ________

b. How much would that employee have paid this year if her medical bills were $7,480? ________

8. An employer provides group health coverage with the following monthly premiums: employee only, $350; employee with one dependent, $450; and employee with multiple dependents, $550.

a. How much does the employer pay over a 5-year period for an employee with multiple dependents? ________

b. If that employee had a dependent with a catastrophic illness that cost $97,000 for hospitalization and treatments during that 5-year period, how much did the insurance company lose on that employee, assuming he had no other medical claims? ________

c. If an employee with no dependents had no illnesses during that same 5-year period, how much did the insurance company make on that employee? ________

____
Score for B (50)

Notes

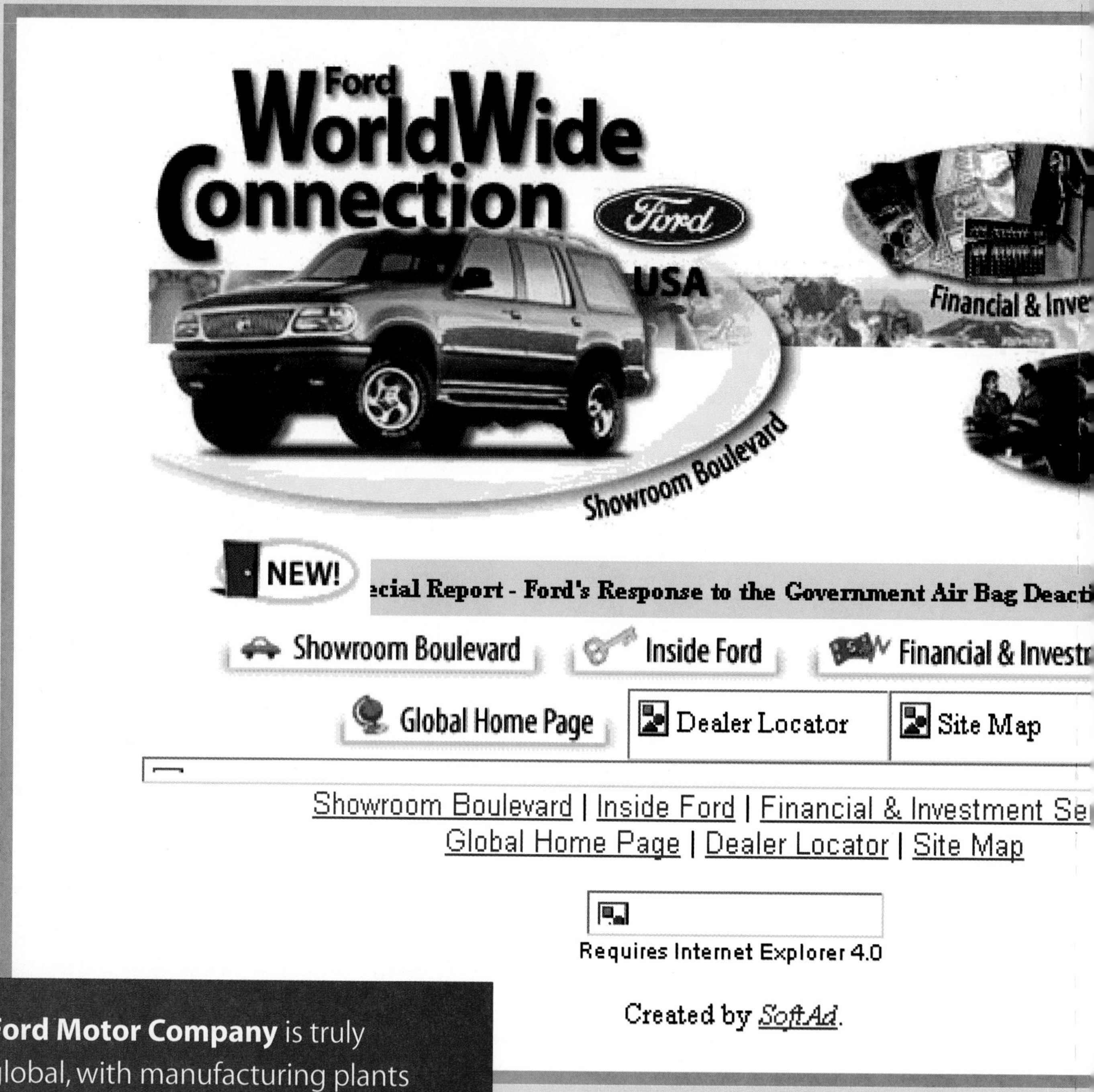

Ford Motor Company is truly global, with manufacturing plants and sales offices throughout the world. It produces cars, trucks, and automobile parts that go into thousands of individual company inventories. Look at its GLOBAL site at www.ford.com or its CAREER CENTER page at www.ford.com/corporate-info/index.html for a wide array of inventory-related jobs all over the world.

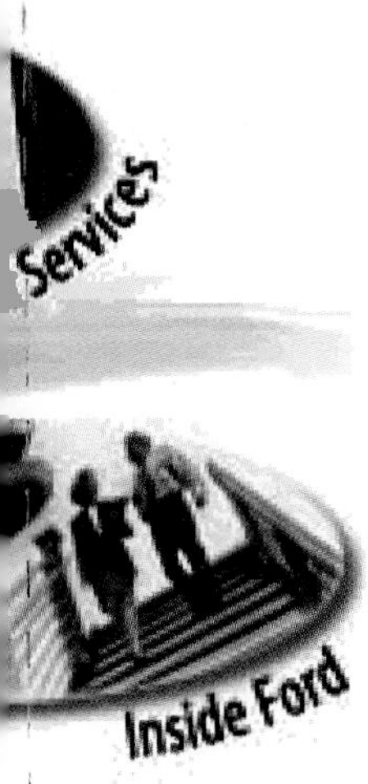

21 Business Inventory and Turnover

Learning Objectives

By studying this chapter and completing all the assignments, you will learn to:

1. Account for inventory by inventory sheets and reports from a perpetual inventory system.
2. Compute inventory value by the average cost, LIFO, and FIFO methods.
3. Compute inventory using the lower of cost or market value.
4. Estimate inventory by computing an estimated cost of goods sold.
5. Compute inventory turnover using cost or retail values.

Large retail outlets have dominant positions in retailing because they carry huge inventories. Computing inventory and the rate of turnover is vital to these enterprises. Many methods are used to keep track of inventories.

A company's inventory is the amount of goods it has on hand at a given point in time. Retail stores and wholesale companies have only one kind of inventory: *merchandise,* those goods they sell that are manufactured by some other firm.

Accounting for Inventory

LEARNING OBJECTIVES 1

Account for inventory by inventory sheets and reports from a perpetual inventory system.

Inventory Sheets

At least once each year, businesses undertake a *physical inventory*—an actual counting of the merchandise on hand. Some stores that require close control take a physical inventory every six months, quarterly, or even monthly.

When inventory is counted, a description of each item, the quantity, the unit cost or retail price, and the *extension* (quantity × price) are recorded on an *inventory sheet,* as shown in Figure 21-1. The inventory value is then compared with accounting records, and any needed adjustments are made at this time.

Figure 21-1: Inventory Sheet

BIG SKY AUTO PARTS HOUSE
Inventory Sheet
April 30, 19—

Description	Quantity	Unit Price (Average Cost)	Extension
Ignition Terminals—#746083	318	$36.14	$11,492.52
Odometer Cables—#007614	73	9.97	727.81
Wiper Blades: Compact—#417654	38	4.71	178.98
Spark Plugs: 0.14—#772034	354	2.34	828.36
Hood/Truck Latches—#476508	58	13.42	778.36
Total			$14,006.03

Figure 21-2: Inventory Record Sheet

BIG SKY AUTO PARTS HOUSE
Inventory Record Sheet

ITEM: QUICKSTART SPARK PLUG: 0.14

PART NUMBER: #772034

LOCATION: Aisle 72, Bin 4, Box C

MINIMUM STOCK: 200 MAXIMUM STOCK: 800

ORDER FROM:
Northwest Distributors
2337 Colfax Avenue
Milbrae, CA 93233
Phone—(415) 345-7654

ORDER: 100–800

Purchase Orders (PO)			Inventory Control					
Date	PO No.	Quantity	Date	Source Code	Units In	Unit Cost	Units Out	Balance on hand
2/03	F0129	400	1/01	—		$2.10		350
3/15	M1678	300	1/31	SJ01			120	230
3/22	M2076	200	2/28	SJ02			58	172
4/26	A3210	400	3/02	F0129	400	2.36		572
			3/31	SJ03			315	257
			4/03	M1678	300	2.40		557
			4/20	M2076	200	2.64		757
			4/30	SJ04			403	354

Perpetual Inventory Systems

Some firms keep a *perpetual inventory*—a running count of all inventory items, based on tracking of each item as it comes into and goes out of inventory. In businesses that handle high-cost items such as cars or large appliances, the perpetual system keeps track of each item by serial number and price.

Businesses that handle small items—such as candy bars or shoes—have difficulty identifying the cost or serial number of each specific item. Their perpetual inventory systems keep a count of the number of units on hand, not individual prices and serial numbers. The use of electronic scanners has simplified application of this type of perpetual inventory system.

Data for a perpetual inventory system are usually kept on a computer. Figure 21-2 illustrates a computer printout of an inventory record sheet. The last item in the Balance on Hand column tells how many units are on hand on the 4/30 recording date—354 Quickstart Spark Plugs: 0.14, part number 772034.

CONCEPT CHECK 21.1

The CompuParts wholesale computer store maintains a perpetual inventory of computer parts received and shipped. The following inventory record sheet shows the data for May. Compute the Balance on Hand after each transaction.

COMPUPARTS WHOLESALE
Inventory Record Sheet

Order From:
Myers Distributors
1422 Oak Drive
Stockton, CA 97777
Fax: 209-775-7823

ITEM: Monitor Cord #A718
Location: Bin #C7
Minimum Stock: 250 **Maximum Stock: 1,000**

	Units In	Unit Cost	Units Out	Balance on Hand
5/01		$15.40		390
5/11	470	$15.80		860
5/15			260	600
5/28	320	$15.90		920
5/31			410	510

Computing Inventory Using the Average Cost, FIFO, and LIFO Methods

LEARNING OBJECTIVES 2

Compute inventory value by the average cost, LIFO, and FIFO methods.

In all inventory systems, the cost of the inventory on hand at the end of the period is called *ending inventory (EI)*. The ending inventory must be computed before financial statements can be prepared.

To compute ending inventory, a business usually adopts one of three cost methods: average cost, FIFO, or LIFO. Once selected, the method must be followed consistently. Figure 21-2 shows a typical inventory record sheet; these cost data are used to illustrate computations for the three cost methods.

The Average Cost Method

The *average cost method* assumes that the costs of all items on hand are averaged and shared evenly among all units.

EXAMPLE A

The average cost of the units on the inventory record sheet for stock part #772034 (Quickstart Spark Plugs: 0.14), illustrated in Figure 21-2, is computed as follows:

Date	Units Purchased	Cost	Extension
1/01	350	$2.10	$ 735.00
3/02	400	2.36	944.00
4/03	300	2.40	720.00
4/20	200	2.64	528.00
	1,250		$2,927.00

Average cost per unit: $2,927 ÷ 1,250 = $2.34
From Figure 21-2, ending inventory at average cost: 354 units × $2.34 = $828.36

The FIFO Method

The *first-in, first-out (FIFO) method* assumes that the costs for units used are charged according to the order in which the units were purchased. Thus, the inventory remaining is assumed to be composed of the units received most recently.

EXAMPLE B

Under the FIFO method, the inventory of 354 units shown in Figure 21-2 would consist of the 200 units last purchased plus 154 units from the preceding purchase.

200 units × $2.64 = $528.00
154 units × $2.40 = $369.60
354 $897.60 Ending inventory at FIFO cost

The LIFO Method

The *last-in, first-out (LIFO) method* assumes that the inventory remaining is composed of the units received first.

EXAMPLE C

Under the LIFO method, the 354 units shown on the inventory record in Figure 21-2 would consist of the 350 units on hand on 1/01 plus 4 units from the first purchase on 3/02.

350 units × $2.10 = $735.00
4 units × $2.36 = $ 9.44
354 $744.44 Ending inventory at LIFO cost

CONCEPT CHECK 21.2

The inventory record sheets for C/K Hairbrushes at Debbie's Beauty Supply show 7,422 units purchased at a total cost of $15,183.79. The inventory at year's end was 3,390 units. Compute the value of the ending inventory by each of the three methods: average cost, FIFO, and LIFO.

Date	Units Purchased	Cost	Extension
1/17	3,113	$2.00	$ 6,226.00
1/30	200	2.07	414.00
2/20	950	2.09	1,985.50
3/17	2,044	2.11	4,312.84
10/30	600	2.00	1,200.00
11/17	515	2.03	1,045.45
	7,422		$15,183.79

Average cost: $15,183.79 ÷ 7,422 = $2.046
3,390 × $2.05 = $6,949.50

FIFO: (515 × $2.03) + (600 × $2.00)
+ (2,044 × $2.11) + (231 × $2.09) = $7,041.08

LIFO: (3,113 × $2.00) + (200 × $2.07)
+ (77 × $2.09) = $6,800.93

Computing Inventory at the Lower of Cost or Market Value

Financial statements usually present the ending inventory at its cost value, either average, FIFO, or LIFO. However, in some cases the *market value* of goods is lower than their original or average cost. Most companies prefer to show the *lower of cost or market value* in their inventories. When market value exceeds the cost, the cost is used; when the cost exceeds market value, market value is used.

Compute inventory using the lower of cost or market value.

STEPS to Determine the Lower of Cost or Market (LCM) Inventory Value

1. Compute the unit or total cost for each type of inventory item using either the average, FIFO, or LIFO costing method.
2. Determine the market value for each inventory item.
3. Compare the cost value from Step 1 with the market value from Step 2 and choose the lower of the two.
4. Compute the extension amount for each item based on the lower amount.
5. Sum the amounts in Step 4 to determine the total inventory value under LCM.

EXAMPLE D

Under LCM using the average cost method, the total inventory shown in Figure 21-1 would be valued at $13,802.13.

		STEP 1	STEP 2	STEP 3	STEP 4	
Description	**(A) Quantity**	**(B) Unit Price (Average Cost)**	**(C) Unit Price at Market**	**(D) Lower of (B) or (C)**	**Extension (A × D)**	
Ignition Terminals—#746083	318	$36.14	$35.50	$35.50	$11,289.00	market
Odometer Cables—#007614	73	9.97	11.00	9.97	727.81	cost
Wiper Blades: Compact—#417654	38	4.71	4.70	4.70	178.60	market
Spark Plugs: 0.14—#772034	354	2.34	2.64	2.34	828.36	cost
Hood/Trunk Latches—#476508	58	13.42	14.10	13.42	778.36	cost
Total					$13,802.13	STEP 5

EXAMPLE E

Under LCM using the FIFO cost method, the total inventory shown in Figure 21-1 would be valued at $13,905.46

		STEP 1	STEP 2	STEP 3	STEP 4	
			Market Value (D)			
Description	**(A) Quantity**	**(B) FIFO Cost**	**(C) Unit Price**	**Total (A × C)**	**Lower of (B) or (D)**	
Ignition Terminals—#746083	318	$11,321.67	$35.50	$11,289.00	$11,289.00	market
Odometer Cables—#007614	73	727.81	11.00	803.00	727.81	cost
Wiper Blades: Compact—#417654	38	192.15	4.70	178.60	178.60	market
Spark Plugs: 0.14—#772034	354	897.60	2.64	934.56	897.60	cost
Hood/Trunk Latches—#476508	58	812.45	14.10	817.80	812.45	cost
Total					$13,905.46	STEP 5

CONCEPT CHECK 21.3

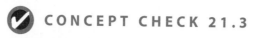

L & L Records' inventory shows the following. Compute the inventory value at the lower of cost or market.

Description	Quantity	Cost	Market	Extension
Classical #3	300	$ 7.07	$10.10	$2,121.00
Western #8	180	9.10	8.07	1,452.60
Modern–Light #11	410	11.17	12.08	4,579.70
Rock–New #4	89	12.10	12.10	1,076.90
Total				$9,230.20

Estimating Inventory Value

LEARNING OBJECTIVES 4

Estimate inventory by computing an estimated cost of goods sold.

For monthly financial statements, inventory frequently is estimated, without a physical count or a perpetual inventory system. The method usually used to estimate month-end inventory is called the *gross profit method.* This method involves estimating the cost of goods sold and subtracting this amount from the sum of the opening inventory and purchases made during the month. Note that *beginning inventory* is the ending inventory from the month before and *purchases* are those goods for sale that have been acquired during the current month. The gross profit method is based on the following formula:

Beginning inventory (BI)
+ Purchases (P)
Cost of goods available for sale
− Cost of goods sold (CGS) (estimated)
Ending inventory (EI) (estimate)

Without a physical inventory, a precise cost of goods sold is not known. In this case, it is estimated by applying a markup percentage rate to *net sales* (total sales less sales returned and adjustments for the period). The net sales (100%) less this markup percentage rate equals the cost of goods sold. For instance, if the markup rate were 30%, the cost of goods sold would be 100% − 30% = 70%. If the rate of markup were 40%, the cost of goods sold would be 100% − 40% = 60%.

EXAMPLE F

Assume Big Sky Auto Parts had a beginning inventory of $80,000. During the month, the company purchased and received $50,000 in goods and had net sales of $90,000. Throughout the month, Big Sky maintained a 40% markup on all sales. Its cost of goods sold would be computed as follows:

Net sales for the month	$90,000	
Cost of goods sold (estimated)	$54,000	($90,000 × [100% − 40%] = $90,000 × 0.60)

Big Sky Auto Parts would then determine its ending inventory (estimated) as follows:

Inventory, beginning of month	$ 80,000
Purchases for month	+ 50,000
Goods available for sale	$130,000
Cost of goods sold (estimated)	− 54,000
Ending inventory (estimated)	$ 76,000

Sometimes a company's markup percentage rate is based on cost rather than selling price. In this case, if the markup on cost were 30%, the cost of goods sold would be net sales divided by 130%. If the markup on cost were 40%, the cost of goods sold would be net sales divided by 140%.

EXAMPLE G

Assume Big Sky Auto Parts had a beginning inventory of $80,000. During the month, it had purchases of $50,000 and net sales of $90,000. Throughout the month, Big Sky maintained a markup of 40% based on cost. What were Big Sky's cost of goods sold and ending inventory?

Beginning inventory	$ 80,000.00	
Purchases	+ 50,000.00	
Cost of goods available for sale	$130,000.00	
Cost of goods sold (estimated)	− 64,285.71	($90,000 ÷ 140%)
Ending inventory (estimated)	$ 65,714.29	

CONCEPT CHECK 21.4

C & S Electronics shows the following. Compute the ending inventory at cost.

Beginning inventory	$24,000	Net sales for period	$90,000
Purchases for period	$33,000	Markup based on retail	40%

$24,000 + $33,000 = $57,000 cost of goods available
$90,000 × 60% = $54,000 cost of goods sold
$57,000 − $54,000 = $3,000 ending inventory

Computing Inventory Turnover

LEARNING OBJECTIVES 5

Compute inventory turnover using cost or retail values.

Inventory turnover is the number of times the average inventory is converted into sales during the year. Inventory turnover is very high for a grocery store or ice cream parlor; it is very low for a specialty jewelry store or an antique shop.

Before turnover can be determined, average inventory must be calculated. *Average inventory* is the average of the inventories taken over a given period of time—annually, semiannually, quarterly, or monthly.

Inventory is taken:	Average inventory (at retail or cost)
Annually (once a year)	(Beginning inventory + Ending inventory) ÷ 2
Semiannually (every six months)	(BI + end of 6 months + EI) ÷ 3
Quarterly (every three months)	(BI + 3 quarterlys + EI) ÷ 5
Monthly (every month)	(BI + 11 monthlys + EI) ÷ 13

Inventory turnover can be computed based on either retail (selling) price or cost, following the steps below.

STEPS to Compute Inventory Turnover at Retail

1. Determine net sales.
2. Compute average inventory using retail price.
3. Compute inventory *turnover at retail:* Net sales ÷ Average inventory at retail.

EXAMPLE H

Assume the inventories for the year, based on selling price, are as follows: beginning, \$90,000; end of month 3, \$80,000; end of month 6, \$100,000; end of month 9, \$70,000; and end of month 12 (ending), \$60,000. Net sales for the year equal \$520,000. Compute the inventory turnover at retail.

STEP 2 Average inventory = (\$90,000 + \$80,000 + \$100,000 + \$70,000 + \$60,000) ÷ 5
= \$400,000 ÷ 5 = \$80,000

STEP 3 Inventory turnover at retail = \$520,000 net sales ÷ \$80,000 average inventory = 6.5 times

NOTE: The value of net sales and average inventory must both be figured at retail.

Some retail businesses prefer to express their rate of inventory turnover in terms of cost. *Inventory turnover at cost* is obtained by dividing the *cost of goods sold (CGS)* during a period by the average inventory for the same period computed at cost prices. (CGS is simply net sales at cost.)

STEPS to Compute Inventory Turnover at Cost

1. Compute the cost of goods sold using the formula BI + P − EI = CGS.
2. Compute the average inventory at cost.
3. Compute inventory turnover at cost: Cost of goods sold ÷ Average inventory at cost.

EXAMPLE I

Assuming beginning inventory, purchases, and ending inventory are \$60,000, \$300,000, and \$80,000, respectively, compute the inventory turnover at cost.

STEP 1 Cost of goods sold:

Inventory at beginning of year	\$ 60,000
Purchases during year	+ 300,000
Goods available for sale	\$360,000
Inventory at end of year	− 80,000
Cost of goods sold	\$280,000

STEP 2 Average inventory = (\$60,000 BI + \$80,00 EI) ÷ 2
= \$140,000 ÷ 2 = \$70,000

STEP 3 Inventory turnover at cost = \$280,000 cost of goods sold ÷ \$70,000 average inventory = 4.0 times

NOTE: The value of goods sold and average inventory must both be figured at cost.

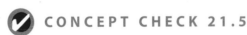

CONCEPT CHECK 21.5

Brinkman Scooter Shop has two branches (A and B), each using a markup of 50% of cost. Last year's data follow. Compute ending inventory, average inventory, and inventory turnover based on retail for each branch.

	Branch A	Branch B
Net sales	$1,400,000	$1,300,000
Beginning inventory—retail	220,000	375,000
Purchases (cost)	900,000	750,000
Inventory—retail (March 31)	190,000	410,000
Inventory—retail (June 30)	280,000	370,000
Inventory—retail (September 30)	280,000	360,000

Ending inventory: A—$220,000 + ($900,000 × 150%) − $1,400,000 = $170,000
B—$375,000 + ($750,000 × 150%) − $1,300,000 = $200,000

Average inventory: A—($220,000 + 190,000 + 280,000 + 280,000 + 170,000) ÷ 5 = $228,000
B—($375,000 + 410,000 + 370,000 + 360,000 + 200,000) ÷ 5 = $343,000

Retail turnover: A—$1,400,000 ÷ $228,000 = 6.14
B—$1,300,000 ÷ $343,000 = 3.79

COMPLETE ASSIGNMENTS 21.1 and 21.2.

Chapter Terms for Review

average cost method
average inventory
beginning inventory (BI)
cost of goods sold (CGS)
ending inventory (EI)
extension
first-in, first-out (FIFO) costing method
gross profit method
inventory sheet
inventory turnover
inventory turnover at cost
inventory turnover at retail
last-in, first-out (LIFO) costing method
lower of cost or market value (LCM)
market value
merchandise inventory
net sales
perpetual inventory
physical inventory
purchases (P)

The Bottom Line

Summary of chapter learning objectives:

Learning Objective	Summary	Example
21.1	Accounting for inventory by inventory sheets and reports from a perpetual inventory system	1. Compute the Balance on Hand after each transaction: (see table below)
21.2	Computing inventory value by the average cost, LIFO, and FIFO methods	2. From the data shown, compute the ending inventory by the average cost, FIFO, and LIFO methods for Redwood Stove Company's stove part #717. The ending inventory, by physical count, was 750. (see table below)
21.3	Computing inventory using the lower of cost or market value	3. Compute Redwood Stove Company's inventory value at the lower of cost or market value. (see table below)
21.4	Estimating inventory by computing an estimated cost of goods sold	4. Redwood Stove Company has a markup of 50% of retail. Last year it had total sales of $400,000. It had a beginning inventory of $150,000 based on cost. It purchased merchandise for $180,000 during the year. Compute the ending inventory at cost.
21.5	Computing inventory turnover using cost or retail values	5. Two years ago Redwood Stove Company used a markup of 70% of cost. That year's data are shown below. Compute ending inventory, average inventory, and inventory turnover at retail. (see table below)

21.1 — Example 1

Date	Units In	Units Out	Balance on Hand
12/01			34,768
12/17	7,789		_____
12/19	11,789		_____
12/20		17,072	_____
12/31		14,490	_____

21.2 — Example 2

Stove Part #717

Date	Units In	Cost	Extension
1/12	200	$22.40	$4,480
1/14	150	20.00	3,000
1/15	700	21.00	14,700
1/17	300	21.50	6,450
1/18	200	22.10	4,420
Total	1,550		

Average Cost:
FIFO: ____
LIFO: ____

21.3 — Example 3

Description	Quantity	Cost	Market	Extension
Stoves	24	$277.50	$350.50	_____
Piping	90	34.50	27.00	_____
Hearths	75	78.00	78.00	_____
Screens	50	105.00	125.00	_____
Tool Sets	28	65.50	55.00	_____
Total				_____

21.5 — Example 5

Net sales	$900,000	Purchases (cost)	600,000
Beginning inventory—retail	300,000	Inventory—retail (June 30)	400,000

Answers: 1. 42,557; 54,346; 37,274; 22,784 **2.** Average cost, $15,990; FIFO, $16,120; LIFO, $15,880 **3.** $6,660; $2,430; $5,850; $5,250; $1,540; $21,730 **4.** Inventory $130,000 **5.** Ending inventory at retail, $420,000; average inventory, $373,333; turnover, 2.41

Assignment 21.1: Inventory Cost

LEARNING OBJECTIVES 1 2 3

Name ______________________

Date ______________ Score ______________

A (40 points) Compute the extensions and totals. (1 point for each correct answer)

1. The inventory of Jim Sutton's Radio-Television shop shows the following items, to be figured at the lower of cost or market price. Compute the total value.

Description	Quantity	Unit Cost Price	Unit Market Price	Extension at Lower of Cost or Market
Quartz clock and pen set	22	$36.00	$34.80	
Travel alarm clock	30	15.60	29.70	
Ultrasonic travel clock	16	23.00	23.70	
Digital alarm clock	40	19.80	18.60	
AM/FM clock radio	112	21.00	17.80	
Digital clock radio	9	54.00	57.50	
Total				

2. A retail furniture dealer counted the following goods in inventory on December 31. An accountant recommended that the inventory items be valued at the lower of cost or market price. Compute the total value of the inventory based on the lower of cost or market price.

Article	Quantity	Unit Cost Price	Extension at Cost	Unit Market Price	Extension at Market	Inventory Value at Lower of Cost or Market
Armchairs, wood	24	$ 40.00		$ 68.50		
Armchairs, tapestry	6	75.00		105.00		
Armchairs, Windsor	12	115.00		85.00		
Beds, Hollywood	8	52.50		35.00		
Bedroom suites	3	297.50		410.00		
Chairs, period	30	63.00		84.50		
Chairs, kitchen	24	23.00		32.00		
Dining tables	8	117.40		87.00		
Dining suites	5	288.80		395.00		
Sofa sets	9	479.60		325.00		
Total						

Score for A (40) ______________

B **(60 points) Compute the value of ending inventory. (10 points for each correct answer)**

3. Garcia Manufacturing Company made purchases of a material as shown in the following listing. The inventory at the end of the year was 3,750 units. Compute the value of the inventory by each of the three methods: (a) average cost; (b) first-in, first-out; and (c) last-in, first-out.

Date	Units	Unit Cost	Total Cost
Jan 5	3,600	$6.20	$ 22,320
Mar. 11	3,000	5.80	17,400
May 14	5,300	6.00	31,800
July 8	1,600	6.30	10,080
Sept. 7	4,000	6.20	24,800
Nov. 10	2,500	6.40	16,000
Total	20,000		$122,400

a. Average cost: ________

b. First-in, first-out: ________

c. Last-in, first-out: ________

4. The Willand Company had 320 units of item number 345 on hand at the beginning of the year, with a cost of $4.20. The number and per-unit cost of units purchased and the number of units sold are listed below. What would be the value of the ending inventory of 380 units based on (a) average cost; (b) first-in, first-out; and (c) last-in, first-out?

Date	Units Purchased	Unit Cost	Units Sold	Units on Hand
Jan. 1				320
Feb. 2			190	130
Mar. 28	200	$4.32		330
Apr. 6	300	4.40		630
May 14			280	350
June 9	250	4.48		600
June 30			220	380

a. Average cost: ________

b. First-in, first-out: ________

c. Last-in, first-out: ________

____

Score for B (60)

Assignment 21.2: Inventory Estimating and Turnover

Name

Date Score

A (50 points) Solve the following problems. (2 points for each correct answer)

1. Fill in the blanks in each of the following calculations with the correct amount. Use the following formulas:

Beginning inventory + Purchases = Goods available for sale
Goods available for sale − Cost of goods sold = Ending inventory

	Store A	Store B	Store C	Store D	Store E
Beginning inventory	$ 80,000	________	$ 37,000	________	$42,000
Purchases	________	97,000	________	21,000	________
Goods available for sale	200,000	215,000	109,000	117,000	89,000
Less cost of goods sold	125,000	72,000	________	27,000	74,000
Ending inventory	________	________	$ 23,000	________	________

2. Each of the five stores in problem 1 had net sales as shown. What was the average percent of markup, based on cost, for each of the five stores? What was the average percent of markup, based on selling price, for each of the five stores?

	Store A	Store B	Store C	Store D	Store E
Net sales	$200,000	$100,000	$172,000	$40,000	$100,000
Markup—cost	________	________	________	________	________
Markup—selling price	________	________	________	________	________

3. The Myrick Record Shop takes inventory at retail sales price every three months. Its inventory at the beginning of last year was $39,482; at three months, it was $46,693; at six months, $53,000; at nine months, $56,500; and at the end of the year, $40,410. Net sales for the year were $203,033.10

a. What was the average inventory? ________

b. What was the turnover? ________

4. Brewer & Adams, a tire shop, began the year with an inventory of \$159,700. Purchases during the year totaled \$278,182. The inventory at the end of the year was \$109,400.

a. What was the cost of goods sold? __________

b. What was the average inventory? __________

c. What was the turnover? __________

____
Score for A (50)

B (50 points) Solve the following problems. (Points for each correct answer as marked)

5. The records of Robinson Auto Parts showed the figures below. ($2\frac{1}{2}$ points for each correct answer)

	Cost	Retail Price
Beginning inventory	\$19,794	\$32,990
Purchases for the year	\$47,200	\$78,667

Net sales for the year	\$61,450
Markup based on sales	40%

Compute the inventory:

a. At cost: __________

b. At retail price: __________

6. The JM Clothing store kept all merchandise records in terms of selling price. On July 1, the JM books showed the following information.

Beginning inventory, January 1:	$23,500
6-month purchases:	99,000
6-month net sales:	87,800

What was the estimated ending inventory on July 1? (5 points) ________

7. The JM Clothing store kept all purchase and inventory records on the basis of the cost price. The owner marked up all goods at 37.5% of the cost price. On July 1, the JM books showed the following information:

Beginning inventory, January 1:	$104,500
6-month purchases:	215,500
6-month net sales:	220,000

What was the estimated inventory, at cost, on July 1? (5 points) ________

8. The AB Art Shop kept all inventory and sales records on the basis of retail prices. It recorded purchases at cost and marked up its merchandise at 120% of cost. On January 1, its inventory of art was $260,000. During the year its purchases amounted to $300,000. Its net sales for the year were $730,000. What was its ending inventory? (5 points)

____

9. From the information given below, calculate estimated cost of goods sold and ending inventory. Round to the nearest dollar. (1 point for each correct answer)

	Cost of Goods Available for Sale	Net Sales	Markup Based on Cost	Markup Based on Sales	Estimated Cost of Goods Sold	Estimated Ending Inventory
a.	$204,000	$260,000	30%		______	______
b.	404,000	260,000		30%	______	______
c.	444,000	350,000		27%	______	______
d.	444,000	350,000	27%		______	______
e.	58,000	50,000	20%		______	______
f.	368,000	400,000		60%	______	______
g.	420,000	600,000		40%	______	______
h.	440,000	360,000	15%		______	______
i.	115,000	180,000	60%		______	______
j.	130,000	200,000	100%		______	______

10. Lathrop Company sold hair products. From the following inventory record sheets for Joy Shampoo, determine the unit and amount totals and the value of the ending inventory of 300 bottles based on average cost, FIFO, and LIFO. (2 points for each correct answer)

Date	Units In	Cost	Amount
1/11	400	$3.40	$1,360
1/23	50	3.00	150
2/10	100	3.20	320
2/20	200	3.30	660
2/25	80	3.50	280
	___		______

Average cost: ______

FIFO: ______

LIFO: ______

Score for B (50)

Notes

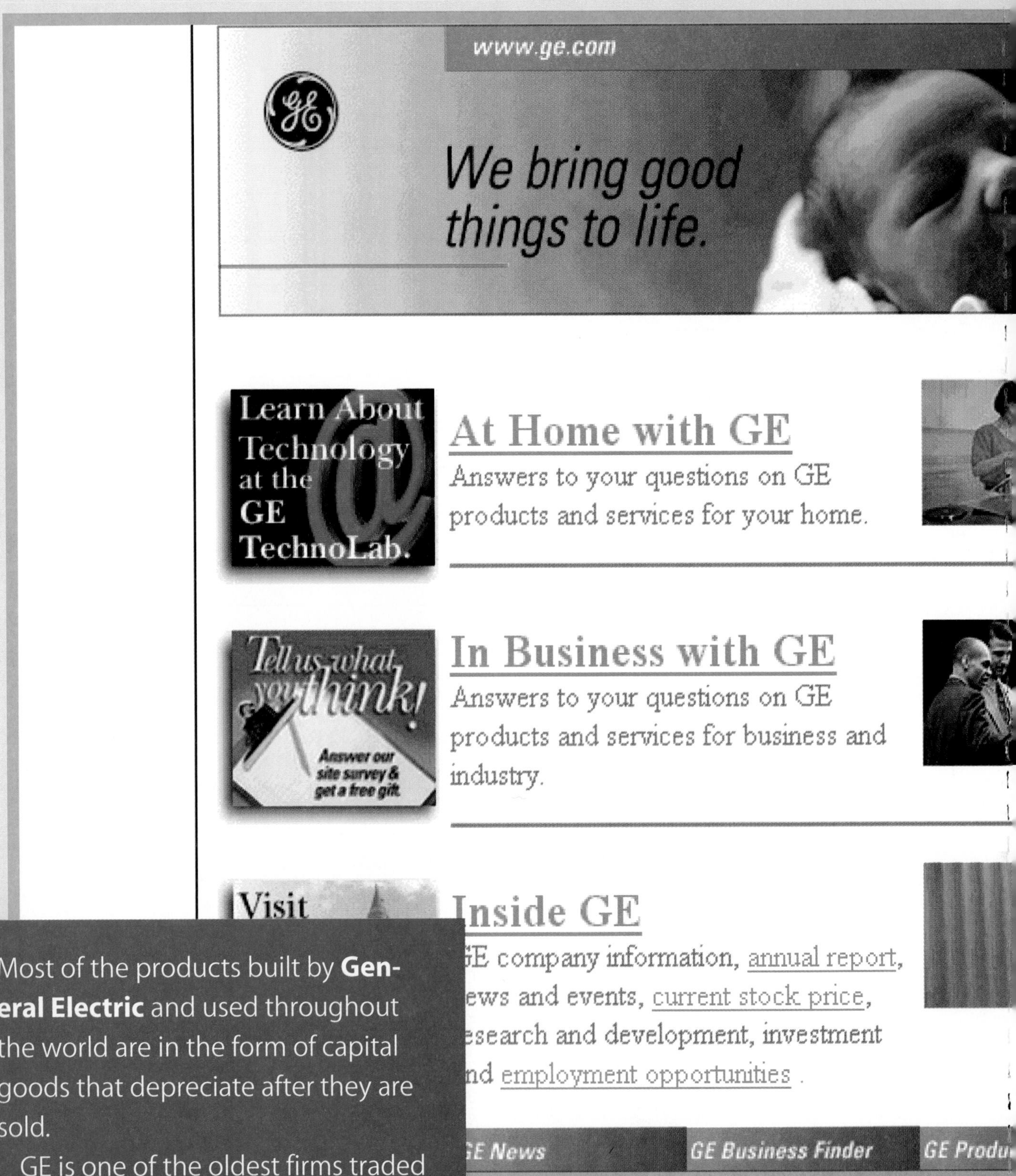

www.ge.com
We bring good things to life.
Learn About Technology at the GE TechnoLab.
At Home with GE
Answers to your questions on GE products and services for your home.
Tell us what you think!
Answer our site survey & get a free gift.
In Business with GE
Answers to your questions on GE products and services for business and industry.
Visit
Inside GE
GE company information, annual report, news and events, current stock price, research and development, investment and employment opportunities.
GE News
GE Business Finder

Most of the products built by **General Electric** and used throughout the world are in the form of capital goods that depreciate after they are sold.

GE is one of the oldest firms traded on the New York Stock Exchange. The company has thousands of employees and offers many exciting and rewarding career opportunities in all parts of the world. Check them out at GE's home page at www.GE.com.

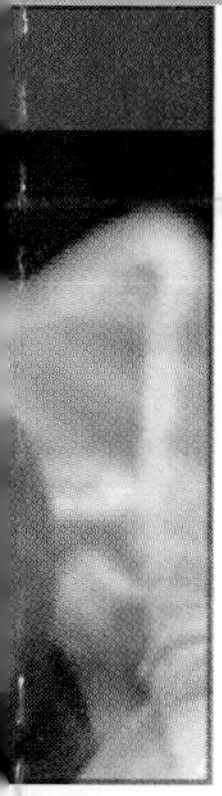

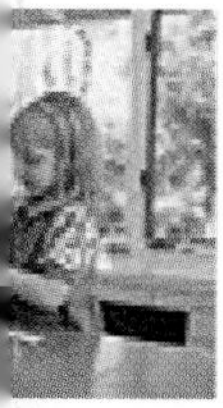

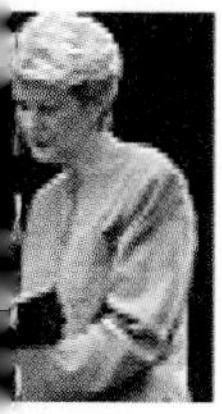

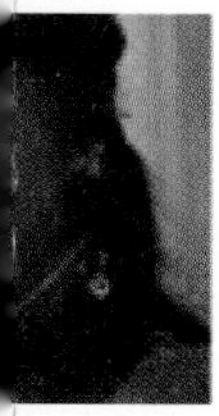

22 Business Depreciation

Learning Objectives

By studying this chapter and completing all the assignments, you will learn to:

1. Compute depreciation using the straight-line method.
2. Compute depreciation using the declining-balance method.
3. Compute depreciation using the sum-of-the-years-digits method.
4. Compute depreciation for income tax purposes using the Modified Accelerated Cost Recovery System (MACRS).
5. Compute partial-year depreciation using the four different depreciation methods covered in this chapter.

Over time and with use, a "usable" commodity loses some of its original value, a process called depreciation. A three-year-old car that sits idle loses some value; the same car, if driven 100,000 miles, loses even more. Other commodities that depreciate include oil, gas, and mineral reserves.

Depreciation is the decrease in the value of assets owned by a business, such as automobiles, buildings, and computers. Depreciation is caused by wear and tear or by *obsolescence* (becoming out-of-date). In the toy manufacturing industry, some dies and tools last only one or two years because of changing fads. An automobile will wear out after a number of years or miles of use. Buildings lose value as wood, electrical wiring, and fixtures deteriorate and as design characteristics and owners' needs change. A business computer frequently becomes obsolete in three to five years.

In business, depreciation is figured on almost all physical assets owned and in use. Depreciation is deducted from gross profits as an expense. This chapter presents four common methods of calculating depreciation.

Computing Depreciation with the Straight-Line Method

LEARNING OBJECTIVES 1

Compute depreciation using the straight-line method.

The *straight-line method* of determining depreciation is the easiest and most frequently used method. The straight-line method distributes depreciation evenly over the useful life of the asset, assigning equal amounts to designated units (miles, number of items made, etc.) or periods (usually months or years). It assumes that wear and obsolescence occur evenly over the life of the property. The straight-line method requires three factors to compute depreciation:

1. The *original cost,* which includes not only the price paid for the item but also any freight charges and expenses for installation.
2. The *estimated physical* or *service life*, which is the length of time the buyer expects to be able to use the asset or the amount of usefulness the buyer expects to get from the asset. The estimated service life may be stated in terms of years of usefulness or number of units (miles) that normally may be expected during the life of the asset.
3. The estimated *scrap value (SV)*, which is the amount the owner of the asset expects to receive upon disposing of it at the end of its estimated service life.

The basic formula for computing the amount of depreciation under the straight-line method is

Depreciation amount for 1 unit or period = (Original cost − Scrap value) ÷ Estimated (physical or service) life in units or periods of time

EXAMPLE A

An office computer costing $12,500 has an estimated life of 5 years and an estimated scrap value of $900. What is the annual depreciation amount?

$12,500 cost − $900 SV = $11,600 estimated total depreciation
$11,600 ÷ 5 estimated total years = $2,320 annual depreciation

NOTE: An annual percentage rate of depreciation can be computed by dividing the annual depreciation amount by the cost. For this example, this rate would be 18.56% ($2,320 ÷ $12,500).

Example B shows depreciation based on the number of hours used. First you must find the hourly depreciation, then multiply it by the number of hours operated during a particular month or year.

EXAMPLE B

A machine costing $10,000 has an estimated 60,000 hours of operation and an estimated scrap value of $400. If it was operated for 2,800 hours in the first year, how much depreciation expense will be shown for the first year?

$10,000 cost − $400 SV = $9,600 estimated total depreciation
$9,600 ÷ 60,000 estimated total hours = $0.16 hourly depreciation
2,800 hours operated × $0.16 = $448 first year's depreciation.

If the life of the machine is stated in terms of the number of units that it will produce during its lifetime, that number should be divided into the estimated total depreciation amount to get the depreciation per unit.

EXAMPLE C

A press that costs $38,000 will produce an estimated 3,500,000 units in its life and has an estimated scrap value of $3,000. If it produced 626,000 units this year, how much depreciation will be shown for the year?

$38,000 cost − $3,000 SV = $35,000 estimated total depreciation
$35,000 ÷ 3,500,000 estimated total units = $0.01 depreciation per unit
626,000 units produced × $0.01 = $6,260 first year's depreciation

Book Value

The *book value* of an asset is the original cost minus the *accumulated depreciation*, the total of all of the depreciation up to that time.

EXAMPLE D

At the end of the first year, the book value of the press in example C would be

$38,000 cost − $6,260 accumulated depreciation = $31,740

The book value can be determined at any time in the life of an asset.

EXAMPLE E

At the end of the third year, the book value of the computer in example A would be computed as follows:

$2,320 annual depreciation × 3 years = $6,960 accumulated depreciation
$12,500 cost − $6,960 = $5,540.

CONCEPT CHECK 22.1

On January 1, Acme Delivery Service bought a new delivery truck for $48,000. Acme estimated a truck life of 200,000 miles and a scrap value of $4,000. In the first year, the truck was driven 38,000 miles; in the second year, it was driven 46,000 miles. Compute the depreciation and book value for the first 2 years.

$48,000 cost − $4,000 SV = $44,000 estimated total depreciation
$44,000 ÷ 200,000 miles = $0.22 depreciation per mile
Year 1: 38,000 miles × $0.22 per mile = $8,360 depreciation
$48,000 cost − $8,360 = $39,640 book value
Year 2: 46,000 miles × $0.22 per mile = $10,120 depreciation
$39,640 value − $10,120 = $29,520 book value

Computing Depreciation with the Declining-Balance Method

Compute depreciation using the declining-balance method.

The *declining-balance (DB) method* is based on the theory that depreciation is greatest in the first year and less in each succeeding year.

STEPS to Compute Depreciation Using the DB Method

1. Divide 100% by the estimated years of useful life to determine the *basic depreciation rate.*
2. Multiply the basic depreciation rate by 2 (*double-declining-balance*) or by 1.5 (*150%-declining-balance*) to determine the *declining-balance depreciation rate.*
3. Multiply the declining-balance depreciation rate by the book value of the asset at the beginning of the year to determine the depreciation amount for that year. (For the first year, the book value at the beginning of the year equals the asset cost.)

Note that Step 3 must be repeated each year, using the new (declined) book value (last year's beginning book value minus last year's depreciation amount). The same rate is used each year. The declining-balance rate continues to apply until the scrap value is reached. The item may not be depreciated below its scrap value.

EXAMPLE F

Use the declining-balance method with an annual double-declining balance to depreciate the office computer from example A.

STEP 1 100% ÷ 5 years = 20%

STEP 2 20% × 2 = 40% annual double-declining-balance rate.

Year		Beginning Book Value		Rate		STEP 3 Depreciation
1		$12,500	×	40%	=	$5,000
2	$12,500 − $5,000 =	7,500	×	40%	=	3,000
3	7,500 − 3,000 =	4,500	×	40%	=	1,800
4	4,500 − 1,800 =	2,700	×	40%	=	1,080
5	2,700 − 1,080 =	1,620	×	40%	=	648
6	1,620 − 648 =	972	×	40%	=	~~388.80~~ $72*

*Since book value ($972) is larger than estimated scrap value ($900), there is some depreciation in the sixth year. However, the calculated depreciation ($388.80) is greater than book value minus scrap value ($972 − $900 = $72). Thus, depreciation is limited to the smaller amount ($72).

CONCEPT CHECK 22.2

On January 1, Acme Delivery Services bought a new delivery truck for $48,000. Acme estimated a truck life of 4 years and a scrap value of $4,000. Compute the depreciation for the first 2 years using the 150%-declining-balance method.

$48,000 cost − $4,000 SV = $44,000 to be depreciated
100% ÷ 4 years = 25%
25% × 1.5 = 37.5% annual 150%-declining-balance rate
Year 1: $44,000 × 37.5% = $16,500 depreciation
$44,000 − $16,500 = $27,500 book value
Year 2: $27,500 × 37.5% = $10,312.50 depreciation

Computing Depreciation with the Sum-of-the-Years-Digits Method

The *sum-of-the-years-digits method* also computes a greater depreciation amount in the earlier years of an asset's life. The decrease in the book value is less rapid than it is under the declining-balance method. This method's name comes from the calculation done in Step 1.

LEARNING 3 OBJECTIVES

Compute depreciation using the sum-of-the-years-digits method.

STEPS to Compute Depreciation Using the Sum-of-the-Years-Digits

1. Compute the sum of all of the years digits in the estimated life of the asset. Use this short-cut formula:
$$\frac{(n + 1) \times n}{2}$$
where n = number of years in the estimated life.
2. Determine the current year's depreciation fraction by using this formula: Estimated total years of life remaining at the beginning of the current year ÷ Sum of all digits from Step 1.
3. Multiply the total depreciation amount (Cost − SV) of the asset by the depreciation fraction from Step 2 to determine depreciation for the current year.

Note that each year a new depreciation fraction from Step 2 is determined and Step 3 is repeated. The sum of all digits in Step 1 and the total depreciation amount in Step 3 are the same every year.

EXAMPLE G

Under the sum-of-the-years-digits method, the office computer from example A would be depreciated as follows:

STEP 1 $\frac{(5 + 1) \times 5}{2} = 15 \text{ (or } 1 + 2 + 3 + 4 + 5 = 15)$

Year	STEP 2 Fraction		Depreciation Total Amount		STEP 3 Depreciation
1	$\frac{5}{15}$	×	$11,600	=	$3,866.67
2	$\frac{4}{15}$	×	11,600	=	3,093.33
3	$\frac{3}{15}$	×	11,600	=	2,320.00
4	$\frac{2}{15}$	×	11,600	=	1,546.67
5	$\frac{1}{15}$	×	11,600	=	773.33
			Total depreciation		$11,600.00

CONCEPT CHECK 22.3

On January 1, Acme Delivery Services bought a new delivery truck for $48,000. Acme estimated a truck life of 4 years and a scrap value of $4,000. Compute the depreciation for the first 2 years using the sum-of-the-years-digits method.

$48,000 cost − $4,000 SV = $44,000 to be depreciated

$\frac{(4 + 1) \times 4}{2} = 10 \text{ (or } 1 + 2 + 3 + 4 = 10)$

Year 1: $\frac{4}{10} \times \$44{,}000 = \$17{,}600$ depreciation

Year 2: $\frac{3}{10} \times \$44{,}000 = \$13{,}200$ depreciation

Computing Depreciation with the Modified Accelerated Cost Recovery System

LEARNING OBJECTIVES 4

Compute depreciation for income tax purposes using the Modified Accelerated Cost Recovery System (MACRS).

Businesses use the depreciation methods described above for financial reporting. However, federal tax laws regulate how depreciation must be taken for income tax purposes. The Internal Revenue Service (IRS) requires that the *Modified Accelerated Cost Recovery System (MACRS)* be used for depreciation of property purchased and put into service after 1986. MACRS "recovers" the entire cost of depreciable property over the allowable period. No scrap value is permitted.

For common business assets, MACRS provides depreciation periods of 3, 5, 7, 10, 15, and 20 years. Examples of assets from each of these categories are as follows:

3 years: Property with a life of 4 years or less—some types of equipment used for research and development, some machine tools, some tractors, and racehorses more than 2 years old when placed into service.

5 years: Property with a life of 4 to 10 years—computers, cars and light trucks, office machines, semiconductor manufacturing equipment, certain telephone equipment, and general-purpose heavy-duty trucks.

7 years: Property with a life of 10 to 15 years—office furniture and fixtures, some agricultural and horticultural structures, and railroad track.

10 years: Property with a life of 16 to 19 years—tugboats, vessels, and barges.

15 years: Property with a life of 20 to 24 years—this category usually contains certain municipal, public utility, and telephone distribution plants.

20 years: Property with a life of 25 or more years—farm buildings and certain municipal infrastructure items such as sewers.

Figure 22-1 shows IRS annual percentages used to compute depreciation by MACRS.

Figure 22-1: MACRS Depreciation Schedule

	Appropriate Percentage					
Year	**3-Year Class**	**5-Year Class**	**7-Year Class**	**10-Year Class**	**15-Year Class**	**20-Year Class**
1	33.33	20.00	14.29	10.00	5.00	3.750
2	44.45	32.00	24.49	18.00	9.50	7.219
3	14.81	19.20	17.49	14.40	8.55	6.677
4	7.41	11.52	12.49	11.52	7.70	6.177
5		11.52	8.93	9.22	6.93	5.713
6		5.76	8.92	7.37	6.23	5.285
7			8.93	6.55	5.90	4.888
8			4.46	6.55	5.90	4.522
9				6.56	5.91	4.462
10				6.55	5.90	4.461
11				3.28	5.91	4.462
12					5.90	4.461
13					5.91	4.462
14					5.90	4.461
15					5.91	4.462
16					2.95	4.461
17						4.462
18						4.461
19						4.462
20						4.461
21						2.231

Note: The MACRS percentage for the first year is applicable to a partial or full year.

EXAMPLE H

Use the MACRS Depreciation Schedule in Figure 22-1 to depreciate the office computer in example A for tax purposes.

Year	Rate (%)	Cost		Depreciation (Rounded)	Beginning Book Value		Current Depreciation		Ending Book Value
1	20.00 ×	$12,500	=	$2,500	$12,500	−	$2,500	=	$10,000
2	32.00 ×	12,500	=	4,000	10,000	−	4,000	=	6,000
3	19.20 ×	12,500	=	2,400	6,000	−	2,400	=	3,600
4	11.52 ×	12,500	=	1,440	3,600	−	1,440	=	2,160
5	11.52 ×	12,500	=	1,440	2,160	−	1,440	=	720
6	5.76 ×	12,500	=	720	720	−	720	=	0

CONCEPT CHECK 22.4

On July 1, Acme Delivery Services bought a new delivery truck for $48,000. Compute the depreciation for the remainder of the first year and for the second full year using the MACRS table (5-year class).

MACRS depreciation first half year: $48,000 × 20.00% = $9,600
MACRS depreciation second full year: $48,000 × 32.00% = $15,360

Computing Partial-Year Depreciation

Frequently, businesses are faced with the need to compute depreciation for only part of the year. Partial-year depreciation is easily computed using any of the methods described in this chapter.

With the straight-line method, the depreciation amount for a partial year is computed by dividing the annual depreciation amount by 12 and then multiplying that result by the number of months of use.

With the declining-balance method, the current year's annual depreciation is found and then divided by 12, and that result is multiplied by the number of months of use.

With the sum-of-the-years-digits method, the overlapping years must be considered. The annual depreciation for the first partial year is found by dividing by 12 and multiplying the result by the number of months of use. From then on, every year will include the remaining fraction of the prior year's depreciation and the partial-year depreciation for the remainder of the current year.

MACRS tables automatically consider partial-year depreciation for the first year.

LEARNING OBJECTIVES 5

Compute partial-year depreciation using the four different depreciation methods covered in this chapter.

EXAMPLE I

Office furniture costing $6,000 and put into use on July 1 is expected to have a useful life of 10 years. Its estimated resale value is $400. Using each of the four methods, compute the depreciation expense for July 1 through December 31 of the first tax year and all 12 months of the second year.

Method	Year	Calculation (rounded to the nearest dollar)
SL	1st	$(\$6{,}000 - \$400) \div 10 \times \frac{6}{12} = \$280$
	2nd	$(\$6{,}000 - \$400) \div 10 = \$560$
DB (150%)	1st	$\left(\frac{100\%}{10}\right) \times 1.5 \times \$6{,}000 \times \frac{6}{12} = \$450$
	2nd	$(\$6{,}000 - \$450) \times 15\% = \$832.50$

SYD	1st	$\frac{(10 + 1) \times 10}{2} = 55$
		$(\$6{,}000 - \$400) \times \frac{10}{55} \times \frac{6}{12} = \$509$
	2nd	$(\$6{,}000 - \$400) \times \frac{10}{55} \times \frac{6}{12} = \$509$
		$(\$6{,}000 - \$400) \times \frac{9}{55} \times \frac{6}{12} = \$458$
MACRS	1st	$\$6{,}000 \times 14.29\% = \$857$
	2nd	$\$6{,}000 \times 24.49\% = \$1{,}469$

CONCEPT CHECK 22.5

In November, Acme Delivery Services bought a new mid-size van for $34,000. It had an estimated scrap value of $4,000 and useful life of 5 years. Compute the depreciation expense for the two months of the first year and for the full second year using the 150%-declining-balance and the sum-of-the-years-digits methods.

$34,000 cost − $4,000 scrap value = $30,000 to be depreciated

Declining Balance

$100\% \div 5 \text{ years} \times 1.5 = 30\%$

$30\% \times \$30{,}000 = \$9{,}000$

Year 1: $\$9{,}000 \times \frac{2}{12} = \$1{,}500$ (2 months)

Year 2: $(\$30{,}000 - \$1{,}500) \times 30\% = \$8{,}550$ (full year)

Sum-of-the-Years-Digits

$\frac{(5 + 1) \times 5}{2} = 15$ (or $1 + 2 + 3 + 4 + 5 = 15$)

$\frac{5}{15} \times \$30{,}000 = \$10{,}000$

Year 1: $\$10{,}000 \times \frac{2}{12} = \$1{,}667$ (2 months)

Year 2: $\$10{,}000 \times \frac{10}{12} = \$8{,}333$ (10 months)

$\frac{4}{15} \times \$30{,}000 = \$8{,}000$

$\$8{,}000 \times \frac{2}{12} = \$1{,}333$ (2 months)

$\$8{,}333 + \$1{,}333 = \$9{,}666$ in year 2

COMPLETE ASSIGNMENTS 22.1 AND 22.2.

Chapter Terms for Review

accumulated depreciation
basic depreciation rate
book value
declining-balance depreciation rate
declining-balance (DB) method
depreciation
double-declining-balance
estimated physical life
estimated service life
Modified Accelerated Cost Recovery System (MACRS)
obsolescence
150%-declining-balance
original cost
scrap value (SV)
straight-line method
sum-of-the-years-digits method

The Bottom Line

Summary of chapter learning objectives:

Learning Objective	Summary	Example
22.1	Computing depreciation using the straight-line method	1. On January 1, 1996, the local Pepsi-Cola bottling franchise purchased a bottling machine for $320,000. Freight was added for $12,000. The cost of installation was $68,000. It was estimated that the machine could be used for 800,000 hours, after which there would be no resale value. The machine was used 92,000 hours the first year, 86,000 hours the second year, and 104,000 hours the third year. Determine the straight-line depreciation and the book value at the end of each year.
22.2	Computing depreciation using the declining-balance method	2. For $56,000, a Gap clothing store bought display racks with an estimated life of 20 years and a scrap value of $4,000. After 3 years, this store closed and sold the display racks for $32,000. If the racks were depreciated by the declining-balance method (150% annual rate), how much less than the book value did the company receive? Round to the nearest dollar.
22.3	Computing depreciation using the sum-of-the-years-digits method	3. A local Ford dealership purchased, for $60,000, a hydraulic lift unit with an estimated life of 7 years and a scrap value of $4,000. Compute the depreciation for each of the first two years using the sum-of-the-digits method. Round to the nearest dollar.
22.4	Computing depreciation for income tax purposes using the Modified Accelerated Recovery Systems (MACRS)	4. Bank One bought new calculators in July for $12,000. Using the MACRS method (5-year class) show the rate, depreciation, and ending book value for the first two years.
22.5	Computing partial-year depreciation using the four different depreciation methods covered in this chapter	5. On October 1, 1997, Ashland Flowers, Inc. bought and installed a new cash register for $1,400. It has an estimated service life of 6 years and an estimated scrap value of $200. The company decided to use the straight-line method of depreciation. What was the depreciation for 1997? What was it for 1998?

Answers: 1. 1996: $46,000/$354,000; 1997: $43,000/$311,000; 1998: $52,000/$259,000 **2.** $12,321 **3.** First year: $14,000; Second year: $12,000 **4.** First year: 20.00% rate, $2,400 depreciation, $9,600 EBV; Second year: 32.00% rate, $3,840 depreciation, $5,760 EBV **5.** 1997: $50; 1998: $200

Notes

Assignment 22.1: Business Depreciation

LEARNING OBJECTIVES 1
LEARNING OBJECTIVES 2
LEARNING OBJECTIVES 3

Name

Date Score

A (30 points) Solve the following depreciation problems. (points for correct answers as marked)

1. An ice cream company has fast-freeze yogurt machines on which it estimates depreciation by the straight-line method. The following table shows cost, estimated life, years used, and scrap value for each machine. Find the annual depreciation, total depreciation, and book value after the indicated number of years of use. ($\frac{1}{2}$ point for each correct answer)

	Original Cost	Estimated Life (years)	Years Used	Scrap Value	Annual Depreciation	Total Depreciation to Date	Book Value
a.	$ 6,000	10	4	$ 350	________	________	________
b.	6,400	7	4	800	________	________	________
c.	8,400	12	3	none	________	________	________
d.	34,600	15	13	1,000	________	________	________

2. United Parcel Service bought two new trucks. The following table shows the cost, scrap value, estimated life (in miles), and mileage for the first year. Using the straight-line method based on mileage driven, compute the first year's depreciation and the book value at the end of the first year for each truck. (2 points for each correct depreciation amount and 1 point for each correct book value)

	Original Cost	Scrap Value	Estimated Life (miles)	Mileage for First Year	Depreciation for First Year	Book Value after 1 Year
a.	$19,800	$800	76,000	15,000	________	________
b.	$27,800	$600	80,000	9,500	________	________

3. The Indiana Chemical Company's equipment cost $214,000 in 1998. Its useful life is estimated to be 15 years, and its scrap value is $4,000. The company uses straight-line depreciation. (2 points for each correct answer)

a. What is the annual depreciation? ________

b. What is the book value of the equipment at the end of 14 years? ________

4. The Jarvis Manufacturing Company purchased a machine for $6,115 on January 1. The freight was $243.80, and the cost of installation was $162. It was estimated that the machine could be operated for 22,800 hours, after which its resale value would be $570. Determine the straight-line depreciation and the book value at the end of each year. (1 point for each correct answer)

Year	Hours of Operation	Depreciation	Book Value
1	2,300	______	______
2	2,750	______	______
3	2,500	______	______
4	2,480	______	______
5	2,800	______	______
6	3,100	______	______
7	2,950	______	______

______
Score for A (30)

B (56 points) Solve the following depreciation problems. Round dollar amounts to two decimal places. (points for correct answers as marked)

5. The Holmes Wholesale Videotape Manufacturing Company owns a group of machines, the details of which are shown in the following table. Holmes uses the double-declining-balance method of calculating depreciation. Compute the depreciation of each machine for the specific years indicated. (2 points for each correct answer)

	Original Cost	Estimated Life (years)	Scrap Value	Year	Depreciation	Year	Depreciation
a.	$ 4,000	10	$ 400	2	______	4	______
b.	8,000	4	300	1	______	3	______
c.	5,940	5	100	3	______	5	______
d.	7,750	10	none	2	______	3	______
e.	18,800	8	1,225	4	______	5	______
f.	980,000	20	none	2	______	4	______

6. Machinery purchased from General Electric by the Ali Dugan Company cost $69,800. Depreciation was determined by the double-declining-balance method for an estimated life of 16 years. Compute the following:

a. Book value after 4 years (8 points): __________

b. Total depreciation after 6 years (4 points): __________

7. The Harris Manufacturing Company bought an engine for $31,500. The engine had an estimated life of 20 years and a scrap value of $5,250. After 7 years, the company went out of business and sold the engine for $15,000. If the machine was depreciated by the double-declining-balance method, how much did the company lose on the sale (the difference between the book value and the selling price)? (20 points) __________

____
Score for B (56)

C (14 points) Solve the following depreciation problems. (1 point for each correct answer)

8. The Western Salvage Service bought three trucks. The table below shows the cost, estimated life, and resale estimate for each truck. Use the sum-of-the-years-digits method to find each truck's depreciation for the first and second years of use. Round answers to the nearest dollar.

Original Cost	Estimated Life	Resale Estimate	Depreciation for First Year	Depreciation for Second Year
a. $46,000	6 yr	$4,000	________	________
b. 54,000	5 yr	6,000	________	________
c. 88,000	7 yr	8,000	________	________

9. Using the information in problem 8b, compute the amount of depreciation for years 3 through 5.

Year 3: ________

Year 4: ________

Year 5: ________

10. Using the information in problem 8, compute the amount of depreciation for each vehicle for 2 years using the straight-line method. Round to the nearest dollar.

________ ________ ________

11. Which method of depreciation would give the smaller amount of write-off, and how much less would it be for the three vehicles for the two years? ________________

____

Score for C (14)

Assignment 22.2: Business Depreciation

LEARNING OBJECTIVES 4

LEARNING OBJECTIVES 5

Name

Date Score

A (43 points) Solve the following depreciation problems. Round dollar amounts to two decimal places. (points for correct answers as marked)

1. Early in 1998, a building contractor bought a cement mixer for $9,000. Its estimated life was 6 years, and its scrap value was $600. At the end of 4 years, the machine wears out and is sold for scrap for $225. (4 points for each correct answer)

a. By the straight-line method, how much difference is there between the book value and the cash value of the machine on the date of the sale? __________

b. In April 1999, a mixer costing $18,000 is purchased. Its estimated life is 5 years. What is the book value of the new mixer on December 31, 2000? Use MACRS. __________

2. E, F, and G were partners in a small textile company. In 1997, they spent $54,000 for equipment that they agreed would last 8 years and have a resale value of 5% of cost. The three partners could not agree on the depreciation method to use. E was in favor of using the double-declining-balance system, F insisted on the 150%-declining-balance method, and G was sure the sum-of-the-years-digits method would be better. Show the three sets of annual depreciation in the table below. At the end of 4 years, what would be the book value under each of the three methods? (2 points for each correct depreciation amount, 1 point for each correct total, and 1 point for the correct book value)

Year	Double-DB	150%-DB	SYD
1	__________	__________	__________
2	__________	__________	__________
3	__________	__________	__________
4	__________	__________	__________
Total	__________	__________	__________
Book value	__________	__________	__________

3. The Wilcox Company owned assets that cost $1,600,000. Depreciation was figured at a straight-line rate of 3% per year. After 16 years, the company sold the assets for $2,350,000. How much greater was the selling price than the book value at the time of the sale? (5 points) __________

Score for A (43)

B (57 points) Solve the following depreciation problems. (points for correct answers as marked)

4. On March 1, Botts Realty spent $16,000 for a new company car with an estimated life of 4 years and an estimated scrap value of $4,000. Botts Realty elected to use the straight-line method for depreciation. On the same date, Wayne Realty bought an identical car at the same price and also estimated the car's life and scrap value to be 4 years and $4,000, respectively. Wayne Realty, however, chose the sum-of-the-years-digits method for depreciation.

a. At the end of the first year (10 months of use) and second year, how much depreciation did each company calculate? (3 points for each correct answer)

Botts: Year 1 ________ Wayne: Year 1 ________

Year 2 ________ Year 2 ________

b. At the end of the second year, which company had more recorded accumulated depreciation, and what was the difference in the amounts? (5 points) ________________

c. True or false: At the end of the fourth year, Wayne Realty will have recorded more accumulated depreciation than Botts Realty. Explain your answer. (4 points) ________

5. In May 1997, Brown & Flynn bought a light-duty truck for $20,800. One year later, they bought an additional truck for $21,800. In June 1999, a third truck was purchased for $23,500. Use MACRS (5-year class) to determine the total allowable cost recovery for 1999. (12 points) ________

6. Travis Marcus purchased new office furniture July 15, 1998, for $28,100. Use MACRS (7-year class) to show the rate, depreciation, and beginning and ending book values for 1998, 1999, and 2000. Round to the nearest dollar. (2 points for each correct answer)

Year	Rate		Cost		Depreciation	Beginning Book Value	Ending Book Value
1998	______	×	$28,100	=	______	______	______
1999	______	×	$28,100	=	______	______	______
2000	______	×	$28,100	=	______	______	______

____
Score for B (57)

Notes

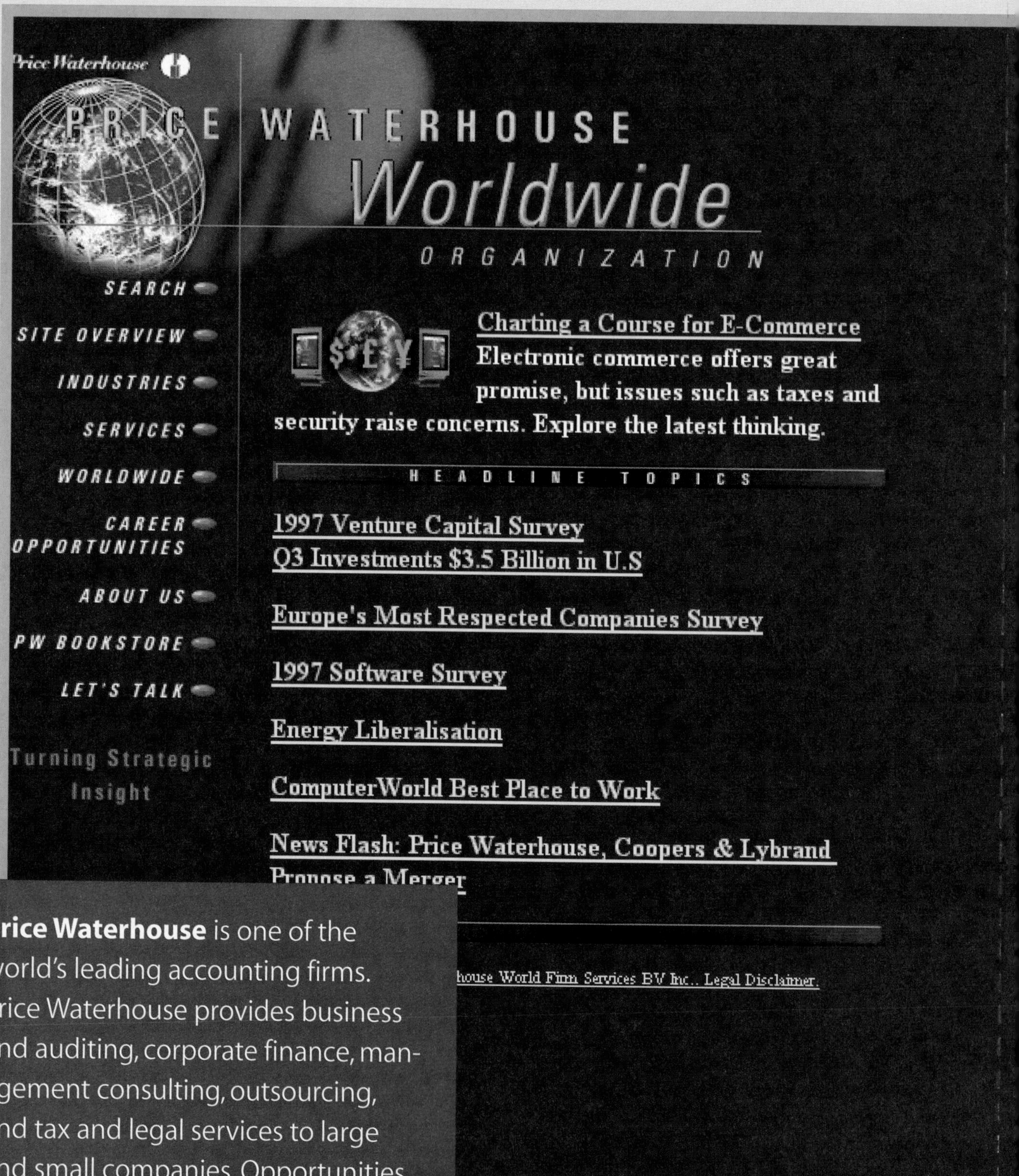

Price Waterhouse
PRICE WATERHOUSE
Worldwide
ORGANIZATION
SEARCH
SITE OVERVIEW
INDUSTRIES
SERVICES
WORLDWIDE
CAREER OPPORTUNITIES
ABOUT US
PW BOOKSTORE
LET'S TALK
Turning Strategic Insight
Charting a Course for E-Commerce
Electronic commerce offers great promise, but issues such as taxes and security raise concerns. Explore the latest thinking.
HEADLINE TOPICS
1997 Venture Capital Survey
Q3 Investments $3.5 Billion in U.S
Europe's Most Respected Companies Survey
1997 Software Survey
Energy Liberalisation
ComputerWorld Best Place to Work
News Flash: Price Waterhouse, Coopers & Lybrand Propose a Merger

Price Waterhouse is one of the world's leading accounting firms. Price Waterhouse provides business and auditing, corporate finance, management consulting, outsourcing, and tax and legal services to large and small companies. Opportunities in the field of accounting and auditing are very strong and growing. Price Waterhouse has a site you will want to visit as you complete assignments in this chapter. You can find it at www.pw.com.

23 Business Financial Statements

Learning Objectives

By studying this chapter and completing all the assignments, you will learn to:

1. Analyze balance sheets, comparing items and periods.
2. Analyze income statements, comparing items and periods.
3. Compute commonly used business operating ratios.

Physicians, dentists, and mechanics use diagnostic tests to determine the condition of patients and cars. In business, financial statements are used to measure the health of a company. Knowing how to read and interpret them is a vital skill in business operations.

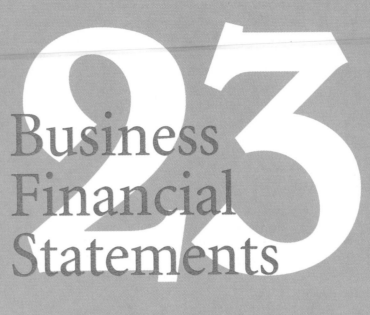

Financial statements provide information that allows owners, managers, and others interested in a business to evaluate its current condition and past operating results. Two important financial statements are the balance sheet and income statement. The *balance sheet* shows the current condition of a business at a definite point in time. It lists what a business owns *(assets)*, how much it owes *(liabilities)*, and the difference between the two *(net worth)*, usually referred to as owners' or stockholders' equity. The *income statement* shows the past operating results for a given period of time. It lists the revenues, the expenses, and the net income or loss for the period.

Analyzing Balance Sheets

LEARNING OBJECTIVES 1

Analyze balance sheets, comparing items and periods.

On a balance sheet, the total assets must always equal the total liabilities plus owners' or stockholders' equity. Balance sheets are analyzed to compare individual items with other items and with the same item on different dates, usually one year apart. Many businesses use the form of balance sheet illustrated in Figure 23-1.

Figure 23-1: Balance Sheet

Dolphin Water Sports Stores

Balance Sheet as of December 31, 1997 and 1996

	1997 Amount	1997 Percent	1996 Amount	1996 Percent	Increase/Decrease Amount	Increase/Decrease Percent
ASSETS						
Current assets:						
Cash	90,000	12.64%	86,000	13.15%	4,000	4.65%
Accounts receivable	134,000	18.82%	98,000	14.98%	36,000	36.73%
Notes receivable	28,000	3.93%	32,000	4.89%	(4,000)	−12.50%
Merchandise inventory	180,000	25.28%	148,000	22.63%	32,000	21.62%
Total current assets	432,000	60.67%	364,000	55.66%	68,000	18.68%
Fixed assets:						
Equipment	220,000	30.90%	190,000	29.05%	30,000	15.79%
Less depreciation	(60,000)	−8.43%	(50,000)	−7.65%	(10,000)	20.00%
Equipment net	160,000	22.47%	140,000	21.41%	20,000	14.29%
Buildings	300,000	42.13%	300,000	45.87%	—	0.00%
Less depreciation	(180,000)	−25.28%	(150,000)	−22.94%	(30,000)	−20.00%
Buildings net	120,000	16.85%	150,000	22.94%	(30,000)	−20.00%
Total fixed assets	280,000	39.33%	290,000	44.34%	(10,000)	−3.45%
TOTAL ASSETS	712,000	100.00%	654,000	100.00%	58,000	8.87%
LIABILITIES AND STOCKHOLDERS' EQUITY						
Current liabilities:						
Accounts payable	18,000	2.53%	24,000	3.67%	(6,000)	−25.00%
Accrued payroll	38,000	5.34%	30,000	4.59%	8,000	26.67%
Payroll taxes payable	6,000	0.84%	4,000	0.61%	2,000	50.00%
Notes payable	42,000	5.90%	48,000	7.34%	(6,000)	−12.50%
Total current liabilities	104,000	14.61%	106,000	16.21%	(2,000)	−1.89%

Figure 23-1: Balance Sheet (continued)

	1997 Amount	1997 Percent	1996 Amount	1996 Percent	Increase/Decrease Amount	Increase/Decrease Percent
Long-term liabilities:						
Mortgage payable	90,000	12.64%	120,000	18.35%	(30,000)	–25.00%
Notes payable (over 1 year)	36,000	5.06%	30,000	4.59%	6,000	20.00%
Total long-term liabilities	126,000	17.70%	150,000	22.94%	(24,000)	–16.00%
Total liabilities	230,000	32.30%	256,000	39.14%	(26,000)	–10.16%
Stockholders' equity:						
Common stock	359,000	50.42%	359,000	54.89%	—	0.00%
Retained earnings	123,000	17.28%	39,000	5.96%	84,000	215.38%
Total stockholders' equity	482,000	67.70%	398,000	60.86%	84,000	21.11%
TOTAL LIABILITIES AND STOCKHOLDERS' EQUITY	712,000	100.00%	654,000	100.00%	58,000	8.87%

In Figure 23-1, the amounts for various items such as cash and accounts payable are compared to total assets and total liabilities and stockholders' equity. Also, the amounts for 1997 are compared with the corresponding amounts for 1996, and the amounts and percents of increase or decrease are shown. When two statements are compared, the earlier period, usually a prior year, is **always** used as the base. The changes in balance sheet items between two periods measure the growth or decline of the business.

The first step in analyzing a balance sheet is to compute the percent each item is of the total assets or of the total liabilities and stockholders' equity (net worth). The second step is to compute the amount and percent of change between two dates being compared. Note three facts:

1. The totals for assets and for liabilities and stockholders' equity are equal.
2. The percent listed for each item under assets is of the total assets; the percent listed for each item under liabilities and stockholders' equity is of the total liabilities and stockholders' equity.
3. The percent of increase or decrease between the two years is based on 1996, the **earlier** year.

CONCEPT CHECK 23.1

In its next year, 1998, Dolphin Water Sports Stores had total assets of \$600,000, total liabilities of \$240,000, cash of \$140,000, and mortgage payable of \$60,000. Determine the following amounts and percents.

a. What was its total stockholders' equity in 1998?
\$600,000 − \$240,000 = \$360,000

b. What was its balance sheet percent of cash?
\$140,000 ÷ \$600,000 = 23.33%

c. What was its balance sheet percent of mortgage payable?
\$60,000 ÷ \$600,000 = 10.00%

d. What was its percent of increase in cash?
(\$140,000 − \$90,000) ÷ \$90,000 = 55.56%

e. What was its percent of decrease in mortgage payable?
(\$90,000 − \$60,000) ÷ \$90,000 = 33.33%

Analyzing Income Statements

LEARNING OBJECTIVES 2

Analyze income statements, comparing items and periods.

The income statement shows revenue, expenses, and the difference between the two, net income. Income statements are analyzed by comparing all other statement items with the *net revenue,* which is total revenue less any returns and allowances. Net revenue (frequently called *net sales*) is always 100%. All other items on the income statement are reported as a percent of net revenue/sales. The resulting percents are extremely important for all businesspeople. They are compared to budgeted amounts, to percents for competing businesses, and to percents for past periods.

Figure 23-2 shows a typical income statement for one year, in which dollar amounts are converted to percents based on net sales. Percents are rounded to two decimal places, and dollar amounts are rounded to the nearest whole dollar. Cents are seldom used in reporting annual figures.

Figure 23-2: Income Statement

Dolphin Water Sports Stores

Income Statement for Year Ended December 31, 1997

	1997 Amount	1997 Percent
Revenue from sales:		
Sales	988,900	101.43%
Less returns	13,900	1.43%
NET SALES	975,000	100.00%
Cost of goods sold:		
Inventory, January 1	211,000	21.64%
Purchases	423,000	43.38%
Available for sale	634,000	65.02%
Inventory, December 31	226,000	23.18%
Cost of goods sold	408,000	41.85%
Gross profit on sales	567,000	58.15%
Operating expenses:		
Salary and benefits	290,000	29.74%
Rent and utilities	62,000	6.36%
Advertising	32,400	3.32%
Depreciation	40,000	4.10%
Equipment and supplies	15,800	1.62%
Administrative	12,500	1.28%
Total operating expense	452,700	46.42%
Income before tax	114,300	11.72%
Income tax	30,300	3.11%
NET INCOME	84,000	8.61%

Most businesses want to compare the operations of the current year with those of the preceding year. The statement in Figure 23-3 has information for both the current and the preceding year. It also shows the amount and percent of increase or decrease from the preceding year. Frequently, comparative statements will include these differences, since the percent of net change—especially if it is significantly lower—will affect future business decisions.

Figure 23-3: Comparative Income Statement

Dolphin Water Sports Stores

Income Statement for the Years Ended December 31, 1997 and 1996

	1997 Amount	1997 Percent	1996 Amount	1996 Percent	Difference Amount	Difference Percent
Revenue from sales:						
Sales	988,900	101.43%	850,000	104.81%	138,900	16.34%
Less returns	13,900	1.43%	39,000	4.81%	(25,100)	–64.36%
NET SALES	975,000	100.00%	811,000	100.00%	164,000	20.22%
Cost of goods sold:						
Inventory, January 1	211,000	21.64%	193,000	23.80%	18,000	9.33%
Purchases	423,000	43.38%	401,000	49.45%	22,000	5.49%
Available for sale	634,000	65.03%	594,000	73.24%	40,000	6.73%
Inventory, December 31	226,000	23.18%	211,000	26.02%	15,000	7.11%
Cost of goods sold	408,000	41.85%	383,000	47.23%	25,000	6.53%
Gross profit on sales	567,000	58.15%	428,000	52.77%	139,000	32.48%
Operating expenses:						
Salary and benefits	290,000	29.74%	242,000	29.84%	48,000	19.83%
Rent and utilities	62,000	6.36%	61,400	7.57%	600	0.98%
Advertising	32,400	3.32%	25,700	3.17%	6,700	26.07%
Depreciation	40,000	4.10%	32,000	3.95%	8,000	25.00%
Equipment and supplies	15,800	1.62%	10,300	1.27%	5,500	53.40%
Administrative	12,500	1.28%	14,200	1.75%	(1,700)	–11.97%
Total operating expense	452,700	46.43%	385,600	47.55%	67,100	17.40%
Income before tax	114,300	11.72%	42,400	5.23%	71,900	169.58%
Income tax	30,300	3.11%	24,400	3.01%	5,900	24.18%
NET INCOME	84,000	8.62%	18,000	2.22%	66,000	366.67%

Another analysis carried out by many businesses is a comparison between actual results and budgeted figures. Owners and managers note differences between budgeted and actual amounts and make adjustments where necessary. Most businesses and virtually all government entities use monthly and annual budgets to guide and monitor their operations. Figure 23-4 illustrates a monthly and year-to-date budget comparison at the end of June, the sixth month of the year.

To find the percent change, the budgeted amount is subtracted from the actual amount and the difference is divided by the **budgeted** amount.

Figure 23-4: Monthly/Year-to-Date Budget Comparison

Dolphin Water Sports Stores

Income Statement for the Month and the Six-Month Period Ending June 30, 1997

	June 1997				Six Months Year-to-Date			
	Budget	**Actual**	**Amount Difference**	**Percent Difference**	**Budget**	**Actual**	**Amount Difference**	**Percent Difference**
Revenue from sales:								
Sales	$85,000	$86,500	$ 1,500	1.76%	$510,000	$480,000	$(30,000)	−5.88
Sales returns	5,000	3,500	$(1,500)	−30.00%	10,000	6,000	$ (4,000)	−40.00
NET SALES	$80,000	$83,000	$ 3,000	3.75%	$500,000	$474,000	$(26,000)	−5.20
Cost of goods sold	35,000	38,000	$ 3,000	8.57%	225,000	230,000	$ 5,000	2.22
Gross profit	$45,000	$45,000	$ —	0.00%	$275,000	$244,000	$(31,000)	−11.27
Operating expenses	31,000	39,000	$ 8,000	25.81%	185,000	196,000	$ 11,000	5.95
Income before tax	$14,000	$ 6,000	$(8,000)	−57.14%	$ 90,000	$ 48,000	$(42,000)	−46.67
Income tax	6,000	1,000	$(5,000)	−83.33%	40,000	16,000	$(24,000)	−60.00
NET INCOME	$ 8,000	$ 5,000	$(3,000)	−37.50%	$ 50,000	$ 32,000	$(18,000)	−36.00

CONCEPT CHECK 23.2

In its next year, 1998, Dolphin Water Sports Stores had total sales of $1,300,000, net sales of $1,200,000, gross profit of $650,000, and advertising expense of $40,000. In 1998, the company budgeted gross profit of $900,000. Determine the following amounts and percents.

a. Amount of sales returns in 1998
$1,300,000 − $1,200,000 = $100,000

b. Amount of cost of goods sold in 1998
$1,200,000 − $650,000 = $550,000

c. Percent of net sales increase from 1997 to 1998
($1,200,000 − $975,000) ÷ $975,000 = 23.08%

d. Percent of advertising expense in 1998
$40,000 ÷ $1,200,000 = 3.33%

e. Percent gross profit was different from 1998 budgeted amount
($650,000 − $900,000) ÷ $900,000 = −27.78%

Computing Business Operating Ratios

LEARNING OBJECTIVES 3

Compute commonly used business operating ratios.

In addition to comparing dollar amounts and percents on financial statements, business managers and owners frequently want to study relationships between various items on their income statements and balance sheets. These relationships generally are expressed by ratios. A *ratio* is the relation of one amount to another. Thus, the ratio of one dollar to one quarter, or $1 to $0.25, is a ratio of 4 to 1, or 4 : 1.

In analyzing financial statements, six important financial analysis ratios are commonly used: the working capital ratio, the acid test ratio, the ratio of accounts receivable to net sales, the inventory turnover rate, the relation of net income to net sales, and the rate of return on investment (equity).

Working Capital Ratio

The *working capital ratio* comes from the balance sheet. It tells the amount of current assets that would remain if all of the company's current liabilities were paid immediately. This ratio helps the reader of the balance sheet understand how well the company is able to pay its current debts.

Working capital ratio = Total current assets ÷ Total current liabilities

EXAMPLE A

The working capital ratio for Dolphin Water Sports Stores for 1997 from Figure 23-1 is

$432,000 ÷ $104,000 = 4.2 = 4.2 : 1

The ratio 4.2 to 1, or 4.2 : 1, means that the business has $4.20 in current assets to pay for each $1 in current liabilities.

Acid Test Ratio

The *acid test ratio* is used to determine the amount of assets that can be quickly turned into cash to pay current liabilities. Usually, these are cash and accounts receivable, current assets that easily can be turned into cash.

Acid test ratio = (Total of cash + Accounts receivable) ÷ Total current liabilities

EXAMPLE B

The acid test ratio for Dolphin Water Sports Stores for 1997 from Figure 23-1 is found as follows:

Cash	$ 90,000
Accounts receivable	134,000
Total cash and receivables	$224,000

$224,000 ÷ $104,000 = 2.2 = 2.2 : 1

Ratio of Accounts Receivable to Net Sales

When businesses sell on credit, they need to be alert to the amount and quality of their accounts receivable. They need to compare the amount of their current receivables to the amounts for prior years and compare the extent of their receivables to those of similar companies. By computing the *ratio of accounts receivable to net sales* every year, management and investors can keep an eye on the percent of sales that have not yet been paid for by customers. An increasing ratio over the years can indicate problems with collecting payment and should be investigated.

Ratio of accounts receivable to net sales = Accounts receivable ÷ Net sales

EXAMPLE C

The Dolphin Water Sports Stores ratio for 1997 is

Figure 23-1		**Figure 23-3**
$134,000	÷	$975,000 = 0.137 = 0.14 : 1

Inventory Turnover Rate

In retail stores, the cost of inventory often is very high. One way to control inventory costs and increase profit is to maintain a high level of inventory turnover. *Inventory turnover rate* lets management and others know the average number of times inventory is sold during the year. The higher the turnover number, the better the movement of inventory. *Average inventory,* found by averaging either monthly, quarterly, or yearly inventory amounts, must be computed first. The rate is given as the number of times larger, instead of as a ratio to 1.

Average inventory = (Beginning inventory + Ending inventory) ÷ 2 (annual)
Inventory turnover rate = Cost of goods sold ÷ Average inventory

EXAMPLE D

Based on the information in Figures 23-3 and 23-1 the 1997 inventory turnover for Dolphin Water Sports Stores is found as follows:

January1 December 31
($211,000 + $226,000) ÷ 2 = $437,000 ÷ 2 = $218,500 average inventory
$408,000 cost of merchandise sold ÷ $218,500 = 1.9 times inventory turnover rate

Relationship of Net Income to Net Sales

An increase in total sales volume does not necessarily mean that a business is improving, since expenses may be increasing at an equal or greater rate than revenues. It is important to look at the *relationship of net income to net sales.* The relationship is given as a percentage:

Relationship of net income to net sales = Net income ÷ Net sales

EXAMPLE E

Based on information from Figure 23-3 the Dolphin Water Sports Stores' 1997 relationship is $84,000 ÷ $975,000 = 8.6%. Comparison with the relationship for 1996 of 2.2% ($18,000 ÷ $811,000) indicates an improvement.

Rate of Return on Investment

Stockholders and owners want a reasonable return on their investment (equity). A ratio that measures the *rate of return on investment* is the ratio of net income to stockholders'/owners' equity. The rate is given as a percentage:

Rate of return on investment = Net income ÷ Stockholders'/owners' equity

EXAMPLE F

Based on Figures 23-3 and 23-1, the rate of return on the stockholders' investment for Dolphin Water Sports Stores for 1997 is

$84,000 ÷ $482,000 = 0.1742 = 17.4% rate of return

CONCEPT CHECK 23.3

Texas Installations' financial statements showed the following:

Cash	$170,000	Current liabilities	$380,000	Net sales	$900,000
Accounts receivable	300,000	Total liabilities	700,000	Inventory 1/1/1997	400,000
Total current assets	590,000	Net income	72,000	Inventory 12/31/1997	250,000
Total assets	950,000	Stockholders' equity	420,000	Purchases for 1997	600,000

Using the above numbers, compute the following ratios:

a. Working capital ratio $590,000 ÷ $380,000 = 1.6 : 1
b. Acid test ratio $470,000 ÷ $380,000 = 1.2 : 1
c. Average inventory ($400,000 + $250,000) ÷ 2 = $325,000
d. Inventory turnover $400,000 + $600,000 − $250,000 = $750,000
   $750,000 ÷ $325,000 = 2.3 turnovers
e. Net income to net sales ratio $72,000 ÷ $900,000 = 0.08, or 8%
f. Rate of return on investment $72,000 ÷ $420,000 = 0.1714, or 17.1%

COMPLETE ASSIGNMENTS 23.1, 23.2, AND 23.3.

Chapter Terms for Review

acid test ratio
assets
average inventory
balance sheet
financial statements
income statement
inventory turnover rate
liabilities
net revenue
net sales
net worth
rate of return on investment (equity)
ratio
ratio of accounts receivable to net sales
relationship of net income to net sales
working capital ratio

Summary of chapter learning objectives:

Learning Objective	Summary	Example
23.1	Analyze balance sheets comparing items and periods	1. A modified balance sheet for Dolphin Water Sports Stores for December 1997 and 1996 appears below. Compute the percents for 1997 and the percents of increase/decrease between 1997 and 1996.

Dolphin Water Sports Stores

Balance Sheet as of December 31, 1997 and 1996

	1997 Amount	1997 Percent	1996 Amount	1996 Percent	Increase/Decrease Amount	Increase/Decrease Percent
ASSETS						
Current assets:						
Cash	90,000	______	86,000	15.03%	4,000	______
Accounts receivable	134,000	______	98,000	17.13%	36,000	______
Merchandise inventory	180,000	______	148,000	25.87%	32,000	______
Total current assets	404,000	______	332,000	58.04%	72,000	______
Fixed assets:						
Equipment	220,000	______	190,000	33.22%	30,000	______
Less depreciation	(60,000)	______	(50,000)	−8.74%	(10,000)	______
Equipment net	160,000	______	140,000	24.48%	20,000	______
Buildings	100,000	______	100,000	17.48%	—	______
Total fixed assets	260,000	______	240,000	41.96%	20,000	______
TOTAL ASSETS	664,000	______	572,000	100.00%	92,000	______
LIABILITIES AND STOCKHOLDERS' EQUITY						
Current liabilities:						
Accounts payable	18,000	______	24,000	4.20%	(6,000)	______
Accrued payroll	38,000	______	30,000	5.24%	8,000	______
Payroll taxes payable	6,000	______	4,000	0.70%	2,000	______
Total current liabilities	62,000	______	58,000	10.14%	4,000	______
Long-term liabilities:						
Mortgage payable	90,000	______	120,000	20.98%	(30,000)	______
Total liabilities	152,000	______	178,000	31.12%	(26,000)	______
Stockholders' equity:						
Common stock	359,000	______	359,000	62.76%	—	______
Retained earnings	153,000	______	35,000	6.12%	18,000	______
Total stockholders' equity	512,000	______	394,000	68.88%	118,000	______
TOTAL LIABILITIES AND STOCKHOLDERS' EQUITY	664,000	______	572,000	100.00%	92,000	______

Summary of chapter learning objectives:

Learning Objective	Summary	Example
23.2	Analyze income statements, comparing items and periods	2. A modified income statement for Dolphin Water Sports Stores for the years 1997 and 1996 appears below. Compute the percents for 1997 and the percents of difference between 1997 and 1996.

Dolphin Water Sports Stores

Income Statement for the Years Ended December 31, 1997 and 1996

	1997 Amount	1997 Percent	1996 Amount	1996 Percent	Difference Amount	Difference Percent
Revenue from sales:						
Sales	988,900	______	850,000	104.81%	138,900	______
Less returns	13,900	______	39,000	4.81%	(25,100)	______
NET SALES	975,000	______	811,000	100.00%	164,000	______
Cost of goods sold:						
Inventory, January 1	211,000	______	193,000	23.80%	18,000	______
Purchases	423,000	______	401,000	49.45%	22,000	______
Available for sale	634,000	______	594,000	73.24%	40,000	______
Inventory, December 31	226,000	______	211,000	26.02%	15,000	______
Cost of goods sold	408,000	______	383,000	47.23%	25,000	______
Gross profit on sales	567,000	______	428,000	52.77%	139,000	______
Operating expenses:						
Salary and benefits	221,000	______	225,000	27.74%	(4,000)	______
Rent and utilities	62,000	______	61,400	7.57%	600	______
Advertising	32,400	______	25,700	3.17%	6,700	______
Depreciation	40,000	______	32,000	3.95%	8,000	______
Equipment and supplies	15,800	______	10,300	1.27%	5,500	______
Administrative	12,500	______	14,200	1.75%	(1,700)	______
Total operating expense	383,700	______	368,600	45.45%	15,100	______
Income before tax	183,300	______	59,400	7.32%	123,900	______
Income tax	30,300	______	24,400	3.01%	5,900	______
NET INCOME	153,000	______	35,000	4.32%	118,000	______

The Bottom Line *Continued*

Summary of chapter learning objectives:

Learning Objective	Summary	Example
23.3	Computing commonly used business operating ratios	Using the Balance Sheet and Income Statement for 1997 from The Bottom Line problems 1 and 2, compute the following ratios: 3. Acid test 4. Average inventory 5. Net income to net sales 6. Rate of return on investment

Answers: 1. 1997 percent: 13.55%; 20.18%; 27.11%; 60.84%; 33.13%; –9.04%; 24.10%; 15.06%; 39.16%; 100.00%; 2.71%; 5.72%; 0.90%; 9.34%; 13.55%; 22.89%; 54.07%; 7.98%; 77.11%; 100.00%. Increase/decrease percent: 4.65%; 36.73%; 21.62%; 21.69%; 15.79%; 20.00%; 14.29%; 0%; 8.33%; 16.08%; –25.00%; 26.67%; 50.00%; 6.90%; –25.00%; –14.61%; 0%; 51.43%; 29.95%; 16.08% **2.** 1997 percent: 101.43%; 1.43%; 100%; 21.64%; 43.38%; 65.03%; 23.18%; 41.85%; 58.15%; 22.67%; 6.36%; 3.32%; 4.10%; 1.62%; 1.28%; 39.35%; 18.80%; 3.11%; 15.69%. Difference percent: 16.34%; –64.36%; 20.22%; 9.33%; 5.49%; 6.73%; 7.11%; 6.53%; 32.48%; –1.78%; 0.98%; 26.07%; 25.00%; 53.40%; –11.97%; 4.10%; 208.59%; 24.18%; 337.14% **3.** 3.61 **4.** $218,500 **5.** 15.7% **6.** 29.9%

Assignment 23.1: Balance Sheet Analysis

Name

Date Score

A (50 points) Solve the following balance sheet problems. (points for correct answers as marked)

1. In the following balance sheet, find the percent for each 1997 and 1996 item, then find the amount and percent of change. Round percents to two decimal places. ($\frac{1}{2}$ point for each correct answer)

Midwest Products Company—Balance Sheet—As of December 31, 1997 and 1996

	1997 Amount	1997 Percent	1996 Amount	1996 Percent	Increase/Decrease Amount	Increase/Decrease Percent
ASSETS						
Current assets:						
Cash	$ 240,000		$ 210,000			
Accounts receivable	250,000		175,000			
Inventory	300,000		275,000			
Total current assets	790,000		660,000			
Fixed assets:						
Machinery	280,000		280,000			
Less depreciation	120,000		100,000			
Machinery net	160,000		180,000			
Building	350,000		270,000			
Land parcel holdings	210,000		190,000			
Total fixed assets	720,000		640,000			
TOTAL ASSETS	$1,510,000		$1,300,000			
LIABILITIES						
Current liabilities:						
Accounts payable	$ 90,000		$ 65,000			
Accrued payroll	45,000		35,000			
Payroll taxes payable	15,000		20,000			
Total current liabilities	150,000		120,000			
Long-term liabilities:						
Mortgages payable	300,000		310,000			
Notes payable—long term	180,000		210,000			
Total long-term liabilities	480,000		520,000			
Total liabilities	630,000		640,000			
Stockholder's equity:						
Common stock	400,000		400,000			
Preferred stock	330,000		220,000			
Retained earnings	150,000		40,000			
Total stockholders' equity	880,000		660,000			
TOTAL LIABILITIES AND STOCKHOLDERS' EQUITY	$1,510,000		$1,300,000			

2. The Midwest Products bookkeeper overlooked the fact that $15,000 cash had been paid to employees but not deducted from the cash account. Assume that the balance sheet in problem 1 was adjusted to reflect the correction. (1 point for each correct answer)

a. What would be the adjusted amount for 1997 cash? __________

b. What would be the adjusted amount for 1997 accrued payroll? __________

Score for A (50)

B (50 points) Solve the following balance sheet problems. (points for correct answers as marked)

3. In the following balance sheet, find the percent for each 1997 and 1996 item, then find the amount and percent of change. Round percents to **one** decimal place. *Note that totals will sometimes be different from individual amounts because of rounding.* ($\frac{1}{2}$ point for each correct answer)

Major's Music Mart—Balance Sheet—As of December 31, 1997 and 1996

	1997 Amount	1997 Percent	1996 Amount	1996 Percent	Increase/Decrease Amount	Increase/Decrease Percent
ASSETS						
Current assets:						
Cash	$ 44,000	______	$ 34,000	______	______	______
Accounts receivable	28,500	______	24,800	______	______	______
Inventory	33,800	______	32,500	______	______	______
Total current assets	106,300	______	91,300	______	______	______
Fixed assets:						
Machinery	57,500	______	52,000	______	______	______
Less depreciation	14,600	______	13,300	______	______	______
Machinery net	42,900	______	38,700	______	______	______
Building	200,000	______	200,000	______	______	______
Land parcel holdings	65,800	______	50,000	______	______	______
Total fixed assets	308,700	______	288,700	______	______	______
TOTAL ASSETS	$415,000	______	$380,000	______	______	______
LIABILITIES						
Current liabilities:						
Accounts payable	$ 12,600	______	$ 11,000	______	______	______
Accrued payroll	9,200	______	7,000	______	______	______
Payroll taxes payable	1,200	______	1,000	______	______	______
Total current liabilities	23,000	______	19,000	______	______	______
Long-term liabilities:						
Mortgages payable	70,000	______	60,000	______	______	______
Notes payable—long term	26,000	______	30,000	______	______	______
Total long-term liabilities	96,000	______	90,000	______	______	______
Total liabilities	119,000	______	109,000	______	______	______
Stockholders' equity:						
Common stock	180,000	______	180,000	______	______	______
Preferred stock	88,000	______	84,000	______	______	______
Retained earnings	28,000	______	7,000	______	______	______
Total stockholders' equity	296,000	______	271,000	______	______	______
TOTAL LIABILITIES AND STOCKHOLDERS' EQUITY	$415,000	______	$380,000	______	______	______

4. Show what changes would have been made in the cash and preferred stock amount in 1997 if Major's Music Mart had sold an additional $4,000 in preferred stock. ($\frac{1}{2}$ point for each correct answer)

	Amount	Percent
Cash	______	______
Preferred stock	______	______

______

Score for B (50)

Assignment 23.2: Income Statement Analysis

Name

Date Score

A (50 points) Solve the following income statement problems. (points for correct answers as marked)

1. In the following income statement, find the percent for each 1997 and 1996 item, then find the amount and percent of change. Round percents to two decimal places. ($\frac{1}{2}$ point for each correct answer)

Chan Restaurant Supplies
Income Statement
For the Years Ended December 31, 1997 and 1996

	1997 Amount	1997 Percent	1996 Amount	1996 Percent	Difference Amount	Difference Percent
Revenue from sales:						
Sales	$850,000		$725,000			
Less returns	30,000		25,000			
NET SALES	$820,000		$700,000			
Cost of goods sold:						
Inventory, January 1	210,000		190,000			
Purchases	440,000		390,000			
Available for sale	650,000		580,000			
Inventory, December 31	250,000		210,000			
Cost of goods sold	400,000		370,000			
Gross profit	$420,000		$330,000			
Operating expenses:						
Salary	125,000		98,000			
Rent	82,000		78,000			
Advertising	15,000		20,000			
Delivery	4,000		3,500			
Depreciation	3,500		2,800			
Equipment rental	1,400		900			
Administrative	7,000		5,000			
Miscellaneous	2,100		1,800			
Total operating expenses	240,000		210,000			
Income before tax	180,000		120,000			
Income tax	30,000		20,000			
NET INCOME	$150,000		$100,000			

2. Assume that the ending inventory was $220,000 in 1997. Compute the following items. (2 points for each correct answer)

1997 Gross profit amount ________ 1997 Gross profit percent ________

1997 NET INCOME amount ________ 1997 NET INCOME percent ________

Score for A (50)

B (100 points) Solve the following income statement problems. (points for correct answers as marked)

3. In the following income statement, find the percent for each 1997 and 1996 item, then find the amount and percent of change. Round percents (no decimal place). (84 points, 1 point for each correct answer)

Markus Utah Enterprises
Income Statement
For the Years Ended December 31, 1997 and 1996

	1997 Amount	1997 Percent	1996 Amount	1996 Percent	Difference Amount	Difference Percent
Revenue from sales:						
Sales	$85,000		$73,500			
Less Returns	2,000		1,500			
NET SALES	$83,000		72,000			
Cost of goods sold:						
Inventory, January 1	24,500		17,500			
Purchases	38,500		37,000			
Available for sale	63,000		54,500			
Inventory, December 31	26,000		24,500			
Cost of goods sold	37,000		30,000			
Gross profit	$46,000		$42,000			
Operating expenses:						
Salary	11,400		10,100			
Rent	7,100		6,900			
Advertising	800		1,860			
Delivery	200		340			
Depreciation	750		200			
Equipment rental	350		160			
Administrative	980		530			
Miscellaneous	190		220			
Total operating expenses	21,770		20,310			
Income before tax	24,230		21,690			
Income tax	2,630		1,690			
NET INCOME	$21,600		$20,000			

4. Assume that the beginning inventory was $21,500 in 1996 and $28,000 in 1997 and that the rent was $6,400 in 1996 and $6,800 in 1997. Compute the following lines to reflect the revised beginning inventory and rent numbers. (8 points for each correct row)

	1997 Amount	1997 Percent	1996 Amount	1996 Percent	Difference Amount	Difference Percent
Gross profit						
NET INCOME						

Score for B (100)

Assignment 23.3: Financial Statement Ratios

Name

Date Score

A (26 points) Solve the following financial statement ratio problems. ($\frac{1}{2}$ point for each correct answer)

1. Cindy Davis was considering investing in a business. The following statements were used in analyzing the Angel Stationery Store. Compute the net changes in the balance sheet and income statement. Round to one decimal place.

Angel Stationery Store
Comparative Balance Sheet
As of December 31, 1997 and 1996

			Increase/Decrease	
	1997	**1996**	**Amount**	**Percent**
ASSETS				
Current assets:				
Cash	$113,800	$104,200		
Accounts receivable	138,200	112,800		
Merchandise inventory	172,000	133,000		
Total current assets	$424,000	$350,000		
Fixed assets:				
Building improvements	$40,000	$48,000		
Equipment	136,000	115,000		
Total fixed assets	$176,000	$163,000		
TOTAL ASSETS	$600,000	$513,000		
LIABILITIES				
Current liabilities:				
Salaries payable	$34,600	$28,800		
Accounts payable	121,400	113,200		
Total current liabilities	$156,000	$142,000		
Long-term liabilities:				
Notes payable	$159,000	$190,000		
Total liabilities	$315,000	$332,000		
Owner's equity:				
G.A. Star, capital	$285,000	$181,000		
TOTAL LIABILITIES AND OWNER'S EQUITY	$600,000	$513,000		

Angel Stationery Store—Comparative Income Statement—For the Years Ended December 31, 1997 and 1996

	1997	1996	Difference Amount	Difference Percent
Net sales	$747,200	$835,000		
Cost of goods sold:				
Merchandise inventory, January 1	$133,000	$130,000		
Purchases	574,000	689,000		
Merchandise available for sale	$707,000	$819,000		
Merchandise inventory, December 31	172,000	133,000		
Cost of goods sold	$535,000	$686,000		
Gross profit on sales	$212,200	$149,000		
Expenses:				
Selling	$ 81,000	$ 57,300		
Other	27,200	8,100		
Total expenses	$108,200	$ 65,400		
Net income	$104,000	$ 83,600		

Score for A (26)

B (24 points) Solve the following problems. (2 points for each correct answer)

2. Provide the following information for Cindy Davis's consideration. When the ratio is less than 1, give the ratio to three decimal places; otherwise, round to one decimal place.

	1997	1996
a. Working capital ratio		
b. Acid-test ratio		
c. Ratio of accounts receivable to net sales		
d. Inventory turnover rate		
e. Ratio of net income to net sales		
f. Rate of return on investment		

Score for B (24)

C (26 points) Solve the following problems. ($\frac{1}{2}$ point for each correct answer)

3. Cindy Davis was offered a second business. She received the following statements for 1997 and 1996. Complete calculations for a comparative balance sheet and a comparative income statement for Banner Office Supplies, showing the amount and the percent of change.

Banner Office Supplies—Comparative Balance Sheet—As of December 31, 1997 and 1996

	1997		1996		Increase/Decrease	
	Amount	**%**	**Amount**	**%**	**Amount**	**%**
ASSETS						
Current assets:						
Cash	$ 41,000	26.8	$ 16,000	14.7		
Accounts receivable	12,000	7.8	8,000	7.3		
Merchandise inventory	46,000	30.1	31,000	28.4		
Total current assets	$ 99,000	64.7	$ 55,000	50.5		
Fixed assets:						
Building	$ 39,000	25.5	$ 43,000	39.4		
Equipment	15,000	9.8	11,000	10.1		
Total fixed assets	$ 54,000	35.3	$ 54,000	49.5		
TOTAL ASSETS	$153,000	100.0	$109.000	100.0		
LIABILITIES						
Current liabilities:						
Notes payable	$ 4,500	2.9	$ 5,500	5.0		
Accounts payable	9,500	6.2	6,000	5.5		
Total current liabilities	$ 14,000	9.2	$ 11,500	10.6		
Long-term liabilities:						
Mortgage payable	$ 33,000	21.6	$ 38,000	34.9		
Total liabilities	$ 47,000	30.7	$ 49,500	45.4		
Owner's equity						
R. A. Banner, capital	$106,000	69.3	$ 59,500	54.6		
TOTAL LIABILITIES AND OWNER'S EQUITY	$153,000	100.0	$109,000	100.0		

Banner Office Supplies—Comparative Income Statement—For the Years Ended December 31, 1997 and 1996

	1997		1996		Difference	
	Amount	**%**	**Amount**	**%**	**Amount**	**%**
Net sales	$205,000	100.0	$101,000	100.0		
Cost of goods sold:						
Merchandise inventory, January 1	$ 31,000	15.1	$ 27,500	27.2		
Purchases	154,000	75.1	64,500	63.9		
Merchandise available for sale	$185,000	90.2	$ 92,000	91.1		
Merchandise inventory, December 31	46,000	22.4	31,000	30.7		
Cost of goods sold	$139,000	67.8	$ 61,000	60.4		
Gross profit on sales	$ 66,000	32.2	$ 40,000	39.6		
Expenses:						
Selling	$ 31,000	15.1	$ 21,500	21.3		
Other	13,000	6.3	7,250	7.2		
Total expenses	$ 44,000	21.5	$ 28,750	28.5		
Net income	$ 22,000	10.7	$ 11,250	11.1		

Any differences of 0.1% from individual items are due to rounding.

Score for C (26)

D (24 points) Solve the following problems. (points for correct answers as marked)

4. Using the figures from Part C, compute the following ratios and comparisons for Banner Office Supplies. Give ratios to two decimal places. (2 points for each correct answer)

	1997	1996
a. Working capital ratio	______	______
b. Acid-test ratio	______	______
c. Ratio of accounts receivable to net sales	______	______
d. Relationship of net income to net sales	______	______
e. Rate of return on investment	______	______

Refer to Sections B and D of this Assignment to answer the following questions. (2 points for each correct answer)

5. a. As of December 31, 1997, which of the two businesses had the better (larger number) return on the owner's equity? ______________________

b. As of December 31, 1997, which of the two businesses had the stronger (larger number) ability to provide working capital for new investment? ______________________

____
Score for D (24)

Notes

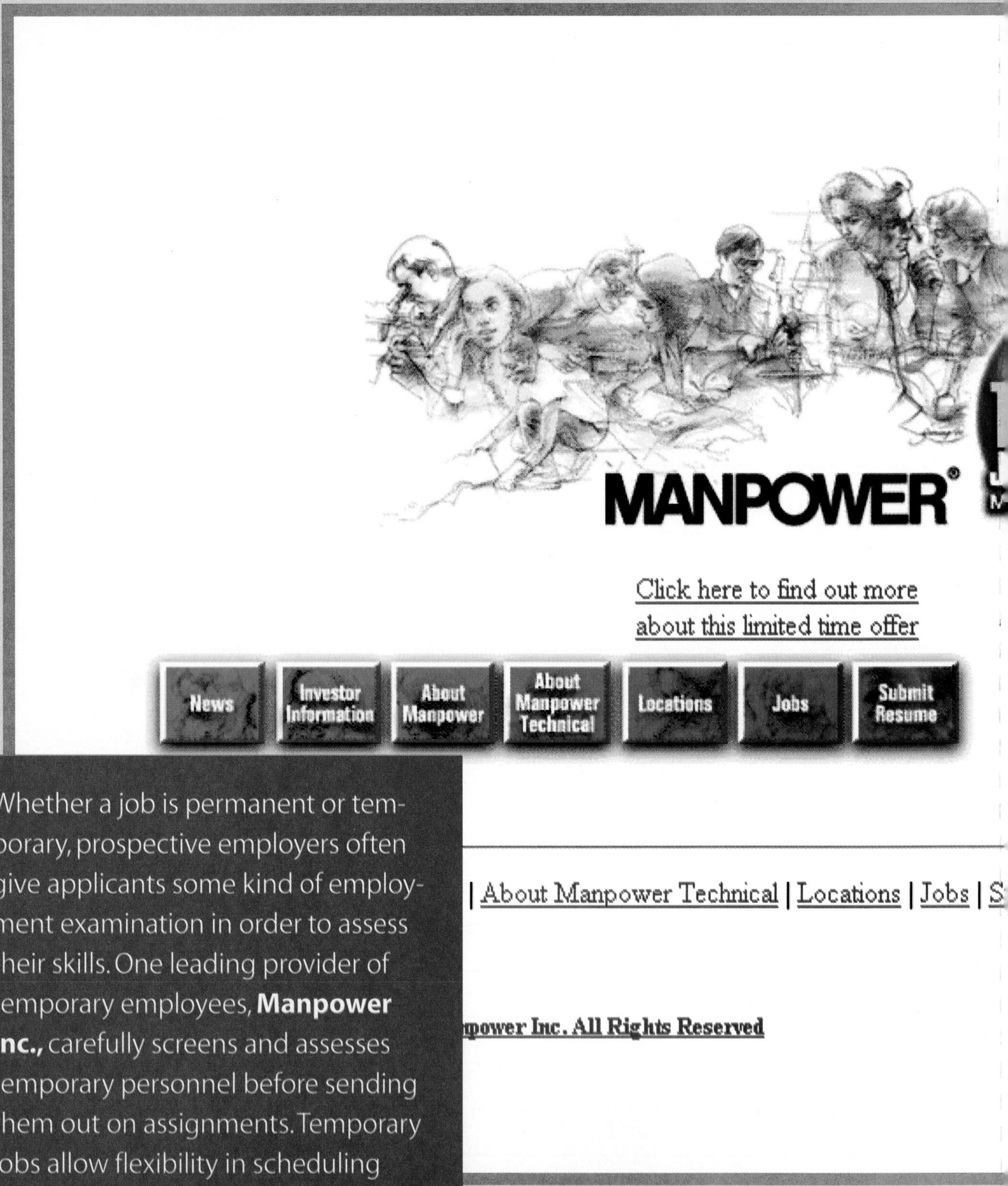

Whether a job is permanent or temporary, prospective employers often give applicants some kind of employment examination in order to assess their skills. One leading provider of temporary employees, **Manpower Inc.,** carefully screens and assesses temporary personnel before sending them out on assignments. Temporary jobs allow flexibility in scheduling times and places to work, and many business school graduates are choosing this option. To learn more about career opportunities and jobs available through temporary placement, see www.manpower.com.

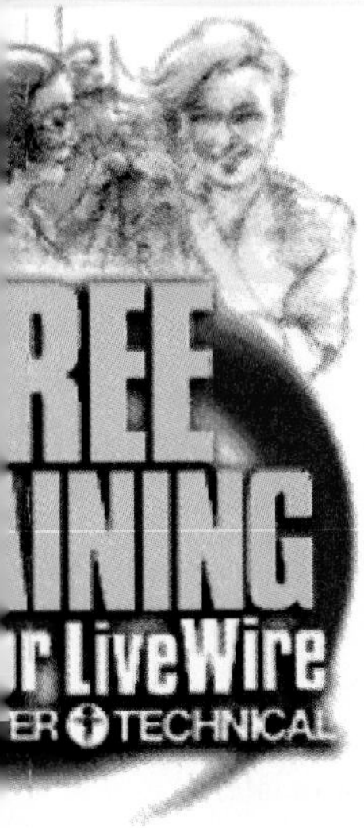

Resume

24 Math in Employment Tests

Learning Objectives

The review in this chapter will strengthen your ability to:

1. Solve rate, time, and distance problems.
2. Solve proportion problems.
3. Solve time and work problems.
4. Solve measurement problems.
5. Solve percentage problems.
6. Solve relationship problems.

Taking employment tests is stressful for many applicants for business and government jobs. Stress can be reduced by confidence, which can be built up through practice and familiarity with the kinds of mathematical problems that often appear on the tests.

A knowledge of business math is important in applying for both business and government jobs. This chapter reviews the types of problems commonly found on employment tests. Previous chapters in this book have introduced each type of problem solution.

Solving Rate, Time, and Distance Problems

LEARNING OBJECTIVES 1

Solve rate, time, and distance problems.

In all rate, time, and distance problems, the formula is simple:

Rate (or Speed) × Time = Distance

Given any two factors, it is easy to find the third:

Rate × Time = Distance
Distance ÷ Time = Rate
Distance ÷ Rate = Time

EXAMPLE A

A train leaves the station traveling at 40 mph. How far has the train traveled 6 hours later?

Rate × Time = Distance
40 mph × 6 hr = 240 mi

EXAMPLE B

A train traveled 550 miles in 11 hours. How fast was the train going?

Distance ÷ Time = Rate
550 mi ÷ 11 hr = 50 mph

EXAMPLE C

A train traveled 300 miles at 60 mph. How many hours did the journey require?

Distance ÷ Rate = Time
300 mi ÷ 60 mph = 5 hr

EXAMPLE D

Train X leaves station X traveling 40 mph on a 400-mile trip to station Y. Train Y leaves station Y traveling 60 mph over the same 400 miles toward station X. How many hours will the trains have traveled when they pass each other?

Distance = 400 mi
Total rate = 40 mph (X) + 60 mph (Y) = 100 mph
Distance ÷ Rate = Time
400 mi ÷ 100 mph = 4 hr

EXAMPLE E

How far will train X in example D have traveled when the two trains pass each other?

Rate × Time = Distance
40 mph × 4 hr = 160 mi

EXAMPLE F

Ellen walks 4 miles per hour. Her brother walks 6 miles per hour. Her brother leaves home an hour after Ellen, going in the same direction. How far ahead of Ellen will her brother be when Ellen has walked 32 miles?

Determine the time required for Ellen to walk 32 miles:

Distance ÷ Rate = Time
32 mi ÷ 4 mph = 8 hr

Determine the distance her brother walks:

Rate × Time = Distance
6 mph × (8 − 1 = 7 hr) = 42 mi

Subtract:

42 mi − 32 mi = 10 mi ahead

EXAMPLE G

Margie types 50 words per minute. Sharon types 75 words per minute. They each typed a page with 300 words. Margie started 1 minute before Sharon. Who finished first?

Margie's time: (300 words ÷ 50 wpm) − 1 min head start = 5 min
Sharon's time: 300 words ÷ 75 wpm = 4 min
Sharon finished first: 4 min vs. 5 min

CONCEPT CHECK 24.1

a. Sam and Mary start traveling toward each other from 360 miles apart. Sam is traveling at 40 miles per hour, Mary at 50 miles per hour. How much time will elapse before they meet?

Distance = 360 mi
Total rate = 40 mph + 50 mph = 90 mph
360 mi ÷ 90 mph = 4 hr

b. Julie types 50 words per minute. Brad types 75 words per minute. They each typed a page with 400 words. Julie started 2 minutes before Brad. Who finished first?

Julie's time: (400 words ÷ 50 wpm) − 2 min head start = 6 min

Brad's time: 400 words ÷ 75 wpm = $5\frac{1}{3}$ min

Brad finished first: $5\frac{1}{3}$ min vs. 6 min

Solving Proportion Problems

Almost all employment tests include proportion problems. The *unit method* is a simple and fast way to solve proportion problems. To use this method, find a single basic unit of 1 in the problem, and then proceed to the answer. These problems may also be solved by proportionate shares (see example J).

LEARNING OBJECTIVES 2

Solve proportion problems.

EXAMPLE H

To sort 360 letters, three clerks require 4 hours. How many letters can seven clerks sort in 2 hours?

$3 \times 4 = 12$ clerk hours to sort 360 letters
$360 \div 12 = 30$ letters per clerk hour (1 unit)
7 clerks $\times$ 2 hours = 14 clerk hours
$14 \times 30 = 420$ letters

EXAMPLE I

The number of pennies in a cash box was twice the number of nickels. There were five times as many nickels as there were dimes. All the coins totaled \$36. How many pennies were there?

Group the coins:

10 pennies + 5 nickels + 1 dime = 45 cents

Determine the number of **single units:**

\$36 ÷ \$0.45 = 80 units

There are 10 pennies in each of the 80 units; therefore, multiply to find the answer:

80 units $\times$ 10 pennies = 800 pennies

EXAMPLE J

X, Y, and Z invest in a business as follows: X, \$150; Y, \$250; Z, \$400. Later, the three divide \$1,200 profit in proportion to their investments. How much does each receive?

Total investment = \$150 + \$250 + \$400 = \$800

X's share: $\frac{150}{800} \times \$1{,}200 = \$225$

Y's share: $\frac{250}{800} \times \$1{,}200 = \$375$

Z's share: $\frac{400}{800} \times \$1{,}200 = \$600$

CONCEPT CHECK 24.2

a. To wash 36 cars, three men require 6 hours. How many cars can nine men wash in 4 hours?

$3 \times 6 = 18$ man hours to wash 36 cars
$36 \div 18 = 2$ cars per man hour (1 unit)
9 men $\times$ 4 hours = 36 man hours
$36 \times 2 = 72$ cars

b. A, B, C, and D invest in a building together, as follows: A, \$4,000; B, \$6,000; C, \$10,000; D, \$12,000. Later, they sell the building for a profit of \$8,000. They divide the profit in proportion to their investments. How much profit does each receive?

Total investment = \$4,000 + \$6,000 + \$10,000 + \$12,000 = \$32,000

A's share: $\frac{4{,}000}{32{,}000} \times \$8{,}000 = \$1{,}000$ B's share: $\frac{6{,}000}{32{,}000} \times \$8{,}000 = \$1{,}500$

C's share: $\frac{10{,}000}{32{,}000} \times \$8{,}000 = \$2{,}500$ D's share: $\frac{12{,}000}{32{,}000} \times \$8{,}000 = \$3{,}000$

Solving Time and Work Problems

Time and work problems are another form of problem frequently included in employment tests. The first and most important step in solving time and work problems is to find the *fraction* of the job that can be completed in one unit of time (a day, for example). Once you have found this amount, divide the *denominator* by the *numerator* to get your answer.

LEARNING OBJECTIVES 3

Solve time and work problems.

EXAMPLE K

X can do a job in 5 days. Y can do the job in 10 days. How long will it take the two of them working together to do the job?

X takes 5 days: 1 day $= \frac{1}{5}$ of job

Y takes 10 days: 1 day $= \frac{1}{10}$ of job

X and Y together do $\frac{1}{5} + \frac{1}{10}$, or $\frac{3}{10}$, of the job in 1 day.

Therefore, they can finish the job in $3\frac{1}{3}$ days ($10 \div 3 = 3\frac{1}{3}$).

EXAMPLE L

X and Y together can do a job in 4 days. X can do the job alone in 16 days. How long would it take Y to do the job alone?

X and Y take 4 days: 1 day $= \frac{1}{4}$ of job

X alone takes 16 days: 1 day $= \frac{1}{16}$ of job

Y alone can do $\frac{1}{4} - \frac{1}{16}$, or $\frac{3}{16}$, of the job in 1 day.

Therefore, Y can complete the job alone in $5\frac{1}{3}$ days ($16 \div 3 = 5\frac{1}{3}$).

CONCEPT CHECK 24.3

a. A can do a job in 6 days. B can do the job in 4 days. C can do the job in 4 days. How long will it take the three of them working together to do the job?

A takes 6 days: 1 day $= \frac{1}{6}$ of job

B takes 4 days: 1 day $= \frac{1}{4}$ of job

C takes 4 days: 1 day $= \frac{1}{4}$ of job

A, B, and C together do $\frac{1}{6} + \frac{1}{4} + \frac{1}{4}$, or $\frac{2}{3}$, of the job in 1 day.

Therefore, they can finish the job in $1\frac{1}{2}$ days ($3 \div 2 = 1\frac{1}{2}$).

b. Carl and Ron together can paint a house in 6 days. Carl can paint the house alone in 10 days. How long would it take Ron to do the job alone?

Carl and Ron take 6 days: 1 day $= \frac{1}{6}$ of job

Carl alone takes 10 days: 1 day $= \frac{1}{10}$ of job

Ron alone can do $\frac{1}{6} - \frac{1}{10}$, or $\frac{1}{15}$, of the job in 1 day.

Therefore, Ron can complete the job in 15 days (15 ÷ 1 = 15).

Solving Measurement Problems

Solve measurement problems.

The traditional measurements shown in Figure 24-1 are commonly included in employment tests. These should be memorized.

Test problems generally involve changing from smaller units to larger ones and vice versa; adding, subtracting, multiplying, and dividing measures; and reasoning to logically apply units of measure. Use Figure 24-1 in working the following examples.

EXAMPLE M

How many hours equal 9,000 seconds?

9,000 ÷ 60 (sec in 1 min) = 150 min

150 ÷ 60 (min in 1 hr) = 2 hr 30 min

$$2 \text{ hr } 30 \text{ min} = 2\frac{30}{60} = 2\frac{1}{2} \text{ hr}$$

Figure 24-1: Traditional Measurements

Weight

16 ounces (oz)	= 1 pound (lb)
2,000 pounds	= 1 ton

Length

12 inches (in.)	= 1 foot (ft)
3 feet	= 1 yard (yd)
5,280 feet	= 1 mile (mi)
1,760 yards	= 1 mile

Time

60 seconds (sec)	= 1 minute (min)
60 minutes	= 1 hour (hr)
24 hours	= 1 day (da)
7 days	= 1 week (wk)
$4\frac{1}{3}$ weeks	= 1 month (mo)
52 weeks	= 1 year (yr)
12 months	= 1 year

Capacity

2 cups	= 1 pint (pt)
2 pints	= 1 quart (qt)
4 quarts	= 1 gallon (gal)
16 ounces (1 lb)	= 1 pint

Area

144 square inches	= 1 square foot (sq ft)
9 square feet	= 1 square yard (sq yd)
43,560 square feet	= 1 acre (a)
640 acres	= 1 square mile (sq mi)

Volume

1,728 cubic inches	= 1 cubic foot (cu ft)
27 cubic feet	= 1 cubic yard (cu yd)
1 cubic foot	= $7\frac{1}{2}$ gallons of water

EXAMPLE N

How many inches are there in 6 yards?

6 yd × 3 ft = 18 ft
18 ft × 12 in. = 216 in.

EXAMPLE O

Add 2 yards, 1 foot, 9 inches and 3 yards, 2 feet, 6 inches.

Yards	Feet	Inches
2	1	9
3	2	6
1	1	
5	3	15
	−3	−12
6	1	3

In the final step, smaller units are changed to the next larger units, where possible.

EXAMPLE P

Subtract 3 yards 10 inches from 15 yards 2 feet 7 inches.

Yards	Feet	Inches
	1	19
15	~~2~~	~~7~~
−3		−10
12	1	9

Because 10 inches cannot be subtracted from 7 inches, 1 foot (12 inches) is taken from the Feet column and added to the 7 to make 19 inches, from which 10 inches can be subtracted.

EXAMPLE Q

How many square yards of linoleum are used for a floor 18 feet wide and 27 feet long?

18 ft × 27 ft = 486 sq ft
486 sq ft ÷ 9 = 54 sq yd

EXAMPLE R

If a 14 foot 9 inch rod were cut into 3 equal pieces, how long would each piece be?

14 ft × 12 in. = 168 in.
168 in. + 9 in. = 177 in.
177 in. ÷ 3 = 59 in.
59 in. ÷ 12 in. = 4 ft 11 in.

EXAMPLE S

Find the gallons in a tank 18 feet long by 6 feet wide with 4 feet of water.

Length × Width × Height = Volume
18 ft × 6 ft × 4 ft = 432 cu ft

432 cu ft × $7\frac{1}{2}$ gal per cu ft = 3,240 gallons

CONCEPT CHECK 24.4

a. Subtract 1 yard 2 feet 11 inches from 4 yards 2 feet 6 inches

Yards	Feet	Inches
	4	
3	~~1~~	18
~~4~~	~~2~~	~~6~~
−1	−2	−11
2	2	7

b. A contractor dug a swimming pool 36 feet long and 20 feet wide and filled it to a depth of 6 feet. What was the volume of water in the pool? (Answer in gallons.)

Find the cubic feet of water:
36 ft × 20 ft × 6 ft = 4,320 cu ft of water

Find the volume of 4,320 cu ft of water:

4,320 cu ft × $7\frac{1}{2}$ gal = 32,400 gal

c. How many minutes are there in 24 hours?

24 hr × 60 min per hr = 1,440 min

d. How many square yards of carpet does it take to carpet a room 24 feet long and 18 feet wide?

24 ft × 18 ft = 432 sq ft
432 sq ft ÷ 9 sq ft per sq yd = 48 sq yd

e. A carpenter saws a board 20 feet 10 inches long into two equal pieces. How long is each piece?

20 ft ÷ 2 = 10 ft
10 in. ÷ 2 = 5 in.

Each piece is 10 ft 5 in. long.

Solving Percentage Problems

LEARNING OBJECTIVES 5

Solve percentage problems.

A percent is a fractional expression whose denominator is 100. Percent may be expressed using a percent sign (%) or a decimal point (.). Fifteen percent, for example, is 15% or 0.15.

EXAMPLE T

A worker earning $400 a week saves 12% of her earnings. How much does she save each week?

Base × Rate = Percentage
$400 × 12% = $48 saved each week

EXAMPLE U

If a customer's 15% discount on a purchase amounted to $30, what was the total amount of the sale?

Percentage ÷ Rate = Base
$30 ÷ 0.15 = $200 total sale

EXAMPLE V

Of 120 employees in an organization, 90 attended the company picnic. What percent of the employees attended the picnic?

Percentage ÷ Base = Rate
90 ÷ 120 = 75% attended

EXAMPLE W

A company earned a profit of $8,000 in 1997 and $6,000 in 1998. What was the rate of decrease?

Find the dollar amount of decrease:

$8,000 − $6,000 = $2,000 decrease

Apply the formula:

Amount of decrease ÷ Original amount = Rate of decrease
$2,000 decrease ÷ $8,000 original amount = 25% rate of decrease

EXAMPLE X

A company had a profit of $9,000 in 1997 and $10,500 in 1998. What was the rate of increase?

Find the dollar amount of increase:

$10,500 (1998) − $9,000 (1997) = $1,500 increase

Apply the formula:

Amount of increase ÷ Original amount = Rate of increase
$1,500 increase ÷ $9,000 original amount = 16.67% rate of increase

CONCEPT CHECK 24.5

a. A customer was given a 15% discount on furniture costing $180. What was the percent of discount?

Base × Rate = Percentage
$180 × 15% = $27

b. Another customer was given a 10% discount of $25 on a dining room set. What was the original cost of the dining room set?

Percentage ÷ Rate = Base
$25 ÷ 10% = $250

c. A third customer was given $30 off on a $200 couch. What was the rate of discount?

Percentage ÷ Base = Rate
$30 ÷ $200 = 15%

d. Three hundred customers purchased season tickets to ball games last year; 250 purchased them this year. What is the rate of decrease?

Find the amount of decrease:
300 − 250 = 50

Apply the formula:
50 decrease ÷ 300 original amount = 16.67% rate of decrease

e. A salesman sold 14 cars last year and 16 this year. What is the rate of increase?

Find the amount of increase:
16 − 14 = 2

Apply the formula:
2 ÷ 14 = 14.29% rate of increase

Solving Relationship Problems

Solve relationship problems.

Relationships in a series of numbers may be found by comparing the first three or four terms in the series.

EXAMPLE Y

Complete the series: 3, 6, 9, 12, 15, _____, _____
Add 3 to the preceding number. The last two terms are 18 and 21.

A series might combine two or more steps.

Complete the series: 4, 8, 6, 10, 8, 12, _____, _____
Alternately add 4 and subtract 2. The last two terms are 10 and 14.

A series might be progressive.

Complete the series: 1, 3, 6, 10, _____, _____
The difference between successive numbers increases by 1. The last two terms are 15 and 21.

Complete the series: 1, 2, 6, 24, _____, _____
Multiply consecutively times 2, times 3, times 4, etc. The last two terms are 120 and 720.

Complete the series: 1, 4, 2, 8, 4, 16, _____, _____
Alternately multiply by 4 and divide by 2. The last two terms are 8 and 32.

Number relationships may be visualized from a verbal description.

EXAMPLE Z

A person walked 2 miles south, then 3 miles east, then 2 miles north, then 4 miles west. How far was he from his starting point?

1 mile

CONCEPT CHECK 24.6

a. Complete the series: 4, 8, 12, 16, _____, _____

Add 4; the last two terms are 20 and 24.

b. Complete the series: 50, 47, 44, 41, _____, _____

Subtract 3; the last two terms are 38 and 35.

c. Complete the series: 5, 10, 7, 12, 9, 14, _____, _____

Alternately add 5 and subtract 3; the last two terms are 11 and 16.

d. Complete the series: 2, 4, 8, 16, _____, _____

Multiply by 2; the last two terms are 32 and 64.

e. Complete the series: 2, 8, 4, 16, 8, 32, _____, _____

Alternately multiply by 4 and divide by 2; the last two terms are 16 and 64.

f. A person drove 4 miles east, then back 3 miles west, then back 2 miles east, then back 1 mile west. How far was she from her starting point?

2 miles

COMPLETE ASSIGNMENTS 24.1, 24.2, AND 24.3.

The Bottom Line

Summary of chapter learning objectives:

Learning Objective	Summary	Example
24.1	Solving rate, time, and distance problems	1. Plane A leaves San Francisco for Honolulu, a distance of 2,600 miles, at a speed of 500 miles an hour. Plane B leaves for the same flight a half hour later, flying at a speed of 600 miles an hour. How far will plane A have flown when plane B overtakes it?
24.2	Solving proportion problems	2. To stuff 600 envelopes, four clerks require 3 hours. How many envelopes can six clerks stuff in 3 hours?
24.3	Solving time and work problems	3. X can do a job in 6 days. Y can do the same job in 5 days, and Z in 4 days. If X, Y, and Z work together on the job, how long will it take them to finish?
24.4	Solving measurement problems	4. A tank is 15 feet by 18 feet and is filled to a depth of 5 feet with water. What is the volume of the water in the tank? (Give your answer in gallons.)
24.5	Solving percentage problems	5. A company employs 480 workers. Half of them drive to work. Of those who drive, 15% drive black cars. How many black cars are in the company parking lot? 6. A store has 2,000 customers with store credit cards. Of these customers, 420 attended a special sale. What percent of credit card customers attended the sale?
24.6	Solving relationship problems	7. Complete the series: 12, 24, 36, 48, ______, ______ 8. Complete the series: 2, 5, 3, 6, ______, ______ 9. Complete the series: 3, 12, 6, 24, ______, ______ 10. Complete the series: 1, 3, 6, 10, ______, ______

Answers: 1. 1,500 miles **2.** 900 **3.** $1\frac{23}{60}$ days, or 1.38 days **4.** 10,125 gal **5.** 36 **6.** 21% **7.** 60, 72 **8.** 4, 7 **9.** 12, 48 **10.** 15, 21

Notes

Assignment 24.1: Math Problems on Employment Tests

Name ____________________

Date ____________________ Score ____________________

A (68 points) Solve the following problems. (4 points for each correct answer)

1. Bob can wash 5 cars per hour. Al can wash 4 cars per hour. Working together, how many cars can they wash in 9 hours? __________

2. Jane can do a job in 8 hours. Martha takes 12 hours to do the same job. How long will it take Jane and Martha working together to do the job? __________

3. Team A can do a project in 10 days. Team B requires 15 days to complete the same project. How long will it take both teams working together to finish the project? __________

4. Betty and Theresa together can do a job in 20 hours. Working alone, Betty can do the job in 60 hours. How long would it take Theresa, working alone, to do the job? __________

5. One bricklayer can lay 450 bricks per day. Another can lay 540 bricks per day. Working together, how many days would it take them to lay 6,435 bricks? __________

6. If Chantall can do a job in 5 days, Colleen in 6 days, and Claire in 10 days, how long would the job take if Chantall, Colleen, and Claire worked together? __________

7. A plane leaves Los Angeles for New York and travels at 600 mph. At the same instant, a plane leaves New York for Los Angeles and travels 480 mph. If the total distance between the two cities is 3,600 miles, how much time will elapse before the planes meet? ________________

8. Refer to problem 7. If the Los Angeles to New York plane departed at 8:30 a.m., how many miles would it have traveled by 2:30 p.m.? (Ignore time zones.) __________

9. Refer to problem 7. Suppose planes both landed in Chicago, which is 1,200 miles from New York and on a straight line between the two cities. What time would the Los Angeles to New York plane arrive in Chicago if it departed from Los Angeles at 12 noon? (Ignore time zones.) __________

10. Faye and Franco start toward each other from 240 miles apart. Faye leaves 1 hour before Franco. Faye travels at 30 miles per hour, Franco at 40 miles per hour. How many miles will Franco have traveled when they meet? __________

11. Al walks at 6 miles per hour; Michael walks at 4 miles per hour. If Michael starts to walk in a certain direction 1 hour before Al, how far behind Al will he be when Al has walked 24 miles? __________

12. Two cars started toward each other from 375 miles apart. The speed of one car was 25 mph. It met the other car after 5 hours. What was the speed of the other car? __________

13. If four postal clerks require 60 minutes to sort 1,200 letters, how many letters can ten clerks sort in 8 hours?

____

14. Three different bakers produce the following numbers of loaves of bread per hour: baker A, 250; baker B, 300; baker C, 350. If they all work the same number of hours and produce a combined total of 12,600 loaves, how many of these loaves does baker B produce? __________

15. Refer to problem 14. How many hours does each baker work? __________

16. X, Y, and Z invest $25,000, $50,000, and $75,000, respectively, in a business. Later, they sell the business for $96,000 and divide the proceeds in proportion to their original investment. How much does Z get? __________

17. A cash box had an equal number of dimes and quarters. It had twice as many pennies and three times as many nickels. The total cash was $416. How many nickels were there? __________

____

Score for A (68)

B (32 points) Solve the following problems. (4 points for each correct answer)

18. Subtract 5 hours 20 minutes 30 seconds from 10 hours 23 minutes. ______________

19. Add 5 yards 2 feet 9 inches, 4 yards 1 foot 7 inches, and 1 yard 6 inches. ______________

20. A room is 24 feet long and 15 feet wide. How much will it cost to cover the floor with carpet costing $18 a square yard if an extra 4 square yards must be purchased for matching? __________

21. A swimming pool is 60 feet long and 30 feet wide. It is 3 feet deep at one end and slopes evenly to a depth of 9 feet at the other end. How many gallons of water will be required to fill it to 1 foot from the top. (**Hint:** $(3 + 9) \div 2 =$ 6 ft average depth of pool.) ____________

22. A customer received a 30% discount on a $200 item, a 20% discount on a $150 item, and a 15% discount on an $80 item. What was the total dollar amount of the discount? __________

23. At a company employing 280 people, 40% of the employees took the bus to work, and 5% lived close enough to walk. The others drove cars. How many employees drove cars to work? __________

24. Complete the following series: 4, 12, 8, 16, 12, __________, __________

25. Complete the following series: 2, 8, 4, 16, 8, __________, __________

Score for B (32)

Assignment 24.2: Math Problems on Employment Tests

Name ____________________

Date ____________ Score ____________

A (55 points) Solve the following problems. (5 points for each correct answer)

1. United Airlines flight A flies 2,000 miles from Minneapolis to New York in 5 hours. United Airlines flight B flies 2,000 miles from Minneapolis to New York in 4 hours. If United flight A starts 1 hour before United flight B, how far ahead of flight B will it be when flight B has flown 1,500 miles? __________

2. A car leaves Cleveland for Albuquerque and travels at 55 mph. Simultaneously, a second car leaves Albuquerque for Cleveland and travels at 50 mph. If the total distance is 1,575 miles, how much time will go by before the two cars meet? __________

3. If the Cleveland to Albuquerque car (from problem 2) left at 9 a.m., how far from Albuquerque would it be at 6 p.m.? __________

4. X and Y start toward each other from 150 miles apart. X leaves 1 hour before Y. X travels at 30 mph, Y at 20 mph. How many miles will Y have traveled when they meet? __________

5. The Swenson nursery plants 14 trees per hour. The Johnson nursery plants 12 trees per hour. Working as a team, how many trees can the two nurseries plant in 22 hours? __________

6. One manufacturer can produce 800 VCRs per day; another can produce 960 per day. Working together, how many days would it take the two manufacturers to produce 39,600 VCRs? __________

7. One computer printer prints at 1,060 words per minute. A second brand prints at 510 words per minute. A third unit prints at 1,430 words per minute. How many words do the three computers produce in 1 hour? __________

8. Alberta can sew a dress in 3 days. Allison requires only 2 days. If they combine efforts to fill one order to sew 30 dresses, how long will they take to fill the order? __________

9. If W can do a job in 4 days, X in 6 days, Y in 6 days, and Z in 12 days, how long would it take to complete the job if all four worked together? __________

10. Refer to problem 9. How long would it take W and Y to do the job? ________

11. Refer to problems 9 and 10. How much more time would it take X and Z than W and Y to complete the job?

____

____
Score for A (55)

B **(45 points) Solve the following problems. (4 points for each correct answer)**

12. How many minutes are there in $1\frac{1}{2}$ days? ________

13. How many inches are there in 32 yards? ________

14. How many gallons of water would it take to fill a swimming pool that was 10 feet wide, 30 feet long, and 5 feet deep? ________

15. Refer to problem 16. If water cost $0.07 per gallon, how much would it cost to fill the pool? ________

16. Subtract 1 yard 2 feet 9 inches from 3 yards 2 feet 2 inches. ________

17. A room measures 21 feet long and 15 feet wide. How much will it cost to carpet the room with carpet that costs $18.50 per square yard? ________

18. If a Jacuzzi that is 5 feet long, 4 feet wide, and 3 feet deep is filled with water, how many gallons of water does it contain? ________

19. Complete the following series: 6, 10, 14, 18, 22, ________

20. Complete the following series: 3, 4, 8, 9, 18, 19, ________

____
Score for B (45)

Assignment 24.3: Practice Employment Test

Name ______________________________

Date ______________ Score ______________

(100 points) Solve the following problems and fill in the blank with the letter of the correct answer. ($2\frac{1}{2}$ points for each correct answer)

Answers

1. Kay typed 50 letters per day for 7 days; Joe typed 50 letters per day for 5 days. What is the total number of letters typed by both?
a. 350; **b.** 600; **c.** 100; **d.** 550 — **1.** _____

2. An automobile traveled for 3 hours 20 minutes at an average speed of 45 mph. How many miles did it travel?
a. 180; **b.** 135; **c.** 157; **d.** 150 — **2.** _____

3. A sales representative received commissions of $39.50 in March, $49.20 in April, $18.00 in May, and $97.70 in June. What was the average monthly commission?
a. $49.20; **b.** $51.10; **c.** $204.40; **d.** $40.00 — **3.** _____

4. If a person receives a 30% discount on a purchase of $96.80, how much will that person pay?
a. $29.04; **b.** $93.90; **c.** $32.27; **d.** $67.76 — **4.** _____

5. Of 465 students in school, 93 went to a ball game. What percent of the students did NOT go to the game?
a. 20%; **b.** 40%; **c.** 60%; **d.** 80% — **5.** _____

6. Two cars are traveling in the same direction, one at 50 mph, one at 55 mph. If the slower car started an hour earlier, how many hours will it take the faster car to catch up to it?
a. 11; **b.** 9; **c.** 10; **d.** 5.5 — **6.** _____

7. A homeowner has enough lawn seed to plant $\frac{2}{3}$ of a backyard that is 90 ft by 20 ft. How many square feet will go unplanted?
a. 330; **b.** 180; **c.** 900; **d.** 600 — **7.** _____

8. X saves twice as much as Y. Y saves twice as much as Z. If X saves a total of $1,500, how much does Z save?
a. $1,500; **b.** $600; **c.** $375; **d.** $500 — **8.** _____

9. If $15,300 is divided among X, Y, and Z in the proportions 3, 5, and 9, respectively, how much will X receive?
a. $2,700; **b.** $5,900; **c.** $5,100; **d.** $900 — **9.** _____

10. Two trains were 780 miles apart. They were headed directly toward each other. One traveled at 30 mph. The other traveled at 35 mph. How many hours did it take for the trains to meet?
a. 26; **b.** 13; **c.** 18; **d.** 12 — **10.** _____

11. At $14.25 per sq yd, how much would it cost to carpet a room 18 ft by 27 ft?
a. $2,308.50; **b.** $692.55; **c.** $769.50; **d.** $6,925.50 — **11.** _____

Answers

12. Two partners, X and Y, own a restaurant. They sell a $\frac{1}{3}$ interest to Z. If the part of the restaurant X and Y still own is worth a total of $15,000, how much was the original value?
a. $22,500; **b.** $30,000; **c.** $45,000; **d.** $7,500 **12.** ____

13. A bus left San Diego at 1:30 and traveled 50 mph. A train left San Diego at 3:30 traveling in the same direction at 70 mph. At what time will the train catch up with the bus?
a. 6:30; **b.** 9:00; **c.** 11:18; **d.** 8:30 **13.** ____

14. If plane X averages 800 mph and plane Y averages 400 mph, how many hours will plane X travel before it overtakes plane Y if plane Y has a 2 hour and 30 minute head start?
a. $1\frac{1}{4}$; **b.** $2\frac{1}{2}$; **c.** 5; **d.** $7\frac{1}{2}$ **14.** ____

15. How long will it take a car to travel 1,100 miles at an average speed of 55 mph?
a. 20 hr; **b.** $18\frac{2}{11}$ hr; **c.** 55 hr; **d.** $16\frac{2}{3}$ hr **15.** ____

16. Two teenagers who were 60 miles apart walked toward each other. They met in 4 hours. One teenager averaged 7 mph. How fast did the other travel?
a. 7 mph; **b.** $8\frac{4}{7}$ mph; **c.** $6\frac{3}{7}$ mph; **d.** 8 mph **16.** ____

17. Two cars started toward each other from 400 miles apart. They met in five hours. Car X averaged 45 mph. How many mph did car Y average?
a. 45; **b.** 55; **c.** 35; **d.** 37 **17.** ____

18. A bus averaging 45 mph leaves New York at 9:30 a.m. How many miles will it have traveled at 4:45 p.m.?
a. 281.25; **b.** 326.25; **c.** 236.25; **d.** 282.5 **18.** ____

19. A submarine travels at a rate of 12 mph under water and 24 mph on top. In a 100 mile trip, it travels 20 miles below and the rest on top. How many hours does the 100 mile trip take?
a. $4\frac{1}{6}$; **b.** $8\frac{1}{2}$; **c.** 5; **d.** $7\frac{1}{24}$ **19.** ____

20. How long will it take a train averaging 60 mph to cover its entire route of 400 miles if it loses 45 minutes travel time in stops?
a. 7 hr 25 min; **b.** 6 hr 40 min; **c.** 5 hr 55 min; **d.** 9 hr **20.** ____

21. If a hiker travels 18 miles in 4 hours, how many miles will be covered in 7.5 days walking 8 hours per day?
a. 240; **b.** 262.5; **c.** 320; **d.** 270 **21.** ____

22. X can do a job in 3 days. Y can do the same job in 2 days. How many days would it take them to do the job together?
a. 1.8; **b.** 1.5; **c.** 1; **d.** 1.2 **22.** ____

Answers

23. Aren, Warner, and Brown invested $1,000, $1,500, and $3,500, respectively, in a business partnership. If the annual profit of $1,500 is divided among them in proportion to their investment, how much will Aren receive?
a. $300; **b.** $250; **c.** $1,000; **d.** $375

23. _____

24. Three salespeople, X, Y, and Z, sold a combined total of $8,400. X sold $3,360; Y and Z split the remainder. If a $300 bonus was divided among the three in proportion to their sales, how much did Z receive?
a. $90; **b.** $180; **c.** $50.40; **d.** $75.60

24. _____

25. From Los Angeles to Dallas, a plane takes 3 hours, 25 minutes. A train takes 11 hours, 10 minutes. How many hours are saved by taking the plane?
a. $7\frac{3}{4}$; **b.** $17\frac{1}{4}$; **c.** $31\frac{3}{4}$; **d.** $19\frac{3}{4}$

25. _____

26. To 7 gallons 3 quarts 1 pint of liquid are added 2 gallons 4 quarts. How many pint jars would the total quantity fill?
a. 87; **b.** 55; **c.** 17; **d.** 173

26. _____

27. Y and Z start traveling toward each other from 600 miles apart. Y is traveling at 35 mph, Z at 40 mph. How many hours will elapse before they meet?
a. 7; **b.** 8; **c.** 9; **d.** 10

27. _____

28. Y and Z start traveling toward each other from 600 miles apart. Y is traveling at 35 mph, Z at 40 mph. How many miles will Y travel before they meet?
a. 400 ; **b.** 320; **c.** 350; **d.** 280

28. _____

29. Departments X, Y, and Z had sales of $1,100, $1,900, and $2,500, respectively. A $700 advertising charge was allocated proportionately. How much is Dept. X's share of the advertising charge?
a. $140; **b.** $350; **c.** $110; **d.** $116.67

29. _____

30. In problem 29, what would Dept. Z's expense be if the advertising charge was increased to $2,200?
a. $100; **b.** $900; **c.** $1,000; **d.** $484

30. _____

31. If X and Y together do a job in 6 hours and X alone does the job in 10 hours, how long does it take Y alone to do the job?
a. 12 hr; **b.** 20 hr; **c.** 15 hr; **d.** 9 hr

31. _____

32. A company had expenses of $15,500 in 1994 and $18,600 in 1995. What was the percent of increase?
a. 15%; **b.** $16\frac{2}{3}$%; **c.** 25%; **d.** 20%

32. _____

Answers

33. This year XYZ company had last year's expenses of $24,000 increased by 20%. If $\frac{1}{8}$ of this year's expenses were charged to overhead, what would be the amount?
a. $2,400 **b.** $3,600 **c.** $4,800 **d.** $3,000

33. ______

34. In an agent's 8% commission for selling a product amounted to $1,200, what was the total amount of the sale?
a. $12,000; **b.** $9,600; **c.** $8,600; **d.** $15,000

34. ______

35. How many days will be required for 5 persons to build 5 machines if 5 persons can build 20 machines in 8 days?
a. 5; **b.** 4; **c.** 2; **d.** 1.6

35. ______

36. Mae Miles drove 231 miles in one day. If this is 40% more than she drove the day before, how many miles were driven the day before?
a. 165; **b.** 162.7; **c.** 323.4; **d.** 57.75

36. ______

37. What is the number of square feet on one wall of a 24 ft by 24 ft room with a 12 ft high ceiling?
a. 48; **b.** 6,912; **c.** 288; **d.** 64

37. ______

38. Add: 2.001 + 3.14 + 280.3 + 0.7
a. 512.5; **b.** 286.141; **c.** 287.007; **d.** 285.611

38. ______

39. A secretary earns $1,400 per month, spends 90% of what is left after deductions of 22%, and saves the rest. How many months will it take the secretary to save $1,528.80?
a. 11; **b.** 12; **c.** 13; **d.** 14

39. ______

40. A $300 lamp is sold at a 40% discount; 15% of the sales price goes for advertising. What is the advertising cost?
a. $180; **b.** $60; **c.** $27; **d.** $18

40. ______

______
Score (100)

Notes

Glossary

A

Account purchase. A detailed statement from the commission merchant to the principal.

Account sales. A detailed statement of the amount of the sales and the various deductions sent by the commission merchant to the consignor.

Accrued interest. Interest earned from the last payment date.

Accumulated depreciation. The total of all the depreciation recognized up to a specified time.

Acid test ratio. Used to determine the amount of assets that can be quickly turned into cash to pay current liabilities; acid test ratio = total of cash plus receivables ÷ total current liabilities.

Ad valorem. Duty that is a percent of the value of the item.

Additional death benefit (ADB). Benefits, available with some life insurance policies, that allow the insured to purchase, at a low rate per thousand dollars of coverage, additional insurance up to the full face value of the policy. In case of death of the insured by accident, both the full value of the policy and the ADB would be paid to the beneficiaries of the insured. If death occurs other than by accident, the full value of the policy is paid but no ADB is paid. Sometimes referred to as accidental death benefit.

Additional discount. Extra trade discount based on purchase volume.

Adjusted bank statement balance. The dollar amount obtained by adding to or subtracting from the bank statement balance checkbook activities not yet known to the bank. This should equal the adjusted checkbook balance.

Adjusted checkbook balance. The dollar amount obtained by adding to or subtracting from the checkbook balance those activities appearing on the bank statement that do not yet appear in the checkbook. This should equal the adjusted bank statement balance.

Adjusted gross income. Gross income minus certain income adjustments.

Algebra. A form of mathematics in which letters as well as numbers are used to represent values.

Allocate. Distribute.

Amortization payment factor. A number which, when multiplied by the per $1,000 loan amount, calculates the amount of each loan payment.

Amortization schedule. A schedule of payments; the schedule shows the amount of interest and the amount of principal in each payment.

Amortization table. Amortization schedule.

Amortizing. The process by which a loan's monthly payments are always equal in dollar amount while the interest amount, which is calculated on the unpaid balance, always varies.

Amount credited. The total amount paid plus the amount of cash discount.

Amount of an annuity. The accumulated cash value at the end of the annuity term (at the end of the last period). The amount includes the sum of all payments plus the accumulated compound interest on all payments.

Amount of decrease. The rate of decrease times the base amount.

Amount of increase. The rate of increase times the base amount.

Annual discount amortization. The spreading of the discount amount evenly over the life of the bonds; annual interest ÷ total cost = average annual yield.

Annual percentage rate (APR). The annual equivalent interest rate charged.

Annual premium amortization. The spreading of the premium amount evenly over the life of the bonds.

Annuity. A series of equal payments that are made at regular equal time intervals.

Annuity due. An annuity in which payment is made at the *beginning* of each time interval.

Annuity factor. A present value factor or a future value factor.

Annuity insurance. Life insurance that pays a certain sum of money to the insured every year after the insured reaches a specified age or until the insured's death.

Assessed valuation. A property value determined by a representative of the local or state government.

Asset. Something of value owned by a business or a person.

Auto collision insurance. Insurance that protects the vehicle of the insured against collision damage.

Auto comprehensive insurance. Insurance that protects the vehicle of the insured against fire, water, theft, vandalism, falling objects, and other damage that is not caused by collision.

Auto liability and property damage insurance. Insurance that protects the insured against claims resulting from personal injuries and property damage.

Average. A single number that represents a group of numbers. The process of determining that single number.

Average annual yield. The average annual income rate from an investment; annual interest ÷ total cost = average annual yield.

Average cost method. A method of valuing inventory that assumes that the costs of all items on hand are averaged and shared evenly among all units.

Average daily balance. The sum of each day's balance divided by the number of days in the month. Payments are usually included; new purchases may or may not be included.

Average principal. The average unpaid balance.

Average inventory. The inventory average calculated by summing each inventory valuation (determined by physical inventory) and divided by the number of physical inventories over a given period of time; average annual inventory = (beginning inventory value + ending inventory value) ÷ 2.

Average principal invested. The maturity value plus the cost price then divided by 2.

B

Balance sheet. The financial statement of what is owned (assets), what is owed (liabilities), and the difference between those two (net worth) on a given date.

Bank discount. The decrease in value of a discounted note.

Bank statement. A formal accounting by a bank of the adding and subtracting activities that have occurred in one bank account over a stated period of time (usually a month).

Bar graph. A diagram similar to the histogram except that there may not be a number scale along the horizontal axis and the bars normally do not touch each other.

Base (B). The whole quantity or 100% of an amount.

Base value. The amount in the first year, month, or other period of time. A value to which another value is compared.

Basic depreciation rate. A rate of depreciation determined by dividing 100% by the estimated total years of useful life of the item.

Bearer bonds. Bonds with interest coupons attached; title to such bonds is not recorded in the name of a person but passes from bearer (holder) to bearer with delivery of the bonds.

Beginning inventory. The cost of inventory on hand at the beginning of a time period.

Beneficiary. A person, a company, or an organization that benefits from the insurance policy.

Board of directors. A group of people elected by the stockholders to oversee the running of the corporation.

Bonds. Long-term notes issued by a corporation or government entity as a means of borrowing money.

Book value. The original cost of an asset minus the accumulated depreciation.

Broker. A person who performs services of buying and/or selling for a commission.

Business statistics. The collection, tabulation, and/or presentation of number information about a business situation.

C

Callable bonds. Bonds that have a provision for the issuer of the bonds to repurchase or call the bonds in at specified dates if the board of directors authorizes the retirement (payoff) of the bonds before their maturity date.

Cancel. "Divide out" common factors that occur in both the numerator and denominator.

Cancellation. Process of dividing out common factors.

Capital stock. The general term applied to the shares of ownership in a corporation.

Cash discount. A reduction in an invoice amount available to the buyer for paying all or part of the amount within a stated period of time.

Cash surrender value. The amount of cash that the company will pay the insured on the surrender, or "cashing-in," of the insurance policy.

Charges. The commission and any other sales expenses, such as transportation, advertising, storage, insurance, etc.

Charter. The basic rules under which the corporation operates.

Check. A written order directing the bank to pay a certain sum to a designated party.

Checkbooks. Checks and check stubs to record deposits, withdrawals, check numbers, dates of transactions, other additions or subtractions, and the account balance.

Check register. A place for recording important information about each cash transaction.

Circle graph. A graph of data presented in circle form; a "pie chart."

Classes of data. Groups of organized individual values.

Coinsurance clause. An insurance policy clause specifying that, if a property is not insured up to a certain percentage of its value, the owner is the bearer of part of the insurance and will not be covered for the full amount of damages.

Commercial paper. Documentation of a promise to repay a loan or pay for merchandise.

Commission. Payment to an employee or to an agent for performing or helping to perform a business transaction or service. A fee charged by the broker for buying or selling stock for a client.

Commission merchant. A person who performs services of buying and/or selling for a commission.

Common denominator. A denominator that is shared by two or more fractions. The product of the denominators of two or more fractions is always a common denominator.

Common divisor. A number by which both the numerator and denominator can be evenly divided in order to arrive at a reduced fraction.

Common multiplier. A number by which both the numerator and the denominator are multiplied to raise the fraction to higher terms.

Common stock. The usual type of stock issued by a corporation. Most common stock gives it owners one vote for each share owned.

Comparative bar graph. Two bar graphs can be drawn together on one grid to make a comparison of statistical data.

Complement method. A method for finding the net price.

Complement rate. A rate equal to 100% minus the discount rate; used with the complement method in determining trade or cash discounts.

Component bar graph. A bar graph that is constructed to show how certain data is composed of various parts.

Compound amount. The original principal multiplied by the compound amount factor.

Compound amount factor. A number factor used to shorten the process of calculating a future value (compound amount).

Compound interest. The accumulation of simple interest applied several times during the term.

Compound interest tables. Tables used to calculate compound interest.

Compounded daily. Computation of interest 365 times a year.

Compounded monthly. Computation of interest twelve times a year.

Compounded quarterly. Computation of interest four times a year.

Consignee. The party to whom a consignment shipment is sent.

Consignment. Goods from a producer to a commission merchant for sale at the best possible price.

Consignor. The party who sends the consignment.

Constant divisors. Divisor is usually the last number entered in and is usually the first number entered in multiplication problems.

Constant multipliers. A calculator feature that provides that a number, once entered, can be automatically repeated as a multiplier by entering the new multiplicand and depressing the equals key.

Convertible bonds. Bonds that have a provision to be converted into a designated number of shares or a designated value of the corporation's stock at the request of the bondholder.

Convertible preferred stock. Preferred stock that gives the owner the option of converting that preferred share into a stated number of common shares.

Cost-based markup. The difference between the price and the seller's cost of an item for sale which is calculated as a percent of that cost.

Cost of goods sold. The seller's cost of items (goods) that have been sold during a certain time.

Coupon bonds. Bonds with interest coupons attached; title to such bonds is not recorded in the name of a person but passes from bearer (holder) to bearer with delivery.

Credit balance. A negative difference.

Credit card. Credit extended by a third party.

Credit rating. The reputation of a buyer.

Cross-checking. Adding columns vertically and then adding these totals horizontally.

Cumulative preferred stock. Preferred stock for which all dividends in arrears must be paid before current period dividends can be paid.

Current yield. The average annual yield (income rate) from an investment.

D

Debenture bonds. Bonds that have the backing of the corporation but do not specify any of the corporation's tangible assets.

Decimal equivalent. The presentation of a nondecimal number in decimal form.

Decimal point. The period between two numerals.

Decimal representation. A number containing a decimal part that represents a coin.

Declare a dividend. The authorized distribution of earnings to stockholders; this is done by the board of directors.

Declining-balance method (DB). A depreciation method that assumes a greater use (and greater productivity) in the earlier years of an asset's life; thus depreciation is greatest in the first year and less in each succeeding year.

Deductible. A cost that must be paid by the employee before any cost is paid by the insurance company.

Deductible clause. An insurance policy clause that stipulates that the insured will pay the first portion of collision damage and the insurance company will pay the remainder up to the value of the insured vehicle.

Denominator. In a fraction, the number below the line.

Deposit slip. A written form that lists cash and checks being deposited into a bank account and cash received from the amount being deposited.

Depreciated. Reduced in value through use.

Depreciation. The decrease in the value of an asset through use.

Derived. Developed.

Difference. The result of subtracting the subtrahend from the minuend.

Discount. A fee charged when someone buys the note before maturity. The difference between a bond's par value and its market value when the market value is less. Rule: When bonds are sold at a discount, the yield rate will be higher than the stated (face) rate.

Discount amount. The decrease in value of a discounted note.

Discount broker. A stockbroker who buys and sells stock according to the clients' instructions.

Discount date. The last day on which a cash discount may be taken. The day on which a note is discounted (sold).

Discount method. Useful when you want to know both the net price and the actual amount of the trade discount.

Discount period. A certain number of days after the invoice date, in which a buyer may receive a cash discount. The time between a note's discount date and its maturity date.

Discount rate. The percent used for calculating a trade or cash discount. The interest percent charged by the buyer of a discounted note.

Discounting a note. Selling a note before its maturity date.

Dividend. The number being divided.

Divisor. The number used to divide another number.

Dollar markup. The total of operating expenses and net profit. Markup expressed as an amount rather than as a percent.

Double-declining-balance method. A declining balance method that determines a depreciation amount for the first year that is approximately twice the straight-line rate.

Down payment. Part of the price of goods paid at the time of purchase.

Due date. The final day by which time an invoice is to be paid. After that day the buyer may be charged interest.

Duty. Charge or tax imposed on imported items by the Customs Agency to protect United States manufacturers against foreign competition in domestic markets.

E

Effective interest rate. The actual annual rate of interest.

Employee's earnings record. Summary by quarter of the employee's gross earnings, deductions, and net pay.

Ending inventory. The cost of the inventory on hand at the end of a time period.

Endowment insurance. Insurance payable upon the insured's death if it occurs within a specified period, and an endowment of the same amount as the policy, payable if the insured is alive at the end of that period.

Equalization. Adjustment of assessments.

Equation. A sentence that is made up of numbers and/or letters that represent numbers, divided into two sections by an equal sign (=).

Equivalent single discount rate. A single trade discount rate that can be used in place of two or more trade discount rates to determine the same discount amount.

Estimated physical life. The amount of usefulness an owner expects to get from an item before it is physically worn out.

Estimated service life. The amount of usefulness an owner expects to get from an item before it will need to be replaced due to obsolescence.

Exact interest method. The calculation of interest assuming a year that is 365 (or 366) days long.

Exemption. A reduction of adjusted gross income that is allowed for each taxpayer, qualifying spouse, and qualifying dependent.

Export. Domestic goods (produced in the United States) for sale in foreign countries.

The Export Administration Regulations. International Trade Administration rules and regulations to which all international trade is subject.

Extend credit. To give a buyer immediate possession or immediate service with payment due in the future.

F

Face value. The dollar amount written on the note; it is the same as the amount borrowed, or the principal (P).

Factors. Term used in multiplication to mean "numbers."

FICA. Federal Insurance Contributions Act or Social Security tax.

Finance charge. The fee that the seller charges for the privilege of buying on credit.

Financial statements. Statements presenting financial information about a company; two of these statements are the balance sheet and the income statement.

Finished goods. Those items that have completed the manufacturing process.

First-in, first-out (FIFO) costing method. A method of valuing inventory that assumes that costs for units used or sold are charged according to the order in which the units were manufactured or purchased.

Fixed costs. Costs that remain the same even though the number of units manufactured varies.

Foreign trade zone. Domestic United States site that is considered to be outside U.S. Customs territory.

Form 1040. One of the basic income tax return forms filed by taxpayers.

Form W-2. The wage and tax statement sent to each employee by the employer at the end of the year.

Form W-4. The form used to inform the government of one's marital status and to claim withholding allowances.

Formulas. Equations written with letters.

For-profit corporations. Businesses that operate for a profit and whose owners are stockholders.

Fraction. A number expression of one or more equal parts of a whole unit.

Fractional equivalent. The presentation of the value of a non-fraction in fraction form.

Frequency table. A schedule of information presenting a tally of data frequency.

Frequency. The number of values in each class of data.

Full service broker. A stockbroker who not only does the buying and selling upon request for clients but also provides investment advice and manages some of the investments.

Future value. The estimated future amount of money being loaned or invested today or over time.

Future value factor. A number factor used to calculate a future value.

Future value of an annuity. A value that will accumulate at a certain time in the future from the investment of annuity payments.

G

Graduated commission rates. A system of rates by which graduated commissions increase as the level of sales increase.

Gross cost. The prime cost and all charges paid by the principal.

Gross income. All income received from any source except for that specifically excluded.

Gross proceeds. Whatever price the commission merchant gets for the consignment; also, the full sales price before any allowances, returns, or other adjustments are considered.

Gross profit. The term used by accountants to describe the difference between the sales price and the cost of the sold goods.

Gross profit method. A method of estimating inventory without a physical count or perpetual inventory system.

Group insurance. Health insurance coverage extended to a group of people. The cost for each person's coverage is less expensive than it would be under an individual policy.

Grouped data. Individual values organized into groups.

H

Health maintenance organization (HMO). Group health insurance coverage with limited options as a means of keeping health insurance costs lower than that of regular group policies.

HI. Hospital Insurance (medicare).

Higher terms. A fraction in which both the numerator and denominator have been multiplied by the same number.

High-risk driver. A driver with a record of numerous citations or accidents.

Histogram. A diagram that presents the grouped data from a frequency table.

I

Import. A good produced in a foreign country and brought into the United States.

Improper fraction. One whole unit or more. The numerator is greater than or equal to the denominator.

In arrears. A term used to describe unpaid dividends on cumulative preferred stock.

Income statement. The financial statement that shows the revenues, the expenses, and the net income for a certain period of time.

Insured. For life insurance, this is the person whose life is being insured; for other types of insurance, it is the person who receives the benefit of the insurance.

Interest. A fee, usually charged for the use of money.

Interest-bearing note. A note that has a maturity value that is greater than its face value.

Interest dollars. The interest stated as an amount of money rather than a percent.

Interest period. The period of time between the loan date and the repayment date.

Inventory sheet. A form used for recording information when taking a physical inventory.

Inventory turnover. The number of times the average inventory is converted into sales during the year.

Inventory turnover rate. A rate that lets management and others know the average number of times inventory is sold during the year; inventory turnover rate = cost of goods sold ÷ average inventory.

Invoice. A document from the seller requesting payment from the buyer; the supplier's bill.

Invoice date. The date stated on an invoice; the beginning of the discount period.

Issue. To offer a stock or bond for sale.

Itemized deductions. Potential reductions to income allowed for certain payments made during the tax year.

J

Junk bond. A bond with a low rating, thus a higher risk.

L

Last-in, first-out (LIFO) costing method. A method of valuing inventory that assumes that the inventory on hand at the end of a period of time is composed of the units received first.

Late charge. A fee for invoice payment after a deadline.

Levy. A government charge or fee.

Limited-payment life insurance. A certain premium to be paid every year for a certain number of years specified at the time of insuring, or until the death of the insured, should that occur during the specified period. The policy is payable on the death of the insured, although there may be some options available at the end of the payment period.

Line graph. Presentation of data on a graph in which the data points are connected by a line.

Liquid. A term used to describe an investment that can be readily sold for, or "converted to" cash.

List price. The price amount listed in the catalog.

Loan initiation fee. A fee charged by a bank or other lender to cover the cost of processing the loan application.

Loan payment schedules. Loan schedules showing each period's beginning unpaid principal balance, its total payment, and the amount of interest and of principal in each payment.

Loan value. The amount that the insured may borrow on the policy from the insurance company.

Long-term credit. Loans that are longer than one year.

Lower of cost or market value (LCM). An inventory valuation method by which the lower amount of either the market value or the cost value is chosen.

Lowest terms. A fraction that cannot be reduced by any common divisor.

Low-risk driver. A driver with a long-standing, clear driving record.

M

Market value. The dollar amount required to replace the inventory as of the inventory date.

Markup. The difference between the price and the seller's cost of an item for sale. In dollars it is the amount added to the cost of the goods in order to have a gross profit high enough to cover operating expenses and to make a net profit.

Markup percent based on cost. When the dollar cost and the dollar markup are known, it is a percent that is calculated by dividing the dollar markup by the cost.

Markup rate. Markup percent.

Maturity date. The final day of a note (or bond) on which the borrower (the maker of the note or bond) pays the face value and any interest due to the holder of the note or bond. The due date.

Maturity value (MV). For an interest-bearing note (or bond), it is the sum of the face value (principal) and the interest dollars; $MV = P + I$. For a non-interest bearing note, it is the same as the face value.

Mean. An "average" that is found by dividing the sum of the group of values by the number of values in the group.

Median. An "average" that is the middle number.

Merchandise. Those goods that the company offers for sale.

Mill. One tenth of one cent or $0.001; a tax rate may be expressed in mills.

Minuend. Number from which subtraction is being made.

Mixed decimals. A number containing a decimal point and both a whole-number part and a decimal part.

Mixed number. A number that represents more than one whole unit by combining a whole number and a proper fraction.

Mode. An "average" that is represented by the number that occurs most often.

Modified Accelerated Cost Recovery System (MACRS). The accelerated depreciation method that is required by the IRS.

Modified complement method. A method for finding the net price when two or more trade discount rates are involved.

Multiplicand. The factor that is multiplied.

Multiplier. The factor that indicates how many times to multiply.

Municipal bonds. Bonds issued by states, cities, school districts, and other public entities.

N

Negotiable note. One that can be sold by the lender.

Negotiable promissory note. A promissory note that may be sold to a third party.

Net price. The price the distributor will charge to his customer after any trade discounts have been subtracted from the list price.

Net proceeds. The amount sent to the consignor as a result of consignment sales; gross proceeds minus charges.

Net profit. The return for the owner after all expenses have been subtracted from sales.

Net purchase. The price of the merchandise actually purchased.

Net sales. Total sales for the time period minus sales returned and adjustments made during the same time.

No-fault insurance. Insurance coverage under which the driver of each vehicle involved in an injury accident submits a claim to his or her own insurance company to cover medical costs for injuries to the driver and passengers in that person's own vehicle. The insurance does not cover damage to either vehicle involved in an accident.

No-par stock. Stock issued without par.

Non-interest-bearing note. A note having a maturity value equal to its face value.

Nonparticipating preferred stock. Preferred stock which has a priority right limited to a specified percentage.

Number of compounding periods. The number of time periods of equal length over which interest is calculated.

Number sentence. Numbers used in sentence form.

Number sentence equations. Number sentences in which both sides of the equal sign contain calculations.

Numerator. In a fraction, the number above the line.

O

OASDI. Old-Age, Survivors, and Disability Insurance.

Obsolescence. Becoming out-of-date.

Odd lot. Any number of stock shares less than 100.

Odd lot differential. A small extra charge by the broker for buying or selling an odd lot.

Of. "Multiply," particularly when "of" is preceded by the Rate and followed by the Base.

150%-declining-balance method. A declining-balance method that determines a depreciation amount for the first year that is approximately one and one-half the straight-line rate.

Operating expenses. The costs of operating the business.

Ordinary annuity. An annuity in which payment is made at the *end* of each time interval.

Ordinary interest method. The calculation of interest assuming a year that is 360 days long.

Original cost. The cost of building or buying an asset and getting it into use.

Overhead costs. General costs not directly related to sales merchandise.

Over-the-counter. A term that means the securities traded are not listed on a stock or bond exchange.

P

Participating preferred stock. Preferred stock that provides for possible dividends greater than a stated percentage.

Partnership. A business that is not incorporated and has more than one owner.

Payee. Party to whom a check is written.

Payment period. The length of time from one payment to the next.

Payroll register. A summary of wages earned, payroll deductions, and final take-home pay.

Percent. A number equal to a fraction whose denominator is 100.

Percentage (P). A portion of the Base.

Percentage method. One of two primary methods for calculating the amount of income tax to withhold from employee paychecks. after the total withholding allowance is subtracted from an employee's gross earnings, the amount to be withheld is determined by taking a percentage of the balance. The percentage to be used is given by the IRS.

Percent key. A calculator key that eliminates the need to convert a percentage to a decimal before multiplying or dividing.

Percent of cost. Markup that is based on the cost of the goods for sale.

Percent of selling price. Markup that is based on the selling price.

Periodic inventory. An inventory system that does not require a continuous physical monitoring of the units and unit costs into and out of the inventory stock. The information about the purchases and sales of items is recorded in the accounting system and compared with the results of the physical inventory; an adjustment to the accounting records is made as needed.

Perpetual inventory. A running count of all inventory units and unit costs based on a physical tracking of every item as it comes into and goes out of inventory.

Physical inventory. An actual counting of the inventory.

Powers of 10. Numbers that are multiples of 10, such as 100 and 1,000. The number 1 followed by one or more zeros.

Preferred Provider Organization (PPO). Group health insurance coverage with benefits based on use of contracted providers as a means of keeping health insurance costs lower than that of regular group policies.

Present value formula. A formula used to calculate present value using a present value factor.

Price-based markup. The difference between the price and the seller's cost of an item for sale that is calculated as a percent of the selling price.

Prime cost. The price commission merchants pay for the merchandise when they purchase goods for their principal.

Principal. Amount that is borrowed using credit. The person (client) for whom a service is performed.

Proceeds. The amount the seller receives from the buyer of a note being discounted; the difference between the maturity value and the discount amount.

Product. The answer to a multiplication problem.

Promissory note. An agreement signed by the borrower that states the conditions of a loan.

Proper fraction. Smaller than one whole unit. The numerator is smaller than the denominator.

Property insurance. Insurance against loss of or damage to property.

Property tax. A tax on real estate or other property owned by the business or an individual.

Prorate. Distribute.

Purchases. Those goods for sale that have been acquired during the current time period.

Pure decimal. A number with no whole-number part.

Q

Quotient. The answer to a division problem.

R

Rate (R). The percent of interest that is stated or calculated.

Rate (percent) of decrease. The negative change in two values stated as a percent.

Rate (percent) of increase. The positive change in two values stated as a percent.

Rate of return on investment. A rate that approximates the interest rate the owners are earning on their investment in the company; rate of return on investment = net income ÷ owner's equity.

Ratio. The relation of one amount to another.

Ratio of accounts receivable to net sales. Indicates the percentage of sales that have not yet bean paid for by customers; ratio of accounts receivable to net sales = accounts receivable ÷ net sales.

Raw materials. Unused items waiting to become part of the goods manufactured.

Reconciliation of the bank balance. Comparison of the check stubs or check register with the bank statement to determine the adjusted bank balance.

Recovery amount. The maximum amount the insurance company will pay.

Registered bonds. Bonds issued to a person whose name is listed or registered with the corporation.

Relationship of net income to net sales. This ratio indicates the portion of sales that is income; relationship of net income to net sales = net income ÷ net sales.

Remainder. A part of a dividend that is left after even division is complete. The leftover part of division into which the divisor cannot go a whole number of times.

Remittance. Amount a buyer actually pays after deducting the cash discount.

Resale, scrap, or salvage value (SV). The amount of value the owner of the item expects to receive from disposing of it at the end of the item's estimated useful life.

Rounding down. The process of dropping unwanted digits to the right of a certain digit.

Rounding off. Rounding up or down.

Rounding up. The process of changing a certain digit to the next larger whole value and dropping unwanted digits to the right.

S

Sales. The revenue realized by the seller for providing a good or service to a buyer in exchange for something else of value, usually money or a promise.

Sales tax. A government charge on retail sales of certain goods and services.

Secured. Guaranteed by certain assets. A bond that is guaranteed by certain of the issuer's assets.

Securities. Stocks, representing ownership, and bonds, representing debt, that usually can be bought and sold, or traded.

Semi-annual. Every 6 months.

Series of discounts. Two or more trade discount rates available to the buyer for different volume purchases.

Short rates. Insurance premium rates charged for less than a full term of insurance.

Short-term credit. Loans that are one year or less in length.

Simple interest. The fundamental interest calculation.

Single-payment interest method. The most direct method of computing interest on loans; the method uses the formula $I = P \times R \times T$.

Sole proprietorship. A business that has only one owner and is not incorporated.

Solution. The value or number that makes the equation true.

Solving the equation. The procedure of finding the solution to an equation.

Standard deductions. Set amounts, provided by the IRS, that may be claimed by those individuals who do not itemize their deductions.

Stated interest rate. The interest rate stated on the note or bond, the par or face rate.

Statement of account. A report that shows an opening balance, all deposits and credits, all checks paid, withdrawals recorded, bank service charges, general information about the account, and the balance at the end of the period. A bank statement.

Statistical data. Number facts or information that is organized, summarized, and interpreted.

Straight (or ordinary) life insurance. Insurance requiring a certain premium to be paid every year until the death of the insured person. The policy then becomes payable to the beneficiary.

Straight-line method. A depreciation method that distributes the depreciable cost of an item in equal amounts to designated units or periods covering its useful life; (original cost − scrap value) ÷ estimated total life in units or periods of time = depreciation amount for 1 unit or period.

Substitution. The replacement of one value for a different but equal value.

Subtrahend. Number being subtracted.

Sum-of-the-years-digits method (SYD). A depreciation method that assumes a greater use (and greater productivity) in the earlier years of an asset's life; the rate of depreciation is greater than the straight-line method but less than the declining-balance method in the earlier years.

T

Tax rate. The percent used to calculate a tax.

Taxable income. The amount of income upon which the income tax is determined.

Term insurance. Insurance protection that is issued for a limited time. A certain premium is paid every year during the specified time period, or "term." The policy is payable only in case of death of the insured during the term. Otherwise, neither the insured nor the specified beneficiaries receive any payment, and the protection stops at the end of the term.

Term of the loan. The period of time between the loan date and the repayment date.

Terms of payment. A statement on the invoice that informs the buyer of any available discount rate and discount date as well as the due date.

Time (T). Stated in terms of all or part of a year, the length of time used for calculating the interest dollars, the rate, or the principal.

Title. Right of ownership.

Total income. Gross income.

Trade discounts. Discounts given to buyers that generally are based on the quantity purchased.

Truth in Lending Act. A federal law to assist consumers in knowing the total cost of credit.

Turnover at cost. Inventory turnover determined using an average inventory based on inventory valued at cost.

Turnover at retail. Inventory turnover determined using an average inventory based on inventory valued at retail.

U

Unknown. The letter part of an equation.

Unpaid balance. The remaining loan principal not yet repaid.

Unpaid-balance interest method. A method of calculating interest on loans in which a new interest amount is determined each payment period; the calculation is based upon the unpaid principal balance at the beginning of each payment period.

Unsecured. Not secured. A bond that is not guaranteed by the issuer's assets.

V

Variable. The letter part of an equation.

W

Wage-bracket method. One of two primary methods for calculating the amount of income tax to withhold from employee paychecks. This method starts by granting a deduction for each withholding allowance claimed. The amount for each withholding allowance is provided by the IRS in a table. This method uses a series of wage-bracket tables published by the IRS.

Working capital ratio. This ratio tells the amount of current assets that would remain if all of the company's current liabilities were paid immediately; total current assets ÷ total current liabilities.

Work-in-process. Partially manufactured goods.

Answers to Odd-Numbered Problems

Chapter 1

Assignment 1.1

1. 347
3. 377
5. 491
7. 639
9. 337
11. 1,823
13. 2,437
15. 1,626
17. 1,589
19. 2,362
21. 1,897.20
23. 1,286.33
25. 1,395.30
27. 1,904.78
29. 7,269.37
31. 175.93
33. 132.44
35. 265.86
37. 296.36
39. 224.25

Assignment 1.2

1. 61
3. 47
5. 5
7. 76
9. 50
11. 9
13. 59
15. 29
17. 14
19. 411; 584
21. 399; 92
23. 283; 616
25. $73.98
27. $60.82
29. $38.61
31. $4,642.81
33. $8,216.01
35. $3,151.61
37. $7,107.91; $6,983.78
39. 61.94; $48.80
41. 1,830,823.85; $1,790,906.69

Assignment 1.3

1. 24
3. 520
5. 90
7. 240
9. 72
11. 144
13. 48
15. 80
17. 36
19. 88
21. 28
23. 136
25. 72,576
27. 317,327,062
29. 1,080,000
31. 4,184,998
33. 548,784
35. 2,266,875
37. 184,200
39. 166,050
41. 34,400
43. 52,640
45. 9,800
47. 1,000
49. 60,264
51. 144.00
53. 366.08
55. 1,787.50
57. 2,352
59. 3,234
61. 26,400

Assignment 1.4

1. 12
3. 12
5. 42
7. 4
9. 13
11. 30
13. 13
15. 28
17. 52
19. 17
21. 7 (41)
23. 587
25. 390
27. 90 (5)
29. 38 (500)
31. 22 (16)
33. 612
35. 178 (28)
37. 184 (137)
39. 1,000 (7)
41. 20 (118)
43. 517 (597)
45. 1,111 (49)
47. $2.20
49. 1 (49)
51. 1,112 (36)
53. 260 (49)
55. 2,000,148 (24)
57. 45
59. 105 (9)

Assignment 1.5

1. 400,000
3. 2,400,000
5. 5,400,000
7. 30,000
9. 2,000,000
11. 640,000
13. 7,000,000
15. 1,000,000
17. 4,000
19. 4,000
21. 270,000; 259,602
23. 10,000,000; 9,822,780
25. 200,000; 200,532
27. 75; 74.64
29. 200; 208.20
31. 20; 19.41
33. 2; 1.76
35. 20; 20.56

Chapter 2

Assignment 2.1

1. 26
3. 7
5. 2
7. 90
9. 23
11. 15
13. 9
15. 114
17. 251
19. 500
21. $9.00
23. 11
25. 11
27. $400
29. $310
31. $28
33. $62.50

35. $74.00
37. 20
39. 385
41. 11
43. 7
45. 3
47. 16
49. 21
51. 50
53. 5
55. 15
57. (a) 30, 25
(b) 36, 31
(c) 66, 60
(d) 510, 460
59. (a) 25, 5
(b) 9, 3
(c) 100, 20
(d) 100, 50

Assignment 2.2

1. $0.72
3. $7.12
5. 103 lb
7. $1.50
9. 900 mi
11. $9.95
13. $79.92
15. $14.85
17. $23.70
19. $760
21. $801
23. $799.60
25. $240
27. $55.79
29. $89.40
31. $6 + 4 + 2 = 17 - 5$
33. $9 - 3 - 1 = 2 + 3$
35. $20 + 1 + 2 = 16 + 7$
37. $12 + 3 - 3 = 7 + 5$
39. $64 - 32 - 8 = 8 + 16$

Chapter 3

Assignment 3.3

1. 21,120
3. 1,620
5. 48
7. 27 yd 0 ft 10 in.
9. 110 lb 4 oz
11. 9 gal 2 qt 0 pt
13. $326,700
15. $63
17. $6 per sq ft
19. $76.80
21. 250 cu ft
23. 15 hr or 900 minutes

Assignment 3.2

1. $1,008
3. $3,888
5. Room A
7. 4 ft
9. 24 mi

Chapter 4

Assignment 4.1

1. 0.613
3. 0.42
5. 860.00098
7. fifteen and seventy-three hundredths
9. four hundred ninety-two and three tenths
11. fifty-eight and nine hundred nine thousands
13. 651.577
15. 353.7662
17. 54.2897
19. 131.5662
21. 9.686
23. 1,037.6589
25. 0.459
27. 2.2309
29. 0.03767
31. 289.874
33. 16.932
35. 0.099
37. 67.8979
39. 0.375 in.

Assignment 4.2

1. 6.3 gal
3. 3.8 qt
5. 4.3 ft
7. $5.43
9. $942.37
11. $0.04
13. 4.373 pt
15. 12.633 oz
17. 8.999 yd
19. $4.63
21. $42.53
23. $11.45
25. 263.8
27. 1.8
29. 41.34
31. 5.32
33. 25.999
35. 0.459
37. 19.6 oz
39. 5.75 ft
41. 15.45 mi
43. 52.9 oz

Chapter 5

Assignment 5.1

1. $798.00
3. $289.46
5. 90.0564
7. 22.8562608
9. $1.85
11. $45.25
13. 1.71
15. 8.76
17. 4.25
19. 3,060.8
21. 972
23. $1,500.00
25. $2.13
27. $30.72
29. $0.21
31. $0.62
33. $56.55

Assignment 5.2

1. (a) 4.0
(b) 0.4
(c) 0.04
(d) 0.004
3. (a) 0.28
(b) 2.8
(c) 28
(d) 280
5. (a) 0.0048
(b) 0.048
(c) 0.48
(d) 4.8
7. (a) 27,000
(b) 2,700
(c) 270
(d) 27
9. (a) 120
(b) 1,200
(c) 12,000
(d) 120,000
11. (a) 0.004
(b) 0.04
(c) 0.4
(d) 4
13. (a) 0.14
(b) 1.4
(c) 14
(d) 140
15. (a) 70
(b) 7
(c) 0.7
(d) 0.07
17. 0.375
19. 0.333
21. 0.5

23. 0.25
25. $456.88
27. $39.16
29. 6.4 recipes
31. 6.25 hr

Chapter 6

Assignment 6.1

1. 1 6/7
3. 1
5. 2 1/4
7. 3 3/4
9. 1 5/6
11. 3 1/5
13. 1 5/7
15. 2 1/4
17. 1 1/3
19. 1 8/25
21. 5/3
23. 41/15
25. 38/15
27. 13/4
29. 35/6
31. 9/7
33. 47/13
35. 94/21
37. 30/7
39. 59/10
41. 3/5
43. 3/5
45. 2/3
47. 2/5
49. 3/5
51. 4/5
53. 2/9
55. 3/5
57. 2/7
59. 2/9
61. 3/18
63. 12/15
65. 6/9
67. 12/28
69. 3/6
71. 32/44
73. 44/48
75. 12/27
77. 21/30
79. 36/42
81. 1 1/2 yd
83. 1/8, 9/64, 3/16, 7/32, 1/4

Assignment 6.2

1. 3/4
3. 3 1/8
5. 1 7/10
7. 5 2/5
9. 6 13/24
11. 9 23/30
13. 1/2
15. 5/16
17. 5/8
19. 2 3/5
21. 5/6
23. 4 5/24
25. 33 7/8
27. 1 5/8
29. 7/8 in.
31. 13 11/12 yd

Chapter 7

Assignment 7.1

1. 2/15
3. 11/20
5. 2/9
7. 5/8
9. 5/12
11. 2 1/3
13. 5 5/8
15. 15 3/4
17. 3 1/5
19. 4 4/9
21. 18 1/3 cu yd
23. 12 min

Assignment 7.2

1. 1 1/9
3. 5/6
5. 1 1/5
7. 2 1/2
9. 5/8
11. 4 2/3
13. 4 1/6
15. 1 1/2
17. 3
19. 3 1/3
21. 6 pieces
23. 7 1/2 loads

Chapter 8

Assignment 8.1

1. 205.00; 4,192.50; 2,449.50; 1,459.50; 1,414.50; 1,342.50; 4,338.25; 4,251.25; 3,401.25; 2,976.25
3. 1,076.82; 1,076.82; 1,076.82; 764.02
5. 886.03; 3,046.03; 3,046.03; 2,962.87
7. $1,251.56
9. 4,020.90; 3,872.70; 4,849.50; 4,035.50; $3,750.33
11. 1,678.36; 1,541.95; 1,177.77; 2,302.62; $1,527.52

Assignment 8.2

1. 802.50; 752.90; 678.71; 904.21; 791.89; 758.56; 746.56; 678.79; 466.79; 328.79; 422.79
3. **(a)** $918.30
   (b) $1,630.27
   (c) $1,013.81
   (d) $942.32
   (e) $934.83

Assignment 8.3

1. Central Heating, Inc.
Reconciliation of Bank Statement,
November 30

Checkbook balance		$ 896.91
Minus unrecorded bank charges:		
Service charge		9.50
		$ 887.41
Plus bank interest credit		12.00
Adjusted checkbook balance		$ 899.41
* * *		
Bank balance on statement		$1,132.46
Minus outstanding checks:		
No. 148	$ 26.62	
No. 156	100.16	
No. 161	77.17	
No. 165	29.10	233.05
Adjusted bank balance		$ 899.41

3. Davis and Davis, Inc.
Reconciliation of Bank Statement,
July 31, 19—

Checkbook balance		$17,940.44
Minus unrecorded bank charges:		
Service charge	$ 18.00	
Automatic transfer—insurance	$1,765.00	
Returned check charged to account	1,500.00	3,283.00
		$14,657.44
Plus bank interest credit		83.20
Adjusted checkbook balance		$ 14,740.64
* * *		
Bank balance on statement		$17,464.54
Plus deposit not recorded by bank		2,004.35
		$19,468.89
Minus outstanding checks:		
No. 730	$ 78.60	
No. 749	2,765.23	
No. 753	556.25	
No. 757	271.84	
No. 761	97.73	
No. 768	958.60	4,728.25
Adjusted bank balance		$14,740.64

Chapter 9

Assignment 9.1

1. Abrams: $360.00; $108.00; $72.00; $540.00
   Aguilar: 320.00; —; —; 320.00
   Kula: 300.00; 90.00; 30.00; 420.00
   Murphy: 360.00; 67.50; —; 427.50
   Norton: 352.00; —; —; 352.00
   Payton: 320.00; —; —; 320.00
   Perry: 320.00; 84.00; —; 404.00
   Polar: 360.00; 13.50; —; 373.50
   Quinn: 352.00; 105.60; 17.60; 475.20
   Reston: 352.00; —; —; 352.00
   Sacco: 300.00; 90.00; 30.00; 420.00
   Warren: 352.00; 52.80; —; 404.80
   Totals: $4,048.00; $611.40; $149.60; $4,809.00
3. $2,253.76
5. $610.54
7. $6.04; $7.00; $0.96
9. $29.86; $30.00; $0.14

Assignment 9.2

1. Black: $400.00; $335.40
   Burns: 418.00; 319.02
   Dawson: 368.00; 303.84
   Frey: 420.00; 352.87
   Muldez: 450.80; 351.31
   Nations: 373.50; 315.92
   Odell: 392.00; 335.02
   Rayder: 546.00; 454.23
   Ridem: 352.00; 275.08
   Totals: $3,720.30; $3,042.69
3. 1/6: $251.79
   1/13: 276.46
   1/20: 276.46
   1/27: 269.19
   2/3: 278.08
   2/10: 279.56
   2/17: 276.62
   2/24: 276.15
   3/3: 277.80
   3/10: 309.42
   3/17: 266.10
   3/24: 274.77
   3/31: 267.26
   Quarter totals: $3,579.66
5. (a) $22,528.40
   (b) $1,396.75
   (c) $326.67
   (d) $2,500.95
   (e) $4,224.37
7. (a) $19,500; $7,000
   (b) $56
   (c) $378
   (d) $434

Chapter 10

Assignment 10.1

1. (a) $12,900
   (b) $35,800
   (c) $11,700
   (d) $ 5,596
   (e) $20,777
3. (a) $4,400
   (b) $ 660
5. (a) $25,400
   (b) $3,810

Assignment 10.2

1. $4
3. Allens $2,287
5. $20,260

Chapter 11

Assignment 11.1

1. $3.82; $0.78; $5.17; $2.00; $0.11; $5.69; $10.00; $20.23; $1.13; $0.64
3. $88.29
5. (a) Gems, Inc.
   (b) $32.63

Assignment 11.2

1. $940,000,000; $412,500,000; $318,000,000
3. $1.80; $1.75
5. $2,565
7. $248
9. (a) 1.6% (0.016); 1.7% (0.017); 1.4% (0.014); 1.5% (0.015)
   (b) 16; 17; 14; 15
11. $972

Chapter 12

Assignment 12.1

1. 0.21
3. 0.0367
5. 400%
7. 12%
9. 125%
11. 3.245
13. 52%
15. 8.33%
17. 500%
19. 0.001
21. 0.24
23. 13.19
25. 0.384
27. $0.28
29. $5
31. 1.6
33. 60
35. 1.12
37. 25%
39. 100%
41. $0.60
43. 225%
45. $44
47. $4,000
49. 88
51. 400
53. 40%
55. $21.00
57. 140%
59. 25

Assignment 12.2

1. 300
3. 104
5. $7,760
7. 542
9. $60
11. 10%
13. 25%
15. 20%
17. +74; +16.9%
19. +230; +12.7%
21. +1,715; +16.0%
23. (189); (17.4%)
25. (608); (21.7%)
27. +$116.47; +19.6%
29. (14.40); (5.9%)
31. +22.74; +15%
33. (806.61); (16.5%)
35. (716.61); (17.6%)

Assignment 12.3

1. 270
3. 5,500
5. 55%
7. 240,000
9. $420
11. $3,000
13. $24,960
15. 15%
17. $50,000
19. 100%

Assignment 12.4

1. (a) 2,100; 28%; $3,360
   (b) 1,800; 24%; 2,880

(c) 2,400; 32%; 3,840
(d) 1,200; 16%; 1,920
Total 7,500; 100%; $12,000

3. East: $7,000
West: $4,000
North: $6,000
South: $8,000
5. East: $3,040
West: $4,160
North: $5,440
South: $3,360

Chapter 13

Assignment 13.1

1. $3,780; $3,780
3. $1,710; $3,310
5. $2,600; $3,800
7. $2,680
9. $3,310
11. $4,400
13. $852; $27,305.75
15. $504; $7,611.35
17. $224; $5,176.00
19. $597; $5,767.00
21. $228; $3,296.80

Assignment 13.2

1. $5,400
3. $3,750
5. $3,620
7. $1,256.85
9. $562
11. $9,000

Chapter 14

Assignment 14.1

1. $375; $875
3. $1,190; $2,210
5. 66%; $1,980
7. $880; $330; —; $990
9. 70%; 85%; —; $1,071
11. 70%; 80%; 95%; 46.8%
13. $466

Assignment 14.2

1. Apr. 2; Apr. 22; $15.55; $502.75
3. June 5; July 5; $59.75; $721.75
5. Feb. 1; 99%; $477.97
7. $507.61; $500; $340.39

Chapter 15

Assignment 15.1

1. $657.68
3. $245.88
5. $280.47
7. $225; $975
9. $960; $2,160
11. $155; $775
13. $2,500; $5,000
15. 130%; $1,000
17. 200%; $55
19. 125%; $688
21. 250%; $420
23. $1,479; $3,944
25. $570; 50%

Assignment 15.2

1. $253.53
3. $2,590.12
5. $37.49
7. $28.80; $35.20
9. $518; $962
11. 75%; $135
13. 20%; $13.20
15. 80%; $500
17. 60%; $4,100
19. $77; 35%
21. $962; 65%
23. $99.20; $148.80
25. $72.96; 60%

Chapter 16

Assignment 16.1

1. $28
3. $14.40
5. $247.50
7. $2,240
9. $850.50
11. $17.55; $17.31; $0.24
13. $7.65; $7.55; $0.10
15. $49.25; $48.58; $0.67
17. $1,833.33; $1,808.22; $25.11
19. $8.50; $8.50; $0.00
21. $14; $14.12; −$0.12
23. $6.25; $6.10; +$0.15
25. $60; $60.32; −$0.32

Assignment 16.2

1. $7.50; $757.50
3. $90; $3,690
5. $1,600; $76,600
7. $565.07; $25,565.07
9. $67.81; $5,067.81

Chapter 17

Assignment 17.1

1. 98
3. 189
5. 126
7. March 2, 2000
9. Nov. 7, 2001
11. Jan. 3, 2000; $120; $8,120
13. Nov. 22, 2000; $350; $24,350
15. 105; $21.88; $866.88
17. 200; $425.75; $9,675.75
19. $180.00
21. $2,400.00
23. 9%
25. 135 days
27. $5.69
29. 8.5%
31. 60 days
33. $1,278.01

Assignment 17.2

1. $95; August 17, 1999
3. 6%; December 20, 2000
5. $1,800; October 3, 2001
7. 150 days; April 28, 2001
9. 5%; July 9, 2002

Chapter 18

Assignment 18.1

1. $60.00; 20; $19.33; $40.67
3. $525.00; 20; $74.41; $450.59
5. $92.00; 30; $67.37; $24.63
7. $650; 20; $118.07; $531.93
9. April 20: 31; $12,000.00; $99.88; $7,000.00; $6,900.12; $5,099.88
May 20: 30; 5,099.88; 41.08; 5,140.96; 5,099.88; 0.00

Assignment 18.2

1. $77; $6,523; 7.08%
3. $28.50; $2,821.50; 12.12%
5. Nov. 12; 63; $72.45; $4,527.55
7. $70; $4,270; Aug. 17; 47; $55.75; $4,214.25
9. $132.30; $6,612.30; Jan. 22; 82; $150.61; $6,461.69

Assignment 18.3

1. Sept. 18; 39; $22.44; $2,077.56
3. Feb. 16; 58; $66.74; $3,433.26
5. $165.70; $5,765.70; Sept. 7; 84; $172.50; $5,593.20
7. $29.59; $1,829.59; June 28; 39; $23.46; $1,806.13

Chapter 19

Assignment 19.1

1. (a) 1%
(b) 1.25%
(c) 1 1/3%
(d) 0.66%
(e) 0.5%

(f) 1 2/3%
(g) 2%
(h) 1.5%
(i) 0.75%
(j) 1.75%
(k) 5/6%

3. $21.75; $1,136.16
5. $42.61; $1,444.67
7. $22.96; $1,567.76
9. $556.42; $6.81; $1,500.43
11. $800.12; $9.25; $1,184.58

Assignment 19.2

1. (a) $60
(b) $1,250
(c) 14.4%
3. $2,000; $15.00; $500; $515.00; $1,500
5. $1,000; 7.50; 500; 507.50; 500
7. (a) $37.50
(b) $1,250
(c) 9%
9. 16.8%

Assignment 19.3

1. 0.25944; $908.04
3. 0.04707; $583.67
5. 0.09026; $690.49
7. $45.00; $1,483.26; $4,516.74
9. 3,022.36; 22.67; 1,505.59; 1,516.77
11. $45.00; $1,155.00; $4,845.00
13. 3,681.34; 27.61; 1,172.39; 2,508.95
15. (a) $562.50
(b) $387.75
(c) $74,612.25

Chapter 20

Assignment 20.1

1. (a) $960
(b) $220
(c) $1,650
(d) $1,430
3. (a) $1,875
(b) $1,250
(c) $220
(d) $3,233
5. (a) $53,340
(b) $50,000
(c) $6,000
(d) $3,440
(e) $56,000

Assignment 20.2

1. (a) $3,000
(b) $2,250
(c) $1,200
3. $170,000
5. (a) $137,500
(b) $82,500
(c) $150,000
(d) $150,000
7. $360,000

Assignment 20.3

1. $289.50; $396.48; $1,081.60; $1,964.00; $1,683.00; $4,039.50
3. $3,200
5. (a) $9,050
(b) $9,500
(c) $6,545
7. (a) $574
(b) $2,524

Chapter 21

Assignment 21.1

1. $765.60; $468.00; $368.00; $744.00; $1,993.60; $486.00; $4,825.20
3. (a) $22,950
(b) $23,750
(c) $23,190

Assignment 21.2

1. **A:** $120,000; $75,000
B: $118,000; $143,000
C: $72,000; $86,000
D: $96,000; $90,000
E: $47,000; $15,000
3. (a) $47,217
(b) 4.3
5. (a) $30,124
(b) $50,207
7. $160,000
9. (a) $200,000; $4,000
(b) $182,000; $222,000
(c) $255,500; $188,500
(d) $275,591; $168,409
(e) $41,667; $16,333
(f) $160,000; $208,000
(g) $360,000; $60,000
(h) $313,043; $126,957
(i) $112,500; $2,500
(j) $100,000; $30,000

Chapter 22

Assignment 22.1

1. (a) $565; $2,260; $3,740
(b) $800; $3,200; $3,200
(c) $700; $2,100; $6,300
(d) $2,240; $29,120; $5,480
3. (a) $14,000
(b) $18,000
5. (a) $640.00; $409.60
(b) $4,000.00; $1,000.00
(c) $855.36; $307.93
(d) $1,240.00; $992.00
(e) $1,982.81; $1,487.11
(f) $88,200.00; $71,442.00
7. $66.35
9. $9,600; $6,400; $3,200
11. straight line; $31,885

Assignment 22.2

1. (a) $3,175
(b) $8,640
3. $1,518,000
5. $15,670

Chapter 23

Assignment 23.1

1. **1997 percent:** 15.89%; 16.56%; 19.87%; 52.32%; 18.54%; 7.95%; 10.60%; 23.18%; 13.91%; 47.68%; 100.00%; 5.96%; 2.98%; 0.99%; 9.93%; 19.87%; 11.92%; 31.79%; 41.72%; 26.49%; 21.85%; 9.93%; 58.28%; 100.00%
1996 percent: 16.15%; 13.46%; 21.15%; 50.77%; 21.54%; 7.69%; 13.85%; 20.77%; 14.62%; 49.23%; 100.00%; 5.00%; 2.69%; 1.54%; 9.23%; 23.85%; 16.15%; 40.00%; 49.23%; 30.77%; 16.92%; 3.08%; 50.77%; 100.00%
Amount of change: 25,000; 20,000; 20,000; 80,000; $210,000; (5,000); (30,000); (10,000); 110,000; 220,000; $210,000
Percent of change: 9.09%; 20.00%; 10.53%; 12.50%; 16.15%; –25.00%; –14.29%; –1.56%; 275.00%; 33.33%; 16.15%
3. **1997 percent:** 10.6%; 6.9%; 8.1%; 25.6%; 13.9%; 3.5%; 10.3%; 48.2%; 15.9%; 74.4%; 100.0%; 3.0%; 2.2%; 0.3%; 5.5%; 16.9%; 6.3%; 23.1%; 28.7%; 43.4%; 21.2%; 6.7%; 71.3%; 100.0%
1996 percent: 8.9%; 6.5%; 8.6%; 24.0%; 13.7%; 3.5%; 10.2%; 52.6%; 13.2%; 76.0%; 100.0%; 2.9%; 1.8%; 0.3%;

5.0%; 15.8%; 7.9%; 23.7%; 28.7%; 47.4%; 22.1%; 1.8%; 71.3%; 100.0%

Amount of change: $10,000; 3,700; 1,300; 15,000; 5,500; 1,300; 4,200; —; 15,800; 20,000; $35,000; $1,600; 2,200; 200; 4,000; $10,000; (4,000); 6,000; 10,000; —; 4,000; 21,000; 25,000; $35,000

Percent of change: 29.4%; 14.9%; 4.0%; 16.4%; 10.6%; 9.8%; 10.9%; 0.0% 31.6%; 6.9%; 9.2%; 14.5%; 31.4%; 20.0%; 21.1%; 16.7%; −13.3%; 6.7%; 9.2%; 0.0%; 4.8%; 300.0%; 9.2%; 9.2%

Assignment 23.2

1. **1997 percent:** 103.66%; 3.66%; 100.00%; 25.61%; 53.66%; 79.27%; 30.49%; 48.78%; 51.22%; 15.24%; 10.00%; 1.83%; 0.49%; 0.43%; 0.17%; 0.85%; 0.26%; 29.27%; 21.95%; 3.66%; 18.29%

1996 percent: 103.57%; 3.57%; 100.00%; 27.14%; 55.71%; 82.86%; 30.00%; 52.86%; 47.14%; 14.00%; 11.14%; 2.86%; 0.50%; 0.40%; 0.13%; 0.71%; 0.26%; 30.00%; 17.14%; 2.86%; 14.29%

Amount of difference: $125,000; 5,000; $120,000; 20,000; 50,000; 70,000; 40,000; 30,000; $90,000; 27,000; 4,000; (5,000); 500; 700; 500; 2,000; 300; 30,000; 60,000; 10,000; $50,000

Percent of difference: 17.24%; 20.00%; 17.14%; 10.53%; 12.82%; 12.07%; 19.05%; 8.11%; 27.27%; 27.55%; 5.13%; −25.00%; 14.29%; 25.00%; 55.56%; 40.00%; 16.67%; 14.29%; 50.00%; 50.00%; 50.00%

3. **1997 percent:** 102%; 2%; 100%; 30%; 46%; 76%; 31%; 45%; 55%; 14%; 9%; 1%; 0%; 1%; 0%; 1%; 0%; 26%; 29%; 3%; 26%

1996 percent: 102%; 2%; 100%; 24%; 51%; 76%; 34%; 42%; 58%; 14%; 10%; 3%; 0%; 0%; 0%; 1%; 0%; 28%; 30%; 2%; 28%

Amount of difference: $11,500; 500; $11,000; 7,000; 1,500; 8,500; 1,500; 7,000; $4,000; 1,300; 200; (1,060); (140); 550; 190; 450; (30); 1,460; 2,540; 940; $1,600

Percent of difference: 16%; 33%; 15%; 40%; 47%; 16%; 6%; 23%; 10%; 13%; 3%; −57%; −41%; 275%; 119%; 85%; −14%; 7%; 12%; 56%; 8%

Assignment 23.3

1. **Amount of change:** $9,600; 25,400; 39,000; $74,000; $(8,000); 21,000; $13,000; $87,000; $5,800; 8,200; $14,000; $(31,000); $(17,000); $104,000; $87,000

Percent of change: 9.2; 22.5; 29.3; 21.1; −16.7; 18.3; 8.0; 17.0; 20.1; 7.2; 9.9; −16.3; −5.1; 57.5; 17.0

Difference/amount: $(87,800); $3,000; (115,000); $(112,000); 39,000; $(151,000); $63,200; $23,700; 19,100; $42,800; $20,400

Difference/percent: −10.5; 2.3; −16.7; −13.7; 29.3; −22.0; 42.4; 41.4; 235.8; 65.4; 24.4

3. **Amount of change:** $25,000; 4,000; 15,000; $44,000; $(4,000); 4,000; $0; $44,000; $(1,000); 3,500; $2,500; $(5,000); $(2,500); $46,500; $44,000

Percent of change: 156.3; 50.0; 48.4; 80.0; −9.3; 36.4; 0.0; 40.4; −18.2; 58.3; 21.7; −13.2; −5.1; 78.2; 40.4

Difference/amount: $104,000; $3,500; 89,500; $93,000; 15,000; $78,000; $26,000; $9,500; 5,750; $15,250; $10,750

Difference/percent: 103.0; 12.7; 138.8; 101.1; 48.4; 127.9; 65.0; 44.2; 79.3; 53.0; 95.6

5. **(a)** Angel Stationery Store, 36.5% vs. 20.8%

(b) Banner Office Supplies, 7.07:1 vs. 2.7:1

Chapter 24

Assignment 24.1

1. 81
3. 6 days
5. 6 1/2 days
7. 3 1/3 hr, or 3 hr 20 min
9. 4:00 p.m.
11. 4 mi
13. 24,000 letters
15. 14 hr
17. 2,400 nickels
19. 11 yd 1 ft 10 in.
21. 67,500 gallons
23. 154
25. 32, 16

Assignment 24.2

1. 100 mi
3. 1,080 mi
5. 572 trees
7. 180,000 words
9. 1 1/2 days
11. 1.6 days more
13. 1,152 in.
15. $787.50
17. $647.50
19. 26

Assignment 24.3

1. b
3. b
5. d
7. d
9. a
11. c
13. d
15. a
17. c
19. c
21. d
23. b
25. a
27. b
29. a
31. c
33. b
35. c
37. c
39. d

Index

A

Accounting, for inventory, 348–349
Account purchase, 214
Account sales, 213
Accounts receivable/net sales ratio, 389–390
Accumulated depreciation, 367. *See also* Business depreciation; Depreciation
Acid test ratio, 389
Addends, 2
Addition, 2–4
  checking, 4
  of decimals, 62–63
  of fractions or mixed numbers, 94–95
  horizontal, 4
  left to right, 3–4
  of weights and measurements, 46–47
Additional death benefit (ADB), 333
Additional discounts, 225
Adjusted bank balance, 124
Adjusted checkbook balance, 124
Adjusted gross income (AGI), 161
ADP Corporation, 136
Agents, 210
Allen, Paul, 26
Allocation, of rents, 195–196
Allstate Insurance Company, 286, 326
Amortization, 313–315
Amortization payment factors, 313
Amortization schedules, 314
Amount credited, 230
Annual interest rates, 306
Annual percentage rate (APR), 256, 307
Annuity insurance, 333
Approximate effective rate, 311–312
Approximation, of products and quotients, 78–80
Area measurements, subtracting, 47
Assessed valuations, computing, 177–178
Assets, 384
  book value of, 367
Auto insurance, 328–329
Automated Clearing House Association, 120
Automatic teller machines (ATMs), 118, 120
Average cost method, 349–350
Average daily balance, 307
Average inventory, 353, 390
Average principal, 310
Average unpaid balance, 310

B

Balances, unpaid, 230–231
Balance sheets, analyzing, 384–385
Bank balances
  continuous, 122
  reconciliation of, 124
Bank charges, 126
Bank credits, 124
Bank discounts, analyzing, 291–292
Banking, 119–126. *See also* Loans
  electronic, 123
  maintaining checkbooks and check registers, 122
  reconciling bank statements, 123–125
  using deposit slips and bank checks, 120–121
Bank loans, 254, 255
Bank of America, 190, 254
Base
  cost as, 241
  finding, 192–194
Base year, 194
Beginning inventory (BI), 352
Beneficiary, 332
Biweekly payroll period, 142
Book value, 367, 369
Borrowing. *See also* Loans
  by businesses, 287–295, 305
  to take cash discounts, 288–289
Brokers, 210
Budget comparisons, year-to-date, 387–388
Burger King Corporation, 42
Business. *See also* Businesses
  mathematical calculations in, 2
  using percents in, 189–196
  use of weights and measurements in, 49–51
Business depreciation, 365–372
  declining-balance method of, 368
  methods used for, 365
  Modified Accelerated Cost Recovery System (MACRS) method of, 370–371
  partial-year, 371–372
  straight-line method of, 366–367
  sum-of-the-years-digits method of, 369
Businesses. *See also* Inventory
  borrowing by, 287–295, 305
  payment of property taxes by, 177
Business financial statements. *See* Financial statements
Business insurance, 327–336
Business loans, 271–277
Business math, 405–414
  measurement problems, 410–412
  percentage problems, 412–413
  proportion problems, 407–408
  rate, time, and distance problems, 406–407
  relationship problems, 414
  time and work problems, 409–410
Business operating ratios. *See* Operating ratios
Business operations, comparing, 387
Business taxes, federal, 166–167. *See also* Taxes
Buying services, 210

C

Calculations, by rounding numbers, 34
Calculators, 78
  use in calculating interest, 259
Cancellation, 106–107, 110
Career Magazine, 136
Cash discounts, 224, 227–231. *See also* Discounts
  borrowing money to take, 288–289
  complement method for, 229
  for fully paid invoices, 227–230
  for partially paid invoices, 230–231
"Cashless" economic system, 287
Cash surrender value, 334
Charges. *See also* Freight charges
  for credit transactions, 306
  defined, 213
Checkbooks, maintaining, 122
Check registers, maintaining, 122
Checks
  outstanding, 124
  using, 120–121
Chevron Corporation, 104
Chevron Mall, 104
Cigarette taxes, 177
Citibank Corporation, 270
Coca-Cola Company, 72
Coinage, decimal, 73
Coinsurance. *See also* Insurance
  owner's share of property loss under, 331
  on property losses, 331–332
Coinsurance clauses, 331
Coldwell Banker Real Estate, 188, 286
Collision insurance, 328
Commission merchants, 210, 212
Commissions, 209–215
  calculating, 210–211
  graduated-sales, 211–212
  use of percents in, 188
Common denominators, 94–95
  in subtraction, 96–97
Common factors, canceling, 106–107
Comparative income statement, 387
Complement method, 224–225
  for cash discounts, 229
  shortcut for, 226
Complement rate, 224
Comprehensive insurance, 328
Computation, mental, 28
Computers, inventory data on, 349
Consignee, 212
Consignments, 212
Consignor, 212
Consumer Credit Protection Act of 1968, 307
Continuous bank balance, 122
Contributions, medical insurance, 335–336
Corporate Tax Rate Schedule, 166, 167
Cost. *See also* Gross cost; Prime cost
  computing directly, 244
  computing from markup percent, 242, 244
  computing from selling price, 242
  computing markup based on, 241–242
  computing markup percent based on, 242–243, 243

computing selling price based on, 241, 244–245
computing selling price directly from, 241–242
inventory turnover at, 354
net sales at, 354
overhead, 195–196
Costing methods, for inventory, 349–350
Cost of goods sold (CGS), 240, 352, 354
Credit, 287
extension of, 256
revolving, 289
Credit balance, 5
Credit cards, 306
Credit charges, 305–315
Credit interest rates, converting, 306
Credit purchases, additional fees for, 310–311
Credit rating, 293
Cross-checking, 4
Cubic yards, 49
Customer accounts, bank credits to, 124

D

Daily interest charges, 307. *See also* Interest
Dean Witter Financial Services, 286
Death benefits, 333
Decimal coinage, 73
Decimal equivalents, 80
Decimal point, 61
Decimals, 59–65
adding, 62–63
changing fractions into, 80–81
changing percents to, 191–192
changing to percents, 190–191
dividing by other decimals, 76–77
dividing by whole numbers, 75–76
electronic displays and, 60–61
multiplying, 74
reading, 61–62
rounding, 64
subtracting, 63
versus fractions, 60
Declining-balance (DB) depreciation method, 368, 371
Declining-balance depreciation rate, 368, 372
Decrease, using percents to measure, 194–195
Deductible clauses, 328
Deductions, 162
employee, 139
Denominators, 90
Dependency exemptions, 160–161
Deposits, outstanding, 124
Deposit slips, using, 120–121
Depreciable assets, book value of, 367
Depreciation. *See also* Business depreciation
accumulated, 367
for tax purposes, 370
Depreciation fraction, 369
Depreciation periods, 370
Depreciation rate, 368
Differences, 5
"Digital Daily, The," 158
Digital displays, 60
Digits
repeated, 3
significant, 79
Discount amount, 291, 294
Discount date, 228, 289
Discounting, 291. *See also* Discounts
of interest-bearing notes, 294–295
of non-interest-bearing notes, 293–294
Discount method, 224, 225
Discount period, 228, 291
Discount rate, 225, 291
equivalent single, 226–227
versus interest rate, 292
Discounts, 223–231. *See also* Additional discounts; Cash discounts; Discounting
single-trade, 224–225
trade, 225–226
Discover Card, 286
Distance measurements
adding, 46
subtracting, 47
Distance problems, solving, 30–31, 406–407
Distribution, of rent, 195–196
Dividend, 9
rounding, 12
Division, 9–11. *See also* Long division
checking, 10
in converting units of measure, 44
of decimals, 76–80
with divisor and dividend ending in zero, 10–11
estimation in, 12
of fractions, 110–112
by powers of 10, 77–78
by 10 and 100, 10
of weights and measurements, 48
Division problems, steps in approximating, 79
Divisor, 9
rounding, 12
Dollar markup, 240, 241
computing from markup percent, 244
Double-declining-balance, 368
Down payments, 256
Drivers, low-versus high-risk, 329–330
Due date, 228, 289
computing, 295
of a promissory note, 272, 273–274

E

Effective rate
alternative formula for estimating, 311–312
computing, 310–312
increasing, 310–311
Elderly persons, tax exemptions for, 180
Electronic banking, 123
Electronic displays, decimals and, 60–61
Electronic fund transfers (EFTs), 120, 123
Electronic scanners, 349
Employee commissions, 209–215
Employee earnings records, 146–147
Employees. *See* Payroll records
Employer quarterly federal tax returns, computing, 147–148
Employer's Tax Guide, 140, 141
Employment tests, math in, 405–414
Ending inventory (EI), 349
Endowment insurance, 333
Equations, 27–34
defined, 32
numeric, 32–33
Equity, owners' and stockholders', 384
Equivalents, fractional and decimal, 80
Equivalent single discount rate, calculating, 226–227
Estimated physical (service) life, 366
Estimations, 11–12
making, 34
Exact interest
comparing with ordinary interest, 258–259
computing, 258
estimating, 260
Exact interest method, 258
Exemptions
computing, 179–181
personal, 160–161
Expenses, overhead, 195–196
Extension, 348

F

Face value, 292, 293
of a note, 272
subtracting loan fees from, 291
Factors, 6
Federal Deposit Insurance Corporation (FDIC), 118
Federal Express (FedEx), 304
Federal income taxes, 159–167. *See also* Taxes
for business, 166–167
computing using Form 1040, 160–166
Federal income tax withholding, computing, 139–144
Federal Insurance Contribution Act (FICA) taxes, 147
Federal Insurance Contributions Act (FICA), 138, 145
Federal tax returns, employer quarterly, 147–148
Federal Unemployment Tax Act (FUTA), 148
Federal unemployment tax liability, computing, 148–149
FIFO (first-in, first-out) method, 350
Finance charges, 306
computing, 307–308
Finance terms, 308
Financial statements, 383–391
balance sheets, 384–385
business operating ratios, 388–391
income statements, 386–388
purpose of, 384
Floor space, allocating overhead costs based on, 195–196
Ford Motor Company, 346
Form 941, 147
Form 1040
Adjustments to Income section of, 161
using, 160–166
Form 1120, 166
Form W-4, 138
For-profit corporations, computing taxes for, 166
Fractional equivalents, 80
Fractions, 89–97. *See also* Mixed numbers
adding, 94–95
changing into decimals, 80–81
changing to percents, 190–191
dividing, 110–112
everyday use of, 105
improper, 90–91, 108
multiplication of, 106–110
numerators and denominators in, 90
on the NY Stock Exchange, 93
proper and improper, 90

raising to higher terms, 92–93
reducing to lowest terms, 92, 106
subtracting, 96–97
versus decimals, 60
Freight charges, 229
Fundamentals, learning, 1

G

Gallons, 49
Gasoline taxes, 177
Gates, William, 26
General Electric (GE) Corporation, 364
Goods, market value of, 351. *See also* Merchandise
Government debt, 160
Government payments, 120
Graduated sales commissions, calculating, 211–212
Gross cost, 214
Gross pay, 209
calculating, 210–211
Gross proceeds, 212, 213
Gross profit method, 352
Gross weight, 49
Group insurance plans, 335

H

Hawaii, 174
Health Maintenance Organizations (HMOs), 335
Higher terms, raising fractions to, 92–93
High-risk insurance rates, computing, 329–330
Home pages
ADP Corporation, 136
Allstate Insurance Company, 326
Bank of America, 254
Burger King, 42
Chevron Corporation, 104
Citibank Corporation, 270
Coca-Cola, 72
Coldwell Banker, 188
Federal Deposit Insurance Corporation (FDIC), 118
Federal Express (FedEx), 304
Ford Motor Company, 346
General Electric (GE) Corporation, 364
Hawaii, 174
Internal Revenue Service (IRS), 158
JCPenney, 58
Manpower Inc., 404
Microsoft, 26
PepsiCo, xvi
Price Waterhouse, 382
Reebok International, Ltd., 88
Sears, 286
Sharper Image, 208
Target stores, 222
Toys "R" Us, 238
Horizontal addition, 4
Horizontal subtraction, 5

I

Improper fractions, 90, 108
changing mixed numbers into, 91
changing to mixed numbers, 90–91
Incentive pay, 210
Incentive plans, graduated, 212
Income, taxable, 161
Income statements, 384
analyzing, 386–388
Income taxation. *See also* Taxes; Withholding
federal, 159–167
federal business, 166–167
state, 145
Income Tax Withholding Percentage Method Tables, 140, 142–144
Increase, using percents to measure, 194–195
Individual retirement accounts (IRAs), 161
Installment purchases, computing costs of, 308–309
Insurance, 327–336
auto, 328–329
computing cash surrender and loan values for, 334
computing coinsurance on property losses, 331–332
computing life insurance premiums, 332–333
computing low- and high-risk rates for, 329–330
computing short rates for, 330
group medical, 145
medical, 335–336
Insurance fees, on credit purchases, 310, 311
Insurance policies, loan value of, 334
Insurance premiums, 328
Insurance rates, computing, 329–330
Insured, defined, 330
Interest. *See also* Exact interest
bank, 254
for credit purchases, 306
defined, 256
for installment purchases, 308–309
ordinary, 257, 258–259
on promissory notes, 271
rate/time combinations for estimating, 259–260
simple, 255–261
unpaid-balance method for computing, 289–291
using calculators to compute, 259
Interest amount, calculating, 275–276
Interest-bearing notes, 272
computing maturity value of, 275
discounting, 294–295
Interest days, calculating, 272–273
Interest dollars, 272
Interest period, 256
calculating, 272–273
Interest rate. *See also* Effective rate
calculating, 275–276
credit, 306
versus discount rate, 292
Interest variables, computing, 275–276
Internal Revenue Service (IRS), 139, 158, 370
International Bureau of Weights and Measures, 43
Inventory
accounting for, 348–349
average, 390
computing, 347
defined, 348
Inventory methods, 349–350
Inventory record sheet, 348
Inventory systems, perpetual, 349
Inventory turnover, computing, 353–355
Inventory turnover at cost, computing, 354
Inventory turnover rate, 390
Inventory value, 348
estimating, 352–353
lower of cost or market value (LCM), 351–352
Inverses. *See* Reciprocals
Investment, rate of return on, 390–391
Invoice date, 227
Invoices
cash discounts for fully paid, 227–230
cash discounts for partially paid, 230–231
Itemized deductions, 162–163

J

JCPenney, 58
Job opportunities, at Burger King, 42

K

Kilogram weight, standard, 43

L

Lending methods, 291–292
Liabilities, 384
long-term, 385
Liability and property damage insurance, 328
Life insurance, 327
computing premiums for, 332–333
Life insurance values, 334
LIFO (last-in, first-out) method, 350
Limited-payment life insurance, 332
Liquid measurements, adding and subtracting, 47
List price, 224
Loan fees, subtracting from face value, 291
Loan origination fee, 311
Loans. *See also* Term of a loan
amortizing, 313–315
bank, 254, 255
long-term, 288
monthly payments on, 289
non-interest-bearing, 292
payment schedules for, 314–315
proceeds of, 291
short-term, 271
Loan value of a policy, 334
Long division
estimating answers in, 12
steps in, 9
Long-term credit, 256
Long-term business loans, 288
Lower of cost or market value (LCM), 351
Lowest terms, reducing fractions to, 92
Low-risk insurance rates, computing, 329–330

M

Macy's Department Store, 256
Manpower Inc., 404
Markdowns, 239
Market value
of goods, 351
of property, 177–178
Markup, 239–246
computing based on cost, 241–242
computing based on selling price, 243–245
computing markup variables, 240
Markup percent, 240, 241–242
computing based on cost, 243
computing cost from, 242

computing dollar markup and cost from, 244
computing from selling price, 245–246
Markup percentage rate, 352–353
Markup rate, 241
Mathematical operations, using weights and measurements, 46–49
Mathematics, in employment tests, 405–414. *See also* Business math
Maturity date, 272
Maturity value, 272, 292, 293
of a note, 291
of promissory notes, 274–275
McDonald's restaurants, 224
Measure, units of, 60
Measurement computations, in business, 49–51
Measurement problems, solving, 410–412
Measurements. *See* Weights and measurements
Medical insurance
computing contributions and reimbursements for, 335–336
group, 145, 335
Medicare, 138
Medicare deductions, 139
Medicare taxes, 145
computing, 145–146
Mental computations, 28
Merchandise
as inventory, 348
returned, 229
Microsoft Corporation, 26
Middle men, 224
Mills, computing tax rates in, 178–179
Minuend, 5, 96
Mixed decimals, 61
Mixed numbers
adding, 94–95
changing improper fractions into, 90–91
changing to improper fractions, 91
multiplying, 108–110
subtracting, 96–97
Modified Accelerated Cost Recovery System (MACRS)
depreciation method, 370–371
depreciation schedule, 370
Monetary system, 60–61
Monthly interest rates, computing, 306–307
Monthly payments, for amortized loans, 313–314
Monthly payroll period, 142
Multiplicand, 6
rounding, 11
Multiplication, 6–8
checking, 6–7
in converting units of measure, 44
of decimals, 74
estimation in, 11–12
of fractions, 106–110, 109–110
of mixed numbers, 108–110
of numbers ending in zero, 7
by powers of 10, 77–78
of the product of two factors, 8
by 10, 8
by 25 and 50, 8
of weights and measurements, 47–48
of a whole number and a fraction, 107–108
with zero in the middle of the multiplier, 7–8
Multiplication answers, estimating, 12
Multiplier, 6
rounding, 11

N

National Basketball Association (NBA), 190
National debt, 160
National Football League (NFL), 190
Negative differences, 5
Negotiable notes, 293, 294
Negotiable promissory notes, 272
Net income, 386
Net income/net sales relationship, 390
Net price, 224
Net proceeds, 213
Net purchases, 229
Net revenue, 386
Net sales, 352. *See also* Net revenue
Net worth, 384
New York Stock Exchange, fractions on, 93
No-fault insurance, 328–329
Non-interest-bearing notes, 272, 292
discounting, 293–294
Nonprofit organizations, property tax exemptions of, 180
Nontaxable items, 177
Notes. *See* Promissory notes
Number combinations, 2–3
Numbers, rounding, 34. *See also* Mixed numbers
Number system, decimal point and, 61
Numerators, 90
Numeric equations, solving, 32–33
Numeric relationships, in a series, 33, 414
Numeric sentences, 32

O

100, multiplication and division by, 77–78
150%-declining balance, 368, 372
1%, combinations of time and interest that yield, 259–260
1,000, multiplying and dividing by, 77–78
Operating ratios, computing, 388–391
Oral communication, multiplication of fractions and, 109–110
Ordinary interest
comparing with exact interest, 258–259
computing, 257
Ordinary interest method, 257
Ordinary life insurance, 332
Original cost, 366
Outstanding checks, 124
Outstanding deposits, 124
Overhead expenses, using percents to allocate, 195–196
Owners' equity, 384

P

Partial-year depreciation, 371–372
Partnerships, computing taxes for, 166
Payee, 120
Payment schedules, for loans, 314–315
Payroll checks, 120
Payroll deductions, 145
Payroll periods, 142–144
Payroll records, 137–149
completing employee earnings records, 146–147
computing employer quarterly tax returns, 147–148
computing federal income tax withholding, 139–144
computing Social Security, Medicare, and withholdings, 145–146
computing unemployment tax liability, 148–149
preparing a payroll register, 139
Pension benefit payments, 120
PepsiCo, Inc., xvi
Percentage rate, 192
annual, 256
Percentages. *See also* Percents
finding, 192–194
problem solving for, 412–413
use in real estate transactions, 188
Percentage withholding method, 140
Percents. *See also* Markup percent
for allocating overhead expenses, 195–196
in business, 189–196
changing fractions and decimals to, 190–192
changing to decimals, 191–192
computing tax rates in, 178–179
in measuring increase and decrease, 194–195
use in business, 194–195
Perpetual inventory systems, 349
Personal exemptions, 160–161
Personal insurance, 327–336
Physical inventory, 348
Place value, 61
Point. *See* Decimal point
Positive differences, 5
Powers of 10, multiplying and dividing by, 77–78
Preferred Provider Organizations (PPOs), 335
Premium rates, 329
for property insurance, 331–332
Premiums
insurance, 328
life insurance, 333
Price. *See also* List price; Selling price
determining, 240
net, 224
sales tax as a percent of, 176–177
Price Waterhouse, 382
Prime cost, 214
Principal, 272. *See also* Average principal
calculating, 275–276
defined, 210, 256
interest charged on, 289
Principals, calculating sales and purchases for, 212–215
Proceeds, 294
gross, 212
of a loan, 291
net, 213
of non-interest-bearing notes, 293
Products, 6
approximating, 78–80
Profits, 240
increasing, 390
Promissory notes, 271, 272, 291. *See also* Interest- bearing notes; Non-interest-bearing notes
calculating interest days of, 272–273
computing maturity value of, 274–275
determining due dates of, 273–274
discounting, 293, 294
Proper fractions, 90
Property, market value of, 177–178

Property insurance, 328, 331–332
Property losses, computing coinsurance on, 331–332
Property taxes, 175
computing, 177–178
computing in percents and mills, 178–179
Property tax exemptions, 180
Proportion problems, solving, 407–408
Prorations, computing, 179–181
Purchases. *See also* Account purchase
calculating for principals, 212–215
defined, 352
installment, 308–309
net, 229
Pure decimals, 61

Q

Quarterly federal tax returns, computing, 147–148
Quotients, 9
approximating, 78–80

R

Rate, finding, 192–194. *See also* Discount rate
Rate problems, solving, 30–31, 406–407
Ratios, 388–391
Real estate transactions, use of percentages in, 188, 194
Reciprocals, 110
Recovery amount, computing, 331
Reebok International Ltd., 88
Reimbursements, medical insurance, 335–336
Relationship problems, solving, 414
Remainder, 9
Remittance
calculating, 227
computing with the complement method, 229
Rents, allocation of, 195–196
Restaurant chains, 224
Retail, computing inventory turnover at, 353
Retail businesses, borrowing by, 288
Retailing, 347
Retail Statement of Account, 308
Returned goods, computing commission on, 210–211
Returned merchandise, 229
Return on investment, rate of, 390–391
Revenue Act, 159
Revolving credit, 289
Rounding, 34
of decimals, 64
net price and, 226
Rounding up, 64

S

Sales
account, 213
calculating for principals, 212–215
net, 352
Sales commissions, 209–215
calculating, 210–211
Sales tax
as an amount per unit, 177
computing, 176–177
as a percent of price, 176–177
state laws concerning, 177
Scanners, electronic, 349
Schedule C, 166–167
Scrap value (SV), 366, 367, 370
Sears Group, 286
Selling price, 241
computing based on cost, 241–242, 244–245
computing cost from, 242
computing markup based on, 243–245
computing markup percent based on, 245–246
Selling services, 210
Semimonthly payroll period, 142
Series, numeric relationships in, 33
Series of discounts, 225
Service life, estimated, 366
Sharper Image, The, 208
Short rates, computing, 330
Short-term credit, 256
Short-term loans, 271
Significant digits, 79
Simple interest, 255–261
computing, 256–257
computing on a monthly basis, 306–307
estimating, 259–260
Single discount rate, equivalent, 226–227
Single-trade discounts, calculating, 224–225
Skills, perfecting, 1
Social Security, 138
Social Security payments, 120
Social Security taxes, 139, 145
computing, 145–146
Sole proprietorships, computing taxes for, 166–167
Special assessments, computing, 179–181
Square yards, 49
Standard deductions, 162
Standard of living, 287
State income tax, 145
State taxes, 175, 176
State Unemployment Tax Act (SUTA), 148
State unemployment tax liability, computing, 148–149
Stockholders' equity, 384, 385
Straight life insurance, 332
Straight-line depreciation method, 366–367, 371
Subtraction, 5–6
by changing numbers, 5–6
checking, 5
of decimals, 63
of fractions or mixed numbers, 96–97
horizontal, 5
of weights and measurements, 47
Subtrahend, 5, 96
Sum-of-the-years-digits depreciation method, 369, 371
Sums, 2

T

Target stores, 222
Taxable income, 161
computing, 164
computing using Form 1040, 160–166
defined, 164
Taxes. *See also* Federal Insurance Contribution Act (FICA) taxes; Medicare taxes; Social Security taxes
federal income, 159–167
federal and state unemployment tax, 148–149
sales, 176–177
Taxpayer filing status, 160
Tax rate, state, 176
Tax Rate Schedules, 164–165
Tax returns, quarterly, 147–148
10
multiplication and division by, 77–79
powers of, 77–78
Term life insurance, 332
Term
of a loan, 256
of a promissory note, 272–273
Terms of payment, 227
360-day method, 257
365-day year, 258
Three-factor multiplication, 7
Time problems, solving, 30–31, 406–407, 409–410
Total assets, 385
Total liabilities, 385
Total pay. *See* Gross pay
Toys "R" Us stores, 238
Trade discounts, calculating a series of, 225–226
Transactions, short- and long-term, 256
Travelers discounts, 223
Truth in Lending, 307, 310
Turnover rate, computing, 347
Two-digit numbers, adding columns of, 3–4
"Twofer" discounts, 223

U

U.S. monetary system, 59
Unemployment tax liability, computing, 148–149
Unit method, 407
Units of measure, changing, 410–412
Unpaid balance, 310
computing, 230–231
Unpaid-balance method, 308
computing interest using, 289–291
Usable commodities, depreciation of, 365

V

Veterans, tax exemptions for, 180

W

Wage-based tax, 145
Wage-bracket withholding method, 140, 141
Web sites. *See* Home pages
Weekly payroll period, 142–144
Weights and measurements, 43–51
converting, 44–46
performing mathematical operations using, 46–49
use in business applications, 49–51
Whole numbers, dividing decimals by, 75–76
Whole numbers and fractions, multiplying, 107–108
Withholding
computing, 145–146
methods of, 140
Withholding allowances, 139
Word problems, 27–34
solving, 28–30
understanding, 109–110
Working capital ratio, 389
Work problems, solving, 409–410

Y

Year-to-date budget comparisons, 387–388

Progress Report

Part	Chapter	Assignment	Title	Page	Date Assigned	Date Completed	Score/ Grade
1	1	1.1	Addition Review	15			
		1.2	Subtraction Review	17			
		1.3	Multiplication Review	19			
		1.4	Division Review	21			
		1.5	Estimating	23			
	2	2.1	Word Problems, Equations, and Series	37			
		2.2	Word Problems, Formulas, and Equations	39			
	3	3.1	Weights and Measurements	53			
		3.2	Business Applications	55			
2	4	4.1	Addition and Subtraction of Decimals	67			
		4.2	Decimals in Business	69			
	5	5.1	Multiplication and Division of Decimals	83			
		5.2	Estimates, Equivalents, and Applications	85			
	6	6.1	Fractions and Mixed Numbers	99			
		6.2	Addition and Subtraction	101			
	7	7.1	Multiplication of Fractions	113			
		7.2	Division of Fractions	115			
3	8	8.1	Check Register and Check Stubs	129			
		8.2	Check Register and Bank Statements	131			
		8.3	Bank Balance Reconciliation Statements	133			
	9	9.1	Payroll Problems	151			
		9.2	Payroll, Earnings Record, Payroll Tax Returns	153			
	10	10.1	Federal Income Tax	169			
		10.2	Federal Income Tax	171			
	11	11.1	Sales Tax	183			
		11.2	Property Taxes	185			
4	12	12.1	Base, Rate and Percentage	199			
		12.2	Rate of Increase and Rate of Decrease	201			
		12.3	Business Applications	203			
		12.4	Distribution of Overhead	205			
	13	13.1	Commission	217			
		13.2	Application with Commission	219			
	14	14.1	Trade Discounts	233			
		14.2	Cash Discounts	235			
	15	15.1	Markup Based on Cost	251			
		15.2	Markup Based on Selling Price	253			
5	16	16.1	Simple Interest	263			
		16.2	Simple Interest Applications	267			
	17	17.1	Dates, Times, and Interest	279			
		17.2	Using Interest in Business	283			

Part	Chapter	Assignment	Title	Page	Date Assigned	Date Completed	Score/ Grade
5	18	18.1	Single and Multiple Payment Interest	297			
		18.2	Bank Discount and Discounting Notes	299			
		18.3	Discounting Notes Using a 365-Day Year	301			
	19	19.1	Monthly Finance Charges	317			
		19.2	Installment Sales and Effective Rates	321			
		19.3	Amortization	323			
6	20	20.1	Auto Insurance	339			
		20.2	Property Insurance	341			
		20.3	Life and Medical Insurance	343			
	21	21.1	Inventory Cost	357			
		21.2	Inventory Estimating and Turnover	359			
	22	22.1	Business Depreciation	375			
		22.2	Business Depreciation	379			
	23	23.1	Balance Sheet Analysis	395			
		23.2	Income Statement Analysis	397			
		23.3	Financial Statement Ratios	399			
	24	24.1	Math Problems on Employment Tests	417			
		24.2	Math Problems on Employment Tests	421			
		24.3	Practice Employment Test	423			